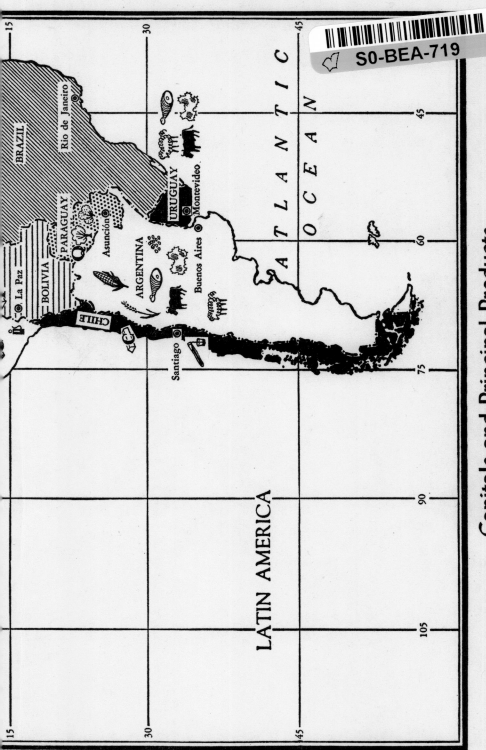

LATIN AMERICA

Capitals and Principal Products

Latin American
Politics and Government

Latin American Politics and Government

Second Edition

AUSTIN F. MACDONALD

Professor of Political Science
University of California

THOMAS Y. CROWELL COMPANY
New York - 1954

Preface

SINCE this book first appeared, in the spring of 1949, the changes in Latin American government have been frequent and often violent. The governments of six nations have been overthrown by revolution. Scores of other rebellions have been repressed with varying degrees of bloodshed. Eight new national constitutions have been adopted. Some countries have abandoned their democratic ways; others have moved steadily closer to well-established democracy.

All these details have been fitted into the description of Latin American political life. In addition, a long chapter has been added on the relations of Latin America with the United States. The number of charts and graphs has been substantially increased. It is hoped that these changes and additions will be regarded with favor by the many persons who gave a kind reception to the first edition.

Acknowledgment should be made of the very substantial assistance rendered by Professor Leslie Lipson, of the University of California, and by Mr. Wesley A. St. John and Mr. Robert D. Hayton, of the staff of the University of California's Political Science Department.

AUSTIN F. MACDONALD

Berkeley, California
January 3, 1954

Contents

CHAPTER I

A General
View

~~~~~~

Latin America is a convenient term to indicate the twenty independent republics of the New World that share a common background of Latin culture. But the use of one name for the entire region must not lead to the mistaken belief that all twenty countries are essentially alike. Quite the contrary is true. In area the Latin American countries range from Brazil, which is larger than the United States, to Haiti, which is smaller than West Virginia. In population there are vast dissimilarities, also. Brazil has more people than Great Britain, whereas Panama has fewer than Liverpool. In one nation of Latin America the inhabitants are almost completely black; in other countries they are principally Indian; and in still others they are almost entirely white. Some Latin American nations are literate and prosperous; others are illiterate and desperately poor. So of course countries that differ so widely will have very different political institutions. The student of Latin American government should always remember this elementary fact. He should bear in mind that virtually every rule of Latin American politics has a long list of exceptions. The whole picture cannot be obtained except by a separate view of every Latin American country. Before we begin our country-by-country analysis, however, it may be worth our while to note some of the general trends. We now understand that they cannot be regarded as universal rules.

Principal Features of Government in Latin America

CAUDILLISMO. One of the most common features of Latin American government, and one of its greatest evils, is the prevalence of what is generally called *caudillismo*. The best translation for it is *bossism*. A *caudillo* is a leader or chief or boss. He may be the leader of a tiny faction in a remote province, or the chief of a group that is seeking to dominate national policies. But whatever the number of his followers, he is their boss and the boss of the territory that they control. From earliest days the Latin Americans have had a fondness for *caudillos*. They have always been more interested in their public men than in their public policies. They have tended to follow colorful leaders, to the subordination of issues. To some extent, of course, this tendency appears in all countries, but it seems to be exaggerated in Latin America. A picturesque demagogue is virtually assured a large following. Once he acquires power, by whatever means, the people are prepared to laud him.

In the early days, when distances were great and the means of communication almost unbelievably poor, the *caudillo* of every section was able to escape a large measure of direct central control. Time was required to transmit orders from the central authorities, and time was required for the central authorities to learn whether their orders had actually been carried out. Incipient revolts were not easily crushed. Even today, in most of the nations of Latin America, government is handicapped by great distances and poor communications. But modern improvements have lessened the effect of distance, and as a result all the central governments have greatly strengthened their position. Local revolutions do not have so much chance of success.

POSITION OF THE PRESIDENT. The greatest *caudillo* of them all is the president. He is the leader of the nation, and this position gives him great prestige. It also gives him vast authority. The average citizen of the United States has no comprehension of the scope of the power placed in the hands of the president of virtually every Latin American state. From our point of view such concentration of authority is dangerous. The Latin Americans are inclined to agree, but they contend that it is necessary. They think of government in terms of crisis—one revolution succeeding another with breath-taking rapidity; and they advance the plausible argument that crises will not await the reasoned deliberations of many men. One man, they say, must have the necessary power to act. His hands must not be tied when emergencies arise.

The president as lawmaker. Especially surprising to citizens of the United States is the part played by a Latin American president in the lawmaking process. He may, of course, propose laws to Congress, and veto the laws that it submits for his signature. But, over and above these

commonplace powers, is his authority to issue decree-laws. When Congress is not in session, which usually means eight or nine months of the year, the president issues decrees that have the force of law. These decrees deal not only with policies already established by Congress, but also with matters that Congress has never considered. If, for example, the president wishes to regulate the exportation of petroleum or the employment of foreigners, he may issue a detailed order covering every aspect of the matter, and running to several thousand words. Exporters of petroleum or employers of foreign labor are bound by this decree quite as much as if it had been enacted into law by Congress. And if, at some future time, Congress should decide to consider the matter, it is confronted by a *fait accompli.*

The constitutional basis for such high-handed presidential action varies from country to country. In the Dominican Republic it is specifically authorized: "The President of the Republic may issue regulations, decrees, and instructions whenever necessary." In Argentina the authorization is not so clear, and most Argentine presidents have tried—with remarkable success—to find some legislative basis for every new policy that they have decided to adopt. Legalists have sometimes objected that the legislative basis was exceedingly flimsy, but their protests have never prevented the chief executive from interpreting the laws in such manner as he saw fit. The presidents of such countries as Bolivia or Nicaragua scarcely bother to find a constitutional basis for anything they desire to do. To them, and to their people, the president and the government are practically indistinguishable. And so, though the procedure may vary from nation to nation, the net result is nearly always the same. The president is the principal lawmaker as well as the chief executive, and Congress plays a definitely subordinate role.

Control of the budget. The president's power to spend money is equally incomprehensible to the Anglo-Saxon mind. True, the process of preparing and adopting the budget is sufficiently orthodox in most countries of Latin America. The president, through his advisers, presents the budget estimates to Congress, which enacts them into law. But at this point orthodoxy ends, for the president does not consider himself bound by Congressional authorizations, even if they happen to agree with his own estimates. He frequently directs the spending of sums considerably in excess of those allotted by Congress; and, since he has no corresponding power to increase taxes, the inevitable result is an unbalanced budget. The president's power to authorize additional payments may rest on some provision of the constitution, on a law of Congress, or merely on custom. It is, of course, an emergency power, to be exercised only in time of special need. But no president ever seems to have difficulty in finding times of special need. They occur, in most countries, several times a year, and to the tune of millions of pesos or bolívars or cruzeiros. And there is no way to challenge the president's decisions. When he says that money

Density of Population in Latin America

(Each figure represents 10 persons per square mile)

Mexico ....

CENTRAL AMERICA
Costa Rica ....

Guatemala ....

Honduras ....

Nicaragua ....

Panama ....

El Salvador ....

ISLANDS OF THE CARIBBEAN
Cuba ....

Dominican Republic ....

Haiti ....

NORTHERN SOUTH AMERICA
Colombia ....

Venezuela ....

WEST COAST OF SOUTH AMERICA
Bolivia ....

Chile ....

Ecuador ....

Peru ....

EAST COAST OF SOUTH AMERICA
Argentina ....

Brazil ....

Paraguay ....

Uruguay ....

And, by way of comparison, the
UNITED STATES

5

must be spent, that is the end of the matter. Some countries try to provide a feeble safeguard by declaring that the president must have the consent of all the members of his cabinet before exceeding the sums appropriated by Congress. But, since the cabinet ministers have been appointed by the president and hold office at his pleasure, their objections are not likely to be very strenuous. In the United States we say that funds shall not be paid from the public treasury except in conformity with the law. In Latin America they say: except in conformity with the law *or presidential decree.* It is a significant addition.

The state of siege. Perhaps most amazing of all the president's powers is his authority to declare an *estado de sitio*—state of siege. Latin American writers usually compare it to our suspension of the writ of *habeas corpus,* but it is something much more extensive, and much more drastic. Our Constitution declares: "The privilege of the writ of *habeas corpus* shall not be suspended [presumably by the president], unless when in cases of invasion or rebellion the public safety may require it." Under such circumstances, then, the president of the United States may suspend the writ of *habeas corpus*—in other words, he may set aside the citizens' protection against arbitrary arrest. The other guarantees of the constitution remain inviolate, of course. But in Latin America a president may set aside all the guarantees of the constitution. He may, for a limited period, make himself virtually an absolute dictator, without violating a single provision of the constitution. He may control the lives and property of private citizens throughout all the territory of the nation or in such areas as he may designate, and for as long a time as he may deem necessary. Obviously such extensive powers must be restricted in some manner, and constitutional restrictions are never lacking. The president may not act except "in case of invasion, grave disturbance of the public peace, or any other emergency that may place society in grave danger or conflict" (Mexico), or "when the security of the state requires it" (Peru). In some countries he may not declare a state of siege without the approval of his cabinet. In others he is obliged to report his actions to Congress at the earliest possible moment. But not one of these conditions really limits the power of a president who desires to be a despot. Crises are always at hand for those who seek them. In fact, government in many Latin American countries is literally government by crisis—an almost continuous succession of declarations of the state of siege. The president and his henchmen run the country as their fancy may dictate, and no one dares oppose them. No one may speak in opposition, for there is no freedom of speech.

No one may write a word of criticism, for there is no freedom of the press. No one may defy the most arbitrary decrees, for there is no freedom from arbitrary arrest. Fortunately, this is by no means a universal state of affairs. Some countries experience a state of siege only when genuine emergencies arise. Some of them—Mexico and Chile, for example—have been able to manage their affairs for several decades without habitual recourse to extraordinary power.[1]

SUBORDINATE ROLE OF CONGRESS. In every Latin American country Congress is inferior to the president in authority and prestige, regardless of what the constitution may say on the subject. The members are likely to be regarded with good-natured contempt, despite the fact that many of them may be distinguished physicians or lawyers or editors. And it must be admitted that this popular attitude is not without foundation. Even the congressmen themselves, in most cases, do not take their work too seriously. They may become embroiled in bitter debates; they may even carry their personal animosities to the point of physical violence, as happens not infrequently; but they would be the first to admit, with typical Latin American cynicism, that they are almost completely dependent upon the president's pleasure. The constitutional provisions do not, as a rule, indicate this fact. Congress is authorized to enact laws, to override presidential vetoes, to declare war. The Senate usually approves at least some presidential appointments. But these clauses shed no light on the practical operation of Latin American politics. The congressmen—or a majority of them—are the president's men. They have been elected with his approval, and his disapproval would mean their almost certain defeat. They would be very hesitant to override a presidential veto, despite the fact that the constitution guarantees them that right. They would seldom dare to institute impeachment proceedings.

Occasionally the newspapers of the United States carry stories that seem to belie these generalizations—stories about a Chilean president whose legislative program has been blocked by a rebellious Congress or an Ecuadorian president who has been impeached. These articles are correct, but the incidents are far from typical. Congress does not usually question the president's leadership.

POSITION OF THE COURTS. The courts, like Congress, are subordinate

[1] For a good discussion of the state of siege in Mexico, see J. Lloyd Mecham's article, "Mexican Federalism—Fact or Fiction?" in the March, 1940, issue of the *Annals of the American Academy of Political and Social Science*, pp. 23–38. The Argentine situation is discussed by Segundo V. Linares Quintana in *Gobierno y Administración de la República Argentina*, Vol. II, Chap. XIX.

to the president.   Even if the judges have been chosen for long terms
and given constitutional guarantees of secure tenure, as is frequently the
case, they know that a determined president can usually find a way to
remove them from office.   Moreover, they share the Latin American tradition that nothing must be permitted to interfere with the chief executive's
principal policies.   To declare a law unconstitutional is definitely not good
form.   Yet it must be recorded, to the credit of the judges in some countries of Latin America, that at times they have declared laws unconstitutional in the face of very strong pressure, and have provided the first—
and almost the last—defense against tyranny.   More than one military
regime has been obliged to face the uncompromising hostility of the courts.

But the struggle between dictator and courts has not often proved equal.
Laws invalidated by the highest tribunal have often been enforced as
rigorously as before, just as if the judges had not spoken.   In fact, judicial
disapproval generally lacks the significance that we attach to it in the
United States.   A distinguished Brazilian commentator on the constitution expressed the opinion, a few years ago, that the president should not
be bound by a single court decision invalidating a law.   If, however, the
highest court should declare the statute unconstitutional in case after case,
the president might properly consider himself bound by these reiterated
opinions.

INTERPRETATION OF THE CONSTITUTION.   The typical Latin American attitude toward the constitution is quite different from ours, and quite difficult for us to comprehend.   Latin Americans do not look upon a constitution as the fundamental law, to be regarded as superior to all other laws and
enforceable under all circumstances.   It is instead an ideal toward which
they are striving—a record of what should be done under ideal conditions.
When those ideal conditions have been achieved, the constitution will be
respected in its entirety.   But, until that happy day arrives, more practical
solutions must be found for pressing problems.

Every constitution specifies the manner in which it may be amended.
Sometimes the amending process is quite difficult.   It may perhaps involve a two-thirds vote in each house of Congress, and then a duplication
of this vote one year later, when Congress meets again.   It may require
also the approval of the state legislatures.   Under such circumstances,
obviously, the will of the majority may be thwarted by various minority
groups.   We, too, have experienced this difficulty, and we have tried to
overcome it in various ways.   Sometimes our presidents have looked to
the Supreme Court for "reinterpretation" of constitutional provisions that

happened to block their plans for reform, and sometimes they have even tried to "purge" the Supreme Court of members who did not prove sufficiently pliable. But in many Latin American countries such indirect methods are found unnecessary. The president simply issues a decree—or Congress passes a law—amending the constitution, and it is thereby amended. The fact that the constitution itself prescribes a much more complicated amending process seems to have nothing whatever to do with the matter. The president, or at least the president and Congress combined, are immune from constitutional limitations whenever the need for prompt action seems to be imperative.

THE SPOILS SYSTEM. The spoils system is the basis of the public administration in nearly all the nations of Latin America. Men are given jobs in the public service because of friendship, or because they are useful cogs in the political organization. Merit seldom plays an important part in the selection of public employees. There are, of course, some important exceptions. Brazil has operated under a fairly efficient merit system for nearly two decades; and, though this system has not excluded politics from the higher brackets, it has safeguarded thousands of minor employees. Mexico has enacted legislation protecting public employees from arbitrary dismissal, though it has given very little thought to the selection of personnel on the basis of proved competence. In many other countries the merit principle has been established in certain departments or for certain offices. But nearly everywhere the keynote is spoils.

There is an important difference, however, between the Latin American and United States versions of the spoils system. In this country the politicians have used the spoils of every political victory to build up tightly controlled political machines. They have organized their followers in amazingly efficient fashion. In the big cities, especially, all the wards and precincts have their leaders and workers, who expect to be rewarded with government jobs for the party services that they perform on election day. But in Latin America no such compact party organization exists. Local parties often change their structure and even their names with bewildering rapidity. National parties are likely to be nothing more than loose federations of these local groups. Therefore jobs in the public service are given, not as a reward for party service, but as a reward for partisan service to outstanding politicians. Every *caudillo* has his following, and its strength depends very little on the party label that he happens to be wearing at the moment. A few countries, of course, follow a somewhat different pattern. In Mexico the official party, the Institutional Revolutionary Party, has established a fairly elaborate organization throughout the republic. In many countries the Socialists, and sometimes the Communists, have succeeded in maintaining efficient organizations, though the number of their followers is relatively small.

GRAFT. Graft is widespread in Latin America. Almost everyone accepts it as a necessary and inevitable aspect of public life. Official salaries are low, and public employees quite commonly expect to supplement their incomes with "gratuities" from private citizens who desire favors from the government, such as a passport issued in violation of the law, an exemption from building restrictions, or a contract to pave a new street.

In one Latin American capital a story was circulated recently concerning a newly constructed motion picture palace. It seems that the owner of the building was summoned to explain why he had constructed it in such a manner as to obstruct a portion of the sidewalk, in violation of the building law. In vain he explained that his builder and his lawyer had interpreted the law quite differently; that they had believed, and still believed, the building to be well within the prescribed limits. Nothing that he could say satisfied the officials, however; they insisted that the building must be moved back from the sidewalk a distance of three meters. Since it was obvious that this demand could not be met, and since the owner could not obtain a permit to operate his theater, he finally sold it at a very substantial loss. The new owner, who was a leading politician, had not the slightest difficulty in obtaining the necessary permit, and nothing more was said about sidewalk obstruction.

Sometimes practices of this sort extend to the very highest officials. The despot Gómez, who died in 1935 after ruling Venezuela for twenty-six years, left a personal fortune valued at two hundred million dollars. He owned cattle ranches, coffee and sugar plantations, industrial plants. Yet he had begun his political career in comparative poverty.[2] Agusto Leguía of Peru, another "perpetual" president, died in prison in 1932 while awaiting trial on charges of having stolen vast sums from the public treasury.[3] Other presidents have managed to acquire great wealth while earning comparatively modest salaries.

As a rule, however, Latin American presidents have kept aloof from such sordid transactions. Many of them have been high-principled statesmen, desiring only the welfare of their people. But even they have had very little success in eliminating graft among the rank and file of public

[2] See pages 429–430.
[3] See page 352.

employees. Some of them have not even tried, for they have realized that it is a part of the established system, and that the system is bigger than any one man. Years ago, when the notorious Tweed Ring was looting the treasury of New York City, Lord Bryce asked his New York friends what they proposed to do. They raised their eyebrows. In Latin America, when respectable citizens are confronted with the evidence of graft in the public service, they usually shrug their shoulders. The gesture is different, but the meaning—and the result—are the same.

INFLUENCE OF THE CONSTITUTION OF THE UNITED STATES. Nearly all the constitutions of Latin America have a familiar ring to the student of government in the United States. Nor is this at all surprising, for our constitution has served more or less as a pattern. In Argentina the supreme court officially recognized this fact a number of years ago when it declared: "The system of government that rules us is not our creation. We have found it in action, tested by long years of experience, and we have appropriated it." One Argentine scholar, after studying the influence of the fundamental law of the United States on the constitution of his own country, pointed out similarities in sixty of the one hundred and ten articles.[4] The story is much the same elsewhere.

But no one must suppose that such similarity in constitutional provisions means similarity in the actual operation of government. The governments of Latin America are not like ours; in fact, they do not even closely resemble it. Their judicial systems are continental European, not Anglo-Saxon. Their local government is based largely on the pattern they inherited from Spain, with certain traces of French influence. Their educational systems, their culture, and their habits of thought are European, and have always been so. No formal clauses of a constitution can alter these fundamental facts.

Government by Revolution

One of the most typical aspects of Latin American life is the tendency to settle political issues by force. Government by revolution might almost be said to be the rule. Since the turn of the present century the governments of the nations to the south have been overthrown by revolt seventy-six times—an average of nearly four successful uprisings per country. No one knows how many unsuccessful rebellions have occurred during these

[4] Padilla, Alberto, *La Constitución de los Estados Unidos como Precedente Argentino*, pp. 111–113.

years because no one has ever taken the trouble to count them, but they certainly run into the hundreds.   Nor does anyone know how many revolts against authority were planned and executed in Latin America during the bloody nineteenth century, but there can be no doubt that they were very much more frequent before 1900 than they have been since.

The history of the present century has seemed more tranquil than that of the nineteenth, but only by comparison.   Revolutions are still the order of the day.   In fact, only Uruguay has escaped a twentieth-century *coup d'état,* and its lot has not been especially fortunate, for it has been plagued by more or less serious uprisings in 1902, 1903, 1904, 1910, 1933, and 1935.[5] Even little Costa Rica, which is justly proud of its reputation as a staunch defender of the democratic faith, has experienced three successful revolutions within recent decades, all arising from popular discontent with the policies of the government.[6]

Some of the Latin American nations seem to be in almost constant ferment.   Bolivia, for example, has had violent changes of government in 1920, 1930, 1934, 1936, 1937, 1943, 1946, and 1952.[7]   More than half of Ecuador's presidents have resigned under pressure or have been forced out of office, sometimes feet first.   Many Latin American statesmen have doubtless been tempted to echo the words that the great liberator, Simón Bolívar, spoke more than a century ago: "There is no faith in America, neither in individuals nor in nations.   Treaties are worthless bits of paper, constitutions are paper and ink, elections are battles, liberty is anarchy, and life is agony." [8]

Scarcity of Democracy

THE LIST OF DEMOCRACIES.   The list of nations accepting the democratic doctrine of free elections is amazingly short.   It includes only Costa Rica, Uruguay, and Chile.   Possibly, since Brazil and Ecuador have held some honest elections within recent years, they too may be listed as candidates for nomination to the roll of honor.   Cuba could once claim at least passing mention.   Even proud Argentina, now bowed under the weight of tyranny, may recall the happier days, from 1914 to 1930, when it could boast of a free government of free men.   Mexico has incorporated certain democratic features in its government.   Colombia is now making changes that may

[5] See pages 484–489.
[6] See pages 638–639.
[7] See pages 532–541.
[8] Quoted by A. Curtis Wilgus in *The Development of Hispanic America,* p. 507.

restore it to its once high place on the democratic roll of honor. But there the list ends. The other nations of Latin America are not democracies, and never have been democracies. Nor is there reason to suppose that they will soon adopt the democratic way of life. They have given abundant evidence of a preference for dictatorship.

INFLUENCE OF THE COLONIAL ERA. It is not difficult to understand why democratic practices have been so rare among our southern neighbors. For one thing, the authoritarian tradition of the colonial era was strong, and its influence has never entirely disappeared. The ideal of freedom, as exemplified by England, France, and the United States, has achieved great popularity in Latin America, but too often it has been interpreted by the ignorant masses as freedom from all restraint, and the resultant anarchy has necessitated strong repressive measures. In most of the countries of Latin America, dictatorship is the only kind of government that has ever been possible.

LACK OF EDUCATION. The close relationship between education and democracy is so generally understood that it scarcely merits comment. The vast majority of Latin Americans have always been unlettered; they are unlettered today, despite the valiant efforts of some of their farseeing statesmen; and their ignorance is an unsurmountable barrier to democratic progress. Government by the people is unthinkable unless the people are sufficiently well informed to accept the responsibilities of such a system. Unfortunately, it is not necessarily true that a well-educated nation will be a democratic nation, as witness Germany; but it *is* true that a poorly educated nation lacks the essentials of popular self-government. In Latin America illiteracy is so widespread that it might almost be called a universal characteristic. There are, of course, exceptions—some countries that have a proud educational record, and some people in every country who are highly cultured and sophisticated. But for the most part the indictment of illiteracy stands unchallenged.

Nearly everywhere in Latin America the educational pattern is the same. The masses of the people receive at best six years of elementary schooling, and at worst no schooling whatever. Only a tiny handful advance beyond the primary grades, and these few receive a training in the liberal arts, designed to fit them for admission to college. Then, in college or university, these select students are given professional training. They become lawyers or doctors or dentists or architects, and eventually they may drift into politics. They are highly cultured sophisticates, disciples and patrons of the arts. But they are *not* the people. They are the sons and daughters of the "best" people—the landed aristocrats whose families have played a dominant role since colonial days. It may fairly be said, without forgetting the exceptions, that good education in Latin America is the heritage of a select few. Small wonder, therefore, that democracy has not flourished in such a soil!

TRADITION OF FORCE AND FRAUD. Another serious handicap to democracy is the Latin American tradition of force and fraud. Once a "man on horseback" has seized the reins of power, there is a temptation for him to retain control indefinitely, or pass it on to one of his intimate associates, who will be sure to follow a similar policy. Constitutions and laws have been prepared with great care to prevent illegal retention of power by a single man or group, but they seldom accomplish their announced purpose. The president may brazenly flout the constitutional decree that elections shall be held every four years or every six with the explanation that the existing state of emergency makes necessary the postponement of elections until some more tranquil time. Perhaps the state of emergency exists only in the president's imagination. Perhaps it has been created by popular dissatisfaction with the president's policies. But it can still provide an excuse for indefinite delays in setting the date of elections. And no one can seriously challenge the president's decision, unless prepared to meet armed force with armed force.[9]

Absolute dictators. In Nicaragua General Anastacio Somoza has ruled as absolute despot, though not always as president, since 1937. Fulgencio Batista, the dictator of Cuba from 1936 to 1944, has once again seized control of his country's government by force of arms. Higinio Morínigo, who ruled Paraguay until 1948, has been replaced after a brief interregnum by another dictator, Federico Chaves. The dictator of the Dominican Republic, General Rafael Leonidas Trujillo, has held power since 1930. Only part of that time has he actually been president of the country, but meanwhile he has taken care to fill the presidency with hand-picked subordinates.

Dishonest elections. There are many countries of Latin America, however, where other means, less flagrant than the use of force but equally successful, are used to keep control out of the hands of the people. The constitutional provisions prohibiting any president from serving more than one term, or serving two consecutive terms, may be respected with scrupulous care. Elections may be held at regular intervals. *But the party in power always wins.* It makes no difference how the people cast their votes; the

---

[9] There is an interesting, though somewhat unorthodox, discussion of the problem in William S. Stokes' article, "Violence as a Power Factor in Latin American Politics," in the September, 1952, issue of the *Western Political Quarterly,* pp. 445–468.

elections are always manipulated in such a way as to bring victory to the party that does the counting. Sometimes voters are intimidated. Sometimes they are told that they may not vote because they are not properly registered. Sometimes the polling places are changed on short notice, and located in such unlikely spots as to discourage all but the most persistent. Sometimes, on the other hand, everything is managed correctly at the polls, but the votes are then miscounted. The technique varies from place to place, and even from election to election. The result, however, is almost always the same.

The masses of the people, in most of Latin America, are profoundly indifferent to fraudulent tactics as a means of securing and retaining public power. They have had little or no experience with honest democratic government, and they feel no urgent impulse to change the existing state of affairs. On the other hand, there is nearly always an opposition party or coalition, which objects most violently to the use of fraud. Sometimes it may even allege fraud when none exists. In any event, its leaders contend that they have been kept from office illegally, and that the will of the people has been shamelessly flouted.

What, under the circumstances, can the opposition leaders do about the use of fraud? They might carry their charges to the courts, but experience has taught them that their time would be wasted. They can urge their followers to protest by boycotting future elections, a course that the opposition parties of several countries have actually followed from time to time, although it is not entirely clear that they have hurt anyone except themselves. So there is nothing left but revolution. Force must be met with force.

The revolutionary habit. Now, there is nothing inherently wrong about revolution. If used by honest men to right grievous wrongs, it may be the highest form of patriotism. But there is always the danger that revolution may get to be a habit—that it may be used by every defeated candidate to reverse the results of the election, regardless of the merits of the case. In many Latin American elections no one, except of course the election officials who did the counting, really knows how the people cast their ballots. Therefore it is always possible for a disappointed office seeker to claim that he was cheated, and to attempt to overthrow the government on the basis of this claim.

In the United States we accept without question the result of an election, assuming that it represents the will of the majority, as it normally does. In some cities and at some elections there may be fraud or even intimidation, but for the most part the American people are accustomed to having their votes counted as they have cast them. Therefore the minority party accepts the people's decision, secure in the knowledge that it will acquire power as soon as it can win the support of a majority of the voters. In Latin America the defeated party has no such assurance; on the contrary, in most countries, it has every reason to believe that it will be excluded from control of the government indefinitely, regardless of its popular support, unless it can muster greater armed strength than the party in power. So of course it thinks in terms of force.

Many Latin American politicians, when they speak freely of their trade, admit that the elections have been fixed in advance. "But," they ask, "what can we do? If we once relinquished power, we could never regain control except by a revolution because the other crowd won't play fair. It will cling to power year after year, regardless of the way the votes are cast." And the spokesmen for the "other crowd" justify themselves in some such words as these: "Why shouldn't we cling to power year after year? Isn't that what our opponents are doing right now? It will take a revolution to get them out." And so it goes, decade after decade, in country after country. It is a vicious circle, from which there seems to be no easy way of escape.[10]

The military class. The governments of most of our southern neighbors are run by the generals, with the aid of the colonels and a few civilians. A military man may or may not serve as president, though at the moment these lines are written the presidents of thirteen of the Latin American republics are professional soldiers. But, regardless of such details, the army almost always has the power and shows no hesitancy in making it felt. Every president, whether soldier or civilian, knows that he can remain in office as long as the army supports him, but not one hour longer. He might perhaps disregard widespread civilian discontent. But dissatisfaction within the army is something that he cannot possibly afford to ignore, for revolutions, when they come, are not usually popular movements. They are plotted and carried out by army officers—sometimes by the officers who happen to control a strategic military establishment, such as the Campo de Mayo garrison on the outskirts of Buenos Aires. The president and his associates may be rounded up and executed or deported after the exchange of a few shots and the wounding of a few civilian bystanders. Or a few days of bloody fighting may be required to accomplish this re-

[10] See Frank Tannenbaum's *Peace by Revolution*.

sult. If, on the other hand, the president acts decisively, and if most of the army is still loyal to him, the story may have a very different ending, with the revolutionary leaders in full flight or in hastily dug graves. But, in any event, it is force that usually determines the result rather than the will of the people. The people are not armed; they are in no position to enforce their will against machine guns and rifles, and, if necessary, airplanes and tanks.

Many men and women in the United States overlook this elementary fact. "Why," they ask, "do the Latin Americans permit their dictators to continue in power? Why don't they do something about it?" To "do something" about a machine gun, when you happen to be on the wrong end, is not easy. It takes a special brand of courage, and perhaps a large dose of foolhardiness. So the dictators continue to dictate, with army support. Even those Latin American presidents who are confirmed democrats have no illusions as to the source of their power. Each knows that an army united against him could turn him out overnight, so he strives to keep the army united in his behalf. This retention of unified army support is likely to involve consultations with high-ranking army officers before making any decisions regarding major matters of national policy, and it is certain to require relatively high army salaries and relatively rapid promotions. But these things are generally considered a small price for keeping the army in line. In 1937, when Getulio Vargas decreed a new constitution for Brazil, he explained (in the constitution itself) that he was doing so "with the support of the armed forces, and yielding to the dictates of public opinion." Most presidents are not so frank as to list the support of the armed forces ahead of the dictates of public opinion.

DEMOCRACY AS AN IDEAL. Admiration for the democratic way of life is deeply instilled in the masses of Latin America. They respond with profound emotion to such words as "democracia" and "libertad," and as a result their political leaders use them often. Even the most cynical tyrants usually find it wise to speak of the will of the people, identifying their own regimes with the democratic cause. Occasionally a dictator violates this simple rule. In 1940 Getulio Vargas took occasion to praise Mussolini's brand of fascism in these words: "We are marching toward a future different from all we know in economic, political, and social organization; and we feel that old systems and antiquated formulas have entered a decline. It is the beginning of a new era." In 1943 Higinio Morínigo, who was then the president-dictator of Paraguay, officially pronounced old-fashioned democracy dead, and put himself on record as favoring "selective" democracy. But such statements are rare, and not usually well advised. Vargas later endorsed democracy in very emphatic terms. Morínigo never explained the meaning of "selective" democracy, though it could reasonably be assumed that he would do the selecting. It seems that the people of Latin America like to think of their governments as democratic. When they cannot shut their eyes to existing dictatorial practices, they think of democracy as the goal toward which they are striving. In many parts of the world the democratic tradition has been cast aside as unworthy, but not in Latin America. The men and women of that area hold firmly to the ideal, if not the practice, of free government.

DICTATORSHIP BUT NOT FASCISM. Many books published in the United States speak loosely of fascism in Latin America.[11] Now, it must be clearly understood that fascism and dictatorship are not synonymous. Fascism is a way of life—a system of government with its own theories and standards. It substitutes order for liberty, it places the welfare of the state above the welfare of its citizens, and it glorifies the ideal of war. It seeks to perpetuate itself by systematically indoctrinating the men and women of the nation, and especially the children. That is fascism as it was practiced in Italy and Germany and as it still exists in Franco's Spain. It has no place in Latin America, except to some extent in Argentina. There are, of course, a number of characteristics that many of the Latin American countries share with fascist nations—arbitrary government by one man or a few men, censorship of the press, suppression of individual liberties. But these things are not new. They existed in Latin America long before European fascism came into being. They are nothing more nor less than old-fashioned dictatorship. Latin Americans have experienced its evils for many long years.

THE THREAT OF COMMUNISM. Communism is potentially dangerous in Latin America, though it has not yet made great headway except in Bolivia and Guatemala. In most Latin American countries the communists are extremely noisy and relatively ineffective. Yet occasionally they make spectacular gains at unexpected times and places. They have held cabinet posts in Chile, and have controlled the municipal council in Rio de Janeiro. They will undoubtedly continue to win some converts, despite the determined opposition of the Roman Catholic Church. The Latin American masses are too poor and too hungry to be completely indifferent to communism's seductive appeals.

[11] See, for example, *The State of Latin America,* by Germán Arciniegas.

The Roman Catholic Church

PREDOMINANCE OF ROMAN CATHOLICISM. The Roman Catholic Church is able to exert great influence in Latin American politics, because the overwhelming majority of Latin Americans are Roman Catholic, at least by inheritance. Many of them, especially the men, regard the church with open contempt and refuse to enter any place of worship. But even they look to the church during the great moments in the lives of their families—births, weddings, deaths. Many of them, though adopting attitudes of agnostic skepticism, look without disfavor or even with secret approval upon the devotions of their womenfolk.

EARLY POSITION OF THE CHURCH. The church is or has been a burning issue in every country of Latin America, not because of its devotional activities, but because of its political connections. It must be remembered that church and state were closely united in Spanish America during the colonial period. The Roman Catholic religion was the official faith, and the king of Spain appointed the archbishops and bishops. The church was in a most favored position, holding vast estates in every colony. In Peru, for example, at the end of the colonial era it owned nearly forty per cent of all the houses and arable land. In Mexico, it was even more strongly entrenched. Throughout Spanish America church money was loaned to private persons at high rates of interest. Great cathedrals and churches possessed ornate furnishings. The church enjoyed a virtual monopoly of education. Royal favor had made it prosperous. When, therefore, the colonists rose in rebellion against Spanish authority, it was not at all surprising that the Roman Catholic Church should support this authority and do everything in its power to crush the tide of revolt. Priests blessed the Spanish arms. They preached from their pulpits that the Spanish cause was the cause of God. In the early years of the struggle for independence a severe earthquake devastated the rebellious provinces of what is now Venezuela, leaving the loyalist provinces largely unscathed. The Catholic clergy thereupon declared that this was an evidence of the Almighty's disapproval of rebel activities.

There were, of course, some priests who espoused the independence movement. Two great leaders of the Mexican fight against the Spanish royalists were Father Hidalgo and his friend and disciple, Father Morelos. But these men did not speak for the church. Both of them were excommunicated and, eventually, found guilty of heresy and put to death. In 1824, when the independence of most of the nations of Latin America had already been definitely assured, the Pope issued an encyclical to the archbishops and bishops of America, asking them to support the cause of "our very dear son Ferdinand, Catholic King of Spain, whose sublime and solid virtues cause him to place before the splendor of his greatness the luster of religion and the happiness of his subjects."

THE CHURCH CONTROVERSY. Because the church had identified itself so unmistakably with the royalist cause in America, thousands of patriots regarded the representatives of the church as their sworn enemies. They were determined to secure revenge—in some cases by putting priests to death but in all cases by stripping the church of its lands and prerogatives. Had the church been a purely political institution, such plans would doubtless have encountered very little opposition, but the church was not solely or even primarily political. In the minds of many other patriots it was the sole repository of spiritual truth and the keeper of the keys of the Kingdom of God. This group, admitting readily enough that the church had been on the losing side and regretting the indiscretion, preferred to forget the whole matter as speedily as possible and leave the church's power as great as before.

Here, certainly, was the basis for a bitter controversy, and it became extremely bitter in nearly every nation of Latin America. The conservatives lined up in support of the church, and the liberals united against it. Clericalism became the issue in hotly contested elections; it furnished the excuse, if not always the reason, for bloody revolutions. When the liberals won, they usually confiscated church properties, secularized education, and refused further appropriations from the public treasury for the support of the church. When the conservatives triumphed, they commonly restored church lands, put education once more under religious control, and made additional public appropriations for the maintenance of church activities.

The pendulum often swung from one extreme to the other within a few years. In some countries of Latin America it still does. Mexico is now experiencing an era of religious toleration, after a period of persecution marked by such extremes as the requirement, in one state, that every priest must be over forty *and a married man*. Argentina is governed at present by a strongly pro-church group, which has set out to restore to the clergy an influence long denied to them. Compulsory religious instruction, removed from the school curriculum many decades ago, has now been replaced.

On the other hand, a few countries have approached the religious problem with wisdom and tolerance. They have separated church and state, but without depriving the church of all its means of support. Brazil adopted such a policy as long ago as 1890. The church was permitted to retain its extensive land holdings and was exempted from the payment of taxes on property actually used for religious purposes. Thus conservative opposition was lessened to such measures as the secularization of education and the marriage ceremony. In Uruguay, which disestablished the church in 1919, the people promptly subscribed to a large popular endowment fund in order that church revenues should not be materially reduced by loss of government support.[12]

The United States, fortunately, has largely escaped the religious issue in politics. There have been some examples of religious prejudice, of course, but they have been kept to a minimum. The major political parties have not divided on the issue of what to do with the church. Instead, they have agreed that all churches should be equal before the law. No other policy would be expedient in this country because no one faith can claim the allegiance of more than a small percentage of the entire population. Neither Catholics nor Methodists nor Presbyterians nor Baptists can hope to achieve for their sect the status of an official religion; the united opposition would be overwhelming. But in Latin America, when the question of a state religion is raised, no one has to ask "Which religion?" It is Roman Catholicism or none.

* * * * * *

Here, then, is the pattern of Latin American politics. But the pattern is woven from many different threads—twenty of them, to be exact. Let us consider each one separately. First, Argentina.

SELECTED REFERENCES

Arciniegas, Germán, *The State of Latin America*, New York, Knopf, 1950.

Beals, Carleton, *Lands of the Dawning Morrow*, Indianapolis, Bobbs-Merrill, 1948.

———, *Rio Grande to Cape Horn*, Boston, Houghton Mifflin, 1943.

Beals, Carleton, *et al.*, *What the South Americans Think of Us*, New York, McBride, 1945.

Bemis, Samuel F., *The Latin American Policy of the United States*, New York, Harcourt, Brace, 1943.

Blanshard, Paul, *Democracy and Empire in the Caribbean*, New York, Macmillan, 1949.

[12] The church controversy is ably discussed in J. Lloyd Mecham's *Church and State in Latin America*.

Brown, Harriett M., and Helen M. Bailey, *Our Latin American Neighbors*, Boston, Houghton Mifflin, 1944.

Christensen, Asher N., ed., *The Evolution of Latin American Government: A Book of Readings*, New York, Holt, 1951.

Davis, Harold E., *Government and Politics of Latin America*, Washington, D.C., American University, 1950.

———, *Makers of Democracy in Latin America*, New York, Wilson, 1945.

Dunne, Peter M., *A Padre Views South America*, Milwaukee, Bruce, 1945.

Fitzgibbon, Russell H., ed., *Constitutions of Latin America*, Chicago, Univ. of Chicago Press, 1948.

Gordon, Wendell C., *The Economy of Latin America*, New York, Columbia University Press, 1950.

Guerra Iniguez, Daniel, *La Revolución Americana*, Caracas, Editorial Avila Gráfica, 1949.

Hanson, Simon, *Economic Development in Latin America*, Washington, D.C., American Affairs Press, 1951.

Horn, Paul V., *Latin American Trade and Economics*, New York, Prentice-Hall, 1949.

Howard, George P., *Religious Liberty in Latin America?*, Philadelphia, Westminster Press, 1944.

Humphrey, John T. P., *The Inter-American System*, Toronto, Macmillan Co. of Canada, 1942.

James, Preston E., *Latin America*, rev. ed., New York, Odyssey Press, 1950.

Josephs, Ray, *Latin America: Continent in Crisis*, New York, Random House, 1948.

Mecham, J. Lloyd, *Church and State in Latin America*, Chapel Hill, N.C., Univ. of North Carolina Press, 1934.

Prewett, Virginia, *The Americas and Tomorrow*, New York, Dutton, 1944.

Privitera, Joseph F., *The Latin American Front*, Milwaukee, Bruce, 1945.

Quintanilla, Luis, *A Latin American Speaks*, Macmillan, 1943.

Rippy, J. Fred, *Historical Evolution of Latin America*, 3rd ed., New York, Crofts, 1945.

Sands, William F., and Joseph M. Lalley, *Our Jungle Diplomacy*, Chapel Hill, N.C., Univ. of North Carolina Press, 1944.

Schurz, William L., *Latin America: A Descriptive Survey*, rev. ed., New York, Dutton, 1949.

Severin, Kurt, and Lenore Sorsby, *To the South*, New York, Duell, Sloan & Pearce, 1944.

Soule, George H., *et al.*, *Latin America in the Future World*, New York, Farrar & Rinehart, 1945.

Stuart, Graham H., *Latin America and the United States*, 4th ed., New York, Appleton-Century, 1943.

Whitaker, Arthur P., *The United States and South America: The Northern Republics*, Cambridge, Mass., Harvard Univ. Press, 1948.

Wilgus, A. Curtis, ed., *The Caribbean at Mid-Century*, Gainesville, University of Florida Press, 1951.

Wythe, George, *Industry in Latin America*, rev. ed., New York, Columbia Univ. Press, 1949.

CHAPTER 2

ARGENTINA
The Rise of Democracy

The Land and the People

ARGENTINA is the leading nation of Latin America. It has more motor cars, more miles of railroads, more radios, more telephones, more bank deposits than any of the other countries. Its exports have a considerably higher value. Its people have a much higher living standard than the people of almost any other Latin American country. It is the principal agricultural nation, the leader in livestock, and the most highly developed in manufacturing. It boasts of the largest city. Moreover, the Argentine rate of illiteracy is much lower than that of almost any other part of Latin America. The mortality record is considerably better than that of France or Italy, and compares not unfavorably with that of Great Britain or the United States.[1]

AREA AND POPULATION. Argentina is not a large country. It has one million square miles to Brazil's three million. It is exceeded in population by both Brazil and Mexico. Brazil, in fact, has nearly three times as many people as Argentina. But the Argentine Republic's eighteen millions are alert, wide-awake, progressive. They work harder, play harder, accomplish more than most other Latin Americans. Their neighbors often refer to them as the "Yankees of the South," and though the phrase is not intended as a compliment, it does indicate the driving power of the Argentine people.

[1] See the second edition of *Geografía Económica y Política Argentina*, by Lorenzo Dagnino Pastore. See also Austin F. Macdonald's *Government of the Argentine Republic*, Chap. I.

CHARACTER OF THE POPULATION. One factor that makes Argentina very different from most of Latin America is the character of its population. *It is a white nation.* By way of contrast, considerably more than half of the people of Brazil have Indian or Negro blood in their veins. Not more than ten per cent of the people of Mexico are of pure white stock, and very nearly the same percentage applies to Venezuela, Colombia, Peru, Ecuador, and many another Latin American republic. In Argentina, however, only about three per cent of the people have Indian blood. There are virtually no Negroes.

The Argentine Republic was not always white. Its people were a mixed race during the colonial era, and well into the nineteenth century. The gauchos, those hardy cowboys of the *pampa,* were the descendants of Spanish conquerors and Indian women. When Charles Darwin visited Argentina in 1833, he commented upon the blending of the races and the comparative scarcity of white blood.[2] But the years since Darwin's visit have been years of great European immigration. The white race has taken Argentina for its own. The greatest tide of immigration came between 1885 and the outbreak of the First World War—the very years when immigration to the United States was also at its peak. After the war it continued at a more moderate pace until the depression years of the thirties, when it was slowed to a mere trickle by a combination of economic forces and restrictive Argentine immigration. But Argentine policy has changed recently in this regard. The welcome sign is out once more for large numbers of European immigrants, and the announced goal is a population of forty millions within a very few years.[3]

The Italians. As might be expected, Spanish stock predominates, but many Argentines—perhaps one third of all the people in the country—are of Italian ancestry. At the turn of the present century many Italians used to make the long voyage from their homeland to Argentina just to aid in harvesting the wheat crop. Their expectation was to return home after the harvest, and many of them did so. But many others liked the new country so well that they stayed on, or returned later as immigrants. Today, therefore, Italian influence is everywhere. It is evident in the names of the people, the food they eat, and the way they speak. Argentina has been described as an American nation financed with British capital, and peopled

[2] *Journal of Researches into the Natural History and Geology of the Countries Visited during the Voyage of* H.M.S. Beagle *Round the World,* Vol. I, p. 85.

[3] There is a good discussion of the character of the Argentine population in A. E. Bunge's *Una Nueva Argentina,* Chap. VI.

Latin American Standards of Living
As Reflected in the Number of Telephones per 1,000 Persons

Mexico

CENTRAL AMERICA

Costa Rica

Guatemala

Honduras

Nicaragua

Panama

El Salvador

ISLANDS OF THE CARIBBEAN

Cuba

Dominican Republic

Haiti

NORTHERN SOUTH AMERICA

Colombia

Venezuela

WEST COAST OF SOUTH AMERICA

Bolivia

Chile

Ecuador

Peru

EAST COAST OF SOUTH AMERICA

Argentina

Brazil

Paraguay

Uruguay

And, by way of comparison, the
UNITED STATES

Based on the most recent estimate of the American Telephone and Telegraph Company, as published in the *World Almanac*.

with Italians who speak bad Spanish.   There is more than a little truth in this observation.

It must not be supposed, however, that the Italians form a completely alien element in the population, as they have so often done in the large cities of the United States.   There are no "little Italys" in Argentina.   The Italians find the Argentines very much like themselves, and they blend readily with the general population.   Second-generation Italians are not Italian; they are Argentine.   In the United States we often speak of Italian-Americans and German-Americans, but almost never do we hear of English-Americans, despite the vast number of persons of English stock. The English have been thoroughly assimilated.   The situation is similar with the Italians of Argentina.

The British.   British influence in the Argentine Republic is out of all proportion to the number of Britishers who live there.   This is all the more surprising when we understand that the Anglo-Argentines consider themselves a race apart—exiles in a foreign land.   They may marry Argentine women; some of them do.   But they continue their British habits and traditions, and carefully instill them in the younger generation.   If they can afford it, they send their children "home" to school in England. They speak Spanish with an English accent, and, it must be confessed, English with a Spanish accent.

The ties that bind Britain and the Argentine Republic are primarily economic.   British investments in Argentina totaled about two billion dollars at the outbreak of the Second World War.   They were cut drastically during the six years of war, as the British desperately liquidated their foreign holdings in order to meet the stupendous cost of maintaining their victorious armed forces.   But many factories, stores, and refrigerator plants are still British-owned; so were many street car lines until 1943, and most of the railroads until 1947.   The British are still good customers for Argentine beef, despite recent arguments over beef prices.   They supply the Argentine market with cotton and woolens; coal, iron, and steel; machinery, chemicals, papers.   Britons fondly (and smugly) refer to Argentina as "the other Dominion." [4]

The Germans.   Like the English, the Argentine Germans also have tended to cling to their own culture and traditions.   They publish their own newspapers in their own language and stubbornly resist all attempts at "Argentinization."   Numerically they are not very important, but they

[4] The story of the British in Argentina is well told by Ysabel F. Rennie in *The Argentine Republic*, pp. 230–265.

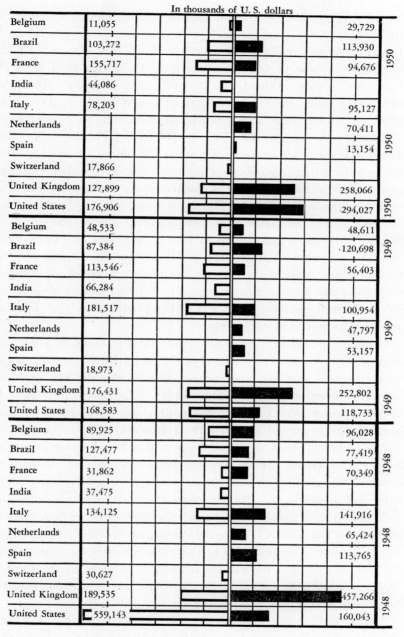

IMPORTS   EXPORTS

In thousands of U. S. dollars

Country	Imports	Exports	Year
Belgium	11,055	29,729	1950
Brazil	103,272	113,930	1950
France	155,717	94,676	1950
India	44,086		1950
Italy	78,203	95,127	1950
Netherlands		70,411	1950
Spain		13,154	1950
Switzerland	17,866		1950
United Kingdom	127,899	258,066	1950
United States	176,906	294,027	1950
Belgium	48,533	48,611	1949
Brazil	87,384	120,698	1949
France	113,546	56,403	1949
India	66,284		1949
Italy	181,517	100,954	1949
Netherlands		47,797	1949
Spain		53,157	1949
Switzerland	18,973		1949
United Kingdom	176,431	252,802	1949
United States	168,583	118,733	1949
Belgium	89,925	96,028	1948
Brazil	127,477	77,419	1948
France	31,862	70,349	1948
India	37,475		1948
Italy	134,125	141,916	1948
Netherlands		65,424	1948
Spain		113,765	1948
Switzerland	30,627		1948
United Kingdom	189,535	457,266	1948
United States	559,143	160,043	1948

Argentine Trade with Principal Countries

Based on figures from *Foreign Commerce Yearbook, 1950*, a 1952 publication of the United
States Department of Commerce.

are largely concentrated in two sections—the northeastern territory of Misiones, where they mingle freely with German colonists just across the border in Brazil; and the southern lake district, where their Chilean neighbors are also of German extraction. These two areas are really Germanic "islands" in the Argentine "sea"; the inhabitants still maintain their own schools, where their small fry are taught the glories of Germanic literature and Germanic arms. Just before and during the Second World War they were taught the glories of Hitler and National Socialism. Hitler-type youth organizations flourished. "Cultural" societies for their elders attracted large numbers of persons. Not all German-Argentines accepted this propaganda, some of them speaking out earnestly and often against Hitler and his kind. There was a strongly anti-Nazi German-language newspaper published in Buenos Aires. But no one can doubt that strong pressure was exerted to force all Germans into line. When democratically minded Argentines in the national Chamber of Deputies finally became aware of the situation and made a thorough investigation, they uncovered an extensive propaganda machine, with its headquarters in the German embassy, which was flooding the country with pro-Nazi truths, half-truths, and whole lies.[5]

In the decade before the war Germany managed to obtain a very substantial slice of Argentine trade, chiefly through barter agreements that very effectively shut out other nations. Then came the war years and the almost complete ruin of German industry and commerce. More recently, however, West Germany has made a determined effort to regain some of the lost ground, though without great success.

The French. The Argentines have a deep and abiding admiration for France. French has always been the second language of cultured Argentines, though English now threatens to replace it. Paris has always been their second home. The wealthiest families have sent their children to France to be educated, and frequently they have followed their children, establishing fine residences along the Parisian boulevards. Poorer Argentines may never have been able to earn enough money for a trip abroad, but they, too, know of the wonders of France. They believe that French literature is the highest form of literature, and that French art is the last word in art.

The fall of France in 1940 was a tragic event for Argentina. It was bemoaned in high homes and low. And when Paris was finally liberated in

---

[5] See Roland H. Sharp's *South America Uncensored*, pp. 9–27. See also Hubert Herring's *Good Neighbors*, pp. 67–78.

August of 1944, Buenos Aires had such a celebration as it had seldom witnessed in all the years of its history. The officials of the military clique, then ruling Argentina with an iron hand, were determined to suppress any such demonstration, lest the cheers for French democracy be transformed into a protest against the lack of democracy at home. The police were ordered to enforce strictly the decrees against unauthorized processions and speeches, and they carried out those orders by riding their horses into the crowds, knocking down men, women, and children indiscriminately. Even tear gas was used. One cartoonist for a Mexico City newspaper captioned his drawing: "Paris has fallen, but the fighting continues in the streets—of Buenos Aires." The people of Buenos Aires were undaunted, however. They filled the downtown thoroughfares, the bars, restaurants, and motion picture theaters, singing the "Marseillaise." French flags were everywhere. Such enthusiasm would have been aroused by the liberation of no other capital—not London or Madrid or Rome, and certainly not Washington or Berlin or Moscow.

Yet the attachment to France is largely sentimental. France has never been one of the two or three leading customers of Argentina, except for a very short period during the unsettled years that followed the Second World War. Frenchmen form but a small part of the population, and they have never attempted a systematic drive to spread their culture. They are content to let it speak for itself.

The Americans. The number of Americans in Argentina is exceedingly small, but American investments are substantial. American firms dominate or play an important role in such industries as meat packing, chemicals, tires. Some of the public utilities are in American hands. We supply motor cars, agricultural and other machinery, dyes, and paints—to mention only a few of the more important items in a long list. American products are always in favor with the buying public.

But, though we export so much to Argentina, we do not begin to meet the Argentine demand for American products. The Argentine government determinedly restricts imports of United States goods, because it cannot pay for larger quantities without going into debt. The truth of the matter is that we do not buy enough from Argentina. Its chief export products, beef and wheat, are directly competitive with our own, and we have no intention of permitting them to enter our markets on equal terms. We have, in fact, absolutely prohibited the importation of fresh Argentine beef. The Argentines, who are very sensitive, resent this treatment bitterly. They say, with reason, that Argentine beef is as fine as any in the world; and they imply that our prohibition is based on the fear that we cannot compete with meat of such high quality. The usual reply of United States officials to this charge is that some Argentine cattle are afflicted with the dread hoof-and-mouth disease and that the only way we can protect ourselves is to impose an embargo on all Argentine beef. The Argentines admit readily enough that some of their animals are diseased, but they contend that there are large areas of the republic in which there is no trace of the malady. So, they ask, why should beef from these areas be excluded from the United States? They have even proposed that a fact-finding commission be appointed to determine the regions that might safely be regarded as disease-free. To date, however, these proposals have accomplished exactly nothing. The political influence of American cattle-men has been too great. In all probability the Argentines do not really think that they could sell a great deal of meat in the United States even if the embargo were removed. They doubtless understand that high tariff and freight rates would prove virtually insurmountable barriers even under the most favorable circumstances. But with them it is a matter of principle. They view with indignation our official viewpoint that Argentine beef, which is consumed with great eagerness by millions of Europeans, is nonetheless unfit for human consumption.

There are, of course, some Argentine products that we can and do buy. We take considerable quantities of flaxseed, tung oil, wool, hides, and skin, as well as quebracho extract, which is used in tanning. These articles are important, but they cannot replace beef and wheat in the Argentine economy.

The United States is not really popular in any Latin American nation, but its unpopularity reaches a peak in Argentina. The Argentines say that we are aggressive, materialistic, and immoral. They point to our nineteenth-century expansion at the expense of Mexico and our twentieth-century intervention in the affairs of a number of Caribbean countries as conclusive evidence that we are a giant octopus—"the octopus of the North" —reaching out great tentacles to crush every nation that happens to lie across our path of empire. They talk bitterly about our worship of money and our preoccupation with the things that money can buy. They say that we have no appreciation of the things of the spirit—that we are interested in motor cars and bathtubs and night clubs and cocktail bars to the exclusion of art and literature and music. They say that we are too busy making money to understand the art of gracious and leisurely living. And they base their charge of immorality chiefly on our high divorce rate and the freedom that we allow our women. Some of these Argentine ideas about us have at least a measure of truth. Some are based entirely on misunderstanding. But no matter how accurate or inaccurate they may be, they all play a part in shaping Argentine–United States relations.[6]

THE CLIMATE AND THE LAND SYSTEM. Argentina is a temperate-zone nation. There are only two other countries of Latin America—Chile and Uruguay—that do not lie wholly or largely within the tropics, and neither of them has the land, the people, or the resources to be a leader in Latin American affairs. But Argentina has the land, the people, and the resources, and its location in the temperate zone gives it a great advantage over its tropical neighbors. Its great *pampa* or central plain, well-watered and highly fertile, provides an ideal home for many millions of persons. Its sugar and tobacco lands in the north and its sheep country in the south, though not so attractive as the *pampa,* are well able to support millions of others. In fact, there would be no land problem in Argentina if the land were distributed in a reasonably equitable manner. But there has never been a serious attempt to make such a distribution, although the government has taken some halting steps during the last four or five years. It has expropriated some tracts of land, with suitable compensation, and has sold them to landless workers, to the applause of the government-controlled press. But these expropriations seem to have been political rather than economic, and they have been carried out on such a small scale as to leave the picture virtually unchanged. Land is still concentrated in the hands of a comparatively few families. Some of them own vast empires. Properties of less than twenty-five hundred acres are the exception in the richest agricultural section of the nation, and not even one third of the farming families of the nation own the lands they till.

Perhaps the worst feature of the land system is the tendency of the rich proprietors to abandon their *estancias* for the great metropolis of Buenos Aires or even for the pleasure resorts of Europe, leaving paid overseers in charge. The natural result is that these owners lose interest in the land and its development, except to the extent that it can be made to yield still larger profits. Because so much of the land is in a few hands, agricultural immigrants have found great difficulty in securing suitable farms. Most of them must work as tenants.[7]

[6] See Luis Quintanilla's interesting little volume, *A Latin American Speaks.*
[7] See Miguel A. Cárcano's comprehensive work, *Evolución Histórica del Régimen de la Tierra Pública.* See also Carl C. Taylor's more recent work, *Rural Life in Argentina.*

Until less than a decade ago the great landowners were Argentina's un-challenged ruling class. They dominated the nation—economically, so-cially, politically. They developed strains of the world's finest cattle; they grew wheat and corn and linseed; and their financial reward was almost fabulous. At one time they had almost a monopoly on higher education. Their sons, and sometimes their daughters, studied at the national uni-versities of Buenos Aires, La Plata, Córdoba, and Tucumán, and at the Sorbonne and Oxford and Cambridge. They set the social standards of the nation, and rigidly excluded from their little group all persons not be-longing to the landholding elite. Not unnaturally, they used their great influence to shape the course of Argentine public policy, both foreign and domestic. Everything was done for beef and wheat; little or nothing was done to encourage the development of manufacturing.

DEVELOPMENT OF INDUSTRY. Despite the long-time policy of govern-mental neglect, which only recently has been reversed, manufacturing be-came increasingly important from the very first years of the present cen-tury. Today more than half of the wage earners of the republic are employed in industrial establishments, and more than half of the taxable in-comes are derived from industry. This is a far cry from the Argentina of half a century ago, when even flour was imported because there was no way of transforming the country's wheat into bread.

It must be understood, however, that much of the manufacturing is directly related to agriculture. Meat-packing plants handle the livestock as it is brought in from the *estancias*. Other industrial establishments take the products of the soil, and transform them into food, beverages, textiles, and chemicals. Until very recently there was almost no heavy industry, and even today heavy industry labors under a great handicap because Ar-gentina has only low-grade supplies of coal, and almost no readily accessible iron. But recent governments have decreed that, as a part of the program of national defense, the nation must make its own planes and tanks, re-gardless of cost. So some planes and tanks have actually been made in Argentine factories.[8]

The development of industry has, of course, brought with it the growth of a large class of industrial laborers. Many of them are highly skilled, and earn reasonably good wages. Their sons sometimes attend the uni-versities, and become physicians or lawyers. More of the workmen are semiskilled or unskilled, however, and their wages reflect that fact. Yet

[8] George Wythe, *Industry in Latin America*, rev. ed., pp. 83–122.

they are much better off than larger numbers of their countrymen, who still work for almost nominal wages under semifeudal conditions in the vineyards of Mendoza or the sugar plantations of Tucumán. Labor unions have attracted many members, but they have never become a major force in Argentine politics. Lacking the legal advantages bestowed upon American labor unions, they have never been able to make such an impressive showing for their members. Yet labor is a great potential force, as Juan Perón realized when he seized control of the unions and turned them to his own purposes.

INFLUENCE OF BUENOS AIRES. Anyone who would understand the intricacies of Argentine life must understand that there are two Argentinas—Buenos Aires and the interior. There are, in fact, two areas that go by the name Buenos Aires—the national capital, a great metropolis with a population of more than three million and most of the nation's wealth; and the adjoining province of which it was once a part. It might be added that the province of Buenos Aires has far more than its share of the wealth not concentrated in the capital itself. Its crop and pasture lands are the richest of any province in the nation; its density of population is the greatest; its literacy rate is the highest; its motor cars are the most numerous. Between them, therefore, the province and the city of Buenos Aires dominate Argentina.

The city itself is a magnificent center of civilization, able—and willing—to boast of its fine hotels and homes, its theaters and art galleries and museums. It has almost a strangle hold on the country's imports and a firm control of its exports. Nearly one third of all Argentines live within its borders or in neighboring suburbs. Here, too, is most of the industry. Argentines from the provinces regard this great concentration of population and wealth with something akin to dismay. They often say: "The head is too big for the body." President Perón has announced his intention of decentralizing industry and thus weakening the power of the metropolis. But neither Perón nor anyone else has been able to accomplish this aim.

The struggle for power between Buenos Aires (city and province) and the rest of the nation has had a profound influence upon the whole course of Argentine history. It has inspired countless orators to deliver countless perorations; it has led to bloodshed and even to civil war. In 1880 this struggle was finally decided, to the extent that any such decision can ever be said to be final. The capital city was taken from the province of

Buenos Aires and placed directly under the control of the national government. But the game for economic power still continues, with the metropolis holding most of the cards.[9]

Here, then, is a brief sketch of some of the more significant forces that underlie Argentine politics. Let us now observe the swiftly moving political scene.

The Democratic Era

SÁENZ PEÑA: *Early career.* The story of modern Argentina, politically speaking, may well be dated from 1909. In that year a scholarly statesman with a long record of public service was nominated for the presidency by a Conservative coalition. His name was Roque Sáenz Peña. He had, in fact, been nominated for the presidency eighteen years earlier, when he was only forty years of age. But at that time he had learned that his father was to be the choice of a rival group, and, rather than run in opposition, he had withdrawn his candidacy. Later he served his country in Spain and Italy. He was in Italy when he received word that he had again been given the presidential nomination; he promptly resigned his position as minister and returned home to conduct his campaign for election.

Government by the Conservatives. In the early twentieth century Argentina's political campaigns were never decided on the basis of broad issues of public policy. The Conservatives owned the country body and soul, and not for a moment did they weaken their grip. They were the large landowners, together with their political satellites, working always for their own interest in the smug belief that their welfare and the welfare of Argentina were synonymous. Occasionally they might disagree violently with one another over certain issues or candidates, but they were always in complete agreement concerning their class rights and privileges. To be sure, an opposition party—the Radical Civic Union—had been formed in 1890 to represent the growing liberal element in the Argentine population. Despite its name this group was not radical. It was just about dead center politically, and it represented the new middle class. Its primary aim was honest government—certainly a reasonable goal but one very difficult of achievement in Argentina in those days. In fact, dishonesty had beaten the U.C.R. (*Unión Cívica Radical*) time after time, despite its strong and constantly increasing popular appeal. There was

---

[9] See A. E. Bunge's previously cited work, Chap. X.

also a Socialist Party, which had been organized in 1896 but had consistently failed to gain many adherents except among the workers of the city of Buenos Aires.

Triumph of Sáenz Peña. By the year 1909, when the Conservatives nominated Roque Sáenz Peña, liberal sentiment was strong in Argentina. Many persons went so far as to declare that the U.C.R. could win an honest election. But no one went so far as to claim that the election would be honest. Never in the whole history of the country had there been an election free from fraud. And the Conservatives saw no reason to alter the situation. They were determined to hang on to power by fair means or foul. The U.C.R., seemingly, could not shake their grip. It had tried every device within its power—propaganda, political strategy, even revolution—without success.

It was at this time that Sáenz Peña began to fill his campaign speeches with ringing denunciations of fraudulent elections and promises of electoral reforms that would put control of the government in the hands of the people. No one, apparently, took him seriously—least of all the members of his own party. They assumed that no one in his right mind would really interfere with the means of his own rise to power. Had not the same promises been made in other elections, only to be conveniently forgotten when the echoes of the campaign had died away? This election, they thought, would be no different from the others. But they reckoned without their candidate. Dr. Sáenz Peña was not only a scholar, he was also a gentleman; and when he gave a promise he kept it. As soon as he had attained the presidency—by force and fraud, to be sure—he set about the task of modifying the vicious electoral law. He entrusted to his minister of the interior the task of framing the kind of legislation that he deemed essential to honest elections. This legislation included provisions for a secret ballot, which had never been used in Argentina, and for a new registry of voters. Minorities were to be represented for the first time, and voting was to be compulsory. When this bill was introduced in Congress, which had overwhelming Conservative majorities in both houses, it met with bitter opposition. Conservative congressmen were understandably averse to enacting a law that might well spell their own ruin at the next election. Such was the power of the President, however, that they finally did his bidding.

The Radicals were jubilant, though their happiness was tempered by a "wait-and-see" skepticism. The new policy of the government seemed too good to be true. Yet the Radical leaders could see no harm in taking the

President at his word. They abandoned their plans for revolution. They also told their adherents to vote. This was a complete reversal of policy, for they had boycotted every election held in the past twenty years. The first test of the President's good intentions, and of Radical strength, was the Buenos Aires municipal election of 1912. The U.C.R. easily won a majority of the seats in the council. This event so shocked the Conservatives, who had been fighting among themselves as usual, that they united in the province of Santa Fe to oppose the candidacy of an obscure country doctor who was seeking the governorship on the Radical ticket. The doctor was elected by a substantial majority. Thus the people learned for the first time that it was possible to elect to public office men who did not bear the endorsement of the first families.

Death of Sáenz Peña. In October, 1913, President Sáenz Peña became seriously ill. He surrendered his authority to the Vice-President, Dr. Victorino de la Plaza, and moved to the country to regain his health. By the middle of the following July he had improved sufficiently to justify hope of a complete recovery, and he even made plans to assume the presidency. But he had a sudden relapse, and died on August 9, 1914. The leaders of the U.C.R. were greatly distressed. They knew that a word from the new President, de la Plaza, would suffice to initiate a fresh campaign of fraud and violence, in which the Radical gains would probably be lost. But de la Plaza never spoke the word. To his credit it must be recorded that he enforced the new election law faithfully and conducted himself with scrupulous impartiality during the campaign to choose his successor.

Irigoyen: *Election of 1916.* There were several presidential candidates, but by far the most important was a tall, swarthy politician, sixty-six years of age, whose name was Hipólito Irigoyen. He had long been the acknowledged leader of the Radicals, and everyone assumed that he would be their candidate in the 1916 campaign. But he had said repeatedly that he did not wish the presidency. Perhaps he meant what he said; more probably he felt that a certain reluctance would strengthen his position. In any event he declined the nomination when the convention of the U.C.R. offered it to him. But the convention refused to take no for an answer, and finally Irigoyen consented.

He was the idol of the masses, and by far the strongest candidate that his party could have selected. Like every strong man, however, he had numerous enemies. Some of them, within his own party, were so incensed at his nomination that they bolted the party ticket. Irigoyen won the election, nonetheless, though by a very slim margin. On October 12, 1916, he was inaugurated president of Argentina—the first president ever to be chosen in a free election. The people left no doubt as to how they felt. They unhitched the horses from his carriage as soon as he entered it, and pulled it through the streets of Buenos Aires in a triumphant procession.

Neutrality in First World War. After the political honeymoon, however, President Irigoyen found himself faced with many disturbing problems. For one thing, he had to decide what attitude Argentina would take in the European War. Germany was sinking Argentine ships, and there were many Argentines who believed that their country should cast its lot with France and England. After the United States and Brazil entered the conflict and the European war became a world war, the pressure for Argentine participation on the side of the Allies became almost irresistible. But Irigoyen managed to resist it. His argument was that a neutral Argentina could contribute more to the cause of peace than an Argentina at war—and that, moreover, it could be much more prosperous. Whether Argentine neutrality actually contributed anything to a peaceful world may perhaps be doubted, but that it stimulated Argentine prosperity is beyond question.

Labor problems. In the domestic economy the problem of labor was the biggest question mark. Conservative governments had never tried to do very much for the masses, though they had adopted certain parts of a broad labor code that had been proposed in 1904. With Irigoyen it was a very different story. He owed his election in no small measure to labor votes, and labor expected to be suitably rewarded. In this it was disappointed. It did indeed receive many of the reforms for which it asked— collective bargaining, public housing projects, the removal of many restrictions on union activity. But Irigoyen refused to identify himself as an exclusively labor man. He was, in fact, more nearly the representative of the middle classes—the professional men and merchants and white-collar workers. He believed in the necessity of maintaining public order; and when a general strike was called in 1919, he permitted the police to interfere, with the result that many persons were killed or injured.

Arbitrary tactics. One of the charges frequently made against Irigoyen was that his acts were arbitrary, ruthless, and at times illegal. The charge was not without foundation. As boss of the U.C.R. he had built up his power by whatever means came to hand, and as president he saw no reason to change his ways. He intervened frequently in provincial affairs, removing provincial officials and replacing them with his own trustworthy subordinates. There was, however, considerable justification for this highhanded procedure. Irigoyen could and did say that he had received a popular mandate from the people for liberal government and that the Conservatives who still controlled many of the provinces were determined not to yield an inch unless forcibly removed from office. So he removed them.

ALVEAR. As the year 1922 approached, and with it the end of Irigoyen's term, he began to ponder the question of a successor. This was necessary, because the constitution of Argentina follows the usual Latin American practice of prohibiting two presidential terms in a row. The man who seemed most suitable was a fifty-four-year-old aristocrat named Marcelo T. de Alvear, whose distinguished family name and vast estates could be forgiven because of his long record of faithful labor for the Radicals. Alvear was in Paris as the ambassador of his country at the time that the finger of fate was placed upon him, but he hastened home to make his bid for popular support. The convention of the U.C.R. had nominated him as a matter of course; no one thought to question the word of the great Irigoyen. Nor did the voters question it. Even the workers, who had been disappointed by Irigoyen's lukewarm support of their cause, rallied around the man he named as his successor. It was obvious that they would have nothing to do with the Conservatives. They might perhaps have voted for the Socialists. Some of them, in fact, did so, but not enough to make socialism a major force in Argentine politics. Argentine socialism had always been an intellectual movement rather than a popular one, and outside of the federal capital it had no great strength.

Alvear became president of his country at almost the same time that Coolidge attained the presidency of the United States. Like Coolidge, he was safe and sane. And, like Coolidge, he had the good fortune to take over the reins of government in an era of unparalleled prosperity. He made reasonable concessions to labor, as Irigoyen had done, but for the most part he tried to please the middle classes. His was a middle-of-the-road policy. It was very much like the policy that Irigoyen had pursued before him, and most persons supposed that the two men would continue to see eye to eye. But in less than two years they had an open break. Alvear said that Irigoyen was a despot, who still tried to run the country though he no longer had the title of president. Irigoyen said that Alvear was a little man with big ideas, who forgot to be grateful for the favor that had been bestowed upon him when he received the presidency. Perhaps both men were right.

IRIGOYEN'S SECOND TERM. In any event a fight to the finish was inevitable.

It occurred in 1928, when Irigoyen indicated that he would like to be president for a second term. He was then seventy-eight years of age and in failing health, but the magic of his name was such that he secured the Radical nomination without much difficulty. Alvear led his followers out of the party and formed the Antipersonalist U.C.R. The name of the new group was somewhat misleading. Its members were not opposed to personalities in politics, but only to the personality of Hipólito Irigoyen. The party name continued in use, however, even after Irigoyen's death. In the 1928 election the Antipersonalists chose a distinguished lawyer named Leopoldo Melo to oppose Irigoyen. The conservatives, who had found the Alvear group reasonably sympathetic to their ideas, endorsed Melo's candidacy. But the people preferred Irigoyen and gave him a large popular majority. The U.C.R. was still the dominant party.

Within a short time, however, the world crisis of 1930 began to affect Argentina. Irigoyen did almost nothing to improve the situation; within a short while it became painfully evident that he was physically and mentally incapable of doing so. He was infirm, and his mind had deteriorated badly. At the age of eighty he was no longer president in anything but name. Meanwhile, a number of his more unscrupulous subordinates proceeded to run the country for their own benefit. They added thousands of their friends and relatives to the public payroll and robbed the public treasury with callous indifference. It was an unpleasant spectacle.

Popular dissatisfaction. As might well have been anticipated, the people began to tire of their onetime idol. Most of them did not know how helpless the man really was, but they did know that matters were going from bad to worse. In the provincial elections of 1930 they elected many candidates who were pledged to oppose the president's policies. At this point the U.C.R. suddenly lost its long-standing enthusiasm for honest elections. It still controlled the Chamber of Deputies—the lower house of the national Congress—and it used this control for the purpose of preventing the seating of the opposition's newly elected members. Properly authenticated credentials were rejected on every conceivable pretext. These political maneuvers wasted a great deal of time. Congress met on May first; four months later it had not completed the preliminary organization necessary to do business. In early August a number of deputies belonging to the opposition party signed the so-called "Manifesto of the Forty-Four," calling attention to the flagrant violations of the law and demanding that the situation be corrected. Still the government did nothing. Meanwhile the nation's exports sank to new lows, and the peso dropped steadily. The ineptitude of those in power could no longer be concealed.

The opposition lost no time in seizing its opportunity. It united its supporters in various patriotic organizations bearing such names as "Republican League" and "May Legion." Talk of revolution was everywhere. In the public press and even on the floor of Congress it was freely declared that only an organized military revolt could save the nation. Even among the leaders of the dominant U.C.R. there were many who realized that a storm must soon break over their heads unless drastic steps were taken to avert it. The Vice-President of the nation, a well-intentioned party wheel horse named Enrique V. Martínez, proposed that the ministers resign in a body, so that they might be replaced by other leaders who possessed the confidence of the people. His suggestion was ignored. The Minister of War then issued a number of decrees that might perhaps have eased the tension, but they were promptly countermanded by the President. Irigoyen was too senile to take decisive action, yet even at this late date he would not permit the necessary steps to be taken by others. When the Minister of War learned that his orders had been rescinded, he submitted his resignation, and Irigoyen accepted it.

These arbitrary acts led to widespread denunciation of the President. Many persons, even among his former ardent supporters, openly declared that he should resign. The students of the universities, who have always played an active part in politics in Argentina as elsewhere in Latin America, organized demonstrations against the government. The police were ordered to break up these meetings and they did so, but only after bloody rioting. Finally President Irigoyen was made to understand the seriousness of the situation. At long last he performed the final act for which the nation had been waiting; he submitted his resignation to Congress. Vice-President Martínez assumed the presidential authority, which he was destined to exercise only a few hours.[10]

THE REVOLUTION: *The plot.* While Irigoyen was being persuaded to resign, the army was quietly preparing its own solution of Argentina's problems. The leader of the plot was General José F. Uriburu, a man with a distinguished record and an even more distinguished ancestry. His uncle had served as president of the nation; his father and grandfather had been governors of the province of Salta. At the age of nineteen he had graduated from the national military college, and had embarked upon a military career. He had been a member of the Supreme War and Navy

---

[10] The Irigoyen era is traced by Ysabel F. Rennie in her previously cited work, pp. 188–228.

Council and the army's first inspector general. Like most of his fellow officers, he was a Conservative and deeply distrustful of Irigoyen's policies, even in the days when the old man was still a popular hero. But he saw no way to restore Conservative control until mid-1930, when the government was obviously crumbling.

The military uprising. The revolution was set for September 6, 1930, and it proceeded on schedule, regardless of the resignation of the now-despised Irigoyen, which had been submitted the preceding afternoon. Troops began to move in the early morning hours. Soon they were pouring into the city of Buenos Aires, well armed and ready for any opposition that might develop. General Uriburu sent a telegram to the Acting President, calling on him to resign. "If you do not," he declared, "I shall hold you responsible for any blood that may be shed." At first it seemed that bloodshed might be entirely avoided. The crowds gathered along the streets were for the most part enthusiastic. They cheered and waved their handkerchiefs; some threw flowers at the marching columns. Though they had no possible way of knowing what the program of the revolutionary government would be, most of them believed that any change from Irigoyen and his cronies would be a change for the better. Later many of them decided that they had been mistaken.

Mob violence. The revolutionary forces met their first real opposition in the Plaza del Congreso, the great square on which the national capitol faces. At this point some loyalist troops opened fire, but their chief accomplishment was the killing and wounding of a considerable number of bystanders. Soon the loyalists were routed, and the revolutionary troops were in complete control of the city. Meanwhile civilian mobs got out of hand. They overturned automobiles and street cars, and sacked a number of hotels, restaurants, and even private homes. Ostensibly their wrath was directed against the Radicals—against hotels and restaurants frequented by Radical politicians, and the houses where they lived. But, as so often happens in such cases, the mobs were not too careful to distinguish between friend and foe. Fortunately, however, they were dispersed without doing a great deal of damage, and order was soon restored.

Overthrow of the government. While the tumult of the revolution was at its worst, Irigoyen fled by motor car to the nearby provincial capital of La Plata, accompanied by his physician and a few friends. Even at this late hour he seems to have believed that all was not lost. If disloyal troops had temporary control of the federal capital, perhaps they would soon be overthrown by his supporters in the provinces. When, however, he reached

La Plata, he discovered to his chagrin that his supporters had apparently vanished into thin air. So he permitted himself to be placed under technical arrest. A little later he was sent to the island of Martín García, in the Plata estuary, where he was kept under guard for seventeen months. By that time a new election had been held, and it was thought safe to release him. He lived quietly until July, 1932, when death mercifully released him from his pain and sorrow.

But let us return to that eventful day of revolution, September 6, 1930. Acting President Martínez received Uriburu's ultimatum in midmorning and immediately went into conference with his advisers. They debated for more than eight hours and finally decided that Martínez should follow Irigoyen's example by resigning. The wisdom of this course was quite apparent, since the government no longer had troops with which to defend itself. So Martínez and his Radical friends moved out of the *Casa Rosada*—Argentina's "pink house," where the presidential offices were located—and Uriburu and his staff moved in. It was all over in less than twenty-four hours. There was, in fact, an attempt at counter-revolution by some of Irigoyen's partisans two days later, but it collapsed almost before it began. As usual, most of the victims were spectators.

URIBURU. From the outset General Uriburu strove to surround his regime with an aura of respectability. It was to be no iron-fisted dictatorship, he explained, but a constitutional government that carefully respected the rights of the people. One of the General's first acts was to issue a manifesto, declaring adherence to the constitution and laws of the land. Unfortunately, however, his deeds did not always match his words. The day after protesting his loyalty to constitutional government he dissolved Congress, thus making himself in effect an unchallenged dictator. But he found no difficulty in explaining this apparent inconsistency. Did not everyone know that Congress was filled with venal politicians? Had not everyone seen Congress brazenly flout the will of the people by refusing to seat deputies who had been honestly elected? Obviously no revolutionary government could permit its reform program to be blocked by such a group of men. The only remedy, as General Uriburu carefully explained to the nation, was to liquidate the Congress that had been so unfaithful to its trust and send its members back to the oblivion they so richly deserved. When the proper time came, he promised, there would be another election for new members of Congress, who would faithfully execute the mandate of the people.

The purge. As it turned out, the members of Congress were not the only ones to lose their jobs. The national administration was systematically purged of all members of the Radical Party in order to make way for deserving Conservatives. General Uriburu might talk as much as he pleased about a government for all the people, but his appointments soon made abundantly clear that his government was for the Conservatives and no one else. Prominent Radicals were persecuted unmercifully. Many were beaten, and some were imprisoned or exiled. The General was determined to stamp out Argentine liberalism.

Preparation for the 1931 election. In fighting liberalism, Uriburu believed that he had the support of the masses. He soon learned his mistake, however, when a Buenos Aires provincial election gave victory to the U.C.R. by a substantial margin. That the Radicals could win an election so soon after they had been discredited was a surprise to all concerned. Radical leaders in all parts of the country began to dream of a return to power, but General Uriburu was determined to shatter that dream at whatever cost and by whatever means. His first step was to declare the election void. Then, fearful of further Radical success, he postponed indefinitely the elections that had been scheduled in a number of other provinces. But there was a presidential election in the offing; it was scheduled for November of 1931. How could the Conservatives be assured of victory at that time? Uriburu would have liked to cancel that election, too, but wiser counsel prevailed, and in the end he agreed to permit it to be held as announced. He did his best to stifle all opposition, however, by systematically eliminating leading contenders from the political scene. The Radicals had already held a convention and selected as their presidential candidate Marcelo de Alvear, who had been chiefly responsible for the establishment of the Antipersonalists four years earlier but was now ready to return to the Radical fold following Irigoyen's downfall and death. As their choice for vice-president the Radicals had named Adolfo Güemes. Thereupon Uriburu declared both candidates ineligible—Alvear, because he had not completed the six years between presidential terms required by the constitution, and Güemes, because he had been too closely associated with the old regime. So the U.C.R. ordered its supporters to boycott the election.

Force or fraud? During its year in office the Uriburu administration had been steadily losing prestige. It had failed to restore prosperity to the nation as it had promised. Exports were still at a low ebb; unemployment was widespread. The government's stock answer to all criticism was to jail its opponents or drive them into exile. Everyone could now see that, despite its loud protestations, the Uriburu regime was not a constitutional government. It was a heavy-handed military oligarchy. Everyone could understand that it was not trying to promote the interests of the masses as it had promised. It was working for the large landholding aristocracy every hour of the day. Even among the Conservatives Uriburu had lost a great deal of prestige. Many of them believed that his methods were entirely too crude. The way to keep control of the government, they argued, was not to suspend elections and throw opposition leaders into jail, but to hold elections and maintain a semblance of honesty, while encouraging sufficient fraud to insure the desired result. That was the traditional Conservative method; it had never failed until Sáenz Peña had foolishly insisted upon an honest election law. Well, Sáenz Peña was in his grave, and his election law, though still on the statute books, could be manipulated to give surprising results in the hands of skillful and unscrupulous officials. So why not use finesse instead of an iron fist? [11]

JUSTO: *Nomination and election.* The leader of the Conservative group favoring fraud instead of force was a retired general named Agustín P. Justo, who had once served as minister of war. He had been a member of the Radical Party, but had followed Alvear into the ranks of the Antipersonalists. Later, when Alvear once more resumed his leadership of the U.C.R., Justo stayed with the Antipersonalists, whose political views were by this time so close to the Conservative party line that the two groups could work together without difficulty. To many Conservatives Justo seemed an ideal choice for president. He was a pleasant, tactful man in the prime of life (fifty-six years of age), reasonably popular with the masses despite his conservative views, and not too much of a militarist. Undoubtedly he wanted to be president. Uriburu was opposed to the Justo candidacy, but his own prestige had reached such a low point that scarcely anyone paid attention to his wishes. When, therefore, the Conservatives met in party convention, they named Agustín Justo as their presidential candidate and Dr. Julio A. Roca as their choice for vice-president. The Antipersonalists had already nominated Justo, though they had made another selection for the vice-presidency. For all practical purposes, therefore, the election was already won. How could anyone hope to defeat General Justo, who had the support of both the Conservatives—or National Democrats, as they now called themselves—and Antipersonalist Radicals, especially in view of the U.C.R.'s decision to boycott the election? It must be recorded, however, that two groups did try to block Justo's election.

[11] Julio A. Quesada, *Orígenes de la Revolución del 6 de Septiembre de 1930.*

They were the Progressive Democrats, a relatively unimportant party of mildly liberal tendencies, and the Socialists. They combined forces to nominate a distinguished liberal for president and a scholarly socialist for vice-president. These two men waged an earnest and dignified campaign but accomplished nothing. How the votes were actually cast in this election will always be a matter of conjecture. There can be no doubt, however, that the Conservatives used every trick of the trade to ensure the victory of their candidates. They bribed some voters, terrorized others into staying away, and arranged for gangs of "repeaters" to travel from polling place to polling place. By such means Agustín Justo became president of Argentina.

Protection of the Conservatives. Once in office, General Justo set out to improve his country's desperate financial condition. He negotiated with Great Britain a treaty virtually guaranteeing large British purchases of Argentine beef. In exchange for this concession the British extracted a heavy price. They secured Argentina's promise to reduce her tariffs on British goods and to turn over a large part of her meat-packing business to British-owned refrigerator plants. These clauses of the treaty were bad news for the United States, whose manufacturers had been capturing a growing share of Argentine business. They were bad news for Argentine manufacturers, also, whose infant industries could scarcely hope to compete with the industries of Great Britain or the United States unless given a considerable measure of protection. But neither President Justo nor any of his intimates really cared what happened to Argentine industry. They were determined to protect the interests of the great Conservative landowners—the beef and wheat kings, who wished to be assured of a good European market for their products. As long as the price of beef and wheat were high, nothing else really mattered.

Labor laws. President Justo was too shrewd a man, however, to suppose that any twentieth-century nation could be run exclusively for the benefit of a single class. If the Conservatives were to remain in power, they must show that their self-interest could be an enlightened self-interest that brought benefits to the poor as well as the rich. With this thought in mind, the President recommended a number of sweeping changes in the labor laws—vacations with pay for workers, compensation for those injured in industrial accidents, protection against arbitrary dismissal. Most of these proposals were enacted into law. But it is interesting to note that they were designed primarily to safeguard the rights of workers in commerce and industry. The agricultural laborers could look for their protection to their masters, the owners of the great *estancias,* just as they had done from earliest times.   And if this protection was something less than adequate—well, after all, what could one expect in the semifeudal economy of rural Argentina?

Increased prosperity.   General Justo proved to be a strong president and, in many respects, a good one.   He strengthened the nation's financial position, consolidating the huge floating debt that the Radicals had permitted to accumulate.   He succeeded in raising the prices of meat and agricultural products by restricting their production.   To all levels of Argentine life he brought an increased measure of prosperity, though it must be admitted that his efforts were greatly aided by the improved tone of world trade.   On the debit side of the ledger must be placed the widespread graft that flourished in high and low places, as well as the systematic election frauds that made a mockery of democratic government.   All things considered, the masses of the people were not greatly impressed with the Justo regime.   Most of them had not voted for him in 1931—the official count to the contrary notwithstanding—and they had no intention of voting for his hand-picked successor in 1937.   They admitted readily enough that the Justo labor program had been a step in the right direction, but most of them regarded it as nothing more than a Conservative trick to win labor votes.[12]

ORTIZ: *Nomination.*   The man picked by General Justo to be the next president of Argentina was a well-known corporation lawyer named Roberto M. Ortiz, who, like Justo, had followed Alvear out of the Radical Party in 1928; also like Justo he had stayed with the Antipersonalists in 1931 instead of returning to the Radical fold.   Under Alvear, Ortiz had been minister of public works; later, under Justo, he had served as minister of finance.   He was sufficiently conservative to satisfy the great landowners who ran the country, but they insisted that since the presidency was to go to an Antipersonalist Radical (who by definition was an ally rather than a member of their own group), the vice-presidency must be given to a member of their own National Democratic Party.   The matter was speedily arranged, and soon the Conservative coalition of National Democrats and Antipersonalists officially named its slate—Roberto M. Ortiz for president and Ramón S. Castillo for vice-president.   Castillo was the dean of the faculty of law of the University of Buenos Aires, a distinguished man whose highly conservative views were generally known.

[12] For contrasting views of the Justo administration, see Ricardo Levene's *History of Argentina,* pp. 514–515, and Ysabel F. Rennie's previously cited work, pp. 258–262.

Election of 1937. The parties opposing the coalition slate had little hope of success, but they went about the business of nominating candidates as seriously as if they really expected to win. The Radical choice for president was obvious—Marcelo de Alvear, the one-time Irigoyen follower, who now held the party in the palm of his hand. He was sixty-nine years of age and his early vigor was gone, yet the masses of the people still had faith in him. They would undoubtedly have elected him if given half a chance. But they never had the smallest fraction of a chance. The Conservatives saw to that. Fraud was the order of the day just as it had been in 1931. All kinds of tricks were used to defeat the popular will. Leaders of the U.C.R. were "quarantined" on suspicion of harboring the germs of yellow fever, and kept safely out of the way until after election day, when it was discovered that the yellow fever scare was all a mistake. Thousands of voters suspected of liberal tendencies were deprived of their enrolment booklets, without which they could not establish their identity at the polling places. When the news was released that Ortiz had won the election, the people were disgusted but not particularly surprised. What else could have been expected, as long as the Conservatives were in a position to count the votes?

Restoration of honest government. President Ortiz was inaugurated on February 20, 1938. Six months later he began to use his influence strongly for honest elections. He wrote a letter to one provincial governor indicating that electoral frauds would no longer be tolerated, and shortly afterward he annulled a local election that obviously had ignored the popular will. Such tactics aroused the entire nation. The Conservatives foresaw a possible end to their regime, and the Radicals recognized the possibility of returning to power. Both groups were anxious to know whether Ortiz really meant what he said. Was he another Sáenz Peña, elected by fraud but determined to restore honest government? Apparently he was. He intervened in province after province, setting aside all elections that were tainted with dishonesty. Several of his cabinet ministers resigned in protest against such "disloyalty" to the Conservative cause, and were replaced with men who had a higher regard for free elections.

The natural result of the President's policy was a resurgence of activity within the Radical Party. Party leaders worked feverishly to elect their candidates, and with marked success. By 1940 there were enough Radical members of the national Chamber of Deputies to outvote the Conservatives. In the Senate the Conservatives still had a substantial majority, because senators served for six years, with only one third of their membership chosen every other year. But time was with the Radicals. They could afford to wait. In four years at most they would again have control of the government, barring a very unkind blow of fate.

Ortiz and Castillo. In the first months of 1940 the unkind blow of fate fell. It came in the form of a serious illness, which eventually forced Ortiz to relinquish the powers of the presidency. The man had been diabetic for many years; finally his eyesight began to fail. It went rapidly from bad to worse, until he was totally incapable of performing the functions of his office. And yet for a time he clung desperately to his job, not because he loved power but because he feared that Vice-President Castillo would hand the country back to the Conservatives and use fraud to restore them to power. There is, however, a limit to human endurance. By July of 1940 Roberto Ortiz knew that he could go on no longer. On the third day of that month he signed a decree surrendering his authority, and Castillo took over. He lost no time in justifying the worst fears of Ortiz and his Radical friends. He interfered systematically in provincial elections, just as Ortiz had done, but for the purpose of preventing honest elections instead of guaranteeing them. He replaced the cabinet ministers who had been loyal to Ortiz with men of his own stripe. The Conservatives were on top again, and the trick had been turned without firing a shot.

Death of Ortiz. The Radicals were understandably loath to admit that all was lost. After all, Ortiz was still president of the nation. Perhaps he could recover from his illness, regain his eyesight, and assume the presidency once more. Prominent eye specialists were summoned to the President's bedside, but they advised against an operation on the ground that the state of his health would not permit it. The Senate, top-heavy with Conservatives, appointed a committee to ascertain the possibility that Ortiz might make a return from darkness, and the committee report indicated that no such return was possible. The committee members were probably determined to reach this conclusion regardless of the facts; but there can be little doubt that they told the truth. Even a famous eye specialist sent by President Roosevelt to examine the stricken man concurred in the opinion that nothing could be done. In the middle of 1942 Roberto Ortiz died. In a way his death came as an anticlimax. He had lost his fight two years earlier.

ARGENTINE NEUTRALITY. But let us return to 1939, when President Ortiz was still the master of his fate and of his nation. The march of the German armies into Poland, followed by the outbreak of a general European war, brought many problems for Argentina. Ortiz decided that his country would solve those problems as a neutral, and there was little disagreement with this policy. The people of Argentina, like the people of the United States, were prosperous and contented in 1939, and not at all disposed to participate in a quarrel that seemed to be none of their business. They had remained neutral during the First World War and prospered greatly as a result. Perhaps this new war would bring an increased demand and higher prices for Argentine beef and wheat. There was general sympathy for England, which, after all, was Argentina's best customer, and for France, which was Argentina's spiritual motherland. But scarcely any Argentines thought that their country should take an active part in the struggle.

That was in 1939. But on December 7, 1941, the picture changed suddenly, as a result of the Japanese treachery at Pearl Harbor. It changed, at least, as far as the United States was concerned. Ramón Castillo, who was guiding the affairs of Argentina by this time, professed his complete inability to see any reason for change in his country's policy of neutrality. As he carefully pointed out, Argentina had not fought a foreign war in nearly three quarters of a century. It was devoted to the cause of peace. Why, then, should it abandon its traditional policy unless actually attacked?

Among the Argentine people there were sharp differences of opinion as to the wisdom of President Castillo's policy. The masses were strongly democratic, and fervently hopeful of an Allied victory. They were led by such men as Marcelo de Alvear, the Radical leader, and Nicolás Repetto, the chief of the Socialists. Even many of the Conservatives were in the Allied camp as a result of their strong commercial ties with Great Britain.

But not all those who favored the Allied cause were ready to endorse a policy of active co-operation with the Allied nations. Far from it. Many of them believed that Argentina could serve the Allied cause well enough, and its own interests best, by continuing to ship its foodstuffs to Europe for the use of the Allied armies and people—receiving, of course, a good price for these shipments. Then there were other persons—a smaller group, but not without influence—who hoped openly and loudly for a triumph of German arms. Included in this group were not only those of German extraction but also large numbers of very devout persons whose Catholic sympathies led them to regard Franco and his Falangist Spain, and therefore Hitler and his Nazi Germany, as the last bulwarks of Christian civilization against the spreading influence of the pagan Russians.

Many army officers also sympathized with Germany's ambitions. They had studied their profession in Germany; they spoke the German language; and they had been greatly impressed with the might of the German army. At the outbreak of the war many of them had believed that a German victory was inevitable, and this belief was strengthened by the British rout at Dunkirk and the fall of France. If they did not favor active intervention on the German side—and few actually did go so far—at least they believed that Argentina should keep as friendly as possible with both sides, so as to be able to do business with the victor.

German propaganda. The German government spent vast sums in Argentina in an attempt to influence public opinion. It maintained a news service that supplied news free of charge to those newspapers and magazines willing to use it. Meanwhile, of course, American news services, like the Associated Press and the United Press, were continuing to do business at their regularly established rates. The result was that many of the smaller newspapers, especially in the interior of the country, published the German version of all news stories, saying frankly that they could not afford American prices. A number of German-controlled radio stations broadcast the news. At least one newspaper, *El Pampero* (or Big Wind, as it was named with unconscious humor), was indirectly subsidized with German funds. German newsreels were shown in some of the motion picture theaters.

Perhaps this outlay by the German government was not entirely wasted, but it certainly accomplished far less than its sponsors had hoped. Most of the Argentine people continued to read the news as supplied by the Associated Press and the United Press to their favorite newspapers. They continued to attend motion picture theaters where American films were shown. And, in general, they continued to favor an Argentine policy that did not take sides in the conflict.[13]

Argentina and the United States. It must be clearly understood that even among those Argentines who warmly espoused the Allied cause, the sympathy was for Great Britain and France, not for the United States or the Soviet Union. The United States was a longtime rival; it was regarded as a greedy nation whose entry into the war had doubtless been prompted by a desire to protect its own interests. The Soviet Union was thought to be a godless state, ruthlessly seeking to destroy the way of life that most Argentines held dear. Between Hitler's Germany and Stalin's

[13] Hubert Herring describes German propaganda in Argentina in his previously cited work, pp. 67–78.

Russia, said many Argentines, there really wasn't a great deal to choose. It would be a sorry day for the world when either of those nations overran Europe.

Until the United States entered the war, most Americans were not even aware of Argentine foreign policy. They had no ready way of knowing what was happening in Argentina, and no reason to care. When, however, Japanese bombs fell on Pearl Harbor, the people of the United States expected the other nations of the Western Hemisphere to rally swiftly to their support. Most of them did so. But Argentina was a noteworthy exception, and the American people demanded to know why. Why should any nation remain callously indifferent when the United States had been attacked? Forgotten was American indifference to the attack on Poland and to the fate of France. Now Americans were at war, and there should no longer be such a thing as neutrality in the world. Neutrality must be a mask for German sympathies. Those who were not for us must be against us. So most Americans reasoned. But Castillo continued his policy of neutrality, while the Argentine people continued to debate it as vociferously as Americans had quarreled before Pearl Harbor.

CASTILLO'S DOMESTIC PROBLEMS. In addition to strained relations with the United States, domestic troubles were plaguing the Castillo administration. British purchases of beef for military and civilian use had driven meat prices to very high levels; and, while this pleased the great landowners who were Castillo's chief supporters, it created a serious problem for the workers. In Argentina even the very poorest people eat meat; and when its price is almost beyond their reach, there is bound to be widespread discontent. The cost of other essentials was also rising rapidly, and wages were not keeping pace with the spiral of inflation. The influence of the government was used to protect British investments in the railways and in the municipal street car system of Buenos Aires, which had long been known for their high charges and poor service. Not unnaturally, therefore, many persons said that President Castillo was more interested in serving his wealthy friends and their British associates than in safeguarding the interests of the Argentine nation.

State of siege. Castillo's reply to this charge, and to dozens of others that were hurled against him by the newspapers and by his political opponents in Congress, was to declare a state of siege, thus sweeping away all the ordinary constitutional guarantees of individual liberty. Meetings could not be held to discuss public policy without the consent of the police. Newspapers could not print editorial comment, or even news stories, without the approval of the censors. Castillo imposed the state of siege one week after the United States entered the Second World War; and he maintained it for nearly eighteen months, until he was finally and forcibly removed from office. Congress had the constitutional power to override him and lift the state of siege; but since the Senate was still dominated by the Conservatives, no action was taken. And while the people complained more bitterly than ever, Castillo continued his conservative policies.

ELECTION PLANS. 1943 was an election year. Early in the year the rumor began circulating that the Conservative candidate was to be a wealthy landholding politician named Robustiano Patrón Costas. Probably no one in all Argentina could have been more acceptable to the little pro-British clique of wealthy men who dominated the Conservative coalition, or more unacceptable to the masses of the people. Patrón Costas was said to have built his fortune on the misery of thousands of peons, who worked on his sugar plantations at starvation wages and never managed to get out of debt. Against such a candidate the opposition could easily have won—assuming, of course, imaginative leadership and an honest election. Actually, however, the leadership of the opposition was singularly unimaginative. The Radicals, the most important group, had never recovered from the death of Alvear. Minor party chieftains were squabbling with one another, instead of presenting a united front for the coming campaign. The Socialists were still led by Nicolás Repetto, a mild-mannered scholar in his early seventies. And as to the possibility of an honest election, everyone knew the answer. Ortiz and Castillo had split over that very issue; now that Ortiz was dead, Castillo would never permit the votes to be counted in such a way as to jeopardize the interests of his own party. Patrón Costas was as good as elected unless there should be a miracle. The Argentine people prayed for a miracle, but with very little hope that their prayer would be heard. It was answered in the early morning of June 4, though not exactly in the way that they had anticipated. Patrón Costas never became president of Argentina.

SELECTED REFERENCES

See references at end of Chapter 3.

ARGENTINA
The Rise of Perón

The Revolution

FIRST HOURS. In the early hours of June 4, 1943, the army moved against the government, for the second time in less than thirteen years. The uprising was precipitated by the rumor that the U.C.R. was about to name General Pedro P. Ramírez as its presidential candidate, in opposition to Patrón Costas. Ramírez, a professional soldier who had openly expressed admiration for the tactics of the German army, if not its ideals, was scarcely the man to rekindle the flame of Argentine liberalism, but the Radicals knew that they had much to gain by bidding for army support. They understood that Ramírez, one of the acknowledged leaders in the military clique, could swing a substantial segment of the army to their side.

But if the rumor pleased many Radicals, it disturbed many Conservatives. President Castillo, especially, was annoyed, for Ramírez was his minister of war. Could it be that the man was actually flirting with the Radicals while ostensibly giving his loyalty to a Conservative administration? Castillo wanted an immediate answer. When the answer came, however, it did not satisfy him. Ramírez did indeed deny that he was seeking the presidential nomination, but he failed to say what he would do if the nomination were pressed upon him. Moreover, he did not tender his resignation as minister of war, though propriety seemed to suggest such a step. Castillo awaited the resignation for two days, but it did not come.

During the two days following Castillo's demand for an explanation Ramírez was exceedingly busy. He called together his fellow officers, and proposed revolution. The plans were laid hurriedly, but with care,

Nothing was left to chance. Finally, however, Castillo got wind of the plot, and called a cabinet meeting at two in the morning. It was a stormy affair, and at its close Ramírez was ordered placed under arrest. He had to act fast, and he did. Within two hours well-disciplined troops were moving toward the heart of Buenos Aires.

OVERTHROW OF THE GOVERNMENT. Upon hearing of the approaching troops, President Castillo hurried from the *Casa Rosada* to make a personal appeal for the support of soldiers in a nearby garrison, but without avail. When he returned, a representative of the army greeted him with a demand for his resignation. Castillo refused in no uncertain terms, though he must have known that he could not long stand out against armed force. The first revolutionary troops from the Campo de Mayo reached the city about seven in the morning, and encountered no immediate resistance. They proceeded to take over strategic points, while the people of the capital engaged in a wild demonstration against the hated Castillo regime. *"Viva la libertad!"* they shouted. *"Viva la democracia!"* Meanwhile the forces of the Navy Mechanical School decided to enliven the affair by firing on the revolutionary troops. There was a sharp exchange of shots, and more than one hundred people were killed or wounded. In other parts of the city there were occasional riots. But in a few hours it was all over. The fate of the nation had been decided once more by a brief display of armed might in the capital city. Castillo and his cabinet fled from the *Casa Rosada,* and took refuge on a minesweeper, which steamed out into the Plata estuary.

THE NEW REGIME. All the day of Castillo's flight and well into the night the people continued to celebrate, though they had no idea what they were celebrating. The one indisputable fact was that Castillo and his crowd no longer controlled the nation. Who did control it? That was anybody's guess. The next day, however, the question was answered. The new provisional president was not General Ramírez, but General Arturo Rawson, the longtime proponent of a bigger and better army. Ramírez was to continue as minister of war.

As for the other cabinet ministers, the announcement of their names was disappointing to the friends of democracy. The portfolio of finance went to the proprietor of the German-subsidized newspaper *El Pampero*. The ministry of agriculture was entrusted to a general who had been closely associated with the discredited Castillo regime. Nearly all the ministers were generals, and most of them were known to be conservative, if not reactionary. The new government immediately suspended publication of communist newspapers, but made no attempt to interfere with papers of known fascist sympathies. Congress was dissolved, and martial law was invoked to enable the army to crush any incipient opposition with the least possible trouble. Meanwhile the government issued a series of proclamations that were evidently designed to secure public confidence. Argentina would co-operate with the other nations of the Western Hemisphere. It would stamp out dishonesty in the public service. It would protect the liberties of the Argentine people.[1]

Ramírez

General Rawson had virtually no opportunity to prove what he could do. Two days after taking office he resigned and turned over his powers to War Minister Ramírez. The cabinet was reshuffled and some of the most notorious Nazi sympathizers were dropped. But the government did not lose its predominantly military appearance; on the contrary, every cabinet post except one went to an army or navy man. An admiral became vice-president of the nation. The September elections were suspended indefinitely. The word "provisional" was dropped from the title of the government. Evidently General Ramírez intended to make his regime secure before trusting to the vagaries of popular fancy.

POPULAR CONFUSION. In the first days of the revolution there was considerable confusion in the minds of the Argentine people as to just what had actually occurred. Was the new government really in favor of closer co-operation with the Allies and with the other nations of the Americas? Confirmed democrats thought so, and pointed to the pro-Ally speeches of the Minister of Foreign Relations. Axis sympathizers thought not, and nodded with approval while the Minister of the Interior banned a number of democratic organizations. Was the government really going to respect the liberties of the people? Its spokesmen said it was, even though their acts seemed to belie their promises. Nobody really knew what to believe, but everyone hoped for the best. Most of the newspapers published laudatory editorials, contrasting the honesty of the new regime with the venality of the Castillo administration. Most of the political parties pledged their allegiance to the new order, though the Conservatives remained sulkily aloof.

[1] See *Argentine Diary*, by Ray Josephs, pp. 3–15.

In the United States the news of Argentina's revolution was received with delight. Most Americans assumed that this uprising against Castillo was based on impatience at his failure to break with the Axis powers. Even our State Department jumped to this conclusion, and extended recognition to the new regime in less than a week. Great Britain recognized it the same day. But Germany and Italy had granted recognition twenty-four hours earlier. Apparently no one knew whether to class the new government as friend or foe—or just another neutral.

THE REVOLUTIONARY LEADERS DISAGREE. The contradictions in Argentina's foreign and domestic policy during these first weeks of the new regime arose from sharp differences of opinion within the military junta that had seized control of the nation. General Rawson, who was thought by many persons to have been forced out of the presidency because of his unwillingness to sever relations with the Axis powers, was actually the leader of the pro-Ally clique. He had favored much closer co-operation with Great Britain and the United States, on the ground that the war was swinging slowly but surely in their favor and that Argentina had best be on the winning side. In the privacy of the barracks he had pointed out that Argentina badly needed arms and military equipment, and that the United States—the great arsenal of democracy—certainly would not supply them to any nation whose loyalty to the allied cause was in considerable doubt.

But most of the leaders of the revolution were unwilling to support a break with the Axis. Some of them were Axis sympathizers; many more were simply ardent nationalists who refused to concede that Argentina should follow the lead of any other power. These army nationalists had formed an association, which they called the G.O.U. (Group of United Officials). Their goal was some sort of totalitarian state, and they took as their motto *Government, Order, Unity*—corresponding to the initials of their organization. The G.O.U. opposed both major political parties— the Radicals, because they favored liberal democracy, and the Conservatives, because they stood for continued subservience to Great Britain in order to insure a good market for Argentine beef. Rawson and his friends would certainly have liked to turn the government back to the Radicals at the earliest possible moment. So, perhaps, would Ramírez. But Ramírez was not the boss of the nation, despite the fact that he held the title of president. He was only one of the group, which was trying desperately to establish a coherent policy. His one insistent cry, in the days when the revolution was taking shape, had been that the Conservatives must be overthrown. And the other army chiefs who comprised the junta had gladly accepted this premise. It had been almost their only point of agreement.

MILITARY DICTATORSHIP. As the days passed, and the Ramírez government flooded the country with decrees on almost every conceivable subject, the nature of this new regime became increasingly clear. It was a military dictatorship, and it believed in a military type of discipline for all the people. Men and women must do what they were told because the government in its superior wisdom had so decreed. Order was to replace liberty. And anyone who fomented disorder would speedily be taught the error of his ways. Anyone who even questioned the right of the government to act in such an arbitrary manner would speedily be made to understand that it no longer paid to think. Some of the acts of the government subjected it to ridicule. When it undertook to eliminate slang from the radio, some announcers went to the other extreme and used such stilted phrases that the point was not lost on their listeners. When some women were arrested for wearing their skirts too short, others proceeded to lengthen their skirts to the ankle. Generally speaking, however, the government's orders were taken very seriously. Those who poked fun at its humorless decrees speedily regretted their temerity. A famous comedian was dragged off to jail because he declared that the initials of Pedro P. Ramírez stood for *Presidente para rato* (president for a little while).

As might have been expected, one of the first acts of the new government was to strengthen its position by intervening in all the provinces. Military men were sent to replace the civilian administrators and were told to keep a sharp lookout for any possible troublemakers. Shortly afterward the mayors of most of the leading cities were summarily dismissed. Their places were taken, for the most part, by promising young colonels who were members of the G.O.U. A general was placed in charge of the city government of Buenos Aires. Provincial legislatures and city councils ceased to function.

ECONOMIC REFORMS. As soon as the Ramírez regime was firmly in the saddle, it began to devote its attention to some of the serious economic problems that confronted the nation. Rents, which had been rising steadily for many months, were reduced by decree. Telephone, light, and power rates were lowered, also. Minimum wages were established for farm laborers, whose desperate plight had never roused the Radicals to action— much less the Conservatives! Salaries were increased throughout the government service and married men with children were given substantial bonuses. General Ramírez announced that he and the military members of his cabinet would continue to live on their salaries as army or navy officers, instead of drawing the much larger salaries to which they were entitled by law. Economy, an ever-popular word with taxpayers, was said to be the order of the day.

The masses of the Argentine people were delighted. At last they faced the prospect of some small measure of relief from the constantly rising spiral of inflation. They were pleased, also, by a number of decrees directed at foreign capital. The British-controlled corporation which had a monopoly of street transportation facilities in the city of Buenos Aires was dissolved. A little later an American company which had been operating the street cars in the northern city of Tucumán was treated to a dose of the same medicine, and thereupon banners were placed upon all the street cars reading: "This car is Argentine." [2]   The termination of the British monopoly was especially good news to the people of Buenos Aires, for they had suffered from inadequate transportation for many years while the British made a substantial profit on obsolete equipment. British-owned street cars had been the butt of innumerable jokes, and the basis of innumerable complaints. They had been the center of attack whenever unruly mobs wished to show their disapproval of almost anybody or anything. To single out the transportation corporation as one of the first victims of the new regime was an almost certain way to win a measure of popular support.

CONTINUED NEUTRALITY. As the days passed, it became increasingly clear that the Ramírez government intended to continue Castillo's neutrality policy, despite increasing pressure by the United States to break relations with the Axis. Ramírez himself spoke of the need for closer ties with the other nations of the hemisphere, including the United States, and Foreign Minister Storni put the matter even more strongly. "The time has come for deeds, not words," he declared. A committee was appointed to study the whole question. But nothing happened. And in the meantime the German propaganda campaign continued at full blast. German soldiers from the pocket battleship *Graf Spee,* who had been interned in Argentina since 1940 when their vessel had been scuttled in the Plata estuary, were still enjoying the liberty of the country. Against this hypocrisy General Rawson spoke out in no uncertain terms. He was no longer a member of the government, but as the leader of the June revolt his words still carried a great deal of weight. So Ramírez decided to get him

[2] See *The Argentine Republic,* by Ysabel F. Rennie, pp. 375–383.

out of the country by making him ambassador to Brazil. Rawson did not want to go; he found one excuse after another to delay his departure, and finally resigned his ambassadorship. But his resignation was not accepted and Ramírez had his way. In Rio, however, Rawson continued to cause trouble. He made speech after speech in support of the Allied cause— truly an amazing performance for the official representative of a neutral country.

In October, four months after the rise to power of the Ramírez regime, a manifesto was published in the leading newspapers of Argentina, calling upon the government to take its rightful place at the side of the Allies, and criticising it for its disregard of civil liberties. This manifesto was signed by more than one hundred and fifty of the nation's most distinguished citizens—lawyers, physicians, industrialists, merchants, scientists. Included in the list was the president of the University of La Plata. The government replied by dismissing every one of the signers who held public office—a much larger number than might be supposed, because of the Argentine practice of staffing its universities with outstanding professional men who devote only two or three hours a week to their university duties. The loss of their teaching salaries meant very little to these men, but the loss of their services was a heavy blow to the universities.

THE REIGN OF TERROR. The democratic manifesto published by protesting citizens stood on solid ground when it deplored the loss of civil liberties. Under Ramírez and his friends the guarantees of the constitution had been utterly disregarded from the day that they seized power. Argentines soon discovered that they were living under a tyranny as ruthless as that of the nineteenth-century despot Rosas. The tactics of the Ramírez crowd were much the same, but with twentieth-century refinements. Persons suspected of being too friendly to the Castillo regime, persons who spoke too freely in criticism of the new administration, persons known to be Communists or suspected of communist tendencies—all these and hundreds of others were arrested and taken to jail. Some of them got out again after a few days or weeks; the less fortunate were sent to concentration camps in such places as Neuquén in the southern part of the country or Martín García Island in the Río de la Plata. In virtually all cases they were held incommunicado, at least until the police had questioned them at length, and satisfied themselves that there were no more secrets to be learned.

Many prominent leaders of the opposition simply disappeared, and the police blandly expressed complete ignorance of their whereabouts. A "special section" of the federal police of Buenos Aires was entrusted with

the task of making these arrests, and it did its work with an efficiency
worthy of the German *Gestapo*. Conditions in the concentration camps
for political prisoners were said to beggar description. Poor food and
unsanitary accommodations took a heavy toll of the inmates. Some
women, many of them from prominent families but all suspected of lacking sympathy for the new government, were sent to houses of correction
for street walkers and degenerates. As stories of these atrocities spread,
the people became genuinely frightened. Few could be certain that they
were not next on the wanted list of the police. Spies were everywhere—
waiters in the restaurants, servants in the homes. Men and women began
to say to themselves what they did not dare to say aloud—that even the
Castillo regime, with all its faults, had never tried to institute a campaign
of terror.

SUPPORTERS OF THE REGIME. In spite of widespread opposition the Ramírez administration had its staunch supporters. Among them were
thousands of unorganized workers who applauded the government's drastic action to reduce rents and utility charges. Some industrialists who had
won special favors from the new regime also endorsed it, though most of
the nation's businessmen were definitely in the opposition camp. The
Roman Catholic Church maintained a consistently sympathetic attitude—
not unnaturally, in view of the new government's pro-church policies.
From the very beginning Ramírez and his friends set out to win the
church's support. They reversed the traditional Argentine viewpoint
that religious education should be excluded from the schools, and decreed
instead that instruction in the fundamentals of the Catholic faith must be
given to every school child, regardless of the wishes of the child or his
parents. This policy had long been urged without success by the Catholic
Church; in fact, the Pope's direct representative in Argentina had been
expelled from the country in 1884 for pressing the matter too vigorously.
But now at last a revolutionary government had accepted the church's
point of view—spontaneously, without the slightest pressure from church
leaders, who had long assumed that the question was closed. Small wonder that many leading Roman Catholics condoned the violence of the
new regime. The violence was not directed against them!

INTERFERENCE WITH THE PRESS. At first the full extent of the new government's abuse of power was not realized by the masses of the people.
The newspapers printed only fragmentary accounts, or carefully avoided
the subject. If they tried to speak out against the new tyranny they were
ruthlessly suppressed. Editors were told that they might "comment on

the government's acts, decisions, and policies with freedom and frankness," but that they must "spontaneously adjust their criticism to constructive ends." Argentine newspaper men had no difficulty in understanding just what was meant. Some of them, however, persisted in speaking out boldly against dictatorship. They were soon made to feel the government's displeasure. Editors were sent to jail or to concentration camps. Entire issues of great dailies were confiscated, and the publishers cautioned that they must mend their ways if they expected to continue in business. Eventually this treatment began to produce results. The newspapers printed what they were told to print, and nothing else. Stories of government tyranny and popular protests ceased to appear. Even Buenos Aires' great newspaper, *La Prensa,* which had a long and distinguished record of successful opposition to press censorship, almost gave up the fight. Its subsequent sparks of defiance, in critical but ambiguous editorials, served only to emphasize the low estate to which it had fallen.

The excuse given most frequently by the government for its interference with freedom of the press and individual liberties was that these steps were necessary to combat the growing communist menace in Argentina. Until the 1943 revolution no one had supposed that communism presented a serious threat to the Argentine way of life. The Communist Party had never been able to win a single election in any province or city, and in some of the provinces it had even been outlawed. But Ramírez and his gang suddenly discovered Communists beneath every bush and in the offices of nearly every newspaper. Thousands of opponents of the new regime were suspected of communist tendencies, and treated as if the suspicion had actually been proved.

INTERFERENCE WITH LABOR. Many labor leaders were victims of Ramírez' anti-communist campaign. Their headquarters were padlocked as "notorious centers of communist activity" and they were sent off to concentration camps without the opportunity to defend themselves. The government was not anti-labor; on the contrary, it courted the labor groups and frequently intervened to settle strikes in their favor. But it was definitely opposed to the powerful labor leaders, just as it was opposed to any men who were powerful enough to challenge its authority. Though it was prepared to improve the lot of Argentina's workers, it did not propose to permit them to insist on better conditions *as a matter of right.* If in its own good time it should decide to raise wages, it expected to receive the humble thanks of a docile proletariat. It wanted no labor organizers who might claim that they, rather than the government, had brought about the desired result. So it proceeded to bribe, cajole, imprison, or otherwise remove them from the political scene. Yet the government's labor troubles did not cease. The closing months of 1943 witnessed a wave of strikes in Buenos Aires and the other industrial centers of the nation. New leaders arose to continue the fight. The labor unions were undoubtedly a thorn in the side of the government, and a difficult thorn to remove.[3]

INTERFERENCE WITH THE UNIVERSITIES. Among the critics of the revolutionary government the most vocal were probably the students of the universities. There are six principal universities in Argentina and all are controlled by the national government. These universities have a monopoly on the granting of degrees in law, medicine, engineering, and the other professions, and they can therefore make or break the professional careers of aspiring young people. Many previous Argentine governments had used this power to force students into line, and the Ramírez regime followed these time-honored tactics, adding some innovations of its own. It dismissed university rectors and deans, replacing them with professors who promised to be more tractable. Thereupon the students, who had been in the forefront of almost every demonstration against the government, rioted with renewed vigor. They paraded with large signs praising democracy and condemning dictatorship. When mounted police charged them with swinging clubs, they threw hundreds of marbles into the streets, causing the horses to lose their footing. The government responded by suspending classes. It also threatened to expel all students who stayed away from examinations "without adequate reasons." Yet most of the students did stay away as a protest against such dictatorial practices, though they knew that in all probability they were forfeiting their careers.

SPARKS OF ANTI-SEMITISM. The Ramírez government was not officially anti-Semitic, but some of its strong supporters left no doubt that they would like to see an Argentine pogrom. Nationalist newspapers ranted against the Jews without government interference, while pro-democratic dailies were closed for "spreading dissension among the people." Even some of the cabinet ministers were known to favor a campaign of Jew-baiting. Unruly mobs, acting with the tacit approval of the police, attacked the homes and offices of "Jews, Communists, and bankers"—surely an odd assortment of targets. Gradually, however, the fire of anti-Semitism burned out. The mobs were told to direct their energies against more dangerous enemies. The more notorious Jew haters in the cabinet were

---

[3] Ernesto Galarza discusses the labor situation of this period in "Argentine Labor under Perón," No. 2 of *Inter-American Reports*, March, 1948.

forced out, or obliged to mend their ways. And the government made clear that it did not favor the persecution of any racial group.

GROWING IMPORTANCE OF PERÓN. By October of 1943 Colonel Juan D. Perón had become an important figure in the revolutionary government. An acknowledged leader of the younger army officers, he had at first received only the relatively insignificant post of undersecretary of war. But he managed to place his friends in numerous key positions and before long he was able to give orders to his nominal superiors. Even President Ramírez, who seems to have regarded Perón as a possible rival, adopted many of his "suggestions." In October Colonel Perón took over the affairs of the ministry of labor, though without cabinet status. Shortly afterward he was made a full-fledged member of the cabinet, with the title of minister of labor. A few months later he became minister of war, without surrendering his labor portfolio.

Undoubtedly he was a natural leader of men. Young (forty-eight), handsome, and charming, he knew the secret of yielding graciously on minor points in order to minimize the opposition to his important plans. He wanted to be president of the nation, and he went quietly about the task of winning support in every likely quarter. To the people he promised a "new phase" of the revolution, in which the power of the masses would replace the power of the army, and the officers would return to their barracks. The revolution, he explained, had social significance; it was designed to improve the lot of the common men of Argentina. Though not anti-capitalistic, it was determined to end the exploitation of man by man. Thus Perón spoke, but his actions were very different. While he talked of returning the government to the people, he worked continuously for more repressive measures to keep the army in control. While he stressed his love of the workers, he strove with all his might to break the backs of the independent labor unions which had worked so long and so hard for the workers' welfare. Perón was an opportunist. He favored any person or any cause that might further his ambition. At a moment's notice he would discard any person or any cause that seemed to stand in his path. Before and above all else, he was in favor of Juan D. Perón.

THE UNDERGROUND OPPOSITION. While Perón and his rivals were struggling for power within the Ramírez government, thousands of plain citizens were still struggling for liberty. Secret societies sprang up almost overnight, publishing newspapers, magazines, and handbills. The chief problem was to get them past the police and into the hands of the people for whom they were intended. Some were sent boldly through the mails, but the postal authorities began to examine all letters and packages, and put a stop to this practice. Copies of illegal newspapers were left in the workers' washrooms at the factories and refrigerator plants in the hope that they would be widely circulated before coming to the attention of the police. Some copies were even distributed furtively along the principal thoroughfares of Buenos Aires during rush hours.

Probably the most important of the underground organizations was *Patria Libre*—Free Motherland—which tried to unite all democratically minded Argentines, regardless of party, in opposition to the dictatorship. But there were dozens of others. The Communists had their own organization, and even a separate youth movement. The Socialists worked with the Communists at times, but more often preferred to go their separate way. It was inevitable that the Communists and Socialists should play an important part in the underground movement because they had been forced to bear the brunt of the government's displeasure. But persons of every political faith were included. The police made a desperate effort to discover the places where democratic literature was published. Sometimes they succeeded, and as a result printing presses were smashed and editors were hurried off to jail. But somehow the newspapers and leaflets continued to appear. Not all the efforts of the police could stamp out the love of liberty in the Argentine people.

Some of the literature of the underground movement was published in Montevideo, the Uruguayan capital on the eastern side of the Río de la Plata, only one hundred and twenty-five miles from Buenos Aires. Many of Argentina's leading political figures fled to Montevideo immediately after the Rawson-Ramírez revolution; others came a little later, as their unwillingness to bow to dictatorship made life at home increasingly uncomfortable, not to say dangerous. They were a strangely assorted group— Communists, Socialists, Radicals, Progressive Democrats, Conservatives. Back in Argentina they had spent much of their time quarreling with one another, and it took a while for them to learn the habit of co-operation. In fact, they never succeeded in burying their differences sufficiently to permit the formation of a single organization. But eventually they did work together very effectively. In addition to publishing newspapers and magazines for circulation in Argentina, they maintained regular news broadcasts over a Montevideo radio station. These broadcasts gave to the people of Argentina an opportunity to learn what was happening in the outside world—and even in their own country, for the Montevideo exiles' contacts with the underground at home enabled them to report Argentine news promptly and accurately. Every fresh act of oppression by the dictatorship was described over the Montevideo radio, though no word of it appeared in the Argentine papers. Naturally the Ramírez government was greatly disturbed. It protested to Uruguay against its "unfriendly" attitude, only to be told that the Uruguayan government believed in free speech, and would permit any man to have his say, either for or against the Ramírez regime. Then a Buenos Aires radio station, operating on the same wave length as the Montevideo station, tried to drown out the exiles' broadcasts. Meanwhile Argentine secret police, thinly disguised as tourists, swarmed over Montevideo, prying into the exiles' affairs, but accomplishing very little. The government was more successful in cutting off the exiles' funds, which were still largely in Argentina. Only with great difficulty could they raise the money necessary to continue their opposition activities.[4]

ALLIED PRESSURE. In Argentina the government was being forced nearer and nearer to a break with the Axis powers. United States pressure was strong, and had been increasing for several months. American-made motor cars were breaking down in the streets of Buenos Aires and Rosario and Santa Fe for lack of parts. American-made tractors were standing idle on the *estancias*. And, when Argentina protested that it needed these things in larger quantities at once, it was told that larger quantities were not available. There was scarcely enough, said the United States government, to supply its own needs and those of its allies. Surely Argentina understood that neutrals would have to wait. Argentina did understand. It understood, too, when there was no American film for its young motion picture industry, while American film flowed to Mexico in a steady stream for the use of the rival Mexican cinema business and American technicians instructed Mexicans in the finer points of motion picture production.

But these things were minor annoyances. What really worried the Argentine government was that Great Britain might join the United States in bringing pressure to bear. It might even—crowning misfortune!—shut off its purchases of Argentine beef. The prospect of a British boycott of Argentine meat supplies was admittedly remote. After all, Allied troops in Europe had to be fed, and British civilians could not be permitted to starve. The United States could have made up the deficit

---

[4] See the interesting article by L. and S. Martin, "Argentina's Underground Press," in the August, 1944, issue of *Inter-American*, pp. 14–15. See also "Argentine Underground *versus* a New Fascist Empire," *Free World*, October, 1944, pp. 6 ff.

from its own meat resources, but in order to do so it would have had to curtail domestic meat supplies much more drastically. And the average American civilian was probably not ready to tighten his own belt merely to force a recalcitrant Argentine government into line. While Ramírez and his advisers debated these matters, an incident occurred that hastened the need for a rupture with the Axis. A man named Hellmuth, the Argentine son of German immigrants, had been appointed vice-consul to Barcelona, but on his way to his new post he fell into the hands of the British, and apparently gave them a great deal of information on the operation of Axis espionage within Argentina. The British government, thoroughly aroused at last, was prepared to support more strongly the demand of the United States that Argentina change its foreign policy and line up with the Allies. When this news reached Ramírez, he realized that the time had come to yield to Allied pressure. On January 24, 1944, he called a cabinet meeting, and announced his decision. Nothing was made public, however. Colonel Perón was not present at the cabinet meeting, and when he learned what was happening he called together his fellow officers of the G.O.U. Should they permit Ramírez to go through with his plan? All night they argued it out, only to find themselves hopelessly at odds. It was this lack of unity within the Group of United Officials that enabled Ramírez to have his way. Against a really united military clique he could not have stood for an hour.

SEVERANCE OF DIPLOMATIC RELATIONS WITH THE AXIS. On January 26, 1944, the Argentine government formally severed diplomatic relations with Germany and Japan. In justifying its stand it explained that the representatives of these countries in Argentina had abused their diplomatic immunity and had actively encouraged the operation of spy rings. These facts, which had been generally known for many months, were scarcely valid reasons for breaking relations *at such a late date*. By failing to act sooner, the Argentine government had made itself virtually an accessory after the fact. Argentines of every political faith knew that there must be other reasons for this sudden change of heart. Moreover, they knew what those other reasons were. They understood that they were being high-pressured by the United States and Great Britain into a move that they would never have taken of their own accord. And, because they were highly resentful of outside influence, they condemned the Ramírez regime for its subservience. There was no general rejoicing such as there would have been if the government had acted immediately after the Japanese attack at Pearl Harbor, when the cause of Pan American unity furnished a sufficient and obvious reason. Even those who had prayed fervently for an Allied victory expressed their regret that Argentina had not taken the step of its own accord.

But General Rawson, still making pro-democratic speeches in Rio de Janeiro, received with delight the news of his country's change of heart, and, "as chieftain of the revolution," cabled to President Ramírez his warmest congratulations on the government's decision to "comply with the revolution's principal purpose." Ramírez wired back that Rawson was not the chieftain of the revolution, and that its principal purpose had been "the reaffirmation of Argentine sovereignty." The national intervenor of Tucumán probably expressed the popular mood more accurately when he ordered all flags in the province flown at half-mast for a period of ten days in recognition of the nation's humiliation. It was widely suggested that the *Casa Rosada* (Pink House) was being turned into a White House.[5]

Farrell

SUBSTITUTION OF FARRELL FOR RAMÍREZ. After President Ramírez took matters into his own hands and broke relations with the Axis, his days as president were numbered. Many of his subordinates resigned in protest, and two members of his cabinet were forced out by the G.O.U. By February 24 the "Colonels' clique" of young army officers within the G.O.U. was ready to strike. Perón was an important member of this group, but not yet its undisputed leader. When Ramírez tried to fill the vacant cabinet posts with men who were known to be unfriendly to the colonels, the clique took decisive action. Shortly before midnight its members seized the Buenos Aires post office and the main police station. Colonel Emilio Ramírez, a distant relative of the president who had been placed in charge of the police, was "relieved of duty." From that hour President Ramírez was virtually a prisoner. Early the next morning he signed a dictated statement which declared that he was suffering from utter exhaustion, and for that reason was transferring the executive power to his minister of war, General Edelmiro Farrell. Admittedly Farrell was not a strong man. He became acting president because the warring factions within the G.O.U. could not agree on someone they really wanted. Farrell himself understood the situation perfectly. "They won't fire me," he is said to have

---

[5] See Richard Pattee's article, "The Argentine Question: The War Stage," in the October, 1946, issue of the *Review of Politics*, pp. 475–500.

boasted. "I'm the only man in Argentina who doesn't want to be president."

The new government tried hard to give the impression that its *coup d'état* had been nothing more than a routine change. The president was tired, it explained to all who would listen. His war minister was carrying on. No change in policy. Nothing to get excited about. Farrell underlined this attitude with a "business as usual" statement. He released from jail a number of Nazi sympathizers, but almost immediately balanced this act by releasing several prominent democrats. Meanwhile the Communists, real and alleged, stayed behind the bars. The United States, which had hurriedly recognized the Ramírez government in the fond belief that it would take a strong stand in favor of the Allies, saw a chance to rectify its error by withholding recognition from Farrell. Great Britain and most of the Latin American nations followed its lead, but Bolivia and Paraguay, whose governments were only pale reflections of the Buenos Aires military regime, hastened to extend recognition. So did Chile.

CONTINUED AMERICAN PRESSURE. As the months following the break with the Axis passed and it became increasingly clear that the Farrell government had no intention of taking drastic action against the pro-Axis groups still operating within the country, Cordell Hull spoke out sharply. Evidently the men who controlled Argentina were fascist-minded, he said. But he wanted it clearly understood that he had no quarrel with the Argentine people. They were surely a lot better than their leaders. This was strong language, coming from the secretary of state of the United States. Its principal effect, as far as the Argentine people were concerned, was to unite them behind their government to a degree that would otherwise have been impossible. Even the Socialists spoke out against Secretary Hull's remarks, which they termed an unwarranted interference with Argentina's domestic affairs. The leaders of virtually all the political groups took a similar attitude. Perhaps their government was unsatisfactory. Perhaps it was even destroying their liberties. But it was *their* government, and *their* liberties that were being destroyed. By what right did the representative of a foreign power question Argentina's integrity, and tell it what to do? The incident led to dozens of anti-United States demonstrations, some of which ended with attacks on the offices of the leading democratic newspapers of Buenos Aires. "We are Argentines, not colonists!" screamed the rioters. When the Argentine foreign minister made a speech pointing out that the nation had in fact made substantial contributions to the war effort—at a fair price, of course—and that in any event it was the master of its own destiny, thousands of men and women declared: "Argentina has put on long pants."

Not to be deterred by this unexpected reception of his first statement, Secretary Hull later amplified his charges. He listed a number of incidents that he regarded as evidence of Argentina's unfriendly attitude, and declared that the United States would not recognize the Farrell regime until "it is conclusively demonstrated that there has been a fundamental change in Argentina's policy." While the United States thus formally condemned the Argentine government, Great Britain tacitly approved it. Prime Minister Churchill did in fact say a few mild words in support of the United States position, but the British press threw its weight strongly on Argentina's side of the argument. Yet the United States continued to apply such pressure as it could without British assistance. On August 15, 1944, it froze Argentine gold stocks in New York. Six weeks later it announced that American ships would no longer call at Argentine ports. These measures were little more than petty annoyances, however. As long as Argentina could sell its beef and wheat to the Allies at a substantial profit, it had no real cause to worry.[6]

Perón

NEW HONORS FOR PERÓN. The struggle for power within the G.O.U. had ended in a decisive victory for Colonel Perón. He had become vice-president of the nation, as well as minister of labor and minister of war. More and more his orders were being recognized as law. President Farrell, who seems to have regarded Perón with favor from the outset, certainly made no effort to check his growing prestige. And Perón himself managed to turn every trivial incident to account in conducting his personal publicity campaign. When an earthquake almost destroyed the city of San Juan, he paraded the streets of Buenos Aires in the company of movie stars, begging donations for the unfortunate victims. When strikes threatened to disrupt industry, he fraternized with the workers, promising them full support while he continued to crush their unions and jail their leaders. New unions were soon created with his blessing, and the men who organized them proved ready to take his orders.

STIFLING OF THE PRESS. When the Farrell crowd first took over the government, Perón made it his business to announce that the unpopular

[6] See Hubert Herring's article, "Can We Run Argentina?" in the October, 1946, issue of *Harper's Magazine*, pp. 298–305.

Ramírez decree gagging the press was officially dead. From that moment, he explained, the newspapers were free to print what they pleased. A few editors took this statement literally, and soon found themselves in jail. But the large majority knew better than to suppose that the militarists had really experienced a change of heart. They printed the news with great caution, and limited their editorials to meaningless generalizations. As the months passed, it became increasingly clear that the censorship was really as ironclad as ever. Newspapers were told to avoid such "controversial" subjects as liberty or the constitution. In April *La Prensa,* the stouthearted champion of liberty which had published uninterruptedly for nearly three-quarters of a century, was closed by presidential order. Five days later it was permitted to resume publication, but not until its editor had come to terms with the administration. Liberty was dead in the Argentine Republic.

INCREASED MILITARY STRENGTH. One of the chief concerns of the Farrell-Perón regime was the strengthening of the Argentine army. Within a few months the number of troops was tripled, and plans were under way for the development of heavy industries that would supply the nation's needs in time of war. On July 9 Argentine-made Nahuel tanks (from the Indian word for *tiger*) rolled down the streets of Buenos Aires for the first time, as giant military parades celebrated the national holiday. Announcement was made that military training of all citizens would begin at the age of twelve years, instead of eighteen, as formerly. Army appropriations skyrocketed. Most Argentines, who had never seen a war and had not the slightest desire to engage in one, were justifiably apprehensive. But Colonel Perón explained that war was the farthest thing from his mind. His sole desire was to place Argentina on an equal footing with its neighbors (meaning Brazil, which had greatly increased its military strength, with the aid of the United States, after entering the Second World War). His single purpose was to make Argentina so strong that no nation would dare to attack. And as for the lowering of the age for compulsory military service, did anyone suppose that the government was planning to put twelve-year-old boys in uniform? Its purpose was to supervise their physical education, so that there would be no weaklings in the Argentine army. The people of Argentina listened to Perón's reassurances, but many of them continued to ask one another why large armaments had suddenly become so necessary to the nation's welfare. Had Argentina's neighbors acquired warlike designs? Or was Argentina itself developing warlike aspirations? These questions were asked not only in Argentina, but also in Brazil and Chile. And, as Argentina continued to arm, they remained unanswered.

The Farrell-Perón military program involved huge expenditures. By 1945 it called for larger sums for armaments than for all the other functions of government combined. It called for a budget in which expenditures were twice as large as revenues. In 1942 the Castillo regime had appropriated only very modest sums for military purposes. It had, in fact, spent as much for education as for the army and navy. But the colonels' clique had other ideas. Educational expenditures remained at about the same level, while public funds were devoted unstintedly to the task of building up a powerful military machine. For a supposedly peaceful nation, Argentina had surprisingly warlike ideas.

FRIENDLINESS TOWARD RUSSIA. While the government continued to hunt down "Communists" and urge the nation's industrialists to support the revolutionary regime on the ground that it was the best protection against the Communist menace, Vice-President Perón unexpectedly developed an interest in the Soviet Union. "I have long believed," he said in a speech delivered in late February, 1945, "that we should take steps toward formal relations with Moscow. As a nation we cannot ignore the fact that Russia is a great factor in the world." Some of the Colonel's critics immediately replied that Argentina had successfully ignored this fact for more than a quarter of a century—in fact, ever since the fall of the czars; and they suggested that a few more years probably would make no great difference. But most Argentines preserved a discreet silence. They had learned that this was the safest plan, unless they were prepared to praise the government and all its works.

In the field of international relations, Argentina's position was becoming steadily more difficult. An inter-American conference was held in Mexico City in late February, 1945, and Argentina was excluded at the insistence of the United States. Most of the Latin American countries would undoubtedly have preferred to invite Argentina—not because they approved of its military dictatorship, but because they realized that it was the leading nation among them, without whose presence there could be no genuine Pan Americanism. They deferred to the wishes of the United States, however. As the conference neared its close, there was general agreement that the Argentine Republic should be given another opportunity to demonstrate its willingness to co-operate with the other nations of the western hemisphere. A resolution was adopted mildly deploring the fact that Argentina had chosen to go its separate way, and hinting that a declaration of war against the Axis would be sufficient to square the account.

WAR AGAINST THE AXIS. A declaration of war was not at all to the liking of the colonels' clique. They had stood firmly on a platform of Argentine neutrality (or at worst a severance of diplomatic relations) for nearly two years, and many of them dreaded the admission that their policy had been mistaken. President Farrell is said to have declared that if the cabinet should decide on a declaration of war, he would resign. But Colonel Perón, more adaptable than the others, shifted his position with remarkable agility. He was now as strongly in favor of war as he had formerly been against it. As he pointed out again and again to his colleagues, there was no longer any question concerning the outcome of the war. Germany and Japan were almost ready to admit defeat, and certainly could not attempt retaliation against Argentina. Then, too, manufactured goods to maintain the nation's economy were becoming desperately scarce, and apparently the only way to get them in a hurry was to placate the United States. But the clinching argument was that only a declaration of war would obtain for Argentina a seat at the conference table of the United Nations, when the charter of the new world organization was written.

At last Perón had his way. On March 27, 1945, after a protracted cabinet session, President Farrell announced that his country was at war with Germany and Japan. He did not carry out his threat to resign. There were few demonstrations. Most Argentines felt that they had been forced into war by outside pressure, just as they had been compelled to sever diplomatic relations fourteen months earlier. But they had to admit that some tangible benefits followed promptly. American representatives arrived to discuss the availability of high-priority industrial equipment. And in the San Francisco Conference Argentina was admitted as a full-fledged member, with the wholehearted co-operation of the United States and against the determined opposition of the Soviet Union. Since the die had been cast, the Argentine government tried to give at least the appearance of doing a thorough job in ridding itself of Axis propaganda. It suppressed the pro-Axis foreign language newspapers, and interned enemy diplomats. The property of many German firms was confiscated.

OPPOSITION TO PERÓN. Colonel Perón had encountered a number of unexpected difficulties in his effort to make himself the strong man of Argentina. On June 16 most of the nation's leading industrialists and merchants united to publish a signed manifesto in which they accused the Vice-President of ruining the country with his economic policies. The huge and rapidly mounting debt disturbed them most, but other matters also received their critical attention. A few days later nearly all the principal societies of cattle breeders signed a similar declaration. The democratic press, which had been shackled so long that it had almost forgotten the taste of freedom, took courage and added a number of charges of its own. Students in all the universities began to demonstrate against the government. "Down with dictatorship!" was their slogan. It was interesting to note that virtually all the hue and cry was directed against Perón. Farrell was president, but no one thought to hold him responsible for anything. Perón was the man who was ruining the country; Perón was the evil genius of all men who loved freedom. And, when the time came for elections, Perón would try to make himself president. Few Argentines doubted it.

While Perón's enemies tried to destroy his political career, the Colonel fought back energetically. He inspired a number of the labor unions, now controlled by his henchmen, to issue a full-page eulogy of "the loyal friend of labor, Juan D. Perón." The government paid for this touching expression of labor's support. The pro-Axis and nationalist press tried to soften the charges against Perón, and made countercharges against his opponents. The Colonel made advances to the U.C.R. and actually succeeded in winning the support of a few minor politicians, who set up their own organization and brazenly called themselves *the* Radical Party. In the universities some of the students, who regarded Perón as the chief defender of their nation against "Yankee imperialism," fought it out with the Colonel's detractors. The encounters were frequent, and sometimes bloody. Argentina was a nation divided against itself.

PERÓN *versus* BRADEN. Perón's attempt to picture himself as an Argentine knight in shining armor, meeting the onslaughts of the Yankee dragon, received unexpected supporting evidence when the new American ambassador in Buenos Aires, Spruille Braden, began to speak out in no uncertain terms against the failure of the Argentine government to fulfill its solemn pledges. It had, he said, promised to liquidate pro-Axis firms within its borders, but most of them were still doing business. It had agreed to restore freedom of the press, yet censorship was as strict as ever. Every time that Braden delivered an address, he spoke out strongly against dictatorships. Usually he spoke in general terms, or in parables, but no one could miss his point, which was that the United States did not like the Argentine government and would regard its collapse with extreme pleasure. This was not the conventional language of diplomacy. Perón and his friends insisted that it was not even the language of good neighborliness. They said that Braden's persistent criticisms were an unwarranted interference with Argentina's conduct of its own affairs. And they were probably right, just as Braden was right when he called them demagogues.

The Farrell-Perón crowd did everything possible to discredit Braden, though without great success. It encouraged the Perón-dominated labor unions to call a memorial service for the workers killed in a mine accident of the Braden Copper Company in Chile. Ambassador Braden had no connection with the company, but the memorial service turned out to be an excuse for attacking the ambassador and his policies. As the weeks passed, the attacks continued. Anti-Braden circulars and pamphlets were widely distributed. Of course the Argentine government took no official part in this campaign, but Perón's fine Italian hand was only thinly concealed. As Braden spoke his mind more and more freely, many of the opponents of the government rallied around him. Crowds cheered him at unexpected times and places. But there is serious reason to doubt that he served his country's cause in Argentina. Thoughtful Argentines, even those who had been fighting the colonels' clique for years, questioned the propriety of Braden's tactics. They remembered too well the days when direct interference in Latin American affairs had been an established part of United States diplomacy, and they feared that the old interventionist policy was about to be revived.

CONCESSIONS TO THE OPPOSITION. Early in July, 1945, President Farrell promised that the army would retire to its barracks in the near future. A free election to choose the new rulers of Argentina would be held, he said, before the end of the year. A committee was appointed to study the old Sáenz Peña election law and determine what changes would be necessary to draft it into a modern statute. One of the nation's leading scholars was made secretary of the committee. When its report was made public, the United States press almost unanimously condemned it as a "fascist document" because it provided for public regulation of political parties. But some form of regulation was necessary and had long been urged by virtually all Argentine students of government. The cabinet approved the proposed law in August, and it began to seem that the Farrell-Perón regime was really preparing to end its "trusteeship," as it liked to call its military rule.

PERÓN AND LABOR. Few persons supposed, however, that even with a free election the nation was likely to be rid of Perón. The astute Colonel was busy with public appearances and public speeches. He promised everything to everybody, but most of all he cultivated the labor groups. Apparently they could write their own terms in return for their support of his still-unannounced candidacy. Although the Colonel was careful not to say that he wanted to be president, his followers said it for him. "Viva Perón!" and "Perón for president!" were cries often heard, as mobs roamed the streets attacking American and British stores and the offices of the pro-democratic newspapers. The opponents of the dictatorship formed their own groups and there were a number of pitched battles between these two factions. The weapons were sticks and stones, and even small arms. The police seldom intervened unless Perón's supporters were getting the worst of it. When they did take a hand, they used such brutal methods that protests flowed in to the *Casa Rosada* from many quarters. Argentina seemed to be on the brink of civil war.

ARREST OF PERÓN. At this point of violent pre-election conflict a group of army officers located in the strategic *Campo de Mayo* decided to take matters into their own hands. They called a general meeting of the G.O.U. and within a few days it was decided that Perón must go. On October 12 the Colonel was arrested and sent to the prison on Martín García Island in the Plata estuary where so many of his political opponents had spent months or years. But Perón's visit turned out to be only a matter of days. Hardly had he arrived before he complained of his health and announced that he must go back to Buenos Aires to be near his physician. So back he went—this time to the luxurious military hospital. Meanwhile the army officers who had seized control of the government were proving their ineptitude. They could not agree on a cabinet, and while they quarreled the public services remained virtually at a standstill. Farrell was still president, but only in name. Undoubtedly his loyalty was to Perón, and he gave these newcomers only the most reluctant co-operation.

THE "RETURN FROM ELBA." While Perón, still under arrest, continued to safeguard his health at the military hospital, his interests were protected by the amazingly efficient political organization he had developed. The heart of that organization was the Ministry of Labor, and its muscles were the thousands of ignorant workers who had been paid five pesos a day for many months to go about Buenos Aires and neighboring cities stirring up agitation for Perón. These were the *gritones,* or criers, who would cry loudly and often for the Colonel and his friends, or against any of his enemies, as long as they received their daily five pesos. Yelling, looting, and spreading terror were more interesting than regular employment and also more profitable. Of course, the maintenance of such an organization required a considerable outlay, but Perón had taken care of that. Large pension funds had been set up, but none of the money had ever been paid out in pensions. Then, too, the appropriations to the Ministry of Labor had been increased out of all proportion to its legitimate needs. With all this money at his command, Perón had not found difficulty in paying the wages of his hoodlums. With his arrest the payments stopped, and the hoodlums decided that their best plan was to get him back into power at the earliest possible moment. They instituted a virtual reign of terror.

The army officers in charge of the government continued, meanwhile, in their do-nothing policy. Then, on the evening of October 17, the news came over the radio that Colonel Perón was about to address the nation from a hotel room. No, he would deliver his address from the *Casa Rosada*

The Casa Rosada, where the presidents of Argentina do business.   (Photograph by the author)

itself. He would speak within two hours. No, he would go on the air in just one more hour. The Colonel did indeed speak within an hour, and from the *Casa Rosada's* balcony. With him was President Farrell, who embraced him warmly. The speech left no doubt as to the meaning of the dramatic turn of events. Perón was back; he was the master of the nation.

ELECTION PLANS. President Farrell, who had originally promised free elections before the end of 1945, later announced that they would not be held until the following April. Then, without warning, he suddenly advanced the election date to February 24. If his purpose was to take the anti-Perón forces by surprise, he certainly succeeded. They had expected to prepare careful plans in leisurely fashion, but the earlier date made delay impossible. Hurriedly the party leaders met. They were against Perón, almost to a man, and they decided that their best strategy was to unite all the parties in a single Democratic Union. The Radicals, the Progressive Democrats, the Socialists, the Communists—every group except the Conservatives—expressed willingness to support a single set of candidates for president and vice-president. Never before in the history of Argentina had there been such unanimity.

The failure of the Conservatives to join forces with the other parties was less significant than might be supposed. Most of the Conservatives were prepared to vote for anyone who had a reasonable chance of keeping Perón out of office. In the early days of the campaign the story got around that the Conservative leaders had been asked not to join the coalition, lest their bad record prejudice many voters. This story gained wide credence when the Conservatives decided not to name candidates of their own, thus leaving the field clear for the candidates of the Democratic Union. The parties were united only in their choice for president and vice-president. At the lower levels they continued to name their separate candidates and wage their separate campaigns. After all, they belonged to very different political faiths, and their union was admittedly a matter of temporary expediency. Its one purpose was to defeat Juan D. Perón.[7]

TAMBORINI AND MOSCA. There was general agreement that the candidates of the anti-Perón forces should be members of the Radical Party, which was by far the strongest element in the coalition. So the leader of the U.C.R., José Tamborini, became the Democratic Union's choice for president. He had a long record of public service, and a spotless reputation. He had served creditably as minister of the interior and as senator. There was nothing that could be said against him. Nor, for that matter, was there very much that could be said for him. He was completely honest, and completely colorless—hardly a match for the dashing Colonel Perón. His running mate, Enrique Mosca, was a man of the same stripe. Not just the candidates, but even the platform of the Democratic Union showed a lack of imagination. It promised, in negative fashion, that labor would lose none of its gains, and made reference to additional unspecified benefits that might be expected in the future. It urged honest elections, which it undoubtedly

[7] See H. B. Murkland's article, "Argentine Battleground," in the October, 1945, issue of *Current History*, pp. 299–304.

wanted, since the other side controlled the government and counted the ballots. And, in the field of international relations, it managed to say very little very charmingly, in order to give the least possible offense to all potential supporters.

THE PERÓN CAMPAIGN: *Pro-labor policies.* While the Democratic Union continued its cautious bid for votes from both ends of the political scale, the Perón forces concentrated on the labor vote. The leaders of Perón's puppet unions got together and formed a new Labor Party. Petty politicians were dragged from obscurity to set up a separate Argentine Labor Party, which could scarcely be distinguished from the Labor Party, since both groups had been founded for the express purpose of furthering the Colonel's candidacy. A third Perón party also appeared, headed by a minor politician named J. Hortensio Quijano, who had deserted the Radical fold to throw in his lot with the ambitious Colonel. This new group was to be called the Radical Party, though it had been able to attract none of the important leaders of the U.C.R. Perón, who had resigned from his government posts in October, did not make formal announcement of his candidacy until two months later, but then he began a whirlwind campaign to win the support of the masses. His methods were those of a typical demagogue. He promised everything. Whatever labor wanted, it could have. Wages must go up; prices must come down. The Colonel's agents circulated among the peons of the northern provinces, asking them to indicate the portions of the large estates on which they worked that they would like to have for their very own. And, when the astonished workers tremblingly indicated their choices, the agents solemnly entered their words in impressive ledgers. "There you are," they said. "The land will be yours when Perón becomes president." In the larger cities the workers were encouraged to strike against the foreign-owned meat-packing plants, and strong government pressure was exerted to obtain compliance with union demands.

Even though Perón was officially out of the government, his friends in the *Casa Rosada* continued his pro-labor policies, and the Colonel himself did not hesitate to take full credit for everything that was done. Ten days before Christmas the wages of all employed persons in the nation were arbitrarily increased by government decree. At the same time employers were directed to pay to every worker a Christmas "bonus" equivalent to one month's salary. As might well have been expected, the result was a long wail of anguish from Argentina's industrialists and shopkeepers. They emphasized their protests by closing the doors of their factories and stores, and keeping them closed for three days. But when they opened them again the decree was still in effect. Perón had demonstrated his power, and—far more important—he had given the workers a taste of the benefits that might be expected when he became president.

Many laborers who had been planning to support the Democratic Union began to question the wisdom of their course. Would the Democratic Union increase their wages fifteen or twenty per cent? Its leaders did not say so. But Perón had already made the increase a reality! To thousands of poor, ignorant workers those few additional pesos in the weekly pay envelope meant considerably more than the four freedoms. Speakers for the Democratic Union tried to make light of the Colonel's handiwork. "What if you do have a few more pesos every week?" they challenged. "Prices are so high that you're really worse off than before." But the Perón forces had an answer. "Look at Brazil or Chile," they said. "In those countries the inflation is worse than here, but the government hasn't raised all wages. That's because they don't have a Perón." In January, 1946, with the election only about a month away, the Farrell administration decreed the expropriation of two vast *estancias*. Explaining that the land was needed for colonization, it offered to pay a small fraction of its real worth. The owner of one of these estates was Patrón Costas, the Conservative whose presidential yearnings had prompted the 1943 revolution. It began to look as if the government might really be planning to give land to the landless.[8]

Perón's speeches were models of demagoguery. He proudly hailed his followers as *descamisados*—shirtless ones—and identified himself with the "sweaty class." "You're dirty and I'm dirty," he would announce to cheering throngs. "We're all dirty together." And then his hired *gritones,* intent on earning their five pesos a day, would parade the streets, ready to do battle with any person who had the temerity to wear a coat and necktie. Whenever the Democratic Union held a mass meeting, these hoodlums would try to break it up. If the anti-Perón forces fought back, the resulting riot would soon assume serious proportions. The police would stand quietly on the side lines unless the *gritones* seemed to be losing ground. At that point they would take a hand, swinging their clubs relentlessly at the heads of Democratic Union supporters.

Violence. Violence was the keynote of the campaign. Every time a crowd gathered to hear anti-Perón speeches, the Colonel's followers turned the affair into a free-for-all. On one occasion they commandeered several street cars and drove them at full speed through a parading group of Tamborini supporters, killing one person and injuring many others. When

[8] See Ernesto Galarza's previously cited report, *Argentina under Perón.*

Tamborini and Mosca set out by train from Buenos Aires for a tour of the provinces, their departure was made the signal for a serious riot. Everywhere that they tried to speak they were drowned out by Perón's rowdies. Their train was riddled with bullets on several occasions, and twice set afire. Flames swept the baggage car, destroying large quantities of campaign literature. Everywhere the posters of the Democratic Union were systematically torn down, or covered over with rival posters bearing Perón's face or slogans. The offices of newspapers supporting Tamborini were attacked time after time. Some of them were wrecked. Perón's ruffians were determined that the opposition should not be given a hearing.

Sources of Perón's strength. Just how many votes Perón would receive in an honest election seemed to be anybody's guess. Certainly his strength was considerable. The farm workers and the unskilled laborers in the cities generally regarded him as their champion. Many government employees were prepared to vote for him because of the tangible benefits they had received at his hands. Nazi sympathizers remembered his valiant service to their cause. And, in addition, Perón had the support of the Catholic Church. Cardinal Copello and several archbishops signed a pastoral letter in his behalf, which was read in Catholic churches throughout the nation. This letter did not mention the Colonel by name, but it warned Argentine Catholics not to vote for any candidate or group that opposed religious instruction in the public schools. Since Perón favored religious instruction and the Democratic Union opposed it, this was equivalent to an endorsement of Perón's candidacy. Some members of the Catholic clergy spoke out courageously against Perón and his tactics, despite the official stand taken by their superiors, but there can be no doubt that the weight of the church was thrown strongly in favor of the Colonel. Some few dissident members of the Radical Party also climbed on the Perón bandwagon. They were the followers of Hortensio Quijano, whose desertion of the Radicals had been rewarded with nomination as Perón's running mate. These, then, were the principal sources of the Colonel's strength. They seemed to be scarcely enough *in an honest election*. But few people expected the election to be honest.

American interference. On February 12, just twelve days before the election, the State Department of the United States entered the campaign by issuing a one-hundred-and-thirty-one-page Blue Book, in which it formally charged Argentina with collaborating with Nazi Germany, and carefully documented its charges with captured papers from the German Foreign Office. Prominently mentioned as a collaborationist was Juan D. Perón.

This information had been in the possession of the United States government for some time; the decision to release it just before election was evidently made by Spruille Braden, who had left Argentina several months earlier to become assistant secretary of state.

As soon as the news reached Argentina it was given wide circulation by the democratic press, which had been permitted relative freedom from censorship during the campaign. Perón's reply was characteristically shrewd. He said that the charges were not true; that Braden himself was the head of a vast Yankee spy ring in Argentina; and that, entirely aside from the truth or falsity of the document, it was an intolerable interference with Argentina's internal affairs. Why, asked the Colonel, had the United States waited until this particular moment to release the Blue Book? There could be only one possible answer—it wanted to ensure his defeat. It was trying to tell Argentines how to vote! Here was a ready-made issue, and Perón took the fullest possible advantage of it. He told the voters that they must decide whether to support their own nation or the United States. To put the matter even more concretely, they must decide whether to vote for Perón or Braden. In the excitement, Presidential Candidate Tamborini seemed to be almost forgotten. Whether the Blue Book actually influenced large numbers of voters is a moot question. Many friends of the Democratic Union said that it merely confirmed what they had always suspected. Many Perón supporters condemned it as an unwarranted personal attack on their candidate. Thousands of Argentines of all political faiths undoubtedly resented the action of our State Department, and called it an example of bad manners. Whether many of them voted for Perón at the last moment as an expression of their resentment is something that will never be known. The kindest thing to be said for the State Department's blunder is that Perón would probably have been elected anyway.

AN HONEST ELECTION. Just before election day the army announced that it was guaranteeing a fair election, and would not permit either side to resort to force or fraud. Apparently it meant what it said, for the votes were honestly cast and honestly counted. Watchers from all the parties were permitted to inspect the process. Everyone admitted that it was one of the fairest elections in Argentine history. The leaders of the Democratic Union, who had never really expected to be given a fair chance, expressed their delight in no uncertain terms. And, as the early returns seemed to indicate victory for their candidates, they publicly congratulated the army on the way the election had been handled. But as the returns from the outlying provinces were counted, the tide began to swing in Perón's favor. By the end of the second day it was clear that he had won. Too late the leaders of the Democratic Union began to talk about the violence that had characterized the campaign. Too late they complained that they had never had a free opportunity to present their case to the voters. They were already on record as accepting the election returns.

REVERSAL OF AMERICAN POLICY. Perón's election to the presidency placed the State Department of the United States in a most unenviable position. It had done everything possible to defeat him, but he was now the president-elect of Argentina, chosen by the people in an admittedly free election. What should the next move be? At first the United States government continued to hold aloof; then it gradually bowed to the inevitable. It sent a new ambassador to Buenos Aires. It released Argentine gold stocks in the United States, which had been frozen for nearly two years. It rescinded numerous export restrictions. It discussed with the Argentine chief of staff the possibility of making American military equipment available to Argentina, in order to increase the efficiency of inter-American defense. And in other ways also it showed its willingness to accept the situation. Eventually it "permitted" Spruille Braden to resign from the State Department, thus indicating its abandonment of the Braden policy of fighting Perón at any cost.

LABOR REFORMS. As president of the nation, Perón continued the policies that he had already established. He strengthened his control of labor by offering additional favors to those few labor leaders who still dared to show sparks of independence. If they did not succumb to these blandishments, they were sent to join their fellow labor leaders in jail, where they had ample time to contemplate their folly. Meanwhile their places were taken by interventors appointed by the government. Not all the forces of labor were brought into Perón's camp, of course, but the dissenters could scarcely make themselves heard above the enthusiastic shouts of government supporters. This enthusiasm was sustained by a veritable torrent of new social security laws. The minimum wage statute was amended to provide for increases with every rise in the cost of living. Paid vacations for workers were assured, and the pension plan greatly strengthened. The system of compensation for industrial accidents was completely overhauled. The right of employers to dismiss unsatisfactory workers was reduced almost to the vanishing point. A national housing administration was established, with power to supervise an extensive long-range program of public and private housing. To millions of Argentine laborers these reforms meant more than the right to vote freely for the heads of their own unions.

SUPPRESSION OF OPPOSITION. While Perón, by force and favors, thus gained control of organized labor, he strengthened his grip on the life of the nation in many other ways. He reorganized the six national universities for the purpose of bringing them directly under his authority. Presidents, deans, and professors were dismissed in great numbers, and more pliant persons appointed in their stead. Newspapers were forced into line by the threat of shutting off their supplies of newsprint. *La Prensa* still continued its opposition, but most of the other dailies were compelled to accept the government's policies as their own. The government took charge of two of the largest radio stations, and imposed a strict censorship on the others. Perón's control of the judiciary was assured when Congress impeached and convicted four of the five judges of the supreme court. The debt to the Catholic Church, which had contributed in no small part to a Perón victory, was paid by a law making religious instruction compulsory in all primary and secondary schools. This policy had been in effect, of course, since the rise of the dictatorship in 1943; the new law of Congress merely gave validity to the earlier decree.

THE FIVE-YEAR PLAN. It must not be supposed, however, that Perón spent most of his early months as president persecuting his enemies and placating his friends. These matters were of secondary importance. First came the gigantic task of developing the great resources of the nation. Perón had definite ideas as to the manner in which this should be accomplished, and he embraced them in a Five-Year Plan, which was explained in two volumes and two hundred thousand words. The plan was sent to Congress in October, 1946, and became law shortly afterward. It included many features, but its keynote was industrialization. This result was to be accomplished by extensive government participation in industry and increased government control of private business. Many of these plans were soon put into effect. Millions of pesos were poured into the construction of highways, the development of harbors, and the improvement of sanitary facilities. Protection was provided for new industries. The Argentine dream of freedom from the domination of foreign capital was achieved in large measure. The railroads and the telephone system were bought from their foreign owners. Debts to other countries were paid. For a time it seemed that the goals of the Five-Year Plan might actually be achieved in five years. The cost of the plan was met largely by manipulation of wheat and beef exports. The government bought these products at a fixed low price—much to the dismay of the great landowners who used to dominate Argentine politics—and then sold them at a much higher figure in the world market.

CONGRESSIONAL ELECTIONS. In March of 1948 congressional elections were held throughout the country. As Perón had promised, the laws were altered to permit women to vote. The government followed the same tactics that had proved so successful in the campaign of 1946. It used every possible device to intimidate the opposition until the very day of the election, and then permitted free voting and an honest count of the ballots. The scheme worked even better than before. Perón's forces strengthened their position, securing more than two thirds of the seats in both houses of Congress. Thus they had enough votes to amend the constitution.

THE NEW CONSTITUTION: *A second presidential term.* Immediately after the 1948 congressional elections Perón's intimates began to suggest that the constitutional prohibition against two successive presidential terms should be removed. Such a change, they explained, would promote greater democracy; it would permit a popular executive to serve for more than a single term if the people so desired. Perón's opponents promptly pointed out that the proposed modification would also permit a ruthless president to keep himself in power indefinitely through his control of the election machinery, regardless of what the people really wished. But opposition arguments were to no avail. The pro-Perón majority was determined to have its way, and it speedily laid plans for a constitutional convention to draft a new fundamental law. Delegates to the convention were chosen in December, 1948. They met a few weeks later, and after two months of deliberations they adopted a new constitution which authorized the president to serve any number of successive terms. The Radicals, a lonely minority, walked out of the convention hall when this decision was reached, but their absence merely simplified the task of the Peronista majority.[9]

LOSS OF JUDICIAL FREEDOM. One of the direct results of the adoption of the new constitution was the complete destruction of judicial freedom in Argentina. The new fundamental law, like the old, made provision for Senate confirmation of judges appointed by the president. Most people assumed that this clause referred to new appointments, but the Senate

[9] For a good summary of the other changes wrought by the new constitution, see Robert J. Alexander's *The Perón Era*, pp. 75–83.

promptly announced that it would consider all federal judges, even though they had been appointed and confirmed many years earlier. This maneuver, which was clearly in defiance of constitutional tradition, opened the way for removal of anti-Perón judges. It ignored the plain declaration of both old and new constitutions that judges should serve during good behavior. Within a few months more than seventy federal judges were dismissed—that is, they were told that the Senate had refused to ratify their appointment. Some had served for more than twenty years. All had refused to take orders from the Peronistas.

EVA PERÓN: *Rise to power.* One of the most surprising aspects of the Perón regime, in its early years, was the amount of political power wielded by the wife of the dictator. Eva Perón—*Evita,* or Little Eva, as she commonly called herself—was a remarkable woman. Raised in poverty as the daughter of a widowed boardinghouse keeper, she finally became a minor radio actress. Then came her friendship with Perón, and her marriage to him in October of 1943. At that time Juan Perón was forty-eight years old, and Evita was twenty-six. Admittedly Evita was a beautiful woman, and it seems that she was politically ambitious. She held audiences for people in all walks of life; she made speeches in places that her husband was too busy to visit; and she campaigned actively for a number of causes, such as woman suffrage. Through the María Eva Duarte de Perón Welfare Foundation, which was established in June of 1947, she distributed food, medicine, and money to thousands of needy people throughout the country, and thus established herself as a Lady Bountiful. Through her constant intervention in labor affairs—almost invariably as the champion of labor—she gained the affection of the "shirtless ones" to whom her husband so often turned for support. Some foreign observers even pictured Evita as a rival of Perón himself for mastery of the nation. But this thought seems never to have occurred to the President's lady. In the Foreword to her book, *The Reason for My Life* (*La Razón de Mi Vida*), which was published in 1951, she declared: "I was not and am not anything but a simple woman . . . . a sparrow in an immense bevy of swallows. . . . . And he [Perón] was and is the giant condor who flies so high and safe amidst the peaks and close to God. If it had not been for him [Perón] who descended to me and taught me to fly in another manner, I should never have known the life of a condor, nor have been able to contemplate the marvelous and magnificent immensity of my people. Therefore neither my life nor my heart belongs to me, and nothing of

what I am or have is mine.   All I am, all I have, all I think and all I feel,
is of Perón." [10]   Despite the excessive modesty of these lines, however,
the book managed to convey the impression that Evita Perón, in her own
right, was a tireless champion of the underprivileged.   One of the photo-
graphs used to illustrate the volume showed her allegedly leaving the
offices of the Ministry of Labor at three in the morning, still beautifully
dressed and quite alert after eighteen exhausting hours of work in behalf
of the people of Argentina.

Rejection of the vice-presidency.   As early as November, 1948, a Peronista newspaper proposed Eva Perón's name as a candidate for governor
of the province of Buenos Aires.   A year and a half later a provincial political convention announced its opinion that she should be considered for
"high office."   Then, in August, 1951, the stage was set for the nomination
of Evita to the post of vice-president of the nation.   A Peronista party
rally in Buenos Aires displayed side by side huge posters of Perón and
his wife, while speaker after speaker demanded that Evita be given the
vice-presidential nomination.   Meanwhile the crowds were given free food
and entertainment, and, if they had come from the provinces, free lodging.
Everything seems to have been done to whip up popular enthusiasm for
Eva Perón's candidacy.   But then Eva herself asked for time to consider
the matter.   Provincial party leaders rushed to Buenos Aires, and endless
secret conferences were held.   For more than a week the atmosphere of
suspense thickened, while rumors multiplied on every street corner and
in every café.   Finally Evita addressed the nation by radio, saying that
she would not be a candidate.   The reasons for that decision may never
be fully known, but most impartial observers believe that it was the result
of pressure from several influential groups.   The army seems to have been
bitterly opposed to the possibility, however remote, of a woman as
commander-in-chief.   Many party workers, especially from the provinces,
undoubtedly shuddered at the prospect of a woman in high public office.
In any event, Evita's name was withdrawn from consideration as a vice-
presidential candidate of the Peronistas, and the honor went to Hortensio
Quijano, the incumbent vice-president who had long suffered from serious
illness.[11]

PRESIDENTIAL CAMPAIGN OF 1951: *The rivals.*   In July, 1951, Congress
passed a law fixing November of that year as the time of the next presidential election, three months ahead of schedule.   The Radicals promptly

[10] Page 10.
[11] Vice-President Quijano died on April 3, 1952.

SUPPRESSION OF *La Prensa*. The great Buenos Aires newspaper, *La Prensa*, had been thoroughly crushed several months before the election. As early as January of 1951 the news vendors were encouraged to present a long list of utterly unreasonable demands to the management of *La Prensa*, and to climax this action with a long and bloody strike. Gasoline bombs were hurled into the offices of the newspaper. The police did nothing, of course. Finally the employees of *La Prensa*, who had remained loyal throughout the dispute but had been forced to stay away from work by threats of violence, decided to take matters into their own hands. More than one thousand of them gathered in a body and tried to force their way into the newspaper plant for the purpose of resuming their jobs. Their lives were threatened by hoodlums, who actually killed one employee. But most of *La Prensa*'s workers managed to get inside, only to be arrested by the police, who had stayed at a discreet distance during the fighting. It was now abundantly clear that the government would not permit *La Prensa* to continue as an independent newspaper. The publisher was threatened with arrest, but managed to escape to Uruguay. In April, 1951, Congress passed a law expropriating *La Prensa*. Provision was made for compensating the owners, but at the same time the government instituted lawsuits against the newspaper, asking for fantastic penalties that were sure to exceed the compensation. On November 19, just eight days after the presidential election, *La Prensa* reappeared on the newsstands. But in the meantime it had been turned over to the government-controlled Labor Federation, and had been transformed into a mouthpiece of the Perón regime. The last great champion of Argentine liberty was dead.[14]

DEATH OF LITTLE EVA. On July 26, 1952, the Argentine nation was officially notified of the death of Eva Perón. Followers and sycophants of Perón, as well as thousands of plain people, went to extravagant lengths to demonstrate their grief. Eight persons were killed and thousands injured in the crush of mourners. For a time Evita's body lay in state in the offices of the Ministry of Labor; later it was transferred to the Palace of Congress, and then to the headquarters of the Labor Federation. Eventually it will be placed in a magnificent mausoleum that is now under construction. Every worker in Argentina has "voluntarily" contributed one day's pay to help finance this burial place. Stamps have been issued bearing Evita's portrait; cities, streets, and schools have been re-

[14] See *Perón's Argentina*, by George I. Blanksten, pp. 209–214. See also Robert J. Alexander's previously cited work, pp. 62–68.

named in her honor; her book, *The Reason for My Life,* has been made required reading in all the public schools; a perpetual flame has been lighted in her honor; and one ardent group has even turned to the Vatican with the request that she be made a saint. To what extent this adulation and grief are genuine is an interesting question, but one not readily answered. Dissent is a luxury that few Argentines can now afford. One public employee who came to work without the black necktie and arm-band prescribed by the authorities was promptly dismissed, and told that he was on the government's blacklist for life.[15]

ECONOMIC PROBLEMS. The Perón regime has survived a number of economic crises, but only with great difficulty. The sharply rising cost of living has caused great dissatisfaction among the workers, despite frequent wage increases. Waves of strikes have swept the country from time to time, and the government has alternated between cajolery and force in restoring industrial peace. The effort to industrialize Argentina at a headlong pace, as contemplated in the Five-Year Plan of 1946, proved too great a strain on the nation's economy and had to be modified. The at-tempt to compel the great landowners to sell their beef, wheat, and corn at unreasonably low prices, in order to enable the government to reap a rich profit in the world market, led to a very substantial cut in the production of these commodities. Black bread replaced white in Argentine bakeries. Argentines were told that they must accustom themselves to meatless days—at the outset, one day a week, but later two. This was sheer tragedy, for it involved a complete change in the eating habits of the nation. The people of Argentina had long consumed more meat per capita than the people of any other nation.

Perón had explanations for these misfortunes, of course. They were due to the two-year drought, to the increased meat consumption of the more prosperous working class, to the evil schemes of hostile nations (principally the United States)—but not in any case to the mistakes of the Argentine government. And on the positive side of the ledger there were a number of entries, for which Perón took full credit. Industrialization had un-doubtedly made substantial strides. The foreign debt had been paid off almost completely. Illiteracy had been greatly reduced. And public works—especially highways and irrigation projects—had received greater attention than ever before.

Today the government is trying, with some success, to restore agricul-

---

[15] *Hispanic American Report,* September, 1952, pp. 33–34. See also Robert J. Alexander's article, "Perón Rules Alone," in the March, 1953, issue of *Current History,* pp. 159–164.

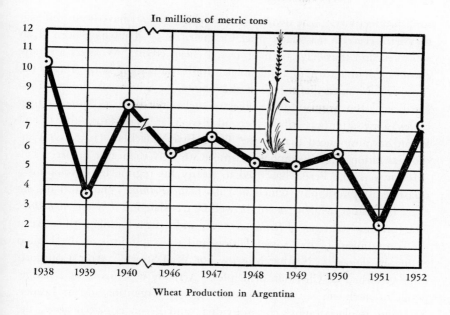

In millions of metric tons

Wheat Production in Argentina

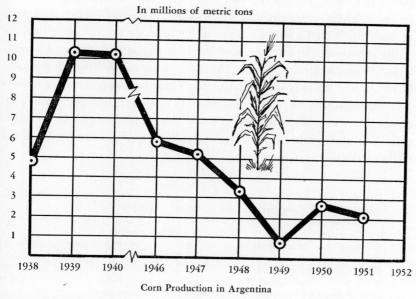

In millions of metric tons

Corn Production in Argentina

Based on information in the May, 1953, issue of *International Financial Statistics*, a publication of the International Monetary Fund.

tural productivity. The owners of the great *estancias* have been told that they will receive a reasonable price for their crops. They have been given subsidies, and they have been promised cheap credit. Workers are now encouraged to return to rural areas. Industrialization is no longer the primary and immediate goal of the nation, to which all else must be sacrificed. But as an ultimate objective it has not been forgotten. It receives some attention in the Second Five-Year Plan (1953–1958), and Perón has announced that in the Third Five-Year Plan (1958–1963) industrialization will be emphasized more strongly than ever before.

JUSTICIALISMO. Perón has tried to justify his regime by developing a quasi-fascist philosophy, which he calls *Justicialismo*. The word has no exact English equivalent; it might well be translated as *The era of justice*. The fundamental tenet of *Justicialismo* is said to be a middle path between the communism of the Soviet Union and the capitalism of the United States; its slogan is "Neither Moscow nor Wall Street." And it purports to be governed by Christian principles. Actually it seems to be a hodge-podge of catch phrases, all designed to glorify Argentina and its Leader. The state is placed above the individual, and Perón is placed above the state. In October of 1950 the Dictator made a balcony speech in which he set forth "twenty fundamental truths of *Justicialismo*." The movement, he said, established a balance between law and society. It placed capital at the service of the economy, and the economy at the service of society. It assured social justice for all. And of course it was truly democratic. In fact, it was the only real democracy. Those who opposed *Justicialismo* —in other words, those who opposed Perón—were by definition anti-democratic and traitors to their country. As a philosophy, *Justicialismo* may leave much to be desired, but as a collection of glittering generalities its political value is unquestioned.[16]

[16] The "Twenty Truths" of *Justicialismo,* as set forth by Perón in 1950, are:

1. True democracy is the system by which the government carries out the will of the people, defending a single objective: the interests of the people.
2. Peronism is an eminently popular movement. Every political clique is opposed to the popular interests and, therefore, it cannot be a Peronist organization.
3. A Peronist must be at the service of the cause. He who serves a clique or *caudillo* in the name of Peronism is a Peronist in name only.
4. There is only one class of men for the Peronist cause: the workers.
5. In the New Argentina, work is a right because it dignifies man, and a duty because it is only fair that each one should produce at least what he consumes.
6. There can be nothing better for a Peronist than another Peronist.
7. No Peronist should presume to be more than he really is, nor adopt a position inferior to his true social status. When a Peronist begins to think himself more important than he really is, he is on the way to becoming an oligarch.

SELECTED REFERENCES

Alexander, Robert J., *The Perón Era*, New York, Columbia University Press, 1951.

Blanksten, George I., *Perón's Argentina*, Chicago, University of Chicago Press, 1953.

Bradford, Saxtone E., *The Battle for Buenos Aires*, New York, Harcourt, Brace, 1943.

Bunge, Alejandro, *La Economía Argentina*, 4 Vols., Buenos Aires, Agencia General de Librerías y Publicaciones, 1928–1930.

—————— *Una Nueva Argentina*, Buenos Aires, Kraft, 1940.

Carril, Bonifacio del, *Buenos Aires frente al País*, Buenos Aires, Emecé Editores, 1944.

Congress of Industrial Organizations, *The Argentine Regime*, New York, C.I.O., 1946.

Cumberland, Charles C., *Mexican Revolution: Genesis under Madero*, Austin, University of Texas Press, 1952.

Dagnino Pastore, Lorenzo, *Geografía Económica y Política Argentina*, rev. ed., Buenos Aires, Crespillo, 1947.

Dickmann, Enrique, *Recuerdos de un Militante Socialista*, Buenos Aires, La Vanguardia, 1947.

Dorfman, Adolfo, *Historia de la Industria Argentina*, Buenos Aires, Escuela de Estudios Argentinos, 1942.

Editors of *La Prensa, Defense of Freedom*, New York, John Day, 1952.

Errecaborde, Alberto, *La Tierra y el Hombre; Nueva Legislación Agraria*, Buenos Aires, Editorial Perlado, 1948.

Flores, María, *The Woman with the Whip: Eva Perón*, New York, Doubleday, 1952.

---

8. With regard to political action the scale of values for all Peronists is: first, the homeland; second, the cause; third, mankind.

9. Politics do not constitute for us a definite objective, but only a means of achieving the homeland's welfare as represented by the happiness of the people and the greatness of the nation.

10. The two main branches of Peronism are social justice and social welfare. With these we envelop the people in an embrace of justice and love.

11. Peronism desires the establishment of national unity and the abolition of civil strife. It welcomes heroes but it does not want martyrs.

12. In the New Argentina the only privileged ones are the children.

13. A government without a doctrine is a body without a soul. That is why Peronism has established its own political, economic, and social doctrine: *Justicialismo*.

14. *Justicialismo* is a new philosophical school of life. It is simple, practical, popular, and endowed with deeply Christian and humanitarian sentiments.

15. As a political doctrine, *Justicialismo* establishes a fair balance between law and society.

16. As an economic doctrine, *Justicialismo* achieves a true form of social economy by placing capital at the service of the economy and the economy at the service of society.

17. As a social doctrine, *Justicialismo* assures an adequate distribution of social justice, giving to each person the rights to which he is entitled.

18. We desire a socially just, an economically free, and a politically independent Argentina.

19. We are an organized state and a free people ruled by a central government.

20. The best of this land is its people.

See *El Justicialismo: Doctrina y Realidad Peronista*, by Raúl A. Mende. See also *Conducción Política*, which is the published record of the lectures delivered by President Perón at the Peronist Superior School in 1951. For an excellent criticism in English of *Justicialismo*, see George I. Blanksten's previously cited work, pp. 276–305. See also *The State of Latin America*, by Germán Arciniegas, pp. 62–78.

Greenup, Ruth and Leonard, *Revolution before Breakfast; Argentina, 1941–1946,* Chapel Hill, N.C., Univ. of North Carolina Press, 1947.

Josephs, Ray, *Argentine Diary,* New York, Random House, 1944.

Kirkpatrick, F. A., *A History of the Argentine Republic,* Cambridge, Eng., Cambridge Univ. Press, 1931.

Levene, Ricardo, *A History of Argentina* (translated by William S. Robertson), Chapel Hill, N.C., Univ. of North Carolina Press, 1937.

Macdonald, Austin F., *Government of the Argentine Republic,* New York, Crowell, 1942.

Mende, Raúl A., *El Justicialismo: Doctrina y Realidad Peronista,* Buenos Aires, Alea, 1950.

Moyano Llerena, Carlos, *Argentina Social y Económica,* Buenos Aires, *Editorial Depalma,* 1950.

Nudelman, Santiago, *El Radicalismo al Servicio de la Libertad,* Buenos Aires, Editorial Jus, 1947.

Partido Peronista, *Manual del Peronista,* Editorial Ateneo, 1949.

Perón, Eva, *La Razón de mi Vida,* Buenos Aires, Ediciones Peuser, 1951.

Perón, Juan, *Conducción Política,* Buenos Aires, Escuela Superior Peronista, 1951.

Phillips, Henry A., *Argentina; Pivot of Pan-American Peace,* New York, Hastings House, 1944.

Rennie, Ysabel F., *The Argentine Republic,* New York, Macmillan, 1945.

Richmond, Leonard T., *Argentina's Third Position and Other Systems Compared,* Buenos Aires, Acme Agency, 1949.

Rodríguez, Carlos J., *Irigoyen; Su Revolución Política y Social,* Buenos Aires, La Facultad, 1943.

Rowe, Leo S., *The Federal System of the Argentine Republic,* Washington, D.C., Carnegie Institution, 1921.

Sammartino, Ernesto, *La Verdad sobre la Situación Argentina,* 2nd ed., Montevideo, 1951.

Sharp, Roland H., *South America Uncensored,* New York, Longmans, Green, 1945.

Smith, C. Edmund, Jr., *Yankee Diplomacy: United States Intervention in Argentina,* Dallas, Southern Methodist University Press, 1952.

Taylor, Carl C., *Rural Life in Argentina,* Baton Rouge, Louisiana State University Press, 1948.

Verde Tello, Pedro, *El Partido Socialista,* Buenos Aires, La Vanguardia, 1952.

Weil, Félix José, *Argentine Riddle,* New York, John Day, 1944.

White, John W., *Argentina: The Life Story of a Nation,* New York, Viking Press, 1942.

CHAPTER 4

ARGENTINA
The Structure of Government

~~~~~~

The Constitution

THE CONSTITUTION adopted by Argentina in 1853, and revised extensively in 1860, served the nation for nearly a century. For many years it was the oldest constitution in Latin America. Since 1949, however, the Argentine Republic has had a new fundamental law. The present constitution differs from its predecessor in a number of important respects, yet fundamentally the two documents are very much alike. Both are based on the constitution of the United States. Juan Bautista Alberdi, who has often been called the father of the Argentine constitution of 1853, took his ideas very liberally from American sources, and the committee that framed the document acknowledged this debt in its report to the constitutional convention. "This project," it explained, "is modeled in the form of the constitution of the United States, the only example of a true federation that exists in the world." [1] The 1949 constitutional convention retained most of the old fundamental law, though adding, substituting, or modifying many clauses. So even the present constitution of Argentina strongly reflects American influence. There are, however, substantial differences between the fundamental laws of the two nations. The president of Argentina, for example, is given considerably more authority than the chief executive of the United States. In Argentina Roman Catholicism is declared to be the official state-supported religion, and the president and vice-president are required to be members of its communion. [2]

[1] González Calderón, Juan A., *Derecho Constitucional Argentino*, 3rd ed., Vol. 1, p. 278.
[2] Constitution of 1949, Arts. 2 and 77.

THE BILL OF RIGHTS. The constitution of 1853 contained a substantial list of guarantees of individual freedom. The 1949 model follows the same general plan. It assures freedom of speech and press, freedom of religion, and the right to petition for the redress of grievances, to hold and dispose of property, and to travel freely within the territory of the nation. It declares that there shall be no arbitrary arrests, no convictions for crime except in the manner specified by law, and no unreasonable violation of the sanctity of the home. In addition to these traditional guarantees, however, the 1949 document includes many of the "social rights" that have become so popular in modern constitutions. The laborer is assured an adequate moral and material return for his work; the family is guaranteed protection by the state; old age is promised special consideration; and youth is told that it may receive education to the limit of its capacity. It must be understood, however, that these sweeping generalizations are merely broad statements of policy, to be carried out "in conformity with the laws." The president and Congress decide when they shall become effective, and to what extent.

SUSPENSION OF GUARANTEES. The value of any bill of rights depends, of course, on its interpretation. It is no better than the officials who enforce it. In Argentina, prior to the revolution of 1943, the tradition of individual liberty had become well established. Men said what they thought, without fear of reprisals by the government. The great metropolitan dailies of the city of Buenos Aires, as well as the newspapers of the provincial cities, were free to criticize cabinet ministers, leaders of Congress, or even the president himself. Although the papers sometimes took advantage of this freedom to print untruths or half truths, public officials displayed admirable restraint. They were justifiably proud of Argentina's reputation as a protector of individual liberty.

Ramírez, Farrell, and Perón changed all that. They speedily made a mockery of the more important constitutional guarantees. People could no longer speak their minds for fear of arbitrary arrest. Newspapers could not criticize the government without danger of serious repercussions.[3] Since Perón's election to the presidency the guarantees of liberty have been ignored just as systematically as in the first days of the military dictatorship. The present administration has succeeded in making the bill of rights virtually a dead letter.

The constitution itself provides a means by which the guarantees of

3 See page 89.

individual liberty may be set aside in times of emergency. This is the *state of siege*, the temporary annulment of all constitutional guarantees and privileges. Originally borrowed from the French, it has been accepted almost everywhere in Latin America.[4] It is regarded as a useful device for strengthening governmental authority in times of national peril, and there can be no doubt that it has proved its value. But, like every such measure, it is subject to abuse. The framers of the constitution of 1853 tried to prevent the misuse of the state of siege by imposing a number of restrictions, which have been retained in the present document: the president must have the consent of the Senate, if Congress is in session; he may not impose sentence or inflict punishment on persons accused of crime; he may not suspend constitutional guarantees for an indefinite period. The 1949 constitution recognizes not only the state of siege but also another device with an imposing name: *state of prevention and alarm.* It may be imposed whenever "the normal course of life or the fundamental activities of the population" are threatened. Its effect is not to suspend constitutional guarantees, but merely to limit them temporarily if necessary.[5] Just what the state of prevention and alarm adds to—or takes from—the state of siege is not entirely clear; the two powers seem to overlap. But this much is reasonably certain: any constitutional restrictions on the use of either power may be regarded lightly. They are no real handicap to Juan Perón or his police.

AMENDMENT OF THE CONSTITUTION. The Argentine constitution may be amended much more easily than the constitution of the United States. The 1853 document, also, was capable of easy amendment, yet it was altered but twice after 1860. This infrequency of amendment may have been due to the fact that Argentine constitutional provisions were regarded as somewhat elastic. The president acted in accordance with his own interpretation of the fundamental law, or even more or less in open defiance of it. Congressmen sometimes objected to this presidential abuse of authority, but speedily changed their minds if their own interests were favored. The courts, though empowered to declare laws unconstitutional, were always loath to do so. Since the Perón purge of the supreme court [6] they have been still less inclined to challenge any government policy. Within reasonable limits, therefore, it might almost be said that the con-

---

[4] See pages 6–7.
[5] Constitution, Art. 34; Art. 83, Cl. 19.
[6] See page 83.

stitution has always meant what the president wanted it to mean. Formal amendment seemed scarcely necessary. Yet an entirely new constitution was adopted in 1949.

The method of reforming the 1949 constitution, which follows the 1853 model in this respect, is set forth in Article 21: "Either the whole or any part . . . may be amended. The necessity for such amendment must be declared by Congress by a vote of at least two thirds of the members present, but the amendment shall not be made except by a convention summoned for that purpose." When Congress summons a constitutional convention, it indicates the articles of the constitution that seem to need reformation, and the convention may consider no others. But Congress may not indicate the exact nature of the changes to be made or compel the adoption of any reforms.[7]

Suffrage and Elections

WHO MAY VOTE. The constitution makes no attempt to establish qualifications for voting. This matter is therefore regulated by federal law for federal elections, and by the laws of the provinces for provincial and municipal elections. There used to be considerable diversity, but now the vote is generally extended to all persons who have attained the age of eighteen years, provided they do not fall into certain categories that have been specifically excluded, such as convicted criminals, insane persons, deserters from the armed forces, or—for very different reasons—clergymen and members of the regular army. Women did not vote in national elections until 1948, but they have now been placed on a par with men in this regard.

The theory of Argentine government makes voting not only a right but a definite obligation. Eligible persons must vote, according to the law, and penalties are prescribed for failure to do so. In practice, however, the compulsory features of the election law are almost never enforced. They are too complicated for ready application to large numbers of persons. Therefore, men and women go to the polls or stay at home on election day according to their individual desires, without fear that failure to vote will bring punishment.

ELECTION PROCEDURE. The polls are open on election day from eight in the morning until six in the evening. Each voting place is in charge

---

[7] There is a good discussion of the amending process in Segundo V. Linares Quintana's *Gobierno y Administración de la República Argentina*, Vol. I, pp. 215–221.

of a president of elections who is designated by higher authorities. The several political parties are represented by watchers, whose presence is authorized by law. When an elector enters the voting place, he gives his name to the president of elections and presents evidence of his identity. He is then handed an unsealed blank envelope and invited to retire to the privacy of an adjoining room in order to indicate his choice. Although the government provides the official envelopes in which the ballots are placed, it does not provide the ballots. These are prepared by the parties at their own expense in conformity with government regulations concerning size, shape, and color. The texture of the paper is not identical for the ballots of all parties, but this detail is trivial, since every ballot is enclosed in a heavy envelope before it reaches the ballot box. Stacks of ballots are placed in the private room adjoining the main polling place. In privacy, therefore, the voter selects the ballot of his choice. It is obvious that each party will include only the names of its own candidates; splitting the ticket therefore becomes somewhat difficult. But it is not impossible, for the law authorizes the voter to cross out names and write in other names, provided he does not "scratch" more than one half of his chosen party's candidates. A system of limited voting is used for the election of members of the Chamber of Deputies, the lower house of the national Congress. Each voter may mark his ballot for but two thirds of the total number of vacancies. If, therefore, nine deputies are to be elected, each voter may express only six preferences. But if there are eleven vacancies, thus entitling the elector to vote for seven and one-third candidates, he may indicate eight choices. And if only two offices are to be filled, he may vote for the full number. This plan was adopted in the hope of insuring adequate representation to minorities. In practice, however, it has sometimes produced grotesque results—a single party once gained two thirds of the representation of a province by capturing twenty-seven per cent of the total vote.[8]

The President

IMPORTANCE OF THE PRESIDENT. "The president," declares the constitution, "is the supreme head of the nation, and has the general administration of the country in his charge." [9] In the scheme of Argentine political life he is more important than Congress or the courts, or the two combined. His authority is greater than that of the president of the United States

---

[8] Crespo, Eduardo, *Nuevos Ensayos Políticos y Administrativos,* p. 55.
[9] Art. 83, Cl. 1.

or the chiefs of state of most democratic nations. The framers of the Argentine constitutions of both 1853 and 1949 were impressed with the need for a strong executive. They authorized the president to appoint and remove almost the entire personnel of the national administration without the necessity of securing Senate approval. They permitted him not only to call special sessions of Congress, but also to extend regular sessions beyond the usual five-months period. They entrusted him with the power to declare a state of siege when Congress was not in session.

The years since the adoption of the constitution of 1853 have witnessed the development of other presidential powers, based largely on custom. Many matters of public policy are now determined by presidential decree instead of congressional action, and many expenditures are ordered by the president without reference to law. These are not new developments, having become a regularly accepted part of Argentine government long before the days of Perón and his military friends. Although it is true that President Perón has raised the presidency to a new peak of power—he has secured a strangle hold on Congress [10] and reduced the judiciary to virtual impotence [11]—the president of Argentina has always been a strong man.

QUALIFICATIONS. The constitution declares that the president must be a natural-born citizen, not less than thirty years of age. Mention has already been made of the fact that the president, as head of a Roman Catholic state, must be a member of that faith.[12] In addition to these formal requirements there are, of course, political specifications that cannot always be met so easily: the successful candidate must be one of the party leaders or a dominant figure in the army, and he should be a native of Buenos Aires because of that city's great political influence.

METHOD OF SELECTION. Until 1949 the president was elected indirectly, as in the United States. Today, however, he is chosen directly by the people, by a simple plurality of votes. "For the purpose of electing the president . . . the provinces, the federal capital, and the national territories shall form a single district." [13]

TERM. The president serves for six years. According to the constitution of 1853, he could not be re-elected "except with an interval of one term." The men who prepared that document were vividly impressed by the seventeen-year tyranny of Juan Manuel de Rosas, whom they had

[10] See page 88.
[11] See page 85.
[12] See page 95.
[13] Constitution, Art. 82.

overthrown the previous year, and they were determined that no other leader should establish a "perpetual despotism." Until the advent of Juan Perón their efforts were strikingly successful. Second presidential terms were almost unknown in Argentina. Only two presidents assumed office a second time under the 1853 constitution, and only one completed two terms. But today all is changed. The present constitution specifically declares that the president is eligible for re-election. In fact, it imposes no limit on the number of terms that may be served.[14] So apparently there is no reason, short of revolution, why Perón should not equal the record of the tyrant Rosas.

SALARY AND PLACE OF RESIDENCE. The salary of the president, translated into American currency, is about thirty thousand dollars a year, in addition to which he receives substantial sums for entertainment, travel, and the like. He is also supplied with an official residence. Until a few years ago it was the *Casa Rosada,* which fronts the Plaza de Mayo in the heart of Buenos Aires. Now, however, the *Casa Rosada* is used for presidential and other offices, and the president has an official home in another part of the city.

POWERS: *Executive head of the nation.* The powers of the president fall naturally into three main groups—executive, legislative, and judicial. Among the executive powers is the general authority to enforce the laws and direct the public administration. "The president issues the instructions and regulations necessary for putting the laws of the nation into effect," declares the constitution, "but shall see to it that their spirit is not altered by exceptions made by the regulations."[15] The appointing power of the president, as previously indicated,[16] is very extensive. He names the members of the civil and military services of the nation, federal judges, diplomats, and high-ranking ecclesiastics. For the most part he acts without the necessity of consulting any other person or body. There are, however, some exceptions to this general rule. Senate approval is necessary for members of the judiciary and the diplomatic corps, and for certain high officers of the army and navy. It may also be required for offices created by law, if Congress sees fit to impose this condition. And though the president names the bishops and archbishops of the Catholic Church, he does so from lists of three submitted by the Senate. These exceptions are important, of course, but they leave the president ample discretion in

[14] Art. 78.
[15] Art. 83, Cl. 2.
[16] See page 100.

the selection of his subordinates. His power of removal is absolute, except for ambassadors and ministers plenipotentiary, whose cases must be presented for Senate consent.

The president is commander-in-chief of the armed forces of the nation, and the officer responsible for its defense. This does not mean that he is expected to assume active command of military campaigns, though in the early days some Argentine presidents actually took the field at the head of their troops. More commonly the details of military strategy are left to the professional militarists, while the civilian president occupies himself with the broader aspects of army and navy administration, supplementing the laws of Congress with necessary regulations. In time of war, or when a state of siege has been declared, these presidential powers assume major proportions.

The conduct of foreign relations falls within the scope of the president's authority. Since he names ambassadors and foreign ministers, they are virtually his personal representatives. He receives the diplomats accredited by other nations, and in this way grants or withholds recognition of newly established governments. The treaties that he negotiates must receive the approval of a majority of both houses of Congress, instead of a two-thirds Senate majority, as in the United States.

Power to summon Congress. The president possesses a considerable measure of control over legislation. The constitution expressly declares that Congress shall assemble in ordinary session every year on the first day of May, but in practice Congress does not begin its session until the president is ready to appear before the two chambers for the purpose of presenting his annual message on the state of the nation. The message is seldom ready by May 1, so Congress marks time while it awaits the pleasure of the chief executive.

Under the authority of the constitution the president calls special sessions of Congress, as in the United States, and also extends the regular sessions. Therefore the decision as to whether congressional activity shall extend beyond the official deadline of September 30 rests, not with the members of Congress, but with the president. In fact, the president may even dissolve the sessions of Congress whenever he desires to do so. In 1908 President Alcorta told the congressmen to return to their homes, and enforced this demand with federal troops. Even Juan Perón has not taken such a drastic step since his election to the presidency.

Introduction of bills. "Laws may originate in either chamber of Congress," declares the constitution, "by means of bills presented by their members *or by the executive power."* [17]   Thus the president is specifically given the right to participate in the process of framing legislation.   He possesses no more actual authority, in this regard, than the president of the United States, who may introduce so-called "administration" measures through friendly congressmen.   But at least the president of the Argentine Republic is spared the necessity of resorting to subterfuge; he sends directly to Congress, in his own name, the final drafts of the bills he regards as necessary for the national welfare.

Veto power.   When a bill has been enacted by both houses of Congress, it goes to the president for his signature.   The president has twenty days in which to decide whether he will approve or veto, but failure to sign within the twenty-day limit is regarded as a tacit indication of consent, regardless of whether Congress is still in session; there is no pocket veto, as in the United States.[18]   A two-thirds vote in each chamber is necessary to override a presidential veto, and in Argentina it is seldom obtained.   Today, with Perón's strangle hold on both houses of Congress, it would be unthinkable.   The constitution of 1853 made no reference to the power of item veto, and therefore presumably denied such authority, yet several presidents vetoed certain items in budget bills, and then put the remainder into effect.   The present constitution specifically authorizes the chief executive to veto portions of bills, and does not limit this power to budget measures.[19]

Decree-laws.   Every modern nation has experienced the trend toward a multiplication of administrative regulations interpreting and enforcing the general rules established by the legislative body.   A well-ordered legislature no longer attempts to provide for every conceivable circumstance; it has learned that better results can be obtained by authorizing the executive branch to supply the details and make the exceptions.   But, as pointed out in an earlier chapter,[20] Latin Americans have carried to extremes the practice of government by decree.   Argentina is an outstanding example. The president not only regulates the details of established policies by executive order; he actually makes many of the policies that govern the nation, and puts them into effect without consulting Congress.   He is a lawmaker in his own right.

[17] Art. 69.
[18] In the United States the president may veto a bill by simply "pocketing" it (that is, failing to take any action concerning it), if Congress adjourns within the ten-day period permitted for presidential consideration.
[19] Art. 73.
[20] See pages 3–4.

Pardons. "The president of the nation," states the constitution, "may grant pardons or commute penalties for crimes subject to federal jurisdiction, after obtaining a report from the tribunal in question, except in cases of impeachment by the Chamber of Deputies." [21]   Although the president must first consult the court that imposed sentence in order to be certain that he understands all the facts involved, he is under no obligation to follow the court's recommendation.   The question of granting or withholding pardon is solely within his discretion.

Expulsion of foreigners. A law enacted by Congress in 1902, and still on the statute books, authorizes the president to expel from the country any aliens who have been convicted of crime by the courts of a foreign nation, or whose presence compromises the public security or perturbs the public order. This is a far-reaching power. It enables the chief executive to impose upon foreigners the severe penalty of expulsion without judicial trial. From his decision they have no appeal. The constitutionality of this law was challenged a number of years ago, but was upheld by the supreme court.

THE VICE-PRESIDENT. The vice-president of the nation occupies approximately the same position as in the United States. He presides over the Senate, but his most important function is conditional—to assume the duties of the presidency if for some reason the president should be incapable of performing them. The qualifications of the vice-president are the same as those of the president. This is necessarily so, since he may be called upon to assume the presidency. He receives an annual salary of approximately fifteen thousand dollars a year. Since he normally belongs to the same party as the president, it is commonly assumed that he will continue the administration's policies if he should inherit the executive authority. In past years this assumption has not always been justified, however.

SUCCESSION TO THE PRESIDENCY. The constitution provides that Congress shall determine the succession to the presidency in the event of the death or incapacity of both president and vice-president. In 1868 Congress enacted the necessary legislation, which is still in force. It specifies that the order of presidential succession shall be: (1) the provisional president of the Senate, (2) the president of the Chamber of Deputies, and (3) the president of the supreme court. The occasion for the operation of this law has not yet arisen, since both the president and vice-president have not been removed by death or other cause during a single term.

21 Art. 83, Cl. 6.

The National Administration

THE CABINET.   When the constitution of 1853 was adopted, it made the mistake of specifying the exact number of cabinet ministers—five—and indicating their titles.   Apparently the founding fathers did not foresee the vast growth of governmental activity, necessitating a larger number of ministers and a rearrangement of functions.   The result was that this portion of the constitution had to be amended.   As revised in 1898, it provided for eight cabinet members and did not mention the exact phases of the public business to come under their direction, thereby permitting greater flexibility in the organization of the national administration.   The present constitution does not attempt to specify the number of cabinet officers.   It merely declares that the matter shall be fixed by "a law of the nation, upon the proposal of the executive power." [22]   Today there are twenty-one cabinet ministers—a larger number than in any other nation of the Americas.[23]   These ministers are chosen by the president and are responsible solely to him.

CABINET MINISTERS AND CONGRESS.   "The ministers may attend the joint or separate sessions of the Senate and the Chamber of Deputies, in order to present reports and take part in the debates, without the right to vote." [24]   In practice, however, they almost never go to the legislative chambers unless sent by the president to explain matters of importance.   One clause of the 1853 constitution declared: "Each chamber may cause the ministers of the executive power to appear before it in order to receive such explanation and information as may be deemed advisable." [25]   The exact meaning of these words was never entirely clear.   Obviously they authorized Congress to demand that the department heads appear before it to explain their policies and their conduct.   But suppose Congress was not satisfied with the explanations offered?   Might it adopt a resolution of censure?   And, if so, what was the effect of such a motion?   Did it imply that the ministers thus criticized had lost the legislature's confidence, and must therefore resign?   Obviously it did not.   In the Argentine scheme of government the members of the president's cabinet are and have always been responsible solely to him.   They are under no obligation whatever

[22] Art. 84.

[23] Here is the imposing list of cabinet posts: Foreign Affairs and Worship, Interior, Justice, Education, Public Health, Communications, Political Affairs, Economic Affairs, Treasury, Foreign Trade, Finance, Industry and Commerce, Public Works, Agriculture and Husbandry, Labor and Welfare, Transport, Defense, Army, Navy, Aeronautics, Technical Affairs.

[24] Art. 88.

[25] Art. 63.

to please the legislature, except as political expediency may suggest; and if either chamber expresses dissatisfaction with their conduct, it does no more than any private citizen might do, with equal effect. The present constitution seems to be quite explicit on this score. Instead of speaking of the power of Congress to summon cabinet ministers, it merely states: "Each of the chambers may ask the chief executive to supply information on matters within the scope of its authority. The chief executive may answer in person or by means of a written report, or he may send one of his ministers to convey the information." [26]

ORGANIZATION OF THE MINISTRIES. The cabinet ministers—the heads of the principal departments—are chosen for political reasons, so it is obvious that they have no knowledge, unless by chance, of the administrative routine they are supposed to direct. Under such circumstances it is desirable to have permanent undersecretaries who are trained administrators, capable of advising their nominal superiors and maintaining continuity of ministerial policy, regardless of the political changes that mark the rise and fall of party fortunes. With this thought in mind, the office of undersecretary for each ministry was established by decree, and the newly appointed undersecretaries were given the task of advising the ministers and the president on all technical aspects of government activity. Unfortunately, however, this plan has never worked as its framers intended, because the men appointed as undersecretaries have not been trained administrators. Instead they have been promising young politicians, subject as much as the ministers themselves to the vicissitudes of party politics. The results have frequently been evident in the low quality of the public services.

SELECTION OF PERSONNEL. There is no uniform system of selecting public personnel in the federal service—or, for that matter, in the administrative services of the several provinces. No central personnel agency exists, and there is no central control over employment, promotion, discipline, or dismissal. There are, to be sure, a few general rules that Congress has extended to the entire federal service, but no department or bureau is responsible for their enforcement. In practice, therefore, there are virtually no restrictions on the authority of every federal agency to hire such persons as it may desire, with or without examination, and to dismiss them whenever it is so inclined, with or without reasons. Some employees, especially in the technical and clerical groups, are chosen by competitive examinations, which are required by the rules of the bureau

[26] Art. 64.

directly concerned—not by general law. In such cases the bureau chief appoints examining committees, usually naming his immediate subordinates. It is probably no exaggeration, however, to say that ninety-nine per cent of the men and women in the service of the government have been chosen more or less directly for political reasons. Loyalty to Perón is the primary test.

Congress

THEORY VERSUS PRACTICE. The Congress of the Argentine Republic still functions, at least in theory, in just about the same way that it did prior to the rise of Perón. It debates and adopts legislative proposals; it passes upon presidential nominations to administrative and judicial posts. In fact, it goes through all the motions of a co-ordinate branch of the government. But since both houses of Congress are completely dominated by Perón's followers, who servilely accept his orders, the theory of legislative independence gives way in practice to the reality of the Perón dictatorship.

TERMS AND QUALIFICATIONS. Congress is composed of two houses. The upper house, the Senate, is composed of thirty-four members, two from each of the sixteen provinces and two from the federal capital. Senators are elected by direct vote of the people for a term of six years, and one half of the Senate's membership is renewed every three years. Every senator must be at least thirty years of age, and must have been a citizen of the nation for at least ten years, as well as a native or two-year resident of the province from which he is chosen. Senators serve for six years, and are not restricted to any given number of terms. Vacancies are filled by special elections, rather than by the American plan of gubernatorial appointment.

The Chamber of Deputies has a membership of one hundred and fifty-eight, apportioned among the provinces and the federal capital on the basis of population. Deputies are chosen by direct popular vote. The constitution declares that "every deputy is required to have attained the age of twenty-five years, to have enjoyed four years' citizenship, and to be a native of the province in which elected, or have been resident therein for the two years next preceding election." [27]   The term of office is six years, one half of the total membership retiring every third year.

SALARIES AND PERQUISITES. Every senator and deputy is paid a salary of about nine thousand dollars a year. In addition he is entitled to unlimited railroad travel. No special allowance is made for clerical or stenographic

[27] Art. 43.

assistance, except to chairmen of important committees. Nor is provision made for office space, though a few of the party leaders sometimes manage to convert into offices the unused corners of committee or caucus rooms.

THE PALACE OF CONGRESS. The Palace of Congress, where the national legislature holds its sessions, is a handsome domed structure somewhat reminiscent of the capitol of the United States. It stands at the far end of the Avenida de Mayo, which was once the proudest street in Buenos Aires. At the other end of the avenue is the *Casa Rosada,* from whose windows the president may obtain an unrestricted view of the congressional palace, and perhaps keep a figurative eye on legislative activities. The meeting place of the Chamber of Deputies is in the western end of the building. The room is semicircular. On a raised platform sits the president of the Chamber, facing the members. The senior secretary is at his right, and the junior secretary at his left. Directly below in front of the president are the stenographers, who busily record the debates. A long table, not far from the stenographers, has eight chairs; here the cabinet ministers sit when they attend. A few seats on the raised platform, on either side of the president and the secretaries, are reserved for senators and other distinguished visitors who may wish to attend the Chamber's sessions. There are, in addition, three galleries for ordinary visitors, arranged in tiers around the semicircle. And finally there is the press gallery, which is situated behind and above the president. Every deputy has a desk to which he has been specially assigned, and these desks occupy most of the main floor. The Senate arrangement is much the same, except that the room is very small.

CONGRESSIONAL SESSIONS. The constitution specifies that there shall be five months of regular congressional sessions every year, from the first day of May until the last day of September. As already noted, the president may extend a regular session, or call a special session, whenever he deems such action expedient.[28]

Both houses hold regular meetings three days a week—the Chamber on Wednesday, Thursday, and Friday, and the Senate on Tuesday, Thursday, and Friday. The usual hours are from three-thirty in the afternoon until nine in the evening; this arrangement causes no inconvenience, since nine-thirty is the Argentine dinner hour (formal dinners commonly begin at ten or even later). At times, when the pressure of business is great or passions are running high, congressmen may completely ignore the call of home or club and continue in session until midnight, and meetings have

[28] See page 102.

been known to extend completely around the clock. But such devotion to duty is not the rule.

OFFICERS AND COMMITTEES. The presiding officer of the Chamber of Deputies bears the title of president. He is chosen by the Chamber from its own membership by a plurality of votes. He serves for only one year, but according to the rules he may be re-elected for any number of terms. In practice, however, he is almost invariably replaced at the end of a single period by some other party leader. In the Senate the vice-president of the nation presides, but without the right to vote unless there is a tie.

Each house has a number of permanent standing committees—nineteen in the Chamber of Deputies and eleven in the Senate. Each party prepares its own list of committee memberships, and receives representation in proportion to its strength. At present, of course, the Perón forces command the situation so completely that other parties have virtually no voice in the affairs of the committees. The rules of the Chamber of Deputies provide that the president of that body shall appoint the members of the standing committees, but in practice he merely follows the recommendations of the party caucus. In the Senate the presiding officer has not had even nominal control of committee appointments since 1923.

WORK OF COMMITTEES. A committee chooses its own president, who presides over its deliberations and directs the day-by-day routine. In both houses of Congress all the regular standing committees function for three years—in other words, until there is another congressional election necessitating a substantial turnover in committee memberships. Committee meetings are almost invariably secret. Cabinet members may be summoned to explain the measures for which they are responsible, or to give information concerning various aspects of the nation's needs, but outsiders are almost never asked to attend. A committee is not obliged to consider all the proposals that are submitted to it, or to report to the entire chamber concerning its views. It does not, in fact, report on measures unless it intends to recommend their enactment. There are, however, a few exceptions to the general rule that a measure need not be reported unless the committee so desires. Most important is the budget bill, which must be returned within one month.

As soon as a bill is reported favorably by a committee, it is printed for the use of the membership of the house. In this form, of course, it contains all committee amendments. The committee's statement of reasons for making these changes—or reporting the measure without alterations—is not printed, however; instead, it is presented orally to the chamber when the bill finally reaches the discussion stage. The committee designates one of its own number to perform this duty, presumably selecting the best-informed or most interested member as informant. The minority may give a dissenting report, if it so desires, and this statement also is oral.

THE CALENDAR. Each house maintains a calendar of business, and bills are placed on this calendar in the order that they are received from the several committees. They are not permitted to remain in this order, however, nor are they arranged according to their relative importance. Instead the party leaders sort the measures on the calendar—only a small fraction of which can possibly hope to receive legislative consideration—and indicate the ones to be given preference. Some years ago the decisions of the leaders were occasionally challenged by the rank and file of the party membership, and then the various questions of precedence were thrashed out in debate. Such challenges have been virtually unknown since the rise of Perón.

DEBATE AND VOTING. After a bill has been favorably reported by committee, and has finally been made the order of the day, it receives two readings—one for the purpose of discussing in general terms the fundamental principles involved, and the other to consider in detail every article and section. There are fairly rigid time limits on debate in both houses of Congress, but in the larger Chamber of Deputies they are necessarily more severe. Voting may be *viva voce*—that is, by the mere sound of voices; it may be nominal—each member responding to his name as it is called; or it may be by sign—by rising or a show of hands. Since 1936 the Chamber of Deputies has used an electric voting machine, which records accurately and instantaneously the opinion of every member. The Senate still commonly votes *viva voce,* or by a show of hands, for its small membership and still smaller attendance make an electric machine unnecessary.

DISAGREEMENTS BETWEEN THE HOUSES. The constitutional provisions concerning disagreements between the two houses of Congress differ widely from those of the constitution of the United States. In Argentina it is not necessary that both chambers reach complete unanimity on all points before a measure goes to the president. After it has been approved by one house, a bill passes automatically to the other. If the other chamber rejects it completely or fails to take any action, it may not be reintroduced during the session of that year. If, however, the other house merely makes additions or amendments, the proposal returns to the chamber where it originated. Here the amendments may be accepted, in which case the bill is ready for the presidential signature. Otherwise it returns to the revising chamber, which may insist by a two-thirds vote upon retaining the amended form. Then the bill goes back to the chamber of origin, whose members are deemed to approve the changes unless they reject them by a two-thirds majority. No attempt is made to compromise the opinions of the two houses by means of conference committees. This complicated arrangement undoubtedly tends to reduce the number of legislative deadlocks, but in some instances it does so by compelling the majority in one chamber to accept against its will the desires of a strong majority in the other.

SPECIAL POWERS OF EACH HOUSE. In general it may be said that both houses of Congress perform the same functions and exercise the same powers. They are co-ordinate bodies—equal partners in the task of framing legislation for the Argentine nation. However, each chamber does have certain powers that it does not share with the other. The Chamber of Deputies institutes impeachment proceedings, by a two-thirds vote. Until 1949 it initiated measures relating to taxation or the raising of troops, but the present constitution does not recognize its preferred status in these matters. The Senate has the power to try impeachments. The Argentine constitution, more specific in this regard than the constitution of the United States, enumerates the persons who may be impeached—the president and vice-president, cabinet ministers, and judges of the federal courts; and also lists the charges on which impeachment may be based—malfeasance, criminal offenses committed in the discharge of public functions, and common crimes.[29] During impeachment proceedings the Senate sits as a court, and gives judgment by a two-thirds vote. The president of the supreme court presides if the president of the nation is on trial. Conviction leads no further than to removal from office and disqualification from further service in the federal government. Only a few persons have been impeached in all the years of Argentine history. It remained for the Perón-dominated government to make virtually a clean sweep of the supreme court for reasons of politics.[30]

Another power granted only to the Senate is to pass upon the president's nominations to certain high offices in the federal service—judges, diplomats, and the like. When the president submits a name for one of these positions, his recommendation goes directly to the Committee on Confir-

[29] Art. 46.
[30] See page 84.

mations, which studies the record of the nominee and then reports to the Senate in secret session. Rejection of a presidential selection is virtually unknown.

CONGRESSIONAL IMMUNITY. Members of both houses of Congress are guaranteed complete freedom from arrest or other official interference because of opinions expressed in the course of legislative debate. The Argentine constitution goes much further than the constitution of the United States by granting to senators and deputies complete immunity from arrest during the entire period of their official terms, unless they are surprised in the actual commission of serious criminal acts. Complaints may be filed in the ordinary courts, but are without effect unless the Senate or the Chamber of Deputies, as the case may be, votes by a two-thirds majority to suspend the member concerned and deliver him for trial. Although the guarantee in the constitution of 1853 for many years protected the members of Congress from arrest on charges trumped up by the executive, today's constitutional section has no value—there is no real immunity for congressmen who dare to criticize Perón.

The Courts

THE LEGAL SYSTEM. Although the constitution of the Argentine Republic was borrowed largely from the United States, the nation's legal system shows little trace of American or English influence. Argentine legal theories come principally from France, Italy, Spain, and Germany. Judicial procedure has been inherited in considerable part from Spain. But it is the Spanish procedure of colonial times, long since abandoned by the country of its origin—though considerably modified, of course, to meet the needs of another nation and a new day. There is no Argentine common law comparable to the judge-made law of the Anglo-Saxon countries. Not that the courts are completely indifferent to earlier decisions; rather these decisions are not always accepted as binding precedents. They are merely links in the chain of judicial reasoning. Other links, to be given equal weight, are the writings of the accepted commentators. The jury system is not used.

JURISDICTION OF THE FEDERAL COURTS. The jurisdiction of the federal courts, set forth in the constitution, covers three classes of cases. The first class includes those disputes that have been placed under federal control because of their subject matter; they involve the constitution or laws of the nation, or treaties with foreign powers, or they are cases of admiralty or maritime or aeronautical jurisdiction, or bankruptcy. The second class lies within the federal sphere because of the persons concerned: the nation or one of the provinces is a party; or an ambassador, public minister, or foreign consul is a participant. In this category, also, are actions involving citizens of different provinces and citizens versus foreign states. Then there is the third class—cases that fall within federal jurisdiction because of place. These arise through the commission of criminal acts in territory that is under the exclusive control of the nation. After the constitution has thus outlined federal jurisdiction, it declares: "The supreme court shall have original and exclusive jurisdiction in disputes between the nation or a province or its inhabitants and a foreign state; in matters concerning ambassadors, ministers plenipotentiary, or foreign consuls; and in cases between the nation and one or more provinces, or between provinces." [31] Other classes of federal disputes begin in the lower courts, and reach the supreme court on appeal, if at all.

SUPREME COURT. The supreme court has five members—a president and four associates—appointed by the president of the nation with the approval of the Senate. They serve during good behavior and may be removed only by process of impeachment. This method of appointment and this tenure apply to all judges in the federal hierarchy. Every member of the supreme court must be a natural-born citizen, at least thirty years of age, a graduate of one of the national universities, and a practicing attorney for at least ten years.

ATTORNEY GENERAL. Among the important officers in the scheme of federal justice is the attorney general (*procurador general*) of the nation. He has the same qualifications as the members of the supreme court, and is chosen in the same manner. He is, of course, the legal adviser of the president—and also of the several ministers, at least in name, though most of the ministries have their own legal staffs. One of the functions of the attorney general is to give his opinion on all cases that come before the supreme court, even if the nation is not a party or otherwise directly concerned. The court is not bound by the attorney general's advice, and most students think that this arrangement wastes time without serving any useful purpose.

APPELLATE COURTS. Until 1902 there were no intermediate tribunals between the lowest federal courts and the supreme court of the nation. Within the federal system the supreme court was obliged to hear all appellate cases, and with the passing years the burden became very great.

[31] Art. 96.

So at last Congress established four courts of appeal to receive cases from the lowest tribunals and thus provide a measure of relief for the supreme court. Later the number of appellate courts was substantially increased. Today, as a result of sweeping changes made in 1950, there are six courts of appeal in the federal capital and nine in other parts of the nation. The appellate tribunals in the federal capital are highly specialized. One handles nothing but civil cases; others hear only criminal disputes, or matters relating to commerce or labor or the national administration. In the provinces, however, an appellate court normally accepts all classes of cases. An appellate tribunal usually has three members, but additional judges are added when necessary. For example, the appellate court for labor disputes in the federal capital has twelve members. Judges of the appellate courts must have the same qualifications as the justices of the high tribunal, except that the minimum number of years of legal practice is set at six instead of ten.

COURTS OF FIRST INSTANCE. Below the appellate tribunals are the courts of first instance, where most cases are begun. Six such courts have been established in the federal capital, and thirty-three in other parts of the country. The judges must be natural-born Argentine citizens, at least twenty-five years of age, with not less than four years of legal practice.

THE *fiscal.* The *fiscal* of a court is an officer whose exact equivalent is not to be found in Anglo-Saxon jurisprudence. Roughly the word *fiscal,* as used in this sense, may be translated *public prosecutor.* But the *fiscal* is something more than a prosecuting attorney; he represents the government and gives his opinion in all cases involving the public interest. He takes a hand in civil as well as criminal cases, preparing statements that form a part of the official records used by the trial judges. *Fiscales* are chosen by the president of the nation with the consent of the Senate. They must have the same qualifications as the judges of the courts they serve.

National-Provincial Relations

DIVISION OF POWERS. The first constitutions of the United Provinces of La Plata, as Argentina was originally called, were unitary; that is, they concentrated all public power in the national government. But they never proved satisfactory for Argentina's sprawling territory and diverse needs, so the constitution of 1853 adopted instead the principle of federalism. This principle is still retained, at least in theory. Authority is

divided between a nation and sixteen provinces. The national government is supposed to possess only the powers that are expressly delegated by
the constitution, or those that may reasonably be implied. As in the
United States, therefore, it is a government of delegated powers. The
provinces, on the other hand, possess the residue of governmental authority; they may do anything that is not forbidden to them or delegated exclusively to the nation.[32]

BROAD NATIONAL POWERS. The power of the national government, however, is considerably broader than in the United States. For example,
federal jurisdiction extends over the entire field of civil and criminal law.
Congress may define and provide penalties for all crimes—not merely for
those crimes that happen to bear on other federal powers, as in our system
of government. And civil litigation, too, may be made the subject of
federal laws, without inquiry as to whether it borders on some delegated
authority. The Argentine constitution contains a general welfare clause
which begins: "Congress shall have power to provide for everything conducive to the prosperity of the country, its hygiene, morality, health, and
social aid, and the advancement and welfare of all the provinces. . . ."[33]
Even the constitution of 1853 contained a general welfare clause that was
worded almost as broadly, but it was never interpreted in such a way
as to destroy the very fundamentals of Argentine federalism. Today
Perón seems bent on accomplishing that destruction. He declares that
his goal is a "practical federalism," which will bring about national unity
through the integration of the provinces."[34]

INTERVENTION. The right to intervene in provincial affairs has always
been one of the most important of federal powers. It has virtually nullified many of the rights presumably reserved to the provinces, and has
given the national authorities a measure of control scarcely suggested by
the literal words of the constitution. It must be clearly understood, therefore, that Perón did not invent the doctrine of intervention. He merely
borrowed it and made it his own. Intervention may, and sometimes does,
originate at the request of the authorities of a province. Usually, however, the national government takes the initiative. It may intervene in any
province at any time, even though the authorities of the province are
united in their opposition to such a course. The decision rests with the
president or Congress. In most cases the president assumes the responsi-

---

[32] Constitution, Art. 97.
[33] Art. 68, Cl. 16.
[34] Quoted by George I. Blanksten in his previously cited work, p. 147.

bility. He may act for a number of reasons, but the one most commonly assigned is the preservation of the republican form of government. The exact meaning of the words "republican form of government" has never been determined, and for that reason a president who is anxious to intervene in provincial affairs can almost always find some circumstance that destroys the republican form of government, and therefore makes intervention necessary. A provincial election may be fraudulent (or may be said to be). Provincial courts may be unduly subordinated to the influence of the governor. They may give preferences to some men that they deny to others in the same category. For these reasons, or for dozens of others, the "republican form of government" in a province may be "jeopardized," and apparently its only salvation is intervention by the federal authorities.

When the president has decided to intervene in the affairs of some province, he issues the necessary decree bringing the provincial government under federal control. He then appoints a federal commissioner who takes charge of provincial affairs. This commissioner supplants the governor and the legislature, and perhaps also the courts, as well as the officers of all municipalities. He issues such decrees as may be necessary to replace or supplement existing legislation, and supervises all the administrative functions. He acts in conformity with the provincial constitution and laws, to the extent that they do not interfere with the purposes of his assignment. But these purposes come first; he is a federal officer, and responsible only to the nation—not to the people of the province whose destiny he temporarily controls. The authority of the commissioner is upheld by federal troops.[35]

Provincial Government

THE GOVERNOR. Each province has a governor, who is chosen by the people. His term is six years; usually he is forbidden to serve two terms in succession. His authority is somewhat more restricted than in the early days, but he is still the dominant figure in provincial government. As a practical matter he must be an ardent supporter of Perón; otherwise he will not long retain his post. Like the president of the nation, he makes most appointments without the necessity of securing the consent of the

[35] The standard work on federal intervention is Luis H. Sommariva's La Intervención Federal Argentina Comparada con la Norteamericana y la Suiza, published in Buenos Aires in 1935. For a good discussion of intervention since the advent of Perón, see George I. Blanksten's previously cited work, pp. 139–143.

Senate. But in the province of Buenos Aires [36] the governor is required to obtain Senate confirmation of his nominations to practically all important positions in the administrative service. Even the members of the governor's cabinet must be approved. The Buenos Aires constitution also declares that persons other than cabinet ministers who are appointed by the governor with Senate approval must be removed in the same manner. The other provinces give the governor virtually a free hand in making removals. His legislative powers require no special comment. In every province he may veto the acts of the legislature and may be overridden only by a two-thirds vote. He may extend the sessions of the legislatures or call special sessions. His power of pardon is somewhat more restricted than that of the president.

THE LEGISLATURE. In the early days of Argentine independence nearly all the provincial legislatures were unicameral—in other words, all the members sat as one group. Gradually, however, interest developed in bicameral or two-chamber deliberative bodies. Today twelve provinces have two-house legislatures. The four provinces still retaining the unicameral plan are sparsely populated and poor; three of them receive subsidies from the federal treasury because they cannot meet their ordinary costs of government. The four single-chamber legislatures are small, none having more than twenty-five members. In the other provinces the size of the Chamber of Deputies ranges from twenty to seventy-six. Provincial Senates are considerably smaller. Until recently the provincial legislators served without pay. Now, however, they are commonly remunerated, on the basis of the number of days they work. The two newest Argentine provinces—President Perón Province (1951) and Eva Perón Province (1952)—have adopted a form of double voting reminiscent of Mussolini's Italy. Members of the Argentine Labor Federation vote like other citizens for provincial legislators, but in addition they choose their own special representatives in the legislatures of these two provinces.

THE JUDICIAL SYSTEM. The judicial systems of the several provinces all conform to a more or less uniform pattern, though there are numerous local variations. The supreme court is composed of five members in half of the provinces, and three members in the other half. The judges of the high tribunal are invariably appointed by the governor. Usually the constitution requires the approval of the Senate—or of the legislature, in those four provinces that have unicameral legislative bodies. Only four

[36] It will be remembered that there is a province of Buenos Aires, separate from the city of the same name.

provinces have followed the federal plan of permanent tenure for judges; most of the others agree on six years. Appellate courts, standing midway between the lowest courts and the supreme tribunal, are found in only four provinces. In the others the volume of judicial business is not sufficiently heavy to warrant such an arrangement. The judges of the appellate tribunals are chosen in the same manner and for the same terms as the members of the provincial supreme court. So, too, in most cases, are the judges of the courts of first instance. For petty disputes there are justices of the peace, who are commonly appointed by the governor and serve for one year without pay. They are not required to possess any special qualifications, other than the ability to read and write.

Territorial Government

In addition to the sixteen provinces there are eight territories,[37] which contain thirty-five per cent of the nation's territory but less than five per cent of its population. These sparsely populated lands, which lie on the fringe of the highly developed regions, are controlled directly by the national government. Two territories are administered by the armed services. Each of the other six territories has a governor appointed by the president with Senate approval for a term of three years, and a secretary who serves as the governor's assistant and handles most of the administrative details. There is no territorial legislature.

Municipal Government

POWERS OF THE CITIES. In Argentina the cities are the creatures of their respective provinces. They have only a small measure of control over their own affairs, and any authority that they happen to possess is a gift from the provincial government. Municipal home rule, in the American sense, does not exist. Cities do not frame their own charters. In fact, they do not even have charters. They are governed by such general and special statutes as the legislature may see fit to enact, and such regulations as the governor and the heads of the administrative departments may choose to issue. There are, of course, local officials, but virtually everything they do is limited by laws and decrees originating at the provincial capital.

[37] Until recently there were ten territories, but Chaco Territory became President Perón Province in 1951, and La Pampa Territory became Eva Perón Province in 1952.

ORGANIZATION OF CITY GOVERNMENT. In more than half of the provinces the municipal chief executive—the *intendente*—is chosen by the governor with Senate approval. This arrangement has produced more or less continuous conflict between the *intendente* and the city council, because the members of that body are popularly elected and consider themselves the anointed crusaders in a holy war to protect local interests from central interference. The *intendente* names the heads of the administrative departments, and dismisses them at his pleasure. Therefore he has a ready means of controlling every aspect of the municipal administration. There are a few provinces that provide for the selection of the *intendente* by the city council or by the voters, but in such cases he usually lacks authority over important administrative services.

BUENOS AIRES. In 1880 the city of Buenos Aires was taken from the province of the same name, and made a federal district under the direct control of the national authorities. Since that date it has experienced many changes in its government. Four times an elective city council has been established, and four times it has been abolished. Today the people of the capital city have no voice in their own affairs.[38] The official head of the federal district is an *intendente* appointed by the president with Senate approval. He names the entire personnel of the municipal service and issues necessary decrees relating to the city's affairs. Congress serves as the local lawmaking body.

SELECTED REFERENCES

Alvarez, Juan C., *Derecho Federal y Municipal,* Buenos Aires, Editorial Sanná, 1943.
Amadeo, Santos P., *Argentine Constitutional Law,* New York, Columbia Univ. Press, 1943.
Baldassarre, Pedro, *Los Derechos del Habitante ante una Doctrina Económica-Política-Social Universal,* Buenos Aires, Editorial Viracocha, 1949.
Bielsa, Rafael, *El Orden Político y las Garantías Jurisdiccionales,* Buenos Aires, Universidad Nacional del Litoral, 1943.
———— *Principios de Derecho Administrativo; Legislación Administrativa Argentina,* Buenos Aires, Universidad Nacional del Litoral, 1942.
Cabral Texo, Jorge, *El Régimen de los Decretos—Leyes en el Derecho Público Argentino,* Buenos Aires, Librería Jurídica, 1949.
Cooke, John, and Ricardo Guardo, *Reforma de la Constitución Nacional, Proyecto de Ley y Fundamentos,* Buenos Aires, Impr. del Congreso de la Nación, 1948.
Dana Montaño, Salvador M., *Justicia Social y Reforma Constitucional,* Santa Fe, Argentina, Instituto de Investigaciones Jurídico—Políticas de la Universidad del Litoral, 1948.

[38] Except, of course, through their representation in the national Congress.

Dana Montaño, Salvador M., *Principios de Derecho Público,* 2 Vols., Santa Fe, Argentina, La Unión, 1931, 1937.

González Calderón, Juan A., *Derecho Constitucional Argentino,* 3rd ed., 3 Vols., Buenos Aires, Laiouane, 1931.

—— *Instrucción Cívica,* 6th ed., Buenos Aires, Kraft, 1947.

Ibarguren, Carlos, *La Reforma Constitucional; Sus Fundamentos y su Estructura,* Buenos Aires, Abelado, 1948.

Lafont, Julio B., *Historia de la Constitución Argentina,* 2nd ed., Buenos Aires, Editorial F.V.D., 1950.

Linares Quintana, Segundo V., *Derecho Público de los Territorios Nacionales,* Buenos Aires, Porter Hnos., 1937.

—— *Gobierno y Administración de la República Argentina,* 2 Vols., Buenos Aires, Tip. Editora Argentina, 1946.

—— *Los Partidos Políticos, Instrumentos de Gobierno,* Buenos Aires, Alfa, 1945.

Longhi, Luis Ricardo, *Derecho Constitucional Argentino y Comparado,* Buenos Aires, Editorial Bibliográfica Argentina, 1945.

Macdonald, Austin F., *Government of the Argentine Republic,* New York, Crowell, 1942.

Melo, Carlos R., *Los Partidos Políticos Argentinos,* Córdoba, Arg., Imp. de la Universidad, 1945.

Moreno, Ismael, *Una Nueva Constitución para la Nación Argentina,* Avellaneda, Argentina, Editorial Nueva Vida, 1949.

Ossorio y Gallardo, Angel, *Nociones de Derecho Político,* Buenos Aires, Editorial Atlántida, 1944.

Rodríguez de la Torre, Miguel, *Ante el Problema de la Reforma Constitucional,* Córdoba, Argentina, Impr. de la Universidad, 1948.

Rowe, Leo S., *The Federal System of the Argentine Republic,* Washington, D.C., Carnegie Institution, 1921.

Salcedo, Saturnino, *Las Primeras Formas de Elegir y los Actuales Sistemas Electorales; Régimen Político de las Provincias Argentinas,* Buenos Aires, E.T.G.L.A., 1948.

Sánchez Viamonte, Carlos, *Derecho Constitucional,* Buenos Aires, Kapelusz y Cía., 1945.

Santa Cruz, M., *Síntesis de Derecho Constitucional Argentino y Comparado,* Buenos Aires, Editorial Licurgo, 1944.

Sastre, Pastor, *Derecho Constitucional Argentino,* Buenos Aires, Accinelli Hnos., 1945.

—— *Manual de la Constitución,* Buenos Aires, Ciordia y Rodr'guez, 1950.

Sommariva, Luis H., *La Intervención Federal Comparada con la Norteamericana y la Suiza,* Buenos Aires, El Ateneo, 1935.

Storni, Gabriel F., *Suspensión de las Garantías Constitucionales,* Santa Fe, Arg., Castellví, 1945.

Tagle, Carlos A., *Estado de Derecho y Equilibrio de Poderes en la Constitución Argentina,* Santa Fe, Arg., Imprenta de la Universidad Nacional del Litoral, 1944.

Villegas Basavilbaso, Benjamín, *Derecho Administrativo,* Buenos Aires, Tip Editora Argentina, 1949.

CHAPTER 5

BRAZIL
From Empire to Republic

The Land and the People

ONE of Brazil's most conspicuous characteristics is its great size. It is larger than the United States. It has almost as much territory as the other nine nations of South America combined, and almost as many people. But the people are concentrated in a relatively small area—the eastern plateau, which parallels the coast from Salvador in the north to Porto Alegre in the far south. Back of the eastern plateau lies the great Amazon basin, with its two million square miles of luxuriant jungles, wild animals and reptiles, and fewer people than the state of Minnesota. Back of the eastern plateau also, but farther south, lies the Matto Grosso (literally, dense forest) which is mostly grazing land instead of forest and may some day become the center of a great civilization. At present, however, it is cursed by inaccessibility. It has no convenient outlet to the sea and its single-track railroad serves only a small section in the extreme south. Consequently most Brazilians stay near the coast. But the "relatively small area" where they make their home is small only by comparison with the rest of the nation. It sprawls beside the South Atlantic for two thousand miles and comprises as much territory as Great Britain, France, and Germany. It extends from the heart of the tropics well into the Temperate Zone. It boasts of such great metropolitan centers as Rio de Janeiro, with its world-famed harbor; São Paulo, which is larger than Detroit and growing faster; and Recife, whose history dates from 1504.

NEED FOR LARGER POPULATION. Some professional geographers and professional optimists contend that Brazil could support a population of eight hundred million, instead of its present fifty-two million. They indicate that vast sections of the southern interior have reasonably good climatic conditions and very cheap land—an attractive combination for the pioneer. They declare that even the Amazon basin may provide a home for many millions of persons when the problem of combating tropical diseases has finally been solved. And they point out that even the rich lands near the coast have not been fully developed. The answer to many of Brazil's difficulties, they emphasize, is a larger population. And they are right. They may be too enthusiastic when they speak of eight hundred million. But there can be no question that Brazil needs more people.

São Paulo: *The coffee empire.* The Republic of the United States of Brazil, as it is officially called, has twenty states, but two of them dominate the nation's political and social life. Those two, São Paulo and Minas Geraes, have about one third of all the people in the country, and far more than one third of the national wealth. São Paulo alone accounts for at least half of Brazil's agricultural production. It is slightly larger than New England, and has about as many people. Lying along the southeastern coastal strip, it is readily accessible to the sea. Within its borders is the world's greatest coffee empire. The dry mild climate and fertile red soil are ideally suited to coffee cultivation. São Paulo lies partly within the tropics, but most of its area has an elevation of two or three thousand feet above sea level, and it is on this plateau that the great coffee *fazendas,* or plantations, are found. After the coffee has been harvested, dried, and packed, it is shipped to the capital city of the state, which also bears the name of São Paulo, and which is some twenty-five miles distant from the sea at an elevation of twenty-eight hundred feet. From there it is sent, over the most profitable railroad in South America, to Santos, "coffee port of the world." Some coffee is shipped from Rio de Janeiro, but not enough to challenge the supremacy of Santos. The Brazilian coffee crop decreased somewhat during the war years, but today it is larger than ever. Brazil continues to be the world's largest producer of coffee.[1]

Cotton. Cotton also is grown principally in São Paulo, and it is Brazil's number two export crop. For many years Brazilian cotton was known chiefly for its broken fibers and improper grading, but about thirty years ago the government decided to correct this unsatisfactory situation. It sent promising young students to the United States, where they took special courses in cotton growing and grading. The results were spectacu-

---

[1] See *Brazil; An Expanding Economy,* by George Wythe. See also *The Brazilian Economy,* by Henry W. Spiegel, and *Brazil,* by Preston James.

lar. In São Paulo alone the production increased from thirty thousand bales to nearly two million bales within a period of ten years. The prejudice against Brazilian cotton in the world markets speedily disappeared. Many of São Paulo's coffee growers have now set aside large portions of their land for cotton. They find that it provides a convenient income when the bottom drops out of the coffee market, as it does from time to time.

Industry. São Paulo has still another claim to fame: it is the center of Brazilian manufacturing. Large numbers of Italian immigrants have settled in São Paulo within the last few decades, coming mostly from the industrial regions of northern Italy and bringing with them their technical skill. They have aided considerably in the phenomenal rise of Brazilian industry. The number of industrial establishments in the entire nation has increased ninefold since 1920. Most of these "factories" are small plants, relying largely on hand labor. They are designed primarily for light industry—the making of flour from Brazilian wheat; the packing of Brazilian beef, pork, and lamb; the weaving of textiles from Brazilian cotton, silk, and rayon; the production of shoes from Brazilian leather; the making of drugs and chemicals from Brazilian raw materials.

But some heavy industry has developed within the last few years. This movement was given strong impetus by the Second World War, which closed the normal channels of trade with Europe and greatly increased the difficulty of obtaining manufactured goods from the United States. Brazilian officials thereupon arranged for the construction, at a cost of more than seventy-five million dollars, of the great Volta Redonda steel plant. Part of the money came from the Brazilian treasury, and part of it from the Export-Import Bank of the United States. The United States government was more than willing to make this gesture of good neighborliness toward a friendly nation at a time when the impact of war was emphasizing sharply the need for friends. The Volta Redonda plant is located on the Paraiba River in the small state of Rio de Janeiro, a few miles north of the borders of São Paulo. It should play an important part in the development of Brazilian heavy industry.[2]

The city of São Paulo. São Paulo, the capital city of the state, is an amazing metropolis. Its population of two million, two hundred thousand places it second among Brazil's cities, but all good Paulistas are cer-

---

[2] See the revised edition of George Wythe's *Industry in Latin America*, pp. 141–195. See also Morris L. Cooke's enthusiastic *Brazil on the March*, and José Jobim's *Brazil in the Making*.

tain that it will soon overtake Rio de Janeiro, the national capital, and recent estimates indicate that it may already have done so. It has the spirit of a boom town. It thinks nothing of removing mountains to make way for boulevards. New construction is everywhere. One of São Paulo's favorite stories concerns a man who answered an advertisement describing a new apartment, only to discover a vacant lot at the address given. But an agent on the premises assured him that there was no mistake; the foundation would be dug that afternoon, and by the following week the apartment would be ready for occupancy. So the Paulistas vie in telling tall stories and constructing tall buildings. There can be no doubt that they live in one of the world's most thriving cities.

MINAS GERAES. Minas Geraes, the only state that even pretends to challenge São Paulo's leadership, lies northeast of its rival and a short distance back from the coast. It is almost as big as Texas, and has just about as many people. Like Texas, therefore, it is a land of wide-open spaces. It has great ranches where cattle, hogs, horses, and mules are raised. It has cities where industry is developing at a rapid pace. But its chief claim to fame is based on its vast and varied mineral resources. *Minas Geraes* means general mines, and the name is richly deserved. Most of Brazil's rich mineral resources are concentrated in this one state. There is iron ore in abundance, including the famous iron mountain at Itabira. There is still a great deal of gold, though not in the quantities that once made Brazil the world's leading producer of the precious metal. There are large deposits of manganese, chrome, and mica. Diamonds, chiefly for industrial purposes, are plentiful. Coal is available in large quantities, also, but its quality is poor and it is located mostly in remote regions. The lack of more satisfactory coal supplies has undoubtedly been largely responsible for the slow growth of Brazil's heavy industries, but it need not remain a major handicap. Water power, of which Brazil has an abundance, can readily be substituted for coal. Less than ten per cent of the nation's potential hydroelectric power has been developed to date, but the electric power industry is growing rapidly. The future of Brazilian heavy industry seems to be assured, and its center seems likely to be the state of Minas Geraes.

Belo Horizonte, the capital city of Minas Geraes, is only a little more than half a century old. Like Washington, D.C., it was laid out according to a master plan, with many parks and broad boulevards. Today it is an impressive city of three hundred and forty thousand population—the only Brazilian city of that size to lie so far from the coast. The two hundred

In thousands of metric tons

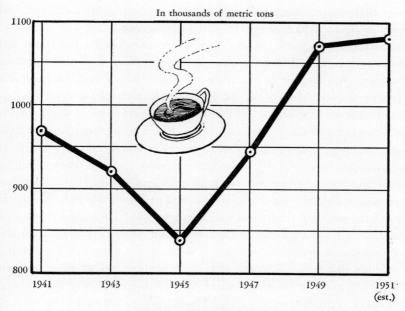

| | 1941 | 1943 | 1945 | 1947 | 1949 | 1951 (est.) |

Coffee Production in Brazil

In thousands of metric tons

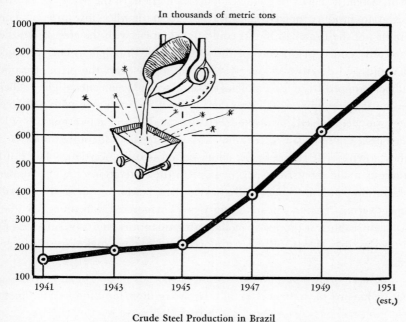

| | 1941 | 1943 | 1945 | 1947 | 1949 | 1951 (est.) |

Crude Steel Production in Brazil

Based on information in the *United Nations Statistical Yearbook, 1952.*

miles that separate it from Rio de Janeiro are covered by a railroad and also a broad modern highway.[3]

OTHER STATES. There are, of course, other states besides São Paulo and Minas Geraes that deserve at least honorable mention in the Brazilian economy. Rio Grande do Sul, in the far south, which has about as much territory as New Mexico but six times as many people, is the center of Brazil's livestock industry. Millions of sheep and cattle graze upon its grass-covered tablelands. Baía, in the north, has great plantations of cacao, whose beans provide the chocolate of world commerce.

Amazonas, in the heart of the Amazon basin, is three times as big as Texas and has only one half as many people as Rhode Island. Its vast forests once yielded a fortune in rubber, and permitted Manáos, the capital city of the state, to mushroom into a metropolis. The rubber barons of Manáos really believed that their boom town would become one of the great urban centers of the world, and they spent a fortune in beautifying it. Huge mansions along the river were constructed of stone brought from Europe. A magnificent opera house was erected at great expense, and opera companies were brought from Italy to entertain the wealthy families of Manáos. But the bubble burst shortly after the First World War, when the newly developed rubber plantations of the Malay Peninsula began to produce great quantities of rubber at very low prices. The product of the Brazilian forests could not compete with the crops from the carefully tended plantations of the Orient, and Brazilian rubber production plunged downward sharply. Within a few years the price of crude rubber dropped from three dollars a pound to eighteen cents. The rubber barons deserted their fine homes, and most of the workmen who gathered the crop were forced out of the forests by the threat of starvation. Slowly the opera house began to crumble. Manáos took on the appearance of a ghost town. The future of the entire region is still uncertain. The Ford interests made extensive experiments with the cultivation of rubber under plantation conditions, but finally turned their holdings over to the Brazilian government after encountering many unexpected difficulties. Today Amazon rubber is produced in moderate quantities, but not sufficient to meet Brazilian needs. Rubber imports from Malaya make up the difference.

THE CITY OF RIO DE JANEIRO. Most glamorous of all Brazilian cities is Rio de Janeiro, the national capital. Its two million, four hundred thousand

[3] There is a great deal of information about all the major cities of Brazil in Vera Kelsey's *Brazil in Capitals.*

inhabitants make it the second city of Latin America and one of the great metropolitan centers of the New World. Three hundred miles northeast of São Paulo, it stretches along the southern shore of the world's most beautiful harbor. Its inhabitants—the *cariocas,* as they call themselves—have spared no expense to make their city equal the majesty of its environs. They have constructed impressive public buildings, fine apartment houses, and beautiful homes; they have laid out broad tree-lined boulevards and

The famous harbor of Rio de Janeiro, as seen from Corcovado (the Hunchback). (Photograph by the author)

magnificent parks. But Rio is more than a show place. It is the principal commercial city of the nation. Nearly forty per cent of Brazil's imports pass through its harbor. It is important also as a manufacturing and distributing center. Like Washington, D.C., it lies within a federal district, whose four hundred square miles make it six times as large as the District of Columbia. Just to the north is the small state of Rio de Janeiro, whose capital, Niteroi, lies across the bay from the capital city of the nation.[4]

RACIAL COMPOSITION. In the United States we often refer to our country as a melting pot because we have fused successfully the white races of

[4] See Hugh Gibson's sympathetic volume, *Rio.*

Europe. But Brazil has carried its racial amalgamation much farther. Its people are a product of many races—white, red, black. The early settlers from Portugal did not bring their families with them, and they intermingled freely with the Indian women. A little later, as African slaves were imported, the process was repeated. During the last hundred years more than four million European immigrants have come to Brazil, and even two hundred thousand Japanese have established homes. These many races have intermarried with very little regard to color, and the result is a very loosely drawn color line. Some writers even go so far as to say that a color line does not exist. But that is too strong a statement. The leading families are white, for the most part, and most of the wealth is in their hands. Yet there certainly is not the race prejudice that exists in most parts of the United States. A person with Negro blood may stay at any hotel, eat in any restaurant, travel in any public conveyance. He may even aspire to high political office, if he possesses the necessary qualifications. He may, and sometimes does, travel in the best social circles. It must be admitted, however, that the Negroes largely constitute the poorer classes, and that they have somewhat more than their share of disease and illiteracy. But this state of affairs does not exist because of any official policy or because of popular antipathy to colored persons. Color is, to some extent, a matter of social status. An American was greatly mystified by the statement that a plantation foreman *used to be* a colored man. He expostulated that race was not something to be changed from time to time, like a suit of clothes. But his informant explained that the man used to be one of the laborers on the plantation; therefore he was black. Later, by hard work, he rose to be foreman; that made him white.

The racial composition is by no means uniform throughout Brazil. In the north, which used to be the heart of the nation during the first years of slavery, Negro blood is much in evidence. The people are short, with swarthy complexions. In and around Rio there is a great deal more white blood. The men and women are taller and heavier, and their features more commonly reflect European ancestry. South of Rio, from São Paulo to Rio Grande do Sul, the white races are strongly entrenched. In the interior of the country the people are still mostly of Indian stock.[5]

Germans and Japanese. In 1942, when Brazil declared war on Germany and Italy, there was some uncertainty as to the loyalty of many Brazilians of German birth or ancestry. The Italians, for the most part, were un-

[5] See Donald Pierson's *Negroes in Brazil.*

sympathetic to Mussolini's regime, but many Germans in Rio Grande do Sul and neighboring Santa Catarina brazenly flaunted their loyalty to Hitler. Germany had carried on an extensive propaganda campaign in an effort to control Brazil's German population, and had succeeded in no small measure. Nazi *Schützenbünde,* or shooting societies, had been established in southern Brazil and were parading in Nazi-like uniforms and arm bands. But the Brazilian government bore down heavily, and the shooting societies disappeared. There was no serious trouble. Nor did the Japanese immigrants disturb the public order throughout the war, though many of them expressed bitter regret when Brazil declared war on Japan in the spring of 1945. Most of the trouble occurred, oddly enough, after Japan had surrendered. Japanese secret societies in the neighborhood of São Paulo took the position that talk of Japanese defeat was merely Allied propaganda, and that any person of Japanese ancestry who believed such a rumor was disloyal to the Japanese homeland. Several men and women who seemed inclined to accept the "lie" of an Allied victory were murdered. Eventually, of course, even the members of the secret societies came to the belated realization that Japan had not won the war.[6]

BRAZILIAN-AMERICAN RELATIONS. Brazil's relations with the United States have always been very friendly. It followed the United States into the First World War, while most of the other important Latin American nations remained neutral. At the Rio conference of 1942, held less than six weeks after the attack at Pearl Harbor, Brazil's Foreign Minister Oswaldo Aranha worked unceasingly to rally the delegates to the support of the United States, and his own country severed relations with the Axis powers before the end of the conference. Pro-Axis newspapers and news agencies operating in Brazil were suppressed, and prompt action was taken against Axis nationals and active Axis sympathizers. In August, 1942, after a number of Brazilian ships had been sunk by German submarines, Brazil officially entered the war. It rendered valuable assistance to the Allies by providing bases for the defense of the Americas, and furnishing both men and supplies for the assault on Europe. Brazilian and American troops fought side by side in the Italian campaign.

On June 11, 1940, before the tides of war had engulfed the New World, Brazil's President Vargas made a speech praising the ideology of fascism. He did not say in so many words that he admired Hitler and Mussolini, but he did talk about the "aspirations of virile peoples" and the decline of "old systems and antiquated formulas." On numerous other occasions he

[6] See Gilberto Freyre's *Brazil, an Interpretation.*

had expressed substantially the same ideas, and his remarks had passed virtually unnoticed.   But this speech received world-wide attention because Vargas happened to deliver it the day after President Roosevelt bitterly assailed Italy's unjustified attack on France, describing it as a "stab in the back."   Many persons thought that the Vargas address was a defense of Mussolini in direct answer to Roosevelt's charges.   One of the leading newspapers of Buenos Aires headlined: "Vargas, with fascist language, justifies the aggression of the barbarians."   Other newspapers throughout the hemisphere said the same thing in different ways.   All this was very distressing to President Vargas, who apparently had no idea that his words would create such a startling effect.   He cabled President Roosevelt, saying that he had not even read President Roosevelt's address, that his own speech had been misinterpreted, and that of course the United States could count on the friendship of Brazil in any emergency.   He did not add, though he might well have done so, that his own speech was intended strictly for home consumption.   Only a short time afterward, in the emergency of war, Vargas was called upon to fulfill his promise of cooperation, and he fulfilled it handsomely.

The friendship of Brazil and the United States rests upon a solid commercial basis.   We buy most of Brazil's coffee and cacao, and large quantities of its manganese, woods, and nuts.   In exchange Brazil buys our motor cars and radios, machinery, tools, and chemicals.   No other nation of South America buys as much from the United States, or sells as much to this country.   Obviously such good customers cannot afford to be bad neighbors.[7]

The Brazilian Empire

INDEPENDENCE.   Brazil's history has been relatively untroubled.   It achieved independence from Portugal without firing a single shot or shedding a single drop of blood.   For a number of years Brazil had been the center of the Portuguese Empire, because Napoleon's armies had overrun Portugal and driven the royal family into exile.   When, however, Napoleon was finally defeated, the king returned to the mother country.   But he left his son, Dom Pedro, in charge of Brazilian affairs.   The young prince, who had just passed his twenty-second birthday, was a dashing figure and highly popular.   Everyone was sure that he would make a good ruler.   So there was general disappointment when the prince re-

---

[7] See *Brazil, Bulwark of Inter-American Relations,* by Henry A. Phillips.

ceived word from his father in Portugal that he must return home at once. Brazilians in high office urged the young man to disregard his father's command and stay in Rio. Popular demonstrations made clear that this was the desire of the people. At last, on January 9, 1822, Dom Pedro gave his answer. He said: "If it be for the good of all and the general happiness of the nation, tell the people that I remain." Eleven months later he was crowned emperor of Brazil. January 9 has since been celebrated as "I remain" day, the day of national independence.

PEDRO I. Unfortunately, however, Dom Pedro did not fulfill his early promise of becoming a good ruler. He governed with almost no regard for public opinion, and maintained a secret police to uncover any opposition. Newspapers that dared to criticize his policies were ruthlessly suppressed. A convention called to draft a constitution for the nation was told that the new document must be "an insurmountable barrier against any invasion of the imperial prerogative," and when the delegates ignored this command they were summarily dismissed. Nine years of this kind of treatment were enough to convince the Brazilians that something drastic must be done. On April 6, 1831, they did it. A mob gathered in front of the imperial palace, loudly demanding that the emperor abdicate. Soldiers called to the scene refused to suppress the rioters. When Dom Pedro found that he could no longer count on the support of his own troops, he realized that his career was at an end. Early in the morning of April 7 he signed the abdication papers, naming his son Pedro as his successor. Young Pedro was then six years of age.

PEDRO II. After the ex-emperor had sailed away on an English warship, Congress set up a regency to govern the nation during young Pedro's minority. There was some talk of establishing a republic, and republican sympathizers even staged minor revolts in different parts of the country, but the general sentiment favored retention of the monarchy. In 1840, when young Pedro reached his fifteenth birthday, Congress officially declared him of age and asked him to assume the duties of his position. On July 23 he was crowned as Emperor Dom Pedro II. Thus began one of the longest and most tranquil reigns in history. Dom Pedro remained upon the throne of Brazil for almost half a century.

A benevolent despot. The new emperor was very different from his father. In many ways he was an ideal monarch. He was alert, intelligent, conscientious. Instead of indulging in the vices that seemed to be characteristic of European royal families, he conducted himself in a highly respectable manner. Though not a devout Catholic, he showed sufficient respect for the church to satisfy public opinion. He was democratic in his habits; in fact, he deliberately shunned display. As a tolerant monarch, he permitted criticism of his regime. But on one very important point he stood firm. He was determined to be emperor in fact, and not merely in name. Actually he never said so in just those words. On the contrary, he studiously avoided the appearance of trying to make himself an absolute monarch. Never did he question the desirability of constitutional government. He named prime ministers to rule the country, choosing them in each instance from the leadership of the majority party. He permitted the prime ministers to choose their colleagues in the cabinet. He was graciously pleased to sign the laws that Congress presented for his approval. But he maintained an election system that usually assured the election of his friends. He sometimes used the great prestige of his office to prevent the enactment of laws that he did not wish to sign. And, since he appointed the members of the Senate, control of legislation was not difficult. Dom Pedro was somewhat of an autocrat. There can be no doubt, however, that he was a wise and benevolent one. Brazil prospered under his rule.

Growing opposition. As the years passed, the position of the emperor gradually became less secure. A newly formed Republican Party advocated the abolition of the monarchy and the establishment of a republic. Dom Pedro, who prided himself on his tolerance, extended protection to the men who were openly advocating this change. He also used his influence against certain measures advanced by the Catholic Church, and thus forfeited the support of some of his staunchest followers. In 1888, while the emperor was temporarily absent from the country, his daughter Isabel, who was serving as regent, was persuaded to sign a law of Congress freeing the slaves and making no provision for compensation to their former owners. The proposal was not new; it had long been endorsed by nearly all liberal Brazilians. But the conservative slave owners, who had always opposed most strongly any proposal to abolish the monarchy, had assumed that they could count on the monarch to protect their interests. When they suddenly found themselves deprived, with royal approval, of the manpower necessary to operate their great estates, most of them lost interest in politics. Some actually joined the Republicans. The days of the monarchy were numbered. The situation was aggravated by the serious illness of Dom Pedro. He suffered from diabetes, and it was generally known that he could not live many years. Unpleasant rumors circulated concerning his daughter Isabel and her husband, who was the grandson of Louis Philippe of France. These rumors seem to have been entirely without foundation, but they received wide acceptance nonetheless. The prospect of Isabel upon the throne of Brazil was sufficient to weaken the convictions of many determined monarchists.

Fall of the empire. Finally, in November of 1889, the storm broke. It was not a people's movement in any sense. On the contrary, it was a military *coup d'état,* plotted and carried out by the leaders of the armed forces. But if the people could have been consulted, there is no reason to suppose that they would have withheld their blessing. Everyone knew that it was time for a change. The uprising had been scheduled for November 20, but almost at the last minute the date was advanced because of rumors that certain military leaders were to be imprisoned. Troops began to gather at their appointed places early in the morning of November 15. Within a few hours all major strategic points had been seized, and the cabinet had been placed under guard. The only casualty was the minister of marine, who was shot in the leg when he tried to resist. The news reached Dom Pedro in Petropolis, the summer capital in the highlands back of Rio, about twenty miles away. He returned to Rio in great haste, only to find that the revolutionaries were completely in control of the government. No one offered to do him harm; on the contrary, he was treated with the greatest respect. But he was made to understand that he and his family must leave Brazil, never to return. The monarchy had outlived its usefulness.

Apparently Dom Pedro did not even entertain the idea of resistance. His first thought was for the welfare of Brazil, as it had always been. When informed that a vessel was standing by to carry him into exile, he uttered no word of protest. In Paris, where he spent his last few years, he strengthened the hand of the newborn republic by refusing to lend his name to a counter-revolutionary movement. When Brazilian diplomats in France and other European countries visited him to pay their respects and offer their resignations, he told them that their first duty was to their country, rather than their emperor. He refused a grant of money from the Brazilian treasury. When he died, in 1891, Brazilians of all classes mourned the loss of a true friend, as well they might have done. Nearly thirty years later the mortal remains of Dom Pedro and his empress were brought from Lisbon to Rio de Janeiro, to find their final resting place on Brazilian soil.[8]

[8] The era of Pedro II is traced with care and skill by João Pandiá Calogeras in his *History of Brazil,* Chaps. VIII–XII.

First Years of the Republic

DEODORO DA FONSECA.   On November 16, 1889, the day that Dom Pedro sailed into exile, the leaders of the revolution officially declared Brazil a republic.   The provinces were to become states, with considerably greater authority to regulate their own affairs.   Marshal Manoel Deodoro da Fonseca, who had headed the uprising, became provisional president.   He was a brave man, and no one ever questioned his integrity or loyalty. Even in the dying hours of the empire, when old Dom Pedro was hurrying from Petropolis to Rio in a vain effort to save his throne, Deodoro still talked of submitting a list of new ministers to the emperor, and was with difficulty persuaded to throw the full weight of his influence behind the republic.   Despite the new president's many fine qualities, however, he was scarcely the man to undertake the responsibility of establishing a new regime.   His intelligence was limited, his temper was short, and he possessed virtually no experience in the management of public affairs. Moreover, he seemed unable to accept criticism with good grace.   Every objection to his proposals seemed to him a deliberate insult.   Therefore he was constantly quarreling with his advisers, and replacing one group with another.

RUY BARBOSA.   Fortunately for the new republic, there were some able men who possessed great influence with Deodoro.   One of them was Ruy Barbosa, the brilliant jurist who became minister of finance in the provisional government.   He drafted the decree separating church and state, which was issued on January 7, 1890, only a little more than seven weeks after the overthrow of the empire.   This decree was a model of tolerance. Though stripping the church of most of the prerogatives that it had enjoyed for centuries, it did so in a moderate spirit and without bitterness. Thus Brazil escaped religious strife, such as has marred so much of Mexico's history.   Barbosa was responsible also for the adoption of an excellent new criminal code and for numerous improvements in the organization of the courts.

But Ruy Barbosa was not successful in everything he attempted.   His management of the nation's finances produced near disaster.   By granting special privileges to favored banks, he encouraged wild speculation.   Soon the nation was flooded with paper money.   Within a year and a half the milreis, the official unit of currency, had dropped to less than half of its former value in pounds sterling.   The credit of the nation was seriously weakened.   Some of Barbosa's apologists have pointed out that he inherited an unsound financial policy from the empire in its death struggle. They have emphasized also that Barbosa was not entirely his own master. He was constantly under pressure from his friends within the provisional government, and from special interests of all kinds, to issue decrees that did not have his wholehearted approval. But it must be admitted that Barbosa was the responsible head of the ministry of finance, and the director of a financial policy that created serious difficulties for the nation.

A NEW CONSTITUTION. On November 15, 1890, one year to the day after the overthrow of the empire, a popularly elected convention met to prepare and adopt a new constitution for the republic. As a basis for its deliberations it was given the draft of a constitution prepared largely by Ruy Barbosa. Provisional President Deodoro evidently expected the convention to adopt this draft virtually unchanged, and when it proceeded to make numerous amendments, he chose to regard every amendment as a personal affront. Small wonder, therefore, that a rift soon developed between the President and the members of the convention. It grew steadily as the days passed. In due time, however, the convention finished its work. The new constitution, adopted on February 24, 1891, was an excellent document. It fixed the general course of Brazilian policy for nearly half a century.

ELECTION OF DEODORO. As the new constitution went into effect and the constitutional convention became the first Congress under the republic, the rift between its members and Marshal Deodoro widened steadily. The Marshal stubbornly insisted on his own policies, and surrounded himself with his old military cronies, many of whom still cherished nostalgic memories of the empire. Chief among them was the Baron of Lucena, whose open contempt for the republicans won him few friends. The time had come for the election of a constitutional president, and Congress was to make the choice. Deodoro's name was mentioned first, as might well have been expected. He was the recognized leader of the revolution and the nation's first citizen. Many persons thought that no other name should even be considered. But there was strong opposition to Deodoro in Congress and throughout the country. Eventually the opposition leaders narrowed down their various preferences to a single choice—Senator Prudente de Moraes, who had served as presiding officer of the constitutional convention. Prudente was undoubtedly a distinguished man, but the point most commonly made in his favor was that he was a civilian. Brazil, said his supporters, needed a civilian rather than a soldier to guide it in the paths of peace. As might have been anticipated, Marshal Deodoro bitterly resented any opposition to his own candidacy and regarded those who voted against him as his personal enemies. When the vote in Congress was finally taken, it stood: 129 for Deodoro and 97 for Prudente. Thus Manoel Deodoro became the first constitutional president of Brazil.

DEODORO AND CONGRESS. Almost from the outset of his term the new President found himself at loggerheads with Congress. Many of those who had voted in his favor were repelled by his imperious manner. The opposition gathered momentum, and soon Congress was spending most of its time in the preparation of measures designed primarily to embarrass the President. Deodoro could scarcely restrain his fury. Finally, on November 3, 1891, less than a year after his election, he answered his critics in the one way that he knew. He dissolved both houses of Congress and announced his intention of governing the country without further interference. Thus Deodoro transformed the government into a dictatorship. He felt strongly that the members of Congress had persecuted him for their own political advantage, and that his only recourse was to strip them of their authority. There seems to be little doubt that his motives were good. Less can be said, however, for his judgment. By dissolving Congress and thus violating the plain letter of the constitution, he destroyed the fundamental spirit of the new system of government that had been so recently established. Such a course of action could have only one result. It alienated most of Deodoro's remaining friends and threw the weight of public opinion strongly against him. Revolts flared simultaneously in several parts of the country. The army wavered in its loyalty to its commander-in-chief. Clearly Deodoro could no longer retain the presidency without plunging the country into civil war, and that he was unwilling to do. He issued a manifesto resigning his high office and placing all the blame for this unfortunate turn of events upon "the ingratitude of those for whom I sacrificed myself." Deodoro was one of the noblest souls in Brazilian history, and one of the poorest administrators.

PEIXOTO. With the resignation of Marshal Deodoro, Vice-President Floriano Peixoto assumed the responsibilities of the presidency. But he had many enemies, and he made others by using his authority to force Deodoro's friends from their positions of influence. Revolt was in the air. In September of 1893 the Brazilian fleet openly broke with the government and threatened to shell Rio de Janeiro, a threat that it would almost certainly have carried out but for the prompt intervention of foreign squadrons stationed in the harbor. Meanwhile a revolution had broken out in the south, and the frustrated commanders of Brazil's navy threw in their lot with the revolutionary leaders. The fighting continued for many months, and some bloody encounters took place. But eventually the rebellion was crushed. The young government had survived a major crisis, and became much stronger as a result of its triumph.

PRESIDENT PRUDENTE. The election of 1894 proved to be a milestone in Brazilian history, for it resulted in the choice of a civilian president— Prudente de Moraes, who had unsuccessfully opposed the candidacy of Marshal Deodoro in 1891. At that time Prudente had spoken out vigorously against the evils of military rule, and he made abundantly clear in 1894 that his views had not changed. Not unnaturally, therefore, the army was almost solidly against him. Even after his election, and almost to the very day of his inauguration as president, the air was filled with rumors of a military *coup d'état* that would bar him from the presidency. But the threatened uprising never materialized, and Prudente was permitted to assume the duties of his office without incident.

Tranquility was only surface-deep, however. In the south there were still some rebels who had not laid down their arms. In the north a group of religious fanatics openly defied the government and won several unexpected military victories before they were finally dispersed. Many of the leaders of Congress were hostile to Prudente and anxious to block his proposals at every opportunity. The people began to lose their confidence in him. There seemed to be considerable doubt that he would be permitted to serve his full four-year term. But at this moment the President suddenly regained a large part of his lost popularity as the direct result of a tragic incident. He had set out from the presidential palace to review some troops when, without warning, he was attacked by a common soldier. Prudente himself escaped injury, but his minister of war was killed and another high military officer received serious wounds. There seems to be no reason to believe that the assassin acted for anyone but himself, yet the masses immediately jumped to the conclusion that the leaders of the opposition were involved in a plot to kill the President. Public opinion veered sharply in his favor, and he finished his term in an atmosphere of general good will.

Growth of the Republican Tradition

The next three presidents of Brazil were all civilians. Under them the nation moved steadily toward political maturity. Brazil's finances were put in order, and thus the foundation was laid for an era of prosperity.

Railroads and harbors were developed, and the nation's national resources were exploited as never before. In 1902 a brilliant young physician named Oswaldo Cruz was named minister of public health. He inaugurated a vast sanitary program and eventually, despite the obstacles placed in his path by professional politicians and professional militarists, he succeeded in virtually eliminating such dread diseases as yellow fever, bubonic plague, and smallpox, which had ravaged the country for many years.

FRAUDULENT ELECTIONS. Since the establishment of the republic there had never been "free and unfettered elections," in our sense of the term. Each outgoing president named his successor, who was subsequently ratified at the polls as a matter of course. In theory the chief executive had nothing whatever to do with the selection of the next chief executive, but in practice his decision was final. When, therefore, in 1910 the acting president threw his support to the candidacy of Marshal Hermes Rodrigues da Fonseca, the nephew of Father of the Republic Deodoro, it was generally assumed that any other candidates would be wasting their time. One person who refused to make such an assumption, however, was Ruy Barbosa, the eminent jurist who had prepared the original draft of the 1891 constitution. He stumped the country in an unprecedented political campaign, pointing out that Brazil had made great strides under civilian rule and calling upon the people to refuse to elect another military man to the presidency. Whether the people ignored his advice or whether the votes were not honestly counted is still an unsettled question, but in any event Marshal Hermes was officially declared the winner by a large majority.

PRESIDENCY OF MARSHAL HERMES. The presidency of Marshal Hermes justified the worst fears of his opponents. At times he supported the scheming manipulations of his army friends; at other times he seemed determined to block them. He meekly granted the demands of one group of rebels in the navy, but crushed another naval uprising without mercy. He allowed himself to be influenced by every politician who chanced to catch his ear, and clung to any one policy only until some adviser suggested a change. By such tactics he managed to alienate practically the entire nation. Civil war was in the air before the end of his term, and would almost certainly have broken out if Marshal Hermes had been able to force upon the nation the man whom he had chosen as his successor. Fortunately, however, the "crown prince" possessed enough common sense to realize that his own election would be the signal for a general revolt, and enough patriotism to try to avert such a catastrophe. He withdrew his candidacy. Thus the path was cleared for the election of another civilian who enjoyed the confidence of nearly all the leaders of the nation.[9]

GEOGRAPHICAL SELECTION OF PRESIDENTS. Strong political parties, in the American sense of the term, had never developed in Brazil. Political groups were constantly changing and lacked the organization and discipline necessary to permanent existence. The tradition had gradually developed that Brazil's two great states, São Paulo and Minas Geraes, should have a monopoly on presidential candidates. A statesman from any other part of the country, regardless of his other qualifications, could scarcely hope to be considered. There were occasional exceptions, of course, but as a rule the retiring governor of São Paulo would become president for four years, and would then be succeeded by the retiring governor of Minas Geraes. It was an endless circle, and to the inhabitants of Brazil's other eighteen states it seemed a vicious circle. But by 1930 it had become so firmly established that it was sometimes called an unwritten part of the constitution.

DISREGARD OF TRADITIONS. By 1930, also, the tradition of civilian presidents had become well rooted. And orderly government had become commonplace in Brazil, though there were occasional uprisings—a minor revolt in 1922 and a more serious rebellion in 1924. As the presidential campaign of 1930 got under way, it was generally assumed that the governor of Minas Geraes would be the official candidate. The retiring president, Washington Luis, was from São Paulo, so Minas Geraes was clearly entitled to the election of its favorite son. But at this juncture the governor of Minas Geraes announced that he was not a candidate. His support would go to Getulio Vargas, the young and ambitious governor of the state of Rio Grande do Sul. The unwritten law did not quite cover this situation, but Dr. Vargas regarded himself as the logical heir of the governor of Minas Geraes and therefore entitled to the president's support. President Luis, however, thought otherwise. He threw the full weight of his prestige to Dr. Julio Prestes, who at that time was the governor of São Paulo. Outraged cries were heard in all parts of the country, but especially in Minas Geraes and Rio Grande do Sul. Was the nation to be saddled with two successive presidents from São Paulo? If so, that state might claim the exclusive right to name presidential candidates and might even succeed in dominating the entire nation. The crisis was so serious that virtually all the opponents of Prestes submerged their differences and united in support of Vargas. The campaign promised to be unusually

[9] See *Brazil after a Century of Independence,* by Herman G. James.

exciting and unusually close. Actually Prestes won by a considerable margin. That, at least, was the result of the official count. But Vargas declared that he had won the election, only to be robbed of his triumph by force and fraud. In a fair election, he said, he would have been declared the victor.

THE VARGAS REVOLUTION. The truth of Vargas' charges is difficult to assess. Undoubtedly some fraud occurred; it happened in every election. Undoubtedly some Vargas supporters were intimidated and kept away from the polls. But whether these incidents were sufficiently numerous to affect the result can only be a matter of conjecture. At any rate, millions of Brazilians were convinced that Vargas should have been declared the winner. Dissatisfaction spread throughout the nation. It was fanned by the world depression, which was felt severely in Brazil. Artificially high coffee prices suddenly collapsed, and hundreds of planters were ruined. Foreign trade, which was Brazil's life stream, slowed to a mere trickle. The government was generally blamed for this disastrous state of affairs, and there can be no doubt that its policies had been far from helpful. When, therefore, the supporters of Vargas decided to install him in the presidential palace by force of arms, they encountered surprisingly little opposition. The revolutionary forces struck on October 4, 1930. Wash-ington Luis, who had not yet surrendered the presidential office to his successor, was taken prisoner and given thirty minutes to resign. At the end of the thirty minutes he was still defying his enemies to make him sign anything, but his defiance was an empty gesture. His power was gone. Seven weeks later he sailed for exile in Europe. Getulio Vargas had already been declared president of Brazil, by the grace of God and the Brazilian army.

SELECTED REFERENCES

Amaral, Luis, *Aspectos Fundamentaes da Vida Rural Brasileira,* São Paulo, Brazil, E. G. "Revista dos Tribunaes," 1936.

Bastos, Humberto, *A Marcha do Capitalismo no Brasil,* São Paulo, Brazil, J. Magal-hães, 1944.

Calmon, Pedro, *Historia Diplomática do Brasil,* Belo Horizonte, Brazil, Livraria Editôra P. Bluhm, 1941.

Calogeras, João Pandiá, *A History of Brazil* (translated by Percy A. Martin), Chapel Hill, N.C., Univ. of North Carolina Press, 1939.

Cooke, Morris L., *Brazil on the March,* New York, McGraw-Hill, 1944.

Días Rollemberg, Luiz, *Aspectos e Perspectivas de Economía Nacional,* Rio de Janeiro, Departmento de Imprensa e Propaganda, 1941.

Freyre, Gilberto, *Brazil, an Interpretation,* New York, Knopf, 1945.

Haskins, Caryl P., *The Amazon,* New York, Doubleday, Doran, 1943.

Hehl Neiva, Artur, *O Problema Imigratorio Brasileiro,* Rio de Janeiro, Imp. Nacional, 1945.

James, Herman G., *Brazil after a Century of Independence,* New York, Macmillan, 1925.

James, Preston E., *Brazil,* New York, Odyssey Press, 1946.

Jobim, José, *Brazil in the Making,* New York, Macmillan, 1943.

Kelsey, Vera, *Brazil in Capitals,* New York, Harper, 1942.

——— *Seven Keys to Brazil,* New York, Funk & Wagnalls, 1940.

Lima, Hermes, *Notas à Vida Brasileira,* São Paulo, Brazil, J. Magalhães, 1945.

Palmer, Thomas W., *São Paulo in the Brazilian Federation: A State Out of Balance,* Ann Arbor, University of Michigan Microfilms, 1950.

Phillips, Henry A., *Brazil, Bulwark of Inter-American Relations,* New York, Hastings House, 1945.

Pierson, Donald, *Negroes in Brazil,* Chicago, Univ. of Chicago Press, 1942.

Pierson, Donald, and Others, *Cruz das Almas: A Brazilian Village,* Washington, D.C., Smithsonian Institution, 1951.

Porto, J. Costa, *Pinheiro Machado e su Tempo,* Rio de Janeiro, J. Olympio, 1951.

Sáenz Hayes, Ricardo, *El Brasil Moderno,* Buenos Aires, Edición del Instituto Americano de Investigaciones Sociales y Económicas, 1942.

Smith, T. Lynn, *Brazil; People and Institutions,* Baton Rouge, La., Louisiana State Univ. Press, 1946.

Smith, T. Lynn, and Alexander Marchant, eds., *Brazil: Portrait of Half a Continent,* New York, Dryden Press, 1951.

Spiegel, Henry W., *The Brazilian Economy,* Philadelphia, Blakiston, 1949.

Wythe, George, *Brazil: An Expanding Economy,* New York, Twentieth Century Fund, 1949.

Zweig, Stefan, *Brazil, Land of the Future,* New York, Viking Press, 1941.

CHAPTER 6

BRAZIL
The New State

Early Dictatorial Years

WHEN Getulio Vargas became president of Brazil in October of 1930, he was forty-seven years of age. A short, chubby man with smiling eyes, his glasses gave him somewhat the appearance of a college professor. In his early days he had ridden the range in his native state of Rio Grande do Sul; at sixteen he had entered the army, and studied for a military career. Eventually, however, he abandoned the army for the law. He became a practicing attorney and an energetic participant in the great game of politics. His rise as a politician was steady but not spectacular. First, he was a deputy in the legislature of his state, then a congressman. Washington Luis made him minister of finance in 1926; two years later he was named governor of Rio Grande do Sul. And from that strategic position he moved into the presidency.[1]

SEIZURE OF ABSOLUTE POWER. From the outset of the new regime it was evident that a strong man had seized the reins of power. Vargas left no doubt that he was the master of the nation. He suspended the constitution of 1891 and issued a decree conferring upon himself all the executive and legislative powers of the nation, until such time as a constitutional convention should prepare a new fundamental law. As it turned out, Vargas was in no hurry to summon a convention. He delayed the matter nearly four years. Meanwhile he ruled the country. He dissolved not only the national Congress, but all state legislatures and municipal councils. He suspended all the constitutional guarantees of individual liberty and pro-

[1] For a more detailed discussion of the early years of Vargas, written in a most respectful vein, see Paul Frischauer's *A Biography of President Vargas of Brazil.*

hibited the courts from reviewing the legality of any of the acts of the government. He removed the governors of all the states and appointed interventors in their place. Many of these interventors were junior army officers, whose enthusiasm scarcely compensated for their lack of administrative experience. The mayors of cities were dismissed right and left, and their successors were appointed by the interventors. Loyalty to the new regime was the primary qualification for all public officials.

STIFLING THE OPPOSITION. Here then, under Vargas, was a thoroughgoing dictatorship—no novelty in Latin America, but almost unprecedented in Brazil. The President tried to lessen the shock by governing with moderation. During the first years he made no great changes in the lives of the people. He exiled a few of his political opponents, but granted amnesty to the large majority, and succeeded in converting some into staunch supporters. Firing squads were not a part of his stock in trade. Thus he developed the tradition, which still persists in some quarters, that he was easygoing almost to the point of indifference. Nothing could have been farther from the truth. He soon demonstrated that he would not tolerate opposition, whether from friend or foe, and he consistently followed his own course, though making a great show of listening to advice.

REFORMS. Some of the appointments made by Vargas were outstanding. Oswaldo Aranha, who was later to achieve international stature, became minister of justice. Afraino de Mello Franco, a jurist of wide reputation, was placed in charge of foreign affairs. Every effort was made by the Vargas regime to solve the difficulties growing out of the world depression, and considerable progress was made. The acreage devoted to sugar was reduced drastically, because Brazilian sugar could not compete in the world market. Cotton acreage, on the other hand, was expanded. A National Department of Coffee was established to regulate production and stabilize prices. It cannot be denied that in many ways the new government was good for Brazil. It showed a courage and decisiveness that had been sadly lacking for many years—most of the time, in fact, since Dom Pedro II sailed into exile.

REBELLION. In spite of his good works, many persons could not forgive Vargas for his dictatorial methods. The opposition centered in São Paulo, as might well have been expected. Julio Prestes, the president-elect who never became president because Vargas acted first, had been São Paulo's governor. The rich coffee growers of the state were dissatisfied because of São Paulo's disproportionately heavy contributions to the national treasury. Gradually the plans for a rebellion began to take shape. It was generally understood that Minas Geraes and Rio Grande do Sul would join São Paulo, but at the last moment their forces were used to support the national government. So São Paulo was compelled to carry out its plans unaided. It did so without hesitation. *Paulistas* of every political faith joined in the defense of their state. Volunteers were so numerous that arms could not be found to equip them. Even women and children did everything in their power for the success of the cause. But the effort was in vain. After nearly three months of strenuous fighting the federal forces surrounded the revolutionary armies and forced them to yield. The cost of the uprising, in men and money, was very great on both sides. As usual, President Vargas adopted a general policy of clemency for the rebels. He had no desire to transform his vanquished enemies into martyrs.[2]

CONSTITUTION OF 1934. To some extent the São Paulo uprising strengthened Vargas' hand. Its collapse left the nation without any effective opposition. But the opposition still existed, no matter how scattered and disorganized it might be. Vargas was too shrewd a politician to disregard the signs of widespread dissatisfaction. He decided, at long last, to fulfill his implied promise to call a constitutional convention, so that popular government might be restored. The convention assembled in November of 1933. Many of its members were men of national caliber, distinguished in their several professions. An overwhelming majority were pro-Vargas. It could scarcely have been otherwise, for President Vargas controlled the election machinery. All things considered, however, the constitution that emerged from the labors of this convention was a good document, reflecting the generally accepted traditions of liberal democracy. There was to be a Congress of two houses, representing the people and the states, respectively, in the American tradition. There was to be a president with strictly limited powers. And there was to be a system of national courts, headed by a supreme court with the final power to pass upon the constitutionality of laws. The powers of the states were to be restored, and the cities were to have their popularly elected municipal councils, as they had possessed them before 1930. This, then, was the work of the liberally minded constitutional convention. And, to crown its work, it named as president for the term 1934–1938 that great democrat and liberal statesman, Getulio Vargas![3]

---

[2] This period is well covered by Ernest Hambloch in *His Majesty the President*.

[3] For a discussion of the 1934 constitution, see Pedro Calmon's *Curso de Direito Constitucional Brasileiro*.

ANOTHER TERM FOR VARGAS. To many persons the very idea of Vargas as a defender of the liberal faith was absurd. The thought of Vargas as president for another term was anathema. They contended that the man was ineligible. Had not the outmoded constitution of 1891 prohibited two successive terms for any president? Did not the new constitution of 1934 contain the same restriction? How, then, could Vargas be eligible for a term beginning in 1934, when he had been the nation's chief executive since 1930? To this Vargas replied that the years from 1930 to 1934 should not properly be considered a presidential term. They were an interregnum, a period of transition between the old order and the new. Vargas himself was merely provisional president during the period, serving as trustee for the new order. Now that the new order had arrived, its representatives assembled in constituent congress should certainly have the right to name as president anyone they pleased. And, though Vargas did not say so, he clearly intimated that they might have done much worse.

The "First Regular Term"

At the beginning of his "first regular term," as President Vargas invariably called the continuation of his regime in 1934, he took care to live within both the letter and the spirit of the new constitution. President and Congress co-operated wholeheartedly in furthering the social reform program which had already been partially established by decree. The constitution's guarantees of individual liberty were carefully respected. But there can be no doubt that Vargas chafed under the restrictions of a parliamentary regime. As president-dictator he had not been compelled to await the pleasure of a slow-moving legislative assembly. There were others, also, who disliked existing conditions, though for different reasons. Among them were many low-ranking officers of the army and navy, who were dissatisfied with their low pay and inadequate opportunities for promotion. And there were many dissatisfied civilians, especially among the factory workers, who were rapidly becoming more numerous.

One of the leaders of these dissidents was a former army captain named Luis Carlos Prestes, who had openly espoused communism and assumed the role of professional agitator. The entire movement was tinged with radicalism. In November of 1935 these various groups united to stage a revolt, which lasted just three days. It was not much of a rebellion, judged by Latin American standards, but it gave Vargas an excuse to cry "emergency" and establish emergency government—in other words, a government in which he was recognized as absolute master. He forced through Congress a constitutional amendment giving him the right to declare "a state of grave internal commotion," and thus suspend all the guarantees of the constitution. For all practical purposes this was martial law. It continued in effect for more than a year.

THE COMMUNIST THREAT. The justification offered by President Vargas for this fresh seizure of dictatorial power was that communism threatened to engulf the country, and that he must fight it with every available means. Like many another dictator, he proceeded to discover communists behind every rock and tree. He made wholesale arrests of men and women suspected of having radical tendencies. The list of arrested persons included university professors, members of Congress, and even the prefect of the federal district. More than ten thousand were thrown into jail, and were subsequently tried by specially created "tribunals of national security." Throughout Brazil the feeling was widespread that no real danger of a communist uprising existed. Vargas, it was said, merely used the communist menace as an excuse to punish his political opponents. When the prefect of the federal district was found not guilty and freed by the courts, he was given an ovation by the people of Rio. Many of those who had been arrested were subsequently released for lack of evidence. But several thousand men and women were convicted. The known or suspected ringleaders of the 1935 revolt were given long prison terms. Persons of known communist leanings were treated most severely. Luis Prestes, who had recently returned from Russia as an avowed disciple of Stalin, was sentenced to seventeen years at hard labor. Later he was made to stand trial for complicity in a murder which had been committed while he was in jail, and thirty additional years were added to his sentence. Some of his associates were accorded equally severe treatment.[4]

THE FASCIST THREAT. While Vargas was driving the communists underground, another movement of a very different kind presented a much more serious menace to Brazil's way of life. It was a kind of homegrown fascism, whose members called themselves *Integralistas*. The leader of this movement was Plinio Salgado, an undernourished neurotic in his mid-thirties who had been greatly influenced by the success of Mussolini's regime in Italy. As much as possible, Salgado tried to follow the Mussolini technique. He equipped his followers with green shirts and armbands bearing the Greek letter sigma, which of course had no significance and therefore required no explanation. The fascist salute with upraised arm was

[4] For a good sketch of Luis Prestes, see John Gunther's *Inside Latin America*, pp. 406 ff.

adopted. Integralists began to train with military precision. Salgado, who was a writer of no mean ability, used his literary talents to explain the significance of the movement. It stood for order and progress, which was certainly a reasonable ideal, and its slogan was *God, Country, Family*. Beyond these vague generalities, it was all things to all men. When *Integralismo* first began to attract public attention, most Brazilians regarded it as a good joke. But as the number of its recruits grew steadily, the joke seemed much less funny. Businessmen, workers, and even some public officials joined the movement. There were monster parades and great mass meetings. Money began to flow into the party treasury, and a substantial part of it came from the German embassy, though this fact was not known at the time. Brazilian fascism was in full flower.[5]

POLITICAL CAMPAIGN OF 1937. The year 1937 was one of great political activity. Vargas' "first regular term" was drawing to a close, and speculation was rife as to his successor. The democratic forces of the nation, who were strongly opposed to the president's highhanded tactics, chose as their candidate a former governor of São Paulo. This man was progressive, energetic, and an outspoken critic of dictatorship in any form. It was generally assumed that he would have the support of Brazilian liberals and radicals, and even of the communists, who could not put a candidate of their own in the field. To oppose this outstanding liberal the conservatives named a well-known novelist from the north, who had acquired some experience with public affairs by serving as minister of communications under Vargas. He was generally regarded as the official apologist for the existing regime, and though Vargas himself never gave his official endorsement, there seemed to be little doubt as to his sympathies. Salgado, the Integralist *Führer,* also announced his candidacy. No one expected him to win, but he had a definite nuisance value. In a very close election he might even hold the balance of power. Both of the major candidates campaigned vigorously, and Brazilians took an unprecedented interest in the issues presented for their consideration. They awaited eagerly the day of the election, January 3, 1938.

Later Dictatorial Years

THE VARGAS *coup d'état.* On November 10, 1937, a scant eight weeks before election day, the people of Brazil learned with shocked surprise that the choice of a new president had been indefinitely postponed. Mem-

5 See Reinhold Maack's article, "The Germans in South Brazil," in the *Inter-American Quarterly,* July, 1938, pp. 5 *ff.*

bers of Congress arriving at the *Palacio Tiradentes* for their regular session were turned away by a detachment of cavalry. The regularly elected governors of the states were notified that they had been removed from office by presidential decree. Vargas and the army leaders had planned this *coup d'état* with great care. Troops were stationed at strategic points, ready to suppress any opposition. But none was offered. Vargas held the nation in the palm of his hand. Before the end of the day he addressed the people by radio. His sudden action had been necessary, he explained, to save the country from communism. These were desperate times, and only desperate measures would suffice. So Congress had been dissolved. So, too, had the state legislatures and municipal councils. Representatives of the President would administer the affairs of the states and cities. The constitution of 1934, over which the best brains in Brazil had labored for many months, was not merely suspended; it was annulled. In its place the President was promulgating a new constitution, which of course had been prepared long in advance.

JUSTIFICATION OF THE *coup d'état.* Vargas' constitution of 1937 began with an attempted justification of the new seizure of absolute power:

Whereas, the legitimate aspirations of the Brazilian people for political and social peace, seriously disturbed by manifest factors of disorder, created by growing party dissensions, which a malicious demagogic propaganda attempted to transform into class warfare, and which, through the extreme force attained by the ideological conflicts, tended, in its natural process of development, to solve itself by violence, thus subjecting the nation to the imminent threat of a disastrous civil war;

Whereas, the state of apprehension caused throughout the country by the infiltration of communism, which was growing daily more widespread and deeper, calls for a remedy, both radical and permanent in character;

Whereas, the previously existing institutions did not furnish the state with the normal means for preserving and defending the peace, the safety, and well-being of the people;

With the support of the armed forces and yielding to the dictates of public opinion, both justifiably apprehensive of the dangers threatening the Union and of the swiftness with which our civil and political institutions were being undermined;

Now, therefore, it is resolved to insure to the nation its unity, its honor, and its independence; and to the people of Brazil, under a regime of political and social peace, the necessary conditions for their security, their welfare, and their prosperity;

The president of the Republic of the United States of Brazil decrees the following constitution, which comes into effect, as from this date, throughout the country.[6]

Vargas, it will be noted, declared his reliance on two sources of support: the armed forces, and public opinion. *And he put the armed forces first.* Well he might, for without their aid he could never have insured the "unity, honor, and independence" of the Brazilian nation, and the security of his own dictatorship.

SUPPRESSION OF THE INTEGRALISTS. Salgado and his Integralists seem to have assumed that they would play an important part in the new regime. They had previously offered Vargas one hundred thousand well-trained men from their private army to aid his well-publicized fight against communism, and they may have been given assurances that their party would become the official party of the nation. In any event, they were gravely disappointed by the President's uncompromising attitude. Almost at once he set out to crush the Integralist movement. He issued a decree outlawing all political parties; and, since the Integralists were the only party maintaining a thorough organization throughout the entire country, they were hardest hit. Their offices were padlocked, and their leaders were denied permission to hold public meetings. Thereupon Salgado announced that the political purposes of the Integralists had already been achieved, and that the organization would henceforth be known as the Brazilian Association of Culture. Twenty-four hours later the police descended upon the offices of the Brazilian Association of Culture, and closed them permanently. It was clear that Vargas had no intention of permitting a rival dictatorship in Brazil.

THE INTEGRALIST UPRISING. But the Integralists did not submit quietly to this dismemberment of their organization. Early in the morning of May 11, 1938, green-clad troopers attacked Guanabara Palace, the official residence of the president. They disarmed the marines who were on guard, swarmed over the palace grounds, and actually broke into the president's study, where Vargas, assisted by his daughter Alzira, was still working. A man of lesser caliber than Getulio Vargas would have been cowed into instant submission. But the president and his daughter seized revolvers—the only weapons at hand—and opened fire on their assailants. Soon they were joined by Benjamin Vargas, the president's brother, who brought a sub-machine gun, and by several government officials and palace guards. This little group then proceeded to hold the attackers at bay.

[6] Constitution of 1937, Preamble.

As it turned out, their task was not an easy one. They attempted to tele-phone for help, only to discover that the wires had been cut. So one of the group managed to leave the palace grounds unmolested and make his way to a nearby telephone, where he made an urgent appeal for help to the Ministry of War. The troops who came in response to that call did not arrive until five hours later, though they were stationed only a short dis-tance away. No satisfactory public explanation of that long delay has ever been given.

While Vargas and the Integralists were shooting it out, other Green-shirts were busily occupying strategic points throughout the city. Even a part of the Ministry of Marine fell into their hands. They also seized two radio stations, and broadcast to the world that the Vargas government had fallen. But eventually the laggard relief troops arrived at Guanabara Palace and forced the Greenshirts to flee in panic. Other Integralists were systematically routed out of the strategic buildings that they had captured only a few hours before. By seven o'clock in the morning the victory of the government forces was complete. Some of the President's attackers were shot down while trying to make their escape. Others managed to get away into the nearby forest, only to be hunted like wild animals. Thousands of known or suspected Integralists were rounded up and sent to prison camps, where they joined the communists whose influence they had so loudly decried. Salgado himself, who may or may not have been the moving spirit in the assassination plot, boarded a German ship and escaped to Portugal. His followers frantically burned or buried their arms, uniforms, and flags, hoping to escape any connection with the move-ment. *Integralismo* was dead.[7]

CONSTITUTION OF 1937. The 1937 constitution decreed by Vargas for the nation was a remarkable document. It left no doubt as to the suprem-acy of the president. Nearly all the conventional checks on the executive power were conspicuously absent. The president might appoint almost anyone in the public service, without the necessity of securing the approval of any other branch of the government. He might dismiss almost anyone, for whatever reason he deemed adequate. He might dismiss the Parlia-ment—as the new legislative body was to be called—at any time and solely on the basis of his own judgment. He might introduce bills in the Parlia-ment, and such bills should take precedence over measures introduced by the legislators themselves. In fact, proposed laws might not be presented

[7] See Frederico de Villar's interesting article, "Life and Death of Brazilian Fascism," in the June, 1943, issue of *Inter-American*, pp. 16 ff.

by individual legislators, but only by one third of the entire membership of each house. Presidential vetoes might be overridden only by a two-thirds vote of each house—an almost impossible condition, in view of the fact that one third of the members of the upper chamber of the Parliament were to be appointed directly by the president. Under these provisions Vargas would certainly have been the absolute master of Parliament, if there had been any Parliament for him to master. But, as it turned out, Parliament was never permitted to meet from the day the constitution was decreed until the end of the Vargas regime, nearly eight years later. No elections were ever held for members of the Parliament, or, for that matter, for anyone else. Vargas simply ruled by decree. From time to time the judges of the supreme court, who occasionally displayed surprising independence, declared some of his acts unconstitutional. Vargas, with a tolerance rare in dictators, made no attempt to force them to change their opinion, but of course the unconstitutional acts remained in force.

Meaningless guarantees. The new constitution increased the president's term from four years to six, and removed the prohibition against two successive terms. Actually Vargas served for eight years after 1937, without permitting an election to be held at the end of the six-year period, and he was finally removed from office by force. He promised, at the time the 1937 constitution went into effect, that a plebiscite would soon be held to determine whether the people approved of its provisions. That plebiscite was never held. Several thousand words of the new constitution were devoted to the usual guarantees of individual liberty, but the president was authorized to sweep them all away "in the event of a foreign menace or the imminence of internal disturbance." Note that the president did not even have to wait for the internal disturbance to occur; if his crystal ball revealed that trouble was at hand, he might act without further delay. Actually, during those later years of the Vargas regime, Brazil was almost continuously in a state of emergency, and all the guarantees of the constitution were valueless. First the communists furnished the pretext for emergency—that is, dictatorial—government. Then the Integralists were held responsible. And afterward it was the war. But reasons could always be found to keep the rights of Brazilians more or less permanently suspended.

A meaningless constitution. Perhaps the most remarkable aspect of the 1937 constitution was the manner in which it was systematically ignored. Large sections of it never went into effect. Vargas decreed it, after it had been written to his order, but he seems never to have had the faintest intention of respecting his own handiwork. Why should he outline in considerable detail the powers and duties of a Parliament that was never to meet? Why should he take care to include constitutional provisions that would assure his domination of Parliament, if he never expected it to be in session? Why should he even mention a plebiscite, if he never intended it to be held? Those questions long puzzled the people of Brazil. They soon discovered, after the 1937 *coup d'état*, that they were living in a maze of constitutional hocus-pocus. The constitution was in effect, but it was not in effect. It was a difficult conundrum, and only Vargas knew the answer.

Features of the New State: *Supernationalism.* The regime established in 1937 had a grandiloquent title—*O Estado Novo,* the New State. There was, in fact, nothing very new about it, though it did have some fascist overtones. One of its features was a strident supernationalism. Brazil should be for the Brazilians. Foreign nationals and foreign capital would still be welcome, but they must accept fairly strict regulation. At least two thirds of the employees of every foreign company doing business in Brazil must be Brazilians. Moreover, two thirds of the workers in every job category must be natives. Therefore it would be impossible to meet the requirement by giving all the lowest-paid jobs to Brazilians, and saving the high-salaried positions for Americans or Britons or Germans. There were other nationalistic decrees, also. At least twenty per cent of all the coal bought by factories must be Brazilian coal. Some alcohol from Brazilian sugar must be mixed with all gasoline. Manioc flour must be mixed with wheat flour. In these ways the government lent a helping hand to struggling Brazilian industries.

Few symbols. In setting up his New State, Vargas made relatively little use of symbols. There were no official uniforms, except for those in the armed forces. There was no official greeting of "Viva Vargas!" and no outstretched arm. The Integralists had used these devices, and that was a sufficient reason for Vargas to avoid them. No new flag was created to symbolize the New State. But the flag of the republic was shown everywhere on every conceivable occasion, thus arousing the patriotic fervor of Brazilians. Every shop and every office was expected to display a portrait of Vargas. Some shopkeepers did in fact ignore this decree, and they were not punished, but the large majority made certain that the presidential portrait was prominently displayed. The radio was used to some extent to stimulate patriotic emotions, though most of the radio stations were left in private hands and were permitted to broadcast more or less what they pleased, provided they did not actively criticize the regime. Motion pictures might not be shown until they had received the stamp of approval of the Department of Press and Propaganda. Newsreels invariably showed Vargas' latest activities, and of course they always presented him in the most favorable light. Some changes were ordered in school textbooks, and a few professors in the universities lost their positions. But for the most part the school programs continued unchanged, and the universities managed to retain their freedom of speech and thought. For a dictator, Vargas was a mild and reasonable man.

Press censorship. The censorship which he imposed upon the press was thoroughgoing, however, and sometimes it was very drastic. Journalists who criticized the regime too openly were cautioned, in the first instance; if they persisted in their criticism, they might be required to submit in advance to the Department of Press and Propaganda everything that they expected to print. If, after numerous warnings, they still proved intractable, they might be removed from their posts or even excluded from the profession of journalism. In practice it was seldom necessary to resort to the more drastic penalties. A reporter or editor could usually be kept in line by the threat of losing his job; a publisher could generally be forced to take orders by the hint of confiscation of his newspaper. Moreover, there were other and more subtle ways of getting results. The newspapers all relied on imported newsprint, and they had to obtain licenses to import it. If, therefore, their licenses were revoked or even suspended for any considerable period of time, they could be forced out of business. So the Brazilian press generally followed the Vargas line. Foreign-language newspapers were told that they might no longer continue publication. Newspapers and magazines from foreign countries might still be sold in Brazil, but subject to continuous censorship. Individual issues were sometimes confiscated, or individual stories blacked out.

The severity of press censorship varied considerably during the Vargas regime. When Vargas first came to power in 1930, he bore down heavily on all who used the printed word to express their opposition. After 1934, while the "liberal" constitution was in effect, censorship was very mild. From 1937 until 1942 it was more drastic than anything the nation had ever known. The officials of the Department of Press and Propaganda, many of whom were greatly impressed with their authority, established themselves as official arbiters of manners and morals. On one occasion, when a Bolivian woman lost her pet dog and thereupon committed suicide, Brazilian newspapers were forbidden to print the story, lest it lead to a wave of suicides among impressionable dog lovers who had been so unfortunate as to lose their pets.

There were other examples, also, of absurd abuses of authority, but it cannot be denied that many journalists had previously abused their freedom. In the German language press, before its suppression, and in Portuguese language newspapers read by persons of German descent, many of the editors had screamed their wrath against England and France, and even the United States, while lauding Germany and Italy to the skies. As the United States became more and more involved in the European struggle in the days just prior to Pearl Harbor, and as it became increasingly clear that Brazil would eventually cast its lot with the foes of the Axis, German-Brazilian criticism of the government's policy became increasingly bitter and increasingly unfair. To Vargas this situation seemed to call for drastic treatment. Curiously enough, however, he first placed the Department of Press and Propaganda in charge of a man whose fascist sympathies were fairly well known, but eventually he replaced him with a trusted friend of the Allies. After the confiscation or closing of the pro-German segment of the press in 1942, when Brazil went to war, the censorship was relaxed, especially with regard to criticism of domestic policies. Newspaper editors were told that they might print what they pleased, and some of them who took Vargas at his word found that he meant what he said—within reasonable limits, of course. Even during the period of most drastic censorship foreign correspondents experienced little difficulty in sending out their stories. Vargas was extremely sensitive to foreign opinion, and anxious to create the impression abroad that Brazil had a liberal government.[8]

Interference with freedom of speech. Although Brazilians could not always read what their favorite editors really thought of the Vargas regime, most of them could express their own opinions with relative freedom in their homes or at their sidewalk cafes. No widespread purges were ever undertaken, as in Germany and the Soviet Union. There was, however, a secret police force responsible to the President, and it managed to make life miserable for many persons whose prominence and outspoken opposition could not be overlooked. The secret police also arrested thousands of real or supposed communists, who were later sent to prison camps. They accorded the same treatment to thousands of real or supposed In-

---

[8] See "Brazil—and Dictatorship," by S. Harcourt-Rivington, in the *National Review*, February, 1942, pp. 168–174. See also his article in the March, 1942, issue, pp. 274–279; this article is entitled "Brazil under Vargas."

tegralists. And, later, they acted against influential Nazi sympathizers who seemed intent on interfering with the war effort. It was often said in Brazil that a man could be against Vargas, if he were so unimportant that his opinion really didn't count, but that any person of prominence who displayed real independence would sooner or later find himself listed as a communist or Integralist, and subject to arrest. Just how many persons were actually arrested and made to stand trial for actions *or thoughts* detrimental to the public welfare is uncertain. It cannot possibly have been very great, but it may well have included a large proportion of prominent opposition leaders. Vargas was too shrewd a dictator to remain inactive while his enemies gathered strength.

Labor legislation. From the time that Getulio Vargas first came into power in 1930, he undertook to win the support of the masses of the people. He soon issued a series of decrees embodying the main features of a comprehensive system of social security. In 1934 and 1935 he forced additional labor laws through Congress. And in 1937 and 1938, after Congress had ceased to function, he completed his scheme of labor benefits. Maximum hours were decreed for industrial workers, with additional pay for overtime. Minimum wages were established, and local commissions were set up to determine the proper minimum in each community. Employees might not be dismissed without proper compensation, except for just cause as determined by public officials; and the amount of "proper compensation" for employees of long standing was fixed so high as virtually to guarantee them life tenure. A system of old age pensions was established. Syndicates of workers, and also of employers, somewhat along the lines of Mussolini's fascist corporations, were authorized by law. But the workers were denied the fundamental right of all free labor, the right to strike. The 1937 constitution declared, in no uncertain terms, that strikes were "antisocial, harmful to labor and capital, and incompatible with the supreme interests of national production." When, therefore, the workers had a grievance, they were required to submit it to arbitration. Special labor courts were established to handle these and other labor problems.

A victory for the workers. Although this program of social reform deprived labor of its cherished right to strike, it was generally regarded as a victory for the working classes. The minimum wages established in the various parts of the country were admittedly low, but in many cases they represented a substantial increase. The maximum hours decree prevented many abuses that had formerly been widespread. The decisions of the labor courts were generally favorable to the workers—a result that might easily have been foreseen, in view of the fact that most of the large-scale employers of labor were foreigners, and therefore unpopular. But this wooing of labor did not completely alienate capital, as might have been supposed. Vargas left the factory and store owners in charge of their own businesses and tried to assure them continued opportunities for profit. He constantly reiterated his belief in free enterprise. And since farm and domestic workers were excluded from most of the benefits of the labor code, the great plantation owners were affected scarcely at all. Outside of the larger cities—and the overwhelming majority of Brazilians live outside of the larger cities—life was very much the same as before. But Vargas had succeeded in establishing himself as labor's knight in shining armor. The masses were favorably disposed toward his regime.

WAR AGAINST THE AXIS. December 7, 1941, that "day of infamy" in the calendar of history, found the United States suddenly plunged into war. Getulio Vargas did not take long to decide what course his nation would follow. He broke off diplomatic relations with the Axis powers within a few weeks and declared war against them seven months later. He cleaned out nests of European fascism within the country. He arranged for use by the armed forces of the United States of badly needed bases within Brazilian territory. His stand at the side of the Allies contributed in no small measure to the ultimate victory. Some writers, reluctant to give credit to Vargas for any good thing because of his dictatorial methods, have said that he did not lead Brazil into war; the democratically minded Brazilian people did it for him, and he merely permitted himself to be swept along. The most that can be said for him, they insist, is that he did not try to stem the tide. But that is an unfair perversion of the record. Getulio Vargas never faltered in his unwavering support of the United States, and he declared war as soon as Brazilian public opinion was ready for the step. Those who say that he was merely an opportunist may be right. Perhaps he saw which way the wind was blowing and set his sails accordingly. Certainly he reaped a rich reward in the form of American help for his armament program and for his scheme to industrialize Brazil. But no one supposes that Vargas was a confirmed democrat. If he joined the ranks of the Allies primarily for the purpose of benefiting his own country, it may well be said that other men have been hailed as great patriots for displaying similar motives.

OSWALDO ARANHA. During most of the war the President had at his side an able diplomat whose friendship for the United States could not be questioned. His name was Oswaldo Aranha, and he had been a loyal Vargas follower since the uprising in 1930. As minister of justice and minister of finance he served his country well and was rewarded with the coveted post of ambassador to the United States. In Washington thousands of Americans felt the spell of his personality, and he in turn acquired a great admiration for the American people. When, therefore, he was called home to head the Ministry of Foreign Affairs, Americans knew that in the Brazilian government they could be sure of at least one staunch friend. Together Vargas and Aranha charted the course of Brazilian foreign policy in the days prior to Pearl Harbor. Together they decided upon the fateful break with the Axis. Together they led the nation into war. And then, in August of 1944, their friendship was abruptly terminated.

Aranha had served as vice-president of the Brazilian Society of Friends of the United States, and in 1944 he was re-elected to that post. His scheduled speech of acceptance was to have been an important political and social event. But less than twenty-four hours before the appointed time, without a word of notice or explanation, Vargas closed the Society's premises. If this act was intended as a public rebuke to the Foreign Minister, it certainly accomplished its purpose. Aranha submitted his resignation, and the President accepted it with alacrity. In the United States the news of Aranha's dismissal—for it amounted to that—was received with dismay. Some persons thought that perhaps Vargas was ready to embark upon a different foreign policy, more favorable to the Axis. But their fears were soon allayed. Aranha had not been too pro-American. Apparently he had acquired too fine a reputation for his own good. Brazilians were talking about him as a suitable candidate for the presidency, and that automatically made him *persona non grata* in the Vargas regime.

SELECTED REFERENCES

See references at end of Chapter 7.

CHAPTER 7

BRAZIL
From Vargas to Vargas

End of the Dictatorship

RESTORATION OF PRESS FREEDOM. In the early days of 1945 there was growing unrest in Brazil. The inevitable scarcities and high prices of war were spreading dissatisfaction among the people. The rigidity of the dictatorship was causing many leaders to long for a more liberal state of affairs. President Vargas, who never kept his ear far from the ground, finally decided that the time had come to restore the freedom of the press. On February 22 he announced that censorship was dead. From that time on the newspapers might print what they pleased. Actually the press was not quite so free as this decree indicated. A few papers were soon closed for taking undue advantage of their liberty, and others were warned not to engage in "excessive" abuse of the government. Moreover, the radio remained under government control, and several presumably anti-Vargas broadcasts were canceled at the last minute.

For the most part, however, the President seems to have meant what he said. Nearly all the newspapers were permitted to print their stories and editorials without interference from the police. They lost no time in taking advantage of their new freedom. Criticism and abuse were heaped upon the regime from every quarter. The leading dailies attacked the coffee policy, the sugar policy, the labor policy—in fact, almost everything that Vargas had done. There were, in fact, few to support the man who had ruled Brazil for nearly a decade.

THE CALL FOR AN ELECTION. In all probability Getulio Vargas had no idea that a free press would accord him such unkind treatment. Certainly many of his associates were totally unprepared for the blast. But they recovered quickly from their astonishment and prepared to trim their sails to the new wind. The President's cabinet handed him a recommendation that elections be held at the earliest possible moment, "in order to satisfy the evident desire of the people for a restoration of democratic institutions." Vargas considered this proposal for a week, and then announced that he would set a date for elections within ninety days. Almost at the end of that period he made the long-awaited announcement: the elections would be held on December 2, a date nearly seven months away. Both men and women would be permitted—in fact, required—to vote, and the minimum voting age would be eighteen years. But Vargas and his subordinates would remain in office until the inauguration of the new president and the new governors of the states. In other words, they would count the ballots, and in this way they could control the result.[1]

CANDIDATE EDUARDO GOMES. The leaders of the nation did not wait until the formal announcement of the 1945 election date before beginning their political activity. In a surprisingly short time the opposition forces were able to agree on a candidate for the presidency. He was Brigadier Eduardo Gomes, the man who had taken the Brazilian air force when it was almost non-existent and built it into a highly effective and powerful organization. Gomes himself seems to have had very little political ambition. Certainly he was no professional politician. But he lent an attentive ear when the leaders of the opposition assured him that the magic of his name would be sufficient to overcome the handicap faced by anyone who tried to beat the Vargas machine.

In many respects Gomes was an excellent choice. He was unquestionably honest and a sincere patriot. His courage had been proved beyond all doubt. He was a bachelor, a devoted son, and a devout Catholic who neither smoked nor drank. Hard-working and intelligent, he was an excellent administrator, but hardly the man to kindle the popular imagination. As an orator he was mediocre. He made no sweeping denunciations and promised no startling results. The platform of his group somewhat resembled its candidate; it was solid and substantial, but not breathtaking. It promised a greatly expanded educational program, a reduction of taxes on basic necessities, a larger measure of respect for the rights of the states, greater development of natural resources with the aid of foreign capital, and due respect for Brazil's established foreign policy as an active

---

[1] See "Brazilian Politics," by P. Carr, in the *New Statesman and Nation,* November 10, 1945, pp. 313–314.

member of the United Nations. With such a program few Brazilians could quarrel. But many of them could and did object to Gomes himself. They said that he was reactionary, and had been too closely associated with the old regime.

CANDIDATE EURICO DUTRA. Even more reactionary than Gomes, however, and even more closely associated with Vargas, was the "official" candidate for president, General Eurico Dutra. Vargas had called him "the candidate deserving the confidence of the Brazilian people," and it was generally assumed that the government's powerful political machine would be used to further his candidacy. Dutra was a singularly unspectacular man, with a record of mediocrity that may actually have been refreshing to some Brazilians after fifteen years of the brilliant and unpredictable Vargas. As a youth of seventeen, Eurico Dutra had enlisted in the army. Time and perseverance had done the rest. Eight years later he was a second lieutenant, twenty-one years after that he became a colonel, and eventually he rose to be brigadier general and minister of war. In his sixtieth year at the time of his nomination to the presidency, he evidently regarded a strenuous campaign as too taxing or too undignified. His party's platform promised just about the same things that had already been promised by the followers of Gomes. But democratically minded Brazilians could not forget that Dutra had once been an open admirer of Germany, and had climbed on the Allied bandwagon at a very late date. Rio's wits declared that Dutra's office in the war ministry was on the fifth floor, *behind the fifth column.*

THE ROLE OF THE COMMUNISTS. Early in the presidential campaign the Communist leader, Luis Prestes, appeared once more on the scene. He had been given jail sentences totaling nearly half a century and was not scheduled for release until 1983. But Vargas ordered him freed at this opportune moment, and Prestes reciprocated by making pro-Vargas speeches before large crowds. During his years in prison, it seemed, he had come to the conclusion that the man who put him behind the bars was really a very reasonable fellow and must be kept in power until after the elections had been held, in order to insure their honesty. Coming from Prestes, such sentiments were truly amazing. They undoubtedly influenced thousands of poor, ignorant men and women, who drank in their hero Prestes' words and decided that perhaps they had misjudged poor Getulio. More sophisticated Brazilians wondered what kind of a deal Vargas had made with the Communist leader.[2]

[2] See "The Prestes Saga," by John Nasht, in the December, 1945, issue of *Inter-American,* pp. 14 ff.

Vargas himself was not officially a candidate for re-election. On the contrary, he stated in clear and unambiguous terms that he was not a candidate. But he did not say that he would refuse to run if drafted by the people, and some politicians regarded this omission as significant. They speedily organized their own political group, designed to keep him in power for at least another six years, and blanketed the country with their propaganda. They called themselves *Queremistas,* or "We want-ers," and of course the man they wanted was Vargas. Before the campaign had progressed very far, Luis Prestes announced flatly that he would welcome another term for Getulio. "Vargas is a very flexible man," he was quoted as saying. "When it was fashionable to be fascistic, he was a Fascist. Now that it is fashionable to be democratic, Vargas will be a democrat." In return for these kind words, Vargas legalized the Communist Party, and it promptly began a strenuous campaign, choosing candidates for state and local offices and for the national Congress, but carefully refraining from nominating anyone to the presidency.

CANDIDATE VARGAS? As the months before the election passed, the *Queremistas* became increasingly noisy in their demands that Vargas offer himself for another term. They staged mass meetings and monster parades, which democratically minded students and other groups sometimes tried to break up. On such occasions the police promptly intervened, and always on the side of the *Queremistas.* Gomes and Dutra were still campaigning in their stolid way, but they attracted very little attention. The main issue seemed to be whether Vargas, the man who was not even a candidate, should continue to serve as president of the nation. Brazilians who hated dictatorship were frankly worried. They could not forget the last scheduled election, eight years earlier, which Getulio had canceled almost at the last moment. He had taken that action, he said, in the face of a desperate emergency—the threat of communism; and he had promised a plebiscite to determine the popular will. But now, after eight long years, he was still dictator, and the Communist Party had been recognized as a legitimate political group. What was Vargas really planning to do? Was he scheming to repeat his earlier performance, canceling the elections without notice and thus perpetuating his own regime?

The signs seemed to point in that direction. On October 29 Vargas summarily removed the police chief of Rio de Janeiro and installed his own brother in that key post. Something was in the air. The chiefs of the armed forces met hurriedly, and decided that they must take prompt action to forestall another Vargas *coup d'état.* Within a few hours troops and tanks were patrolling the streets of the capital. The government radio station suddenly went off the air. All sorts of rumors swept Rio, but the masses of the people could only guess what was really happening. The next morning they knew. General Pedro Goes Monteiro, the Minister of War, announced that Vargas had been removed from power, and that the presidency had been turned over temporarily to José Linhares, the president of the supreme court. Not a shot had been fired. Vargas, it was learned, had wept when first he received the generals' ultimatum, but by the next day he was able to greet the representatives of the press with his usual smile and with the assurance that a rest was just what he needed. Within a few days he left the capital for his ranch in Rio Grande do Sul. The Vargas regime, which had survived fifteen exciting years, was finally at an end.

The 1945 Campaign

Almost as soon as Acting President Linhares had been installed, he announced that the *coup d'état* would not affect the election schedule in any way. Elections would be held on December 2, as originally planned. It might, perhaps, have been better to announce a postponement of several months. After all, the Vargas political machine still controlled virtually all the states and cities, and was in a position to exert strong pressure on the voters. Not all the Vargas henchmen could be removed in a few weeks. In six months or so it might be another story. By that time all the leading politicians of the old order could probably be swept out of power, and the elections could be held with greater assurance that undue influence would not be used. But the army men who had engineered the uprising were in a difficult position. Their chief criticism of Vargas was that he had not honestly intended to hold the elections as scheduled. Pointing to his brazen sabotaging of the 1937 campaign, they had declared that 1945 was to be the same story all over again. If, then, they took power away from Vargas only to postpone the elections as they had accused him of plotting to do, there would be thousands of national and local leaders to raise the cry of hypocrisy, and millions of ordinary citizens to believe it. So the date was permitted to stand.

OVERHAULING THE BUREAUCRACY. President Linhares lost no time, however, in giving the Brazilian bureaucracy a thorough overhauling. He dismissed the interventors of the states, whom Vargas had appointed, and replaced them with men of his own choosing. He made sweeping shifts in his cabinet. On November 20, just twelve days before the election, he suspended the mayors of all cities for a period of two weeks. In their place he appointed judges of the courts to manage municipal affairs and—most important of all—to supervise the counting of the ballots. During those two weeks, therefore, the Brazilian courts practically ceased to function. But the nation was given the best possible guarantee that its votes would be honestly counted.

THE NATIONAL DEMOCRATIC UNION. With Vargas out of the way, the presidential campaign moved forward at a somewhat accelerated pace. Gomes' supporters, who called themselves the National Democratic Union, favored a policy of economic liberalism. They publicly endorsed the gradual elimination of all customs barriers, with continuing tariff protection on a temporary basis for only "modern and efficient" industries. But many of their spokesmen explained that "temporary" protection might continue for a long, long time, and that it might prove extremely difficult to distinguish between efficient and inefficient industries. Read in the light of these interpretations, Gomes' so-called low tariff policy may not have differed so markedly from the frankly high tariff doctrines of Dutra and his associates.[3]

THE SOCIAL DEMOCRATIC PARTY. The Dutra presidential campaign supporters took the name of Social Democratic Party. Prior to the downfall of Vargas they had exploited his support to the utmost; afterward they took care to emphasize their abhorrence of dictators and all their works. Like their principal opponents, they appealed chiefly to the upper classes, the Roman Catholic Church, and the Army. Communist Prestes was not very far wrong when he said in effect that the difference between the two candidates was the difference between tweedledum and tweedleDutra.

THE CHRISTIAN SOCIALISTS. There were indeed two other presidential candidates besides Gomes and Dutra, but they deserve no more than passing mention. One of them was a high-priced criminal lawyer who offered himself as the head of a group called the Christian Socialists. These men were closely associated with a Bishop Carlos Duarte, who had been excommunicated by the Roman Catholic Church for his insistence upon radical changes in church organization and procedure. After the excommunication, Bishop Duarte had established his own Brazilian Catholic Church, with married men as priests and recognition of the right of divorce. The new church was generally regarded by Brazilians as a freak, and its support certainly added nothing to the chances of the Christian Socialist candidate.

[3] See Virgilio Melo Franco's interesting little work, *A Campanha da U.D.N.*

THE COMMUNISTS. The fourth aspirant to the presidency was a political
unknown whom Luis Prestes produced almost at the last moment as the
nominee of the Communist Party. The man himself was not a Communist, though he accepted Communist support. He was, in fact, too
conservative for the extreme radicals, and too radical for the extreme conservatives. Why Prestes even bothered to present a presidential candidate
within two weeks of the election was somewhat of a mystery. Apparently
the fall of Vargas released him from whatever deal he may have had with
the Dictator, and he decided that the Communists might just as well have
their own nominee to receive the votes of staunch party members.

THE ODDS ON GOMES. Practically all the foreign correspondents reported
that Gomes would win the presidency easily. They pointed out that Dutra
was Vargas' man, and that both the people and the army were glad to be
rid of Vargas. They would scarcely sweep into power the very candidate
who had received Getulio's official blessing. By so doing they might nullify
the recent *coup d'état,* and make Vargas the real power behind the throne.
If these predictions of an easy Gomes victory discouraged Eurico Dutra,
he managed to conceal his emotions. He plodded steadily through the campaign, attending uninspired rallies and making uninspired speeches. Acting President Linhares took great care to preserve his official attitude of impartiality. His one concern seemed to be the maintenance of an atmosphere
in which the issues of the campaign could be openly discussed, and the votes
freely cast and fairly counted.

Election of 1945

DUTRA'S ELECTION. December 2 was election day, as the army had promised. It was the first election in fifteen years, and undoubtedly the most
honest election in the nation's history. Even United States Ambassador
Adolf Berle went out of his way to congratulate the government on its
scrupulous fairness. The results came in slowly, but almost from the first
the trend was unmistakable. Dutra was winning, and by a big margin.
When all the votes had finally been counted, his margin over Gomes was
nearly one million. He was inaugurated as president of Brazil on January
31, 1946.

Explanation of Dutra's victory. The foreign correspondents were hard
pressed to find a reasonable explanation of Dutra's victory. Actually it was
not difficult to explain. The voters had been asked to choose between an
unqualified conservative and a conservative with some liberal tendencies.

Their only other possible choices were a Communist-supported candidate and a political nonentity. Virtally all the conservatives voted for Dutra, not because they actively opposed Gomes but because they considered Dutra somewhat more "dependable." The liberals, on the other hand, were in a quandary. Most of them voted for Gomes, but not a few marked their ballots for the Communist candidate in protest against the stand-pat attitude of the major parties. Among the conservative supporters of Eurico Dutra there were several well-defined groups. The pro-Vargas elements regarded Dutra as the heir apparent, and voted for him almost to a man. The *Integralistas,* many of whom still clung to their political faith despite the official dissolution of their party, generally favored Dutra. They expected no favors from him; in fact, they remembered that he had played an active part in their overthrow. But they hated Communism, and they knew that he shared their hate. He would never compromise with the Communist Prestes, as Vargas had done. Dutra derived additional strength from the farmers and cattle raisers of the interior. He was one of them, having been born and raised on a ranch in the frontier state of Matto Grosso. He knew their way of life and their habits of thought, despite his many years in the army, and he talked in a way that appealed to them.

One of the major sources of Dutra's support was the Catholic Church, which still exercises a great influence in Brazil despite the fact that church and state have been separated for more than half a century. The Catholic clergy of the country campaigned openly for Dutra, and advised their congregations to vote for him. There were, of course, some exceptions, but Dutra must have received the endorsement of at least ninety per cent of the nation's priests. Eduardo Gomes, the candidate of the National Democratic Union, was by no means anti-Catholic. On the contrary, he was very devout and very orthodox. But he had never gone out of his way, as had his opponent, to affirm his Catholicism. In one interview, granted during the course of the campaign, Dutra had declared that the principles of the Roman Catholic Church were indispensable to clear thinking. Another time, in the course of a public address, he had called the Catholic Church "a genuine force interested in the democratization of the world." Moreover, his deeds had matched his words. The chaplain's corps of the Brazilian army was his creation. So, too, was the Catholic chapel at the national military academy. All things considered, therefore, the Catholic Church had reason to believe that it could count on Dutra. So had the new manufacturing interests of São Paulo. They greatly preferred the high tariff ideas of Dutra's Social Democratic Party to the low tariff theories of Gomes' National Democratic Union. The coffee growers of São Paulo, on the other hand, favored Gomes and low tariffs. They were anxious to encourage the United States and other industrial nations to send large quantities of their manufactured goods to Brazil in exchange for Brazilian coffee. When Dutra won the election, it was generally recognized that an intensive effort would be made to industrialize the nation. The coffee growers could no longer hope to dominate the Brazilian economy so completely as in the past.[4]

DUTRA HIS OWN BOSS. No fear seems to have existed that Dutra would be merely a Vargas puppet. The army had just rid the nation of its longtime dictator, and it certainly had no intention of permitting Vargas to stand in the wings and pull the strings while a new president danced. Yet army officers guarded the polls on election day, and made not the slightest effort to interfere while Dutra was voted into power. The inescapable conclusion was that Eurico Dutra—Vargas' official choice—had assured the army of his intention to be his own boss, and that the army believed him. Its confidence was fully justified, for the new president's subsequent relations with his onetime boss were coolly correct. Not by any stretch of the imagination could they have been called intimate.

VARGAS ELECTED TO SENATE. Vargas was determined not to be counted out of the political arena, however. He had scarcely been expelled from the presidency when he announced his candidacy for the office of senator from his native state of Rio Grande do Sul. He was elected by a large majority, despite the frenzied opposition of thousands of persons who feared that he was planning a return to power. A few months later when he arrived in Rio to claim his seat in the Senate, he bought space in the leading newspapers to announce the event. More than fifty thousand persons swarmed to the airport to greet him, almost wrecking two airplanes parked on the field and virtually disrobing a number of policemen who tried to check their triumphant progress. It was a great day for Getulio. But the following afternoon, when he appeared in the Senate, his reception was quite different. One of the Senate leaders presented a resolution of thanks to the army for kicking Vargas out and, as he put it, "making democracy possible." Other senators spoke in similar vein. The newspapers took up the cry, reminding themselves in leading editorials how glad they were to be rid of dictatorship. Getulio Vargas was not at all abashed, however. He went placidly about his business, lining up support for his Labor Party

---

[4] See Frederico de Villar's article, "What Happened in Brazil," in the February, 1946, issue of *Inter-American*, pp. 19 ff.

and arranging deals that might prove highly profitable at some future time.

COMMUNIST STRENGTH. A major surprise of the 1945 election was the relatively strong showing of the Communists. They received more than 600,000 popular votes and won fourteen seats in the Chamber of Deputies, the lower house of Congress. They succeeded in electing their leader, Luis Prestes, to the Senate. Less than a year earlier the Communist Party had made the modest claim of 3,000 members, and many persons had charged it with boasting. The sudden shift from persecution and impotence to official recognition and relative importance was almost too much for the aplomb of the Party's leaders. They began to talk as if they had actually won the election, instead of running a bad fourth. Some of them openly boasted of the day when they would take over the government of the nation. Indeed, it could not be denied that Brazil had acquired the largest Communist Party of any country in the New World.

The Dutra Administration

LACK OF A DUTRA MAJORITY IN CONGRESS. President Dutra was badly handicapped from the very beginning of his administration by the fact that his Social Democratic Party had been unable to win a majority in Congress. It did indeed have one hundred and fifteen seats, as compared with the ninety seats of the Gomes group (National Democratic Union). But the simplest arithmetic would show that a coalition of the ninety Gomes deputies with the thirty supporters of Vargas would yield one hundred and twenty votes to override the government's one hundred and fifteen. If the Communists also joined forces with the opposition, the united front could defeat the government on every issue. Dutra's salvation was that the opposition was far from united. National Democrats, Labor Party members, and Communists had very little in common. In fact, the National Democrats, who were by far the largest single group in the opposition, found themselves much more sympathetic to the aims of the conservative Dutra government than to the radical proposals of the Labor and Communist factions. So it was not at all surprising that the leaders of both the National Democratic Union and the Social Democratic Party should look with favor upon the proposal to join forces in some sort of coalition regime. Such a condition was actually set up, and while it lasted it gave the government forces overwhelming majorities in both houses of Congress. But it collapsed after a couple of months, and President Dutra was forced to continue his government by minority. It was a very unsatisfactory situation, because both the Labor and Communist congressmen used their strength to embarrass the government whenever an opportunity presented itself.

POLICIES OF THE DUTRA ADMINISTRATION. Even before Dutra was inaugurated as president he made clear the general lines of his public policy. The fascist overtones of the Vargas regime would be swept away. The rights of the states would be restored. There would be a new constitution, fashioned in the democratic pattern. The immigration laws would be liberalized, and foreign capital would be welcomed. The co-operation between Brazil and the United States, which had been so successful in time of war, would be continued in the era of peace. Dutra went on to explain, in an interview with a United States correspondent, that those stories about his Nazi sympathies had been totally without foundation. He had been in charge of the purchase of some German artillery, and when the deal was finished the Germans had decorated him. That was all there was to it.

CONSTITUTION OF 1946. All parties were agreed that one of the nation's first orders of business must be the preparation of a new constitution. The curious charter of 1937, which Vargas had lovingly presented to the nation and then largely ignored, could no longer serve as Brazil's fundamental law. Something like the democratic constitution of 1891 would be more appropriate. Almost as soon as Congress met, on February 2, 1946, it declared itself a constitutional convention, and set about the serious task of writing the new document. It was promptly presented with a tentative draft prepared, at Dutra's request, by the acting chief justice of the Supreme court, but not even the members of Dutra's own party paid too much attention to this proposal. When at last the task was finished and the constitution was presented to the nation in September of 1946, it proved to be a fairly liberal document. The president was to be elected directly by the people—that is, by both men and women; he could not hold office for two consecutive terms, and could not be succeeded immediately by any of his blood relatives. He was no longer given the extraordinary powers that Vargas had seen fit to confer upon himself, such as the virtual right to name his own successor and a strangle hold on legislation. Congress was to assume once more the normal role of a lawmaking body. The 1937 constitution was not discarded entirely, however. Many of its labor provisions were retained. So were the ultranationalistic declarations that only Brazilians might own newspapers or mines. But the clauses deliberately designed to foster dictatorship had been swept away. Brazil was assured a democratic way of life, to the extent that any constitution could guarantee it.

There was protracted debate in the constitutional convention over the proposal authorizing the government to outlaw any political party that opposed democracy or "fundamental human rights." The Communists suspected, not without reason, that this clause was aimed directly at them, and they sought to prevent its adoption or at least to modify its phraseology. But the Dutra and Gomes forces united to support the suggestion, and it was passed without difficulty. Another fight was stirred up by the proposal to legalize divorce. Devout Catholics finally won, and marriage was solemnly declared an "indissoluble union."

ECONOMIC UNREST. Almost from the day that President Dutra took office he was forced to grapple with grave economic problems. Prices were rising steadily, and wages were lagging behind. The inevitable result was a disastrous drop in the already low standard of living of the Brazilian masses. Poor people were obliged to stand in line for hours, just for the privilege of buying the barest necessities at fantastically high prices, while the rich patronized the thriving black markets. Government attempts to control prices proved largely ineffectual. The fact that these conditions were duplicated in other countries did not relieve the misery of the Brazilian people or lessen their resentment. Riots broke out in many cities. In early September of 1946 a two-day riot in Rio de Janeiro resulted in the death of one person and the injury of at least one hundred others. Martial law was decreed, and five hundred rioters were thrown into jail. Among them was a Communist member of Congress. He was released after a few hours because of the congressional immunity from arrest guaranteed by the constitution, but the incident brought into sharp focus the part played by the Communists in fomenting dissatisfaction among the people. Through their control of the labor unions they manipulated strikes at times and places best calculated to disrupt the nation's economy. The stevedores at the great coffee port of Santos walked off the job twice in a month. Railroad workers refused to work until their demands for higher wages were met. When the employees of the Rio street railway, light, and power company announced their intention of going out on strike, the government retaliated by calling out troops to maintain the essential services.

Throughout this period of industrial unrest the Dutra regime did very little to remove the basic cause of popular dissatisfaction—high prices. Instead it blamed everything on the Communists, as Vargas had done in previous years. The Communist influence was certainly clear enough;

more than four thousand persons lined the docks to roar a welcome to the new ambassador of the Soviet Union when he arrived in Rio. But it may well be doubted whether Communism could have found such a fertile soil if some way had been found to increase the real wages of the Brazilian workers.

DEVELOPMENT OF INDUSTRY. As an ultimate solution of the country's economic problems the government relied heavily on the development of industry. Large loans were obtained from the Export-Import bank of the United States for the purpose of exploiting new deposits of iron ore and other raw materials, and also for the purchase of industrial equipment. Many American engineers and other technicians were brought to Brazil to speed the process of industrialization. American and other foreign firms were given to understand that they might expect greater encouragement than they had received under Vargas, and greater freedom to pursue their own policies, if only they would make their finished products in Brazilian factories with Brazilian labor, instead of exporting the raw materials and perpetuating Brazil's colonial status.

CONGRESSIONAL ELECTIONS OF 1947. Elections were called for January 19, 1947, to choose state and local officers and some members of Congress. The politicians promptly went into action. Vargas made numerous speeches contrasting the prosperous condition of the nation during his administration (that is, during the early boom years of the Second World War) with its shortages, inflation, and governmental inaction in the Dutra postwar era. He aimed his remarks straight at the workers, evidently hoping to build his Labor Party into a major political force. In his anxiety to win votes he abandoned his earlier pro-American policy, and began to denounce the people of the United States as gross barbarians who could never hope to understand the culture of a great nation like Brazil. This was a frank theft of Communist thunder. The Brazilian Communists, like their fellows in other parts of Latin America, were currently crying out against American "imperialism," and blaming the United States for all the world's troubles. By showing that the United States was always wrong, they probably hoped to demonstrate that Moscow was always right.

Vargas and the Communists. Perhaps Vargas believed that the Communists would co-operate with him throughout the campaign, as they had in the months immediately before his overthrow. If so, he was doomed to disappointment. Prestes and his followers were no longer ready to co-operate. They named their own candidates in opposition to the candidates of the Labor Party; and, in those communities where they seemed

to have no chance of winning, they actually threw their support to followers of Dutra or Gomes, rather than permit victories by the Vargas
Labor Party. Nobody supposed for an instant that the Communists would
sweep the country, but nearly everyone knew that they had an unparalleled
opportunity to strengthen their position. The nation's economy was in
bad shape, the workers were dissatisfied, and many non-Communists
thought that perhaps Communism should be given a chance to show what
it could do.

Dutra and the Communists. The government forces were frankly worried. President Dutra issued a statement calling the Communist Party a
menace to Brazilian democracy and asking all voters to boycott it. The
Catholic Church took a similar stand, urging its members to vote and
reminding them that "every abstention is a vote for Communism." Meanwhile Communist leader Luis Prestes declared that his party would win
one million votes out of perhaps five or six million.

Moderate Communist success. When all the votes were counted, it was
found that the Communists had come within striking distance of their
announced goal. They had received eight hundred thousand votes—about
sixteen per cent of the total. They succeeded in electing two senators,
fourteen deputies, and nearly seventy members of state legislatures. In
the city council of Rio de Janeiro they proved stronger than any other
party, though falling considerably short of a majority. In the important
state of São Paulo the governor was elected with their support, but he
was a wealthy industrialist who had frequently opposed their activities.

SUPPRESSION OF THE COMMUNISTS. President Dutra seems to have been
greatly disturbed by this moderate success of the Communists, even though
it offered no immediate threat to the security of his own regime. He
began to seek ways of destroying Communist influence. In mid-February,
less than a month after the election, his public prosecutor presented to the
Supreme Electoral Tribunal a petition requesting the suppression of the
Communist Party, on the ground that it opposed democracy and took orders
from a foreign power. Luis Prestes himself had unwittingly laid the basis
for this charge several months earlier, when he publicly told a group of
fellow Communists that in case of war between the Soviet Union and
Brazil he would of course expect them to fight on the side of the Soviet
Union. The Electoral Tribunal took nearly three months to decide the
issue. In the meantime Dutra suspended the Communist Youth Union
as an organization harmful to the public welfare. All known Communists
had previously been removed from positions in the public administration,

despite their strenuous protests that they had a right to belong to a recognized political group.

DISSOLUTION OF THE COMMUNIST PARTY. Early in May the Supreme Electoral Tribunal handed down its long-awaited decision. By a vote of three to two it ruled that the Communist Party was illegal and should be dissolved. President Dutra promptly ordered the army and the police to close all Communist quarters throughout the country. Nearly five hundred local clubs were padlocked in Rio by the security police, who patrolled the city in fast cars on the alert for trouble. The trouble did not come. Communists refrained from mass demonstrations, and the party's attorney announced that the decision would be respected, pending an appeal to the supreme court of the nation. Party leader Luis Prestes dismissed the matter with a shrug of the shoulders. "It is not the first time that we have been officially annihilated," he said. "But somehow we always manage to be a little stronger than before." Many persons wondered whether he meant that a new party would be formed, using democratic slogans but following the official Moscow party line.

EXPULSION OF COMMUNIST CONGRESSMEN. Meanwhile the government had to decide what to do with the congressmen and state legislators who had been duly elected on the Communist platform. Dutra believed that the simplest plan would be to have each house expel the Communists within its own membership, so that new members might be named. But at this point he encountered unexpected opposition. The National Democratic Union, which had co-operated with his own followers in so many matters, refused to vote for the expulsion of legally elected representatives of the people. So there seemed to be no way to prevent the Communists from filling out their unexpired terms as men without a party, unless the President should declare martial law and dissolve Congress. This he was unwilling to do. He could not forget the abuse that had been heaped on Vargas for similar tactics. Nor did Dutra himself escape bitter criticism, even from conservative sources. "Brazil is tired of its dictatorial experiences," declared a leading Rio newspaper. "If this time fate has in store for us a return to governmental arbitrariness, we can expect darker days. The specter of civil war will arise in this unhappy home of Brazilian democracy." The Communists themselves blamed the United States for their plight. They contended—without any shadow of proof, of course— that President Truman had brought pressure to bear on Dutra and the Supreme Electoral Tribunal. While the Communists continued their anguished complaints, the Dutra regime systematically carried out its campaign of suppression. The Brazilian Workers' Confederation and its affiliated unions were suspended for six months on the ground that they were Communist-controlled and "sources of agitation among the workers of the nation." Then, in January of 1948, the members of the National Democratic Union reversed their earlier position and agreed to the expulsion of the Communist congressmen. Communism was as dead in Brazil as the law could make it.

ELECTION CAMPAIGN OF 1950. As the end of President Dutra's term drew near, Brazil's political parties began a round of frenzied activity. Party leaders tried to arrange deals that would assure them advantageous positions in the presidential race. The National Democratic Union chose as its presidential candidate Eduardo Gomes, the air force brigadier who had been Dutra's principal opponent in 1945. The Integralistas, who had tried to achieve new respectability by discarding their Fascist green shirts and changing their name, also endorsed Gomes, but many people regarded their support as a doubtful blessing. Meanwhile the Social Democratic Party nominated for the presidency a lawyer named Cristiano Machado, who had held a number of important public offices. Machado was generally regarded as an honest man with strong democratic convictions. Almost certainly he was Dutra's personal choice, but the President took care to maintain at least an appearance of neutrality until the nomination had been made. Then he gave Machado his enthusiastic support. The small Republican Party also endorsed Machado, and in return was permitted to name the vice-presidential candidate of this coalition. In the early days of the campaign the name of Adhemar de Barros was frequently mentioned for the presidency. Adhemar was governor of São Paulo, and a wealthy radical who sometimes walked dangerously close to the Communist line. At first he seemed tempted to announce his candidacy, but eventually he decided to remain as governor of São Paulo, rather than turn the government over to the lieutenant governor, a political opponent who happened to be President Dutra's son-in-law. On June 18 came the announcement for which many persons had been waiting. The Brazilian Workers' Party proclaimed that its candidate would be the old master of Brazilian politics, Getulio Vargas. Almost at once Adhemar de Barros declared that his political group, which called itself the Social Progressive Party, would give Vargas its support. The Social Progressives were thereupon permitted to choose Vargas' running mate, and they selected João Café Filho, a brilliant but controversial figure whose anti-clerical views earned him the outspoken opposition of the Catholic Electoral

League. President Dutra had promised that the government would assure equal treatment to all political groups during the campaign, and that the votes would be counted honestly. He kept his word to the letter.

Return of Vargas

RESULTS OF THE 1950 ELECTION. The election was a great personal triumph for Getulio Vargas, the ex-dictator whom the army had kicked out of power. He received a million and a half more votes than Eduardo Gomes, his nearest opponent, and two million more votes than Cristiano Machado, the government candidate. Vargas carried sixteen of the twenty states and also the federal district. His running mate, Café Filho, also won, though only by a small margin. But the remaining candidates on the Vargas slate fared rather badly. In contests for Congress they ran a poor third. The Social Democratic Party won the greatest number of seats in both the Senate and the Chamber of Deputies.

THE NEW VARGAS REGIME: *Coalition government.* In order to secure the co-operation of Congress, some kind of coalition government was clearly necessary. The Social Democrats indicated their willingness to co-operate, and they were promptly rewarded with four important posts in the new President's cabinet. The Social Progressive Party, led by Adhemar de Barros and Vice President Café Filho, was eager to work with President Vargas. In fact, the only opposition party was the National Democratic Union, and it was not united in its opposition, for within its ranks was a dissident faction that desired to join the government coalition. From the very outset it was clear, therefore, that Vargas could get a substantial majority in Congress; but it was equally clear that he must satisfy a number of diverse groups in order to retain congressional support.

Acceptance of democracy. During the days when Getulio Vargas had been president-dictator of Brazil he had never spent much time trying to win the favor of Congress. In fact, he had not permitted Congress to meet from 1937 until the end of his regime in 1945. But the Vargas of 1950 was a changed man. One can only speculate as to whether his five-year enforced vacation had given him sufficient time to meditate upon the merits of democracy, or whether he feared another army *coup* if he should resume his dictatorial ways. But this much is certain: since his election in 1950 he has adhered strictly to the theory and practice of Brazil's democratic constitution. Congress has been permitted to play its proper role in the scheme of constitutional government. Guarantees of individual liberty have been respected. Vargas is once again president of the nation, but no one can fairly call him dictator.

Public works. The Dutra administration had tried to raise Brazil's standard of living by means of an ambitious plan known as SALTE (the letters representing the Portuguese words for Health, Food, Transportation, and Power). But Getulio Vargas had been in office only a short time before he announced that the SALTE plan, scheduled to run until 1953, must be greatly modified for lack of public funds. And there can be no doubt that the nation's financial picture was far from bright. A year and a half later, however, Vargas proposed a new and very extensive program of public works. Railroads and highways were to be greatly improved, hydroelectric power was to be developed on a more extensive scale than ever before, agriculture was to be mechanized, additional packing plants were to be constructed, the merchant marine was to be enlarged, and port facilities were to be modernized. Almost all factions in Congress heartily endorsed this comprehensive plan, despite continuing uncertainty as to the nation's ability to finance it.

PROBLEMS OF THE VARGAS REGIME. Almost from its very beginning the current Vargas regime has been beset with difficulties. The cost of living has continued to rise at a rapid rate, and wages have not kept up with this increase. Government efforts to check the inflationary spiral have proved ineffective. Coffee production, on which Brazil depends so heavily for its foreign exchange, has been disappointingly low, and the government has had to curtail purchases from abroad. The result has been a severe shortage of many of the essentials of modern Brazilian living. The difficulty of getting necessary foreign capital has been greatly increased by a series of laws excluding foreigners from certain industries, restricting the export of profits, and the like. These laws have been passed at the insistence of extreme patriots and supernationalists, and anyone who suggests their modification is likely to be branded as a tool of foreign interests. Another problem has been the spread of communism. Communist sympathizers seem to be everywhere, despite the statute outlawing the Communist Party. In 1952 they almost secured control of the Rio Military Club, whose membership includes many high army officers. Communist magazines circulate freely. Vargas seems to be surprisingly indifferent to this danger, but he does not follow the Communist Party line. On the contrary, he remains what he has always been—a sincere friend of the United States. And in addition he seems to have become what he never was— a sincere democrat.[5]

SELECTED REFERENCES

Barros, Jayme de, *A Política Exterior do Brasil, 1930–1942,* 2nd ed., Rio de Janeiro, Zelio Valverde, 1943.

Campos, Francisco, *Antecipacoes à Reforma Política,* Rio de Janeiro, J. Olympio, 1940.

Caó, José, *Dutra, o Presidentes e a Restauracão Democrática,* São Paulo, Instituto Progresso Editorial, 1949.

Carvalho Brito, Manuel, *O Civilismo em Minas,* Rio de Janeiro, Casa de Rui Barbosa, 1949.

Dantas Lacombe, Mercedes, *A Força Nacionalizadora du Estado Nacional,* Rio de Janeiro, D.I.P., 1942.

Devinelli, Carlos, *Política Brasileira,* Rio de Janeiro, Zelio Valverde, 1942.

Fontenelle, Walter, *Uma Democracia em Panico,* São Paulo, Editora "Jornal dos Livros," 1950.

Frischauer, Paul, *A Biography of President Vargas of Brazil,* New York, Random House, 1942.

Klinghoffer, Hans, comp., *La Pensée Politique du President Getulio Vargas,* Rio de Janeiro, Imp. Nacional, 1942.

Loewenstein, Karl, *Brazil under Vargas,* New York, Macmillan, 1942.

Melo Franco, Virgilio Alvim de, *A Campanha da U.D.N.,* Rio de Janeiro, Zelio Valverde, 1946.

Monte Arraes, Raymundo de, *O Brasil e os Regimes Ocidentais,* Rio de Janeiro, Tip. do Patronato, 1943.

Phillips, Henry A., *Brazil, Bulwark of Inter-American Relations,* New York, Hastings House, 1945.

Pimpão, Hirose, *Getulio Vargas e o Direito Social Trabalhista,* Rio de Janeiro, Gráfica Guarany, 1942.

Santos, José María dos, *Notas à História Recente,* São Paulo, Brazil, J. Magalhães, 1944.

Smith, T. Lynn, *Brazil; People and Institutions,* Baton Rouge, La., Louisiana State Univ. Press, 1946.

Sobral Pinto, Heraclito, *As Forças Armadas en Face do Momento Político,* Rio de Janeiro, Rodrigues, 1945.

Vargas, Getulio, *A Campanha Presidencial,* Rio de Janeiro, J. Olympio, 1951.

[5] See Benjamin H. Hunnicutt's article, "Brazil: Financial Difficulties," in the March, 1953, issue of *Current History,* pp. 156–158.

CHAPTER 8

BRAZIL
The Structure of Government

The Constitution

BRAZIL's first constitution was adopted in 1824. Unlike most of the constitutions of that period, it borrowed very little from the fundamental law of the United States. Instead it established a parliamentary regime, headed by a monarch who possessed limited powers. This constitution served until the abdication of Dom Pedro and the establishment of the republic in 1889. Then, after a brief period of provisional government, came the constitution of 1891. Its author was a close student of American government and politics, and the draft that he submitted to the constitutional convention was almost a replica of the constitution of the United States. The convention made a number of minor changes, of course, but it maintained all the principal features of the document. For many years, therefore, American influence was predominant in Brazilian constitutional law and theory.

In 1930 Vargas completely changed the pattern. One of his first acts was to suspend the constitution of 1891, substituting a lengthy provisional "decree-constitution" which conferred all executive and legislative powers on the president. Thus the first stage of the Vargas dictatorship began. The second stage was the election of a constituent assembly, which prepared a new fundamental law for the nation. But this constitution was not adopted until 1934, and it was annulled three years later. It had little chance, therefore, to influence the life of the nation. In large part, of course, it followed the Vargas pattern of strong presidential government, but with interesting variations. The discretionary powers of the president were

177

somewhat restricted. Cabinet ministers were said to be responsible to Congress. On the whole, the constitution of 1934 resembled the fundamental law of 1891 more closely than might have been expected.[1] The third and final stage of the Vargas dictatorship began with the adoption of the constitution of 1937, which the Dictator presented to the nation in a decree signed November 10. This authoritarian document was remarkable enough, but even more remarkable was the manner in which large parts of it remained permanently suspended. The constitution said that there should be a Parliament; the constitution was the law of the land; yet there was no Parliament. The constitution imposed a number of restrictions on the authority of the president, but not one of these restrictions was ever enforced. There was, in fact, no one except the president who possessed the power to enforce them. And so Brazil lived for nearly eight years in a constitutional twilight zone, unable to solve the perplexing riddle: When is a constitution not a constitution?[2] But at last Vargas fell from power, and a popularly elected Congress assumed the task of writing a new fundamental law for the nation. The present constitution, promulgated on September 18, 1946, is its handiwork. It retains some features of the 1934 and 1937 constitutions, but to a much larger degree it resembles the fundamental law of 1891. It represents a return to the liberal democratic tradition that avowedly guided Brazilian statesmen in the days before the Vargas dictatorship. And it has been carefully respected by Vargas since his return to power as a constitutional president.

NEEDLESS LENGTH OF CONSTITUTION: *Inclusion of details.* The present constitution is three times as long as the constitution of the United States. Part of this excess length is caused by the inclusion of matters that should properly be entrusted to the discretion of Congress. The constitution specifies, for example, that cemeteries shall be secular, and then immediately nullifies this clause by authorizing religious groups to maintain their own cemeteries.[3] It prohibits child labor in very detailed terms—children may not be employed until they are fourteen years of age, and they may not work at night or in unhealthful industries until they are eighteen. There is, of course, the possibility that such blanket proscriptions may work hardship in individual cases. The constitution recognizes this danger, and tries to avoid it by adding that exceptions may be made by

---

[1] For a good analysis of the 1934 constitution, see Pedro Calmon's *Curso des Direito Constitucional Brasileiro,* pp. 10 *ff.* The earlier period is well covered by Herman G. James in his 1923 work, *The Constitutional System of Brazil.*

[2] See pages 150–152.

[3] Art. 141, Cl. 10.

law or by the competent authorities.[4] Thus it permits Congress to use its own judgment, a result that could have been achieved equally well by omitting the matter altogether.

Verbosity. The great length of the present constitution is due in part to the verbose tendencies of its authors. For example, seven hundred words are devoted to "general principles" concerning the organization of the state courts. Another seven hundred words prescribe the method of preparing and adopting the federal budget. Neither of these matters is even mentioned in the constitution of the United States.

THE BILL OF RIGHTS: *In the constitution of 1891.* In the constitution of 1891 the bill of rights occupied relatively little space. It was taken largely from its American model and referred exclusively to the traditional guarantees, such as freedom of religion, freedom of speech, and the like.

In the constitution of 1937. Under Vargas, however, the bill of rights became a formidable affair. It expanded to several times its former length and followed the trend of the newer constitutions in other countries by including many detailed provisions concerning the family, education, property, social security, and labor. Some of the clauses purporting to insure individual liberties were so worded as virtually to deny any real measure of freedom. The section dealing with freedom of the press, for example, began in fine fashion. "All citizens," it declared, "shall have the right to express their thoughts, orally, in writing, in print, or pictorially, within the limits and conditions fixed by law."[5] Following paragraphs then deprived this declaration of all meaning. They specifically authorized censorship of the press, the theater, the cinema, and the radio; they provided fines and jail sentences for any persons violating the censor's edicts; and they decreed that newspapers must publish all government communications. Many other dictators have permitted constitutional provisions guaranteeing freedom of the press in fairly broad terms, knowing that they could always violate or "interpret" these guarantees to suit their own convenience. Vargas preferred to have his dictatorial powers expressed in unmistakable terms.

The 1937 constitution contained an entire section entitled *The Economic and Social Order.* These paragraphs reflected the Dictator's economic philosophy. Their very first words indicated that Brazil was to remain a capitalist country. "In private initiative, in the creative power of the individual to organize and to invent, exercised within the limits of the public

[4] Art. 157, Cl. 9.
[5] Constitution of 1937, Art. 122.

welfare, lie the richness and prosperity of the nation. The intervention of the state in the economic field is legitimate only so far as it supplies the deficiencies of private initiative and co-ordinates the factors of production, in such a manner as to avoid or solve their conflicts and to introduce, into the play of individual competition, the thought of the interests of the nation." [6] Within the framework of capitalism, however, workers were given many guarantees. They were assured collective labor contracts, annual holidays with pay, minimum wages, an eight-hour day, and necessary medical assistance. But the right to strike was prohibited, on the ground that it was antisocial.[7]

In the constitution of 1946. The bill of rights of the present constitution retains somewhat the form of the 1937 document, but returns to the spirit of 1891. It contains the conventional assurances concerning liberty of conscience, the inviolability of the home, freedom from arbitrary arrest, the right of property. Freedom of speech and press are guaranteed, "without dependence on censorship." [8] There is an unusual clause prohibiting political parties whose programs or activities are "contrary to the democratic form of government." [9] It was this paragraph that provided the basis for the suppression of the Communist Party in 1947.[10]

The provisions of the 1937 constitution dealing with economic and social matters have been largely retained in the present document. There are the same guarantees of maximum hours and minimum wages, holidays with pay, collective bargaining, and the like. But the right to strike is recognized, subject to the inevitable proviso that it shall be regulated by law. Work is declared to be a social obligation, which, as Professor Loewenstein aptly observes, is "a rather platonic postulate if one knows Brazilian habits and climate." [11] There are a number of clauses that seem to show scant respect for the institution of private property. The government may monopolize any industry or activity; it may repress any abuse of economic power; it may regulate the utilization of property, on the basis of the social welfare.[12] The casual reader must not assume, however, that the framers of the 1946 constitution contemplated the speedy adoption of a socialist regime. Their arrows were directed, not against property in

[6] Art. 135.
[7] Arts. 138 and 139.
[8] Constitution of 1946, Art. 141.
[9] Art. 141, Cl. 13.
[10] See pages 172–173.
[11] Karl Loewenstein, *Brazil under Vargas,* p. 57. This is the standard work in English on the Vargas regime.
[12] Arts. 146–148.

general, but against property owned by foreign individuals and corporations. They were intent on keeping Brazil for the Brazilians.

STATE OF SIEGE: *In the constitution of 1937.* All the constitutions of Brazil have recognized the necessity of suspending constitutional guarantees in time of emergency. The declaration of a state of siege has usually been considered a prerogative of Congress, or of the president when Congress is not in session. Vargas, however, made the state of siege virtually a matter of presidential discretion. His personally decreed constitution of 1937 authorized the chief executive (in other words, himself) to suspend the guarantees of individual liberty for a number of different reasons, including "the imminence of internal disturbance." It then went on to declare that "the authorization of the national Parliament will not be necessary to carry out any of these measures, nor may the Parliament suspend a state of siege . . . decreed by the president of the Republic." [13] There were, of course, some restrictions on the president's authority during the existence of a state of siege, but these restrictions could not be enforced, because of another interesting clause: "During the state of siege, the acts practiced by the public authorities, by virtue of its existence, may not be brought before the courts." [14] No dictator could have asked for more sweeping authority.

In the constitution of 1946. The framers of the constitution of 1946 had no thought of prohibiting such a useful device as the state of siege. Their attention was focused instead on the problem of bringing it within reasonable limits and preventing its abuse by the chief executive. To accomplish this result they returned to the earlier concept of the state of siege as primarily a prerogative of Congress. If that body is in session, it enacts the legislation suspending constitutional guarantees. If it is not in session, the president may issue the necessary decree, but in that case the president of the Senate (in other words, the vice-president of the nation) must issue a call for Congress to meet in special session within fifteen days. As soon as it meets, the president must submit a message explaining his action, and justifying the measures that he has taken. Congress then considers the matter, and takes such action as may seem appropriate. Neither the president nor Congress may declare a state of siege unless the country is engaged in foreign war or threatened with serious internal disorder. The law or decree shall not cover a period in excess of thirty days, and may not be extended for more than an additional thirty days, unless

[13] Constitution of 1937, Art. 168.
[14] Art. 170.

Brazil is at war with another nation. The president's powers during a state of siege are not unlimited; on the contrary, the constitution specifies the rights that may be suspended, and the punishments that may be imposed.[15] These limitations are not an absolute protection against dictatorship—no mere scrap of paper can give such a guarantee—but certainly the framers of the present constitution took every precaution to prevent abuse of power while the state of siege is in force.

AMENDMENT OF THE CONSTITUTION. The constitution is easily amended. Proposals for change may be made by one fourth of the membership of either house of Congress, or by a majority of the state legislatures. In either case, the proposed amendment is then considered by Congress and must receive a majority vote in two successive legislative sessions, thus involving a delay of nearly a year. If, however, it is approved by two thirds of the total membership of each house of Congress, it becomes a part of the constitution at once, instead of requiring subsequent action. In the federal system of the United States every constitutional amendment must receive the approval of the state legislatures, on the theory that the states are parties to the federal compact. Brazil, too, has a federal form of government,[16] but has not given its states the power to prevent the amendment of the constitution.

Suffrage and Elections

WHO MAY VOTE. The right to vote extends to both men and women when they reach the age of eighteen. The only exceptions are officers of the armed forces, persons who have been deprived of political rights for conviction of crime or other reason, those who cannot express themselves in Portuguese, and those who cannot read and write. The illiterates, of course, are very numerous, representing well over half of the population; but they are not generally kept from voting, despite the plain words of the constitution, except in the larger cities. Voting is declared to be an obligation, and the law prescribes fines for failure to appear at the polls on election day without a suitable excuse. As in so many countries of Latin America, however, compulsory voting is just a pleasant theory. Lists of non-voters are never compiled, and fines are never imposed.

SUPREME ELECTORAL TRIBUNAL. The judges of the regular courts of law have been made primarily responsible for the honesty of elections. There

[15] Constitution of 1946, Arts. 206–215.
[16] See page 194.

is a supreme electoral tribunal—a supreme court of the election system—which has seven members. Two of them are justices of the supreme court, two are judges of the federal court of appeal, and one is a judge of the court of appeal of the federal district. All five are chosen by the courts of which they are members. The remaining two judges of the supreme electoral tribunal are "citizens of notable juridical learning and unsullied reputation," [17] appointed by the president of the nation from a list of names submitted by the supreme court. This tribunal exercises general supervision over the entire election system. Specifically it registers the political parties and annuls their registration (as it did in the case of the Communists); [18] fixes the dates of elections, unless this matter has already been arranged by law; decides cases involving the alleged ineligibility of candidates; and awards certificates of election to those persons officially declared the winners. The decisions of the supreme electoral tribunal may not be appealed—not even to the supreme court of the nation—except in cases involving allegedly unconstitutional acts or denial of the writ of *habeas corpus*.

ELECTORAL BOARDS. Below the supreme electoral tribunal are regional electoral boards—one for each state, one for the federal district, and one for the territory of Acre, which lies in the Amazon basin. These regional boards are organized in much the same manner as the high tribunal. A majority of their members are judges, but a minority consists of laymen appointed by the president on the recommendation of the courts. Then there are the local election boards. Every community has its local board, presided over by a magistrate of one of the lower courts. The other members are named by the regional election board. When the judges of the regular courts are chosen to serve as presiding officers or members of electoral tribunals, they do not thereby escape the necessity of performing their regular judicial duties. The appointment involves additional obligations. It provides also additional compensation, but not enough to make it popular. The election service of judges is restricted to two years, however, in order to compel a reasonably equitable distribution of the burden.

THE PROCESS OF VOTING. Candidates for public offices are named by the various political groups, of course, and the voters have no direct part in the process. Each party prepares its own ballot, which conforms to legal specifications concerning size, color, and shape. The government provides an official envelope, as in most of the Latin American countries. A

[17] Constitution, Art. 110, Cl. 2.
[18] See page 172.

system of proportional representation is used for the election of congressmen and state legislators, each party receiving the number of seats to which it is entitled on the basis of its earned vote. The electors have no chance to express their preferences among the several candidates presented by a party; instead they must accept or reject the entire slate.

The President

EXECUTIVE POWERS. The extraordinary position of the president under the constitution of 1937 has already been indicated.[19] He could govern the country virtually without interference, even assuming the existence of a functioning legislative body, though in fact the Parliament never met. He could play a decisive part in the selection of his successor, and thus perhaps continue to dominate the government after his term had expired. Within the letter of the fundamental law he could do what other dictators did by extraconstitutional means. The present constitution sweeps away the arbitrary powers of the president but still leaves him in a position of great authority. He appoints the members of his cabinet, other important public administrators, members of the diplomatic corps, high officers of the armed services, and judges of the federal courts. He must, however, have the consent of the Senate in naming all these officials except cabinet ministers. Senate approval is not necessary in making removals.

The president plays a leading part in the conduct of foreign relations. Through the nation's diplomatic and consular officers, who are almost his personal representatives, he becomes the voice of Brazil in foreign lands. He cannot declare war [20] or make peace unless authorized by Congress; but of course he can maneuver the country into a position from which it can scarcely be extricated short of war. The president is authorized to decree the total or partial mobilization of the armed forces. He may also assume command of them, but only through the intermediary of the competent authorities. The Brazilian constitution does not contemplate the possibility of the nation's president deserting his other duties to undertake the active management of a campaign of battle, even though he may sometimes be a general.

Mention should be made at this point of the president's pardoning power. He may grant pardons and commute penalties for federal offenses, after first receiving the recommendations of the courts directly involved.[21]

[19] See pages 150–152.
[20] Except in case of foreign aggression.
[21] The powers of the president are enumerated in Art. 87 of the constitution.

LEGISLATIVE POWERS. Although Congress is the nation's lawmaking body, the president has an influential part in the legislative process. He may introduce bills relating to any matter that falls within the jurisdiction of the federal government. In fact, he has exclusive authority to propose measures dealing with certain subjects—the creation of new positions in the public administration, increases in administrative salaries, or changes in the organization of the armed forces. His suggestions must be made an early order of business, first in the Chamber of Deputies and then in the Senate. The president has ten days to consider every bill enacted by Congress and submitted for his signature. If he does not approve, he returns the measure, together with a veto message. The two houses of Congress then sit as a single body to weigh his objections. They may override his veto by a two-thirds vote of those present. The president is not obliged to say *yes* or *no* to all the clauses of a legislative proposal. Instead he may veto one or two paragraphs of a bill, submitting them to Congress for reconsideration and promulgating the rest of the measure. In Brazil, therefore, it is useless for Congress to attach objectionable "riders" to otherwise acceptable legislation, in the manner of the Congress of the United States. Bills are very seldom passed over the president's veto. The tradition of executive supremacy is too strong.

Decree-laws. The constitution does not recognize legislation by executive order. It merely authorizes the president to issue such decrees and regulations as may be necessary for the execution of the laws of Congress. In many cases, however, presidential decrees go far beyond this limit. They not only interpret the laws, but include many matters that bear little or no relation to the subject matter of existing legislation. In some instances they apply totally different standards from those contemplated by Congress. Vargas, of course, carried decree-legislation to extremes during his first period of power; for want of a legislative body all lawmaking took the form of executive orders.[22] But even in the early years of the republic nearly every president overstepped the restrictions of the constitution. Supreme court decisions sometimes lent encouragement to this practice.[23] During his term President Dutra continued it as a matter of course, and the now democratically minded Vargas has followed his example.

QUALIFICATIONS AND TERM. The president must be a natural-born Brazilian at least thirty-five years of age. He must not be, at the time of his

22 Loewenstein, *op. cit.,* pp. 80–82.
23 James, *op. cit.,* p. 96.

election, a cabinet minister, governor of a state, or a judge of the federal supreme court or one of the electoral courts. The term of the president is five years, and he is not eligible for immediate re-election. Neither may his blood relatives succeed him immediately. It is unfortunate that the presidential period has been set at five years, for this term fails to coincide with the terms of deputies or senators. Only occasionally, therefore, will the chief executive be elected at the same time as the members of Congress. Such an arrangement is not conducive to harmonious relations between these two branches of the government.

SALARY AND RESIDENCE. The constitution provides for direct popular election of the president. His salary is about forty-five thousand dollars a year, in terms of American currency. This is scarcely sufficient to cover the expenses of his office. He is aided, however, by a generous allowance for the maintenance of his official residence. For many years the presidents of Brazil lived in Guanabara Palace, a great mansion surrounded by an immense park. This edifice had been built during the empire for Princess Isabel and her husband, and furnished in a style befitting royalty. Its splendor later provided a suitable background for the chief executives of a great nation. After President Dutra lived in it a short time, however, he moved to the smaller and less attractive Catete Palace, which had been used for cabinet meetings and official receptions. Some persons said that he was influenced in this decision by his wife, who held the superstitious belief that Guanabara Palace was unlucky. In any event, Catete Palace proved unlucky for Senhora Dutra. She died only a few months after taking up her residence there. But the palace is still used as the official home of the presidents of Brazil.

VICE-PRESIDENT AND PRESIDENTIAL SUCCESSION. There is a vice-president, chosen at the same time as the president and in the same manner. He must also have the same qualifications. His only important duty is to preside over the Senate of the nation, without the right to vote except in case of a tie. Should both the president and vice-president die or become incapacitated, the president of the Chamber of Deputies succeeds to the presidency. The vice-president of the Senate is next, and after him comes the president of the federal supreme court.

National Administration

THE CABINET. The constitution makes no mention of the number of cabinet ministries, thus permitting this matter to be fixed by law. At present there are ten ministries: Justice and Interior; Foreign Relations; Finance; War; Marine; Education and Health; Agriculture; Labor, Industry, and Commerce; Aeronautics; Communications and Public Works. Most of these names are self-explanatory, but there should be a few words of explanation concerning the work of the Ministry of Justice and Interior. It has two major functions. One is the general supervision of the judicial system and the penal institutions of the nation: the ministry takes the preliminary steps in cases of pardon; it maintains judicial statistics; and it publishes court records. The other principal function of this ministry is the supervision of state activities and the maintenance of a large number of federal-state relationships. Communications from state officials to officers of the federal government usually pass through this ministry.

THE MINISTERS AND CONGRESS. During the empire Brazil had a parliamentary system which made the ministers of state nominally responsible to Congress; a congressional vote of censure was supposed to force their resignation. Actually the parliamentary system was a sham. The emperor and his immediate advisers controlled the country, and brooked no serious interference with their plans. Through the election system they dominated Congress. Ministries were not permitted to fall until the emperor was through with them.[24] Small wonder that the men who framed the constitution of 1891 were determined to root out all vestiges of the parliamentary system! They not only forbade cabinet ministers to hold seats in Congress simultaneously, but also denied them the right to appear before Congress for the purpose of presenting proposals or answering questions concerning their official activities.[25] Thus they greatly increased the difficulty of maintaining close relationships between the executive and legislative branches of the government.

The present constitution, without attempting to return to the parliamentary form of government, does remove this unnecessary barrier. It declares that cabinet ministers *must* appear before the Senate or the Chamber of Deputies, or any committee of either house, when formally requested to do so; and it makes failure to appear a proper ground for impeachment.[26] This might well be mistaken for parliamentary responsibility, especially if taken in conjunction with the clauses directing the ministers of state to countersign the president's official orders, and declaring them to be "responsible for the acts which they subscribe."[27] Actually these

[24] See page 132.
[25] Constitution of 1891, Art. 51.
[26] Constitution of 1946, Art. 54.
[27] Art. 93.

words have no such significance. Cabinet ministers are responsible to the president—not to Congress. They are the president's personal advisers and hold office as long as they give him satisfaction. Congress could not get rid of them by a vote of *no confidence;* such a vote would be merely an expression of congressional opinion and would have no binding effect. The only way to remove a cabinet minister from office, in the face of presidential objections, would be by process of impeachment. Although Congress could indeed impeach and convict a cabinet minister, just as it could impeach and convict the president of the nation or any high administrative or judicial officer, such a step could not be taken unless the officer was charged with a serious crime against the nation—not merely because his policies differed from those of Congress. Latin American constitutions commonly contain clauses dealing with ministerial responsibility and countersignature of presidential acts, but these clauses usually refer to the form instead of the substance of government.[28]

PERSONNEL POLICIES. Brazil is one of the few countries of Latin America that has attempted to set up a merit system for the selection of public employees. The system applies only to certain groups, and has not been very successful in eliminating incompetents, but at least it has given government workers a reasonable measure of security in their jobs. The present plan was inaugurated by President Vargas in 1936. It established the principle of competitive examinations in the selection of public employees, and set up a personnel agency to administer the law. Vargas had already been in power for six years and had of course found ample time to install his own followers in every branch of the public service. These followers were "blanketed in"—that is, exempted from the necessity of taking examinations in order to retain their jobs. Since 1936, however, the merit system has been generally respected. Some departments have even arranged for the in-service training of their employees. The 1946 constitution contains a number of clauses designed to protect government workers against arbitrary dismissal. It also provides for retirement at full salary after thirty years of service. There are, however, thousands of so-called temporary employees who are excluded from these benefits. Some of them remain on the "temporary" list after years of service.[29] During 1953 experts from the United States spent many months studying the per-

[28] See, for example, page 267.
[29] See Henry Reining, Jr.'s article, "The Brazilian Program of Administrative Reform," in the June, 1945, issue of the *American Political Science Review* (Vol. XXXIX, No. 3), pp. 536–547.

sonnel policies of the Brazilian government, and were expected to recommend an extensive reclassification of public employees.

During the first Vargas regime the number of public employees increased almost every year. By the end of the era the payroll of the government was swollen out of all proportion to actual need. Since then neither Dutra nor Vargas has made any serious effort to reduce the size of this unwieldy bureaucracy. Ways have been found to keep employees busy by multiplying the red tape that was already so characteristic of Brazilian public administration. The government now takes a hand in almost every activity, public or private. Private citizens may not accept private employment or engage in private business of any kind without first obtaining permission from some government agency. Permission is not difficult to obtain, but it involves some expense and, frequently, interminable delay. There are now many lawyers who make their living by helping ordinary citizens to get necessary permits and licenses from the proper departments in the shortest possible time.

Congress

SELECTION AND TERMS: *Senators.* The Senate—the upper house of the national Congress—has experienced a number of changes in the course of Brazilian history. Under the empire its members were chosen for life, the provinces being represented on the basis of population. The constitution of 1891 reduced the term of senators to nine years, and decreed that each state (as the provinces were renamed) should have three senators, regardless of its population. Substantially this plan was followed in the short-lived fundamental law of 1934. When, however, Vargas presented to the nation his made-to-order constitution, it contained a number of remarkable features. Not the least of these were the characteristics of the Federal Council, as the upper house was to be known. It was to have thirty members—one from each of the twenty states, and ten appointed by the president. If the Federal Council had ever met, these ten appointees would undoubtedly have provided a little nucleus of "president's men," ready to endorse all executive proposals and prevent the overriding of an executive veto. Their four-year term was sufficiently short to enable the president, who was elected for a longer period, to replace them if they failed to give satisfaction.

Today's arrangements are much more conventional. The upper chamber is known once more as the Senate; its members are chosen by direct popular vote for terms of eight years. There are three senators from each state and three from the federal district, making a total of sixty-three. Part of the Senate's membership is renewed every four years. Every member must be a natural-born Brazilian, at least thirty-five years old. These qualifications, it will be noted, are the same as for the office of president.[30]

Deputies. The Chamber of Deputies has suffered less than the upper house from experimentation, though the 1937 constitution did provide for the indirect election of its members. In its present form the Chamber has a membership of three hundred and four, popularly elected for four-year terms, and representing the states, the territory of Acre, and the federal district. Deputies, like senators, must be native Brazilians, but the minimum age is twenty-one years. There is no system of partial renewal. Alternates are elected at the same time and in the same manner as the deputies and senators, in order to avoid the necessity of special elections if any members fail to complete their terms.

PLACES OF MEETING, SALARIES, AND SESSIONS. Unlike most countries, Brazil maintains two separate buildings for the two chambers of its Congress. The Senate occupies the Monroe Palace, a small but beautiful gold-domed building. The Chamber of Deputies sits in the Tiradentes Palace, a more imposing structure completed in 1930. There are offices for committees, but not for members of Congress. Secretaries are not regularly provided. Salaries of senators and deputies are small—about nine hundred dollars a year, in terms of American money, plus three dollars for each day of actual attendance. Both houses of Congress meet in regular session each year on the fifteenth day of March, and continue to do business for six months. Because the regular session is so long, special sessions are virtually unnecessary. Provision is made for them, however. They may be called by the president on his own initiative, or at the request of one third of the members of either house. Joint sessions of the Senate and the Chamber of Deputies are held occasionally for certain specific purposes—to inaugurate the legislative session and receive the president's message, to consider the repassage of measures that have been vetoed, to draw up the joint rules of procedure, and to witness the exercises involving the administration of the oath of office to the newly elected president and vice-president.

ORGANIZATION OF CONGRESS. Although the rules are adopted jointly, there are some differences in the organization of the two chambers. The

[30] See page 185.

Senate has ten committees, whose names correspond closely—though not exactly—to the names of the major administrative departments. Thus legislation relating to the ministries of War and Marine is handled by a single Senate committee whose title is Armed Forces. On the other hand, education and health are united in a single ministry, but given separate committees of the Senate. The Chamber of Deputies has fourteen committees, thus largely avoiding the necessity of combining unrelated subjects. Each committee of the Senate has five members, with the exception of the Finance Committee, which has nine. Committees of the Chamber of Deputies are larger, of course; they average seventeen members. In both houses the committees are chosen by a steering committee (*mesa directiva*), which is composed of the presiding officer (president) and four secretaries. There are two vice-presidents also, but they have no duties except to serve in case of the absence or disability of the presiding officer. Each house chooses its own officers, except of course the president of the Senate, who is the vice-president of the nation.

ENACTMENT OF LAWS. As in other countries, every bill must be passed by both houses in exactly the same form before it is submitted to the president for his signature. Differences between the two houses are adjusted by joint meetings of the appropriate standing committees. The influence of the committees is greater at that time than in the earlier stages of discussion, for no committee is permitted to bury a bill that has been entrusted to its care. It must report on every proposal, giving the reasons for its decision. Minority committee members may submit dissenting reports. Such dissents are not unusual.

The Courts

THE LEGAL SYSTEM. The legal system of Brazil, like that of its Spanish-American neighbors, is based on continental European principles. The courts pay relatively little attention to the precedents established in earlier cases, but try instead to judge each case on its merits.[31] One important Anglo-American institution has been borrowed, however: the jury system. It has been used for more than one hundred years, though only in criminal cases. A jury has twelve members, chosen by lot from qualified citizens of the community. A majority vote is sufficient to convict, and a tie is considered the equivalent of acquittal. In recent years the tendency has been to reduce the number of classes of cases requiring the use of juries.

[31] See page 112.

Brazilians seem to be generally convinced that the jury system is unsuited to their needs.

JURISDICTION OF THE COURTS. Because Brazil has a federal form of government, there are two sets of courts—federal and state. In the United States, where a similar situation prevails, the federal courts have jurisdiction over all cases arising under the constitution, laws, or treaties of the nation. Such a grant of authority to the federal courts of Brazil would virtually strip the state courts of power to decide anything, for the Congress of the nation has enacted the codes of criminal, civil, and commercial law. Every criminal act, almost without exception, constitutes a federal offense. Every dispute concerning the terms of a contract or a will centers around some federal statute. Under the circumstances, it has been necessary to restrict the power of the federal courts much more narrowly. The federal courts will not accept original jurisdiction merely because a law of Congress is involved. There must be some other factor, such as the necessity of interpreting the constitution or determining the rights of some government official or agency.

SELECTION AND TENURE OF JUDGES. All judges of the federal courts are appointed by the president of the nation with Senate approval. They are given life tenure, with retirement at the age of seventy, or at any age for proven disability. Retirement is optional after thirty years. Judicial salaries may not be reduced and must be paid in full, even after retirement.[32] Earlier constitutions contained somewhat similar provisions, and were partly responsible for the high grade of men attracted to the judicial service of the nation. Even Vargas respected the principle of permanent judicial tenure, though continuing to enforce regulations that had been declared unconstitutional by the supreme court. The right of the courts to invalidate unconstitutional statutes and decrees has been recognized by every one of Brazil's fundamental laws since the establishment of the republic.

THE SUPREME COURT. The federal supreme court is composed of thirteen judges. The constitution prescribes a minimum of eleven, but provides that judges may be added by law, upon the recommendation of the court. All the judges sit as one body, instead of dividing themselves into two or three groups for the consideration of different kinds of cases, as is so often done in Latin America. Judgments are rendered by majority vote, one of the members being designated to write the opinion of the court, though the other justices may submit concurring or dissenting opinions

[32] Constitution of 1946, Art. 95.

if they so desire. The court chooses its own president, who presides over its deliberations but has no more authority than any other member.

Most of the supreme court's cases come to it on appeal. There are many classes of cases that may be carried from the lower federal courts, or from the highest tribunals of the states, to the supreme court of the nation. If the decision of a lower court is alleged to be contrary to the constitution or to the literal interpretation of a federal law or treaty; if lower tribunals interpret the federal constitution or laws or treaties in different ways; if a writ of *habeas corpus* has been denied by all inferior courts of competent jurisdiction; if a case involves a foreign power; if a political crime is charged—under such circumstances the matter may finally be decided by the supreme court. However, some cases go directly to the highest tribunal: conflicts of jurisdiction between lower tribunals; requests by foreign nations for the extradition of criminals; cases involving the nation, the states, the federal district, or the municipalities; and accusations of common crime made against the president, cabinet ministers, and other high dignitaries of the nation.[33] In most instances, of course, a president or cabinet minister guilty of malfeasance in office would be impeached by the Chamber of Deputies and convicted by the Senate. But such conviction would result only in removal from office, and would not be a bar to subsequent criminal proceedings.

LOWER COURTS. In nearly every large nation there is a group of appellate courts serving as buffers between the supreme court and the district tribunals. Brazil, however, has only one such court. The federal court of appeal—which, like the supreme court, sits in Rio de Janeiro—has nine judges. In many kinds of cases—for example, criminal convictions not involving constitutional issues—its decisions are final. Its original jurisdiction is very narrowly restricted. Below the court of appeal are the district courts. One or more of these courts have been established in every state and in the federal district. They are the first tribunals to hear most of the civil and criminal cases arising under the jurisdiction of the nation.

SPECIAL TRIBUNALS. In addition to the ordinary courts of law, there are a number of other tribunals handling specialized types of cases. Military courts try members of the armed forces for violations of the military laws or offenses against the national security. Under some circumstances, and especially in time of war, their jurisdiction may extend to civilians. There are also election courts, to which reference has already been made.[34] And,

[33] Constitution, Art. 101.
[34] See pages 182–183.

in addition, there is an entire hierarchy of labor courts. Disputes involving working conditions, terms of employment—in fact, any matters concerning labor relations—go to these tribunals. A labor high court serves as the supreme tribunal of the system, and below it are eight regional courts. In every community where labor disputes are numerous there is also a board of conciliation and judgment. This board has representatives of labor and management, appointed by the minister of labor. Its presiding officer is a judge who has specialized in labor matters. The system of labor courts has not prevented strikes, as it was originally supposed to do. It seems, however, to have reduced some of the friction in labor disputes.

Federal-State Relations

FLUCTUATING FEDERALISM. Brazilian federalism has had a checkered history. Under the empire the nation was divided into provinces, which were little more than administrative areas. Each province did indeed have its own popularly chosen assembly, but this body had virtually no power. It was authorized merely to "propose, discuss, and deliberate on measures of local interest." The powerful figure in provincial government was the president of the province, appointed by the emperor and removable at his pleasure. Moreover, the fiscal powers of the provinces were narrowly restricted. The entire scheme of central control was designed to strengthen the authority of the emperor. When, therefore, the empire was swept away, the framers of Brazil's first republican constitution decided to reduce the likelihood of future dictatorship by adopting a federal form of government. The twenty provinces were transformed into states, without any change in their boundaries, and each new state was given the right to adopt its own constitution, elect its own officials, and regulate its own affairs. The Empire of Brazil became the Republic of the United States of Brazil; this is now its official title.

The constitution of the United States of America was copied rather closely, as we have already pointed out.[35] But there were some differences, which almost inevitably gave Brazil a stronger central government and weaker states than its American counterpart. The states of the American Union were in existence before the nation; they fought their war of independence under an extremely loose federation; and it was not until several years later that they finally agreed to adopt "a more perfect union." Naturally they were loath to sacrifice their own rights and privileges. They agreed to transfer to the nation only those powers that clearly could

[35] See page 177.

not be exercised by state officials without injury to the national welfare. And they adopted the fundamental principle that powers not delegated to the central government should, in general, be reserved to the states. In Brazil the situation was completely different. The nation came first, by a great many years. The states were almost an afterthought. Their powers were the gift of the nation—not the inherent right of sovereign entities. So of course the central government retained a generous measure of authority. Yet Brazil accepted the basic principle of American constitutional law concerning the distribution of public power. Its fundamental law of 1891 authorized the states "to exercise in general any and every power and right not denied them by express provisions of the constitution or contained by implication in such express provisions." [36] The present constitution expresses the same thought in almost exactly the same language.[37] During most of the Vargas dictatorship, however, Brazil's federal system completely disappeared. Federal interventors replaced the governors of the states. State legislatures were summarily abolished, and state constitutions set aside. Representatives of the president assumed control of the municipalities. All authority centered in the office of the nation's chief executive. But with the fall of Vargas the extreme centralism of the new state also disappeared, and has not been restored since Vargas' return to power.

DIVISION OF POWERS. The federal government of Brazil not only possesses all the powers that have been attributed to the nation in the American Union but also exercises control over a number of matters that have been reserved to the American states. As previously pointed out,[38] Congress has power to enact general codes of law for the entire nation. The constitution authorizes it to legislate concerning "civil, commercial, penal, electoral, aeronautic and labor law, and legal procedure." [39] It will be noted that this grant of power places elections directly under federal control. It also enables the nation to regulate labor matters directly, instead of relying on implied powers, as must be done in the United States. Congress is permitted to enact necessary legislation dealing with education and natural resources, and to organize a permanent scheme of defense against the effects of drought, epidemics, and floods. It may establish "standards of competence for the practice of the technical, scientific and liberal professions." [40] And, in addition, it may legislate concerning "pro-

[36] Art. 65, Cl. 2.
[37] Art. 18, Cl. 1.
[38] See page 192.
[39] Art. 5, Cl. 15a.
[40] Art. 5, Cl. 15p.

duction and consumption"—a broad grant covering a multitude of matters.

Concurrent powers. In the United States the power of the states to enact concurrent legislation concerning matters of joint interest is implied rather than expressed. Court decisions are sometimes necessary to decide whether national laws in certain fields are exclusive by their very nature, or whether they permit additional state legislation. The Brazilian constitution leaves no doubt on this point. It declares that the federal power to enact laws does not exclude supplementary or complementary state laws in certain fields; then it enumerates these fields, making the list as broad as possible.

Taxation. The taxing powers of the nation and the states are enumerated in the constitution in considerable detail. Most of the important taxes are assigned to the nation—customs revenues, taxes on incomes, production and consumption, business transactions and documents. These levies are the bulwark of the Brazilian tax system; therefore the states are left without a sufficient number of major sources of revenue. This situation is partially corrected, however, by a constitutional provision requiring the federal government to share certain revenues with the states, apportioning the money on the basis of population, area, and a number of other factors. The municipalities also receive a small share of federal funds. Three per cent of federal tax receipts for the next twenty years must be devoted to the development of the Amazon basin. The states and municipalities within the area are required to set aside a similar percentage of their own revenues for this purpose.

INTERVENTION. One of the major differences between the Brazilian and American federal systems is the right of the Brazilian central government to intervene in the affairs of the states. The system is much the same as in Argentina;[41] in fact, the constitutional basis for intervention has been borrowed very largely from the Argentine fundamental law. The power is phrased in such terms as to make it seem a prohibition. "The federal government shall not intervene in the states," declares the constitution, "except. . . ."[42] Then follows a list of the reasons for which intervention will be permitted. It includes the maintenance of the national integrity, the protection of a state from invasion or civil war, the reorganization of state finances when a state defaults on its debt for more than a limited period. Most important, however, because it most commonly provides the excuse for intervention, is the maintenance of the republican representative form of government. No one can say with assurance just what is

[41] See pages 115–116.
[42] Art. 7.

meant by this term; therefore it gives federal officials the greatest possible leeway.

The framers of the present constitution tried to prevent the abuse of the power of intervention by imposing numerous restrictions on its use. The president may not take the initiative except in times of grave emergency, when Congress is not in session; and then he must summon Congress at the earliest possible moment. If the justification for intervention is the maintenance of the republican representative form of government (or a number of other matters), the step must be authorized by a law of Congress. Despite these constitutional provisions, the president usually plays a leading part in the process of intervention. He may demand immediate authority from Congress, on the ground that the public safety is in jeopardy; and Congress is not likely to refuse. Or the president may act during the recess of the legislative branch, knowing that it will almost certainly uphold his action when it meets again. After the decision has been made to intervene in the affairs of any state, the president appoints an interventor, who takes whatever steps may be necessary to restore normal conditions. He replaces the duly constituted authorities of the state, governing in their stead until the emergency is over. If necessary, he may call on federal troops to enforce his decrees and maintain order. Except during the first Vargas regime, intervention has not been used so widely in Brazil as in Argentina. Yet it remains a potent weapon in the hands of the federal government.

State and Local Government

THE STATE GOVERNOR. Brazil's twenty states vary somewhat in governmental organization, but it is possible nonetheless to give a general picture. Each state has a chief executive—president or governor, as he is variously known—who is elected by direct vote of the people. His term is commonly four years, and, like the president of the nation, he is ineligible for immediate re-election in most states. The chief executive of a state is so similar to the president of the nation in powers and duties that he might almost be called the president in miniature. He names all important administrative officers, including of course the members of his own cabinet, usually without the necessity of securing legislative approval. In the lawmaking process his authority follows more or less the generally accepted pattern. He presents annual and special messages to the legislature, introduces bills, and vetoes legislative proposals that fail to meet his approval. His veto may be overridden, usually by a two-thirds vote. In

most cases he is not only the chief executive of the state but also the recognized leader of the political machine. This dual position carries great
prestige; it assures respectful consideration, if not certain adoption, of
every executive proposal.

OTHER FEATURES OF STATE GOVERNMENT. Most of the Brazilian states
have unicameral legislatures. The bicameral principle has generally been
accepted, however, by the larger states. Members are popularly elected;
the most common term is three years. The state judicial system must
conform to a number of principles established in the federal constitution.
Judges are chosen by competitive examination; they serve for life; their
compensation is required to be at least equal to that of cabinet secretaries.
State constitutions are shorter than the fundamental law of the nation;
they can be amended with equal ease. Many of them contain detailed bills
of rights, despite the obvious fact that these provisions merely duplicate
the guarantees of the federal constitution.

MUNICIPAL GOVERNMENT. A certain degree of municipal self-government
is assured by the federal constitution and also by the fundamental laws of
the states. It must not be assumed, however, that these clauses guarantee
home rule in the American sense. They do not permit the municipalities
to frame their own charters. On the contrary, the subject matter of the
charter is covered by general state laws. But some local officials are popularly chosen in every municipality. The members of the municipal council are invariably elected by the voters. The municipal executive—prefect,
as he is called—is selected in a similar manner, unless there are special
reasons for some different method of choice. Special reasons have been
found in many cases, however. The constitution permits the governor of
the state to name the prefect in every state capital, in every district where
there are mineral springs, and in every municipality designated by the
National Defense Council as essential to national defense. Almost every
important city in the nation falls into one or more of these categories. In
the metropolitan centers, therefore, the prefect is usually the direct representative of the state governor, executing his policies and holding office at
his pleasure. It should be explained at this point that the term "municipality" as used in Brazil does not necessarily mean a city. Only a few
municipalities are cities in the American sense; most are rural areas. In
Brazil, and generally throughout Latin America, the municipality corresponds to our county.

RIO DE JANEIRO. Since 1762 Rio de Janeiro has been the capital of Brazil.
As the seat of government and the largest city, it has been placed directly
under the control of the national authorities. In 1834 it was separated

from the Province of Rio de Janeiro; it now constitutes a federal district. The prefect of the district is named by the president of the nation, with Senate approval, and assumes direct responsibility for the management of the local administrative services. Congress enacts a large part of the local legislation. There is, however, a district council, whose members are elected by direct vote of the people. Moreover, the district has representation in both houses of Congress. Its inhabitants are more fortunate, therefore, than the residents of the national capital of the United States, who have no direct voice in the government of their city or their nation.

SELECTED REFERENCES

Brandão Cavalcanti, Themistocles, *A Constituição Federal Comentada,* Rio de Janeiro, J. Konfino, 1948.
Calmon, Pedro, *Curso de Direito Constitucional Brasileiro,* Rio de Janeiro, Freitas Bastos, 1937.
Carvalho, Orlando M., *Problemas Fundamentales do Municipio,* São Paulo, Brazil, Companhia Editora Nacional, 1937.
Castro Filho, J. Ribeiro, *O Problema da Jurisdicão no Direito do Trabalho,* Belo Horizonte, Brazil, Tip. Brasil, 1942.
Cavalcanti de Carvalho, Manoel, *Evolução do Estado Brasileiro,* Rio de Janeiro, A. Coelho Branco F.°, 1941.
Devinelli, Carlos, *Política Brasileira,* Rio de Janeiro, Zelio Valverde, 1942.
Duarte, Gil, *A Paisagem Legal do Estado Novo,* Rio de Janeiro, J. Olympio, 1941.
Duarte, José, *A Constituição Brasileira de 1946; Exegese dos Textos a Luz dos Trabalhos da Assembléia Constituinte,* 3 Vols., Rio de Janeiro, Freitas Bastos, 1947.
Ferreira, Pinto, *Principios Gerais do Direito Constitucional Moderno,* Recife, Jornal de Comércio, 1948.
James, Herman G., *The Constitutional System of Brazil,* Washington, D.C., Carnegie Institution, 1923.
Loewenstein, Karl, *Brazil under Vargas,* New York, Macmillan, 1942.
Oliveira, Yves Orlando, *Doutrinacão Municipalista,* Cidade do Salvador, Liviraria Progresso, 1947.
Oliveira Vianna, Francisco José de, *Idealismo da Constituição,* 2nd ed., São Paulo, Brazil, Companhia Editora Nacional, 1939.
——— *Problemas de Política Objectiva,* 2nd ed., São Paulo, Brazil, Companhia Editora Nacional, 1947.
Silveira, Murilo, *Pontos de Direito Constitucional Civil e Administrativo,* 2nd ed., Rio de Janeiro, Efreddo e Gravina, 1940.
Sousa, Iguatimozy, *Tratado de Administração Municipal,* Rio de Janeiro, Editor Borsoi, 1948.
Timotheo, Pedro, *O Poder Judiciario sobre Nova Constituição,* Rio de Janeiro, 1938.
Vivacqua, Attilio, *A Nova Política do Subsolo e o Regime Legal das Minas,* Rio de Janeiro, Editora Pan-Americana, 1942.

CHAPTER 9

MEXICO
Revolutionary Years

~~~~~~

The Land and the People

MEXICO's seven hundred and fifty thousand square miles place it third in area among the nations of Latin America. In population it stands second, with twenty-six million inhabitants to Brazil's fifty-two millions. Most of the people live on the cold central plateau, which varies in altitude from six to eight thousand feet. Mexico City, the capital, is on this plateau, on the western side of the mountain-rimmed plain known as the Valley of Mexico. It has a population of nearly two millions; no other Mexican city is even one fifth as large. Because the capital is seventy-three hundred feet above sea level, there is nearly always a chill in the air, but snow is practically unknown except on the surrounding mountains.

SPANISH CONQUEST. One of history's most dramatic expeditions was the conquest of Aztec Mexico in the early sixteenth century by a bankrupt Spaniard named Hernán Cortés, whose forces included only six hundred white men and sixteen horses. That so small a group could have conquered a great nation of builders and artisans is almost incredible. When the Cortés party finally reached the heights above the City of Mexico and stood looking down on the Aztec capital, one of the men wrote in his diary: "Gazing on such wonderful sights, we did not know what to say, or whether what appeared before us was real. I stood looking at it and thought that never in the world would there be discovered such lands as these." [1] In some respects, it must be admitted, the Aztec civilization was actually more advanced than that of Europe. It could boast of learned

[1] Bancroft, H. H., *History of Mexico,* Vol. II, p. 148.

architects and astronomers. It was a land of artists and poets. But in military matters its people were no match for the invaders, and they were conquered in less than two years.

The Spaniards were not at all concerned with the preservation of the Aztec civilization. They were interested solely in gold and they went after it with a single-mindedness worthy of a better cause. Soon they were shipping great quantities of it to the mother country. For generations the golden stream continued to flow from Mexican soil. Later, when

The cathedral of Mexico City. In the foreground is the Zócalo, or central plaza. (Photograph by the author)

only a little gold was left, the Spaniards of another age exported silver, which was available in fantastic amounts. Primarily these precious metals enriched the Spanish crown. During the centuries of Spanish control they were never used for the benefit of the people of Mexico.

THE FABLE OF WEALTH—AND THE FACT OF POVERTY. Past discoveries of great fortunes in gold and silver have given rise to the fable that Mexico is an immensely wealthy country. Although it seems to be very poor, many travelers assume that the Mexicans themselves are responsible for this state of affairs. Perhaps, they say, Mexicans lack natural enterprise and fail to utilize the great resources at their disposal. Perhaps they don't know how to make the most of their opportunities. American tourists especially like this idea, for it gives them a feeling of great superiority. They sometimes compare the Mexican to a beggar sitting on a bag of gold.

Holding the Mexicans chiefly responsible for their circumstances is not fair, however. The legend of great natural wealth is far from the truth; Mexico is a poor country, judged by almost any standard. The poverty is obvious to the most casual visitor. It is a bitter poverty, almost intolerable. It is the destitution of a people who have great difficulty in getting enough to eat and do not always succeed in this elemental struggle. And before they can hope to make any substantial improvement in their pitifully low level of living, the people must overcome great handicaps.

The basic reason for Mexico's poverty is the adverse terrain. Not much more than half of the land has any possible agricultural use. The remainder is mountain or desert. And of the fifty-four or fifty-five per cent that can serve an agricultural people, a great deal is forest or pasture, or not readily available to irrigation. Not more than eight per cent of the total area can be used for raising crops, and a large part of this available land lies fallow every year. So it is not difficult to understand why the Mexicans, an agriculturally minded people, have difficulty in making a living. Corn is the principal crop—the basis of the popular diet—yet substantial quantities of corn were imported every year until 1950. Vast irrigation projects are now making new land available, and the government is pushing these projects at great speed, using in part money obtained from the Export-Import Bank of the United States. But only a small fraction of Mexico's arid wastes can be reclaimed. On the central plateau where most Mexicans live there are few places where the rainfall exceeds fourteen inches a year. And since most of this rainfall is concentrated in the summer months, extensive irrigation is an absolute necessity. The truth is that Nature has bestowed a very scanty heritage upon the Mexican people. They must struggle constantly for mere existence.[2]

THE LAND SYSTEM: *Early policies.* For many centuries the situation of Mexico's masses was complicated by the system of land tenure. Even today the problem has not been entirely solved. When the Spaniards first came to America, they found that many of the Indians were practicing communists. The land of every small village was held in common and worked jointly by all the villagers. Real property was not bought or sold; it was communal property and could not be alienated. Some of these communal villages were respected by the Spaniards, but the large majority

[2] A great deal of information concerning Mexican economic conditions may be found in the periodical, *Review of the Economic Situation in Mexico*, published by the Banco Nacional de México.

of them were not. The land became the property of the conquerors or of the Catholic Church. And the Indians, of course, went with the land. They were serfs, without liberty or the means of acquiring it. Thus was laid the foundation of the hacienda system—the division of the country into great estates. A comparatively few families owned Mexico. Or, to be exact, they owned that part of Mexico not in the possession of the Church, which amounted to perhaps one half of the territory of the nation at the close of the struggle for independence. That conflict brought very little change in the economic status of the vast majority of Mexicans. A little group of wealthy aristocrats still owned the great haciendas and still determined the course of public policy.

Juárez and Díaz. In the middle of the past century the masses finally found an articulate champion. His name was Benito Juárez, and he was a full-blooded Indian who rose from poverty to become the governor of his state and eventually president of the nation. Juárez and his friends thought that they would win land for the landless by breaking up the great estates of the Church, but their reforms accomplished very little. And only a few years later their policies were completely reversed by Porfirio Díaz, the Spanish-descended aristocrat who made himself the master of Mexico and ruled the nation from 1876 to 1911. Díaz thought that the attempt to distribute land among the poverty-stricken masses was a glaring mistake. Why give farms to these millions of Indians who would never learn to cultivate them efficiently? Why not put them in the hands of men who understood the duties and privileges of ownership? It was a hard, cynical doctrine, but Díaz unhesitatingly put it into effect. He dispossessed the people of their lands—those small landholders who were so fortunate as to own property—and he turned Mexico into a nation of great haciendas. At the end of his regime one per cent of the population possessed about eighty-five per cent of the land. Three brothers owned virtually the entire state of Hidalgo. Haciendas of a million acres or more were not uncommon. The masses worked at starvation wages, with no hope of improving their lot.

Revolutionary land policies. Then came revolution and a new group of men who were pledged to a complete reversal of the Díaz policies. Not all the successors of Díaz have seen eye to eye, but nearly all have agreed upon the importance of the land problem. They have taken millions of acres of land from the great haciendas and distributed it to the landless. In some cases these properties have been handed out in small parcels to individual owners. More commonly they have been given to the little villages to be used communally, as in Aztec days. Some of these communal projects operate on a very large scale. One of the most ambitious, La Laguna, is a rich agricultural region formerly owned by about two hundred families. Now its four million acres are worked co-operatively by fifty thousand families. There are co-operative stores, as well as co-operative cotton gins, power plants, and railroad systems. Credit is provided by the national government.

Assessment of the land policy. The success of Mexico's land policy is difficult to measure. It is often criticized as flagrant confiscation, which indeed it is. The theory of the land seizures is that they will be accompanied by compensation to the former owners, but this is only a theory. The government finds difficulty in raising sufficient funds to pay the cost of necessary public functions, and under such circumstances it is not likely to worry too much about its promises to a little group of men who now possess neither land nor political influence. So very little has actually been paid, and the great families of the Díaz regime have been reduced to poverty. Their place in the social order has been taken by a group of politicians—a tight little clique of civilians and army officers who now run the country. Together with a small number of wealthy industrialists they form the new aristocracy. They are the top men of Mexico. Below them, in the social and economic order, we find a small middle class, composed of professional men, small industrialists and merchants, and government workers. And at the bottom of the scale remain the incredibly poor peasants, still struggling to obtain the bare necessities of life. These families represent ninety per cent of the nation's population. Has land reform really improved their condition? It is a difficult question. The answer probably is: Yes, but not much. The production of corn, Mexico's staple, is not much greater than it was in 1910.[3]

DIETARY DEFICIENCY. Because the people eat chiefly corn, spicing it with red pepper in the form of chili, they suffer from dietary deficiency. And this is partly responsible for giving Mexico a death rate that is still very high, despite marked improvement in recent years. The Mexican government, acutely conscious of this state of affairs, has undertaken an energetic campaign to change the eating habits of the people. It has long stressed

---

[3] The standard work on Mexico's land problem, *The Ejido, Mexico's Way Out*, by Eyler N. Simpson, is now somewhat out of date. For a more recent discussion, see Frank Tannenbaum's recent work, *Mexico: The Struggle for Peace and Bread*.

the importance of milk and fresh fruits and vegetables. But the masses change their habits very slowly, especially in a country like Mexico where there is so much illiteracy. Large segments of the population still live in just about the way that they did before the ¬¬nquest.

RACES. Mexico is an Indian nation. Ninety per cent of the people have some Indian blood in their veins. Nearly one third are of pure Indian blood. It is a striking fact that Mexico has had so little immigration. European immigrants have been attracted to the United States or Argentina or Brazil, but not Mexico. And as a result almost all Mexicans are descended from the Spaniards of colonial times or the Indians who lived in the land before white men ever came to America. There are, of course, a few thousand Americans and Britons, and smaller numbers of Germans and Frenchmen and Italians. But they comprise less than one per cent of the population. The number of Negroes is negligible. Therefore the population is quite homogeneous, at least from the standpoint of race.

However, large groups of Indians have never been assimilated into the general pattern of national life. Millions are still scattered throughout the country in their remote villages, almost completely isolated from the influences of modern civilization. They live their communal village life as in Aztec days; they speak their own Indian dialects, knowing scarcely a word of Spanish. They are sheltered from the rest of the world by the inaccessibility of the areas in which they live. In these sections roads are almost nonexistent, and the topography makes their construction very difficult. So visitors from civilization are infrequent. The government tries to establish schools, but it has great difficulty in finding teachers. The problem could be solved more easily if these millions of unassimilated Indians were in one part of the country. Unfortunately, however, they are scattered throughout all Mexico. Some are in the backlands of the high plateau, some are in the tropical forests of Yucatán, others live in the southern coastal areas bordering the Pacific. The improvement of their lot is not easy.[4]

CLIMATE AND RESOURCES. The coastal plains of Mexico are hot, and their vegetation varies with the amount of rainfall. In some coastal areas desert conditions prevail; in others there are dense forests. The slopes of the mountains, at elevations of three to five thousand feet, provide a "temperate zone" between the two extremes of seacoast heat and plateau cold.

[4] See Ernest Gruening's *Mexico and Its Heritage*, pp. 69–90.

The products of Mexico display a variety to match the climate. Wheat, beans, rice and sugar are grown in considerable quantities, though they cannot challenge the supremacy of corn. Cotton is a crop of increasing importance. Nearly one half of the world's supply of sisal, the raw material of rope and binder twine, comes from the tropic lowlands of Yucatán and Campeche. Some coffee and tobacco is grown. The livestock industry is important. Several hundred thousand head of cattle are exported every year, principally to the United States.

In the export field, however, minerals have always been most important by a wide margin. Silver is produced in great quantities again, after a lapse of several centuries. The supplies of gold have not been entirely exhausted. And there are other metals that have acquired substantial importance in more recent years—copper, zinc, lead, and iron. In the northern state of Durango there is a famous iron mountain. Large coal deposits have been found. Oil, which exists in great quantities, is an important export, though it is used increasingly by the domestic market.

TRANSPORTATION FACILITIES. Mexico has always been handicapped by inadequate transportation facilities, and even today, despite substantial improvement, this handicap persists. Railway mileage is extensive—fifteen thousand miles in all—but the roadbed and equipment have been permitted to deteriorate, and badly needed large-scale improvements have only just begun, after many years of delay. The highway system, on the other hand, has been greatly improved. Many new roads have been built, and many others have been completely reconstructed. Yet Mexico, which is one fourth as large as the United States, has only about one seventieth as many roads, and most of them are not suitable for use by motor vehicles during the wet season. Air traffic has developed greatly in recent years, but of course this provides only a partial solution of the transportation problem.

INDUSTRIALIZATION. Many Mexicans view with envy the great factories of the United States, and conclude that a similar development within their own country would bring similar prosperity. Perhaps they are right. In any event, they are determined to find out. Manufacturing has increased by leaps and bounds and now provides nearly one fourth of the national income. The textile industry is of prime importance. Leather goods, twine, and cordage are produced on a large scale. Mexico now produces a large part of the tires used by its motor cars. The long list of manufactured goods includes chemicals, electrical appliances, paper, clothing, jewelry. Heavy industry is becoming increasingly important. Steel

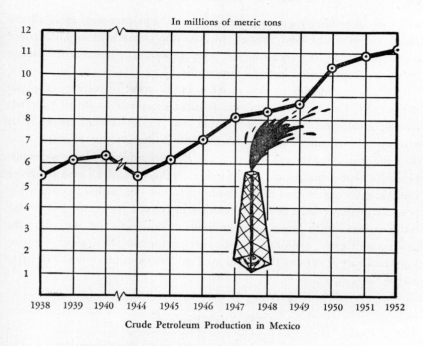

In millions of metric tons

Crude Petroleum Production in Mexico

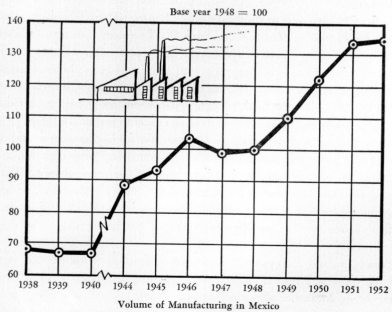

Base year 1948 = 100

Volume of Manufacturing in Mexico

Based on information obtained from the *United Nations Statistical Yearbook, 1952*, and the *United Nations Monthly Bulletin of Statistics*, May, 1953.

mills are increasing their capacity every year and expect to meet all domestic needs in the near future. Most of the radios sold in Mexico are made there. Food processing is very important. There are modern breweries, sugar refineries, and flour mills.

In the long run Mexico may prove to be the most important industrial nation of Latin America, with the possible exception of Brazil.[5] It has iron in great quantities and substantial coal deposits of fair quality. Its water power resources are extensive. One of the greatest handicaps has been the attitude of the government, which has championed labor so whole-heartedly that it has discouraged foreign capitalists seeking new fields for the profitable investment of their surplus funds. A further deterrent has been the widely publicized expropriation in 1938 of American and British oil properties worth hundreds of millions of dollars.[6] But nowadays the government turns a smiling face to foreign capital. It is especially anxious to attract American dollars, as well as American machinery and techniques.

The Díaz Regime

PROSPERITY AND SERFDOM. In Mexico the word *Revolution* has a special significance. It refers to the Revolution of 1910. There have been many other revolutions in Mexico's long and bloody history, but all the others seem to pale into insignificance beside the happenings of that fateful year. Porfirio Díaz was then president, as he had been almost continuously for thirty-four years. During his long regime—*reign,* it might more properly be called—he had brought peace and prosperity to Mexico. Banditry had been checked by means of an efficient rural police force. The railway mileage had been increased twenty-five-fold. Commerce and industry had prospered, and a huge national deficit had been turned into a surplus. Foreign obligations had been met with scrupulous care. Time and again Díaz had proved his administrative ability. Moreover, he had surrounded himself with a group of able statesmen—*Los Científicos,* they called themselves, because they insisted that everything should be done scientifically.

American and European businessmen who dealt with Mexico were greatly impressed by the evident skill and integrity of Díaz. But there were many Mexicans who failed to share their enthusiasm. They were

---

[5] See Sanford Mosk's recent volume, *Industrial Revolution in Mexico.*
[6] See Mexican Oil, by Harlow S. Person.

the Indian masses who had been forced into virtual slavery. For a few *centavos* a day they had to toil from sun to sun, making their few necessary purchases at the plantation stores at unbelievably high prices, and thus perpetuating their own serfdom. For them there was no opportunity, no hope, and no escape. Díaz did nothing to alleviate their misery. On the contrary, he accentuated it by seizing Indian lands and transferring title to men who already owned great haciendas. On more than one occasion Díaz expressed his belief that Mexico would be better off if all the Indians were dead. He never seemed to understand that they *were* Mexico.[7]

MADERO, LEADER OF THE OPPOSITION. Of course, the vocal opposition to Díaz and his scientific friends did not come from the Indian masses. They were inarticulate and totally without any effective means of helping themselves. But there were other Mexicans who knew quite well how to put their objections into words. One of them was Francisco I. Madero, a small, nervous man, thirty-seven years of age, who possessed almost a zealot's faith in the trappings of democracy. What Mexico needed, he said, was an honest election law, so that the people might really have the opportunity to express their opinions; and, above all, it needed the assurance that no president should serve more than one term.

The doctrine of a single term was not new; it had been the law of the land when Díaz first achieved the presidency. But it had been changed to suit the convenience of the great man, and every four years for several decades he had gone through the form of offering himself to the people as a presidential candidate, though taking care to make certain that the votes would always be counted in his favor. So the idea of a single term, with no re-election, had almost been forgotten until Madero revived it. He even wrote a book on the subject, which he published in 1908.[8] The book attracted a great deal of attention. All the opponents of Díaz—those landholders and business and professional men who had received fewer favors than they thought their due—began to ask one another whether the time might not indeed be ripe to get rid of the old despot. After all, he was eighty years of age and no longer able to face his enemies with the vigor he had shown in earlier days.

It must be admitted, however, that Francisco Madero was a strange

[7] See *Díaz, Czar of Mexico* by Carlos de Fornaro. The second (and final) edition of this work was published in 1908, while Díaz was still president. A less impassioned view will be found in Herbert I. Priestley's standard work, *The Mexican Nation, A History.* See also *Porfirio Díaz*, by Carleton Beals.

[8] *La Sucesión Presidencial en 1910.*

man to lead the opposition to the great Díaz. Physically he was unprepossessing, though his eyes burned with an almost magic fire. His family was rich, and he himself had a considerable share of the family estates. He was somewhat of a dreamer, yet it seems that he had a touch of greatness. The people felt it. They knew that he was sincere and honest. Whenever he talked to them he kindled a wave of popular enthusiasm that threatened to sweep all before it.

PREPARATIONS FOR THE ELECTION OF 1910. The next presidential election was set for 1910. Díaz had previously declared that he would not again be a candidate, and as a result several potential successors appeared on the political horizon. But as election day drew near it became increasingly evident that the Díaz renunciation had been merely a political trick. Apparently the old man never intended for an instant to give up his power. He was going to run again, for the eighth time, and few persons supposed that anything could be done to prevent his re-election. He controlled the government, and his subordinates would produce the result he desired. Interest centered in the choice of a vice-president. After all, Díaz might never live to reach his eighty-sixth birthday, and in that case the new vice-president would become president of Mexico. There were many eager aspirants to the vice-presidential nomination, but at last Díaz gave the nod to Ramón Corral, who already held the office of vice-president. Nothing could have been better calculated to arouse popular fury. Corral was said to be the most hated man in Mexico. He had made his vast fortune, according to rumor, in the Indian slave trade and other illegitimate enterprises. As vice-president he had accepted responsibility for some of Díaz' most unpopular acts. Practically no one really liked the man. But Díaz had spoken, and of course his word was law. So *Díaz* and *Corral* became the official ticket.

ARREST OF MADERO. The opposition in the 1910 election was more vocal than it had dared to be in many years. Díaz himself was largely responsible for this state of affairs. In his early days he had suppressed his enemies ruthlessly. Firing squads had worked overtime to smooth the Dictator's path. But old age had mellowed him. At the beginning of the campaign he actually seemed to enjoy Madero's attacks. Later, however, as the little orator's impassioned words struck a responsive chord in the minds of large numbers of Mexicans, Díaz apparently decided that the joke had gone far enough. He gave orders for the arrest of Madero, who was thrown into jail at San Luis Potosí.

CANDIDATE MADERO. Madero's only crime, of course, was that he campaigned too vigorously. He had been nominated for the presidency by a group of persons who named themselves the Anti-Re-electionist Party. Their platform called for a restoration of the constitution—free elections, free speech, a free press, more education, better working conditions. Not all the men who joined forces with Madero really wanted these reforms. They were primarily concerned with getting rid of the Díaz political machine so that they might set up their own political machine in its place. But none of them wanted to be the top man of the opposition. It was too dangerous a post. So Madero became a presidential candidate almost by default. And soon the ranks of his party were joined by thousands of nobodies who desperately desired to make a better Mexico—or longed to make themselves somebodies.

REPERCUSSIONS OF THE ELECTION. On October 4, 1910, the results of the election were announced. Díaz and Corral were declared the victors, of course, and preparations were made for an elaborate inaugural. But three days later Madero escaped from his jail cell and managed to cross the American border disguised as a workman. From the safety of the United States he declared the election fraudulent—which was certainly the case—and proclaimed himself provisional president of Mexico. His *Plan of San Luis Potosí,* written while he was in jail, called for the general establishment of the principle of no re-election, not only for the president and vice-president, but also for governors of states and mayors of cities. It also demanded the return of lands taken from the people to enrich the owners of great estates. It was a formal call to revolution.

THE CALL TO ARMS. The response to that call was immediate and effective. Uprisings occurred in many scattered parts of Mexico. Armed bands roamed the countryside, stopping now and then to plunder, but ready to join any serious movement to oust Díaz. Federal troops sent to disperse these revolutionaries sometimes deserted and joined the other side. After a few months the governor of Chihuahua withdrew his support from Díaz, taking all his state troops with him. When Madero returned to Mexico in February, 1911, he found himself the idol of the hour. Cries of "¡Viva Madero! ¡Viva la Revolución!" filled the air. By this time Díaz was thoroughly frightened. He sent a message to Congress promising that he would reform everything—the system of elections, the judicial system, the concentration of land in great estates. But it was too late. No one believed him. No one ever believes the promises made by a man when a pistol is held at his head.

OVERTHROW OF DÍAZ. Francisco Madero's father and brothers were not so greatly impressed by his impassioned pleas for political reform. What they really desired was a stable government, so that they might have ample opportunity to protect their vested interests. But as close relatives of the Revolution's leader they must perforce be revolutionaries. The turn of events allowed them no choice. Yet they actually conducted negotiations with representatives of the Díaz government, first in New York and later in Ciudad Juárez, where Francisco and a number of other revolutionary leaders joined the conference. The result of these discussions was an agreement that Díaz should resign and leave the country. The government would be turned over to Francisco de la Barra, a moderate who had held the post of Mexican ambassador to the United States. De la Barra would include in his cabinet representatives of both sides, and at the earliest possible moment he would schedule an election to choose his successor. These conditions were met honestly. Díaz, seriously ill from an infected jaw, resigned and left the country. Two Madero brothers were included in the de la Barra cabinet.[9]

Francisco Madero

DISSENSION AMONG THE VICTORS. The promised presidential election was held in October, 1911. A prominent general who had long been a leader in the anti-Díaz movement announced that he would oppose Francisco Madero, but everyone knew that the popular Madero would win. He did, by a landslide. Yet in winning he made a number of influential enemies. His running mate in the 1910 election had been a wealthy landowner named Francisco Vásquez Gómez, who naturally assumed that in 1911 he would again be the vice-presidential candidate. But Madero said no. He chose instead a little-known newspaper editor from Yucatán. There were, of course, some valid reasons for thus cutting short the promising political career of Vásquez Gómez. The man and his brother had undoubtedly intrigued to their own profit, instead of striving for the ideals of the Revolution. To this charge they might indeed have made cynical reply that brothers Gustavo and Ernesto Madero had set them a good example in this respect. But such a reply would scarcely have won them Francisco Madero's favor. So the brothers Vásquez Gómez drifted into the ranks of the opposition. They were a powerful pair, and their hostility cost Madero no small part of his support.

[9] The story of the Revolution is told briefly but interestingly in Anita Brenner's little book, *The Wind That Swept Mexico.*

THE HETEROGENEOUS OPPOSITION. The former supporters of Díaz were against Madero's candidacy, of course, almost to a man. So were the large business interests. There were many American businessmen in this group, and their spokesman was the American ambassador. They were the representatives of a privileged class which had long profited from Mexico's cheap labor system and dreaded any dislocation of the *status quo*. And at the other end of the economic scale, curiously enough, were other opponents of Francisco Madero. They were the landless peasants, who thought that Madero was not doing enough to fulfill his promises of land reform. As a matter of fact, he was doing virtually nothing. He was not even thinking about the land problem. There were other matters that seemed to him much more urgent. Madero had never been primarily concerned with economic remedies for Mexico's plight, though he did in fact promise a reform of the land system. His solutions were almost exclusively political. There must be free speech, he said, and a free press. Elections must be honest. Men must not seek re-election to public office.

EMILIANO ZAPATA. To some of Madero's followers, his proposed political reforms seemed relatively inconsequential. What they wanted was free land, not free elections. And they wanted the land right away, not at some distant time. The leader of this group was an ignorant peon named Emiliano Zapata, who lived in the state of Morelos. Zapata had been greatly impressed by the excellent care given the horses on the large estates, and he contrasted their fine stables with the miserable hovels in which he and his family and friends had always lived. When he heard that a man called Madero was promising land for the landless, he joined the movement right away. He became an important local chieftain, and his men played a part in Madero's triumph. But the months passed, and no land was distributed to the poor. When the matter was called to President Madero's attention, he explained that the matter was complicated and would require a great deal of study. But it seemed very simple indeed to Emiliano Zapata. The rich had the land; the poor did not. The government's troops could take it from the rich and give it to the poor. Why should there be delays? As the Madero administration continued to do nothing, Zapata became more and more impatient. Finally, in November of 1911, he issued his own scheme—the *Plan de Ayala*—which called for immediate expropriation of one third of the land of the great estates and its distribution among the landless. When Madero made no attempt to put this plan into effect, Zapata and his men rose in open revolt. In Chihuahua General Orozco had already begun a rebellion against the central government, and he sent word to Zapata that he too was fighting for the *Plan de Ayala* against the betrayers of the Revolution. To complicate matters still further, an uprising led by the nephew of old Porfirio Díaz broke out in the garrison at Vera Cruz, but it was quickly suppressed.

GROWING UNREST. With rebellion against the government increasing daily, the situation was exceedingly difficult. Perhaps President Díaz would have known how to handle it, but President Madero certainly did not. He scrupulously respected all the guarantees of the constitution, at a time when he would certainly have been justified in declaring martial law. He insisted on free speech, and his enemies used the opportunity to press their campaign of vilification. He maintained a free press, and irresponsible journalists showed their appreciation by printing scandalous reports about the President and his family. When Madero ordered captured plotters placed in jail, instead of lining them up before a firing squad, they continued to plot from their jail cells. The President was like a boxer trying to use Marquis of Queensberry rules against a professional killer. It was an unequal struggle and was made more so by Madero's obvious defects as an administrator. He made bad decisions, trusted men who should not have been trusted, and talked piously while the government ran down like an unwound clock. He placed his own relatives in important positions, and persistent rumor declared that they took full advantage of this excellent opportunity to increase the family fortunes. Francisco Madero himself was certainly an honest man, whatever his relatives may have been; but no one can deny that he was amazingly naive.

As guerrilla bands became increasingly active throughout Mexico, threatening the property and lives of both Mexicans and foreigners, the American ambassador became more and more insistent in his demands that President Madero take the necessary steps to restore order. He also took every occasion to press the claims for damages of Americans and other foreigners, until Madero demanded to know why the United States was persecuting him. Meanwhile a new strong man appeared on the scene. His name was Victoriano Huerta, and he had been one of the moving spirits in the fight to oust Porfirio Díaz. He asked for and received command of the northern armies and defeated the rebel Orozco in a whirlwind campaign. Here at last was a man who knew how to get things done! Madero recognized his talents as a fighter, yet hesitated to give him a full measure of authority.

Huerta and His Enemies

HUERTA'S TREACHERY. On February 9, 1913 began the uprising that was to mark the end of Madero's regime. It was in no sense a popular revolt. Instead it was a palace plot—a *coup d'état* engineered by a little group of disgruntled army officers. One of its leaders was Porfirio Díaz' nephew, who had been released from his prison cell by the plotters. Another was the man who had opposed Madero for the presidency in 1911. It was a grim fight, and it lasted ten days—the Tragic Ten, as Mexicans call it. The battleground was the heart of Mexico City. The people crouched in their homes while bullets and even artillery shells whizzed through the streets. Those who ventured out for food sometimes failed to return. Huerta was placed in charge of the government forces, over the protests of some of the loyal generals. It seems that their fears were justified, for Huerta finally sold out to the rebels. In return they agreed to support him as president. Thereupon troops seized President Madero and the Vice-President, and placed them under guard.

The American ambassador urged immediate recognition of the Huerta government, on the ground that it could restore order to the strife-torn nation. But while Washington hesitated, the world was shocked by the news that Madero was dead. He had been shot, said a cynical bulletin from the Presidential Palace, while trying to escape. Apparently Huerta had never intended to keep his promise, made only two days before, that Madero's life would be spared. President Taft, rapidly nearing the end of his term, ignored the American ambassador's advice to recognize the Huerta government, and passed the problem on to the incoming president, Woodrow Wilson. Meanwhile most of the European nations extended recognition to the new regime. They were happy to do so, for Huerta seemed to be the kind of man they could trust—almost a carbon copy of Porfirio Díaz, with the old dictator's high regard for big business, foreign interests, and the Catholic Church. But Woodrow Wilson was unconvinced. He sent his own special representative to Mexico to obtain the real story.

That story, it turned out, was not very flattering to Huerta. The new dictator was using all the old tricks to crush the opposition. Known or suspected enemies disappeared every day, and when their bodies were later found along some lonely road, the same threadbare explanation was offered: "Shot while trying to escape." There was no freedom of speech; the press did not dare to print the truth. Huerta's friends looted the public treasury on a scale that was unprecedented even in Mexico. And Huerta himself consumed great quantities of alcohol while he managed the affairs of state from one of the back rooms of a little café. When Woodrow Wilson received this sordid report, he flatly refused to recognize the new regime. "Huerta must go," he said. But Huerta had no intention of going anywhere. He managed to obtain necessary funds through a European loan. And when Congress assembled amidst dire threats of a searching investigation, he simply dissolved it after ordering the arrest of more than one hundred of its members.[10]

LEADERS OF REBELLION. Huerta's dismissal of Congress was highly unacceptable to the Mexican people. Revolt flared in many different parts of the country. There were four major revolutionary chiefs, and dozens of minor ones. Emiliano Zapata was still campaigning in the southwest for his *Plan de Ayala*—especially its principal point, the free distribution of land. The northeast corner of the country was controlled more or less securely by Venustiano Carranza, the fifty-two-year-old white-bearded governor of Coahuila, who was a champion of the middle classes. As a senator in the days of Díaz, he had never raised his voice against the old dictator's regime. But he was firmly determined that Huerta must go. As a lawyer and large landowner he wanted to make the country safe for the landowners and businessmen and industrialists. He was wise enough, however, to know that some concessions would have to be made to the workers and peasants. The days of feudalism were gone forever.

Another of the leaders in the fight against Huerta was an ignorant outlaw called Pancho Villa, whose real name was Doroteo Arango. As a boy he had killed an official who outraged his sister, and thereupon he became a bandit, roaming the countryside with a little group of followers and living on the fruits of others' toil. In 1910, when he was thirty-three years old, he offered his services to Madero in exchange for a pardon. Madero accepted, and soon Villa was an important figure in the Mexican army. But he had no part in the *coup d'état* that made Huerta president, and he was determined to overthrow the new government. The other important anti-Huerta chieftain was Alvaro Obregón, a young, well-educated rancher whose primary interest was scientific agriculture. On more than one occasion he had displayed active sympathy for the poverty-stricken Indians and had tried to improve their educational opportunities. He took no interest in military matters until 1912, when rebellion in the

[10] The story of Victoriano Huerta's unhappy regime is well told by Luis Bustamente in *Bajo el Terror Huertista*.

north jeopardized Madero's position. At that time Obregón had recruited and equipped a force of several hundred Yaqui Indians and had played a major part in crushing an uprising. He had, of course, served under Huerta in that fight. But now he was wholeheartedly against Huerta.

THE REBELLION SPREADS. As the campaign for the overthrow of the government progressed, Carranza came to be generally regarded as the principal revolutionary leader. Obregón recognized his overlordship. So did Villa, in an agreement made in the summer of 1914. But Zapata never accepted Carranza's authority, nor did dozens of minor guerrilla chiefs. The so-called revolutionary "army" was really a vast number of independent bands, each fighting at its own time and in its own way, and bound to other bands by nothing more tangible than a common hatred of Victoriano Huerta. Some of these troops were uniformed more or less completely and equipped with modern arms. Others wore the traditional white of the Mexican peon, and carried whatever guns or knives they could pick up in their homes. The women generally accompanied the men—to forage, to cook, or even to fight. Food was taken wherever it could be found, usually in the stores of the towns or in the well-stocked larders of the great haciendas. A few chiefs issued business-like receipts for all the supplies they seized, but most of them ignored such formalities and let their followers help themselves.

There was no clear understanding of the principles behind this mass movement. Carranza and Villa had indeed signed an agreement in which they tried to set forth the things for which they were fighting. These things included the establishment of democratic institutions, the improvement of labor conditions, the distribution of land to the landless, the punishment of those priests who had used their authority in behalf of Huerta—and, of course, the overthrow of Huerta himself. But most of the revolutionary troops never read this statement. Most of them, in fact, could not read. They only knew that they were fighting against the hated dictator and his foreign friends. "Death to Huerta! Death to the gringos!" Those two cries summed up the philosophy of the Mexican masses.

AMERICAN INTERFERENCE. Huerta's respectful treatment of American and other foreign business interests had indeed brought him substantial support among American businessmen in Mexico. But President Wilson persisted in his refusal to recognize the Huerta regime. Through his Secretary of State he directed all American consuls to strive for its "discredit and defeat." The message contained this highly significant statement: *If General Huerta does not retire by force of circumstances, it will become the duty of the United States to use less peaceful means to put him out.* This American policy roused the resentment of practically all Mexicans. Huerta and his friends were especially bitter, and they showed their hatred in many different ways. But even the Dictator's enemies were angered by American interference in Mexican affairs. It was their problem, they said, not ours; and they would handle it in their own way.

The Vera Cruz incident. While the United States continued its disapproval of the Mexican government, there were several incidents that heightened the ill will between the two countries. On April 9, 1914, the paymaster of an American naval vessel went ashore at Tampico to obtain supplies and was promptly arrested by the local authorities. Two sailors who had remained in the small boat were also seized and thrown into jail. When this news reached Huerta he ordered their release, but refused to salute the United States flag. Only a few days later an orderly from an American battleship was arrested while ashore in Vera Cruz and kept in jail for some time. The tension was mounting. When a German ship approached Vera Cruz loaded with arms and munitions for Huerta, the United States fleet cruising in those waters took drastic steps to prevent their delivery. It shelled the city of Vera Cruz and captured it after sharp fighting. Soon the news spread over all Mexico. The nation had been invaded! The gringos were waging war again, as they had done in 1846! Today it was Vera Cruz; tomorrow it would be Mexico City! So the word went from mouth to mouth, and old hatreds stirred in Mexican breasts. Throughout the country American flags were torn down, American business houses were stoned, and American citizens were threatened by mobs.[11]

OVERTHROW OF HUERTA. The menace of Mexican aggression against American lives and property strengthened President Wilson's belief in the wisdom of his non-recognition policy. It was becoming increasingly clear, he said, that Huerta could not maintain order. And, indeed, Huerta's position was becoming very insecure. When he assumed the presidency, in February, 1913, he had a powerful, well-equipped army at his command, and most of Mexico acknowledged his authority. A year later he had lost most of the country and his troops were everywhere on the defensive. In July, 1914, his regime collapsed. Huerta himself sailed away from Mexico into exile, and his troops disbanded. The revolutionaries—the Constitutionalists, as they called themselves—had won. Carranza proclaimed himself Supreme Chief of the Mexican nation.

[11] See J. M. Callahan's excellent study, *American Foreign Policy in Mexican Relations.*

Carranza, Chaos, and the Constitution

MEXICO DISUNITED. Not all Mexicans, however, were willing to grant Carranza the title of Supreme Chief. The revolutionary forces had never been a single, compact organization, and in the moment of victory they seemed less unified than ever before. The enemy who had united them was no longer a threat to their well-being. So they went their separate ways. When a group of generals met in Mexico City and endorsed Carranza, both Villa and Zapata stayed away. Obregón, of course, was present. He was Carranza's right-hand man, and largely responsible for whatever degree of unity had been achieved. When it became clear that Villa would not accept Carranza's overlordship, Obregón arranged for another convention at Aguascalientes, which lay approximately halfway between Villa's headquarters and the capital. The delegates deliberated long and earnestly, and finally reached a compromise which of course pleased nobody. Both Carranza and Villa should retire. The presidency should go to a political unknown, General Eulalio Gutiérrez, whose chief merit was that he had never given full allegiance to either contender. When Carranza and Villa received the news, both sent flowery messages assuring the convention of their willingness to do anything—anything at all—that would further the welfare of their beloved Mexico. Villa even offered to have himself shot. But neither chieftain would recede an inch until the other man moved first. It soon became clear that the convention could accomplish nothing. Mexico was still divided between Carranza and Villa, and no compromise candidate could alter that fact. One by one the leaders of the armed bands that had made up the revolutionary army chose sides in the coming struggle. Most of them cast their lot with Villa, but a considerable number followed Obregón into Carranza's camp. Zapata sat glowering on the sidelines, demanding to know when his plan for the immediate distribution of the land would be put into effect.

CHAOTIC DAYS. The next few years of conflict between the forces of Villa and Carranza were filled with tragedy for Mexico. Armed forces swept across the face of the land, pillaging and killing almost indiscriminately. Every "general" had his own printing press, and turned out his private version of money in fantastic quantities. The inevitable result was the virtually complete collapse of the Mexican economy. Men found it more profitable to wage war than to raise crops or sell goods that would almost certainly be commandeered in exchange for worthless money, so they threw in their lot with one or another of the many guerrilla bands. The number of soldiers grew steadily. Carranza retired with his staff from Mexico City to Vera Cruz, where he established his provisional head-quarters. Thereupon the capital became legitimate prey for anyone who could take and hold it. Time after time it changed hands, and the dazed inhabitants scarcely knew from one day to the next who would be their masters on the morrow.

PROMISES OF REFORM. While guerrilla warfare continued, Carranza made a serious effort to win the support of the Mexican people with something more than guns. He promised that all estates illegally seized by the great landowners would be restored to the masses. He placed himself on record in favor of labor unions and wage and hour laws. He restored self-government to the municipalities in those areas under his control. Few of these promises were made wholeheartedly. Carranza was still funda-mentally conservative, as he had been in the Díaz era, but he had at last been convinced by Obregón that he must guarantee radical reform in order to win popular favor. The plan proved very effective. Organized labor threw in its lot with the Carranza forces and let loose its propaganda in every newly captured town. Slowly but surely Villa seemed to be waging a losing fight.

UNITED STATES RECOGNITION. On October 19, 1915, President Wilson announced that the United States would recognize the Carranza regime as the *de facto* government of Mexico. Huerta had asked in vain for such recognition, when his position seemed much stronger than that of Car-ranza. And the reason officially given for United States failure to recog-nize Huerta—that he had seized power by illegal means—could certainly be advanced with equal force against Carranza. But President Wilson was evidently willing to accept Carranza's assurances that foreign lives and property would be protected and that compensation would be made for the damage caused by the revolution. Once again, after nearly three years, Mexico had a government that was acceptable in the eyes of the United States.

PANCHO VILLA'S BANDITRY. The news of President Wilson's recognition of Carranza hit Pancho Villa like a blow between the eyes. Here, as he saw it, was fresh evidence of unjustifiable American intervention in Mexi-can affairs. And this time the intervention was aimed directly at him. He swore vengeance. In early January, 1916, some of his men stopped a train and took from it eighteen Americans who held passes of safe conduct issued by the Carranza government. Villa ordered them shot without a trial—without, indeed, accusing them of any crime. Two months later he crossed the border into New Mexico, raiding a small town and killing seventeen people. This outrage inflamed public opinion throughout the United States. President Wilson directed American troops to enter Mexico in pursuit of Villa, with orders to kill or capture him and disperse his followers. These orders were never carried out, for the elusive Villa kept retreating farther and farther into the wild country of northern Mexico.

AMERICAN TROOPS IN MEXICO. Carranza made no effort to help the American troops in their search for Villa. On the contrary, he displayed increasing hostility. Nothing would have pleased him more than the destruction of Villa's forces, but he resented the presence of uninvited American soldiers on Mexican soil. And there can be no doubt that he would have had every right to resent this trespassing, if he could have maintained public order within his own country. But, as the American Secretary of State pointed out in a carefully worded note, Villa had to be eliminated as a public nuisance, and the Americans were doing the job simply because the Mexicans had proved themselves unable to do it. This explanation failed to satisfy Carranza, however. His field commander had already forbidden United States troops to move farther into Mexico, and when they did so the Carranza forces attacked, killing a number of American soldiers and capturing several others. War between the two countries seemed inevitable. Eventually, however, a joint conference was arranged to consider the whole situation. American troops were withdrawn from Mexican soil, though Villa still remained at liberty. Carranza had won his point, and thereby increased his political stature throughout all Mexico.[12]

HALFHEARTED REFORM. There can be no doubt that Carranza needed additional prestige at this time of divided loyalties. He had alienated many of his supporters by his wait-and-see policy. To those who demanded immediate large-scale expropriation of lands he said that public order must be established first. To those who proposed sweeping changes in the labor laws he made similar reply. The truth of the matter was that circumstances had placed Venustiano Carranza at the head of a revolution in which he did not really believe. It was a movement of the landless to get land, a drive by labor to change the conditions of employment, a great upsurge of the underprivileged against the privileged class that had long dominated Mexico's economy. And, by a curious twist of fate, the revolution's most powerful leader was a landowner-lawyer whose temperament and training predisposed him to a firm belief in the sanctity of private

[12] The story is well told in *Intervention in Mexico*, by Samuel Guy Inman.

property and the validity of law. Small wonder that his more radical followers grew impatient as they watched reform moving at a snail's pace.

THE CONSTITUTION OF 1917. In September, 1916, Carranza issued a call for a constitutional convention to rewrite the fundamental law which had served the nation since 1857. Delegates were to be popularly chosen and were to assemble in the city of Querétaro, where Mexican independence had been planned a century earlier. Everything went as scheduled, to a certain point. But when the debates began, Carranza soon discovered that he could not control the delegates. Some of them were Zapata's men, some were spokesmen for the new labor movement, some were friends of Obregón, who would fight for Carranza on the battlefield, but preferred more radical company in a parliamentary assembly. Villa and his boys were conspicuously absent.

Carranza was prepared for a somewhat radical document, but certainly he never expected the members of the convention to produce the kind of charter that finally emerged after long weeks of heated debate. It was the most radical constitution of modern times. It declared that "education . . . shall be socialist, and, in addition to excluding all religious doctrine, shall combat all fanaticism and prejudice"—which meant, of course, that it would be taken completely out of the hands of the Catholic Church. All churches, convents, and similar buildings were to become the property of the nation. Charitable and scientific institutions could not be associated with religious bodies. Thus the Catholic Church, which had so often extended its blessing to the privileged classes, was dealt a body blow by the spokesmen of the underprivileged. The constitution also paid its respects to the great landowners. Private property, it said, vested originally in the nation, which transmitted title to individuals. Therefore the nation could impose restrictions on property at any time, in the public interest. Steps should be taken to break up the big estates. As to the mines and petroleum deposits, they belonged to the nation, and could not be alienated. This was, in effect, a notice to the foreign oil companies that they did not have legitimate title to their own lands. They might, indeed, be permitted to continue working their concessions, but only if they agreed to consider themselves "Mexicans in respect to such property, and accordingly not to invoke the protection of their governments in respect to the same." Thus was laid the basis for a long dispute between the foreign oil companies and the Mexican government.

The new constitution also devoted a great deal of space to the protection of labor. There should be maximum hours of work, and minimum wages.

Provision should be made for many forms of social insurance. Proper sanitation should be maintained in all places of work. Strikes should be permitted, but arbitration boards should be established to facilitate the establishment of labor disputes. To the people of the United States, living in this modern age, the clauses of the Mexican constitution dealing with labor matters do not seem so very radical. But to the Mexicans of 1917 they were revolutionary.

CARRANZA'S TRIUMPH AND FINAL OVERTHROW. Elections were held in April of 1917, and Carranza was chosen the first president under the new constitution. Almost at once he requested and received extraordinary financial powers, and he seems to have made some effort to bring order out of the monetary chaos into which the nation had fallen. But he was not very successful, and as a result business conditions remained unsettled. Civil war still flared in widely separated areas, though the government forces under General Obregón were able to record many successes in their pacification of the country. In one battle against Villa's troops Obregón lost his right arm. It was blown off by a grenade. But this unfortunate accident did not affect the course of the campaign, nor did it substantially interfere with Obregón's military and political career. One of the most determined enemies of the Carranza regime, Emiliano Zapata, was killed treacherously in 1918. He had accepted the services of a colonel from the Carranza forces who had announced his conversion to the Zapata cause and "proved" his change of heart by capturing and shooting some Carranza troops. Zapata's suspicions were lulled and he accepted an invitation to visit a neighboring ranch, where he was assassinated. It was a glorious triumph for the treacherous colonel, who was rewarded with fifty thousand pesos and promotion to the rank of brigadier general.

Meanwhile the politicians in Mexico City and in all the state capitals were living well at public expense. Carranza made no serious effort to check this orgy of graft and waste. Nor, for that matter, did he really try to carry out the provisions of the new constitution. He paid only lip worship to those clauses dealing with the expropriation of the great estates. He fought labor at every turn, regardless of the constitution's labor guarantees. He permitted the Catholic Church to continue its normal activities. He did indeed respect the spirit of the constitution concerning foreign capital, but only because such a policy represented his own firm convictions. And when the time came for him to relinquish his authority in 1920, he tried to secure the election of a new president who would take his orders unhesitatingly. The man he picked for this somewhat dubious honor was a pleasant but politically unimportant diplomat, named Ignacio Bonillas, who had served for some time as Mexican ambassador to the United States. But the revolutionary generals would not accept Bonillas—"Mister" Bonillas, as they called him, to emphasize their suspicion that he was too friendly with the Americans. Almost overnight Carranza's support melted away. When General Obregón issued the call for a new uprising, seasoned revolutionaries flocked to him from every part of Mexico. Carranza attempted to escape, but was assassinated by one of his lieutenants. Thus ingloriously died the onetime hero of the Revolution.[13]

OBREGÓN BECOMES PRESIDENT. The man who took over as provisional president following Carranza's death was Adolfo de la Huerta, a close friend of Obregón and one of the leaders of the plot to overthrow Carranza. It was understood that de la Huerta would merely fill out Carranza's unexpired term, and that Obregón would then assume the presidency. There was to be an election, of course, but no one supposed that there would be any real opposition to Obregón's candidacy. Everything was done to smooth his path. Villa, whose private army offered the most direct threat to the new regime, was bought off with assurances of tracts of land for his men and a large hacienda for himself. He retired to enjoy the life of a rich landowner, but not for long. Within four years he was dead from an assassin's bullet. Meanwhile the plans of the new regime proceeded according to schedule. Obregón, who undoubtedly enjoyed great popularity, was elected without difficulty, and assumed the presidency on December 1, 1920. The revolution was over. An uneasy peace had come to Mexico.

SELECTED REFERENCES

Albornoz, Alvaro de, *Páginas del Destierro*, Mexico, D.F., 1941.

Beals, Carleton, *Porfirio Díaz*, Philadelphia, Lippincott, 1932.

Bell, E. I., *The Political Shame of Mexico*, New York, McBride, Nast, 1914.

Brenner, Anita, *The Wind That Swept Mexico*, New York, Harper, 1943.

Bustamante, Luis, *Bajo el Terror Huertista*, San Luis Potosí, El Autor, 1916.

Callahan, J. M., *American Foreign Policy in Mexican Relations*, New York, Macmillan, 1932.

Chávez Orozco, Luis, *La Escuela Mexicana y la Sociedad Mexicana*, Mexico, D.F., Editorial Orientaciones, 1940.

Chico Goerne, Luis, *Hacia una Filosofía Social en el Siglo XX*, Mexico, D.F., Editora del Continente, 1943.

[13] The balance sheet of the Carranza regime is presented by T. E. Gibbon in *Mexico under Carranza*.

Clark, Sydney A., *Mexico, Magnetic Southland*, New York, Dodd, Mead, 1944.

Floyd, Olive, *Doctora in Mexico*, New York, Putnam, 1944.

Hackett, Charles W., *The Mexican Revolution and the United States*, Boston, World Peace Foundation, 1927.

Hardy, Wilfred H., *Liberalism in Mexico, 1857–1917*, Palo Alto, Calif., Stanford Univ. Press, 1931.

Herring, Hubert, *Mexico, the Making of a Nation*, New York, Foreign Policy Association, 1942.

Hudson, Maurice, *Mexico, Yesterday, Today, Tomorrow*, Philadelphia, Dorrance, 1945.

Iturriaga, José E., *El Estructura Social y Cultural de México*, Mexico, D.F., Fondo de Cultura Económica, 1951.

Kneller, George F., *The Education of the Mexican Nation*, New York, Columbia University Press, 1951.

Manning, W. R. *Early Diplomatic Relations between the United States and Mexico*, Baltimore, Johns Hopkins Press, 1916.

Martínez Palafox, Luis, *La Adopción del Federalismo en México*, Mexico, D.F., Escuela Nacional de Jurisprudencia, 1945.

Mosk, Sanford, *Industrial Revolution in Mexico*, Berkeley, University of California Press, 1950.

Niles, Blair, *Passengers to Mexico*, New York, Farrar and Rinehart, 1943.

Parkes, H. B., *A History of Mexico*, Boston, Houghton Mifflin, 1938.

Priestley, Herbert I., *The Mexican Nation*, Macmillan, New York, 1923.

Rosa, Guido, *Mexico Speaks*, New York, John Day, 1944.

Sanchez, George I., *The Development of Higher Education in Mexico*, New York, King's Crown Press, 1944.

Simpson, Lesley B., *Many Mexicos*, 3rd ed., Berkeley, University of California Press, 1952.

Strode, Hudson, *Timeless Mexico*, New York, Harcourt, Brace, 1944.

Tannenbaum, Frank, *Peace by Revolution*, New York, Columbia Univ. Press, 1933.

Teja Zabre, Alfonso, *Panorama Histórica de la Revolución Mexicana*, Mexico, D.F., Ediciones Botas, 1939.

Whetten, Nathan L., *Rural Mexico*, Chicago, University of Chicago Press, 1948.

CHAPTER 10

MEXICO
Evolutionary Years

President Obregón

THE NEW ADMINISTRATION. President Obregón took office with the good wishes of the nation. He was the popular hero, the new strong man of the Revolution, the first unchallenged boss of Mexico in a decade. And he governed the country in the strong man tradition. He appointed his army cronies and other friends to important posts in the new administration. The top job, secretary of government, went to his intimate associate, General Plutarco Calles. General Villareal became secretary of agriculture, and General Hill was named secretary of war and marine. The secretary of the treasury was Adolfo de la Huerta, who had served temporarily as head of the nation after the fall of Carranza and had kept the presidential chair warm for Obregón. Some of the other secretaries and undersecretaries had been generals or lesser lights in the revolutionary forces.

But quite a number of civilians also found their way into the new administration. Most notable of them was José Vasconcelos, who was appointed secretary of education. As rector of the National University of Mexico he had already achieved an enviable reputation, which he enhanced by his wise management of the nation's educational affairs. But all the principal administrators, military and civilian, were made to understand that they could take no action of any consequence without first consulting the President. Every administrative decree must first receive his consent. Every proposed action must be submitted for his approval. Even Vasconcelos, who was permitted greater discretion than any of the others, frequently found himself unable to pass upon urgent matters because he could not arrange a prompt audience with the President.

226

PRESIDENTIAL DOMINATION: *Of Congress.* Obregón dominated Congress completely. There was an opposition, but it had no real power. No bill opposed by the President was ever presented for his signature. No bill actively sponsored by him ever failed to become law. He placed before Congress practically every important measure that received its consideration during his term of office. Obregón's support, at the beginning of his term, came chiefly from the so-called Constitutional Liberal Party, which had been set up by his friends for the purpose of securing his election. It never had a complete organization in all parts of the country, and after the congressional elections of 1922 it fell apart. The Mexican Labor Party included another group of Obregón sympathizers. It too had been established during the 1920 campaign for the purpose of securing his election, after receiving assurances that labor would be given preferential treatment under the new regime. During the four years of the Obregón administration there was a tendency for parties to rise and fall almost overnight. Some of them were created virtually by presidential fiat, and disintegrated when they no longer served the President's needs. The President's influence was felt everywhere.

Of the state governments. Even in the state governments the President was the supreme chief. Candidates for state offices found that their chances of winning an election were greatly increased if they took care to endorse President Obregón and all his works. Some of them neglected that formality, or even indulged in direct criticism of the Obregón regime, only to learn the difficulty of gaining public office without the President's approval. If by any chance they succeeded in winning the election, the secretary of government would speedily discover that it was invalid because of fraud or legal technicalities. The national Senate, acting under orders, would thereupon declare that the state lacked constitutional authorities, and this lack would be supplied by suitable presidential appointments.[1] In some cases federal troops were used to prevent successful candidates from taking office.

EXTRAORDINARY POWERS. Almost at the beginning of his term President Obregón secured from Congress a grant of extraordinary powers to meet the serious financial situation, and from that day he managed the nation's finances as a virtual autocrat of the treasury. He arranged his own budget for 1921 and extended it by executive decree for 1922. He imposed some taxes and abolished others. He changed tax rates from time to time, and

---

[1] The appointments were actually made by the Senate, but from a list of three names supplied in each case by the President.

from his decisions there was no appeal. When he found that the government was not making ends meet, despite all precautions, he issued an order reducing the salaries of all public employees—except, of course, the officers and men of the army. Military expenditures already represented nearly one half of the cost of government, but Obregón knew that he could not long remain in office without army support.

INFLUENCE OF LABOR. Even before the election of Obregón, labor had become a powerful force in Mexico. In 1918 its leaders had formed the Mexican Federation of Labor, or C.R.O.M.,[2] with a membership of about seven thousand. Within two years the total was fifty thousand, and by the end of Obregón's term, in 1924, it had nearly a million and a quarter members, according to its own estimates. The boss of the C.R.O.M. was Luis Morones,[3] who had been jailed by Carranza. As a diligent worker for Obregón's election he was rewarded with an important post in the new government, and he received strong official support in his energetic campaign to unionize all the industrial workers of Mexico. Whenever the C.R.O.M. decided to call a strike against a shop or factory, it simply planted its red and black flag in the building's doorway, and federal troops then enforced the union's edict that no person might enter or leave. Thus the policy of the Díaz regime, which had invariably supported the employers, was completely reversed. Labor, as represented by the C.R.O.M., could count on government backing for all its schemes.

There were other unions also, but without official favor they could scarcely compete against the powerful Morones organization. In 1921, when the independently organized railway workers struck, Obregón declared that their action was a threat against the government, and he used troops to protect the strikebreakers who were running the trains. Again, in 1923, he ordered soldiers to break a strike. This time it was the street car workers, whose violent tactics had tended to alienate public opinion. As Obregón's term drew to a close, he even quarreled with the powerful Luis Morones, blaming him publicly for a political assassination that had recently occurred. But for the most part labor had good reason to be grateful to Obregón. He had helped it mightily in its early days, when such help was essential.

THE LAND PROBLEM. Of all the problems faced by President Obregón, perhaps the most pressing was the distribution of the land. Great haciendas still dotted the face of Mexico, despite the sporadic efforts of Zapata

[2] *Confederación Regional Obrera Mexicana.*
[3] See J. H. Retinger's history of the early Mexican labor movement, *Morones of Mexico.*

and other guerrilla chieftains. The masses of the people were still landless, despite the promises of Madero and his successors. But now it seemed that the time was ripe to take more drastic action.

A law was already on the statute books authorizing the expropriation of portions of the great estates and the issuance of certificates of indemnification to the former owners. This law did not really solve the problem, for it promised several times as much land as it actually made available. But it was a beginning, and for the first time was seriously enforced. The new Department of Agriculture sent out engineers to make surveys and supervise the actual transfer of titles to individuals and villages. Some of the rich landowners who happened to be friends of influential politicians received huge payments for their confiscated properties, but most of them received only trifling compensation or nothing at all. They were told, of course, that more would be paid when the public treasury was full, but they clearly understood the uncertain value of such promises. Some of them actually offered physical resistance to the public officials who came to take their land. A few died while shooting it out with federal troops. Yet Obregón proceeded slowly with the confiscations—too slowly to please many of his radical friends. He argued that the treasury could not possibly bear the burden of very heavy payments until economic conditions were more settled. Thus he placed financial solvency ahead of agrarian reform, to the dismay of those who thought that land reform should come before everything else.

CHURCH AND STATE. Although the constitution of 1917 expressly forbade the church to maintain schools or hospitals or charitable institutions, nothing was done immediately by Obregón to enforce these prohibitions. Catholic schools openly maintained their schedules, and nuns continued to work in the hospitals as they had always done. Many church ceremonies were held on property not owned by the church, though this was in clear defiance of the law. President Obregón at first decided to ignore these violations. He declared that schools and hospitals were still necessary, and the government was not yet in a position to provide them. So, until more funds were available, parochial schools and hospitals must be accepted as a necessary evil. But as the church became more militant, asserting its rights through Catholic labor groups and other newly formed organizations, Obregón's patience finally wore thin. The final straw was a vast religious celebration attended by fifty thousand people, at which the Apostolic Delegate placed the first stone on a monument to Christ the King. This ceremony was held on January 11, 1923. Two days later the Apostolic Delegate was expelled from the country by presidential decree.

Meanwhile a number of incidents showed the anti-clerical trend of the times. Many popular demonstrations were staged against the Catholics, and bombs were thrown at the Archbishop's palace in Mexico City. Church properties were damaged, and the police did virtually nothing to prevent these outbreaks. On one occasion, when a man threw a bomb at the image of the Virgin of Guadalupe, in Mexico's most sacred shrine, he was accompanied by a number of soldiers in uniform. One writer declares that Obregón himself ordered some of these attacks,[4] but the evidence is not convincing. In some of the states the tide of anti-clericalism was running strong. Durango limited to twenty-five the number of priests within its borders, and Yucatán set the maximum at sixteen.[5] Throughout most of Mexico, however, the church displayed astonishing vigor, and actually managed to increase the number of its communicants.

PUBLIC EDUCATION. Public education made rapid strides under the direct guidance of José Vasconcelos and with the strong approval of President Obregón. New schools were opened in all parts of the country, especially in the rural districts, where many Indians could not even speak Spanish. In four years the budget appropriations for education increased three hundred per cent. Volunteer teachers were sent out to assist the regulars in remote areas. Teams of trained educators visited the rural schools, helping the local teachers to improve their cultural and professional background. For the first time in Mexican history the government was waging a determined fight against illiteracy.

RECOGNITION BY FOREIGN POWERS. Shortly after Obregón became president, in December of 1920, his government was recognized by most nations of Europe and Latin America. The United States, however, was in no hurry to extend recognition. First it desired to know something about the new President's policies. Two matters seemed to be especially important—the claims of Americans who had suffered losses during the recent years of civil strife, and the fears of American oil companies that the constitution would be so interpreted as to justify confiscation of their properties.[6] Obregón made a serious effort to satisfy the United States in both matters. He early announced Mexico's intention of paying all

---

[4] Fernández Naranjo, Nicolás, *La Política Religiosa en México, 1917–1937*, p. 128.

[5] The laws always referred to the ministers *of any creed*, but, of course, they were aimed directly at the dominant Catholic Church.

[6] See page 222.

foreign damage claims, and he promised that the constitutional provision nationalizing mineral resources would not be applied retroactively. Not until August of 1923, however, did the United States extend recognition. By that time it was convinced that the rights of its citizens would be properly protected.

GRAFT. In one respect, at least, Obregón continued the ideals and practices of the Díaz regime. He permitted and even encouraged the vicious *mordida* which had long been the curse of Mexican politics. The literal translation of *mordida* is *bite,* and it was so called because every official, high or low, took his "bite" or share from any public money that might happen to pass through his hands. Every private person who wished to do business with public officials must be prepared to pay a little extra for the "bite." The practice was so general that it scarcely aroused comment. Cabinet ministers and bureau chiefs acquired fine homes and luxurious motor cars, while minor officers accepted more modest rewards. But all expected to grow rich at public expense. Even the President, according to current gossip, accepted "loans" from the federal treasury.

THE PRESIDENTIAL SUCCESSION. As Obregón's term drew to a close, he began to give serious thought to the choice of a successor. He himself could not serve a second term without violating the constitution, but he was determined to force the selection of someone who would continue his policies. The man he selected was his old friend and adviser, General Plutarco Calles, the mestizo schoolteacher who had fought at his side against Huerta and later against Carranza. Calles was generally regarded as the strong man of the cabinet, and he had succeeded in retaining the support of labor even after Obregón's open break with Morones. To many persons he seemed an obvious choice, and apparently his chances were greatly strengthened when his chief rival, Adolfo de la Huerta, agreed not to be a candidate. But de la Huerta was far from satisfied. As provisional president in 1920 he had done his share to insure Obregón's election, and more recently as secretary of finance he had played an important part in restoring the nation's solvency. For these reasons he seems to have thought that he should be the next president.

Many prominent Mexicans agreed with him. Among them was the leader of the Co-operatist Party, which had acquired a large following in the brief years of its existence. This man, Jorge Prieto Laurens, openly charged that Obregón was trying to force the election of Calles against the wishes of the people. Obregón retaliated by sending troops to nullify an election that Prieto Laurens had just won as governor of his native state.

After that there was no possibility that the opposition could be bought off quietly. De la Huerta angrily resigned his cabinet post and announced that he would be a presidential candidate. Shortly afterward the breath of scandal touched de la Huerta. It seems that he had been guilty of grossly mismanaging the Department of Finance and even stealing public funds. De la Huerta and his friends insisted, of course, that these charges were trumped up for the occasion. Even his enemies wondered why so incompetent and dishonest a man should have been left in a position of high authority, and even praised for his skill, until he proved a menace to the schemes of the Obregón-Calles faction. In any event, it soon became clear that neither de la Huerta nor any other opposition candidate could beat the smoothly functioning Obregón machine.

BRIEF REBELLION. In December, 1923, the friends of de la Huerta decided to resort to armed rebellion. Several prominent generals joined the rebel forces, taking their troops with them. Obregón was caught by surprise, but he acted with characteristic decisiveness. In a series of swift moves he strengthened his own position and insured the continued support of loyal army officers by rewarding them handsomely with promotions and gifts. The United States aided his cause by permitting him to receive large shipments of arms while preventing such shipments to the rebels. Finally it permitted him to lead his troops across American territory, in order to outflank the forces of de la Huerta. Fighting still continued for some time, but the back of the rebellion had been broken. Insurgents began to lay down their arms. Finally de la Huerta himself fled to the United States, where he took up his residence in Los Angeles. It took four months of strenuous fighting and many millions of pesos to crush the uprising.[7] The organized opposition to the candidacy of Calles was, of course, almost completely destroyed. He won without difficulty, and assumed the presidency on December 1, 1924.

The Calles Era

GREATER LABOR INFLUENCE. As president, Calles soon proved that he was a strong man in his own right. While continuing the general policies of the Revolution, as had Obregón before him, he made a number of important changes in the management of public affairs. Labor was given more power than ever before. Luis Morones, the head of the C.R.O.M. whose recent quarrel with Obregón had temporarily weakened his po-

---

[7] For a detailed account of the de la Huerta uprising, see Vol. III of Jesús Romero Flores' four-volume work, *Anales Históricos de la Revolución Mexicana*.

litical influence,[8] was restored to official favor and placed in charge of the newly established Department of Industry, Commerce, and Labor. He used his authority as a public official to strengthen the position of his own union—against employers, of course, but especially against rival unions. In every move he could count on the backing of President Calles, who intervened personally in a number of labor disputes to force recognition of the C.R.O.M. as labor's bargaining agency. In return Morones and the C.R.O.M. gave the President unqualified support. They even attempted, with considerable success, to establish an unofficial censorship by directing union printers to refuse to work on anti-Calles publications. Yet the Calles administration accomplished very little in the enactment of fundamental labor legislation. It was too busy with practical labor politics.

FISCAL POLICIES. The new regime was scarcely under way before the President took drastic steps to improve the financial condition of the nation, which had been greatly weakened by the recent rebellion. He secured a much needed revision of the income tax law, strengthening its administrative provisions and thus making evasion much more difficult. He made strenuous efforts to reduce federal expenditures, not even sparing the army in his demand for strict economy. Obregón's policy of liberal army salaries and frequent promotions was reversed. The officers grumbled about this change but made no attempt to stage an uprising. The first two years of the Calles regime therefore brought a substantial decrease in public expenditures, which, together with an increase in public revenues, brought a large surplus to the public treasury. Later, however, that surplus began to dwindle as the receipts from the taxes on the oil companies dropped to a new low point.

The basic reason for this drop was that Calles had set out to enforce the strict letter of the constitution concerning public ownership of minerals. Foreign companies, he announced, must have their titles to oil lands confirmed within one year. In exchange for their deeds of ownership they would then be given concessions which would expire within fifty years. And, unless they had begun drilling prior to 1917, they would get nothing at all. The foreign companies protested loudly that this was confiscation, and some of them refused to apply for concessions within the one-year limit. The United States government protested against this interpretation of the constitution, but Calles stood firm. Meanwhile, of course, many of the oil fields stood idle, to the detriment of the Mexican treasury. The dispute was settled temporarily when the Mexican supreme

[8] See page 228.

court upheld in substance the contentions of the oil companies and President Calles mildly accepted this verdict.[9]

PERSECUTION OF THE CHURCH. One of the most controversial policies of the Calles administration was its treatment of the Catholic Church. At first Calles followed his predecessor's example and quietly ignored the church's daily violations of the law. In some of the states, however, a policy of systematic religious persecution was already well under way. The state of Tabasco declared that the ministers of every religious faith must be married men, and arrested several priests for failing to meet this requirement. On January 26, 1926, the Archbishop of Mexico issued a formal protest against such unreasonable treatment of the Catholic clergy, and the next day this protest was published in a leading newspaper of Mexico City.

President Calles chose to regard this protest as a challenge, and acted accordingly. Charges of treason were brought against the Archbishop. Later they were quietly dropped, but in the meantime a number of anti-clerical decrees were issued and strictly enforced. All foreign-born priests were deported and church schools were closed. The Secretary of Government ordered all private schools to register within sixty days, on threat of seizure. The obvious purpose of this decree was to facilitate the enforcement of the constitutional clause prohibiting religious instruction. To these drastic measures the Archbishop replied by ordering the suspension of all religious services requiring the attendance of priests. The churches were to remain open, however, under the supervision of parish members. But the government retaliated by directing municipal authorities throughout the country to inspect the churches and determine whether they would prove more useful as public buildings.

The religious life of Catholic Mexico came almost to a stop. Many devout persons began to hold religious services in their own homes, before their private altars, but they were soon arrested and in many cases their homes were confiscated. Thereupon the Archbishop of Mexico appealed directly to President Calles, only to receive a curt reply placing all blame on the church for its present difficulties. So another appeal was sent to Congress, but without effect. By this time many Catholics had decided to take the law into their own hands. They printed and spread pro-church propaganda, and sometimes they took direct action against the public authorities. Bombs were thrown, public schools were

[9] See William E. Walling's interesting volume, *The Mexican Question; Mexico and Mexican-American Relations under Calles and Obregón.*

mutilated, and in some cases the teachers were murdered. Outlaw bands roamed the country, calling themselves *Cristeros*—followers of Christ— and laying violent hands on all known enemies of religion. Everywhere they left their printed slogan: *Christ is King.* This violence played directly into the hands of the government. It portrayed the followers of the church as lawbreakers—which indeed many of them were—and traitors to their country. It conducted widely publicized trials, and sent several priests to the firing squad. Passions ran high throughout all Mexico.[10]

IMPROVED PUBLIC EDUCATION. The closing of religious schools as part of the anti-clerical campaign made necessary the expansion of public education. President Calles announced that the goal of his administration would be one thousand new rural schools a year. This goal was not reached, but the government's educational program did move steadily forward. Night classes for adults were established in rural areas, with special emphasis on agricultural subjects. A new system of secondary schools was developed to fill the gap between primary and university training. School lunches and free medical care for school children were provided to the extent of the government's limited resources. Public expenditures for education rose steadily, while many other government outlays were being reduced.

DISTRIBUTION OF LAND. Calles was an enthusiastic advocate of land distribution. During his administration the villages and small farmers received nearly three times as much land as they had been given prior to that time. New laws were passed to clarify the tangled land situation. They were partially successful, but some uncertainty still remained as to the kinds of land available for allocation and the persons and groups who might receive it. Contradictory orders and decrees still dealt with the proper procedure to be followed in applying for land and the manner in which it must be worked.

Two conflicting theories of land distribution were in vogue among the intellectuals of the Revolution, and each viewpoint had its staunch champions. One theory favored the apportionment of land to the villages, to be held in trust for the individuals of the community and worked on a communal basis. Many persons favored this system. They said that

[10] There is an extensive literature dealing with the troubles of the Catholic Church in this period of Mexico's history. See J. M. Puig Cassuranc, *La Cuestión Religiosa en Relación con la Educación Pública en México;* J. Pérez Lugo, *La Cuestión Religiosa en México;* Aguiles P. Moctezuma, *El Conflicto Religioso de 1926.* An impartial account in English is given by J. Lloyd Mecham in his *Church and State in Latin America.*

individual holdings would be too small, that the owners would not co-operate in growing and disposing of their crops, and that the inevitable result would be chaos. But there were many other persons who rejected this theory and declared that the interests of the Revolution would be best served by giving each peasant his own small plot of ground. It would indeed be small, but it would be his own, and he would lavish upon it the loving care that he would never give to communal property. Because the leaders of the Revolution could not agree upon either of these theories, both plans were put into effect. Some land was developed communally; some was given directly to individuals.

In practice the communal system developed unexpected defects. It often became the basis for political manipulations. Some village presidents actually demanded and received a substantial share of all the crops grown on the communal land, just as the great landowners had done in former days. Others used their influence to get a large share of the village crops for their own friends and relatives. But these abuses did not discourage the more radical theorists, who still clamored for a more widespread use of the communal system. President Calles recognized both plans but tended to favor individual ownership.[11] One of his most important contributions to the agrarian problem was the establishment of national and regional farm credit banks, from which individuals and co-operatives might borrow the money they needed for implements, animals, fertilizers, and other agricultural necessities. Until this time they had borrowed from speculators, often at usurious rates of interest.

"NO RE-ELECTION" POLICY ABANDONED. Calles had been in power less than a year when prominent politicians began to talk about General Obregón as his successor. The constitution, of course, specifically prohibited such a choice. It said very clearly that no president might serve more than a single term, and this prohibition reflected the spirit of the Revolution. Madero, it will be remembered, had kindled the revolutionary spark with the cry "No re-election!"[12] But Obregón wanted to be president again, and few doubted that ways would be found to gratify his desire. The simplest method of avoiding the charge of unconstitutionality was to change the constitution, so a constitutional amendment was introduced in Congress permitting a president to serve two terms, though not consecutively. The members of Obregón's Agrarian Party

[11] The late Eyler Simpson, who made a careful study of the Mexican land problem, became so firmly convinced of the merits of communal ownership that he entitled his authoritative work *The Ejido* (that is, the community property), *Mexico's Way Out*.

[12] See page 209.

gave strong support to this amendment, but it was resisted by the labor group, which had broken with Obregón before the end of his term.[13] Labor's opposition proved decisive, and the amendment was defeated. That was in October of 1925. But three months later a similar amendment was introduced, and this time labor received direct orders from President Calles: Vote *yes!* Reluctantly it obeyed, and the amendment received sufficient support to insure its passage.[14]

It was a curious situation. Calles was labor's man, but he was also Obregón's man, elected to the presidency through his patron's influence. When, therefore, the time came to pay his political debt, he did so unhesitatingly, and labor did his bidding rather than risk the loss of official favor. Shortly afterward the order came to adopt another constitutional amendment which would increase the president's term from four years to six, beginning with Calles' successor.

ELECTION AND ASSASSINATION OF OBREGÓN. With the amending of the constitution the stage was set for Obregón's return to the presidency in 1928. He was nominated with great fanfare in the spring of 1927 and graciously announced his willingness to become the people's choice. As a matter of fact, there was very little effective opposition. Two high army officers did in fact announce that they too would be candidates, but after several months of futile campaigning and wild talk of revolution they were seized and shot without trial. Meanwhile the Labor Party officially endorsed Obregón. Even Luis Morones, who certainly hated the former President, added his blessing. Later labor withdrew its formal support, but no one really cared. The election was as cut and dried as any in Mexican history. On July 1, 1928, General Obregón became president-elect of his country for the second time. Sixteen days later, before he had opportunity to occupy the presidential chair, he was shot to death.

His assassin was a young Catholic art student who had become involved in the plots of the *Cristeros*. He admitted his guilt readily enough, saying that in this way he had served God and the Catholic Church. Other persons were found to be involved in the plot, including a nun who was given twenty years' imprisonment. The young murderer, of course, was promptly executed. One of the curious results of Obregón's death was the disintegration of the Labor Party. The charge was freely made that Morones and his labor followers had been involved in the plot and, since everyone knew that labor was bitterly opposed to Obregón's re-election,

[13] See page 211.
[14] Seven years later, however, the no re-election clause was restored to the constitution.

this accusation gained considerable credence. Morones and the other labor members of the government were finally forced to resign, and thousands of workers in all parts of Mexico quit the C.R.O.M. It never regained its influence.

ELECTION OF PORTES GIL. On the first day of September, 1928, Calles went before Congress and made the dramatic announcement that he was quitting the presidency. His term of office had already expired, of course, and under such circumstances the constitution specified that a provisional president should be chosen by Congress. Yet there had been considerable doubt that the constitution would be respected. Other Mexican presidents had been extremely loath to relinquish their power. But President Calles said that he proposed to usher in a new era of scrupulous respect for the law. He would step aside and thus prove his integrity.

It soon became clear, however, that he had no intention of leaving the choice of his successor to the whims of fate or the caprice of Congress. He called together the leading generals of the army, and revealed the name of the next president—Emilio Portes Gil, a clever politician of Indian blood and unimpeachable revolutionary antecedents who had served with distinction as governor of Tamaulipas and, more recently, as secretary of government. The generals were aghast, because Portes Gil was not one of themselves. Why, they asked, did Calles insist upon naming a civilian? But President Calles calmed their fears. He assured them that the new administration would be sympathetic to the army. And he explained that, as a guarantee, he personally would supervise and approve everything done by Portes Gil. He intended to be the power behind the throne. Thereupon the generals withdrew their objections and the election of Portes Gil was assured. The vote in Congress was 277 to 0.[15]

CALLES STILL BOSS. Some Mexican writers refer to this period of their history as the era of *Callismo*—in other words, the personal government of Calles. And there is considerable justification for the term, for Calles controlled the nation almost as completely as if it had been his personal domain. Presidents came and went, but always Calles lurked in the background, giving orders, laying plans, manipulating the affairs of state. Those who wanted results did not bother to go to the presidential palace; they went instead to Calles' palatial home. There the decisions were made.

Between 1928 and 1934 Mexico had three presidents. Only one of them

[15] The negotiations that made Portes Gil provisional president are described in detail by Froylan C. Manjárrez in his interesting work, *La Jornada Institucional; la Crisis de la Política*, see Vol. I, pp. 41–67.

was elected; the others were named by Congress. But of course all three were chosen by Calles before either Congress or the people registered their assent. First came Portes Gil, whose provisional term lasted for fourteen months. Then Pascual Ortiz Rubio was elected to the presidency in November of 1929. This choice was not popular with the army or the people, but they had little opportunity to register their disapproval. Some of the generals did in fact stage an abortive revolution, only to discover that Boss Calles was more than a match for them. In 1932 one of Ortiz Rubio's ill-wishers, who believed in direct action, took a shot at him and wounded him in the jaw. Soon afterward he resigned, and went to the United States to recuperate. His place was taken provisionally by Abelardo Rodríguez, a wealthy general of revolutionary days who had served as governor and cabinet minister. Rodríguez rounded out the period to 1934.

CHURCH PERSECUTION CONTINUED. During these years of *Callismo* the Catholic Church was persecuted vigorously. It seemed at first as if the dispute between church and state might be settled amicably, for Portes Gil arranged an agreement with the Vatican by which confiscated churches would be restored, while priests would register with the government as required by law. But this truce was of short duration. Many of the state governments issued new anti-clerical decrees. President Ortiz Rubio, who received frequent complaints from the clergy, explained that he was powerless to interfere in state affairs. When, however, an occasional state governor displayed a sympathetic attitude toward the church, the President's scruples against interference suddenly disappeared. On one occasion the governor of Durango was summarily removed by presidential order, after it had been discovered that he was permitting two hundred priests to function—nearly eight times the maximum fixed by state law. In 1932 the Apostolic Delegate was deported as an "undesirable alien." He was in fact a native Mexican, but the government decided to call him a foreigner because he owed allegiance to a foreign sovereign—in other words, the Pope. The years 1933 and 1934 witnessed a fresh wave of seizures of church property. Calles himself poured oil on the blaze by calling upon all the forces of the Revolution to fight religion.

FURTHER DISTRIBUTION OF LAND. During Portes Gil's presidency the program of land distribution was carried out with considerable vigor. When, however, Calles returned from abroad with the statement that perhaps land reform had gone far enough, President Ortiz Rubio steered his course in the direction thus indicated. He issued a number of decrees making various types of villages ineligible to receive land and protecting the large landowners against further expropriations. He even forced through Congress a law reversing some of the land policies already established. But there were many influential persons who strongly opposed this virtual abandonment of land reform. Though ready to follow the leadership of Calles in most matters, they declared that the Revolution's policy of land expropriation must continue. Many of the leading agrarians in Congress took this stand. So, too, did a number of prominent generals.

Calles, who knew how to dominate the political scene, also knew how to yield gracefully to overwhelming pressure. He permitted the next president, Abelardo Rodríguez, to issue several decrees facilitating the distribution of land. On March 22, 1934, Congress enacted a new agrarian code which improved and expanded the administrative machinery for getting land into the hands of the people. This code was a triumph for the agrarians, but not for their most radical element. Small private land holdings were officially given preference over communal ownership.[16]

LABOR POLICIES. The fall from power of Morones and his labor followers [17] was hastened by the hostility of President Portes Gil. Government patronage was denied to all politicians suspected of sympathy for the C.R.O.M., and federal troops were used against C.R.O.M. agitators on the slightest excuse. The new President was not anti-labor; he was anti-Morones and anti-C.R.O.M. Toward other labor unions he showed a more kindly attitude. For a time he even encouraged a Communist union as a counter-irritant to the Morones group, but when the power of the C.R.O.M. had been completely and finally broken, the Communists soon fell from favor. Meanwhile steps were taken to strengthen the labor laws, and in 1931 a new labor code became effective.

ESTABLISHMENT OF AN OFFICIAL PARTY. One of the most significant events of Portes Gil's administration was the establishment, early in 1929, of an official political party—the National Revolutionary Party, or P.N.R.[18] The idea originated with Calles, of course. For years he had governed with the uncertain support of shifting combinations—agrarians, co-operationists, labor leaders—and he finally decided that the time was ripe to bring them all together in one big party. A convention was called for March 1, 1929, and Querétaro was selected as the place. On the opening day nearly nine hundred delegates were present, representing most shades

<hr>

[16] The events of this period are well covered in the third volume of Alberto M. Carreno's *Páginas de Historia Mexicana.*

[17] See pages 237–238.

[18] *Partido Nacional Revolucionario.*

of political opinion. They speedily signed a pact of union and solidarity, and adopted a declaration of principles phrased in such general terms that it would give offense to no one. Thus the P.N.R. was born. P.N.R. clubs were established in nearly all communities, and soon the word spread that membership in the party was the best way to win official favor—or, in some cases, to avoid official disfavor. Men from all walks of life flocked to the party standard. The P.N.R. newspaper called itself "the official organ of the government," and no one challenged this assertion. Early in 1930 all government employees were notified that seven days' pay would be deducted from their salaries each year, and that this money would be paid into the treasury of the P.N.R. In this way the difficult problem of party financing was solved.

DOMINANCE OF THE P.N.R. Since 1929, therefore, Mexico has been a one-party state. Other political parties have not been forbidden, but they have been unable to compete with the government-controlled and government-financed P.N.R. Candidates lacking the endorsement of the P.N.R. have stood very little chance of election. Policies rejected by the P.N.R. have been defeated as a matter of course. That is the principal reason why Mexico cannot fairly claim that it is a democracy. Its official party stifles all opposition.

RISE OF CÁRDENAS. The next presidential election was set for July 1, 1934. Calles and the other leaders of the P.N.R. put their heads together and finally agreed upon Lázaro Cárdenas, a young mestizo who had joined the Revolution in its early stages and achieved a considerable reputation as a guerrilla leader. His education was meager, for he had been compelled to leave school at an early age to help support his widowed mother and younger brothers and sisters. But after joining the army he soon became a general, and while still a young man he was elected governor of his native state of Michoacán. As governor he balanced the budget and hastened the construction of schools and roads. At the time of his nomination to the presidency he was only thirty-eight years of age. Calles had early marked him as an outstanding leader, and had become his foster father.[19] There is some doubt, however, whether Lázaro Cárdenas was Calles' first choice for the presidency. The young man was known to be very radical. Many times he had placed himself squarely on record in favor of the communal plan of land distribution, despite the known fact

[19] See *Lázaro Cárdenas*, by Djed Borques. Another interesting work is Marcelo A. Villamil's *La Personalidad de Lázaro Cárdenas*.

that Calles preferred a system of individual holdings. But sentiment within the P.N.R. was running strongly toward Cárdenas, and Calles finally gave his approval.

PRESIDENTIAL CAMPAIGN OF 1934. Everyone knew that nomination by the P.N.R. was tantamount to election. All public officers and employees, including the election officials, were members of the Party, and they could not afford to permit the defeat of their own candidate. Cárdenas could have become president without making a single campaign speech. But that easy way did not satisfy him. He undertook the most ambitious political campaign that Mexico had ever seen. By automobile, by train, on horseback, and on foot he covered the country, visiting even the remote Indian villages and talking with the common people who crowded eagerly around him. His formal platform was based on a so-called six-year plan which had been adopted the previous year by the P.N.R. at Calles' insistence. But Cárdenas went far beyond the six-year plan. He told the landless masses that they would get their land without further delay. He promised aid for the isolated Indian communities which no one had bothered to help. He denounced the Catholic Church in very specific terms, calling it a greedy monster and an oppressor of civil liberties. He promised the workers a higher standard of living, but told them they must organize to win their own battles. "Workers of Mexico, unite!" was his cry. There was some opposition, of course. Three other candidates were nominated, and each of them made his bid for popular support. But the official count gave Cárdenas ninety-eight per cent of all the votes cast.

Administration of Lázaro Cárdenas

CÁRDENAS SPLITS WITH CALLES. Calles naturally assumed that the new President would take his orders, just as three preceding presidents had done. And, at the outset, Cárdenas gave no hint of rebellion. He dutifully appointed Calles' followers to important posts. Rudolfo Calles, son of the boss, was made secretary of communications. But Cárdenas had a will of his own. He openly encouraged the wave of strikes that was spreading over the country, including the strike against the Mexican Telephone Company, in which Calles was a large stockholder. Finally, in June of 1935, Calles decided that he could no longer endure the new President's "insubordination." He summoned the press to his home in Cuernavaca and issued an interview placing the blame for Mexico's labor troubles squarely on Cárdenas' shoulders. The companies, he said, were unable to meet the demands of the strikers; the demand for more pay in an hour of depression was unreasonable and savored of treason; and the President deserved the strongest censure for ignoring these plain facts. In a reminiscent mood, Calles alluded to his role as president-maker. "I have selected presidents and I have broken them," he said in effect, "and I can do it again."

TRIUMPH OF CÁRDENAS. Cárdenas quickly accepted the challenge of Calles' criticism. The next day he answered Calles point by point, indicating that he was president of the nation and intended to govern without the help of any outsider. Shortly afterward he demanded and received the resignation of the cabinet ministers friendly to Calles and filled the vacant posts with his own supporters. The members of Congress then had to decide between the two rivals. Many of them were already friendly to Cárdenas, and when it became apparent that he held the balance of power they all flocked to his support. Calles saw that he was beaten and retired to his ranch in Sinaloa. A few months later he left the country. Congress gave President Cárdenas an overwhelming vote of confidence, and army generals assured him of their support. Those few persons who refused to change their allegiance were forced to resign or eliminated from the government in other ways. Lázaro Cárdenas was the new Master of Mexico.

A CHAMPION OF THE PROLETARIAT. President Cárdenas was a determined proletarian. He refused to live in Chapultepec Palace, the imposing castle that had long been the official residence of the presidents of Mexico. He closed the gambling casinos, despite the protests of many prominent politicians. He kept regular office hours and saw the poor before giving audience to the rich. He directed all telegraph offices to receive free of charge, at certain hours, any messages that the people of the country might wish to send him. His first concern was always for the poor and friendless. Tirelessly he traveled from one end of Mexico to the other, visiting remote villages, correcting petty injustices, righting minor wrongs. Personally he investigated hundreds of complaints that otherwise would have received only the cursory attention of local *alcaldes*. His critics said, with some justification, that he was too busy with these minor matters to give proper attention to the major problems of state. The story circulated that "one morning while dispatching business in the capital his secretary laid a list of urgent matters, and a telegram, before him. The list said: *Bank reserves dangerously low*. 'Tell the Treasurer,' said Cárdenas. *Agricultural production failing.* 'Tell the Minister of Agriculture.' *Railways Bankrupt.* 'Tell the Minister of Communications.' *Serious message from Washington.* 'Tell Foreign Affairs.' Then he opened the telegram, which read: 'My corn dried, my burro died, my sow was stolen, my baby is sick. Signed, Pedro Juan, village of Huitzlipituzco.' 'Order the presidential train at once,' said Cárdenas. 'I am leaving for Huitzlipituzco.' " [20]

ACCELERATED PROGRAM OF LAND DISTRIBUTION. The new Cárdenas administration distributed land more extensively than ever before, with emphasis on communal ownership. Many large landowners who had managed to hold on to their properties through nearly a quarter of a century of Revolution and land reform finally gave up the fight and assisted in apportioning them among former tenants. For themselves they kept only the small acreage permitted by law. Some of them went into manufacturing. A few even found their way into politics. Meanwhile many of the peasants found that they were no better off than before. They now owed allegiance to the politicians instead of the landed proprietors. There was not enough land to go around, not enough water to make crops grow, and not enough money to buy even the few essentials of life. President Cárdenas tried desperately to eliminate these difficulties. He established a new bank to finance the communal farmers, and encouraged the establishment of co-operatives. Yet imports of corn and wheat continued to mount, and the total number of acres under cultivation actually decreased during his administration. Mexico's basic problem was still unsolved.[21]

CHURCH PERSECUTION LESS SEVERE. The quarrel between church and state continued during the Cárdenas administration, though its violence was somewhat abated. A decree issued early in 1935 denied the privilege of the mails to any newspaper or magazine circulating religious propaganda or doctrine. This step was taken, according to the official explanation, "to combat fanaticism and religious prejudice, with the firm purpose of obtaining the spiritual freedom of the people." [22] New decrees reaffirmed the well established doctrine that churches and similar buildings were the property of the state. Yet Cárdenas was much more tolerant of the church than Calles had ever been. Several decrees issued during the Cárdenas regime assured to Mexicans their liberty of conscience. The church was permitted to perform its daily routines, though with a greatly reduced number of priests and a minimum of publicity. Men

---

[20] Quoted, with permission, from Anita Brenner's *The Wind That Swept Mexico,* p. 85.

[21] See the survey published in the March, 1941, issue of the *Mexican American Review,* pp. 12–34.

[22] *Diario Oficial,* February 12, 1935.

and women were no longer persecuted for attending mass, as they had been a few years earlier.

INCREASED POWER OF LABOR. When Cárdenas assumed the presidency in 1934, labor was badly disorganized. The C.R.O.M. was practically dead, and the unions comprising its membership had lost many of their followers. There was, indeed, a loosely organized General Confederation of the Workers and Peasants of Mexico, but it had no strong following and no real power. Cárdenas, an active champion of labor, constantly urged the creation of an effective, closely knit labor organization. At his suggestion a Committee of National Proletarian Defense was established in June, 1935.

The moving spirit of this committee was a forty-one-year-old intellectual revolutionary named Vicente Lombardo Toledano, who had begun life as the son of a wealthy copper magnate. The father had been ruined by the Revolution, and young Vicente turned to intellectual pursuits. He had a distinguished university career and served for a time as director of the National Preparatory School. But by this time he had turned to communism and had become an ardent admirer of the Soviet Union. So he abandoned his academic interests and became a labor organizer. He soon became known as a prolific writer and a brilliant orator. This, then, was the man who put new life into the labor movement. His efforts were largely responsible for the creation in 1936 of the Mexican Federation of Labor, or C.T.M.[23] It soon became virtually an unofficial arm of the government, lending support to Cárdenas and carrying out his policies. In return the President worked actively for labor. He issued decrees or sponsored laws increasing wages and making available small loans to workers. Public employees were specifically given the right to organize, and even to strike.[24]

Meanwhile the number of strikes in private industry rose steadily. Major disputes were settled by the National Department of Labor, and almost invariably in favor of the workers, regardless of the merits of the dispute. President Cárdenas made no effort to conceal his pro-labor bias. On one occasion he declared: "Any employers feeling weary of the social struggle may turn their industries over to the workers or the government. Such action would be patriotic; a shutdown would not be." [25] Acting on this theory, the government expropriated the railroads and placed their management in the hands of the workers. Mines, sugar mills, and textile

[23] *Confederación de Trabajadores de México.*
[24] Only the members of the police and armed forces were excluded.
[25] *Los Catorce Puntos de la Política Obrera Presidencial,* p. 29.

factories were accorded the same treatment. After the expropriation of the foreign oil properties, one government corporation was set up to operate the oil fields and another to distribute petroleum throughout Mexico. The workers were given an important part in the management of both agencies. Labor chiefs became powerful and wealthy, using their authority to stifle all opposition.

EDUCATIONAL POLICIES. During the Cárdenas administration the constitutional mandate for "socialist education excluding all religious doctrine" [26] was interpreted strictly. Teachers in many of the states were required to take an oath declaring themselves atheists and "irreconcilable enemies" of the Roman Catholic Church. But education—the kind of socialist education desired by the government—received strong encouragement. Large numbers of new schools were established. Some of them were specifically limited to the families of industrial and farm workers and soldiers. Classes were established in three shifts—morning, afternoon, and evening—so that there would be no interference with regular employment. Emphasis was placed on vocational training.

REORGANIZATION OF THE OFFICIAL PARTY. Late in 1937 President Cárdenas announced that the time had come to reorganize the official party, the P.N.R., and establish it on a broader basis. There should be four sections, he said, representing the four major segments of Mexican life. These segments, as he saw them, were the peasants, the trade unions, the army, and the "popular" group, which was composed chiefly of politicians and government employees. The party leaders met the following March and obediently arranged this reorganization. They also changed the name to *Mexican Revolutionary Party,* or P.R.M.[27] Compulsory contributions from government employees were eliminated, but party resolutions left no doubt that the contributions must continue on a "voluntary" basis. Party organization was perfected, so that it reached every village in Mexico. All the state governors were now members of the official party. So were the overwhelming majority in both houses of Congress, in the state legislatures, and in the municipal councils. Representatives of opposition groups had almost no chance of being elected, and no chance whatever of influencing the course of public policy if, by some strange chance, they should win an election.

NOMINATION OF AVILA CAMACHO. As the time of the 1940 election drew

[26] See page 222.
[27] *Partido Revolucionario Mexicano.* Note that the army section was later abolished, on the theory that Mexico should be freer from military influences.

near, there were several persons who thought that they had a claim to the presidency. Without exception they were generals who had served with more or less distinction in the Revolution. All of them could claim the friendship of Cárdenas. From this group Cárdenas himself picked General Manuel Avila Camacho, who had an unimpeachable record of mediocrity. He came from the same town as the President, and had shown some administrative ability as secretary of national defense. As soon as Cárdenas spoke, the politicians hastened to do his bidding. Lombardo Toledano and his Mexican Labor Federation announced that they would support Avila Camacho. The next day the peasants' section of the P.R.M. selected him as their candidate. Then the army took a similar stand, and the government employees made it virtually unanimous. Avila Camacho had been assured of overwhelming support before the P.R.M. even held its convention to nominate him. But the convention met, nonetheless, and went through the motions of choosing him as the official candidate. That was on November 3, 1939. A second six-year plan was adopted as the party's platform. It differed in no substantial respect from the original plan.

THE UNSUCCESSFUL OPPOSITION. With all the forces of the government solidly behind Avila Camacho's candidacy, it might well have been supposed that no other person would take the trouble to declare himself a candidate. But a dashing army officer with a proud military record decided to fight the P.R.M. His name was Juan Andreu Almazán. He had no organization, of course, but he had a host of friends, and they hastily improvised the *National Action Party,* or P.A.N. Many discontented elements flocked to his standard. Some of them were former followers of Calles, who had never been accepted by the new regime. Some were deposed labor chiefs who had been close to Morones. Others were devout Catholics, attracted by the promise of greater religious freedom.

Almazán's platform was very simple. In addition to advocating a more lenient policy toward the Church, he favored complete freedom of speech and press and a modification of the labor laws to prevent abuses of the right to strike. He went from city to city, reiterating these principles. Everywhere he spoke to large crowds, and thousands of persons were swept away by his impassioned oratory. So successfully did he appeal to the popular imagination that the government forces found themselves no longer able to ignore his campaign. They set in motion the full weight of the party machinery, designed to crush just such mutinies. Force and fraud were used with callous indifference to public opinion. Some of Almazán's supporters were kept away from the polls with bullets and even with hand grenades. No one was greatly surprised, therefore, when Avila Camacho was declared the winner by a margin of ten to one. Almazán charged fraud, as well he might. He even talked of revolution, after first taking the precaution of leaving Mexico. But his words kindled no revolutionary spark, and the threatened uprising never materialized. Avila Camacho became president of Mexico on December 1, 1940.

Avila Camacho, Alemán, and Ruiz Cortines

RELIGIOUS TOLERATION. From the very beginning of his administration Avila Camacho approached public problems with a conservatism that the nation had not experienced for many years. He frowned upon all forms of religious persecution, and in some cases even extended official protection to those who wished to attend church services. "I am a believer," he said, thus causing shocked comment in some quarters. But he made no attempt to repeal the anti-clerical provisions of the constitution and laws. Everyone understood that the church was on probation and must carefully avoid any interference with Mexican politics in order to escape a fresh wave of persecutions. Within a very narrow sphere it might still hope to control the religious life of the people.[28]

MODIFICATION OF THE LAND POLICY. Avila Camacho respected existing communal farms, and even took steps to protect them against burdensome lawsuits by former owners. But he soon made clear that he had greater faith in individual ownership. He gave one million and a half small farmers clear titles to their land, though with certain restrictions designed to prevent them from selling or mortgaging their properties and thus slipping back into the category of landless peasants. The process of land distribution slowed down considerably. The government explained, however, that this indicated no lack of interest in land reform. It meant only that less land was now available for the masses, because so much had already been given away.

WEAKENED POSITION OF LABOR. In labor matters the government's policy was sharply modified. Avila Camacho could scarcely be called anti-labor, but he certainly was not militantly pro-labor, as Cárdenas had been. Instead he tried to maintain a reasonably impartial attitude. He established a system of social security. On the other hand, he secured passage

---

[28] See "The Catholic Revival in Mexico," *Report of the Inter-American Committee of the Catholic Association for International Peace,* Pamphlet No. 35.

of a law making strikes more difficult and penalizing strikers for acts of violence against persons or property. Strikes against the government were declared illegal unless they met certain conditions. Lombardo Toledano protested these restrictions, but to no avail. He was just a labor leader now—not the crony of the President. His C.T.M. began to show signs of falling apart as rival labor groups sought official favor. When war came to Mexico in 1942, the government took firm steps to insure labor peace. It requested and secured a no-strike pledge from nearly all the responsible labor groups, and it acted promptly and decisively against violators of that pledge in a number of essential industries. Some of the more radical labor leaders charged, of course, that the President had sold out to the capitalists. They ignored the obvious fact that the rules had to be different in a nation at war.

Sinarquismo. In 1940 and 1941, as the ground swell of war swept menacingly against the New World, the fanatically Catholic *Cristeros* made themselves felt again, but in a new form and with a new name. They now called their movement *Sinarquismo* (without anarchy). Its goal, they said, was to restore Mexico to its traditional patterns—Catholic faith, Spanish traditions, home, village, Christian political order. The Catholic clergy encouraged it, of course, though no priests were permitted to belong to its organization. It was strongly anti-foreign, which in Mexico meant primarily anti-American. For that reason it received German encouragement and even German funds. Originally called the Anti-Communist Center, it was organized in 1936 by a German engineer named Oscar Schreiter, who taught in a Guanajuato school. But its leaders were nearly all Mexicans, who went about preaching the new order—an authoritarian Utopia, with the Roman Catholic faith installed as the official religion, labor unions reduced to impotence, and the false notions of free speech and free press completely abandoned.

To thousands of devout, illiterate peasants these ideals made a powerful appeal. They gathered to hear rabble-rousing speeches and to sing the official hymn, "Faith, Blood, and Victory." Orators scarcely ever missed an opportunity to attack the United States. The organization acquired a typical fascist character, with uniforms somewhat similar to those of the Nazi storm-troopers. The red armband, worn on the left sleeve, bore a white circle in which was contained a green map of Mexico. The fascist-type salute was made by raising the left arm diagonally across the chest. At first the government regarded these fanatics with amused tolerance. Permission was even given for them to establish a colony in Lower California. When, however, Mexico finally entered the war at the side of the United States, the continued fascist cries of the *Sinarquistas* were little short of treasonable. The government was finally forced to take severe repressive measures.[29]

WAR PROBLEMS. The war brought many changes to Mexico. A so-called "government of national unity" was established, though President Avila Camacho continued his moderate policies without any significant change. On September 16, 1942, the anniversary of Mexico's independence, all five living ex-presidents appeared on the reviewing stand with President Avila Camacho. Even the aging Calles returned from exile in Los Angeles to lend his blessing to the occasion. Throughout the war period prices continued to rise steadily, while wages lagged behind. There were shortages of many things—even corn, which Mexicans must have to live. The government established fixed prices for essential commodities, but seemed totally unable to enforce them. Many businessmen and politicians made fortunes. Meanwhile the United States helped to maintain the Mexican economy by lending large sums of money and sending badly needed technicians. But of course some Mexicans blamed the Americans for continuing shortages, and this explanation was readily accepted by thousands of ignorant peasants.

PRESIDENTIAL CANDIDACY OF ALEMÁN. The political campaign to select a new president of Mexico was in full swing by the summer of 1945, a full year before election day. Avila Camacho finally indicated that he would support Miguel Alemán, a clever forty-three-year-old lawyer who had managed the President's election campaign in 1940 and later served as minister of government. Labor and agrarian groups hastened to pay tribute to the new crown prince. In January, 1946, the P.R.M. ratified the President's choice, as everyone knew that it would. It also changed its name to Institutional Revolutionary Party, or P.R.I.,[30] though the reasons for this change remained obscure. The new party was no different from the old in organization, methods, purposes, or official support. One Mexican cartoonist reflected popular opinion in a cartoon which showed a nurse holding a small baby (the P.R.I.) for the inspection of its proud father (the P.R.M.). Father and son were alike in every respect, despite the disparity in their ages.

[29] An interesting aspect of the Sinarquist movement is presented by Heinz H. F. Eulau in his *"Sinarquismo* in the United States," published in the *Inter-American,* March, 1944. pp. 25–27. In the April, 1944, issue, the *Inter-American* published a long letter by Rev. John A. O'Brien, of Notre Dame University, presenting the Catholic point of view. See pp. 46–47.

[30] *Partido Revolucionario Institucional.*

CANDIDACY AND DEFEAT OF PADILLA. The leading presidential candidate of the opposition was Ezequiel Padilla, who had spent most of his fifty-seven years in Mexican politics. He had served under Zapata and Villa in the Revolution, later becoming a member of Congress, a cabinet minister, and a diplomat. During the war he was a well-known figure at inter-American gatherings, using his remarkable gift of speech to defend the United States and the democratic way of life. Millions of Americans knew Padilla by reputation, and wished him well. But his friendliness for the United States undoubtedly proved a severe handicap in his campaign for the Mexican presidency. People said that he was too subservient to the gringos. When it became clear that Padilla would not receive official support, he turned to the feeble National Action Party, which had represented the opposition in the 1940 election. A few minor politicians signed up. A few businessmen contributed to his campaign fund. Yet almost from the start of the campaign it was clear that Padilla did not have a chance.

The P.R.I. plastered the country with Alemán's name. It appeared at every turn of the road, painted in white letters on houses, barns, and even convenient boulders. Bridges and other public property bore the legend: "Alemán will be president." In the capital his portrait was stamped on all bus tickets. It is probable that millions of Mexicans did not even hear the name of any candidate except Miguel Alemán. So no one was surprised when Alemán won by a margin of three to one. Padilla claimed that the election had been one of the most fraudulent in Mexican history. There can be little doubt, however, that Alemán was the popular choice. The P.R.I.'s widespread, expensive propaganda campaign produced excellent results. Yet there may well have been fraudulent vote counting in the congressional races. Candidates of the National Action Party and the still-active *Sinarquistas* received strong local support in many communities, but were declared the victors in only five districts.[31]

THE CONSERVATISM OF ALEMÁN. Shortly after President Alemán's inaugural he took a number of steps to continue or even expand the conservative policies of Avila Camacho. He appointed moderate businessmen to key posts in his cabinet. He advised workers to avoid illegal strikes. When the workers in the petroleum monopoly walked out in

[31] See the comments of Stephen S. Goodspeed in his unpublished study, *The Role of the Executive in Mexico*, pp. 357-358. This monograph is available in the library of the University of California. It contains a great deal of useful information concerning the recent political life of Mexico, and would have been cited more frequently in this chapter, except for its inaccessibility to most students.

defiance of government orders, the President took swift and decisive action. He sent troops to patrol the oil properties and supported the dismissal of fifty labor leaders who had been responsible for the trouble. Lombardo Toledano probably prevented further government reprisals against the unions by supporting President Alemán, but he thereby weakened the Labor Federation. Many labor groups deserted it soon afterward. Eventually Lombardo Toledano himself was forced out of the Federation, and he promptly began the task of organizing a labor party in opposition to the P.R.I. The ultraconservative *Sinarquistas* also set up an opposition party, under the name of *Fuerza Popular* (Popular Force). Meanwhile the program of land expropriation virtually came to a halt. Small landowners were even guaranteed against nationalization of their last five hundred acres by a newly enacted constitutional amendment.

But Alemán did not ignore the land problem. Instead he attacked it from another angle by trying to increase the total number of arable acres. Water was the answer, of course, though additional water could be supplied only by great hydroelectric units which would require vast sums of money. So in the spring of 1947 the President arranged to borrow from the United States one hundred million dollars, one half of which was to be made available for irrigation projects and other productive purposes. Some of the money was to be used for new factories, roads, and hotels. American industrialists were given to understand that their capital would be welcome, and would be afforded reasonable protection. Since 1947, therefore, American capital, both public and private, has continued to flow into Mexico.

PRESIDENTIAL CAMPAIGN OF 1951–1952. As the end of President Alemán's term drew near, he indicated that his choice for the next president of Mexico was Adolfo Ruiz Cortines, the hardworking but somewhat colorless Minister of the Interior. Ruiz Cortines was then sixty-two years of age, and had spent most of his life working for the government in minor administrative posts. He was virtually assured of the presidency when the P.R.I., the official party, held its national convention and made him its candidate. But opposition groups were by no means ready to concede defeat. The National Action Party, relying largely on the support of devout Catholics, nominated a well-known conservative named Efraín González Luna. The *Sinarquistas,* lacking a candidate of their own, agreed to give González Luna their support. Several dissident groups united to choose General Miguel Henríquez Guzmán, a wealthy and influential former member of the P.R.I. who had stepped aside to permit the nomination of Alemán in 1945, but had finally broken with the official party when he was again passed over in 1951. Although Henríquez Guzmán's platform was quite radical, he seemed unable to gain any substantial following among the labor groups. There was also a fourth presidential candidate—Vicente Lombardo Toledano, the once-powerful Marxist whose influence had been waning for several years. Ruiz Cortines expressed pleasure at the unusually large number of presidential candidates. "This shows that political freedom truly exists in Mexico," he declared.[32] The campaign was comparatively peaceful, though riots and assassinations took a total of fifteen lives. Most of the people seem to have been indifferent to the appeals of the politicians, and the P.R.I. had to work hard to arrange a number of moderately enthusiastic rallies. Ruiz Cortines won, of course, with three times as many votes as all his opponents. Almost all the seats in Congress went to the P.R.I. Henríquez Guzmán charged fraud, but offered virtually no evidence to support his contention. The truth seems to be that the P.R.I. did not need to cheat. Its organization is so nearly perfect that it can keep power in its own hands without resort to force or fraud.

POLICIES OF RUIZ CORTINES. The new President has continued most of Miguel Alemán's middle-of-the-road policies. Industry has been promised the government's active support, and foreign capital has been given to understand that it will receive reasonable treatment. Large sums have been earmarked for the improvement of communications and for other public works. Friendly relations with the Catholic Church have been maintained. In one respect, however, Ruiz Cortines seems to have broken sharply with the tradition maintained by all his predecessors. Instead of condoning the corruption found in virtually all branches of the public service, he has inaugurated a vigorous policy of honesty and morality in government. He has been responsible for a new law requiring every government official and employee to make a public declaration of all his possessions when he assumes public office, and again when he leaves it. Many informed persons wonder whether any one man—even the president of the nation—can compel a complete change in accepted standards of public morality. But the experiment should be worth watching.

Mexico's political leaders still call themselves true sons of the Revolution of 1910. Today, however, the spirit of the Revolution no longer dominates Mexico. Moderation seems to have become the new watchword. Progress, it is said, must be made by evolution. The fiery leaders of the Revolu-

[32] *New York Times*, December 20, 1951.

tion—those who are still alive—may not like the new policy, but they no longer control Mexico. Its destiny has passed into the hands of other men.

SELECTED REFERENCES

Anguiano Equihua, Victoriano, *Lázaro Cárdenas: Su Deudo y la Política Nacional*, Mexico, D.F., Editorial Erédira, 1951.

Beteta, Ramón, *Pensamiento y Dinámica de la Revolución Mexicana*, 2nd ed., Mexico, D.F., Editorial México Nuevo, 1951.

Bojórquez, Juan de Dios, *Lázaro Cárdenas*, Mexico, D.F., Imp. Mundial, 1934.

Botella Asensi, Juan, *La Expropriación en el Derecho Mexicano*, Mexico, D.F., Editorial Moderne, 1941.

Brenner, Anita, *The Wind That Swept Mexico*, New York, Harper, 1943.

Call, Tomme Clark, *The Mexican Venture*, New York, Oxford University Press, 1953.

Casteneda, Andrés Enrique, *Ensayo sobre el Corporativismo*, Mexico, D.F., Escuela Libre de Derecho, 1941.

Chico Goerne, Luis, *Hacia una Filosofía Social en el Siglo XX*, Mexico, D.F., Editora del Continente, 1943.

Correa, Eduardo J., *El Balance del Avila Camachismo*, Mexico, D.F., 1946.

Cuellar, Alfredo B., *Expropriación y Crisis en México*, Mexico, D.F., Universidad Nacional Autónoma de Mexico, 1940.

Daniels, Josephus, *Shirt-Sleeve Diplomat*, Chapel Hill, N.C., Univ. of North Carolina Press, 1947.

Fernández y Fernández, Ramón, *El Problema Creado por la Reforma Agraria de México*, Mexico, D.F., Banco Nacional de Crédito Agrícola, 1941.

Gordon, Wendell C., *The Expropriation of Foreign-Owned Property in Mexico*, Washington, D.C. American Council on Public Affairs, 1941.

Gruening, Ernest H., *Mexico and Its Heritage*, New York, Century Co., 1929.

Herring, Hubert C., *Mexico, the Making of a Nation*, New York, The Foreign Policy Association, 1942.

Kirk, Betty, *Covering the Mexican Front; the Battle of Europe versus America*, Norman, Okla., Univ. of Oklahoma Press, 1942.

López Aparicio, Alfonso, *El Movimiento Obrero en México: Antecedentes, Desarollo y Tendencias*, Mexico, D.F., Editorial Jus, 1952.

Lumen, Enrique, *Almazán: Vida de un Caudillo v Metabolismo de una Revolución*, Mexico, D.F., Editorial "Claridad," 1940.

Martínez Gómez del Campo, Jorge, *Anticonstitucionalidad de la Ley de Nacionalización de Bienes*, Mexico, D.F., Jorge Martínez Gómez del Campo, 1940.

Mecham, J. Lloyd, *Church and State in Latin America*, Chapel Hill, N.C., Univ. of North Carolina Press, 1934.

Mora, José María Luis, *El Clero, la Educación y la Libertad*, Mexico, D.F., Empresas Editoriales, 1949.

Person, Harlow S., *Mexican Oil*, New York, Harper, 1942.

Prewett, Virginia, *Reportage on Mexico*, New York, Dutton & Co., 1941.

Rabassa, O., *Decision Rendered by the Supreme Court of Mexico in the Oil Expropriation Case*, Mexico, D.F., Tall. Gráf. de la Nación, 1940.

Recasens Siches, L., *Vida Humana, Sociedad y Derecho*, 2nd ed., Mexico, D.F., La Casa de España en Mexico, 1945.

Rippy, J. Fred, *The United States and Mexico*, New York, Knopf, 1931.

Salazar Ríos, Santacruz, *La Actual Política Agraria Debe Reformarse Radicalmente*, Mexico, D.F., Universidad Nacional Autónoma de México, Facultad de Jurisprudencia, 1945.

Silva Herzog, Jesús, *La Revolución Mexicana en Crisis*, Mexico, D.F., Ediciones Cuadernos Americanos, 1944.

Simpson, Eyler, *The Ejido, Mexico's Way Out*, Chapel Hill, N.C., Univ. of North Carolina Press, 1937.

Tannenbaum, Frank, *Mexico: The Struggle for Peace and Bread*, New York, Knopf, 1950.

Townsend, William C., *Lázaro Cárdenas: Mexican Democrat*, Ann Arbor, George Wahr Publishing Co., 1952.

Vázquez Pérez, Francisco, *Derecho Agrario*, Mexico, D.F., Ediciones Botas, 1945.

Walling, William E., *The Mexican Question; Mexico and Mexican-American Relations under Calles and Obregón*, Washington, D.C., Robins Press, 1941.

CHAPTER II

MEXICO
The Structure of Government

The Constitution

THE constitution of Mexico is a massive document. It contains about twenty-six thousand words. The general constitutional principles could have been stated in one fourth of that space, but the men of Querétaro were not interested solely in general principles. They preferred to include a vast number of details, in order to make certain that their wishes would not be misunderstood or misinterpreted. Actually, of course, these details have not prevented either misunderstanding or misinterpretation; they have simply added to the bulkiness of the constitution. A single article (the famous Article 27, which deals with public and private property) is almost one half as long as the constitution of the United States.

LABOR PROVISIONS. Article 123, which contains several thousand words, is virtually a labor code. It makes detailed provision for a maximum work day (eight hours), with double pay for emergency overtime work, periodic days of rest (one in seven), equal wages for men and women, regular wages for pregnant women (though they shall not be required to work) during the last three months of pregnancy and for one month afterward. Provision is made for minimum wage commissions in all communities, so as to establish a reasonable relationship between minimum wages and living costs. Employers shall be liable for accidents in their establishments, regardless of actual blame. The right to belong to labor unions and to strike is guaranteed. The constitution even distinguishes between legal and illegal strikes, defining each kind. Penalties are provided for failure to accept government awards. And there are at least two dozen other detailed provisions of a similar character. Obviously they have no place in the fundamental law. They should have been left to the discretion of Congress.

INDIVIDUAL GUARANTEES. There is no preamble—no statement of the reasons for the constitution's adoption and, of course, no invocation of the blessings of God. Instead the first chapter is headed: *Individual Guarantees*. Most of these guarantees of individual liberty were borrowed from the United States and placed in Mexico's fundamental law of 1824. Since that time they have appeared in every Mexican constitution. They include the generally accepted rights of free men—freedom of speech and press, liberty of conscience, freedom from arbitrary arrest and punishment without due process of law, and so on, through a long list. But there are some interesting qualifications. Those who wish to worship God must do so in the privacy of their homes or in churches "which shall always be under the supervision of the public authorities." [1] Open-air services, therefore, are prohibited. It will be remembered that one famous open-air service led directly to the expulsion from Mexico of the Apostolic Delegate.[2] Censorship of books and periodicals is not permitted "except for the purpose of protecting life, morality, and public peace." [3]

SUSPENSION OF GUARANTEES. As in all countries, the constitutional guarantees of individual liberty are worth much or little, according to the policy of the government. Ways can always be found to evade them. The Mexican constitution contains the usual clause permitting the suspension of guarantees in times of stress. "In cases of invasion, grave disturbance of the public peace, or any other emergency that may place society in conflict," it declares, the president shall have the power to suspend "such guarantees as may be a hindrance in meeting the situation promptly and readily." [4] His decree may apply to the whole country, or such parts of the country as he may decide. There are, of course, limits to this broad power. The president must secure the approval of Congress if it is in session, or of its Permanent Committee if Congress is in recess. The suspension of guarantees must be for a limited time and must not be confined to a single individual. But these restrictions do not really hinder any president who is determined to sweep away the protections of the constitution.

In the first years of the Revolution these guarantees were almost in a state of continuous suspension. More recently, however, the presidents

[1] Art. 24.
[2] See page 230.
[3] Art. 7.
[4] Art. 29.

of Mexico have prided themselves on their respect for constitutional liberties. Newspapers print without official interference, except on rare occasions, such criticisms of the government as they desire, though they may have government-inspired labor troubles if they are too outspoken. It is considered good form not to blame the president directly but to aim all complaints at his subordinates, explaining that they have failed to advise him properly. Public gatherings protesting policies of the government are usually permitted without police interference. But the radio is supervised rather strictly, and a fairly rigid censorship of motion pictures is maintained. All things considered, Mexico deserves a fairly high rating for its tolerance of minority opinion. This tolerance has increased as the government has become more stable.

SOCIAL GUARANTEES. In addition to the more common provisions concerning individual liberty, the constitution of 1917 also contains a number of so-called guarantees that are really statements of public policy. All subsoil resources are the property of the nation and may not be exploited except by means of concessions from the national authorities. Steps shall be taken to break up the large estates.[5] Education shall be socialist.[6] These and similar statements represent the philosophy of the revolutionaries who wrote Mexico's fundamental law. They have formed the basis for the nation's vast programs of land expropriation and public ownership. They have served, too, as a justification for the closing of the Catholic schools, which long possessed a virtual monopoly of Mexican education. These social guarantees of the Mexican constitution have influenced constitutional conventions in most of the other countries of Latin America.

AMENDMENT OF THE CONSTITUTION. Amendment of the constitution would seem to be fairly difficult. Every proposed change must have a two-thirds vote in Congress and receive the approval of a majority of the state legislatures. Despite these requirements, however, the fundamental law has been altered over one hundred times since 1917—an average of three amendments a year, as contrasted with one amendment every fourteen years since 1791 in the United States. The president is not supposed to play any part in the amending process, but everyone understands that he and his close advisers are responsible for practically all changes. It may well be wondered how the president can secure the necessary support for so many amendments. The answer is that the one-party system makes

[5] Art. 27.
[6] Art. 3.

opposition almost impossible. The president is head of the party as well as chief of the nation, and when he cracks the party whip his orders are obeyed without delay.

Suffrage and Elections

WHO MAY VOTE. The right to vote in national elections [7] extends to male citizens who have reached the age of eighteen if married, or twenty-one if unmarried. Literacy is not a requirement. The men who framed the constitution of 1917 received a proposal to exclude illiterates from the voting lists but promptly rejected it on the ground that most of the supporters of the Revolution were unable to read and write. Practically every student of the electoral system favors a constitutional amendment restricting the suffrage to literates,[8] but there seems to be little likelihood of its adoption. The movement for woman suffrage has proved much more popular. In 1947 the constitution was amended to permit women to vote in municipal elections, and in 1952 it was changed again to place women on an equal footing with men in all elections.

ELECTION PROCEDURE. The election law of 1918, which remained in force until 1946, was an open invitation to violence. It declared that the first five citizens to arrive at the polls on election day should be the electoral officials. So the strong-armed henchmen of political bosses would appear long before the opening hour—sometimes the night before—and if the agents of other factions were already on the scene, there would be a bloody battle for the control of the polls. In Mexico City, in the 1940 election, the Labor Federation organized its members into battalions, and they made a formidable show of strength as they marched to the polls. Their task was to discourage the opposition and their weapons included not only fists but also guns and hand grenades. Scores of persons were killed in riots before the day was over, and hundreds were wounded.[9] In some cases rival groups set up their own polling places, accepting only the ballots of their supporters. These excesses led to the creation of the 1946 election law, which was adopted in time to control the election of that year. The old system of turning over the polls to the first arrivals was abandoned. Instead, said the law, each polling place should be supervised by an electoral commission composed of representatives of all parties, and the entire elec-

---

[7] The states have their own laws concerning state and municipal elections, but the rules are substantially the same.

[8] See, for example, Felipe Tena Ramírez, *Derecho Constitucional,* pp. 99–102.

[9] See pages 247–248.

tion should be managed by a specially appointed Federal Commission for Supervising Elections.

This new plan undoubtedly eliminated many of the old evils. Enforcement by the army assured relative tranquility. But there were still many defects. Some voters waited in line for hours before they could reach the polling places. Inadequate provisions were made for secrecy, and thousands of persons marked their ballots in full view of their fellow citizens and the election officials. Undoubtedly there were many cases of ballot stuffing. In many precincts the number of votes reported for opposition candidates fell far below the number of voters who openly wore opposition buttons.[10] The provisions of the law specifying multiparty representation on the local election boards proved to be no real assurance of an honest count because all the local officials were named by the P.R.I.-controlled Federal Commission for Supervising Elections. In 1952 the election law was modified in order to remedy these evils. But there is small reason to believe that the P.R.I. has any intention of permitting a serious challenge to its own supremacy. It believes in honest elections only when the people honestly support its candidates.

The President

QUALIFICATIONS AND TENURE. The constitution, like everything else in Mexico, revolves around the president. He is the center of the Mexican solar system. According to the letter of the fundamental law he must be at least thirty-five years of age, a resident of the country for at least one year prior to his election, and not only a native Mexican but also the son of native Mexicans. Members of the clergy are excluded from the presidency, as might well be expected. This prohibition applies also to army officers on active duty, as well as the principal administrative officials of the national government and the governors of the states; persons in these categories who wish to be presidential candidates must resign at least six months prior to election day. The president's term of office, which the constitution of 1917 originally fixed at four years with no re-election, has since been modified several times.[11] Today it is six years, and a second term is not permitted "under any circumstances or for any reason."[12]

METHOD OF SELECTION. The election of the president always follows the

[10] See Stephen S. Goodspeed's previously cited monograph, pp. 356–357. Professor Goodspeed was in Mexico at the time of the 1946 election.

[11] See pages 236–237.

[12] Art. 83.

same pattern. Constitutional and legal provisions declare that he must be chosen by direct vote of the people; in practice he is selected by the outgoing president, and the electors merely ratify this choice. The election is a formality. The official party, the P.R.I., stifles all effective opposition. Six months before a presidential election it holds a formal convention, at which it names its official candidate and adopts a platform. Delegates to the convention are chosen by local conventions. Well in advance of the national convention the leading politicians who have presidential ambitions begin their undercover campaigns, hoping to win the support of influential groups and thus impress the president. When, however, the president finally announces his choice, the delegates to the P.R.I. convention give their approval by acclamation. No other names are presented. There is no contest requiring a number of ballots, such as frequently occurs in party conventions in the United States. The favorite is likely to be a general. He is almost certain to have served as governor of a state.[13] And of course his career must have included a term as cabinet minister, during which time he maintained intimate relations with the president and proved his worthiness to receive the official blessing.

DOMINANCE OF THE OFFICIAL PARTY. In the year before a presidential election there are always a number of prominent politicians seeking the support to the P.R.I. for their presidential ambitions. If, however, they fail to secure the party nomination, they may decide to offer themselves as opposition candidates. But it must be remembered that they are long-time members of the P.R.I. and have built up their political strength within its ranks. When, therefore, they secede from the official party, they must build up their own organizations practically from scratch. The so-called parties thus created at a moment's notice are notoriously inefficient. They cannot match the hierarchy of the P.R.I. in every city and village. They cannot hope to reward their followers with suitable appointments to public office, because they have no reasonable expectation of victory.

Government supporters always find ways to multiply the obstacles along the difficult path of the opposition. Radio stations carrying the words of opposition speakers unaccountably break down. Street cars and buses heading for the meeting places of anti-P.R.I. candidates suddenly develop mechanical difficulties. Public address systems fail to work. Publicity leaflets and posters ordered long in advance are not finished in time. On election day, therefore, ballot box manipulations are scarcely necessary to

---

[13] Avila Camacho was not a state governor, but his brother served as governor for years and built up a powerful political machine.

assure the victory of the P.R.I.   Opposition candidates accept the inevitable
result after charging fraud or perhaps even talking of revolution, and their
party organizations usually disappear from the political scene.   Apparently
the system is unbeatable.

POWERS OF THE PRESIDENT: *Appointment.*   The president of Mexico
possesses broad powers.   He appoints virtually all administrative officers
and employees of the federal government, judges of the supreme court and
certain other federal courts,[14] high-ranking officers [15] of the armed forces,
and members of the diplomatic service.   For some of these appointments
the approval of the Senate is necessary.   This list includes diplomats, supreme court justices, top army officers, and the more important officials of
the Treasury.[16]   Other presidential appointments to judicial positions require the consent of the Chamber of Deputies.   But these restrictions are
not important, for neither house of Congress has ever dared to challenge a
name submitted by the president for its approval.   The overwhelming
majority of appointments to the federal administrative service do not require congressional approval.   The president has unrestricted power to
name his own cabinet secretaries; the heads of departments, bureaus, and
autonomous agencies; and hundreds of others whose work is regarded as
"confidential."   They serve at his pleasure and may be dismissed by him
without any right of appeal.

This broad appointing power enables the president to build up a powerful political machine.   He holds in his hands the political fate of a small
army of government workers—the more important officials and employees,
who direct the activities of the rank and file.   These top men are never
allowed to forget that they owe allegiance directly to the chief executive.
They all belong to the P.R.I., of course, and they form a nucleus of party
strength on which the president can rely at all times.   Minor employees
are protected against arbitrary removal.   Under some circumstances they
may even strike against the government.[17]

Control of foreign relations.   The conduct of foreign affairs is completely in the president's hands.   He decides what Mexico's policies will be
in its relations with other nations, and no one can challenge his judgment
successfully.   Deputies or senators who raise their voices in opposition are
marked for defeat at the next election.   Newspapers that print critical
editorials are likely to be strike-bound.   There is, of course, a secretary of

---

[14] The superior courts of the federal district and the territories.
[15] Colonel and above.
[16] Tena Ramírez, *op. cit.,* p. 407.
[17] See page 245.

foreign affairs who assumes immediate responsibility for the day-to-day routine of the Foreign Office, but to a large extent Mexican presidents take direct control of all important negotiations. Obregón and Calles handled the foreign debt problem personally. Cárdenas made the decision to expropriate the American and British oil properties and carefully supervised the lengthy diplomatic negotiations that followed. The antagonistic attitude of Mexico toward foreign capital during those years was chiefly a reflection of the attitude of President Cárdenas. Later, when Avila Camacho decided to follow a more conciliatory policy, this new attitude became the official viewpoint of the nation.

The constitution provides that treaties negotiated by the chief executive must be submitted to Congress for its approval,[18] but this requirement does not really limit the president's freedom of action. Congress always approves, with a minimum of discussion. It is much easier, of course, to obtain a simple majority in each house of Congress, as specified by the Mexican constitution,[19] than to get the two-thirds Senate majority required by the constitution of the United States. But no one supposes that even a two-thirds clause would seriously handicap the Mexican president. In foreign affairs, as in many other matters, Mexico and its president are indistinguishable.

Introduction and veto of bills. "The legislative power . . . ," declares the constitution, "reposes in a Congress. . . ."[20] Actually most of the legislative power reposes in the president. He possesses the right to introduce bills and uses it freely. Almost all important legislation is prepared and presented to Congress by the president or his principal secretaries. It is then passed by both houses—after extensive debate, perhaps, but almost always without substantial changes. The one-party system has created nearly perfect discipline. So Congress goes through the motions of deliberating the president's suggestions, without ever achieving much more importance than a debating society.

The usual provision is made for the right of presidential veto, following closely the system established in the United States. The president has ten working days in which to decide whether to veto or give his approval; his objections may be overridden by a two-thirds vote in each house of Con-

[18] Art. 89.

[19] The Mexican constitution does not say in so many words that a simple majority is sufficient. It states merely that the president shall make treaties with foreign powers, "submitting them for ratification to the Congress." But this has been interpreted to mean a simple majority.

[20] Art. 50.

gress. But, as in other Latin American countries, there is no pocket veto.[21] The president may veto a bill *in whole or in part*. This power to object to certain sections, without vetoing an entire proposal, might prove very useful to future presidents. To date, however, it has had no significance, because the president does not use his veto power. Measures that would incur presidential displeasure are not enacted by Congress.

Decree-laws. In recent years the laws have given a wide measure of discretion to the administrative departments. This development, which seems to be an almost universal tendency in modern nations, has reduced still further the importance of the legislative branch. Cabinet secretaries and department heads issue the detailed decrees that may be necessary to carry out general statutory provisions. These decrees have the force of law, of course, and in many cases they influence public policy quite as much as the law itself. Sometimes Congress completely abandons its lawmaking power in certain fields for a limited period of time, authorizing the president to act in its stead. The constitution authorizes such an arrangement, but only in times of grave danger to the public welfare, when the constitutional guarantees of individual liberty have been suspended.[22] Despite these restrictions, the presidents of Mexico have requested and received from Congress extraordinary powers covering a wide variety of subjects, or even phrased in such general terms as to bring virtually every aspect of public and private life under presidential control. Sometimes there has been no pretense of grave peril to the nation, and constitutional guarantees have not been suspended, but the special grants of power have been made nonetheless.

The income tax was imposed by executive decree. New codes of civil and criminal procedure were issued. Administrative departments were created, road building programs were carried out, radical changes were made in land reform policies—all without benefit of Congress. Even the annual budgets were issued by executive order. In 1938 the constitution was amended to restrict the practice of legislation by decree, but only four years later Mexico entered the Second World War and found itself face to face with a crisis of the first magnitude. President Avila Camacho appealed for emergency powers and Congress responded by authorizing him to "legislate in all branches of the public administration." In making this sweeping grant Congress imposed only one condition: it should receive annual reports from the President concerning his use of extraordi-

---

[21] For a definition of the term "pocket veto," see page 103.
[22] Arts. 29, 49.

nary powers. Avila Camacho did in fact use his authority sparingly, and relinquished it thirty days after the end of hostilities. Lawmaking by decree, at least in peacetime, seems likely to play a much smaller part in Mexico's future. Some commentators regard this change as an evidence of the nation's political maturity. Others say that it merely reflects the president's omnipotence. He no longer needs to by-pass Congress because Congress is certain to do his bidding.

Other powers. The constitution recognizes the right of the president to pardon persons who have been convicted of federal offenses.[23] Mexican presidents have used this right very freely, especially in political matters. They have been traditionally generous to the small fry involved in revolutions, after making certain of the death of the leaders. The act of pardon does not necessarily remove the stigma of crime; instead it may merely show the president's benevolence. For guilt is a judicial question and has already been determined officially by the courts before a pardon is issued.

As in most Latin American countries, foreigners suspected of illegitimate activities are not always assured a court trial. The constitution authorizes the president to "expel from the territory of the nation, immediately and without judicial process, any foreigner whose presence he may deem inconvenient." [24] This is a far-reaching power, placing every alien in Mexico at the mercy of the chief executive. The constitution establishes no test of a foreigner's undesirability; he may be forced to leave the country merely because of the president's whim. In practice, however, the presidents of Mexico have generally used this authority with restraint. They have expelled only a few foreigners, usually for plotting against the government or interfering with its functions. But when the controversy with the Catholic Church was at its height, a number of priests and even the Apostolic Delegate were deported as "undesirable aliens," though they were native Mexicans born of native parents.[25] Such an "elastic" interpretation of the constitution stretches it virtually beyond recognition.

PRESIDENTIAL SUCCESSION. The Mexican system of government makes no provision for a vice-president. In the early days of Mexican independence there were vice-presidents, but many of them conspired to overthrow the government and seize the presidency for themselves. In 1857, therefore, the office was eliminated. It was restored in 1904, but only for a brief time. Mexican presidents do not look with favor upon any arrangement

---

[23] Art. 89. Offenders against the laws of a state may be pardoned by the state's governor.
[24] Art. 33.
[25] See page 230.

that recognizes an official second-in-command. Some provision must be made, however, for the order of succession to the presidency in case of the chief executive's death, resignation, or disability. The constitution of 1857 placed the chief justice of the supreme court first on the succession list, on the theory that this would keep the matter out of politics. But it had exactly the opposite effect; it dragged the judges into the political mire. During the following quarter of a century three chief justices conspired to foment rebellion and gain the presidency for themselves. So eventually the constitution was amended, eliminating them from the presidential succession.

The present arrangement is complicated and not entirely satisfactory. It establishes two procedures, one to be used if the vacancy occurs during the first two years of the presidential term, and the other, during the last four years. In the first period, Congress sits as an electoral college and chooses, by a two-thirds vote of all its members, an interim president who assumes temporarily the reins of power. But at the earliest possible moment an election must be held so that the voters may name the person who is to fill the unexpired presidential term. Should the vacancy occur during the last four years, however, the substitute president named by Congress rounds out the regular term of office. The people are not consulted. There is always the possibility, of course, that Congress may not be in session when the president dies or resigns. In that case the Permanent Committee of Congress names a provisional president, but he continues in office only until such time as Congress can be called into session and make its own choice.

The grave disadvantage of the entire plan, aside from its complexity, is that it might result in a headless nation in time of crisis. A revolutionary group that had killed the president or forced him to resign might readily prevent the selection of a legitimate successor by dispersing Congress and its Permanent Committee. But this possibility does not greatly disturb Mexicans. They think that more trouble might come from indicating in advance the man who is to succeed to the presidency. He might plot against his chief—a very real possibility, as shown by Mexican history.[26]

National Administration

SECRETARIATS AND DEPARTMENTS. The constitution makes no attempt to fix the number of major administrative departments. It merely declares

---

[26] Tena Ramírez, in his previously cited work, pp. 385–386, develops this argument at some length.

Apparently it is supposed to act as a check on the president. It approves or rejects his nominations to judicial posts and passes upon any proposal that he may make to suspend constitutional guarantees. But these duties are not taken very seriously. The members of the committee, like all the other members of Congress, accept presidential recommendations without criticism or comment. They are not accustomed to challenging the president's leadership. More important is the Permanent Committee's power to name a provisional president if the chief executive should die or resign while Congress is not in session.[34] This situation has never actually occurred since the adoption of the constitution of 1917, but it must be remembered that the life expectancy of Mexican presidents is fairly short. Three of them have been assassinated since the turn of the century.

The Courts .

THE JUDICIAL SYSTEM. The Mexican judicial system reflects the Spanish inheritance, but to some extent it has been influenced by American practice. Court procedure is much the same as in the United States. Witnesses testify and the judge makes notes of what they say. Cross-examination is used regularly. Mexican judges possess greater authority than their American counterparts. They are not merely umpires, enforcing the rules of the game. Instead they have been given sufficient power to guide every trial to a satisfactory result. Juries are no longer used in the federal courts, except in cases involving freedom of the press. Some of the states still retain the jury system for all criminal trials, but the trend is toward its abandonment. There are public defenders, whose salaries are paid by the government, and anyone accused of crime is entitled to their services. Rich people, however, usually hire their own lawyers.

THE WRIT OF *amparo*. An interesting feature of the Mexican system of law is the writ of *amparo* (literally, *protection*), which combines the Anglo-American writ of *habeas corpus* with other court orders.[35] One of its principal purposes is to protect individuals against the abuse of power by public officials. It is a means of enforcing the guarantees of individual liberty set forth at such length in the constitution. Any person who thinks that his rights have been violated—that he has been denied the freedom of conscience, for example, or fined for performing an act not prohibited by law—may go to the courts and request a writ of *amparo*

[34] See page 265.
[35] Chiefly the writs of *mandamus* and *certiorari*.

protecting him from these allegedly illegal acts of the public authorities. The courts will examine the facts and issue the writ if they agree that some constitutional right has been violated. The writ may be directed to the secretary of education, for example, directing him to reinstate a teacher who has been dismissed; or it may command some state or local official, such as a tax collector, to abandon his efforts to collect a tax regarded by the courts as unconstitutional. The writ of *amparo* has another main purpose, also: to maintain the balance of power between the nation and the states. It is the means by which the courts set aside state laws invading the sphere of federal authority or federal statutes interfering with the powers of the states. In practice, the courts take much greater care to protect the authority of the nation than to prevent infringement of the powers of the states. Perhaps this is because the state courts are not permitted to issue the writ of *amparo*. It is exclusively a federal writ.[36]

ORGANIZATION OF THE FEDERAL COURTS. The federal supreme court has twenty-one regular members and five substitutes, all appointed by the president with Senate approval. The judges of the court are assigned to its four main divisions—criminal, civil, administrative, and labor—corresponding to the principal branches of Mexican law. Five judges serve in each division, and the twenty-first man, the chief justice, or *president,* as he is called, supervises the work of all the divisions and directs the details of the court's administration. He presides over the court when it meets in full session to handle general business, such as the adoption of rules of procedure or the determination of a major controversy. The president of the court is designated by its own members, and normally serves for but one year, though he may be re-elected.

Originally the 1917 constitution provided life tenure for judges of the supreme court, but in 1934, at the insistence of President Cárdenas, the term was reduced to six years. Life tenure, said the President in defending this change, would tend to make judges too conservative. What he really meant, of course, was that it might remove them from presidential control. With terms fixed at six years—exactly the same as that of the chief executive—each new president could name his own supreme court. This arrangement continued until 1944, when Avila Camacho sponsored another constitutional amendment which restored the life tenure of the supreme court justices. Perhaps there will be no further assaults on

[36] Mexican scholars have made a number of valuable studies of the law of *amparo*. See Agustín Farrera's *El Juicio de Amparo*. See also the monograph by Romeo León Orantes, which bears the same title.

judicial independence. There is, in fact, no reason for such interference, because the supreme court never challenges the major policies of the chief executive. So consistently does it follow his lead that some Mexican writers even deny the existence of a co-ordinate judicial power.[37]

The constitution establishes qualifications for justices of the supreme court.[38] It also establishes the supreme court's jurisdiction, which is similar to that of the highest tribunal of the United States.[39] Below the supreme court are eleven circuit tribunals. Six of these courts hear almost all classes of cases on appeal; the remaining five have jurisdiction in cases of *amparo*. At the lowest level are forty-two district courts. The judges of both the circuit and district courts are appointed by the supreme court. Any federal judge may be removed for cause by the vote of an absolute majority in each house of Congress, after presentation of charges by the president of the nation. The jurisdiction of the federal courts extends to controversies involving the nation or the states, federal laws or treaties, federal officials or foreign diplomats, or citizens of different states.[40] Other suits, of course, are handled by the state courts.

Federal-State Relations

The official title of the Mexican nation is The United States of Mexico. It is declared to be a federal republic, comprising twenty-eight states, the federal district, and three territories.[41] During the colonial era the Spanish crown instituted a highly centralized system of government, and Mexicans came to associate such a system with despotism. When, therefore, they had the opportunity to govern themselves, they turned naturally to federalism as a protection against the encroachments of a too-powerful central government. Federalism was a basic feature of the constitution of 1824. It was abandoned temporarily in 1835, and again in 1853, but since 1857 it has been accepted without question. The framers of the constitution of 1917 did not even debate the issue.

PARTY CONTROL OF STATE OFFICIALS. There is considerable doubt, however, whether Mexico's so-called federalism really deserves its name. The

---

[37] See, for example, Salvador Azuela's *Derecho Constitucional,* p. 213.

[38] Art. 95. The justices must be native Mexicans, not less than thirty-five or more than sixty-five years old at the time of their appointment, residents of Mexico for the preceding five years (unless absent on affairs of state, and then for a period not to exceed six months), lawyers of at least five years' standing, and not convicted of crime.

[39] Art. 105.

[40] Art. 103.

[41] Arts. 40 and 43.

term *federalism* implies not only a clear-cut constitutional apportionment of powers between the nation and the states, but also a scheme of government that prevents—or at least deters—any substantial modification of this apportionment without the consent of both the nation and the states. If the national government may expand its own authority virtually at will, forcing or cajoling the states into submission whenever a dispute occurs, then the essential element of federalism seems to be lacking. And that is the situation in Mexico. The one-party system is a very useful device for keeping state officials in line. Almost invariably they must be loyal members of the P.R.I. to win election. After taking office they must obey the orders to the party chief—in other words, the president of the nation—in order to remain party members in good standing. Should they ever forget this elementary rule, the party can speedily bring their political careers to a close.

INTERVENTION. There is another and even more drastic way of dealing with state governors or other officials who refuse to take orders from Mexico City. The central government may declare that all the "constitutional powers" of a state have "disappeared"—in other words, that the state does not have a governor, legislators, and other officials—and may then use the army or other means to remove those persons who claim to be the governor and the legislators (but who really are imposters, says the central government, because they have been fraudulently elected or have failed in some other way to meet the requirements of the law). The distinction between a state officer and an impostor is not always clear-cut. One day a governor may exercise all the prerogatives of his office, including the right to ignore presidential "suggestions"; the next day he may discover that he is no longer governor because it has been decided at the national capital that the constitutional powers of the state have disappeared. Under such circumstances a provisional governor is appointed, and he promptly calls for "elections to be held according to the constitution and the law of the said state." [42] These elections are supervised closely by the national government, of course, and if by some strange chance the preceding election resulted in victory for a candidate who was critical of presidential policies, such an accident will not be permitted to happen again.

The formal decision to intervene in the affairs of a state is made by the Senate, and not the president. The constitution says so in very explicit terms. But the Senate does not act on its own initiative. Instead it waits

[42] Art. 76.

for a presidential recommendation. The secretary of government represents the president in such matters. He observes political conditions in the states, and sets in motion the machinery of intervention whenever such drastic action seems necessary.

Intervention sometimes follows a disputed election. The state legislature, performing its constitutional function of tabulating and announcing the vote for governor, may be guided by partisanship instead of arithmetic. So another group of men, claiming to be the legislature because an honest count would have resulted in their election, may meet and declare that their candidate is really the governor. The federal secretary of government usually decides the issue, thus making and breaking political fortunes. Occasionally, however, the disappointed faction may refuse to accept the secretary's decision. So he submits the case, with all relevant documents, to the Senate, and that body promptly declares the disappearance of the state's constitutional powers and the appointment of a provisional governor from a list of three names submitted by the president.

In 1935, after President Cárdenas had broken with Calles, he secured the removal of all the state governors who were known Calles sympathizers. In every one of these states the Senate obediently discovered that constitutional powers had disappeared, and Cárdenas then called on the army to correct the situation. It is not difficult to understand why state officials are subservient to the president. He holds their political careers in his hands.[43]

State and Local Government

PRINCIPAL FEATURES OF STATE GOVERNMENT. Many features of state government are prescribed by the national constitution. It declares that the governor must be Mexican by birth, a native of the state or a resident for at least five years, chosen directly by the people for a term of six years or less, and not eligible to immediate re-election. As to the legislature, the constitution specifies that its members shall be chosen by direct popular vote and may not serve two consecutive terms. The size of the legislature varies with the population of the state, in accordance with a formula fixed by the federal constitution, but the absolute minimum is seven members.[44] Aside from these specific requirements and the general admonition that

[43] See J. Lloyd Mecham's article, "Mexican Federalism—Fact or Fiction?" in the March, 1940, issue of the *Annals of the American Academy of Political and Social Science,* pp. 23–38.
[44] Art. 115.

state regimes must be "popular, representative, republican," each state is free to adopt such a scheme of government as it may desire. There is, however, considerably less diversity among the Mexican states than among the states of the American Union. The governor of a Mexican state is the president in miniature—the head of the local political machine and absolute master of the government. He controls the administration, bullies or cajoles the legislature into submission, and obtains the subservience of the courts.

State legislatures are unicameral bodies, ranging in size from the constitutional minimum of seven to a maximum of thirty-two. Two-year terms are most common, though a number of states have adopted terms of four years. State legislators must be native Mexicans and, as a rule, at least twenty-five years old. The legislative procedure is much the same as in Congress. Judges of the state courts are chosen in a variety of ways— by the governor, the legislature, or direct vote of the people. Judicial terms are relatively short. The powers reserved to the states are fewer and less important than in the United States. Under the terms of the Mexican constitution the nation is given exclusive or concurrent authority over mining, commerce (not just interstate commerce), health, education, religious worship, the production and distribution of electric light and power, and the motion picture industry.[45]

MUNICIPAL GOVERNMENT. The framers of the 1917 constitution took occasion to expound at some length their philosophy of municipal government. They directed the states to adopt the principle of the "free city," including the following points: direct popular election of municipal officials, no immediate re-election, municipal administration of local revenues "derived from the taxes fixed by the state legislature," and corporate existence for cities—in other words, the right to sue and be sued.[46] Of course there was no intention to create municipalities that would be "free" in the sense that they would escape all state supervision and control. Apparently no one thought of granting even municipal home rule, as in some parts of the United States. The cities were to continue as civil subdivisions of their respective states. They were to be governed by state law, as they had always been. Even their right to administer their own revenues was largely nullified by the statement that these revenues should be "derived from taxes fixed by the state legislature." An American city would think that it had been placed in a legal strait jacket if it were not per-

45 Art. 73.
46 Art. 115.

mitted to fix its own tax rate. But to most Mexicans the constitution's limited promise of local self-government doubtless seemed like real freedom for the cities. It was much more generous than any policy previously adopted for municipal government in four centuries of colonial rule and independence. Even today, however, these guarantees of limited autonomy are frequently ignored by the state governments. Some state constitutions authorize the governor to suspend or even repeal the acts of municipal councils, or to suspend or remove the councilmen. Two states [47] have made provision for interventors representing the governor and charged with the responsibility of passing upon local legislation. In nearly half of the states municipal councils may be abolished by a simple stroke of the governor's pen.[48]

There is practically no variation in the organization of municipal government, except for the nation's capital and its suburbs. All other cities have been cut to the same legal pattern. The popularly chosen council enacts the necessary ordinances concerning local affairs; passes upon the acts of the mayor, or municipal president, as he is called; and, through a committee, audits the city's accounts. Only in one state [49] are local budgets locally prepared. The municipal president—elected by the voters, of course, in accordance with the terms of the constitution—assumes responsibility for the local administration. He appoints and removes the heads of the administrative departments. In every state capital, however, the local police chief is responsible to the governor of the state instead of the municipal president. Public administration is not highly developed in Mexican municipalities. It must be remembered that the average Mexican "city" is in reality only a small village. Not more than twenty cities in all Mexico have populations in excess of fifty thousand.

The federal district. Mexico City has always been the great metropolis of the nation. Even in Aztec days it was the capital, and the Spaniards saw no reason to change this arrangement. So all through the colonial period, and into the era of independence, Mexico City remained the center of government as well as the center of culture. Its city council (*cabildo*) was able to exert strong pressure on the colonial viceroys, even though they were the masters of Mexico. When, therefore, in the first days of freedom from Spanish rule, a conflict arose between the authorities of the newly created state of Mexico (of which Mexico City was the heart) and

---

[47] Puebla and San Luis Potosí.

[48] See Salvador González Lobo's excellent study, *El Municipio Mexicano: Antecedentes, Naturaleza, Funciones.*

[49] Sinaloa.

the national government, the nation settled the matter by placing the city in a federal district, whose boundaries were to extend two leagues in every direction from the *Zócalo,* or main plaza. That was in 1824. Later this area was expanded to include twelve small municipalities in addition to the national capital. It now comprises five hundred and seventy-three square miles, making it eight times as large as the District of Columbia.

Over this territory the federal government exercises direct control. The residents of the district have representation in both houses of Congress, but they have no direct voice in their local government. The municipal council, which functioned more or less regularly for four centuries, was abolished in 1928, and a Department of the Federal District was established as one of the major departments of the national administration. The chief of this department is appointed by the president, of course, and serves at his pleasure. He is a member of the president's cabinet. Complete responsibility for all details of the municipal administration vests in the department chief, subject to presidential approval. He manages the public services, directs the construction and maintenance of public works, and supervises the local finances. He issues decrees interpreting and enforcing the laws. The lawmaking body of the federal district is the Congress of the nation. There is also a consultative council, composed of representatives of professional, business, and labor organizations—the Chamber of Commerce, the Association of Small Businessmen, the Landlords' Union, the Association of Tenants, the Union of Professional Men, the groups of workers and farmers and government employees. Even the working women are separately represented. This consultative council has no authority; it merely advises the chief of the district, who is free to accept or reject its suggestions.

The twelve smaller municipalities of the federal district, surrounding Mexico City, used to have their own municipal councils. Now they are merely administrative units. Each of them is headed by a *delegate,* so called because he is the direct representative of the chief of the district, who exercises only such authority as that officer may delegate to him. The delegates are appointed by the district chief, with presidential approval. Within the district Congress has created an elaborate judicial organization, headed by a court of twenty-five members whose imposing title is *Superior Tribunal of Justice of the Federal District.*[50]

---

[50] For a more detailed discussion of the organization and work of the federal district, see the previously cited volume by Lucio Mendieta y Núñez, pp. 127–145. See also *El Gobierno Mexicano,* by José Mijares Palencia, pp. 247–257.

SELECTED REFERENCES

Aguilar Aguilar, Jorge, *El Municipio Libre*, Mexico, D.F., 1946.

Albertos Betancourt, Paúl, *Estudio al Artículo 29 de la Constitución General de la República*, Mexico, D.F., Facultad de Derecho, 1948.

Baltierra Rivera, Leonardo, *Breve Análisis de Evolución Constitucional de México*, Mexico, D.F., Facultad de Derecho y Ciencias Sociales de la Universidad Nacional Autónoma, 1945.

Barrera Fuentes, Florencio, *Historia y Destino del Municipio en México*, Mexico, D.F., Escuela Nacional de Jurisprudencia, 1950.

Castellanos Tena, Fernando, *Nuestras Constituciones*, Mexico, D.F., Facultad de Derecho y Ciencias Sociales de la Universidad Nacional Autónoma, 1944.

Córdoba Ladrón de Guevara, Darío, *Breves Consideraciones sobre el Estado Federal Mexicano*, Mexico, D.F., Facultad de Derecho, 1948.

Farrera, Agustín, *El Juicio de Amparo*, Mexico, D.F., Publicaciones Farrera, 1942.

Fraga, Gambino, *Derecho Administrativo*, 3rd ed., Mexico, D.F., Editorial Porrúa, 1944.

Fuentes Galindo, Fernando, *Organización Constitucional del Distrito Federal*, Mexico, D.F., Facultad de Derecho, 1948.

González Lobo, Salvador, *El Municipio Mexicano*, Mexico, D.F., Escuela Nacional de Jurisprudencia, 1940.

González Torres, Alfonso, *Jurisprudencia Inconstitucional*, Mexico, D.F., Escuela Nacional de Jurisprudencia, 1942.

Hermida Zamudio, Lorenzo, *Democratización del Gobierno Municipal*, Mexico, D.F., Facultad de Derecho, 1949.

Hernández Rodríguez, José, *El Refrendo en el Derecho Mexicano*, Mexico, D.F., Escuela Nacional de Jurisprudencia, 1944.

Herrera Guerrero, Héctor V., *La División de Poderes en la Constitución de 1917*, Mexico, D.F., 1946.

Junco, María Elena, *Irreformabilidad de las Decisiones Políticas Fundamentales de la Constitución*, Mexico, D.F., Escuela Nacional de Jurisprudencia, 1942.

León Gutiérrez, Hugo, *Las Decisiones Políticas Fundamentales en la Constitución Mexicana*, Mexico, D.F., Escuela Nacional de Jurisprudencia, 1944.

López Cárdenas, Fernando, *Compendio de Derecho Constitucional Mexicano*, Mexico, D.F., 1947.

López Moreno, Miguel, *Reformas a la Constitución: La Interpretación del Artículo 135*, Mexico, D.F., Facultad de Derecho, 1949.

Loredo Casteñada, Emma, *El Senado en la Teoría del Estado Federal*, Mexico, D.F., Facultad de Derecho, 1950.

Mendieta y Núñez, Lucio, *La Administración Pública en México*, Mexico, D.F., 1942.

Morales Elizondo, Oscar, *El Principio de la División de Poderes*, Mexico, D.F., Escuela Nacional de Jurisprudencia, 1945.

Moreno, Daniel A., *El Distrito Federal*, Mexico, D.F., Facultad Nacional de Jurisprudencia, 1944.

Muriel de la Maza, Ignacio, *El Municipio en México: Naturaleza y Historia*, Mexico, D.F., Facultad de Derecho, 1948.

Oceguera Ochoa, José María, *La Presidencia de la Cámara*, Mexico, D.F., Facultad de Derecho y Ciencias Sociales de la Universidad Nacional Autónoma, 1945.

Ortiz Cabrera, Jorge, *El Veto en Materia Constitucional*, Mexico, D.F., Editorial Bolívar, 1949.

Robledo Dávila, Francisco, *Necesidad de Reformar el Tribunal de Menores*, Mexico, D.F., Facultad Nacional de Jurisprudencia, 1945.

Santillan Ortiz, Lamberto, *El Sistema de Control Constitucional en México y en los Estados Unidos del Norte*, Facultad de Derecho, Mexico, D.F., 1944.

Tena Ramírez, Felipe, *Derecho Constitucional Mexicano*, Editorial Porrúa, Mexico, D.F., 1944.

Trevino Rodríguez, Francisco, *Los Derechos del Hombre y las Garantías Sociales*, Mexico, D.F., Facultad de Derecho, 1948.

Vallejo y Arizmendi, Jorge, *Estudios de Derecho Constitucional Mexicano*, Mexico, D.F., Editorial Stylo, 1947.

Vega Hernández, Jaime, *La Sucesión Presidencial en México*, Mexico, D.F., Facultad de Derecho, 1949.

Vera Guillén, Guillermo, *Situación Jurídica-Política de los Estados Miembros*, Mexico, D.F., Facultad de Derecho y Ciencias Sociales de la Universidad Nacional Autónoma, 1942.

Villa González, León, *El Principio de la División de Poderes en Nuestras Constituciones*, Mexico, D.F., Mijares y Hno., 1942.

Whetten, Nathan L., *Rural Mexico*, Chicago, Univ. of Chicago Press, 1948.

CHAPTER 12

CHILE
Turbulent Democracy

The Land and the People

THERE is a saying in Chile that God must be Argentine. And indeed it does almost seem that the Almighty has conspired with the Argentines to push the Chileans into the sea. For the Andes, which form the natural boundary between the two nations, lie along the extreme western edge of the continent, giving Chile great length and almost no width. It stretches along the shore of the Pacific for twenty-six hundred miles—practically the same distance as from New York to San Francisco—yet its average width is only a little more than one hundred miles, and in the far south it narrows down to about thirty miles at one point. So the Chileans have an extremely long coastline to defend and great natural handicaps if they seriously try to defend it. They have fought a number of foreign wars, however, with uniformly successful results.

DOMINANCE OF THE CENTRAL VALLEY. Chile has six million inhabitants, more than four million of whom live in the rich Central Valley, which is only about six hundred miles long. This valley lies between the great cordillera of the Andes and a low coastal range. In most places it is no more than twenty-five miles wide. But it is one of the world's richest agricultural regions. It is favored with good soil and a magnificent climate. The northern end of the valley, which lies just north of the geographical center of Chile, is especially fortunate. Its climate resembles that of northern California, and its vegetation is much the same. Irrigation is necessary during the long months of the dry season, but the snow-clad Andes are close at hand. Even the Indians of the valley irrigated their

283

land in the days before white men ever came to the New World. The southern portion of the Central Valley is colder and rainier, but not at all unpleasant. There are, in fact, few parts of the world that possess greater natural charm than the Central Valley of Chile. When Pedro de Valdivia first saw it, in 1540, he exclaimed: "It is truly a valley of Paradise!" Chile's chief seaport is still called Valley of Paradise (Valparaíso).

Crops and livestock. Within the Central Valley are grown most of the temperate zone cereals, but wheat is by far the most important. The climate is ideal for fruits, berries, and melons. Grapes play an important part in the national economy, and Chilean wines are famous throughout the world. There is not much of a cattle industry, though it could be developed without difficulty. In fact, one of the most surprising aspects of Chilean life is the nation's failure to feed itself in normal years. Cattle are regularly imported from Argentina. Even wheat, which is usually exported, must sometimes be bought abroad. The Chilean people, most of whom suffer from malnutrition, do not get enough milk or fruit, though they live in a land where these products could be produced with the greatest ease.

The land system. The basic reason for this unfortunate state of affairs seems to be the land system. Chile is a country of great estates. Nearly two thirds of the nation's farming land is in the hands of one half of one per cent of the people. Most of the remainder is owned by men of considerable wealth—the lesser aristocracy. Big and little aristocrats are powerful politically, and they have combined to perpetuate their virtual monopoly of Chile's agricultural resources. Most of them live in the larger cities, where they can escape the isolation of their great ranches. So the ranches are supervised by paid managers. The average ranch owner asks only a comfortable living for himself and his family. The ranch manager asks only a good salary paid at regular intervals. Very few persons really care whether the ranches are producing their maximum yield. Very few persons take the trouble to inquire. So thousands of acres of fertile land lie fallow every year, while larger quantities of foodstuffs are urgently required. Primitive methods of cultivation are still widely used, despite the obvious advantages of modern techniques. But tractors, threshing machines, and silos are becoming more numerous. Perhaps in time the rich landowners will become more generally interested in scientific farming.

Tenant farmers. Meanwhile the government is making a serious effort to get land into the hands of small farmers. An Agricultural Colonization

Institute, established twenty years ago, has been buying up any great estates offered for sale and has also been dividing government-owned land among the landless. But very few estates are offered for sale, and very little government-owned land is suitable for agriculture. So most of the agricultural workers are *inquilinos* or tenants on the big ranches. Legally they are free to leave whenever they desire, but practically the difficulties are very great. Each tenant has his little home, which shelters his family. It may be, and probably is, a home of unplastered adobe, without modern sanitary facilities and possibly without even a tile floor. But it is home, and not easily replaced. The wages are unbelievably low, yet there are other compensations—two meals a day, a school for the children, a chapel and a visiting priest for all the family, and perhaps an opportunity for the industrious tenant to work another plot of ground on shares with his *patrón*. It is a hard life, and some workers do break away. But most of them are found on the very estates where their fathers and grandfathers lived in other times.[1]

INDUSTRIALIZATION. The Chilean economy has experienced a great change, however, within the last three decades. While farm life continues at its leisurely pace, relatively untouched by modern technology, industrial development has made great strides. Today nearly one third of the workers are engaged in manufacturing. Most of the factories are small, and many of them are merely processing plants for the country's agricultural products. But Chile can now boast of some steel mills, paint and glass factories, and plants for the manufacture of glass, cement, porcelain fixtures, and plastics. The Industrial Revolution has come at last, and Chileans are determined to expand its influence. A Production Development Corporation has been created and charged with the task of "increasing the standard of living of the Chilean people by utilizing the natural resources of the country and lowering production costs." This corporation, whose board of directors includes representatives of government, industry, and labor, has been compared to the Tennessee Valley Authority. It has purchased the securities of some private enterprises and made loans to others. Behind a high protective tariff wall it is trying to make Chile less dependent on other countries for its industrial needs. In time it may have a reasonable measure of success. There are large quantities of readily available high-grade iron ore, and important coal deposits.[2]

[1] For a good account of life on the great ranches of the Central Valley, see George M. McBride's *Chile, Land and Society*.

[2] See Paul T. Ellsworth's *Chile: An Economy in Transition*. See also Gilbert J. Butland's *Chile: An Outline of Its Geography, Economics and Politics*.

PRINCIPAL CITIES. Chile's principal cities are in or near the Central Valley, of course. Santiago, the capital, has a population of one million. It is a curious and charming blending of the very old and the very new. Narrow, dark streets parallel broad, sun-drenched boulevards. Modern office buildings and apartment hotels are only a stone's throw from the elegant mansions of other centuries. Santiago has become a modern metropolis without abandoning its colonial heritage. It is by all odds the nation's largest city. Next in size, but only one fourth as large, is Valparaíso, which is Santiago's seaport, and the principal port of South America's west coast. It lies one hundred and fifteen miles northwest of the capital, and the two cities are connected by railroad and by an excellent highway. Just north of Valparaíso—practically a suburb—is the internationally famous beach resort, Viña del Mar (literally, vineyard of the sea). There are excellent hotels, private homes ranging from modest to magnificent, and a gambling casino which boasts of such standard attractions as cabaret, dinner-dancing, baccarat, and roulette. Because the summer months are cool and practically rainless in Viña del Mar, thousands of persons from other parts of Chile and from neighboring countries have made it a favorite vacation spot. The Argentines especially come in large numbers to escape the heat of Buenos Aires or Rosario, and usually secure the finest homes. Chileans make them welcome, secretly curse their arrogance, and advertise extensively in Argentina to insure their return the following summer.[3]

THE NORTHERN DESERT: *Nitrates*. Beyond the Central Valley, to the north, stretches the vast Atacama Desert, one of the world's most inhospitable regions. Rain is virtually unknown, so there is no vegetation. There is, however, a great natural source of wealth—the nitrate beds that once formed the basis of Chilean economy and paid more than two thirds of the cost of the nation's government. The early Spaniards knew of these nitrate deposits and attempted to use them in the manufacture of gunpowder, but without much success. In fact, it was not until the nineteenth century that someone conceived the idea of selling the nitrates for fertilizer. Not until 1880 could Chile put this idea into practice, because most of the nitrate beds were in Bolivian or Peruvian territory. But Chile defeated Bolivia and Peru in the War of the Pacific and took the nitrate lands as an indemnity.

Within a few years nitrates became Chile's greatest export and a seemingly endless source of wealth. Other countries could furnish no real competition, because Chile held the only known large deposits in the world. The heavy export tax on every barrel of nitrates paid the costs of government and enabled the large landowners to escape taxation almost completely. But the Chilean monopoly was broken at last by a German

Santiago, Chile, taken from Santa Lucia Hill. In the foreground is the Catholic University.
(Photo, Courtesy Grace Line)

chemist named Fritz Haber, who discovered a cheap process for transforming the nitrogen of the air into artificial nitrates. For Chile the result was catastrophic. In 1910 it had supplied two thirds of the world's nitrates; by 1920 it was supplying less than one third. In the year 1932, when the world depression was at its worst, Chile furnished only one twenty-fifth of the world's nitrate supply. By 1938 the Chilean nitrate industry had recovered somewhat, and it made additional gains during the Second World War, when great quantities were used in the manufacture of munitions. But every one understands that Chile can no longer hope to dominate the world nitrate market. If, indeed, it is to sell substantial quantities of its nitrates, it must be prepared to cut the price below the cost of artificial production in other countries. The truth of the matter, however unpalatable it may be from Chile's viewpoint, is that almost any nation can now make its own nitrates or buy them cheaply.

Copper. The northern desert yields a number of other valuable products—copper, iodine (which is a by-product of the nitrate industry), iron, gold, silver, manganese, zinc, and a wide variety of other metals. Copper is by far the most important. It represents more than half of the total value of the nation's exports. Nearly all Chilean copper comes from the mines of three American-owned companies, and two of these companies operate in the desert. They have been forced to overcome serious handicaps in getting out the copper, for the mines are located in very unfavorable territory. No water is available, either for drinking or industrial purposes, unless it is brought long distances. No fuel is at hand. Since there are no trees, there is no timber. All food must be brought from the outside, at great expense. Yet the copper companies have created a number of model mining towns. Living quarters for the workers are better than in other parts of Chile, and of course wages are higher, as they must be to keep men on the job. Good schools and medical facilities are provided. For salaried employees there are tennis courts and football gridirons. The Chilean government approves these progressive steps, of course, but it still looks askance at the foreign mine owners who are reaping a rich reward from Chilean natural resources, despite tax payments representing one third of their net profits. Some Chileans talk of outright confiscation, but the suggestion has not yet received serious consideration.

THE SOUTHERN FORESTLAND. Below the Central Valley, and extending almost to the very tip of the continent, is a land of heavy rain and dense forests, where cold and wet combine to discourage all but the hardiest settlers. An important lumber industry has been established, however, and could be made even more important if transportation facilities were better. In the far south are great sheep ranches. Pasture land is cheap, and the climate is cold enough to produce heavy fleece. But the most important asset of Chile's southern region may be its natural beauty. The territory just south of the Central Valley, and close to the Argentine border, is one of the world's most spectacular beauty spots. It is often called the Switzerland of America—a hackneyed phrase, to be sure, but suggestive of the scenic splendor that awaits the large annual crop of

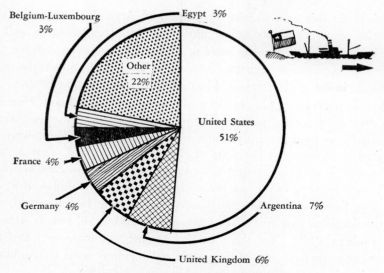

Chilean Exports to Principal Countries (1951)

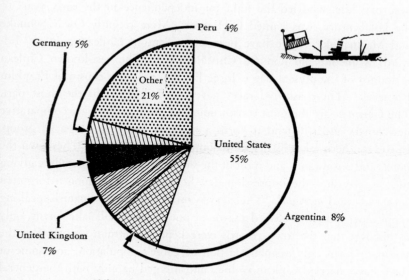

Chilean Imports from Principal Countries (1951)

Based on information obtained from the May, 1953, issue of *International Financial Statistics,* a publication of the International Monetary Fund.

tourists. In this area and in the portion of Argentina just across the frontier are virgin forests and mighty snow-capped volcanoes, as well as placid lakes that reflect the majesty of their surroundings. Some experienced travelers say that the Chilean lake Todos los Santos is the most beautiful in the world. It would be difficult to contradict them.[4]

RACIAL MIXTURE. Chile, unlike most of the nations of Latin America, lies principally within the Temperate Zone. It is one of the few whose population is predominantly white. The Araucanian Indians, who inhabited the country at the time of the Spanish conquest, were savage fighters and not easily conquered. As a result there was comparatively little intermingling of the two races. In the 1870s, when Buffalo Bill was battling the Sioux and General Custer was making his last stand, the Arucanians also were still offering savage resistance in the remote sections of southern Chile. Yet there has been some intermarriage. Perhaps fifteen or twenty per cent of the people of Chile have some Indian blood in their veins. There are almost no Negroes.

Among the whites, Spanish blood predominates, but there is a liberal sprinkling of Italians, French, Germans, English, Irish. The national hero of Chile, who led the fight for independence in the early years of the last century, was named O'Higgins. More recently Oscar Schnake and Marmaduke Grove have been prominent in Chilean politics. Edwards is an old and honored Chilean name. The best-known Chilean cartoonist of the present day is Jorge Délano, a distant cousin of Franklin Roosevelt. These assorted races have blended well, for the most part. The Germans are the most conspicuous exception. They are comparative newcomers and still tend to form a more or less compact racial group. In the southern lake district they dominate certain areas. They own the hotels and restaurants, and most of the shops, in this tourist paradise, giving the casual visitor the impression that he has stumbled upon a forgotten corner of the *Vaterland*. The story is often told of the Spanish-speaking shopkeeper who was elected mayor of one of the small lake towns, only to discover that the town records were kept in German script! But the Germans form only a small fraction of Chile's population, and some of them have married Chilean women and merged happily with the general population. For Chile the German problem is not serious.

THE PROBLEM OF POVERTY. Much more serious, however, is the problem of poverty. The overwhelming majority of Chileans are grindingly, in-

---

[4] See E. J. Sellers' article, *"In Southern Chile,"* in the March, 1947, issue of the *Bulletin of the Pan American Union*, pp. 140–141.

tolerably poor. They work for miserable wages, and spend at least three fourths of what they make on the food necessary for a bare existence. Conditions are bad enough on the farms, but in some of the cities they are even worse. The slums of Santiago and Valparaíso are notorious for their overcrowding and unsanitary conditions. So it is not at all surprising that the nation has one of the highest death rates in the world. Part of the blame for Chile's poverty can be laid at the door of the large landowners, because they are not more interested in increasing the productivity of their estates. Some of the responsibility must be accepted by the foreign mining interests who systematically take from the country every year a considerable part of its natural wealth. Even the masses of the people are partly at fault. They have inherited the Spanish tradition that manual labor is degrading, and thousands of them—members of the so-called white collar class—even scorn positions in stores as below their dignity. They prefer political sinecures, regardless of the small pay involved. But the basic causes of Chilean poverty are two: scarcity of arable land, and excessive dependence on exports of copper and nitrates. Perhaps the rapid growth of industry will prove a major factor in raising the standard of living.[5]

LABOR STRENGTH. Labor unions are strong in Chile. With the encouragement of the government they have greatly expanded their membership in recent years, and have succeeded in enrolling at least fifty per cent of the industrial workers and more than eighty per cent of the miners. Attempts are even being made to unionize the farm workers, though with relatively little success to date. Strikes are fairly frequent, and sometimes paralyze large sections of Chilean industry. Communists have managed to seize control of some of the labor unions, though they are definitely in a minority.

RELATIONS WITH FOREIGN POWERS. Chile's relations with the United States are friendly, but scarcely intimate. After all, the United States is thousands of miles away, and Argentina is just across a long frontier. So the Chileans know that they must be friendly with Argentina. They have frequently followed Argentina's lead, especially in international affairs. In January, 1942, when the foreign ministers of the American republics met in Rio de Janeiro to plan joint action against Axis aggression, Chile supported Argentina's refusal to break diplomatic relations with Germany and Japan. In fact, it did not sever relations with these nations until 1943, just a few months before Argentina was finally forced into

[5] See *Hambre, Miseria e Ignorancia*, by Enrique Zañartu Prieto.

line. When the two countries finally declared war on the Axis powers in 1945, they did so barely in time to become eligible for membership in the United Nations organization that was being created in San Francisco. In 1953 Chile and Argentina signed a comprehensive trade agreement.

It must not be assumed, however, that the Chileans are pliant tools in the hands of Argentina's Perón. On the contrary, they are staunchly democratic. Even President Ibáñez, who has gone much further than most of his countrymen in defending Perón's policies and displaying friendship for the Argentine dictator, is intensely jealous of his nation's honor. But virtually all Chileans remember the fundamental fact that the two nations are close neighbors, whether or not they like the relationship. They do not overlook Argentina's superior economic and military might And they wisely conclude that friendship with Argentina is the better part of valor.

The Rise of Democracy

THE GOVERNING CASTE. The political history of modern Chile really begins in the year 1920, with the election to the presidency of a "man of the people" named Arturo Alessandri. Until that time, nobody in high public office had ever seriously attempted to represent the underprivileged masses. There were, of course, a number of political groups calling themselves "liberal" and "radical," and several parties had combined to form a Liberal Alliance. But both the Conservatives and Liberals represented the same social class, and shared the same economic doctrines. Both owed allegiance to the large landowners—the governing caste that had ruled Chile ever since the early days of independence. This caste had come to regard itself as a God-chosen elite. It blandly assumed that its interests were identical with the interests of the nation. And for many years the masses of the people tended to acquiesce in this point of view. They were unlettered, unambitious, and leaderless. If, indeed, they did produce a man of outstanding genius, the rich were likely to recognize his ability and make him one of themselves.

Manuel Montt, who died in 1880, was such a man. Though born of poor parents, he displayed such talents that he was given the opportunity to study in the National Institute, and was made its rector at the unbelievable age of twenty-six. Five years later he was president of the Chamber of Deputies, and shortly after his forty-second birthday he was elected president of the nation. That was in 1851. He served for two terms totaling ten years, and he strengthened the nation at home and abroad, but never for an instant did he forget his obligation to the landed aristocracy. Through him they ruled the nation. Other men succeeded Montt—some good and some bad—but the story was always the same. The rich were in the saddle, and they meant to stay there.

PARTISANSHIP. It must not be supposed, in spite of the continued dominance of the landed aristocracy, that politics was largely a lost art. The various parties and coalitions worked quite as hard to win elections as if fundamental principles had been at stake. They were determined to gain for themselves the spoils of victory, and they used every artifice in the professional politician's bag of tricks, including large-scale fraud. Bribery eventually became so commonplace that the voters looked with indignation upon any candidate who failed to offer them money. And yet the forms of constitutional government were observed far more scrupulously than in most of the nations of Latin America. Chileans were beginning to understand and appreciate the real meaning of orderly government. Candidates might bribe and cheat, but not often would they try to nullify an election through the use of armed force. The official winner could be reasonably certain of taking office. There were, of course, some exceptions to this general rule. In 1851 and 1859, and again in 1891, there were brief civil wars. But for the most part Chile had a peaceful history, and it profited accordingly.

BEGINNING OF THE MASS MOVEMENT. During the first years of the present century there were indications that the reign of the aristocrats might be drawing to a close. The aristocrats themselves could see none of these signs, of course. They had held power so long that they could not imagine any other state of affairs. But change was in the air. Chile was gradually becoming a literate nation, and for the first time the masses were reading about social and economic reforms in far-off lands. Chile was being industrialized, and the new factory workers were far more radical than the tenant farmers had ever been. Chilean government was undoubtedly corrupt and inefficient, and a ready target for the attacks of the radicals.

GROWING INFLUENCE OF ARTURO ALESSANDRI. One of the principal attackers of the national administration was Arturo Alessandri, whose early career had followed the usual pattern of a conservative politician. In fact, not until he was fifty years of age did he become an ardent advocate of widespread social reform. He had been educated in a Catholic school, and after receiving his license to practice law he had acted as attorney for

Chilean and foreign corporations. As a "liberal-conservative" he had served in Congress and in the cabinets of several presidents. Virtually all his intimate friends were members of the ruling clique. But as the election of 1920 approached, Alessandri began to talk a new language. He denounced the landed aristocracy in no uncertain terms, and emphasized the economic insecurity of the great majority of the people. What was needed, he said, was a full-scale social security program.

The Liberal Alliance made him its presidential candidate. But it was not the Liberal Alliance of other days, whose conservatism had rivaled that of the Conservatives. The Alliance had fallen into the hands of middle class and labor groups, and it was this combination that selected Alessandri as its spokesman. The right-wing factions, meanwhile, had formed a new political organization and called it the National Union. Most of the old-time Liberals were now united with the Conservatives to form its membership. They chose as their candidate a distinguished gentleman of faultless antecedents by the name of Luis Barros Borgoño. The Borgoño campaign was calm and unruffled, in the leisurely conservative manner. But Alessandri stumped the nation from one end to the other, making vigorous speeches in support of his social security program. He was an impressive figure on the public platform, with his great head and mass of heavy hair that suggested a lion's mane. Because of this shock of hair, and also because of his fearless manner in championing the underprivileged, his admirers sometimes called him a lion—the Lion of Tarapacá. Admittedly he was an accomplished orator, and he aroused such fervor in the masses of the people that not even the threats and bribes of their employers could induce them to desert his cause.

Opinions concerning Alessandri differed widely, as might well have been imagined. The workers thought that he was a Messiah, ready to break their chains. His intimate friends said that he was a sincere liberal, whose observation of Chilean poverty had shaken him out of his early conservatism. The right-wing leaders sneeringly pointed out that his conversion to the liberal creed had coincided exactly with the awakening of his presidential ambitions. They called him a demagogue and a charlatan. But whatever men might think of Alessandri, they could not ignore him. He was a skillful political leader.

ALESSANDRI ELECTED PRESIDENT. The presidential campaign was climaxed by an exciting election, in which the partisans of both candidates resorted to unnecessary violence. The police were busy throughout the day suppressing riots. When at last the votes were counted, it seemed that

Alessandri had won by a small margin. But the National Union charged wholesale fraud and threatened to appeal the matter to Congress. Since a majority of the members of Congress were rightists, there seemed little reason to doubt that they would throw out enough Alessandri votes to elect their own candidate. Alessandri and his followers cried to high Heaven against this manifest injustice. They even talked of civil war, and the right wingers knew that these threats were not to be taken lightly. Finally a compromise was reached. A so-called Tribunal of Honor was created and given the difficult task of deciding the election. It awarded victory to Alessandri, but only by a single vote. Thus a champion of the people became president of Chile.[6]

PRESIDENTIAL TROUBLES. But the nation was not yet to reap the fruits of Alessandri's victory. The Senate was still controlled by the National Union, and it refused to approve any portion of the President's social security program. When he suggested laws fixing minimum wages and maximum hours, the Senate turned a deaf ear. It refused even to consider a reasonable compromise. Proposals for workmen's compensation, health and old age insurance, and regulation of child labor all suffered the same fate. The Senate was determined to preserve the old order at any cost. Under the provisions of the 1833 constitution, which still governed Chile, they could censure the President's ministers and force them to resign. This they did time after time. Alessandri spent many weary hours reorganizing his cabinet, when he should have been free to consider the major problems of government.

The Senate was not solely responsible for Alessandri's troubles, however. The bottom had dropped out of Chile's nitrate market just before he assumed the presidency, and the result was a severe depression. Thousands of men lost their jobs as the effect of the nitrate catastrophe was felt throughout the Chilean economy. Within a very short time the peso dropped to one third of its former level, sharply increasing the cost of living. Meanwhile salaries and wages remained substantially unchanged. So the poor *roto*—literally, broken one—Chile's forgotten man, to whom Alessandri owed most of his support, actually found himself worse off than he had been under conservative rule. But he did not waver in his support of the President.

UNFAIR TACTICS. When the time came for new elections, in 1924, Alessandri made a very determined effort to win control of both houses of

[6] For a brief character sketch of Alessandri, see John Gunther's *Inside Latin America*, pp. 245–247.

Congress. He made numerous speeches in behalf of the candidates of the Liberal Alliance, declaring that their election was essential to the success of his program—which indeed it was. In his desire to assure victory he even ordered the police and the army to break up political rallies scheduled by the National Union. Voters desiring to support the National Union's ticket were "induced" to stay away from the polls. These were the very tactics that the rightists had long used to keep themselves in power. They were the tricks that Alessandri himself had bitterly denounced as a shameful mockery of democratic government. Yet he did not hesitate to use them when they suited his own purpose.

PRESSURE BY THE ARMY. In the election of 1924 the Liberal Alliance won control of both the Senate and the Chamber of Deputies. Probably it would have been equally successful without resort to force or fraud, but the Liberals were taking no chances. When Congress next met, however, it proved a bitter disappointment to its friends and well-wishers. Its members spent their time disputing endlessly over trifles. Instead of approving minimum wages for the workers, they voted themselves a substantial compensation, in defiance of the plain declaration of the constitution that congressmen should serve without pay. Even more unwisely, prehaps, they made no effort to increase army salaries in the face of rising prices. This was more than the army could bear. Some of its leaders, knowing that they were strongly supported by public opinion, finally decided to take matters in their own hands. They organized a committee, and named General Luis Altamirano as their spokesman. Altamirano was the chief inspector of the army, and widely known throughout the nation. On September 5, 1924, he took decisive action. He presented to Alessandri a "petition"—*ultimatum* would have been a better word—asking that the congressional pay bill be vetoed, and that something be done at once about higher salaries for the armed forces. He also hinted, not too subtly, that the time had come for Congress to pass the long-promised social security program.

THE ARMY TAKES OVER. The President and Congress fully understood the implications of this "petition." They realized that the army was prepared to have its own way, regardless of civilian opposition. And they accepted as gracefully as possible the obvious fact that the army was really in control of the government. President Alessandri summoned General Altamirano to head the cabinet and gave him almost unlimited responsibility for the conduct of the nation's affairs. Congress responded by meeting all the army's demands. The social security program that had not been able to muster a majority in four years was passed in a few hours. Events were rushing swiftly to a climax. On the evening of September 8 Alessandri resigned and took refuge in the United States embassy. Soon afterward he crossed the Andes into Argentina and from there went into exile in Italy. Altamirano promptly named a military junta, with himself as its head, to run the country. He then dissolved Congress and proceeded to govern by decree. But he allayed to some extent the nation's fear of a military dictatorship when he selected a cabinet of distinguished civilians and made them primarily responsible for the conduct of public affairs.[7]

RETURN OF ALESSANDRI. Altamirano and his friends remained in office less than five months. On January 23, 1925, their regime was overthrown by another group of army officers garrisoned in Santiago. The leader of this clique was Carlos Ibáñez del Campo, a forty-seven-year-old cavalry officer who possessed considerable ability and a consuming ambition. At this time, however, Ibáñez did not try to set up dictatorial government. Instead he protested his loyalty to Alessandri, and proposed that the exiled President be invited to return. This suggestion met with overwhelming popular approval. The people were weary of Altamirano's vacillations and quite ready to believe the charge that he had conspired with the National Union to delay the very reforms he was supposed to promote.

When Alessandri first received the new government's invitation to come back to Chile and assume once more the presidency of the nation, he showed considerable hesitation. After all, he had been forced into exile by one military clique. Was there any reason to suppose that another group of militarists would prove more amenable? Gradually, however, his doubts disappeared as he received increasingly urgent messages from the government, labor leaders, and the chiefs of the Liberal Alliance, all begging him to return and assuring him that the country needed his services. He sailed from Europe and reached Santiago in March, 1925. No one could doubt the delight of the people. They gave him a roaring welcome that he was not likely ever to forget.

A NEW CONSTITUTION. Amidst this popular enthusiasm the Lion of Tarapacá again took up his presidential responsibilities. Carlos Ibáñez, chief of the new military junta, remained in his cabinet as minister of war, but most of the other military men who had engineered the recent *coup d'état* returned to their army duties. Alessandri was convinced that many of his former troubles had been caused by the Chilean constitution, which permitted the Senate to hamstring his administration despite his

---

[7] See *El Golpe de Estado de 1924, Ambiente y Actores*, by Emilio Rodríguez Mendoza.

clear mandate from the people. So he decided that one of his first tasks must be to arrange for the preparation of a new constitution. For this important project he asked the assistance of all the major political groups, as well as business, professional, and labor organizations not directly connected with the government. There can be no doubt that the best brains of the nation participated in the writing of the document. To a very large extent, however, it represented Alessandri's ideas. It ended once and for all the parliamentary scheme of government, which had enabled Congress to force the resignation of a president's ministers. It increased the president's term to six years, though retaining the provision that he should not be immediately eligible to succeed himself. And it gave the president ample authority to match his position as head of the nation.

CHURCH AND STATE. One of the most important reforms of the new constitution was the separation of church and state. This was the culmination of a movement which had torn Chilean society for half a century. It was the logical extension of the principles of religious freedom and secular education. But of course there were many devout Catholics to cry "blasphemy!" at the very thought of what they termed a godless state. Their opposition was weakened by the generous provisions of the constitution. The Roman Catholic Church would be permitted to retain its extensive properties; it would be exempt from taxation on land and buildings devoted directly to religious uses; and during a five-year transitional period it would receive a substantial subsidy from the national treasury. Thus church and state were divorced in a reasonably amicable manner, and Chile escaped the bitterness that has darkened the history of some Latin American nations.[8]

RESIGNATION OF ALESSANDRI. After Alessandri's return from exile he remained in office only seven months. Then he found it necessary to leave the country a second time. Elections were scheduled for October, and the politically ambitious Carlos Ibáñez had announced his candidacy for the presidency, though still retaining his position as minister of war. Alessandri vigorously challenged this strange arrangement. He said that he could not tolerate the spectacle of a presidential candidate continuing to direct the armed forces and, through them, assuming responsibility for the honesty of the elections. Ibáñez must either give up his presidential ambitions—which was of course unthinkable—or else resign from the cabinet. To this virtual ultimatum the Minister of War replied that he

[8] Not all observers are convinced that Chile has escaped serious church troubles, however. See R. C. Moore's interesting but biased *Piety and Poverty in Chile*.

CHILE—TURBULENT DEMOCRACY

would remain a presidential candidate and would not resign his cabinet post.

That answer put the matter squarely up to the President. He had the legal right to dismiss his minister of war or any other cabinet officer, but whether Ibáñez would accept his dismissal was an open question. Perhaps he would call upon his army friends to overthrow the existing regime and establish a government by force. Then, if Alessandri called upon all loyal troops to defend the established order, the result might be a bloody civil war. Rather than accept responsibility for such an uphappy turn of events, the President resigned and turned over the reins of power to his Minister of the Interior. It was indeed a strange situation—a president relinquishing his own office because one of his advisers refused to quit; and it seemed even stranger because the Minister of the Interior who succeeded to the duties of the presidency was Luis Barros Borgoño, the Conservative whom Alessandri defeated in 1920.

PRESIDENT FIGUEROA. Passions were at fever pitch as election day approached. Finally Ibáñez announced that he too would resign if the leaders of the major political parties could agree upon a compromise candidate. They hurriedly canvassed the field and finally selected a sixty-year-old lawyer named Emiliano Figueroa Larraín who had served in Congress, in the cabinet, and in the diplomatic service, and had managed to keep clear of the rough-and-tumble of Chilean politics since the old days of Liberal-Conservative domination. With all the major parties supporting him, Figueroa scarcely needed to do more than wait for the votes to be counted. There was indeed one other candidate, who had the backing of the left-wing labor groups, but he could hardly be considered a serious contender. So no one was surprised at Figueroa's easy victory.

The new President had the very best of intentions, but unfortunately he lacked some of the essential qualities of leadership. While Congress frittered away its own—and the nation's—time, he failed to demand prompt action. Strikes and riots constantly interfered with the country's economy, but he waited patiently for labor to abate its demands. Though the new constitution had strengthened the president's authority, Figueroa was not the man to make full use of his powers. He compromised and placated while the people demanded action. By 1927 it was clear to all that he had accepted a job beyond his capacities.

TRIUMPH OF IBÁÑEZ. Carlos Ibáñez had remained in the cabinet as Minister of War, and as the first months of the Figueroa administration passed he came to be regarded as virtually the head of the government.

He prepared orders and Figueroa signed them. Soon the politicians realized that the President was merely a figurehead and treated him accordingly. Whenever important decisions had to be made, they went directly to the office of the Minister of War. As Figueroa faded into the background and Ibáñez asserted his authority with increasing assurance, Alessandri's dormant reform program received fresh attention. The nation sensed that once again there was a strong hand at the helm. On May 4, 1927, President Figueroa resigned. A series of preliminary steps had moved Ibáñez from the Ministry of War to the Ministry of the Interior, from which post he would be eligible to assume the duties of the presidency. One of his first acts upon Figueroa's resignation was to schedule a new election for May 22—just eighteen days distant. No major party could possibly have selected a candidate and conducted an adequate campaign in so short a time, even if its leaders had been determined to block Ibáñez. Under the circumstances there was only one possible result. Carlos Ibáñez received ninety-seven per cent of the popular vote. At last he became president of the nation, an honor that had been snatched from him two years earlier.

Dictatorship and Chaos

SUPPRESSION OF THE OPPOSITION. By temperament and conviction Ibáñez was a dictator. He had no real love for Chile's democratic constitution, with its separation of powers among the several branches of the government. As Minister of War he had witnessed Alessandri's bitter fights with Congress and Figueroa's complacent acceptance of congressional inaction, and he was determined to avoid such difficulties, regardless of the tactics that must be employed. His tactics were, in fact, quite ruthless and very effective. He filled the jails with political prisoners, arresting both conservatives and radicals who dared to question his policies. Some of the more fortunate leaders of the opposition managed to escape from the country, but those who remained were accorded summary treatment. The newspapers were permitted to print only the government's highly colored version of the news. Existing political parties virtually ceased to function, and in their place the President organized a new party, the Republican Confederation for Civic Action. Politicians of every hue hastened to enroll as members. Chile, like Mussolini's Italy and Stalin's Russia, had become a one-party state.

DESPOTISM AND PROSPERITY. In 1930 members of Congress were to be elected. President Ibáñez "induced" the political leaders to agree upon a single candidate for each district, thereby making elections unnecessary under the terms of the Chilean election law. Needless to say, the candidates thus chosen were all staunch supporters of the President, and ready to take his orders. With all opposition eliminated or driven under cover, therefore, he was able to undertake an extensive program for the correction of Chile's economic and social ills. Highways were built and improved, the railroad lines were extended, irrigation systems were developed on a larger scale than ever before. Agricultural co-operatives and rural credit agencies were established, and greater efforts were made to attract European immigrants. These numerous activities required vast sums of money, but the government solved this difficulty by borrowing abroad. It did not even try to balance the budget. Instead it listed its expenditures in two separate budgets—ordinary and extraordinary—and merely kept the ordinary budget in balance. This dual budget system was financial juggling, of course. Its primary purpose was to draw attention away from the obvious fact that the government was headed for financial trouble.

As a matter of fact, few people understood the situation, and even fewer seemed to care. Chile was prosperous in 1928 and 1929, and available foreign capital seemed to be practically limitless. Moreover, there were a number of solid achievements to the credit of President Ibáñez. He reorganized the nation's educational system, making it much more effective. New schools were built and new teachers employed. A determined attack was made on the problem of illiteracy. The University of Chile was given a larger measure of self-government and its budget was increased. Less defensible was the preferential treatment given the armed forces, but everyone understood that Ibáñez had to keep them satisfied. Without their support he could not have remained in power a single day.

DESPOTISM AND DEPRESSION. In 1930 the Dictator seemed to be well entrenched, although the first signs of trouble had already begun to appear. The primary cause of popular dissatisfaction was the Great Depression, which was sweeping the world and unseating many governments. The demand for Chilean nitrates, already at a low mark, dropped almost to the vanishing point. Foreign capital was no longer available in large quantities. Unemployment was widespread. And many persons who had not worried too much about the dictatorship in prosperous times suddenly remembered the joys of liberty. They complained bitterly about tyranny—and their empty stomachs—as the government tried desperately to remedy the situation by increasing taxes and reducing the number of public employees.

Meanwhile, of course, the program of public works ground to a halt. Payments on the foreign debt had to be suspended. A single corporation was created to control the nitrate industry, but it accomplished very little. Ibáñez shuffled and reshuffled his cabinet, hoping to find a combination of ministers that would be able to restore prosperity to the nation. His hope was vain.

FALL OF THE DESPOT. As the economic situation went from bad to worse, the opposition grew in numbers and determination. Finally, on July 23, 1931, students at the University of Chile took the lead in declaring open defiance. They seized the main building of the university and converted it into a fortress. From the windows they hung large banners inscribed with a single word—LIBERTY. The military police promptly went into action and ultimately succeeded in driving the students from the building, but not until they had killed two persons and wounded a number of others. The repercussions were immediate and startling. All Santiago rose in its wrath against the government that had permitted such brutality. The doctors, lawyers, and teachers went on strike. Ibáñez still had the loyal support of the well-paid and well-fed army, but he found himself powerless to cope with a mass movement of this kind. Three days after the university killings he resigned the presidency and hastily left the country. Thus, after four years, Chile was rid of the man who had done more than any other to weaken its slowly developing democracy.[9]

UNSETTLED CONDITIONS. Troubled times were still ahead, in spite of deliverance from dictatorship. There was no strong man to replace Ibáñez, and no strong tradition of orderly government to prevent chaos. Ministry succeeded ministry with kaleidoscopic rapidity, and several armed uprisings emphasized the important role of the military in Chile's affairs. The President of the Senate, who had received the resignation of Ibáñez and accepted the responsibility of the government, promptly placed all authority in the hands of a distinguished lawyer named Juan Esteban Montero. Most Chileans were relieved to see that he did not turn to the army. Montero, whose career as attorney, author, and university professor had provided no previous political experience, took direct charge of the Ministry of the Interior and governed the nation with the title of vice-president. He announced that a presidential election would be held on October 4, and shortly afterward he permitted his own name to be submitted as a candidate by a group of professional and business men repre-

[9] See Henry Grattan Doyle's article, "Chilean Dictatorship Overthrown," in the September, 1931, issue of *Current History*, pp. 918 ff.

senting most of the parties that had formerly made up the conservative National Union. Unlike Ibáñez, Montero did not try to retain control of the government during the presidential campaign. Instead, he scrupulously resigned from public office the day that he accepted the nomination. There is some evidence to show that he actually preferred not to be a candidate and did not allow his name to be used until influential friends finally persuaded him that the nation needed his services. In any event, he won without difficulty. His only important rival was ex-President Arturo Alessandri, who had the support of a number of left-wing groups.

THE PARADE OF PRESIDENTS. When Montero again returned to power in December, this time as duly elected president, he created a favorable impression by governing strictly in accordance with the constitution. He co-operated closely with Congress, though it was still composed largely of Ibáñez' personal appointees. In every way he seems to have subordinated personal ambition to the welfare of the nation. But economic conditions were still highly unsatisfactory, and apparently the government was incapable of improving them, so many of Montero's friends abandoned him. Every day the opposition gained new recruits. Before the President had served four months of his new term, his rivals were planning ways to discredit him. He clung to power a little longer, however, but on June 4, 1932, six months to the day from the beginning of his regular term, he was suddenly confronted with a *coup d'etat,* and forced to resign.

The leaders of this uprising were left-wing radicals, and they set about the task of transforming Chile into a socialist republic. Their very first decrees were designed to win the support of the masses. Commercial obligations need not be met for thirty days, small businessmen might borrow heavily at the National Savings Bank, and articles pawned at the Bank of Popular Credit should be returned at once to their owners. As might well have been anticipated, the upper classes were greatly alarmed at this turn of events. While they tried to decide what to do, however, the leaders of the new regime were weakening their own position by quarreling with one another. A triumvirate had been named to run the country; within six days one of its members had been forced to withdraw; five days later he was back in power and signing the decree that exiled his two rivals. The man who thus became the head of Chile's government—with army support, it need scarcely be added—was a well-known newspaper editor who had served four years as his country's ambassador to the United States. His name was Carlos Dávila, and he lasted as president exactly eighty-eight days. His program, which he tried to establish by executive decree, was a hodge-podge of ideas known to its ad-mirers as "sane socialism." Perhaps that was the difficulty with it. It was too sane for the far left, and too socialistic for the far right. It made a great many enemies, and not very many friends. Few people were genuinely sorry when a General Blanche of the air corps suddenly seized the reins of power and compelled Dávila to resign. Within three weeks Blanche himself was the victim of another uprising. Troops at strategic garrisons stripped him of authority and turned the government over to the president of the Supreme Court. October 30 was set as the day for choosing a new president and the members of a new Congress.

ELECTION CAMPAIGN OF 1932. The turbulent years under Ibáñez and his successors had wrought major changes in party alliances. The Liberal Party was split into four major groups and a number of minor factions. The Conservatives, though still united among themselves, were unable to merge with other parties in a coalition similar to the old-time National Union. The list of parties included the Radicals, the Socialists, the Radical Socialists, the Democrats, and the Agrarians. There was even a newly organized Communist Party, which gained converts among the factory workers of the Central Valley and especially among the nitrate workers and copper miners of the north. The Radicals held a convention and chose Alessandri as their candidate. His name still held a powerful appeal for the masses, despite his defeat a year earlier. Several of the more powerful liberal groups let it be known that they would support him. The Conservatives named their party leader. Marmaduke Grove, who had helped Dávila establish the socialist republic, became the nominee of the Socialist Party. The Communists also selected a candidate, for the first time in Chilean history. Alessandri's bid for left-of-center liberal support was challenged by Enrique Zañartu, the standard-bearer of the Agrarian Party.

Return to Stable Democracy

ALESSANDRI'S CONSERVATISM. When all the ballots had been counted, it was found that Alessandri was the winner of the presidency by a con-siderable margin. The people had given him more than three times as many votes as Marmaduke Grove, his nearest competitor, and more than all his rivals combined. The Communists ran a poor last. Eight weeks after election day Arturo Alessandri took the oath of office and began his second term as president of Chile. The masses were understandably jubilant. They remembered the valiant manner in which the Lion of Tarapacá had fought their cause in earlier years, and they expected history to repeat itself. For the same reason the Conservatives were frankly worried. They anticipated a fresh rash of social legislation.

Almost from the very beginning of his new term, however, President Alessandri displayed a different—and much more conservative—attitude toward the problems of government. He announced his intention of selecting his cabinet from all major political groups, thus creating a government that would be truly representative of the nation. But, since the Socialists and Communists would not co-operate, only the parties of the left-center, center, and right were included. Gradually, as the President's policies became increasingly conservative, even the members of his own Radical Party grew more dissatisfied, and eventually they withdrew from the coalition, leaving Alessandri to draw his support from the Conservatives and the now united Liberals. Since these two groups had a majority in Congress, the disaffection of the leftist factions did not seriously handicap the government. But everyone marveled at the spectacle of a president elected with left-wing votes who carried out a right-wing program.

ACTION AGAINST LEFT-WING GROUPS. There were, of course, many explanations of Alessandri's change of heart from radicalism to conservatism. The Conservatives said that he had learned a great deal since his first term and had come to realize the danger of too sudden change. The Radicals hinted—and some of them went so far as to state openly—that he had sold out to the enemy. Alessandri himself declared that his sole interest was the maintenance of orderly government. He said that after five years of alternate dictatorship and anarchy the nation was entitled to a stable regime within the letter of the constitution, and that he intended to assure it without regard to parties or personalities. Whatever the President's real motives may have been, he certainly did take drastic steps to maintain order. The Communists and Socialists, which were the groups most likely to disturb the public peace, felt the weight of his displeasure almost immediately. Their quarters were raided by the police, their newspapers ordered to cease publication, and their leaders imprisoned or exiled. Even Marmaduke Grove, who had won sixty thousand votes at the last election, was sent to jail. Labor agitators were accorded summary treatment, and strikes were discouraged as contrary to the public interest.

INFLUENCE OF GUSTAVO ROSS. Many of Alessandri's old-time friends declared that he was unduly influenced by his Minister of Finance, Gustavo Ross. In some respects Ross was an ideal man for his job. Born in Valparaíso of a Scottish family, he had made a fortune in France and had acquired an enviable reputation as a financier. As Minister of Finance he strengthened that reputation; his energetic measures restored the shattered Chilean economy and reduced unemployment. But he was an uncompromising "economic royalist," and he left no doubt as to his views. While Alessandri strove for national unity, Ross seemed to take particular delight in offending the Radicals. He sneered at them openly and scorned all their suggestions. There can be no doubt that among the masses he was one of Chile's most hated men. And, as Alessandri continued to give Ross his full confidence, he too shared a part of the workers' hatred.

CREATION OF THE POPULAR FRONT. While the government aligned itself more and more closely with the right, even using the army to break a strike of railroad workers, the left-wing groups began to lay plans for some sort of coalition, in order to make their opposition more effective. In February, 1936, a Radical member of Congress, speaking before his party's convention in Santiago, proposed a Popular Front composed of "the parties of the Bloc of the Left, the Communist Party, the Labor organizations, employees, farm workers, artisans, students, professionals, intellectuals, cultural and sporting organizations, and all the honest and loyal men and women of the country without distinction as to ideologies, beliefs, or religions." The Popular Front in France was of course a shining example of what might be done. The convention promptly approved the suggestion, and other parties and factions soon fell into line. On March 26, while some left-wing groups were still discussing the matter, a Popular Front organization was actually created after a long session of party leaders in a newspaper office. Officers of the organization were chosen, and the masses were asked to support this new movement for social reform.

The Conservatives said, of course, that the whole scheme was inspired by Moscow. They pointed out, not without reason, that the Russian Comintern had only recently directed the Communist parties in other nations to make common cause with democratic and bourgeois groups against the forces of reaction, and they declared that the more moderate groups were allowing themselves to be duped by the Communists. But the Radicals, Socialists, and other factions within the Popular Front rejected the notion of Communist leadership. The movement was home-grown, they insisted, and had its roots in the natural desire of the people to rid themselves of the hateful Alessandri-Ross administration.[10]

---

[10] The birth of the Popular Front is well described by John Reese Stevenson in his small but excellent volume, *The Chilean Popular Front*, Chap. V.

CONGRESSIONAL ELECTIONS OF 1937. The first test of strength of the Popular Front came in the congressional elections of 1937. The leaders of the several parties were not accustomed to working together. Some of them, in fact, still doubted the wisdom of the new coalition and continued to follow their separate paths with little regard for the official declarations of unity. Meanwhile the Conservatives and Liberals, together with a number of smaller groups, formed a really effective combination of the nation's right-wing elements. Ross seems to have done everything that he could to insure the election of his friends, even resorting to large-scale bribery. But he could not completely nullify the effects of the general enthusiasm for Popular Front candidates. The Socialists made substantial gains, and other leftist parties won a number of seats. It was not a major victory, but it indicated that closer co-operation might produce substantial results.

PRESIDENTIAL NOMINATIONS. As the 1938 presidential election approached, the lines were drawn for what was sure to be a bitter fight. Popular Front leaders had agreed to unite in support of a single candidate, but the choice of this candidate proved to be singularly difficult. The Socialists first held their convention, and indicated that their preference was for their leader, Marmaduke Grove. When the Radicals, the strongest party in the Front, met for the purpose of choosing their candidate, they found themselves divided between two outstanding men, Pedro Aguirre Cerda and Juan Antonio Ríos, both of whom ultimately gained the presidency. Aguirre and Ríos had much in common. Both were born of humble parents, both were well-to-do, distinguished, and members of the moderate wing of the Radical Party. Aguirre had at first opposed Radical participation in the Popular Front because he feared Communist domination, and Ríos made no secret of his dislike of the Communists. Aguirre was an educator and landowner, while Ríos was a prominent attorney. The contest was close, but eventually it was announced that Aguirre had won and would receive the support of the Radicals in the forthcoming Popular Front convention.

When the convention met, in April, 1938, the hope for unity seemed to be slight. The Radicals voiced their determined opposition to Grove, and the Socialists declared themselves equally averse to supporting Aguirre Cerda. Together the two parties could easily dominate the convention, but separately either of them could block any nomination. Ballot after ballot was taken without obtaining the necessary two-thirds majority for either candidate. Then, on the third day, the Socialists unexpectedly gave in. Grove withdrew his name, and Aguirre was acclaimed as the nominee of the Popular Front.

The right-wing parties gave unexpected aid and comfort to their opponents by nominating Gustavo Ross. With almost any other candidate they might have been able to arouse some enthusiasm among the middle classes, who distrusted any presidential aspirant receiving Communist support. But the name of Ross was anathema to all persons claiming even slightly liberal tendencies. The younger, more progressive element within Ross' own party tried to prevent his nomination, but without success. So Ross emerged as the champion of the landed aristocracy and the Catholic Church. These forces were less powerful than they had been in earlier days; but, on the other hand, Ross enjoyed the backing of the government. He was the official candidate—an advantage not to be ignored.

CHILEAN NAZIS. With two hats already in the presidential ring, Carlos Ibáñez made a dramatic re-entry upon the political stage. He had been permitted to return from exile about a year earlier, and he proceeded to make a bid for the support of the Chilean Nazis—*Nacistas,* they called themselves. The leader of this movement was named Jorge González von Marees, and he had followed standard fascist practice, giving his followers smart uniforms, a distinctive insignia (a bolt of lightning), and the usual assortment of meaningless slogans. González von Marees often protested that the movement was not German, despite its close imitation of Hitler's tactics. It was, he said, strictly a home-grown product. It distrusted all foreign influence, and its chief concern was to preserve Chile for the Chileans. That Carlos Ibáñez, the militant liberal, could have made a deal with such an organization was mildly surprising, but could be explained by the fact that both Ibáñez and González von Marees were totalitarians at heart. Both believed in the substitution of order for liberty. So Ibáñez announced that he was a candidate for the presidency, and the Nacistas gave him their blessing.[11]

REBELLION AND MASSACRE. Very few Chileans took the campaign of the Nacistas seriously. It was generally assumed that they would stage a few parades, demonstrate their orderly drilling, and then subside into obscurity after the votes had been counted. Perhaps the Nacistas themselves feared such a result. In any event, they finally moved to take over the government. It was an absurd attempt and foredoomed to failure, for the

[11] Jorge González von Marees presented his philosophy in two small volumes, *El Problema de Hambre* (1937), and *El Mal de Chile* (1940).

Nacistas were few in number and lacked the support of public opinion or—even more important—the armed forces. But apparently González von Marees had decided that it must be then or never.

On September 5, six weeks before the election, a group of young and determined Nacistas gathered before the presidential palace, as their leader gave orders by radio. Without hesitation they opened fire, and one policeman was shot. President Alessandri, who happened to be inside the palace at the time, rushed to the dying man's rescue, dragging him to shelter while Nacista bullets pelted around them. In a very little time the revolutionaries had captured the Social Security Building, which stands next to the palace, and had secured control of the main building of the University of Chile. But their triumph was short-lived. The police counterattacked and soon drove them into the upper stories of the Social Security skyscraper, from which they were dislodged by tear gas and machine guns. There were just sixty-one Nacistas in this group, and after they had surrendered the police shot every one of them in cold blood. Only one badly wounded survivor managed to escape with his life. Chileans are a tolerant people, and when they learned of this massacre they indignantly asked who had ordered it. No one seemed to know. Some said that it was Alessandri. Many were sure that it was Ross. But no one could deny that it was someone in the government, and the Alessandri regime had to bear the responsibility. This incident may have been decisive in the presidential campaign.

REPERCUSSIONS OF THE MASSACRE. González von Marees admitted readily enough that he had issued the command for the abortive uprising of the Nacistas, and he was thrown into jail and sentenced to death. Ibáñez was jailed, also, though he swore that he had not been connected with the plot in any way. Eventually he was released, but not until two days before the election. Meanwhile Aguirre Cerda visited González von Marees in his cell and promised that one of his first official acts, if elected, would be to pardon the Nacista leader. It was smart politics and it won Aguirre a great many votes, for Ibáñez withdrew his own candidacy and directed all his followers to support the nominee of the Popular Front. González von Marees issued similar instructions. Thus Chileans witnessed the curious spectacle of Communists and Nazis endorsing the same candidate. In South America, as elsewhere, politics makes strange bedfellows.[12]

<hr />

[12] The story of the massacre and its aftermath is well told by Juan F. Fernández in his *Pedro Aguirre Cerda y el Frente Popular.*

The Popular Front

TRIUMPH OF AGUIRRE CERDA. Aguirre campaigned for the presidency most aggressively. He traveled from one end of the country to the other, making hundreds of speeches, talking with thousands of persons, and driving home the Popular Front's slogan: *Pan, techo y abrigo* (bread, roof and overcoat). Emphasis was placed on the need for an expansion of the social security program, the further development of education, and the careful maintenance of national defense. Ross made no attempt to match his opponent's zeal in reaching the voters. He relied instead on wholesale bribery. Without doubt he would have liked to use the army to keep Popular Front voters away from the polls and to "safeguard" the ballot boxes while his own friends counted the votes and announced the result. But President Alessandri was not prepared to go so far. To his credit it must be said that he pledged an honest election and kept that promise to the best of his ability. He did not interfere with Ross' lavish and unlawful use of money; perhaps he could not do so. But he tried to make certain that the ballots would be counted exactly as they were cast. That he succeeded in large measure was apparent when the results were made public. Aguirre was declared the winner, though by a scant margin of four thousand votes in a total of nearly half a million. Ross was bitterly disappointed. At first he refused to recognize his rival's triumph, charging— of all things!—that the Popular Front had been guilty of fraud. He had to accept the result, however, when he learned that President Alessandri and the army leaders would not support his claims. On December 24 Pedro Aguirre Cerda took the oath of office as president of the nation. Ross was already on his way to France.

DISSENSION AMONG THE VICTORS. It was evident from the very beginning of Aguirre's administration that troubled times were ahead. The basic difficulty was lack of unity. The President could not count on the support of Congress, since a majority of its members belonged to the Conservative-Liberal opposition. They had been elected in 1937, and another congressional election was not scheduled until 1941. Equally serious was the disunity among the President's own supporters—the members of the Popular Front. This alliance was at best a nebulous thing. It had held together throughout the campaign chiefly because its members shared a bitter hatred of Gustavo Ross. But Ross was gone, the campaign was over, and the various groups comprising the Popular Front no longer felt the same compulsion to work together. After all, they were very heterogeneous.

They included Communists and Socialists, who were traditionally at one another's throats, as well as Radicals and Democrats representing many shades of opinion, some of which were surprisingly far to the right. And it must be remembered that Aguirre owed his triumph not only to his own Popular Front but also to the followers of Ibáñez and González von Marees. Clearly he could not count on the continued help of all those who had endorsed him as a presidential candidate.

ABORTIVE REBELLION. On August 25, 1939, eight months after Aguirre's inauguration, Ibáñez evidently decided that the time was right for another *coup d'état*. For some time he had been increasingly critical of the government's policies, and he evidently hoped that the army would follow his leadership in turning the Popular Front out of power. He did actually secure the support of a group of young army officers, and with their aid he set out to win strategic points and prove himself once more the strong man of Chile. But most of the army remained loyal, and the uprising collapsed almost before it was well under way. Once again Ibáñez was forced to go into exile.

QUARRELS IN CONGRESS. While Ibáñez' plot sputtered and died, the Conservative-Liberal majority in Congress was making life miserable for the President. It refused to pass any important administration measures, thus bringing the government virtually to a standstill. For a short time it actually succeeded in inducing so many members of Congress to stay away that no quorum could be obtained. If it had persisted in this maneuver it might possibly have brought about the downfall of the Popular Front. But even the right-wing Congressmen did not always work together, and when some of them resumed their seats the strategy failed. Nor were the Conservatives successful in their attempts to convict cabinet ministers on impeachment charges. But they did actually impeach one minister (the vote on conviction was two short of the necessary number), and they forced the resignation of a number of others. Their shrewdly worded charges against the leaders of the administration were a constant source of annoyance, even if they proved to be nothing more.

COMMUNIST SQUABBLES. Aguirre's most difficult problems, however, were created by his own followers. Even before he took office the Communists announced that they would accept no positions in the new government. This did not mean a withdrawal of their support, they were careful to explain, but merely a desire not to embarrass the administration. Despite their honeyed words, however, they embarrassed the administration many times and in many different ways. They were constantly quarreling with the Socialist members of the Popular Front. When the Minister of Foreign Affairs, who was a Radical, signed a manifesto deploring attempts to unionize farm labor, the Communists made such a stir that he was forced to withdraw his signature. They ridiculed the "millionaires' cabinet" which included several wealthy landowners. In 1940, when President Aguirre asked for a suspension of strikes and lockouts in the interest of national unity, the Communists attacked him bitterly as a tool of the capitalists.

RADICALS VERSUS SOCIALISTS. Even more serious than the Communists' antagonism in weakening the Popular Front was the rivalry between its two strongest parties, the Radicals and Socialists. Grove and his Socialist followers had made a dramatic gesture of unity in the 1938 convention when they finally switched their strength to Aguirre, but before long they lost their sacrificial spirit. They complained that they were not receiving their proper share of positions in the public service, and they protested that the government was not moving fast enough in its program of social reform. Some of Aguirre's ministers were criticized quite as severely by the far left within the Front's own ranks as by the far right of the opposition. It was clear to all that the Popular Front was a very loose coalition and in imminent danger of collapse. Conservative leaders gleefully predicted that the end would come at any time. President Aguirre must have felt like the tightrope walker whose assistants took delight in distracting his attention and even pricking him with pins.

DISSOLUTION OF THE POPULAR FRONT. The President's own Radical Party was badly split. Some of its members believed that the Communists had been permitted entirely too much freedom and should be suppressed, even if this meant some sort of working agreement with the Conservatives. Others shuddered at the very thought of a Radical-Conservative coalition and talked of disciplining the man who had dared to propose it. But the responsible party leadership was undoubtedly beginning to weary of its Communist associations. More and more Radicals declared that the Communists were an alien group—alien in thoughts and ideals, and taking orders from Moscow. There was considerable evidence to support this assertion. Chilean Communists had consistently followed the party line, as established in the Soviet Union. In 1938, when Hitler was taking over Czechoslovakia and Austria, they could scarcely find words to express their contempt and loathing. But in 1939, after the signing of the Russian-German non-aggression pact, they suddenly discovered that Hitler's acts were motivated by a legitimate desire for the protection of the German people.

It was in 1940, while the Soviet Union was still friendly with Germany, that the Socialists were unwittingly drawn into the anti-Communist fight. One of the most prominent members of their party, Oscar Schnake, had been named Minister of Development, and in this capacity he went to the United States to arrange extensive credits that would bolster the Chilean economy. Then, if ever, was the time to avoid anti-American demonstrations, but the Communists picked that singularly inappropriate moment to stage mammoth protests against "Yankee imperialism." The American capitalists, it seems, had sinister designs on Chile's resources. They were scheming to keep the nation in a state of economic servitude. Even worse, said the Communists, these foreign plotters were receiving active assistance from their pliant tool, Minister of Development Schnake. Here was a man, they charged, who had betrayed his own country for a mess of pottage. This was strong language, and it proved very annoying to Oscar Schnake. As soon as he returned to Chile he made an impassioned speech before a large crowd of party members, defending his own course of action and branding the Communists as disloyal to the workers and the government. Marmaduke Grove and other prominent Socialists endorsed Schnake's words. The end of the Popular Front was now in sight. On January 6, 1941, the Socialist Party formally withdrew from the coalition. Eight days later the Chilean Confederation of Labor followed its example. And only forty-eight hours afterward the Radicals joined the stampede. There was no one left to give the Front decent burial.

CONGRESSIONAL ELECTIONS OF 1941. Even as the Popular Front collapsed, preparations were being made for the congressional elections of 1941. The rightist parties, fearful that they would be defeated and lose control of Congress, had at first announced their intention to boycott the elections. Their official explanation of this policy was that they feared the use of force and fraud by the government and could think of no other way to protect their supporters. But everyone knew exactly what was meant. The Conservatives would have worried less about their followers' welfare if they could have foreseen a reasonable chance of winning. As a matter of fact, their interest in the election rose sharply after the collapse of the Popular Front. When the Aguirre government gave an unconditional guarantee of an honest election and even promised to use the armed forces to preserve order, the last possible objection to participation by the Conservative groups was removed. They entered the campaign and made a serious attempt to retain control of Congress by exploiting the disunity of the leftist parties.

As it turned out, this lack of unity was not so complete as at first anticipated. The Radicals promptly signed an agreement for joint action with two other parties, and later even the Communists were included. Each party was to maintain its own organization and candidates, however. The agreement was nothing more than a friendly alliance, requiring the nominees of any party within the coalition to direct their fire at the Conservative groups, instead of fellow leftists. The Socialists, led by Grove and Schnake, remained proudly aloof. The elections, as Aguirre had promised, were orderly and reasonably honest. When all the votes had been counted, it was clear that the leftist groups had won a substantial victory. In both the Senate and the Chamber of Deputies they gained enough seats to wipe out the Conservative coalition's majority. Both the Radicals and the Socialists won additional places. It was the Communists, however, who made the most spectacular gains. They increased their representation in the Chamber of Deputies from seven to fourteen (out of a total of one hundred and forty-six), and in the Senate from one to four (out of a total of forty-five). Clearly the Chilean Communists could not be ignored.

PRESIDENT VERSUS CONGRESS. If only the parties of the left had been united, President Aguirre might well have expected to receive from the new Congress a reasonable measure of co-operation. But instead he was blocked at every turn. His own Radical Party gave him as much trouble as any. The Minister of the Interior, who was a Radical, precipitated a serious crisis when he suspended two newspapers, one Conservative and one Communist, for attacking the government. His defense of this arbitrary action was that the objectionable editorials were obviously unfair, which indeed they were. But members of Congress insisted that fairness or unfairness could scarcely be the test, since every man was his own judge of what was fair. The only democratic procedure, they said, was to let the newspapers print what they pleased, so that the public might have unrestricted access to sources of information. As for the Minister who ordered the suspension of the papers, it was urged that he should resign at once. The Radicals took the lead in demanding his resignation and, when he remained in the cabinet, they expelled him from the Party.

But President Aguirre refused to be coerced. He pointed out that a cabinet minister was no longer an agent of Congress, as he had been in the days before the adoption of the 1925 constitution. Instead he was the direct personal agent òf the president, and should continue at his post as long as he had the president's confidence. The Minister of the Interior, said Aguirre, had his complete confidence. When the Radicals found that they could not get rid of the defiant Minister, they then ordered the other Radicals in the President's cabinet—five of them in all—to turn in their resignations, and this was done. Aguirre was in a quandary. Should he submit to Radical pressure, or should he try to govern the country without the support of his own party? The latter course seemed to offer fewer objections, so the President replaced the Radical ministers with personal friends who had not been active in politics. His relations with Congress were now so bad that they could scarcely deteriorate further. He could not rely on a single important congressional group to give him consistent support.[13]

DEATH OF AGUIRRE CERDA. On November 10, 1941, President Aguirre suddenly announced that he was seriously ill and would require a long rest before continuing to perform his public duties. He relinquished his office to Jerónimo Méndez, the president of the Radical Party, who had hurriedly been appointed Minister of the Interior in order to become eligible for the succession. In Chile this turn of events caused a great stir. Even in the United States it did not pass unnoticed. *Time,* the news magazine, reported the story in detail. It told about the chaotic state of Chilean politics and described the virtual impossibility of getting anything done. Then it hinted very broadly that Aguirre Cerda's illness was a sham. The real reason for his supposed sickness, said *Time,* was the failure of his followers to co-operate. He would continue to be ill until they learned that they could not get along without him; then he would return to authority in triumph and would have less difficulty in securing team work. This, then, was *Time's* story, and it was reported in masterful fashion.

But scarcely had copies of the magazine reached the newsstands when word came from Chile that Aguirre was dead. There could not have been a more complete or unanswerable refutation of *Time's* charges. The Chilean embassy in Washington made formal protest to the State Department, and President Roosevelt, anxious to play the good neighbor, sent a personal apology for *Time's* lack of good taste and good faith. This apology stirred a fresh tempest. By what right, asked the editors of *Time,* did the President of the United States question the integrity of a reputable American periodical? They readily admitted that the story had been a

[13] There is a good analysis of the administration of Aguirre Cerda in John Reese Stevenson's previously cited work, Chap. VII.

mistake, but they insisted that it had been based on supposedly reliable information. Some newspapers supported *Time* in their editorial columns; others defended the President. But after a short while the incident blew itself away and was forgotten by most people.

ATTEMPTS TO RECREATE THE POPULAR FRONT. In Chile, just before President Aguirre's death, some of the serious breaches among the parties of the left were actually being healed. The Communists, who had fought every attempt of the Radicals and Socialists to foster a strong Pan-Americanism, awoke one morning to find that Germany had invaded Russia. From that moment the war of the western democracies ceased to be an "imperialist struggle." It was Russia's fight, and therefore the fight of all good Communists. The United States, an "arsenal of democracy" providing material and moral encouragement to the democratic powers, must henceforth be considered an ally. Thus one of the most serious obstacles to Communist co-operation with the other parties of the left suddenly disappeared. Not long afterward the Radicals and the Socialists managed to patch up some of their quarrels, largely because of the resignation of the Minister whose retention in the cabinet had created such a storm a few months earlier. If President Aguirre had lived he might actually have been able to resurrect the battered Popular Front. But his death plunged the nation's politics into chaos once more. Acting President Méndez scheduled a presidential election for February 1, as the constitution required him to do, and the parties of the left promptly forgot the ideal of a Popular Front in their haste to select candidates and make their preparations for the campaign.

THE RADICALS' CANDIDATE. In Radical circles two names loomed large as presidential possibilities. One was that of Juan Antonio Ríos, whose name had been prominently mentioned at the 1938 convention of the Radical Party. The other was that of Gabriel González Videla, who had just returned from France where he had served as his country's ambassador to the Vichy government. Each candidate had his admiring partisans and the contest was very close, but eventually it was announced that Ríos had won and would be the standard-bearer of the Radical Party.

In many ways, he was an excellent choice. He could claim to be a man of the people, for he had been born in extreme poverty and had worked his way through secondary school and the University of Concepción, in southern Chile. As a lifelong member of the Radical Party he had labored steadily for his party's success, and had been named to one position after another—secretary of the small municipality where he made his home, then assistant mayor, and later a member of the Chamber of Deputies, a Senator, a cabinet minister. His hatred of the Communists was sincere and well-known; as minister of the interior under Carlos Dávila he had suppressed them ruthlessly, and he never hesitated to speak against the Communist menace. This attitude lost him many friends, of course, among the voters of the extreme left, but on the other hand it endeared him to moderates who could never have been induced to support the more radical González Videla. Ríos was not a great orator, but he had a splendid voice and he always spoke with great conviction. His six-foot-one figure and his impressive manner were assets not easily overlooked. Almost as soon as he received the nomination he called for the support of all true democrats and progressives, taking pains to phrase his invitation in such a way as to make clear that Communists were not wanted.[14]

PRESIDENTIAL CAMPAIGN OF 1942. The former Dictator Carlos Ibáñez had already announced his candidacy and on January 6, 1942, he became the official nominee of the Conservative Party. The next day he received the support of the Liberals and the Nacistas. But there were many Liberals who refused to follow the decision of their party. The party president resigned his office in protest, and carried many Liberals with him into the camp of Ríos. The Socialists were uncertain as to the course they should follow. Their obvious choice was Oscar Schnake, but he was afraid that his candidacy would merely split the leftist vote, thus assuring the victory of Ibáñez. So eventually the Socialist Party gave Ríos its official backing. Even the unwanted Communists worked for Ríos, on the theory that he was less objectionable than the hated Ibáñez. Former President Alessandri added his endorsement. Thus Ríos was assured of formidable support, ranging from the center to the extreme left. Only the rightest groups supported Ibáñez.

The campaign laid greater emphasis on international affairs than any previous political campaign in Chilean history. With the Pearl Harbor attack still fresh in men's minds, and a large part of the hemisphere recently plunged into war, Chile was faced with the question of its position in the world struggle. The followers of Ríos pictured him as a sturdy democrat, sympathetic to the Allied cause and ready to work for the defeat of the totalitarians. Ríos himself never actually promised that Chile would go to war at the side of the Allies, or even that it would break relations with Germany and Japan, but he accepted without protest the pro-

[14] See T. J. Hamilton's article, "Chile's Democratic President," in the November, 1942, issue of *Asia,* pp. 650–652.

democratic plaudits of his supporters. Just before the election he spoke to a great group of Chileans from a platform decorated with pictures of Roosevelt, Churchill, and Stalin. Meanwhile Ibáñez tried to refute the pro-Nazi charges so frequently made against him. But, like Ríos, he was unwilling to go so far as to promise active support to the Allies, and he could scarcely deny that he was the choice of all the pro-Nazi groups in Chile. So Ríos came to be recognized as the champion of the democracies, and there is no doubt that his victory represented to some extent the pro-democratic sentiment of the country. He received about fifty-five per cent of the total vote, and on April 2, 1942, he was inaugurated as president.

Recent Presidents

CHILEAN NEUTRALITY. In his inaugural address President Ríos declared: "The government will faithfully fulfill its duty regarding continental solidarity." This was interpreted by the United States to mean a prompt severance of diplomatic relations with the Axis powers. The Chilean interpretation, however, proved to be quite different. Ríos carefully maintained his country's neutrality, though he did grant non-belligerent status to the United States, thus permitting it to use Chilean ports freely. Great quantities of strategic materials flowed steadily from Chile to the United States. They were paid for, of course, at good prices, but it cannot be denied that they represented a substantial contribution to the Allied war effort. Some pro-Nazi Chilean newspapers went so far as to declare that Chile had abandoned its neutrality and become a war partner of the United States. The Communist dailies, on the other hand, criticized the government for not taking a definite stand against the Axis. But the large majority of Chileans probably approved the President's policy of neutrality. They realized that the country's long coastline would be difficult to defend, and that its economic future would probably be linked with Europe (which might mean a German-dominated Europe). Many political leaders even said that the United States was satisfied with Chile's benevolently neutral attitude.

SEVERANCE OF DIPLOMATIC RELATIONS. The incident that finally jolted the Chileans out of their complacent neutrality was a speech delivered in Boston on October 8 by Sumner Welles, who was then Acting Secretary of State of the United States. Welles spoke of Chile as the center of Axis espionage and, in unusually blunt language, declared that messages sent by clandestine Nazi radio stations on Chilean soil had been responsible for the sinking of Allied vessels. The Chilean government promptly denied these charges and lodged a formal protest with President Roosevelt. President Ríos, who had already accepted an invitation to visit the United States, hastily postponed his trip. Some government circles in Washington expressed surprise that Welles had made his speech so shortly before Ríos' proposed visit. The whole affair, they said, was a flagrant example of careless timing. But government spokesmen explained that the timing had been deliberate. The Boston speech had been made to remove any doubt that the United States was displeased with Chile. Otherwise the visit of President Ríos might well have been construed as an evidence of American approval of Chile's continued neutrality.

As for Chilean protests that the Welles charges were unfounded, the United States government concluded that it should let the world decide. It made public a memorandum that had been delivered to the government of Chile four months earlier, in which attention was called to secret radio messages that had been sent out by Nazi stations in Chile and intercepted by the Federal Communications Commission of the United States. The delivery of that note in June had produced no substantial results, but when it was made public in November the Ríos government suddenly awoke from its lethargy. A number of known German and Italian agents were expelled from the country, and coded messages from Axis diplomatic missions were forbidden. Chilean public opinion veered sharply in favor of a break with the Axis powers. In Santiago, on November 5, cheering throngs paraded in support of the democracies. Not until January 20, however, was the fateful step finally taken. The Senate had just voted, thirty to ten, in favor of severing diplomatic relations, so President Ríos made it official. Thus Chile joined the war effort in the first days of 1943, one year after the Rio Conference of foreign ministers had recommended this action to all the American nations.

ACTION AGAINST THE AXIS. Once the break with the Axis was made, Chile carried out its new policy in good faith. It rounded up three hundred Germans and Japanese who were suspected of subversive activities, and moved them to small towns in the far north or far south, where they would have little opportunity to help the Axis. The use of codes was prohibited, and weather forecasts were discontinued. The permits of Axis nationals to carry firearms were canceled. The offices of German and Italian news agencies were closed, and a notoriously pro-Axis propaganda radio station was shut down.

UNITED STATES AID. The United States gave prompt and tangible evi-

dence of its pleasure at Chilean support of the Allies. It made arrangements for the sale and prompt delivery to Chile of several second-hand
industrial plants that were not being used in the war effort. A few months
later it signed a new contract for the purchase of large quantities of Chilean
copper at a substantially higher price. It also agreed to buy gold and
manganese, which it did not need, in order to bolster the Chilean economy.
And it arranged to ship to Chile substantial quantities of coal, especially
for use in smelting low-grade copper ore. A little later the two countries
signed an agreement calling for the sale of three ten-thousand-ton Chilean
ships to the United States. Payment was to be made in gold bars, and new
vessels from American shipyards would be made available for the Chilean
fleet as soon as possible after the war. Because this treaty was not so
obviously favorable to Chile, it encountered considerable opposition in the
Chilean Senate, but it was finally approved.

ECONOMIC DIFFICULTIES. Almost from the outset the Ríos administration
was beset with difficulties. The war had cut off Chile's usual markets and
created shortages of many necessities. The inevitable result was a sharp
rise in prices, while wages and salaries lagged behind. By 1944 the cost
of living was double the 1939 figure, and food prices were up one hundred
and twenty per cent. President Ríos tried to solve the problem by fixing
price ceilings on hundreds of articles and imposing stiff penalties for violators. But black markets flourished, and many businessmen hoarded their
goods in anticipation of still higher prices. The government seemed
virtually helpless in the grip of these war-borne problems.

POLITICAL DIFFICULTIES. In addition to the economic difficulties, Chile's
political parties were making a bad situation considerably worse by inces-
sant quarrels within their own ranks and with one another. The cabinet
of President Ríos originally included representatives of all the groups that
had supported him, except the Communists, but one by one they drifted
away. First the Socialists became involved in a quarrel over the leadership
of Marmaduke Grove, who had headed the party for many years. The
younger element blamed Grove for the party's declining prestige, and
finally voted to remove him, replacing him with his brother-in-law, Salvador Allende. But Grove refused to accept this verdict and set up a
separate faction which he called the *true* Socialist Party. Since another
group of Socialists had taken a similar action several years earlier, the party
was now split into three factions. Each segment was almost certain to
oppose any action taken by either of the others, and as a result the President's support became less certain than ever. His three Socialist ministers

resigned, and in their stead he named Radicals and Liberals. Since the Liberals were an opposition party, and more conservative than any of the government groups, these appointments marked a definite trend to the right.

The President's troubles multiplied a few months later, when the members of his own Radical Party quarreled violently. Soon the Radical ministers in his cabinet submitted their resignations. Instead of trying to replace them with members of other political groups, Ríos announced that he would get along without politicians, and appoint a group of experts to head the several departments and give him such advice as might be necessary. This was the so-called "administrative cabinet." Several of its most important posts were assigned to members of the armed forces. The President told the country that the arrangement was only temporary, and would be discontinued as soon as the parties gave evidence of their worthiness to be represented in the cabinet. Proof of such worthiness, he explained, would be the subordination of party interests to the national welfare and the enactment of a suitable legislative program.

The "administrative cabinet" was set up early in June, 1943. Three months later Ríos decided that the time had come to give the parties another chance. He dismissed his experts and chose a cabinet which included Radicals, Socialists, and Liberals, as well as representatives of some minor groups. Apparently, however, the President's sanguine expectations of party peace were unjustified. In virtually no time the Ministers were quarreling with one another and with him. At last the Radical members served notice that they expected him to dismiss his other ministers and form an exclusively Radical cabinet. The proposal was unreasonable, since the Radicals held no more than thirty per cent of the seats in either house of Congress. President Ríos refused even to consider it. He declared that his first duty was to his country instead of his party, and that the country must have a stable government. So the Radicals prepared for their party convention the following January, and many of them seriously considered the possibility of choosing an anti-Ríos man as party president.

When the convention opened at Concepción on January 21, it was clear that there would be a major battle. One faction supported Ríos and all his works. The other was determined to repudiate him. At first it seemed that the President's supporters would have little difficulty, especially because they faced a divided opposition. But eventually the opposition managed to heal the breaches within its own ranks, and then it succeeded in carrying the convention. Ríos' candidate for president of the party was beaten, though by the narrow margin of thirteen votes. It was a stinging rebuke. The convention directed President Ríos to make another attempt to form a cabinet from the parties of the left, and, acting upon this command, he finally succeeded. But it was an uneasy truce.

ILLNESS OF RÍOS. The political and economic disorganization of the country during his administration seems to have been too much for the President. Early in January, 1946, he took a six months' leave of absence to try to regain his shattered health. Neither *Time* nor any other magazine suggested that his illness was merely a pretense. The Minister of the Interior, Alfredo Duhalde, became Acting President. He was a moderate Radical, a member of the faction that had tried to uphold the Ríos leadership at the party convention. His political views were perhaps slightly more conservative than those of Ríos. So of course this change boded no good for the parties of the left.

LABOR VIOLENCE. Serious labor trouble broke out in Chile only a short time after President Ríos took his leave of absence. For several months strikes had been increasing in number and violence, despite the President's urgent plea to labor to stay on the job. Finally the government decided on drastic action, and outlawed two of the nitrate unions for their continued strikes, which were said to be illegal. The answer of the Chilean Confederation of Labor was to call a giant protest meeting in Santiago. The meeting was scheduled for January 28. Early in the evening thousands of workers poured into the spacious Plaza Bulnes with banners and signs, all bearing slogans directed against the government. Several hundred armed policemen were stationed at strategic points, to keep an eye on the crowd. This fact greatly annoyed the demonstrators, who were accustomed to holding their meetings with the government's blessing and with a minimum of interference. Some people in the crowd began to boo the police. Then the demonstrators argued with one another over the points made by the different speakers, and soon tried to settle the arguments with their fists. The police moved in, ostensibly to keep order, but with unnecessary roughness, according to the reports of some witnesses. Policemen were dragged from their horses, and several of them were seriously beaten. Thereupon their comrades fired into the air, and when this maneuver failed to restore order, they aimed their shots at the feet of the crowd. Nine persons were killed, and many were injured. It was a bloody affair, and though the government acted within its rights, it outraged labor by daring to use an armed police force against labor agitators.

Two days later the dead were buried, and the labor leaders used the occasion to stage another great mass meeting of protest. This time the police were absent, and no violence occurred. But the Communist elements within the labor unions were determined to show their power. They had called a twenty-four-hour general strike of protest, and scheduled it for January 30, the day of the funerals. It was almost one hundred per cent effective. So they announced another general strike for February 4, fixing no time limit and apparently intending to continue it until the government was brought to its knees. But the Socialists, who controlled a large part of the membership of the unions, refused to join their Communist comrades in this demonstration of labor unity. They said that a prolonged general strike would be harmful to the welfare of the nation, and for that reason they ordered their supporters to stay on the job. The "general" strike began as scheduled, but it was far from general. A number of agitators were arrested by the police on charges of overturning buses, throwing lighted torches into street cars, and committing similar acts of violence. They were released after paying moderate fines. In two or three days the general strike had collapsed. Labor was not united, and without unity it could accomplish nothing.[15]

POLITICAL CRISIS. The labor crisis had caused serious political repercussions. The Radical members of the cabinet had presented to Acting President Duhalde a series of demands, which he refused to grant, so they resigned en masse. Duhalde promptly replaced them with Socialists, and the new Socialist ministers obligingly issued a statement condemning the strike as a Communist plot. The break between Socialists and Communists was now complete. Even Duhalde's own Radicals were in the opposition. Eventually they expelled the Acting President from the party. The Chilean Confederation of Labor split in two, and the government promptly recognized the Socialist faction as the "legitimate representative organ of the working classes."

PRESIDENTIAL CAMPAIGN OF 1946. On June 27, 1946, President Ríos died of cancer of the stomach. Thus two Chilean presidents died in office in less than five years. Nothing could have emphasized more sharply the grueling nature of the job—the cruel physical and mental burden imposed by the necessity of trying to reconcile quarreling parties, factions, and individuals. It was enough to make any man pause before offering himself as a presidential candidate. Apparently, however, politically ambitious

[15] See Moisés Poblete Troncoso's article, "Which Way Chilean Labor?" in the April, 1946, issue of *Inter-American*, pp. 30 ff.

Chileans gave very little thought to the matter. Even before the death of Ríos, when it was known that he could not live for many months, the leaders of the different factions began their informal campaigns, making long speeches in which they explained what was wrong with the country and what should be done to make everything right.

The only effect of the President's death, therefore, was to bring the fight out into the open. The Communists first talked of supporting their party president, but later they united with most of the other leftist groups to support the candidacy of Gabriel González Videla, the forceful, white-haired, forty-seven-year-old Radical who had almost beaten Ríos for the party's nomination in 1942. González Videla was more acceptable to the Communists and left-wing elements than Ríos had ever been. But the Socialist faction led by Marmaduke Grove refused to join a united Popular Front. Instead it threw its strength to Alfredo Duhalde, who resigned as acting president in order to be free to enter the campaign. Duhalde's expulsion from his own Radical Party left him without strong support, but in addition to the Grove Socialists he could count on the Agrarians, a small group of moderate conservatives. The right-wing parties made a desperate effort to unite on a single candidate, but without success. Finally the Conservatives chose Senator Eduardo Cruz Coke, while the Liberals named seventy-seven-year-old Arturo Alessandri.

GONZÁLEZ VIDELA THE NEW PRESIDENT. The campaign of 1946 was bitterly fought. The election had been set for September 4, and when all the votes were counted it was announced that nobody had won the majority required by law. González Videla stood first, with one hundred and ninety thousand votes to Cruz Coke's one hundred and forty thousand, but the other two candidates had prevented a decisive contest. So Congress had to make the final choice. There seemed to be little doubt as to the choice it would make. Its members represented left-wing groups, for the most part, and though they had been unable to present a completely united front during the campaign, few persons thought that they would favor a Conservative over the champion of the left. Cruz Coke's supporters refused to concede defeat, however. Conservative congressmen worked long hours in a feverish attempt to arrange a deal that would insure the selection of their candidate. The Communists threatened revolution if González Videla were not confirmed.

Congress met on October 24 and immediately named González Videla president. It was a triumph for the more radical elements in Chile's political life. The Communists, especially, were in a strategic position, for their votes represented almost exactly the margin of the new President's victory. He offered them three cabinet posts, and they accepted. Thus, for the first time in any country of the Americas, Communists became a part of the government. The news made headlines in the United States and Europe. *Communists run Chile* was a frequently used caption. Actually, the Communists had by no means secured control of the nation. Their three ministries, though important, were not the key posts in the cabinet. The best jobs went to members of the President's own Radical Party.[16]

BREAK WITH THE COMMUNISTS. As the months passed, González Videla began to learn the difficulties of coalition government. The Communists caused the greatest trouble. They seemed to be more interested in spreading discontent among the workers than in keeping the administration on an even keel. When Congress passed a bill restricting the spread of farm unions, the Communists demanded its veto. The bill was undoubtedly too drastic; one of its provisions limited membership in the unions to farm workers who could read and write, thus eliminating a substantial majority of them. González Videla did in fact veto the measure, but not in language sufficiently strong to win Communist approval. So they sent a delegation to demand that he place himself squarely on record against all such conservative proposals. The President replied that he would continue to write his own veto messages and determine his own policies, without coercion by any faction. Thereupon the Communist press attacked him with no apparent regard for the fact that three Communists were members of the government. The Communist Ministers offered their resignations soon afterward and González Videla promptly accepted them, giving the vacant posts to members of the Radical Party. "I am in profound disagreement with the Communists," he declared. "They cannot separate me from the people." Thus the Communists lost their first foothold in a Latin American government, only a few months after they had acquired it.

In October of 1947 they encountered still greater difficulties. A strike had been called in the northern copper mines, and the government announced that Communists were responsible for the miners' unrest. Two members of the Jugoslav embassy were specifically accused of abusing their diplomatic privileges by plotting the strategy of the striking miners. These diplomats were expelled from the country and Chile broke diplomatic relations, not only with Jugoslavia, but also with the Soviet Union and

---

[16] See *Gabriel González Videla, Biografía, Análisis Crítico de su Programa*, by Jorge Guzmán Hernández.

another Soviet puppet state, Czechoslovakia. Then the Chilean police began to make wholesale arrests of Communist leaders. Troops were sent to the mine areas. In Chile, as in Brazil, the official policy is now to make Communism as unpopular as possible.

ANOTHER UNSUCCESSFUL UPRISING. Late in 1948 former President Carlos Ibáñez, who had tried to seize the government by force in 1939, led another uprising. Loyal government forces crushed the rebellion before it reached serious proportions, however, and arrested the principal participants. President González Videla showed his appreciation of the troops' loyalty by ordering a twenty per cent increase in army salaries. Even in democratic Chile the government cannot afford to ignore the welfare of the armed forces.

ECONOMIC DIFFICULTIES. In 1949 the world price of copper dropped sharply, and Chile's revenues suffered a corresponding decline. Meanwhile the cost of living continued to rise, and the government seemed powerless to maintain a reasonable balance between prices and wages. The result was a wave of strikes, accompanied by violence in many instances. When the Santiago bus company raised its fares, its buses were stoned and some were overturned and burned. 1950 and 1951 brought still higher prices and still more strikes. González Videla blamed the outlawed but still active Communists for most of the labor agitation, and asked for additional power to take drastic action against them. Congress responded with a law authorizing the government to arrest and transfer to isolated locations any persons accused of menacing democracy. This statute, officially known as the Law for the Defense of Democracy, was hotly attacked by many persons as a violation of individual rights.

PRESIDENTIAL CAMPAIGN OF 1951–1952. Early in 1951 the leaders of Chile's numerous parties began their usual attempts to form coalitions that might be expected to attract the voters. The groups of the left acted first, and they named seventy-two-year-old Carlos Ibáñez del Campo, who had been the virtual dictator of the nation from 1927 until his overthrow by a spontaneous popular revolution in 1931. In 1938 Ibáñez had been an ardent advocate of the Nazi cause, and in 1942 he had been the candidate of the ultraconservatives. But by 1951 he had veered sufficiently to the left to be entirely acceptable to several leftist parties. Even Radio Moscow endorsed him in a Spanish-language broadcast beamed at Latin America, though Ibáñez himself carefully announced that he had not asked for the support of the Communists and had made no deals with them. Meanwhile the Socialists and some other left-wing groups made their own presidential nomination, instead of endorsing Ibáñez. Several parties of the extreme right agreed upon a candidate, and the center parties, led by the Radicals, finally managed to settle their differences and present a united front. President González Videla announced that the government would remain strictly neutral. All the presidential candidates offered sharp criticisms of government policies. Carlos Ibáñez was especially outspoken in his objections to the Law for the Defense of Democracy, which he attacked as a Law for the Suppression of Liberty.

TRIUMPH OF IBÁÑEZ. The election was held on September 4, 1952. Women voted for the first time in a national contest. When all the votes had been counted, Ibáñez was found to have almost as many as the other three candidates. The parties supporting him did not win enough seats in Congress, however, to assure a majority. Therefore Ibáñez began his term without a friendly legislative body. But he has not yet resorted to dictatorial methods, as he did in 1930. One of the principal achievements of his administration to date has been the signing of a new trade treaty with Argentina. This agreement calls for the exchange of Chilean products, such as copper, iron, and lumber, for Argentine meats and oils. Communist agitation in Chile continues, and perhaps that is why President Ibáñez has not kept his campaign promise to ask for a repeal of the Law for the Defense of Democracy. Authority to transfer labor agitators to remote spots can be very useful to a president who is trying to establish industrial peace without too much regard for the means employed.[17]

SELECTED REFERENCES

Amunátegui y Solar, Domingo, *La Democracia en Chile,* Santiago, Universidad de Chile, 1946.

Butland, Gilbert J., *Chile: An Outline of Its Geography, Economics and Politics,* New York, Royal Institute of International Affairs, 1951.

Contreras Guzmán, Víctor, *Bitácora de la Dictadura; Administración Ibáñez, 1927–1931,* Santiago, Imprenta "Cultura," 1942.

Donoso, Ricardo, *Desarollo Político y Social de Chile desde la Constitución de 1833,* 2nd ed., Santiago, Imp. Universitaria, 1942.

——— *Las Ideas Políticas en Chile,* Mexico, D.F., Fondo de Cultura Económica, 1946.

Edwards, Alberto, *La Fronda Aristocrática, Historia Política de Chile,* Santiago, Editorial del Pacífico, 1945.

——— *Historia de los Partidos Políticos Chilenos,* Santiago, Editorial del Pacífico, 1949.

[17] See Robert N. Burr's article, "Chile: Economic Nationalism," in the March, 1953, issue of *Current History,* pp. 165–169.

Ellorrieta Ferrari, Alicia, *El Problema Indígena en Chile*, Santiago, Tall. Gráf. Casa Nacional del Niño, 1941.

Ellsworth, Paul T., *Chile: An Economy in Transition*, New York, Macmillan, 1945.

Evans, Henry Clay, *Chile and Its Relations with the United States*, Durham, N.C., Duke Univ. Press, 1927.

Fergusson, Erna, *Chile*, New York, Knopf, 1943.

Fernández Larraín, Sergio, *Aspectos de la División del Partido Conservador*, Santiago, Editorial del Pacífico, 1950.

Galdames, Luis, *A History of Chile* (translated by Isaac J. Cox), Chapel Hill, N.C., Univ. of North Carolina Press, 1941.

Guzmán Hernández, Jorge, *Gabriel González Videla, Biografía, Análisis Crítico de su Programa*, Santiago, Imp. Universo, 1946.

Marcó Figueroa, Joaquín, *Chile Marca un Camino*, Buenos Aires, Imp. López, 1946.

Miranda Ramírez, Hugo, *Los Partidos Políticos en el Derecho Constitucional Chileno*, Santiago, Editorial Orbe, 1947.

Moore, R. C., *Piety and Poverty in Chile*, Nashville, Tenn., Broadman Press, 1946.

Pinto, Francisco A., *La Estructura de Nuestra Economía*, Santiago, Editorial del Pacífico, 1948.

Prat, Jorge, *El Fracaso de un Triunfo*, Santiago, Editorial Orbe, 1943.

Seguel C., José Miguel, *La Industria Eléctrica ante la Legislación Chilena*, Santiago, Imp. y Lito. "Leblanc," 1941.

Stevenson, John Reese, *The Chilean Popular Front*, Philadelphia, Univ. of Pennsylvania Press, 1942.

Valdés M., Salvador, *Cinco Años de Gobierno de Izquierda*, Puente Alto, Chile, "La Libertad," 1944.

Vicuña, Carlos, *La Tiranía en Chile*, 2 Vols., Santiago, Soc. Imp. y Lito. Universo, 1939, 1945.

Villalobos Avaria, Guillermo, *De la Subdivisión de la Propiedad y el Problema de la Agricultura*, Santiago, Imp. El Esfuerzo, 1942.

CHAPTER 13

CHILE
The Structure of Government

The Constitution

THE stability of Chilean political life, at least by comparison with other countries of Latin America, is reflected in the small number of its constitutions. The fundamental law of 1833 served, with numerous modifications, until 1925, when the present document was adopted. Though considerably longer than the fundamental laws of Argentina and the United States, the Chilean constitution is a relatively short document. It has no preamble. Instead it begins with a number of declarations—that Chile is a unitary republic; that sovereignty resides in the nation; that no person or assembly may usurp the rights of the people or make demands in the name of the people; that no person or assembly, even under pretext of extraordinary circumstances, may assume powers not expressly granted by the fundamental law.[1] Obviously these clauses are designed to prevent dictatorship. They have not been entirely successful. They did not preclude the dictatorial tactics of Carlos Ibáñez, only a few years after the constitution's adoption. But for the most part these clauses have been obeyed. Chile has become a member of the democratic community in good standing.

BILL OF RIGHTS. The bill of rights contains no special features. All the usual guarantees of individual liberty are included, and for the most part they are carefully respected. But there was a time when Chile was not so careful of personal rights. The constitution of 1833 prescribed the Roman Catholic faith to the exclusion of all others, and for a time this clause was

[1] Arts. 1–4.

vigorously enforced. In 1865, however, Congress passed a law permitting residents of the country to worship as they pleased within the confines of their own property, and even to maintain private schools where other than Catholic religious beliefs might be taught. Today, of course, there is complete separation of church and state, as in the United States.[2] Freedom of speech and press have been violated, even within recent years. But such conditions no longer prevail. Tolerance is the watchword in present-day Chile.[3]

The Anglo-Saxon writ of *habeas corpus* appears in the Chilean constitution as the writ of *amparo*. Most Chilean commentators assume that the two are indistinguishable, but this is far from the truth. The Chilean writ of *amparo,* though designed to prevent arbitrary imprisonment, does not prohibit the police from holding a suspect incommunicado for a limited period of time while they conduct a thorough investigation. Nor does *amparo* mean the same thing as in Mexico;[4] its use in Chile is much more limited.

SUSPENSION OF GUARANTEES. There is the usual provision for suspension of constitutional guarantees by means of a declaration of a state of siege or by the more drastic *estado de asamblea,* which is really martial law. The effect of a declaration of *estado de asamblea* is to suspend the operation of all the civil agencies of the government and to close all the courts. The military commanders have absolute authority. Of course, such harsh action is not to be taken unless Chile has actually been overrun by a foreign army, or is in imminent danger of attack. But the less drastic state of siege may be used either in case of external threats or internal commotion. When it has been declared, the president may order the transfer of any person from one department to another, or the imprisonment of any person—in his own home, if necessary. In times of actual or threatened invasion the president may order the suspension of constitutional guarantees, but he may not do so to meet some internal crisis unless Congress is not in session. It may well be asked whether a state of siege decreed by the president during a recess of Congress automatically terminates when Congress reconvenes. The supreme court has ruled that it does not.[5]

AMENDMENT OF THE CONSTITUTION. The process of amending the constitution is rather complicated. Every proposed amendment must be

[2] See page 298.
[3] See *El Derecho de Reunión*, by Jorge Granada Ostolaza.
[4] See pages 273–274.
[5] This question is considered at some length by Jorge Hörmann Montt in his excellent work, *Derecho Constitucional*, 2nd ed., pp. 44–46.

approved by a majority of the entire membership of each house. Then there must be a delay of sixty days, during which time the matter may be debated by newspaper editors, civic leaders, and all public-spirited citizens. The opposition thus has sufficient opportunity to make its strength felt. At the end of the sixty days the proposal again receives the consideration of Congress. This time, however, the two houses meet jointly, and both senators and deputies vote as members of a single body. A majority of the total membership of the two houses is sufficient for adoption.

The measure then goes to the president, who may sign it and thus make it a part of the constitution. But if the president disapproves, he may return the proposal to the house where it originated, together with a statement of his objections. He may not veto it outright, however, as if it were ordinary legislation; instead he is limited to suggestions for improvement. These suggestions are then considered by each house of Congress. If they are accepted by majority vote, the revised amendment is ready for incorporation in the fundamental law. If, on the other hand, Congress rejects the president's proposals, and does so by a two-thirds vote in each house, the measure then returns to the president in its original form. But the president has one more string to his bow; instead of promulgating the proposed amendment, he may submit the entire question to the people for final decision. Chile has never had such a popular plebiscite, and it may well be doubted whether one will ever be held. But the constitution specifically contemplates such a possibility.[6]

Suffrage and Elections

WHO MAY VOTE. The right to vote in national elections is limited to literate citizens, both men and women, who have reached the age of twenty-one years. But even foreigners may participate in municipal elections under certain circumstances. The list of persons who may not vote includes members of the army and navy and of the national police force, and ministers of religion, as well as those who are mentally incapacitated or have been convicted of crime. Communists, too, may not vote.

ELECTION PROCEDURE. Each party prepares a ballot containing only the names of its own candidates, and the government, as usual, provides an official envelope. A voter may accept the ballot of his party in exactly the form he receives it, or he may indicate his preferences among the various names on the list. But there is no way for him to divide his vote among

[6] Arts. 108–110.

the candidates of several parties. A system of proportional representation is used where feasible. Every candidate must be the representative of some political party. In Chile there is no such thing as an independent candidate, according to the letter of the law. But this clause is no bar to the candidacy of independents, because one hundred persons may form a party. So dozens of new parties spring up at every election, only to sink back into oblivion the day after the votes have been cast.[7]

The President

SELECTION, TERM, QUALIFICATIONS, SALARY. The president of Chile is chosen by direct vote of the people. If no person receives a majority, Congress names one of the two highest candidates.[8] Under the constitution of 1833 the voters named presidential electors who in turn selected the chief executive, but this plan was abandoned in 1925. At the same time the president's term was increased from five years to six. He may not serve two consecutive terms. He must be a native-born Chilean, at least thirty years of age, who has never been convicted of crime—conditions that should not prove difficult for one who aspires to the presidency. The salary of the chief executive, translated into American money, is only a little over four thousand dollars a year. Even though he also receives substantial allowances for travel and entertainment, the total is not sufficient to permit him to live in a style befitting the head of an important nation. His official residence, *La Moneda,* is so called because it once served as the mint. It is a low, rambling building which faces on Santiago's central plaza. A number of government offices share *La Moneda* with the president.

EXECUTIVE POWERS. In Chile the president's powers are extensive, but he is by no means the dominant figure that one might reasonably expect after a study of Latin American politics. Congress is also an important branch of the government and never permits the chief executive to forget that fact. The president's powers of appointment and removal are somewhat restricted. He names and removes the members of his own cabinet at his discretion, but Senate approval is required for the appointment of ambassadors and foreign ministers, high army and navy officers, and important administrative officials below cabinet rank. Judges are appointed by the

---

[7] See *El Sistema Electoral Chileno,* by José Luis Castro A. See also Ricardo Cruz Coke's recent work, *Geografía Electoral de Chile.*

[8] In 1946 there was no popular majority and Congress chose the president.

president, but he must make his selections from lists prepared by the courts.[9] The consent of the Senate is necessary for the removal of most bureau chiefs and other high administrative officers. The president, of course, has full responsibility for the routine conduct of foreign affairs. When treaties are made, however, they must be approved by Congress. And only Congress can authorize a state of war. As commander-in-chief of the army and navy the president is the military head of the nation, though he cannot take personal command of the armed forces without the consent of the Senate.

LEGISLATIVE POWERS. The president has the usual power to propose legislation. Moreover, a constitutional amendment adopted in 1943 gives him exclusive authority to initiate measures dealing with the political or administrative organization of the country, the creation of new public services, or increases in the salaries of government employees.[10] Legislative proposals on any subject marked "urgent" by the chief executive must receive prompt consideration by Congress. The veto power follows the usual lines. The president has thirty days to make up his mind, and his veto may be overridden by a two-thirds majority in each house. There is no pocket veto.[11]

For many years the presidents of Chile regularly authorized payments from the public treasury in excess of the amounts appropriated by Congress. The only restraint on this power was the necessity of securing the consent of all the members of the cabinet. This practice led to financial difficulties, just as it has done in Argentina and Mexico. So in 1943 the president's authority was restricted by constitutional amendment. He may not now order extraordinary expenditures except for emergencies arising from public calamities, foreign aggression, domestic disturbances, or the exhaustion of funds that have been appropriated for absolutely essential public services; and in any case the extraordinary expenditures authorized in one year may not exceed two per cent of that year's budget appropriations.[12] The president has unrestricted power to pardon for all offenses against the nation.[13]

PRESIDENTIAL SUCCESSION. Under ordinary circumstances Chile does not have a vice-president. If, however, the president dies or is incapacitated,

[9] See page 339.
[10] Art. 45. But Congress is specifically permitted to propose increases for its own members and employees.
[11] See El Veto Presidencial, by Fernando Rosselot Bordeu.
[12] Art. 72, Cl. 10.
[13] Art. 72, Cl. 12.

the title of vice-president is assumed by the officer who takes his place. This officer is the minister of the interior. After him the order of succession extends to the other cabinet ministers, as provided by law, and then to the president of the Senate, the president of the Chamber of Deputies, and the president of the supreme court. The vice-president does not fill out the unexpired presidential term. Instead he is required to call presidential elections within sixty days, and the new president thus chosen begins a full term of six years.

National Administration

CABINET MINISTERS. The number of cabinet ministers is fixed by law, thus permitting Congress to make such modifications of the administrative organization as may be necessary from time to time. At present there are thirteen major departments: Interior, Foreign Relations, Finance, National Defense, Justice, Public Education, Agriculture, Economy and Commerce, Labor, Lands and Colonization, Health and Welfare, Public Works and Means of Communication, and Mines. The minister of the interior, who stands just below the president in the public administration, is responsible for the supervision of local government. He manages the postal and telegraph services. He directs the conduct of elections. And he is the responsible head of the *carabineros,* Chile's well-organized national police force. The *carabineros* maintain order in both urban and rural districts. They even direct traffic. Local police forces are unknown, an arrangement that greatly strengthens the position of the national government in any dispute with local authorities.

THE CABINET AND CONGRESS. Chile is one of the few Latin American nations that has experimented with parliamentary government. Troops supporting Congress waged a civil war against the forces of the president in 1891 and won a decisive victory. From that date until 1925 Chile had a parliamentary regime. Presidents took care to select cabinet ministers who would be acceptable to Congress, sometimes even choosing them from the membership of the Senate or Chamber of Deputies. Every presidential order required the signature of the appropriate minister, and every minister was personally and collectively responsible for the acts signed by himself and his cabinet colleagues. He could be forced to resign by a congressional vote of lack of confidence.

Then came the constitution of 1925. One of its major purposes was the abolition of parliamentary government and the restoration of the presidential regime. In this it has not been entirely successful, however. Vestiges of the parliamentary order still remain. Congress vociferously insists that cabinet ministers must command its confidence, and sometimes it is able to compel ministerial resignations through the judicious use of political pressure. Even today, therefore, the president is more dependent on congressional co-operation than in most of the nations of Latin America. President Ríos saw fit to fill his cabinet in part from the membership of Congress, and these ministers continued to serve also as congressmen. This arrangement was possible, under the constitution, only because the nation was at war. When, therefore, Japan's crushing defeat by American forces marked the actual end of hostilities, Chile continued its technical state of war, primarily for the purpose of retaining congressmen in the cabinet. This anomalous situation ended abruptly with the supreme court's decision that a state of war no longer existed in fact.[14]

PUBLIC PERSONNEL. Chile has never adopted a formal merit system for public employees. No central civil service commission supervises the employment, promotion, or dismissal of government workers. These matters are left to the discretion of the several ministries. Some ministries have established rules that provide a considerable measure of protection for the rank and file of the workers against arbitrary dismissal. But politics almost always governs the hiring of employees, except for certain technical posts.

Congress

SELECTION, TERMS, QUALIFICATIONS, SALARIES. The members of both houses of Congress are chosen by direct popular vote. Deputies serve for four years and senators for eight. One half of the senators retire every four years, but all the deputies are chosen at the same time. The constitution declares that there shall be one deputy for every thirty thousand inhabitants; the present membership of the Chamber is one hundred and forty-seven. The size of the Senate has been fixed permanently at forty-five. Chile's twenty-five provinces have been placed in nine groups, with one, two, or three provinces to a group, and each group of provinces is entitled to five senators. No provision is made for alternate deputies and senators, as in so many countries of Latin America. Instead, vacancies are filled by special elections. There are no qualifications for deputies,

[14] See Rodolfo Vio Valdivieso's *Nociones de Derecho Público y Privado*, pp. 81–83. See also Wm. S. Stokes' interesting article, "Parliamentary Government in Latin America," in the *American Political Science Review*, Vol. XXXIX, No. 3 (June, 1945), pp. 522–536.

except that they must be citizens and voters. Senators, in addition, must have a minimum age of thirty-five years. The minimum age for the presidency, it will be remembered, is only thirty years,[15] so a citizen too young for the Senate might conceivably be elected president. Salaries are the same in both houses of Congress—approximately twenty-seven hundred dollars a year (American money) plus some additional allowances.[16]

PLACE OF MEETING. The Palace of Congress is an old building in the center of the city, facing a small but beautiful park. The Senate is housed in one wing and the Chamber of Deputies in the other. Both legislative halls are arranged in a similar manner. There is a raised platform at the front of the hall for a president, two vice-presidents,[17] and two secretaries. Directly below this platform is a table for the stenographers. Then come the members' seats, arranged in semicircular form, with the members sitting from right to left, according to their political views.` Two balconies, one above the other, provide space for visiting diplomats, members of the press, and the general public. To the rear of the hall and at one side are the seats used by cabinet ministers when they attend congressional sessions to present bills or answer questions. Public address systems have been installed in both chambers. There are a number of smaller rooms for the use of committees, but members of Congress do not have private offices. A majority of congressmen have private secretaries but must pay for them out of their own pockets, since no appropriation has been made for this purpose.

SESSIONS. Congress meets in regular session from the 21st of May until the 18th of September. In recent years, however, there have been so many special sessions that it has met almost continuously. Special sessions may be called by the president of the nation or the president of the Senate, but the president of the Senate acts only upon the written request of a majority of the members of either house of Congress. When the president calls a special session he indicates the reasons for the summons, and Congress is forbidden to consider any other matters, except proposals for amending the constitution. But when a special session of Congress has been initiated by the members themselves, they are free to take up any matter within the sphere of legislative authority.[18]

VALIDITY OF ELECTIONS. The constitution of 1833 authorized each house

---

[15] See page 328.

[16] These additional allowances are of minor importance.

[17] There are two vice-presidents in the Chamber of Deputies. The rules of the Senate call for but one vice-president.

[18] Constitution, Art. 57.

to pass judgment upon the validity of the election of its own members, and this clause was interpreted to mean that the election of a new member might be challenged, even though no breath of suspicion had been raised against him. The majority in each house authorized without question the seating of its own adherents, and then proceeded to reject the credentials of most of the new senators or deputies of the opposition, regardless of the merits of the controversy—regardless, in fact, of whether any controversy actually existed. Weeks and sometimes even months were wasted in this manner. The situation became a national scandal.[19] When, therefore, a new constitution was adopted in 1925, it made substantial modifications in the manner of determining the validity of presidential and congressional election returns. The task was turned over to a Qualifying Tribunal, whose five members were to be chosen by lot from the judges of the supreme court, the judges of the court of appeals of Santiago, and the ex-officers of the Senate and Chamber of Deputies. Each house of Congress, however, still retains the right to determine whether its members possess the minimum qualifications established by the constitution. This new plan has given much better results.

OFFICERS AND COMMITTEES. At the beginning of each regular legislative session the two houses of Congress choose their respective officers—a president, a vice-president (two vice-presidents in the Chamber of Deputies), a secretary, an assistant secretary and treasurer, and a controller. Although chosen for but a single year, they may be elected for additional terms. The president and vice-president of the Senate form a directing board, which determines the order of business and makes appointments to committees, subject to such modifications as the membership of the Senate may direct. In the Chamber of Deputies the president and two vice-presidents perform a similar function. The Senate has twelve regular standing committees, each composed of five members; and the Chamber has thirteen standing committees, each with a membership of thirteen. The names of the committees are almost identical in the two houses, and parallel closely the cabinet ministries—Foreign Relations, National Defense, Public Education, and the like. Every bill reported to a committee must be returned with appropriate comments within a given period of time. Bills are never buried in committee.

PROCEDURE. During the legislative period Congress usually meets every Tuesday and Wednesday from four until seven. Measures that have been returned from committee are given the customary two readings, one to

[19] Hörmann Montt, op. cit., pp. 60-72.

consider the general principles and the other to discuss the details. Debate is rather narrowly limited in both houses. The constitution declares that one fourth of the senators shall constitute a quorum, and one fifth of the deputies shall be sufficient to do business. Disagreements between the two houses are settled by a complicated plan, already described for Argentina,[20] which permits one house to override the other by a two-thirds vote.

IMPEACHMENT. Impeachment follows the generally accepted form to some extent, but with a number of different features. The Chamber of Deputies has the usual power to institute impeachment proceedings; it may bring action against the president, cabinet ministers and other important administrators, judges of the courts, and even high officers of the army and navy. The president may be impeached at any time during his term of office *and for six months afterward;* cabinet ministers may be impeached up to three months after they have left office. Just what could be gained by impeaching any public official after the expiration of his term is not entirely clear, for the constitution specifically declares that punishment shall not extend farther than to removal from office.[21] It does add, however, that any public officer found guilty by process of impeachment shall then be tried before a court of competent jurisdiction, in order to answer for his high crimes and misdemeanors, and there can be no doubt that conviction in impeachment proceedings would be an effective method of focusing public attention on the need for a criminal trial. Impeachment cases are tried before the Senate, as in the United States, but a two-thirds vote is not necessary for conviction unless the president of the nation is accused. Otherwise a simple majority suffices.

The Courts

SUPREME COURT. Because Chile is a unitary republic, it escapes the necessity for separate sets of federal and state or provincial courts. One judicial hierarchy serves the entire nation. The head of this hierarchy, of course, is the supreme court, which has thirteen members. Each member must be at least thirty-six years of age, and must have a minimum of fifteen years' experience as attorney or judge. Supreme court justices are named by the president, but he must fill each vacancy from a list of five names prepared by the court itself. The two senior judges of the appellate courts must be included in each list. Justices of the supreme court, like all major

[20] See pages 110–111.
[21] Art. 42, Cl. 1.

court judges in Chile, serve during good behavior. The president of the high tribunal presides over its deliberations for a term of three years. He is named by the president of the nation, who follows the court's wishes in this matter. The supreme court exercises general supervision over all the other tribunals of the nation. By a two-thirds vote it may even recommend that the president remove a judge for improper conduct, and such a recommendation leads automatically to removal. The constitution specifically confers upon the supreme court the right to declare laws unconstitutional.[22] It has used this power with moderation, and usually without serious political repercussions. The president of Chile, unlike the chief executives of so many Latin American nations, is in no position to enforce his will upon the judiciary.

APPELLATE COURTS. Below the supreme court are nine courts of appeal, which have been established in the principal cities of the nation. The number of judges ranges from nineteen in Santiago, where the volume of legal business is very great, to four in some of the smaller centers. The legal qualifications for these justices is somewhat lower than for members of the supreme court—thirty-two years of age, with a minimum of twelve years' experience. For each vacancy in an appellate court the supreme court prepares a list of three names, and from this list the president makes his selection. The law provides that the presidency of each court of appeal shall rotate among its members, in order of seniority of service. Each court president serves for but a single year.

INFERIOR COURTS. At the bottom of the judicial hierarchy are the *jueces letrados*—the "learned judges" who preside over the courts of first instance. There are one hundred and thirty-nine of these judges, and they serve in every small area (*departamento*) of the nation. Seventeen have been assigned to Santiago, seven to Valparaíso, and three each to such larger centers as Valdivia and Concepción. The qualifications required of these judges are legal training and a minimum age of twenty-five years. They are appointed by the president from lists submitted by the appropriate courts of appeal. Their term of office is only one year, but reappointment is common.

Local Government

PROVINCES. The system of local government is highly centralized, as in France. The nation has been divided, primarily for administrative pur-

[22] Art. 86, Cl. 2.

poses, into provinces, departments, subdelegations, and districts.[23] Of
these various units, the provinces are the largest. Chile has twenty-five
provinces. Though they are called *provinces,* as in Argentina, they have
virtually no similarity to the Argentine provinces, which are partners in a
federal union and roughly equivalent to our states. The Chilean concept
of a province is an administrative area established for the convenience of
the national government and serving national ends. Each province is
headed by an *intendente,* who is the direct and immediate representative
of the president of the nation. He is appointed by the president for a term
of three years, but may be removed at any time. He may, on the other
hand, be reappointed indefinitely. His powers are very extensive. He is
authorized to enforce the laws, insure the proper conduct of public employees, and supervise every aspect of provincial administration. The
carabineros within the province are directly responsible to him. Prefects
are appointed on a purely political basis, and are expected to mix politics
with their administrative functions. Each province has a provincial assembly, whose members are chosen for three years by the municipal councils.
The provincial assembly is supposed to advise the *intendente,* but he is
under no obligation to take its advice. In fact, assembly powers have been
so narrowly restricted by law that they scarcely merit the space required
to enumerate them.[24]

DEPARTMENTS. Below the province is the department. Most provinces
have three or four departments apiece, but Santiago has six. Aysen, whose
seventeen thousand people occupy an area as big as Indiana in the far south
of the country, is both a province and a department. The principal officer of each department is a governor, who is appointed for three years
by the president, upon the recommendation of the *intendente.* The governor is a small-scale *intendente,* administering the affairs of the department
and issuing such orders as may be necessary to supplement the decrees
of his superior.

SUBDELEGATIONS AND DISTRICTS. The departments are divided into subdelegations, and the subdelegations into districts. Each subdelegation is
headed—appropriately enough—by a subdelegate, who is appointed for
one year by the governor of the department and made directly responsible
to him. Each district is administered by an inspector, who is named by the
subdelegate and serves at his pleasure. Within the departments, subdele-

---

[23] See *De las Divisiones Territoriales Administrativas,* by Manuel Alvarez Alvarez.
[24] Yet they were thought worthy of a brief monograph. See *Asembleas Provinciales,* by
Raúl Sáenz Vieyra.

gations, and districts there are no assemblies corresponding to the assemblies of the provinces.

MUNICIPALITIES. Although virtually no provision is made for popular participation in the affairs of the provinces and their various subdivisions, the situation is quite different with regard to the cities. Each municipality has a popularly elected council, ranging in size from five to fifteen members, according to population. Literate foreigners may take part in a local election if they are residents of long standing. They may not, however, be elected to public office. The members of a city council are chosen for three years and serve without pay. They enact the ordinances necessary for the conduct of municipal affairs. Administrative activities are in the hands of a mayor, who is chosen by the council from its own membership except in three large cities,[25] where the central government reserves the right of appointment. The mayors of cities receive salaries, which vary with the number and importance of their duties, but are usually nominal. In the smaller communities they are paid only a little over one hundred dollars a year. It should be recognized that neither mayors nor councilmen actually have very much to do. Most administrative matters of any consequence are directed by the *intendentes* and their subordinates. Legislative needs are met, for the most part, by the laws of Congress or the provincial assemblies, or by the decrees of the centrally appointed administrators. Local self-government in the American sense has never seemed very important to Chileans.[26]

SANTIAGO. Within the last two pages passing reference has been made to the *province* of Santiago, and also to the *city* of that name. There are, in fact, three Santiagos—a province, a department, and a municipality. The province of Santiago comprises six departments, but one of them, the department of Santiago, contains nearly eighty-five per cent of the population of the province. Within the department of Santiago are twenty-one municipalities, but the city of Santiago is by all odds the most important. It has sixty per cent of the people who live within the department. Foreigners are often bewildered by the use of the name *Santiago* for several areas of varying size and importance, just as they are confused by the use of the name *New York* for a state as well as a city of the American Union.

[25] Santiago, Valparaíso, and Viña del Mar.
[26] See *La Administración Comunal*, by Gustavo Lorca Rojas.

SELECTED REFERENCES

Alvarez Alvarez, Manuel, *De las Divisiones Territoriales Administrativas*, Santiago, Ancud, Imp. y Enc. "La Cruz del Sur," 1943.

Amunátegui Lecaros, Miguel Luis, *Las Constituciones Liberales*, Santiago, Impresores "La Tarde," 1943.

Bercovich Rosenblut, Raúl, *Agravios Inferidos por Funcionarios Públicos a los Derechos Garantidos por la Constitución*, Santiago, Imp. El Imparcial, 1942.

Bernaschina González, Mario, *Fuentes para el Estudio de la Constitución Política de 1925*, Santiago, Universidad de Chile, 1943.

—— *Síntesis del Derecho Constitucional Chileno*, Santiago, Tall. Gráf. "Valdés Hnos," 1944.

Bustos Acevedo, Julio, *La Seguridad Social*, Santiago, Tall. Gráf. "La Nación," s.a., 1942.

Castro A., José Luis, *El Sistema Electoral Chileno*, Santiago, Nascimento, 1941.

Contreras de la Vega, Humberto, *La Responsabilidad del Estado por los Actos Lesivos de sus Funcionarios*, Santiago, Imp. de Carabineros de Chile, 1942.

Estévez Gazmuri, Carlos, *Derecho Constitucional*, Santiago, Galcón, 1947.

Figueroa Araya, E., *Las Enfermedades Profesionales*, Santiago, Imp. y Lito. "Leblanc," 1943.

Figueroa Carrasco, Ramón Angel, *La Subordinación Legal de los Tribunales ante la Inconstitucionalidad de Forma de las Leyes*, Santiago, Tall. Gráf. "Siamente," 1944.

González Novoa, Guido, *Sindicalización de Funcionarios Públicos*, Santiago, Instituto Geográfico Militar, 1940.

Granada Ostolaza, Jorge, *El Derecho de Reunión*, Santiago, Dirección General de Prisiones, Imp., 1943.

Heise González, Julio, *La Constitución de 1925 y las Nuevas Tendencias Político-Sociales*, Santiago Editorial Universitaría, 1951.

Herrera Aristeguí, Alfredo, *Monografía sobre la Caja Nacional de Empleados Públicos y Periodistas*, Santiago, 1942.

Hörmann Montt, Jorge, *Derecho Constitucional*, 2nd ed., Santiago, Dirección General de Prisiones, Imp., 1942.

Lorca Rojas, Gustavo, *La Administración Comunal*, Valparaíso, Chile, Escuela Tipográfica Salesiana, 1943.

Merino Darrouy, Luis, *Evolucion del Poder Ejecutivo en Chile*, Santiago, Editorial Universitaria, 1949.

Montecinos Rozas, Edmundo, *Apuntaciones para el Estudio de la Evolución de los Partidos Políticos Chilenos y de su Proyección Jurídica*, Santiago, Dirección General de Prisiones, Imp., 1942.

Pardo Zamora, Miguel L., *El Sufragio Universal en Chile*, Santiago, 1946.

Reyes Mason, Carlos, *Jurisprudencia de la Constitución Política de 1925*, Santiago, Imp. El Imparcial, 1944.

Rosselot Bordeu, Fernando, *El Veto Presidencial*, Santiago, Dirección General de Prisiones, Imp., 1942.

Sáenz Vieyra, Raúl, *Asembleas Provinciales,* Valparaíso, Chile, Sociedad Editora Italiana, 1942.

Salas Romo, Julio, *Los Alcaldes, Historia de su Establecimiento y Estudio sobre su Remoción en el Derecho Chileno,* Santiago, Imp. América, 1942.

Silva de la Fuente, Alejandro, *Cuestiones Constitucionales, 1924–1947,* Santiago, Editorial Tegualda, 1948.

Tagle Villarroel, Emilio, *Organización, Atribuciones y Jurisprudencia de los Juzgados Especiales de Menores,* Santiago, Impr. "Roma," 1947.

Torres de la Fuente, Eduardo, *La Elección del Presidente de la República,* Santiago, Impr. "Relámpago," 1948.

Varas Contreras, Guillermo, *Derecho Administrativo,* Santiago, Editorial Nascimento, 1940.

Vio Valdivieso, Rodolfo, *Nociones de Derecho Público y Privado,* Santiago, Imp. El Imparcial, 1943.

CHAPTER 14

PERU

~~~~~~

The Land and the People

THE COASTAL PLAIN. Peru, like ancient Gaul, is divided into three parts. The great backbone of the Andes runs the entire length of the country from northwest to southeast, creating three separate regions that are completely different in climate, crops, and people. To the west, between the Andes and the sea, lies a narrow coastal plain. In some places this plain has a width of but three or four miles; almost nowhere is it more than one hundred miles in width, and the average is about thirty-five miles. Moreover, it is not uniformly level. Cross-ridges of foothills and low mountains —some of them only a few miles apart—run all the way to the edge of the ocean, turning the coastal plain into a series of narrow valleys that are difficult of access except by boat. The prevailing rain-bearing winds, in this part of the world, are on the other side of the Andes, and never get across. Therefore rain is practically unknown in the coastal region. which was as bleak and desolate as the great desert of northern Chile until extensive irrigation projects transformed it into a lovely land.

Today the plain is the heart of Peruvian civilization. It contains the capital city, Lima, which with its seaport (Callao) has a population of more than one million and is nearly eight times as large as any other city of Peru. Lima itself is only six miles from the ocean. Its architecture and gardens make it a most picturesque metropolis. Old churches and temples stand side by side with modern homes and apartment houses. Tree-lined suburbs spread across the valley. Practically all the industries of Peru center around the capital. Here are financial offices, important stores, the two principal universities, the art institutes. Two thirds of the nation's trade passes through Lima's seaport.

When the Spaniards came to Peru, in the early days of the sixteenth century, they found that it was the center of a great Indian civilization known as the Inca Empire. The capital of that empire was Cuzco, high in the Peruvian Andes. It took only a few years for the Spaniards under Francisco Pizarro to destroy the ancient empire and make themselves its masters.[1] Their new domain stretched from northern Ecuador to central Chile. But, like the Incas before them, they made Peru its center. Lima, which Pizarro founded in 1535, soon became virtually the capital of South America. It was certainly the most distinguished city of the continent and probably the most beautiful. Vestiges of that ancient glory still remain.

The agricultural pattern. The agricultural lands of the coastal strip produce an overwhelming share of the nation's export crops. First comes sugar, and then cotton. The area devoted to these crops is relatively small, but soil and climate combine to yield a large return per acre. There are, in fact, a number of factors to offset the geographic handicaps of the coastal plain. One is the Humboldt Current, which carries a steady flow of cold water northward from the Antarctic regions to the Peruvian coast. The winds blowing across this current bring cooling fogs to the entire coastal area and thus provide a pleasant climate. Peru, it must be remembered, is well within the tropics, and under other circumstances might be expected to have very high temperatures. But Lima, which is only twelve degrees from the equator, has a lower average temperature than Los Angeles throughout the year.

The coastal valleys are fortunate, also, to have fertile soil. Much of it is alluvial, carried down from the mountains by hundreds of small streams. There is, of course, the need for constant irrigation, but this presents no insurmountable problems. The high Andes are close at hand and have an annual rainfall of thirty or forty inches. During the rainy season, therefore, mountain torrents race toward the sea and can be harnessed for purposes of irrigation without great expense or labor. Even the necessary fertilizer is readily available. Islands off the Peruvian coast provide a home for great quantities of birds, whose deposits are rich in nitrogen. This is the famous *guano,* which was once exported to Europe at the rate

---

[1] The classic history of Pizarro and his times is Wm. H. Prescott's *History of the Conquest of Peru,* first published a little more than a century ago, and later appearing in many other editions. A comparatively recent work (1939) in Spanish is *Historia del Perú, Descubrimiento, Conquista, Colonia,* by Ricardo Mariategui Oliva.

of hundreds of thousands of tons a year, providing rich fertilizer for European farmers and a rich revenue for the Peruvian government. But eventually the deposits showed danger of depletion. It became necessary to shut off virtually all shipments of guano to foreign countries in order to assure an adequate supply for Peruvian agriculture.

Petroleum. Even more important than sugar or cotton in the national economy is petroleum, which has been produced in large quantities for many years. Peru is the world's twelfth largest producer of petroleum, and was the first nation of South America to exploit its extensive deposits. More recently, however, it has been far outstripped by several other countries. The output of the peak year of 1936 has not since been reached, but the Peruvian government is now offering important inducements to private companies, both domestic and foreign, to search for and develop new oil lands. The present known deposits are located chiefly in the northern part of the coastal strip. Many of them are within sight of the sea, or even below it.

THE HIGH PLATEAU. From the coast the Andes rise steeply to great heights, forming a lofty plateau two hundred miles or more in width. This is the second of Peru's major geographical divisions, and it accounts for nearly thirty-five per cent of the country's area. It is bleak and uninviting, and not well suited to the development of a modern civilization. Its greatest handicap, without doubt, is altitude. Heights of ten thousand feet are common, and fourteen or fifteen thousand feet are not unusual. At such altitudes the cold is always intense. Vegetation is stunted and agriculture presents special problems. Persons who are not accustomed to the rare air of the high plateau suffer from mountain sickness (*soroche*) and find difficulty in leading normal lives. The plateau is not a flat tableland. Instead it is a crisscross of mountain chains, with hundreds of deep valleys. Transportation from one valley to another, or to the coast, is exceedingly difficult. A few railroads and highways do indeed connect the cities of the coastal area with the interior, but they have been built at great expense and great hazard.

Primitive Indian life. The inhabitants of the high plateau are mostly Indians, descendants of the ancient Quechas and Aymarás. Even today their manner of life is very similar to that of their forefathers. They live in mud huts without any of civilization's so-called conveniences. For the most part they are farmers, raising wheat, corn, rye, barley, potatoes, and other temperate zone crops. Peru is the home of the potato; from here it was spread by the Spaniards to all parts of the world. The Indian families have herds of llamas, alpacas, and sheep. Most essential to the economy of this region is the llama, which makes an excellent beast of burden. It has an unpleasant disposition, and it will not carry an unreasonably heavy load. In fact, it will sit down and refuse to move if it thinks that it is being asked to carry too much. But the Indians are used to dealing with these sit-down strikes and know how to use the llamas to best advantage. They use llama wool for clothing, llama skins for leather, and even llama dung for fuel. Without the llama their lives would be almost unbearable.

Even in its present form, life in this area necessitates great hardships. The inhabitants must accept numbing cold most of the time, and gnawing hunger when crops are poor. But they have one compensation—the coca plant, whose leaves they chew almost continuously. This is the plant from which cocaine is derived. It must not be confused with cacao, the source of chocolate. There can be no doubt that coca makes the Indians relatively insensitive to cold, hunger, and pain. It also affects their intelligence, in all probability, and everyone who has studied the Indian problem has recommended that some way be found to wean them from their dependence on the coca plant. But that is more easily said than done, especially in the light of existing conditions. The Indian problem is accentuated by the fact that great numbers of them are unfamiliar with Spanish. After several centuries of life in a Spanish-speaking country they still use their ancient Indian dialects, and thus are cut off from the main current of modern Peruvian civilization. The central government has tried to educate them, but has found the task exceedingly difficult.[2]

Minerals. The high plateau would have very little economic value if it did not possess vast mineral deposits, but these make it of great importance to the nation. In the early days gold and silver were taken from the Peruvian mines in almost fabulous amounts and provided a substantial revenue for the Spanish crown. Today copper has replaced them as a major source of mineral wealth. It stands second only to petroleum. The principal copper mines are in the famous Cerro de Pasco region, which lies northeast of Lima at an elevation of about fourteen thousand feet. Copper is brought from the more remote mines on the backs of llamas and is carried by the Central Railroad down the Andes to the sea at Callao. There are, of course, other metals that deserve at least honorable mention— lead, zinc, vanadium, manganese. Silver and gold are still mined in

[2] See Max H. Minano-García's monograph, *Some Educational Problems in Peru.*

considerable quantities. Important deposits of iron have been discovered in recent years. But none of these has been able to challenge the supremacy of copper.

Cuzco. Cuzco, which the Incas made their capital, is still the principal city of the high plateau, with a population of about fifty thousand. It is difficult to reach, requiring an exhausting two-day train journey from the southern port of Mollendo or a hazardous airplane flight from Lima. But thousands of tourists who visit it every year declare that it is well worth the effort. On every hand are the ruins of Inca temples, fortresses, and palaces. The great Temple of the Sun still broods over the city in majestic splendor. On a nearby hill stand the pre-Inca ruins of the Citadel of Sachsahuaman, built of giant stones that must have been lifted into place by the labor of thousands of slaves. Along the narrow streets of the city plod the Indians in their picturesque garb. Cuzco is a most fascinating place to visit.

EASTERN LOWLANDS. Beyond the high plateau lies the third principal region of Peru—the eastern lowlands. This section, which comprises more than fifty per cent of the nation's area, has very little present economic value. It is really a part of the Amazon basin, and most of it is steaming jungle. Lying on the eastern side of the Andes, it receives all the rain that is denied to the western coastal area. One hundred inches a year are not uncommon in many parts of this territory. It is very inaccessible and most of it has never been explored. The only city of any consequence in the whole region is Iquitos, which lies on a branch of the Amazon River twenty-three hundred miles from its mouth. It has a population of about thirty thousand. As recently as 1940 the journey from Lima in western Peru to Iquitos in the eastern part of the country involved a day's train journey to the high Andes and across the main range, followed by an additional day of motor car travel over the eastern range, and then eight days by pack mules along narrow trails, ending with seven days on the river in canoes and on a small steamer. It can readily be understood why the Peruvian government, anxious to strengthen its garrison at Iquitos during a border dispute with Ecuador, once loaded troops on a transport at Callao and sent them through the Panama Canal, around the northern coast of South America to the mouth of the Amazon, and up the river to their final destination, a total distance of sixty-five hundred miles.

In 1945 a road was finally completed down the eastern slope of the Andes and across the jungle. Air service, too, has helped to reduce the isolation of Iquitos. But it must be remembered that this city is one spot in a great wilderness. Over most of the eastern lowlands savage Indians still roam. There are probably not more than one hundred thousand people in the whole area, which is as big as the state of Texas. Some natural rubber is gathered in the vicinity of Iquitos, and the coca shrub is grown on the eastern slopes of the Andes. These slopes, at altitudes of three to six thousand feet, are sufficiently high to escape the worst inconveniences of the jungle, and some day they may have an important agricultural development. But first their curse of inaccessibility must be overcome.

POPULATION, AREA, RACES. Some historians estimate that Peru may have had ten million inhabitants in the days before the Spanish conquest. To-day, however, it has only about eight million, which places it fifth in population among the nations of Latin America. It is fifth in area, also, with about five hundred thousand square miles. In other words, it is about as large as the United States east of the Alleghenies. Sixty per cent of the people, according to reliable estimates, are full-blooded Indians. Another ten per cent are whites, mostly of Spanish descent. They largely comprise the ruling class. Nearly all the rest of the population is of mixed white and Indian blood. There is, however, a fairly large colony of Japanese. It is larger than in any of the other Latin American nations except Brazil.[3]

FOREIGN ECONOMIC CONTROL. One feature of Peru's economic life is the strong position of foreign enterprises. The British, and also the Italians and Germans, once had substantial investments in Peru, but for many years the United States has dominated the field. American companies now control copper and oil production almost completely and have made large investments in cotton and sugar plantations. Transportation and banking are largely in American hands. Many factories are American-owned. There can be no doubt that these large foreign investments have aided Peru's economic development, but for many years the official Peruvian viewpoint was that this development had been almost exclusively for the benefit of the foreigners. The present government, however, has abandoned this traditional attitude. Foreign capital is given a cordial welcome, and is made to understand that it will not be subjected to unreasonable restrictions.[4]

INDUSTRY. Manufactured goods represent but a small part of the nation's exports. The factories are small and not designed for large-scale production. Indian weavers working in their own homes still account for a substantial part of the textile industry. But many of the newer plants

---

[3] See page 128.
[4] Many American companies are now taking full advantage of their opportunities.

have developed along modern lines.   There are factories turning out food-stuffs and beverages, leather goods, paper, metal products, and chemicals. The government is specially concerned with the establishment of heavy industry, for it shares with many other Latin American governments the belief that industrialization will raise the standard of living.   Although there is virtually no heavy industry at present, extensive plans are on foot. Peru has large deposits of both iron and coal.   The iron, in large quantities and of very high grade, is in the south.   The most important coal deposits, both anthracite and bituminous, are not far from Chimbote, which is on the coast about three hundred miles north of Lima.   Here a steel plant is under construction.   The present port facilities at Chimbote are very meager, but are being steadily improved.   The value of this site for heavy industry is enhanced by the availability of cheap hydroelectric power in great quantities.

The Pattern of Politics

THE ARISTOCRATS IN CONTROL.   Peru has had a turbulent and bloody his-tory.   Not until 1945 did it establish a government that could be called democratic in any proper sense of the term.   Prior to that time it was ruled by a little group of the "best" families and their satellites.   Unfortunately, however, these wealthy families could not always agree among themselves, and their differences fanned the ambitions of unscrupulous military leaders. It is true that public-spirited citizens of great ability sometimes managed to attain high office, but even they had little power to change the system that had dominated Peruvian life for many years.   The army was very power-ful, and most of the nation's presidents came from its ranks.   There were many dictators and would-be dictators, but few of them managed to retain power for any considerable period of time.   One of the exceptions was Ramón Castilla, who ruled the country benevolently but with a hand of iron from 1845 to 1851 and again from 1855 to 1862.   His retirement was followed by a period of almost continuous civil strife, in addition to a brief war with Spain.   In six years there were five revolutions and five new presidents.   Between 1879 and 1883 the country was again plagued with rebellions while it was fighting a foreign war—this time against Chile. Eventually Peru lost the war and made a humiliating peace.   But its civil wars were by no means ended.   Another one began almost at once.

DICTATORSHIP OF LEGUÍA.   The first years of the twentieth century wit-nessed no substantial improvement in Peru's political methods.   In 1909

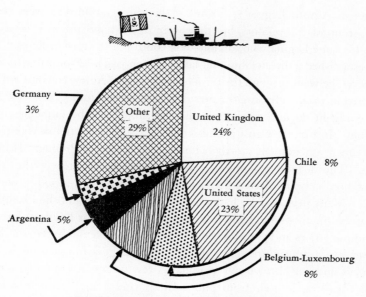

Peruvian Exports to Principal Countries (1951)

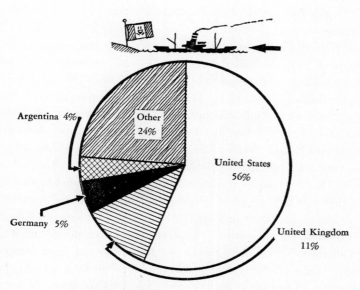

Peruvian Imports from Principal Countries (1951)

Based on information obtained from the May, 1953, issue of *International Financial Statistics*, a publication of the International Monetary Fund.

President Agusto Leguía and some of his cabinet ministers were seized by a group of conspirators, but they were rescued and resumed office. It was this same Leguía who forcibly took control of the government in 1919 and established a dictatorship that lasted eleven years. From time to time, however, he went through the form of re-election. A new constitution was adopted in 1920, increasing the president's term from four years to five, but specifying in no uncertain terms that he should not be immediately re-eligible. In 1923 the clause prohibiting immediate re-election was removed by a timely amendment shortly before the expiration of President Leguía's term. The dictatorship might have continued indefinitely if the world depression had not affected Peru early in 1930, causing a serious economic crisis. Many persons who had accepted without complaint the President's dictatorial methods suddenly rose in protest against his failure to prevent a slump in prices and public revenues. A revolt broke out in the south and spread like a prairie fire across the country. Leguía resigned on August 25, 1930, and was thrown into prison. A few weeks later he was charged with enriching himself from public funds, and after several months of investigation he was ordered to make restitution of about seven million dollars. Almost a year later, still in prison and seriously ill, he was impeached as a traitor to his country.[5] But he died in early February, 1932, before the scheduled date of the impeachment trial. Thus his spectacular career came to its ignominious end.

DESPOTISM AND REVOLUTION. Two days after the resignation of Leguía, in August of 1930, the leader of the revolutionary movement became provisional president. His name was Luis M. Sánchez Cerro, and he was a lieutenant colonel in the army. Many persons were not satisfied with his selection, however. Riots and uprisings broke out afresh and continued sporadically for several months. Finally the revolutionists gained the upper hand and forced Sánchez Cerro to resign. The president of the supreme court was installed as provisional president, only to be overthrown a few days later by counter-revolutionaries. The following October (1931) an election was held to select a new president. Force and fraud played their usual part, and after the votes had been counted it was announced that Sánchez Cerro was the winner. Almost at once he requested and received from Congress extraordinary powers for the purpose of "combating communism"—the excuse prevalent at that time for depriving citizens of their civil liberties. Opposition leaders were exiled. Thereupon the crews of two battleships mutinied, and were not subdued until airplanes and battle-

[5] In Peru, as in Chile, a president may be impeached after he has left office.

ships had been used against them. Only four months later the friends of the late President Leguía attempted to seize the government aeronautics school, but were defeated. The following March another unsuccessful revolt led to the suicide of its chief. In April, 1933, a new constitution was adopted, and three weeks later President Sánchez Cerro was assassinated. Violence was still the keynote of Peruvian political life.

BENAVIDES. The man chosen by Congress as the nation's new president was General Oscar Benavides, a popular military hero who had served briefly as chief executive nearly twenty years earlier. Benavides had very little patience with the delays of congressional procedure. As a military man he was accustomed to giving orders that would be promptly obeyed, and he expected to run the nation in that manner. To a large extent he succeeded. He inspired stringent laws that practically destroyed civil rights, and made it extremely dangerous for anyone to criticize the government. He exiled or imprisoned some of his principal opponents. And his persistent habit of governing by decree made Congress virtually unnecessary. Elections were finally scheduled for October 11, 1936. There were four candidates. When the votes were counted, however, it was discovered that the "wrong" man had won. So the government hastily invalidated the election. Congress then extended the term of President Benavides to 1939 and thoughtfully voted itself out of existence, after directing the chief executive to call a new election "when convenient." After that there was little openly expressed opposition to the Benavides regime. There was, however, one unsuccessful attempt on the president's life, and one abortive revolution.

Benavides was highly conservative, and of course he was a favorite of the landed aristocracy, for whose benefit he ran the country. But he was sufficiently intelligent to recognize the need for social legislation. By law and decree he sponsored a number of measures designed to improve the lot of the workers. A social insurance system, covering most employees except clerical workers and domestic servants, was set up in 1936. Public hospitals and clinics were established in principal cities. Low-cost restaurants were opened, and public housing was undertaken on a modest scale.[6] These were the concessions of the aristocracy to changing conditions. Most of them understood that they could no longer maintain the feudal system inherited from colonial days.

ELECTION OF MANUEL PRADO. In 1939 another presidential election was

[6] See Mary M. Cannon's *Social and Labor Problems of Peru and Uruguay*, published in mimeographed form in 1945 by the Women's Bureau of the U.S. Department of Labor.

held, and this time the government-sponsored candidate won without difficulty. He was Manuel Prado Ugarteche, son of a former president, a highly respected member of an old Spanish family. Trained as an engineer, the new chief executive had served with distinction as a college professor and banker. At fifty he was white-haired but still slender. Most people were pleased by his mild manners and soft speech. The opposition objected less to Prado himself than to the company he kept. He was, they said, the personal choice and more or less the tool of Benavides. He represented the *status quo.*

To a considerable extent President Prado justified these fears, especially in the early part of his administration. He took orders from his predecessor and filled his cabinet with friends of the ex-President. Very gradually, however, he began to assert his own independence. There was no sharp break with Benavides—just a gradual weakening of the ties that bound the two men. Benavides was named ambassador to Spain, and later to Argentina, and in this way he was removed from the domestic political scene. As Benavides men in the government died or resigned, they were replaced by known Prado supporters. The new President did not make any sudden change in the established policies of the government. He retained the Benavides-inspired press law which made any criticism of the government a serious offense. He kept the hated secret police, whose members were commonly known as *soplones* (informers). He continued the systematic persecution of the largest opposition party, whose leaders had been driven into hiding or exile. But in many ways he displayed a spirit of moderation that was new to Peruvian politics. He even worked with Congress, instead of telling its members to go home.

REACTIONARY OPPOSITION. Not all the Conservatives supported President Prado. Some members of the extreme right resented his conciliatory methods and willingness to listen to the complaints of the working class. They regarded his proposals for an extension of the social security system as evidence of dangerous radicalism. This group was not large, but it was highly vocal. Its leaders, the Miró Quesada family, were the owners of Lima's influential newspaper *El Comercio.* They had even objected to the "liberalism" of General Benavides, though in all fairness it must be reported that their quarrel with the General had very little to do with his political and social policies. It sprang from a personal matter—the refusal of the government to execute a young man who had assassinated the head of the Miró Quesada family, together with his wife. Punishment was limited to twenty-five years' imprisonment, on account of the assassin's age, and this comparatively lenient treatment roused the fury of the remaining Miró Quesadas. They helped to finance a semi-fascist organization called the *Civilistas,* whose leader—a sharp-eyed fanatic named Luis Flores—wore a black shirt and introduced the other customary fascist trappings.

BOUNDARY DISPUTE WITH ECUADOR. One cause that united virtually all Peruvians, regardless of their political beliefs, was the undeclared war against Ecuador. The basis of this trouble was a border dispute over a large area of largely unexplored jungle in the Amazon basin. Both countries had claimed this territory for more than a century, but had done almost nothing to make their claims effective. Finally, in July of 1941, shooting broke out in the disputed region. Both sides declared that they had been provoked into action. In any event, the Peruvians were clearly prepared to back up their territorial claims. They sent several thousand men into the field, together with the necessary equipment for a protracted struggle. The government of Ecuador responded as best it could, but it had neither the men nor the material resources to provide effective resistance. The United States, Argentina, and Brazil offered to mediate the controversy, and eventually this offer was accepted by both sides. But in the meantime sporadic fighting continued until the Peruvians were firmly entrenched in the disputed territory. The award ultimately made by the three mediating powers recognized that for the most part Peru's claims were well founded. Ecuador agreed to this decision, though with understandable reluctance.

MULTIPLICITY OF PARTIES. When President Prado was elected in 1939, his support came from a coalition of twelve conservative parties. That situation was typical of Peruvian politics: a great multiplicity of political groups, each bearing some high-sounding name and each able to claim the allegiance of but a small fraction of the voters. Government by coalition has always been necessary, because no one party has been able to obtain a majority. In a recent election one candidate for senator proudly announced that he had been pledged the support of fifteen parties. The present conservative coalition, which calls itself the National Alliance, is made up of the Revolutionary Union, the Republican Socialist Party, the Authentic Socialist Party, the Christian Socialist Party, the groups comprising the National Democratic Coalition, the Liberal Party, the Nationalist Party of Peru, the Constitutional Party, the Radical Party, the Democratic National Union, the National Front of Women, the Democratic Party, the Independent Civic Movement, and various small groups comprising the National Union. To the left of this conservative coalition we have a vast number of parties, groups, and splinters, all adding to the general confusion. Names are totally valueless, of course, in determining the political principles of the various groups. The Democratic National Union is no more democratic than the National Union. The Radicals are highly conservative.

Aprismo. Peru's largest political party is merely one of the factions of the opposition. In fact, it is not even a legally recognized party. The law prohibits its very existence, and its leaders are hounded by the police from one hiding place to another. For many years it was called the American Revolutionary Popular Alliance (*Alianza Popular Revolucionaria Americana*), or *Apra* for short, and the movement was known as *Aprismo*. Today its official title is Party of the People, but almost everyone still calls it Apra. *Aprismo* has become the most loved and most respected name—or the name most hated and feared, according to the point of view—in Peruvian political life.

The acknowledged leader of Apra is a stocky, heavy-set man in his early sixties, whose name is Víctor Raúl Haya de la Torre. He was born in Trujillo, a city of Peru's north coast, and brought up in the middle-class tradition. His father was the publisher of a small newspaper devoted chiefly to the commercial interests of the city. His mother, a devout Catholic, was descended from a distinguished colonial family. The family fortunes had dwindled with the loss of large sugar estates, but Víctor's early years were passed in substantial comfort, if not great luxury. When he was fifteen, however, the remaining family wealth disappeared, and he was forced to support himself by working in a lawyer's office while he studied at the University of San Marcos in Lima. For a time he pursued his studies at the University of Cuzco, and there he had an opportunity to observe at first hand the poverty, hunger, and disease of the highland Indians. It was a sobering experience. But Lima was his home during most of these years, and the place where he met the leaders of Peru's small but rapidly growing group of intellectual liberals. These men, of course, were against the government. They were against all the governments that had controlled the destinies of Peru for many years. From them Haya de la Torre absorbed many radical ideas and adopted them as his own. Students and intellectuals, he decided, must make common cause with the workers. And he decided to put this thought into practice.

As president of the Student Federation he was responsible, more than any other one man, for a general strike in which the students supported the demands of the textile workers for an eight-hour day and won a sur-

prising victory. He took a leading part in the establishment of workers'
colleges throughout the country. These activities earned him the enmity
of two Peruvian presidents. Matters came to a head in May of 1923, when
President Leguía announced a great festival for the purpose of dedicating
the Peruvian nation to the Sacred Heart of Jesus. Haya de la Torre and his
friends objected vigorously to the ceremony. It was, they said, nothing
more than a pre-election maneuver designed to catch the votes of devout
Catholics, and in any event it violated the constitutional guarantee of freedom of religion. So they planned a great demonstration of protest. The
demonstration was held as scheduled, but as the protesting students and
workers came from the meeting they were attacked by the police and three
persons were killed. The students still defied the police, even barricading
themselves in the University. The upshot of this affair was a bitter campaign of persecution, directed against the radical student leaders. Haya
de la Torre was forced into hiding, and for several months he led a shadowy
existence. Finally, however, he was captured and thrown into jail, and a
little later he was deported. President Leguía felt much safer with the
young radical out of the country.

THE APRA PLATFORM. During the next eight years Haya de la Torre
wandered from country to country, observing conditions wherever he went
but thinking mostly about conditions in his own land. He stopped first
at Panama, and then went on to Mexico, where *Aprismo* was given birth.
The program of Apra, according to Haya de la Torre and his friends,
contained five main planks: opposition to Yankee imperialism, maintenance of close economic and political ties among the nations of Latin
America, nationalization of land and industry, internationalization of the
Panama Canal, and solidarity among the oppressed peoples of the world.[7]
Obviously these ideas were not new. Opposition to Yankee imperialism
had become a part of the stock-in-trade of almost all Latin American
politicians, who knew that they could easily arouse their audiences against
the rich and aggressive United States. And of course those who resented
Yankee power would welcome a proposal to internationalize the Panama
Canal. The dream of a close alliance among the Latin American countries
was as old as Bolívar. Nationalization of land and industry and solidarity
among oppressed peoples had a Marxian ring. Haya de la Torre himself
declared that his doctrine was a Marxian theory but not a Marxian dogma—
a distinction too fine for the majority of his listeners. In any event, the

[7] See Haya de la Torre's important work, *El Antimperialismo y el Apra,* in which he
makes a full presentation and defense of his ideas.

disciples of *Aprismo* were not the pliant tools of the Soviet Union. Almost at the very outset the Apristas and the Communists split, and they have been bitter enemies ever since.

BIRTH OF APRA. Though Haya de la Torre may have lacked originality, he certainly possessed flaming conviction. He was a zealot with political sense—a rare combination in any time or place. On May 7, 1924, he unfolded a new red and gold flag before a meeting of students of the University of Mexico. This banner, he explained, was the symbol of the new Indo-America (not *Latin America,* a term of which he disapproved). The name of the new movement was to be the American (not *Peruvian*) Revolutionary Popular Alliance, and separate parties were to be organized in all the Indo-American nations. Actually Apra has met with little success outside of Peru, but Haya de la Torre confidently believed that he was inaugurating a great international crusade.

CANDIDATE HAYA DE LA TORRE. From Mexico Haya de la Torre went briefly to the United States, and then on to Russia, where he spent several months observing conditions and talking with such leaders as Trotzky and Zinoviev. He lived for a time in Paris and later studied at the London School of Economics and at Oxford. Word had reached him meantime of the growing unrest in Peru, and he set out once more for his native land. But his return journey was interrupted at Panama by the authorities of that country, who co-operated with the Leguía government by arresting him and putting him on a boat bound for Europe. He spent the next two years in Germany. Those two years were fateful in Peru's history. They marked the fall of Leguía and the enactment of a new law which was to ensure "free and honest" elections. The delighted Apristas lost no time in presenting a platform and announcing that Haya de la Torre would be their candidate for president. He was still in exile, but he returned immediately to Peru. He made a whirlwind campaign, receiving popular acclaim everywhere. The Apristas were confident that they had won. When, however, the votes were counted, the official tabulation showed one hundred and fifty-two thousand for Sánchez Cerro to one hundred and ten thousand for Haya de la Torre. "We were robbed," cried the Apristas, and offered concrete evidence of the validity of the charge. But they could only protest—without avail, of course—unless they cared to attempt a revolution. Haya de la Torre counseled against violence.

APRA DRIVEN UNDERGROUND. The unexpected popular support of *Aprismo* caused the government a great deal of worry. Sánchez Cerro and his friends decided that their best defense would be a full-scale attack on the movement. Ostensibly the object of this attack was communism,[8] but *Aprismo* bore its full weight. The Apra Party was outlawed, party offices were closed, and party publications were confiscated. Party leaders were jailed or driven into exile. Haya de la Torre spent fifteen months in the penitentiary. Meanwhile Aprista hot-heads increased the difficulties of the party leaders by staging a revolt which was suppressed with considerable bloodshed. One young Aprista tried to kill President Sánchez Cerro, without success, and the next year another party member succeeded in the attempt.[9] Haya de la Torre was nearly lynched in reprisal. But eventually he was freed, and began to lay plans for the election scheduled for 1936.

General Benavides, foreseeing the possibility that even the cleverest political maneuvers might not be able to prevent an Apra victory, had the party declared illegal on the ground that it was an international organization and therefore prohibited by the constitution. Haya de la Torre was told that he could not be a candidate. Thereupon the Apristas threw their support to another candidate of known liberal views, with such success that the government was compelled to annul the election.[10] The secret police were then told to terrorize the Apristas, and they followed their orders to the letter. Some were killed; others went into exile. Haya de la Torre remained in Lima, but was forced to stay in hiding. Only a few of his intimate associates were told where he might be found. Sometimes the police discovered the secret, however, and set out to eliminate this nemesis of conservative politicians. On more than one occasion Haya de la Torre received word that the police were coming only a few moments before they actually arrived. At such times he narrowly escaped with his life. For years he lived this curious half-world existence, sleeping during the day and visiting the secret Apra centers after nightfall. He wrote numerous magazine articles and maintained an extensive correspondence.[11]

BUSTAMANTE FOR PRESIDENT. As President Prado's term drew to a close in 1945, it became increasingly clear that popular sentiment would not tolerate another farcical presidential campaign. There must be an honest election or bloodshed. Not only the Apristas opposed the strongly entrenched conservative machine. Thousands of other liberals were determined to bring about a change in their government. They were par-

---

[8] See page 352.
[9] It is generally believed that the assassin, though admittedly a member of the Apra Party, acted upon personal motives. His brother had been killed by the President's followers.
[10] See page 353.
[11] See the interesting article entitled "The People's Warrior," by Lyn Smith Manduley, in the November, 1946, issue of *Inter-American* (Vol. V, No. 11), p. 18 *et seq.*

ticularly disturbed by a persistent rumor that Prado would arrange for the election of one of his henchmen, so that he might be assured of returning to power after the lapse of a term. The rumor was not only persistent— it was highly credible, and the liberals decided to do something about it. They agreed that their best plan would be to find an extremely popular candidate of their own. He must be a man so well liked and so highly respected that most of the people would rally to his candidacy.

The person who seemed to meet these qualifications most completely was Dr. José Luis Bustamante Rivero, distinguished jurist and diplomat. His record of public service was beyond reproach. Though closely associated with the Benavides and Prado regimes, he was known to have looked with disfavor upon their habitual disregard of civil liberties. He had served as minister of justice, minister to Uruguay, and delegate to the important 1938 Rio conference. In 1945 he was ambassador to Bolivia. No one could claim that Bustamante was a communist. He was perhaps a shade too conservative for the liberals who now offered him the nomination, but this very fact would tend to weaken the force of the government's expected attempt to besmirch his record. He was a devout Catholic, and this would certainly strengthen his position in a strongly Catholic country. Some persons claimed to know that he had been the first choice of President Prado, but had insisted upon so many conditions, such as free elections and respect for constitutional guarantees, that the government finally decided to seek another presidential possibility.

NOMINATION OF BUSTAMANTE. Whether or not Bustamante really rejected nomination by the conservatives because they would not meet his terms, he certainly pursued a cautious policy with the liberals. Their offer of the presidential nomination reached him in La Paz, and he replied that he would have to give some thought to the matter. Finally, the first week in April, 1945, he issued his reply. He would be honored, he said, to be the liberal candidate, but only under certain conditions, which he proceeded to enumerate. Democracy must be established in Peru as rapidly as possible, and those who worked with him must work unceasingly for the democratic cause. In the event of his election he would serve the nation to the best of his ability, and he would put the national welfare first—even before the interests of the group that elected him. To this now-famous Memorandum of La Paz the liberals gave their consent, and Bustamante began his campaign for the presidency.

NATIONAL DEMOCRATIC FRONT. The supporters of Bustamante were a motley crew. They had taken a name—National Democratic Front—

which was intended to emphasize their unity, but actually they were far from united. Some were conservative business and professional men who thought that Bustamante would bring much-needed honest government to Peru. Some were dissident members of the highly conservative Revolutionary Union, looking for a chance to even old scores with their former comrades. Included in the Front were the Communists, who fully understood the impossibility of electing a candidate of their own. Even Marshal Benavides (who had been promoted since the days when he was a plain general) spoke a good word for the Front's candidate, and promised to vote for him. But the Apristas were the largest element in the coalition. Officially, of course, their party was outlawed, and they could not name their own candidate. As individuals, however, they could and did work diligently for Bustamante's success. Their secretly printed newspaper, *La Tribuna,* which passed quietly from hand to hand, gave him unstinted praise. Their agents passed along the word that every good Aprista must vote for the Democratic Front.

NOMINATION OF URETA. Even before Bustamante agreed to accept the invitation of the liberals, the conservatives had their candidate. He was General Eloy Ureta, the hero of the undeclared war against Ecuador in 1941. The liberals could not deny that their opponents had made a wise choice. The General was pleasant and unassuming, and had risen far from humble beginnings. No one had ever questioned his personal integrity. Whether he possessed the ability to administer the affairs of state was an open question, but not the question that caused the most concern to sincere liberals in all parts of the country. They wanted to know whether he could really give honest government with the help of the corrupt conservatives. The answer seemed to be that he could not. Ureta himself had a different viewpoint, however. He said in his speech of acceptance that he wanted to be chosen president in a clean, free election, and that he would govern for the benefit of all his countrymen. His words had the ring of truth. Under other circumstances he might have been generally believed.

LEGALIZATION OF APRA. President Prado lifted the strict newspaper censorship at the beginning of the campaign, and for the first time in many years the newspapers had a chance to print what they really thought about the government and the respective candidates. Then, on May 16, the President went a step further and legalized the Apra Party, which had changed its name to Party of the People for the purpose of escaping the ban on political parties of an international character. The election was less than four weeks away, but the Apristas were not daunted by this lack of time. They scheduled a monster rally for May 20 at the Campo de Marte on the edge of Lima.

Nearly two hundred thousand people answered the summons. By automobile, bus, truck or bicycle, or on foot, they made their way to the meeting place. The field was bright with banners and armbands, and there were great portraits of Bustamante and Haya de la Torre. Bustamante spoke with quiet dignity and was well received. But the great ovation of the day was reserved for Haya de la Torre, making his first public appearance in his native land in more than a decade. The crowd marked his arrival by bursting into wild cheers. Nearly twenty minutes elapsed before Haya could proceed with his scheduled address. When he did begin to speak his listeners soon discovered that he had lost none of his fire. Social justice was his theme, and his text was the Four Freedoms. "We do not desire freedom from want without the other three," he declared. "We do not want bread without liberty, nor liberty without bread. . . . I refer not only to our daily bread, but also to bread of the spirit, that of culture, of education for all, which is a right as sacred as that of nourishment." [12] But social justice should not mean communism. "We do not want the Moscow brand," he said. Evidently his ideas had not changed much in exile. There was, however, one important difference. He was no longer rabidly anti-United States. In fact, he spoke approvingly of the great democracy of the North and its courageous war against totalitarianism. The good neighbor policy was responsible for his change of heart, he explained.

ELECTION OF BUSTAMANTE. Prado's promise of free elections was kept faithfully, to almost everyone's amazement. The tradition of corruption at the polls was so well established that Peruvians could hardly accept the possibility of any other policy. There were, in fact, sporadic instances of violence or attempted fraud. Not all the conservatives in minor positions were willing to take the President's order that everyone be allowed to vote and that the votes be counted as cast. In one small town duplicate sets of ballot boxes were discovered. It was two days before the election, but one set of boxes was already filled to overflowing with ballots marked for Ureta. Some of the polling places in Lima did not open their doors until three hours before closing time, thus depriving several thousand persons of their right to vote. But these cases were by no means typical. The best proof of the government's intentions was the final result. The

12 Quoted in *Inter-American*, July, 1945 (Vol. IV, No. 7), p. 6.

official count gave Bustamante three hundred and five thousand votes to Ureta's one hundred and fifty thousand—a margin of slightly more than two to one. Thus the Prado administration publicly acknowledged and peacefully accepted its own defeat. It was a rare day, as well as a bright one, in Peruvian history.

DEATH OF BENAVIDES. Three weeks after the election Marshal Benavides died suddenly of a heart attack. His record as president certainly did not endear him to Peruvian liberals, but they could not forget that at the end he had put the weight of his personal popularity squarely on the side of the National Democratic Front. So a great funeral was arranged. Even the Apristas, who had suffered more at his hands than any other group, paid their last respects as the body was borne to the cathedral. It was an impressive tribute to a dynamic personality.

POLITICAL DIFFICULTIES. President Bustamante took office on July 8, 1945. At once he began to redeem his campaign promises. He ordered the release of all political prisoners. He pushed through Congress a series of laws repealing the oppressive legislation of earlier administrations—not a difficult task, since a substantial majority of the congressmen were pledged to accomplish this result. In some other matters, however, the President's program did not have such smooth sailing. The Democratic Front had secured control of Congress, just as it had elected the chief executive, but the Front was far from united on a future course of action. The Apristas, the largest political group in the coalition, insisted on immediate and radical legislation to improve the lot of the masses. More moderate members of the Front followed the President's lead in counseling caution. Almost at the outset, therefore, Bustamante discovered that he could not count on consistent congressional support.

In the choice of his first cabinet he had not even given much thought to political considerations. Most of the newly appointed ministers were technicians rather than politicians. Only one was a member of the dominant Democratic Front. Not a single Aprista was included. But this was not a deliberate attempt to rebuff the Apristas, as it might well have seemed to the uninitiated. Haya de la Torre himself had indicated that he and his followers would be quite satisfied to remain outside the administration, so that they might be free to criticize any of the President's plans. But the inevitable result, as more experienced politicians might have foreseen, was frequently a stalemate between the executive and legislative branches of the government. The Minister of Agriculture was called before Congress to explain why there were existing food shortages and how he proposed to eliminate them. When his explanations failed to satisfy the congressmen, he resigned. Then the Minister of Finance was called, and he suffered a similar fate. By the middle of September the whole cabinet had resigned. So President Bustamante made new appointments, this time taking greater care to consult the leaders of the Democratic Front, including Haya de la Torre. Unfortunately, however, these changes did not produce greater harmony. Bustamante might perhaps have forced many of the dissident congressmen into line, but he scorned the pressure politics that had enabled his predecessors to gain the whip hand. He believed firmly in the independence of the legislative branch.

THE FREE PRESS ISSUE. One of the worst quarrels in the new regime arose over freedom of the press. The Apristas, strangely enough, were determined to enact a new censorship law. It might well have been supposed that their experiences with a censored press under Benavides and Prado would have made them eternal champions of press freedom. But they resented the editorial attacks of Lima's two widely read conservative newspapers, *El Comercio* and *La Prensa,* and decided to silence them. So they drafted a bill providing for strict censorship, and forced it through Congress. When it reached the President, he refused flatly to sign it. He himself had been the principal target of conservative attacks, he said, and he was heartily weary of them. But he had always believed in freedom of the press and he did not intend to compromise that belief in order to gain a temporary advantage. The Apristas were impressed by his arguments, but at first they saw no way to accept defeat without losing prestige. Finally they talked the matter over with the President and accepted a curious compromise. The "gag" law would be signed, but not until Congress passed another law removing all its teeth. In that way each side could lay claim to victory. The real triumph was the President's, of course, for the press remained unfettered.

APRA ENTERS THE CABINET. In late January, 1946, the Apristas finally agreed to accept some of the responsibility of directing the executive branch of the government. They were given three important cabinet posts—Development and Public Works, Agriculture, and Finance and Commerce. The first two of these ministries were considered especially desirable, because they provided control of thousands of jobs on the public payroll. Thus *Aprismo* could begin to repay the faithful. But the breach between the President and Congress was not healed. Instead its repercussions were felt in cabinet meetings.

MAJOR ISSUES: *Local self-government.* Another major dispute between Bustamante and the Apristas arose over the method of restoring a measure of self-government to the nation's cities and towns. Before 1920 there had been popularly elected municipal councils, but Leguía had abolished them and arranged to have all local officials chosen by the central authorities. His successors continued this plan for many years. When, however, the Democratic Front came into power, the Apristas insisted upon the reestablishment of the popularly chosen municipal councils. President Bustamante readily agreed. Women were to be permitted to participate in these local elections, under a constitutional clause that had been inoperative until this time. But an unforeseen difficulty immediately arose: the lack of a municipal register, or list of persons eligible to vote. Such a register had to be prepared for each community before local elections could be held.

The task, though apparently simple, proved quite difficult. The people charged with its administration were inexperienced, and some of them may have worked at a snail's pace in order to continue drawing their salaries. In any event, the months dragged by without noticeable results. Finally the Aristas proposed that centrally appointed boards be set up in each community, and that these boards be authorized to choose the local officials. This could scarcely be called self-government, but it would have the obvious merit of replacing local officials appointed by the old regime with new officials chosen by members of the Democratic Front. Undoubtedly it would strengthen the Front's power throughout the country. And it would not be a substitute for self-government—merely a temporary arrangement until the municipal register could be prepared.

Subsidies to municipalities. The Aprista proposal for centrally appointed boards was put into effect, and most of the members of these boards were Apristas. Not unnaturally, therefore, the local officials thus chosen usually bore the Aprista stamp of approval. Thereupon the Aprista-dominated Congress voted to grant large subsidies to the municipal governments, to be used for public works. Much of this money was wasted. No one seemed to be quite certain whether the waste arose from the corruption of local officials or from their admitted inexperience. But everyone could see that the people of the local communities were getting something less than their money's worth. The conservatives, of course, charged that there had been wholesale misappropriation of public funds, and of course the Apristas denied it. Word finally reached the President that the Apristas were spending public money for their own purposes and in some cases directly against his administration. So he informed Congress that in future budgets he would omit subsidies to the municipalities. Haya de la Torre and his followers were furious.

Army reforms. Another dispute arose over certain proposals concerning the army. The Apristas decided to reduce the retirement age of army officers, so that they could move more of their own followers into key positions. They also proposed army pay increases. No one seems to have objected very seriously to the increase in salaries, but there was a great deal of objection to lowering the retirement age. The Minister of War and the Minister of Government, both of whom wanted to protect their old friends in the army, came out strongly against the suggestion, and their arguments carried great weight with the President. Eventually the pay increase was approved, but the age reduction was not.

Debt settlement. While President Bustamante thus quarreled with the Apristas, he also had serious difficulties with his natural opponents, the conservatives. Rising prices had compelled large budget increases and the government finally decided that it must negotiate a substantial loan abroad. Before it could do so, however, it had to put its financial house in order. The dollar debt, most of which had been incurred by President Leguía under scandalous circumstances, had been in default since 1932. President Bustamante had given this matter his serious consideration shortly after taking office, and had managed to reach an agreement with the foreign bondholders, but the Peruvian Senate withheld its approval, largely because of the vociferous objections of the conservatives. So the President tried to make a new settlement. This time his terms were accepted by the Peruvian Senate but rejected by the United States Bondholders' Protective Association. Finally, in desperation, the Peruvian government tried to come to terms directly with the holders of its dollar bonds, and opened an office in New York for that purpose. The conservatives continued to protest, alleging that the proposed settlement was beyond Peru's capacity to pay.

Rising prices. During all this time prices were rising, wages were going up, and strikes were frequent. The unions were becoming stronger and more compact. Wage increases frequently provided a good excuse for working less, and production declined throughout the nation. The conservatives blamed the Apristas for the increased cost of living. But there is little doubt that while the Apristas controlled the Ministry of Finance they made a serious effort to enforce the law fixing maximum prices on necessities. Later, when the Aprista finance minister had been replaced by a more conservative financier who happened to be a wine producer, prices were permitted to spiral upward without interruption.

Freedom of the press. In late 1946 freedom of the press again became an issue. The Apristas were accused of trying to stifle the opposition by sending their rowdies to smash the presses on which the conservative dailies were printed. Several instances of such vandalism occurred. Then the publishers of the conservative newspapers, as well as other important persons on their staffs, received threatening letters and telephone calls. All these messages were anonymous. On January 7, 1947, the president of the board of directors of the influential *La Prensa* was shot and killed as he came out of his office. The assassin was not immediately apprehended, but everyone knew that the victim had been closely associated with the collection of a large campaign fund to beat the Apristas. So suspicion turned toward the leaders of *Aprismo*. After a time one of the Aprista members of Congress was formally accused of having fired the fatal shot. He denied the charge and waived his parliamentary immunity in order that the matter might be cleared up, but years passed without any final decision by the court.

No one seemed to know whether the killing was really the result of an Aprista plot, but nearly all agreed that *Aprismo* itself was under suspicion. The Aprista leaders decided that they could no longer embarrass the government by remaining in important posts, so their three cabinet ministers resigned. President Bustamante accepted the resignations with apparent relief and filled the vacancies with personal friends. In October, 1947, the entire cabinet resigned to give the President a free hand in dealing with the wave of labor agitation that was sweeping the country. Many persons said that the Apristas were behind the agitation for political reasons. Certainly they expressed strong disapproval of the President's firm action against the strikers. The new cabinet was selected primarily for the purpose of facilitating the enforcement of order. It was composed chiefly of high-ranking army and navy officers.

COLLAPSE OF THE DEMOCRATIC FRONT. By mid-July, 1947, the Democratic Front seemed to be falling apart. Many moderates who had joined its ranks were disgusted with the militant tactics of the Apristas, and unwilling to continue a policy of co-operation. The conservatives were quite hopeful, therefore, of electing their own candidate for speaker of the Chamber of Deputies. They had strengthened their own loose coalition and taken a new name—the National Alliance. But their hopes were doomed to failure. The Apristas succeeded in electing their candidate on the second ballot. Thereupon the anti-Apristas in the Senate absented themselves from the day's sessions. That was on July 27. The senators in attendance were unable to organize and do business because they could not obtain a quorum. On succeeding days they had the same difficulty. Days dragged into weeks, and still the Senate was unable to perform any of its functions. The total membership was fifty—forty-nine elected members, plus the former president *ex officio*. But President Prado did not take his seat. One senator was dead. Another was the representative of Peru in the United Nations, and therefore could not take his Senate seat. This reduced the number of working senators to forty-seven. Twenty-two of them—nine from the Democratic Front—were out "on strike." So the Apristas and their friends could never muster an attendance of more than twenty-five, and under the rules they required slightly more than a majority—twenty-eight—to elect officers.

Finally the absentee senators issued a manifesto charging the Apristas with bad faith and deliberate disregard of the public welfare. They also presented a list of conditions that must be met before they would return and permit the Senate to do business. The Apristas then issued their own manifesto, accepting some of these conditions but rejecting others. Manifestoes and counter-manifestoes appeared at frequent intervals, but no agreement was reached. In the Chamber of Deputies the anti-Apristas finally joined the strike. So Congress did nothing the entire session. The Apristas loudly demanded a special session, but the President did not issue the summons. He calmly accepted the situation, even when the anti-Aprista members of Congress continued their policy of abstention, thus preventing the regular legislative session of 1948.

BUSTAMANTE VERSUS APRA. By the middle of 1948, therefore, democratically minded President Bustamante had become a dictator by force of circumstances. Though still accepting the theory of an independent Congress and an executive with limited powers, he had adopted in practice the personal government of his predecessors. He had broken completely with his old friends the Apristas, and thus lacked the support of a congressional majority. So he governed without Congress, relying on the loyalty of the army to keep himself in power. It was an explosive situation, not likely to continue for many months.

In early October the Apristas decided to take direct action against the Bustamante regime. Aided by units of the Peruvian navy they staged a spectacular revolt, fighting hand to hand with loyal troops in the streets of Callao. More than three hundred persons were killed. Within twenty-four hours, however, the uprising was crushed, and Bustamante issued a number of retaliatory decrees. The Apra Party was outlawed, and many of its leaders were arrested.

RETURN OF THE CONSERVATIVES. The conservatives, however, did not consider these measures sufficiently drastic. They plotted with high army officers to seize control of the government. In late October, 1948, only a few weeks after the failure of the Apra uprising, they ordered their forces into action. Everything had been planned with great care. Garrison after garrison threw in its lot with the rebels without firing a shot. When the troops of the strategic Lima garrison also joined the movement, Bustamante knew that his days as president were numbered. He hurriedly surrendered his authority and left the country for Argentina. Thereupon a junta of conservative army officers announced that the government was in its hands. The head of this junta, General Manuel Odría, was a professional soldier whose conservative sympathies were widely known. After assuming the title of provisional president, he spoke vaguely of better times for labor, agriculture, and the army, and promised free elections after "a suitable period of transition." For Apra, however, he indicated that the prospects were bleak. It would be rooted out systematically as a menace to Peruvian life.

THE CASE OF HAYA DE LA TORRE. For more than two months the police searched diligently for Haya de la Torre, while he scurried from one hiding place to another. Then, early in January, 1949, he asked for and received asylum in the Colombian embassy. The practice of granting asylum to political refugees is quite general in Latin America, but the Peruvian government demanded custody of Haya de la Torre on the ground that he was a common criminal seeking to escape punishment. His crime, according to the Odría administration, was the instigation of the unsuccessful October revolt that tried to sweep Apra into power. This line of reasoning completely ignored the obvious fact that General Odría's own government owed its very existence to a similar revolution. The principal difference between Odría and Haya was that one had been successful in rebellion, whereas the other had failed. Not unnaturally, therefore, Colombia refused to admit that Haya was a common criminal. It asked for a guarantee of safe conduct, so that he might leave the embassy and go to Colombian territory. Peru refused to grant such a guarantee. Thereupon Haya de la Torre settled down to the dull routine of life within the Colombian embassy, while Peruvian troops patrolled the neighborhood and even tore up the surrounding streets to make sure that the Apra leader would not slip away unobserved. Finally Colombia and Peru agreed to submit the dispute to the International Court of Justice. The Court rendered a confusing decision in November of 1950, and subsequently handed down two "clarifications" that only muddled the issue more than ever before. Haya, said the Court, was not a common criminal, and Colombia need not turn him over to Peru. But Peru, on the other hand, need not issue a guarantee of safe conduct. How, then, could a practical solution be found? That, said the Court, was beyond the scope of its authority.[13] So Haya de la Torre still resides in the Colombian embassy, and Peruvian troops continue to guard against his escape.

GOVERNMENT BY DECREE. Meanwhile the military junta headed by General Odría set about the task of consolidating its power. It imposed a rigid press censorship, and swept away all guarantees of individual liberty. Police permission was required for meetings of any kind, whether for business or pleasure. The death penalty was imposed for "political crimes," which included not only acts of rebellion but also threats against government officials or their families. Congress was not permitted to meet, so government was solely by decree. But the governing junta gave assurances of an honest election at "an early date." It pleased the merchants by removing most price controls, and it won considerable labor support by ordering a twenty per cent increase in wages.

PRESIDENTIAL ELECTION OF 1950. The promised election was finally scheduled for July 2, 1950. The Apristas were declared an illegal party; so, too, were the Communists. Even the right-wing Revolutionary Union was denied a place on the ballot. It was becoming increasingly clear, therefore, that the people would not be permitted much choice when they went to the polls. General Odría was a presidential candidate, of course. Another general and former senator, Ernesto Montagne, announced that he too would be a candidate, but prudently refused to identify his supporters. Thereupon the government-controlled National Election Board declared that Montagne's candidacy was illegal. The result of these maneuvers was to leave Manuel Odría as the only presidential candidate. Needless to say, he won the election. Eighty per cent of the ballots were marked in his favor, according to the official announcement. The other ballots were returned without indicating any choice for president. The government's candidates won substantial majorities in both houses of Congress, but there were some victorious anti-government

[13] See the judgments of the International Court of Justice, No. 50 (November 20, 1950), No. 52 (November 27, 1950), and No. 60 (June 13, 1952).

congressmen, who called themselves independents. Revolt flared four days after the election, but it was quickly suppressed.

POLICIES OF PRESIDENT ODRÍA. One of the principal aims of the new administration has been the industrialization of Peru. It has adopted a comprehensive Five-Year Plan, which contemplates a great expansion of the infant steel industry. Substantial loans for this purpose have been obtained from the World Bank (the International Bank for Reconstruction and Development), and from the Export-Import Bank of the United States. In contrast with virtually all the rest of Latin America, Peru now emphasizes a free economy. Not only has it permitted prices to seek their own level, but in addition it has abolished currency restrictions. It has balanced the national budget. At the same time it has expanded the system of social security, with increased allowances for maternity care, illness, and total disability. President Odría may be a right-wing dictator, but he evidently intends to justify his dictatorship with a substantial list of material achievements—and, also, with a cloak of constitutionality.

The Structure of Government

CONSTITUTION: *Social guarantees.* Peru has had fifteen constitutions since it declared its independence. The most recent, adopted in 1933, is a short document—not much longer than the constitution of the United States. Many of its clauses are clearly of American origin, but there are evidences of French and even Mexican influence. The constitution has no preamble; instead it begins with a declaration of the nature of the state: "Peru is a democratic republic. The power of the State emanates from the people, and is exercised by the officials of the nation within the limits imposed by the constitution and the laws." [14] Then, after a number of clauses dealing with nationality, we find the inevitable enumeration of guarantees.

The list is very extensive, comprising sixty-three articles. There are national and social guarantees and individual guarantees. In the first category are many statements of national policy: there shall be no industrial or commercial monopolies; private property must be used in conformity with the interests of society; [15] an annual budget shall determine the expenditures and revenues of the government.[16] This chapter also contains a number of "social rights" borrowed more or less directly from the Mexi-

[14] Arts. 1 and 16.
[15] Art. 34.
[16] Art. 9.

can constitution: all mineral property belongs to the state, and may not be exploited by private persons except as permitted by law; [17] the state may assume control of any transportation by land, water, or air, subject to payment of due compensation.[18] The constitution establishes the general outline of Peruvian labor policy: collective bargaining shall be protected; [19] labor contracts shall not restrict the rights of workers; [20] the state favors profit sharing by employees.[21]

Individual guarantees. The individual guarantees follow the usual pattern. Freedom of speech and press shall be inviolable; [22] involuntary servitude is forbidden; [23] individuals or groups may assemble to petition for the redress of their grievances; [24] freedom of religion is assured; [25] and so on through a substantial list. Most of these individual guarantees have appeared in every one of Peru's constitutions, and most of them have been more or less systematically ignored throughout a large part of the nation's history. Freedom of religion, unlike most of the other guarantees, is a comparatively recent innovation. The constitution of 1860 not only recognized Roman Catholicism as the official faith of the nation, but prohibited the public practice of any other religion. This prohibition remained in effect until 1915, when it was removed by constitutional amendment. The fundamental law of 1920 stated simply that "No one may be persecuted because of his ideas or beliefs," [26] but the present constitution is more specific. "Respecting the sentiments of a majority of the people," it declares, "the state protects the Roman Catholic Apostolic religion. But other faiths enjoy liberty for the exercise of their respective cults." [27] Yet non-Catholics have had a difficult time in Peru, even in recent years. In January, 1945, President Prado issued a decree forbidding non-Catholic sects to hold meetings or "acts of religious propaganda" in parks, plazas, and other public places. They were still permitted to hold services within their own church buildings, but this decree seriously hampered missionary work. It was aimed directly at a number of Protestant missionary groups from the United States.

[17] Art. 37.
[18] Art. 38.
[19] Art. 43.
[20] Art. 44.
[21] Art. 45.
[22] Art. 63.
[23] Art. 55.
[24] Art. 60.
[25] Art. 232.
[26] Constitution of 1920, Art. 23.
[27] Constitution of 1933, Art. 232.

Suspension of guarantees. The constitution of 1920 departed from Latin American tradition by making no provision for the suspension of individual rights, even in time of emergency. Apparently these rights were intended to be absolute. The constitution declared in unmistakable language that they might not be set aside "by any law or by any authority." [28] Of course, this was wishful thinking. Presidents accustomed to almost absolute power could not be expected to abandon one of the most useful means of enforcing their power, just because the constitution said so. In 1925 Professor Graham Stuart made this penetrating comment: "Inasmuch as such suspension is bound to occur if the situation demands it, such a prohibition . . . might better have been omitted." [29]

The present constitution takes a more realistic view of the matter by authorizing the suspension of guarantees, but only under certain circumstances and within certain limits. "When the security of the state demands it, the executive power may suspend [certain specified guarantees], either totally or partially, in all or a part of the territory of the nation. If the suspension of guarantees is decreed while Congress is in session, the executive power will report immediately what action has been taken. The decree of suspension shall not be issued for more than thirty days. Its extension shall require a new decree. The powers of the executive during the suspension of guarantees shall be determined by law." [30] In late 1947 President Bustamante suspended constitutional guarantees for thirty days—the maximum time permitted without an appeal to Congress —so that he might have a freer hand in dealing with labor agitators. More recently President Odría decreed a state of siege for a much longer period, without regard to constitutional restrictions.

Amendment of the constitution. Amendment of the Peruvian constitution is very easy. The president or any member of Congress may propose a constitutional change, which must be adopted in each house by a majority of the total membership. Then there must be a delay until the next regular session—that is, approximately one year later—and at this time Congress must again adopt the amendment by vote of an absolute majority in each house. The approval of the president is not necessary.[31] But everyone understands, of course, that in practice the president is the mov-

---

[28] Constitution of 1920, Art. 35.

[29] *The Governmental System of Peru*, p. 25. This monograph, published in 1925, is still the standard work on the Peruvian government of that era. Though long since outdated by the swift onrush of history, it still possesses considerable historical value. A more modern work is *Derecho Constitucional y del Perú*, by Lizardo Alzamora Silva.

[30] Art. 70.

[31] Art. 236.

ing spirit behind every constitutional amendment. The present constitution has been amended a number of times since its adoption in 1933.

SUFFRAGE. Literate male citizens who have attained the age of twenty-one years (or eighteen years, if married) have the right to vote in national elections. In fact, they have the obligation to do so. Many Latin American countries have adopted so-called "compulsory" voting without making any serious attempt to enforce this provision of the constitution. But Peru has adopted a novel method of making voting really compulsory. The election law specifies that any person who stays away from the polls without valid excuse shall suffer a number of penalties. He may not sign a valid contract, for example, or apply for a government concession. The obligation to vote extends only to age sixty; after that the matter is optional. Certain classes of persons are excluded, of course—the physically and mentally unfit, and those who have been convicted of crime. The clergy, also, are denied the franchise, but not members of the armed forces. Women are entitled to vote in municipal elections.

ELECTIONS. Each political party prepares its own ballot in conformity with the election law, which specifies such matters as the ballot's shape, size, and color. As in most Latin American countries, the government provides an official envelope. Voters normally vote a straight ticket for their chosen parties, but are under no legal compulsion to do so. They may select a party ballot, strike out some names, and write in others. Or they may even prepare their own ballots, which will be accepted if they meet the minimum legal requirements as to appearance.

THE PRESIDENT: *Selection and qualifications.* The president is elected by direct vote of the people. If no candidate receives a majority, Congress then makes the selection from the three highest candidates. The president must be a native-born citizen, at least thirty-five years of age, who has resided in the country continuously a minimum of ten years, though not necessarily the ten years immediately preceding his election. He must not be a member of the clergy or the judiciary, or a close relative of the retiring president. Cabinet ministers and members of the armed forces are ineligible, unless they have resigned at least six months before the election.

Term. The president's term is six years.[32] The constitution is very emphatic in its declaration that there shall be no immediate re-election. "This prohibition cannot be amended or repealed. The author or authors of any proposal to amend or repeal it, or those who aid them directly or

---

[32] The constitution of 1933 originally provided for a term of five years, but this was increased to six by a constitutional amendment adopted in 1939.

indirectly, shall automatically lose their status as public officials and shall remain permanently disqualified to hold any public office." [33] These words leave no doubt as to public policy concerning immediate re-election. But it must not be forgotten that the original text of the constitution of 1920, which Leguía himself sponsored, was just as specific in limiting the president to a single term; yet President Leguía was serving his third successive term when a revolution drove him from power. Perhaps future presidents of Peru will show greater respect for the one-term-at-a-time rule.

Salary and residence. The salary of the chief executive is only about five thousand dollars a year, in terms of American money. But to this sum is added another eight thousand dollars for personal expenses, plus eight thousand more for official entertainment. The total is strikingly small. The nation has been more generous, however, in providing an official residence. The presidential palace is a magnificent white marble structure fronting the Plaza de Armas in the center of the city. Directly to the left is the great cathedral, which houses the mortal remains of the conqueror Pizarro.

Role of the cabinet. The president is a strong executive in the fullest sense of the term. The constitution, however, gives very little indication of his true position. It seems to make him more or less of a figurehead, subject to the will of Congress. All his official acts must be countersigned by appropriate cabinet ministers, and these ministers must in turn rely on Congress for their continuance in office. If formally censured by either the Senate or the Chamber of Deputies, they must resign, and the president must accept their resignation.[34] He plays only a minor role, according to the strict letter of the constitution, in the selection of his own cabinet. Indeed, his part is limited to the choice of the prime minister, or president of the council of ministers, as he is officially known. The prime minister then selects his cabinet colleagues, and presents the complete list for the president's approval.[35] On paper that is the French system of parliamentary government. But in France the president graciously gives his assent to the prime minister's proposed cabinet, and then retires to lofty heights above the political struggle while the cabinet directs the affairs of state. The French prime minister is the real head of the nation, and is restricted

[33] Art. 142.

[34] Arts. 172, 173.

[35] The complete list includes twelve ministers: foreign relations and culture, government and police, justice, war, navy, finance and commerce, development and public works, education, public health and social security, aeronautics, agriculture, labor. For a good summary of the organization and activities of the national administration, see *Curso de Derecho Administrativo del Perú,* by Felipe S. Portocarrero.

only by the necessity of securing the co-operation of the other cabinet ministers and, from time to time, the approval of Parliament.

Nothing could be farther removed from the realities of Peruvian politics. The president does indeed name a prime minister, who in turn selects his colleagues. But it must not be supposed that the president maintains an impassive neutrality while the list is being prepared. He virtually dic-

Peruvian sentries guard the presidential palace. (Photograph by the author)

tates the appointment of every member of the cabinet. And when the list is finally presented for his approval, he vetoes without the slightest hesitancy any name that fails to strike his fancy. After the cabinet has been selected, it makes no final decisions concerning important matters of public policy. Neither the prime minister nor any of his colleagues could possibly be called the head of the nation. Cabinet ministers are the president's personal advisers, chosen by him and responsible to him for everything they do. They all countersign the president's orders dealing with their respective departments, but that is just a formality, as it is in most of the other nations of Latin America. There is, of course, the plain statement of the constitution that they must resign on a congressional vote of *no confidence,* and some ministers have actually been forced out of office by congressional disapproval.[36] But the president is under no obligation to consult Congress in naming their successors, and only occasionally does he do so. No one ever forgets that he is the head of the nation.

Presidential appointments. The president makes all appointments in the administrative service. His selections must be approved by the council of ministers—that is, by his cabinet; but of course this restriction does not really restrict his freedom of choice. More significant is the requirement of congressional consent for the promotion of high officers in the armed forces. The president plays an important part in the appointment of archbishops and bishops of the Catholic Church. For every vacancy he presents to Congress a list of three names. The candidate thus chosen by Congress must then be given final approval by the Vatican. This procedure follows the terms of a concordat with the Holy See, which governs the relations of the Roman Catholic Church and the Peruvian nation. Judges of the supreme court are selected by Congress, but from a list of ten names submitted by the president for each vacancy. Not only may the president appoint all persons in the administrative service; he may also remove them at his pleasure. There is no central civil service commission, and no serious attempt has been made to place all government positions on a merit basis. The foreign office, however, maintains a fairly permanent staff, and has used the merit system for many years.

Miscellaneous presidential powers. The conduct of foreign affairs is largely in the hands of the chief executive, of course. He possesses the usual powers—to receive the ambassadors and ministers of foreign powers (thus granting or withholding recognition of their respective countries), to direct the activities of Peruvian diplomats in foreign lands, and to make treaties, which must receive the approval of Congress. The president's power of pardon is less extensive than in most other nations. It is limited to political offenses, and may be exercised only when Congress is not in session. With this exception, Congress grants such pardons as may be necessary to serve the ends of justice.[37] The president directs the armed forces of the nation. But he may not personally take command of troops

[36] See page 364.
[37] Constitution, Art. 123, Cl. 22.

without congressional approval, and even then "he shall be subject to the laws and to military regulations, and shall be responsible for conformity to them." [38]

The veto. The 1920 constitution provided a very weak form of presidential veto. It permitted Congress to override the president's objections by a simple majority in each house. In 1933, however, the new constitution seemingly denied even this weak veto to the chief executive. It said, in apparently unmistakable language, that he *must* promulgate every law passed by Congress, regardless of his own preferences or policies. And it declared that if he should fail to do so within ten days, this task should become the responsibility of the president of Congress.[39] Peruvian presidents have been loath to accept the constitution's plain meaning, however. They have argued that the whole scheme of government is presidential— not parliamentary—and that this implies the right of the chief executive to veto legislative measures. Congress has finally accepted this viewpoint. Its members now recognize the president's authority to reject their proposals. But since the constitution contains no statement that the presidential veto may be overridden by a two-thirds or other majority, the present interpretation of the constitution makes the veto absolute. A bill rejected by the president may not be considered again until the next session of Congress.

Other controls over legislation. The president may introduce bills, of course, and may present his views to Congress in formal messages. He may convoke Congress in special session, indicating what matters require its immediate attention. These matters must be given preferential consideration, but Congress is free to take up such other legislative proposals as it may desire. The call for a special session may also be issued by the president of Congress, upon the request of a majority of the members. All these clauses of the constitution, including the apparent denial of the veto power, seem to relegate the executive to a subordinate position in the lawmaking process. Actually, of course, they have no such effect. The political power and prestige of the president are sufficient to make him a dominant figure in every aspect of Peruvian life.

Presidential succession. The original terms of the present constitution did not establish a regular order of presidential succession. They merely

---

[38] Art. 153.
[39] The presidents of the Senate and the Chamber of Deputies alternate as president of Congress. Each serves for a year.

declared that in the event of the president's death or disability, Congress should name his successor within three days.[40] Executive functions were to be performed by the cabinet in the interim. There was no vice-president. In 1936, however, Peru compensated for this defect by authorizing the election of two vice-presidents. Their qualifications are the same as those of the president. They do not preside over the Senate or the Chamber of Deputies. In fact, they have no duties except to await the unhappy event of the president's death, physical or mental collapse, resignation, conviction on impeachment charges, or absence from the country without congressional permission. If for any reason the president and both of the vice-presidents are unable to serve, the choice of a successor still rests with Congress, and the cabinet is still empowered to act collectively until Congress has acted. The person succeeding to the presidency merely fills out the unexpired term.

CONGRESS: *Selection, term, qualifications, salary.* Congress is composed of the conventional two houses—a Senate of fifty members and a Chamber of Deputies with a membership of one hundred and fifty-three. Both senators and deputies are chosen by direct popular vote, and both serve for six years—the same term as the president. There is no system of partial renewal every two or three years; therefore the nation elects an entirely new Congress at the same time that it chooses a new president. There are no alternates, so vacancies are filled by special elections. Every deputy must be a native-born Peruvian, at least twenty-five years of age, and a native or three-year resident of the department from which he is elected. The minimum age for senators is thirty-five years. Salaries are very small—approximately six hundred dollars a year in American money. No provision is made for secretaries, but some members pay for secretarial help out of their own pockets.

Place of meeting. The Palace of Congress is a beautiful marble building, but it faces a minor park in a poorer section of the city. The meeting place of the deputies contains no noteworthy features; its arrangements follow the usual plan, with space reserved for the cabinet, the press, and the general public. The Senate chamber, however, deserves a word of special comment. Though only a small room, it is one of the most beautiful in the Americas. Everything has been arranged in classic simplicity. Great marble columns stretch from the floor to the very high ceiling.

[40] Unless the vacancy occurred during a recess of Congress, in which case that body should assemble and make its choice within twenty days.

Every senator's desk has its individual microphone. Such an atmosphere should be productive of the very highest statesmanship, though unfortunately it has not always had this result.

Organization and procedure. Congress meets in regular session on the 28th of July of each year and sits for four months. Special sessions, as previously noted,[41] may be called by the president or upon the demand of a majority of the congressmen. The constitution declares that the president of the nation shall attend the opening of each regular session, but adds: "His presence is not essential for Congress to begin its functions." [42] Therefore the chief executive of Peru lacks the Argentine president's power to postpone congressional sessions to suit his own convenience.[43] Each house of Congress chooses its own officers—a president, two vice-presidents, a secretary, and a treasurer. These officers form a steering committee (*mesa directiva*), which conducts the necessary routine and prepares the legislative calendar. The president of each chamber appoints its permanent committees, which play a relatively unimportant part in legislative matters. The rules even permit the committee stage to be eliminated by a majority vote, except for certain measures of major importance. But not many bills become law in this way. Both houses meet five days a week during the legislative period. Meetings usually begin at five o'clock in the afternoon, and continue until nine or ten in the evening. The powers of Congress require no special comment. Impeachment follows the usual form.

REGIONAL LEGISLATURES. Many persons have charged that Congress fails to give due consideration to the needs of all parts of the nation. In the far north and south, especially, it is sometimes said that senators and deputies are blinded by the glitter of Lima; they enact laws best fitted to the requirements of the capital and its environs, with slight regard for their effect on the rest of the country. Some years ago it was proposed that this fault be corrected by the establishment of regional legislatures, and President Leguía accepted this idea. In 1919 he issued a decree establishing three regional legislative bodies—one for the north, with headquarters at Cajamarca, another for the central section, with its meeting place in Ayacucho, and the third for the south, sitting in Cuzco. Members of these regional legislatures were to be chosen by popular vote for terms of five years, and were to meet in regular session for thirty days each year. They were to

[41] See page 378.
[42] Art. 110.
[43] See page 102.

pass laws dealing with local affairs, impose necessary local taxes, supervise local administration, and even request the removal of unsatisfactory local officials named by the central government. President Leguía's decree was incorporated in the constitution of 1920, and the regional legislatures were duly established.

From the very start, however, they were a great disappointment. Their members were usually second-rate men who failed to take any positive action, even on matters of the greatest importance. Even when they did act, their proposals were frequently vetoed by the president on the ground that they conflicted with acts of Congress. The dividing line of authority between the regional legislatures and the national Congress was never clearly drawn, and every difference of opinion was settled in favor of the national authorities. After six years, therefore, the regional legislatures were abolished. Their re-establishment has not been considered seriously since that time.[44]

THE COURTS. The judicial system of Peru follows the customary Latin American pattern. Juries are not used. Some of the earlier constitutions contemplated the adoption of the jury system in criminal cases, but these clauses were never put into effect. The supreme court consists of eleven judges and five solicitors general. The work of these solicitors general is considered so important that they are placed on an equal footing with the justices of the court. They prepare statements in all cases affecting the public interest, and these statements are a part of the official record. The judges place great reliance on them. Constitutional qualifications are the same for both judges and solicitors general of the supreme court: they must be native Peruvians, at least forty years of age, who have had a minimum of twenty years' legal practice or five years on the bench. As previously pointed out,[45] they are chosen by Congress from a list submitted by the president. They serve for life.

The supreme court performs a number of important functions. In addition to its original jurisdiction in certain classes of cases, involving chiefly high officers of the government, it exercises appellate jurisdiction over all litigation considered sufficiently important to warrant its attention. It submits to the president lists of names from which the judges of the superior courts are chosen; it supervises all the inferior courts and directs their work; and it even possesses the right to propose legislation dealing

---

[44] The achievements and failures of the regional legislatures are chronicled in Professor Stuart's previously cited work, pp. 102–105.
[45] See page 377.

with judicial matters.   In some instances all the judges sit as a single body, but usually they are divided into two chambers—civil and criminal.   The court chooses its own president.

Below the supreme court there are nineteen superior courts, whose judges also serve for life, but must be confirmed in office every five years. The superior court of Lima has nineteen justices, but more commonly there are five to a court.   Then there are the courts of first instance, which function in almost every community of any consequence.   Their judges, like the magistrates of the superior courts, serve during good behavior, with ratification at five-year intervals.   They are named by the president from lists submitted by the superior courts.   At the bottom of the judicial hierarchy are the justices of the peace, appointed by the justices of the superior courts from names submitted by the judges of first instance. These justices of the peace are found in every village and town.   They serve for but a single year and receive no compensation.   The honor of holding office is supposed to be a sufficient reward for their services.[46]

INTERNAL ORGANIZATION.   The internal organization of Peru, like that of Chile,[47] is very similar to the French.   The nation is divided into departments, provinces, and districts.   There are twenty-three departments, plus the so-called "constitutional province" of Callao, which is so important that it is treated as a department.   Each of these departments is governed by a prefect appointed directly by the president.   The provinces—four or five to a department, as a rule—are headed by subprefects.   Each province has a number of districts—usually nine or ten—the chiefs of which are called governors.   The entire system is tightly controlled by the central government.   Its head is the minister of government and police, who exercises direct control over the prefects.   The prefects in turn control the subprefects, and the subprefects have full authority over the governors. The people have no voice in the selection of any of these officials, and there are no departmental, provincial, or district assemblies to represent the popular viewpoint.   Proposals to restore to the municipalities their self-government of earlier days have received some attention, but as yet nothing has been done.

SELECTED REFERENCES

Alzamora Silva, Lizardo, *Derecho Constitucional General y del Perú,* Lima, Librería e Imp. Gil, s.a., 1942.

[46] For a good description and analysis of Peru's legal system, see *El Poder Judicial,* by Domingo García Rada, published in 1944.

[47] See page 339.

——— *Programa Razonado de Derecho Constitucional del Perú*, Lima, Librería e Imp. Gil, s.a., 1944.

Barrós, Oscar C., *¿En Donde Está la Justicia?*, Lima, Taller de Linotipía, 1942.

——— *¡Más Allá del Deber!*, Lima, Taller de Linotipía, 1944.

Bernashina, Mario de, *Mi Entrevista con Víctor Raúl Haya de la Torre*, Panama City, Star and Herald Co., 1940.

Bravo Morán, E. T., *Finanzas Administrativas*, Lima, Tip. Lit. Caballero e Hijos, 1935.

Cannon, Mary M., *Social and Labor Problems of Peru and Uruguay*, Washington, D.C., Women's Bureau, U.S. Department of Labor, 1945.

García Rada, D. *El Poder Judicial*, Lima, Talleres de la Editorial Atlántida, 1944.

González Prada, Manuel, *Propaganda y Ataque*, Buenos Aires, Ediciones Imán, 1939.

Lear, John, *Forgotten Front*, New York, Dutton, 1943.

Leguía, Jorge G., *Hombres e Ideas en el Perú*, Santiago, Chile, Ediciones Ercilla, 1941.

Minano García, Max H., *Some Educational Problems in Peru*, Austin, Tex., Univ. of Texas Press, 1945.

Pareja Paz Soldán, José, *Historia de las Constituciones Nacionales*, Lima, Gráf. "Zenit," 1943.

Patrón Faura, Pedro, *Legislación Peruana sobre Empleados Públicos*, Lima, Taller de Linotipía, 1943.

Portocarrero, F., *Curso de Derecho Administrativo del Perú*, Lima, Escuela Tip. Salesiana, 1944.

Ravines, Eudocio, *El Momento Político*, Lima, "Ediciones Perunas," 1945.

Stuart, Graham H., *The Governmental System of Peru*, Washington, D.C., Carnegie Institution of Washington, 1925.

Távara, Santiago, *Historia de los Partidos*, Lima, Editorial Huascarán, 1951.

Ulloa y Sotomayor, Alberto, *Perú y Ecuador*, Lima, Imp. Torres Aguirre, 1942.

——— *Perú y Japón*, Lima, Imp. Torres Aguirre, 1943.

CHAPTER 15

COLOMBIA

~~~~~~

The Land and the People

THE TRADITION OF CULTURE. Colombia is fourth in population among the nations of Latin America. Recent estimates place the number of its inhabitants above the eleven million mark. It is fourth in area, also, with four hundred and forty thousand square miles—in other words, a little larger than California and Texas combined. But Colombians like to boast that their nation stands first in culture, and without doubt they have some basis for their claim. The country is noted for its many authors, scientists, and philosophical writers. It even chose one of its poets to be president of the nation.[1] A popular commentator on life in Latin America was greatly impressed by the "staggeringly intellectual-literary" quality of the conversation at Colombian dinner tables. It dealt with such matters as "the quantum theory, the philosophy of Bertrand Russell, the influence of Rimbaud on Gide, and the works of Waldo Frank." [2] Members of the Chamber of Representatives, he discovered, read their poems aloud to one another.

The preoccupation of the people with cultural matters has a solid foundation. Jorge Isaacs, who died in 1895, wrote the most widely read of all Spanish American novels, *María*. His contemporary, José Silva, was the author of some of the finest modern poems in the Spanish language. The Colombian painter Gregorio Vásquez de Arce y Ceballos has been recognized as one of the outstanding figures of the seventeenth century. Present-day artists like Luis Alberto Acuña have won acclaim as interpreters of modern life. Colombians are proud of their culture. They like to

---

[1] Rafael Núñez, who served from 1879 to 1882.
[2] John Gunther, *Inside Latin America*, p. 160.

refer to their capital city, Bogotá, as the Athens of America, and to point out that it has more bookstores than cafes. Many impartial scholars declare that Colombians speak the best Spanish in Latin America.[3]

MASS EDUCATION. It can scarcely be said, however, that Colombian culture is a mass movement. Most of the people have little or no education. At least half of them, in all probability, cannot even read and write. But the government has made very determined efforts to erase illiteracy. It has set aside ten per cent of the national budget for education, and has increased expenditures for this purpose more than six hundred per cent in the last twenty-five years. Hundreds of new schools have been opened. Trained women are paid a small sum for every person between the ages of seven and twenty years whom they teach to read and write. Only a privileged few, of course, receive university training, but for them Colombia provides excellent facilities. The principal center of higher learning is the National University in Bogotá. Four of the departments maintain universities, however, and there are a number of private institutions providing education of university grade.

IMPORTANCE OF TOPOGRAPHY. Colombia's economic life is conditioned by hard geographic facts. Almost everything in the country depends directly or indirectly on the mountains. The great Andean range that forms the backbone of South America unknots itself in the far south of Colombia and divides into three principal mountain chains. These chains run northward almost to the Caribbean and attain great heights. Some of their peaks rise to eighteen or nineteen thousand feet. The lowland regions are steaming and fever-infested. In some parts they are swamp or jungle; in others they are unhealthful tropical plains. But scarcely anywhere do they provide a comfortable living place for large numbers of persons. The result is that nine tenths of Colombia's population lives in the highlands. Here, too, are eleven of the fourteen major urban centers. Yet the highlands comprise a scant one third of the nation's total area.

TRANSPORTATION PROBLEMS. As in most of South America, the highlands are a criss-cross of mountain peaks, deep valleys, and broad tablelands. Transportation, therefore, presents a major problem. Most Colombians find themselves somewhat isolated from the outside world and even from other sections of their own country. Only about two thousand miles of railroad have been built and much of this mileage is narrow gauge. The highway system is totally inadequate, and great construction difficulties

[3] See S. A. Lewisohn's article, "Colombia, Land of Humanism," in the December, 1943, issue of *Survey Graphic*, pp. 491–492.

prevent its rapid expansion. Even airplane travel, which has proved a great boon to Colombia, faces serious climatic handicaps. The region around Bogotá is frequently shrouded in fog and has been the scene of several major air tragedies. The overwhelming majority of plane passengers travel to and from Bogotá in complete safety, of course, but many timid visitors to the capital, as well as some of its residents, have lost interest in flying. In 1946, when former President Alberto Lleras Camargo was about to leave Bogotá to assume his new duties as director general of the Pan American Union, forty-four persons were killed in a nearby air crash. The new Director General hastily canceled his plane reservation and accepted the tedium of the long journey by train and boat.

The river system. A large part of Colombia's internal commerce is by water. There are a number of important streams, but the principal river is the Magdalena, which flows between the eastern and central cordilleras of the Andes, eventually emptying into the Caribbean. It is the main channel of communication between Bogotá and the coast. This does not mean, however, that Bogotá is situated on its banks. Instead it is located high in the eastern cordillera (8,700 feet) on a small tributary of the Magdalena which is utterly useless for navigation. The Magdalena itself during the dry season is shallow and clogged with sandbars in its upper portion, and there are several stretches of rapids. So the slow and tedious journey from Bogotá to the Caribbean coast is made by a combination of trains and boats. The government is making strenuous efforts to improve this state of affairs, but Bogotá is still one of the most inaccessible capitals of the New World.

There are two other rivers worthy of mention, the Cauca and the Atrato, but they too are badly handicapped by sandbars or other natural obstructions to commerce. The Cauca, a tributary of the Magdalena, is used by shallow-draft steamers to bring gold from one of the richest placer mining regions of the country. The Atrato in the far west rises near important platinum mines.

Bogotá. Bogotá, which stands on a high plateau, is ringed about by still higher mountains. Rain and fog blot out the sun a large part of the year and the average temperature is about fifty degrees, with very little change from season to season. Small wonder, therefore, that it is known as the cool gray city. It is an important metropolis, despite its isolation; its present population is about six hundred and fifty thousand. To the visitor it seems a city of strange contrasts. Most of the houses are low, with eaves projecting over the streets as they did in colonial days, but there are many examples of modernistic architecture. Smartly dressed men and women mingle on the streets with simple country folk. In the markets there are glimpses of Indian life. The great public buildings serve as a reminder that Bogotá is the nation's capital.

MEDELLÍN. Unlike most of the capitals of Latin America, however, Bogotá does not have a virtual monopoly on the intellectual, commercial, and industrial life of the nation. It has an important rival in the city of Medellín, which lies in the central cordillera about two hundred miles northwest of the capital, at an altitude of five thousand feet. The difference in altitude between the two cities is extremely important. It gives to Medellín a summery climate throughout the year, in direct contrast to Bogotá's chilly spring. With its population of three hundred and fifty thousand, Medellín is only half as large as the capital, but it is growing much more rapidly, and its inhabitants confidently predict that some day it will be the nation's principal metropolis. Already it is the chief coffee and mining center of the country and has developed important industries. Moreover, its educational facilities are far above the national average, not more than twenty per cent of its people being illiterate.

A VERTICAL CLIMATE. Altitude is very important in Colombia, as in all tropical lands. It determines the climate, and therefore the crops that can be grown. At or near sea level, where the days and nights are monotonously hot, bananas and sugar and cotton do well. At moderate elevations (three to six thousand feet) it is agreeably mild; here coffee is at home. Still higher the weather is almost invariably cool, or even cold, and temperate zone crops are grown. Visitors from the United States and Europe are perpetually amazed by the relative ease of passing from summer to winter. An ascent of a few thousand feet will accomplish the transformation in a few hours. That is what the Colombians mean when they say that their climate is vertical.[4]

CROPS AND RESOURCES. Colombia is virtually a one-crop country, and the crop is coffee. In value it represents nearly two thirds of the nation's exports. Although Brazil is the largest coffee producer in Latin America, the coffee of Colombia is high in quality and brings an excellent price in the world's markets. Most of it goes to the United States. Other crops are not exported on a large scale.

There are, however, important mineral deposits. Colombia is the

[4] A useful descriptive book is Kathleen Romoli's *Colombia, Gateway to South America.*

world's ninth largest producer of petroleum, though its known deposits do not begin to compare with those of its neighbor, Venezuela. Gold and silver are abundant, and platinum is produced in considerable quantities. Most of the world's emeralds come from the highlands near Bogotá. At least half of the area of Colombia is covered by dense forests. Tropical woods of great value grow in this territory—mahogany, chicle, balsam, dyewoods, and resins.

Industry. There are two manufacturing centers—Medellín and Bogotá. Most of the manufacturing is on a small scale, however, and represents only a fraction of the national wealth. The principal raw materials of industry are imported. But the government is vitally interested in developing manufacturing, and has set up a special agency for this purpose. Public funds have been used to subsidize chemical, steel, and other industries.

Races. Most of the people are of mixed Spanish and Indian blood. But there are a good many Negroes and part-Negroes, especially along the Caribbean coastal strip. Perhaps one fourth of the people are white. They live in the highlands, for the most part, in or near the two great urban centers. The people of Medellín and its vicinity are said to have a large percentage of Jewish blood. Certainly they possess greater energy and a larger measure of business acumen than most of the other inhabitants of the nation.

The Pattern of Politics

Unstable democracy. Colombia was long regarded as one of the few countries of Latin America that could fairly be called a democracy. But this era was succeeded in 1949 by a bloody dictatorship, which has only recently been overthrown.[5] The nation has had a long history of protracted civil wars. Perhaps, however, there has been less fighting for the personal glory of ambitious dictators than in most of the other countries of Latin America. Colombians have shed their blood instead for vital principles.

Great Colombia. Colombia began its independent history with a dictatorship, as did most of Latin America. The dictator was Simón Bolívar, the liberator of the northern half of the continent, and the very magic of his name was sufficient to make thousands of persons accept his

[5] See p. 406.

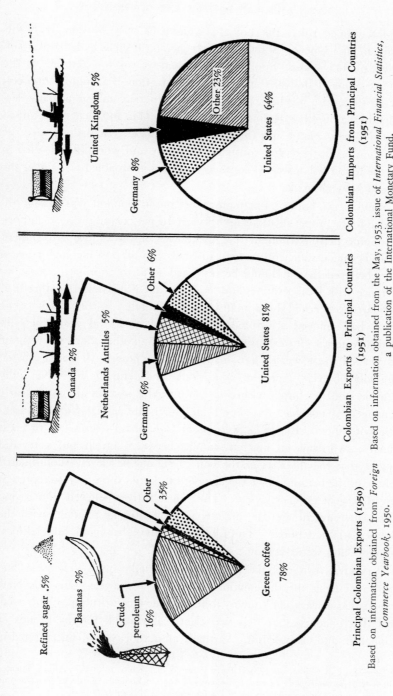

Refined sugar .5%

Bananas 2%

Crude petroleum 16%

Other 3.5%

Green coffee 78%

Principal Colombian Exports (1950)

Based on information obtained from *Foreign Commerce Yearbook*, 1950.

Canada 2%

Netherlands Antilles 5%

Germany 6%

Other 6%

United States 81%

Colombian Exports to Principal Countries (1951)

United Kingdom 5%

Germany 8%

Other 23%

United States 64%

Colombian Imports from Principal Countries (1951)

Based on information obtained from the May, 1953, issue of *International Financial Statistics*, a publication of the International Monetary Fund.

well-intentioned rule. But not all Colombians were satisfied with this arrangement. One of Bolívar's own generals, Francisco de Paula Santander, plotted against him, and subsequently was forced to leave the country. One of Bolívar's dreams was the creation of a single nation embracing the entire northern part of South America, and he actually succeeded in making that dream come true. Colombia and Venezuela united to form Great Colombia in 1819, and three years later Ecuador joined the federation. But there was constant dissension, and when Bolívar died in 1830 the union fell apart. Colombia continued its troubled way under the name of New Granada.

FUNDAMENTAL ISSUES. For many years public opinion was sharply divided as to the proper relationship between the nation and the local authorities. Some persons thought that the power of the central government should be made sufficiently strong to cope with all possible emergencies; others believed that it should be restricted so as to eliminate central interference with local activities and locally granted liberties. Another serious quarrel concerned the Roman Catholic Church. In colonial times the church had enjoyed a favored position, just as it did everywhere in Spanish America. Its extensive land holdings and other sources of revenue had yielded great wealth and made it a vast power. It had a virtual monopoly of every aspect of educational and religious life. Naturally the leaders of the church wished to continue this state of affairs as nearly unchanged as possible, and they found many influential Colombians to agree with them. But there were other Colombians—also men of great influence—who saw an inherent conflict between church and state, and thought that the interests of the church should be clearly subordinated to those of the nation. Two major political parties sprang up to represent these divergent points of view. The Conservatives believed in a strong central government and the maintenance of intimate relations with the Roman Catholic Church. The Liberals, on the other hand, favored local autonomy and secularization.[6]

CENTRALISM AND CONSERVATISM. After Ecuador and Venezuela had withdrawn from the three-nation federation, it was necessary for New Granada (as it was then known) to frame a new constitution. The document that it adopted in 1832 was clearly a triumph for the friends of nationalism and Catholicism. Virtually all authority was concentrated in

---

[6] The history of Colombia's Liberal Party is traced in a bulky volume by Milton Puentes, entitled *Historia del Partido Liberal Colombiano*. Antonio Romero Aguirre performs a similar service for the Conservatives in his *El Partido Conservador ante la Historia*.

a central government. Every important officer—not excepting even the membership of Congress—was to be chosen by indirect election or appointment. Thus the people were denied any real opportunity to make their wishes known through the medium of the ballot box. The Roman Catholic religion was declared the official faith of the nation and the church was permitted to retain most of its ancient privileges. In 1843 another constitution was adopted, but it followed substantially the same lines. In fact, it actually increased the powers of the president. There were several revolutions during this period.

LIBERAL REFORMS. Then came other presidents, other constitutions, and other civil wars. One of the constitutions, adopted in 1853 during a period of Liberal control, made great changes in public policy. It guaranteed freedom of worship for all persons, instead of the compulsory observance of the Catholic faith. It declared that there should be freedom of speech and press. Of course, the freedom of expression ardently desired by advanced Liberals was not permanently won at this time. The Conservatives, and even men who called themselves Liberals, violated this guarantee more than once in later years. Conservatives were frankly shocked at the idea that men should be free to speak and write erroneous thoughts. But the principle of liberty was written into the constitution. It was an important step. There were other major changes, also. Universal suffrage was established, at least in theory, and a federal scheme of government was set up, with power divided between the nation and a number of states.

ADOPTION OF FEDERALISM. The introduction of federalism was a serious mistake. It is always a mistake unless some special factors make it unavoidable. For federalism has numerous disadvantages, such as duplication of governmental machinery and conflicts of authority. It should be used only when diverse conditions exist over a large area, or when people are divided by racial, linguistic, or other barriers. None of these conditions could be found in Colombia. The Liberals made their government unduly complicated when they insisted upon federalism, but they were determined to undermine the power of the central authorities. In 1855 the new constitution was amended to reduce still further the power of the national government, and three years later another constitution was adopted which carried the principle of federalism to absurd lengths. Under its provisions Colombia was less a nation than a federation of semi-independent states. In fact, it was even called *The Granadine Confederation*. Meanwhile there were numerous bloody uprisings and several years of full-scale civil war.

In 1863 the country acquired another constitution, which remained the fundamental law for nearly a quarter of a century. No substantial change was made, however, in the principle of federalism. There were to be nine sovereign states bound to one another in a loose league. The name adopted for this league was *The United States of Colombia,* and its head was to be a president with few powers, elected for only two years. Not long afterward the president declared himself absolute dictator of the nation. The result was another revolution, and he was deposed. By this time civil war had become almost the normal state of affairs, with occasional intervals of peace between the uprisings.[7]

ABANDONMENT OF FEDERALISM. The year 1886 was momentous for Colombia. The Conservatives had already lost control of the government, which they had held for many years, and the Liberal Rafael Núñez was president. Under his influence a national council representing the governors of the several states met in Bogotá and drew up a new constitution. The principle of federalism was discarded, and Colombia became once more a unitary nation with a powerful central government. The states sank to the level of departments, retaining almost none of their former authority. Once again the nation changed its name: it became the Republic of Colombia. The constitution of 1886, though modified many times since its adoption, still remains the basic law of the land. It has been a vast improvement over the documents that immediately preceded it, if only because of its abandonment of the cumbersome federal system. There is considerable doubt, however, whether President Núñez considered primarily the welfare of the nation when he insisted upon a strong central government. His chief concern seems to have been the adoption of a constitution that would make him virtual dictator. But fresh disorders broke out almost immediately, and spread throughout the country.

DISORDER AND BLOODSHED. Even the first years of the present century continued Colombia's bloody saga. The Liberal president elected in 1899 had been seized and imprisoned by Conservative revolutionists the following year, and the Liberals thereupon staged a major civil war. They were finally defeated, but only after several years of bitter fighting and the loss of at least fifty thousand lives. A few months after the end of this struggle came a revolution that resulted in the independence of Panama.[8]

Few persons would have dared to predict at this time that Colombia was

[7] This period of Colombia's history is well covered by Jesús María Henao and Gerardo Arrubia in their *History of Colombia,* which has been translated by Professor J. Fred Rippy.
[8] See the important *Compendio de la Historia de Colombia,* by José Alejandro Bermúdez.

about to enter an era of peace and prosperity, substituting democratic elections for violent revolutions as a means of deciding public policy. Yet such proved to be the case. The president who assumed power in 1904 scarcely seemed to fit into this new pattern. He was a military man, intolerant of opposition, and determined to obtain dictatorial powers. Almost constantly he quarreled with other government officials and with Congress, and he imposed a strict press censorship. But he did initiate a long-range program for the development of the nation, and some of his financial and industrial reforms were highly important. He resigned in 1909 as an expression of his hostility toward the proposed treaty between Colombia and the United States concerning Panama.

CONSERVATIVES AND LIBERALS. From 1900 to 1930 the Conservatives controlled the government. Most of the presidents were lawyers or writers or newspaper publishers, rather than generals. Constitutional guarantees of individual liberty were generally respected. Elections followed the democratic pattern. In 1930 the Liberals finally won control of the government. The successful presidential candidate was Enrique Olaya Herrera, a forty-nine-year-old diplomat who was then serving as minister to the United States. He made few major changes in the established policies of the Conservatives, partly because of his moderate temperament and partly because of his preoccupation with the problems created by world-wide depression. Recovery from the depression seemed to him more important than reform.

NOMINATION OF ALFONSO LÓPEZ. As the time drew near for another presidential election in 1934, the Liberals were sharply divided in their search for a suitable candidate. This was not at all surprising, in view of the divergent groups comprising the party's membership. Many wealthy industrialists called themselves Liberals, either because they opposed the dominance of the Roman Catholic Church or because they thought that the Conservatives were a shade too reactionary. Nearly all the employees of these industrialists, especially those who belonged to trade unions, also claimed membership in the Liberal Party. So did many intellectuals, whose views were far from uniform. In fact, the Liberals could count on the votes of almost everyone except the representatives and followers of the feudal landholding class, plus some very devout Catholics. This overwhelming Liberal support placed the party in a very enviable position, but it was also a source of weakness because it necessitated endless compromise in the selection of party candidates and the preparation of party programs.

In 1934 it was finally decided that the Liberal presidential candidate should be Alfonso López Pumarejo, a businessman and diplomat, forty-nine years of age, whose education had been obtained partly in the United States. His family had been well-to-do, but when he was still a young man the family fortunes were lost in the collapse of the López Bank. So he worked at a number of jobs—coffee merchant, newspaper publisher, representative of various investment houses. For a time he served as his country's minister to the court of St. James. During the years he had veered more and more to the left in his political thinking, until he came to be recognized as a champion of labor. Big business, he thought, was responsible for the failure of his family's bank, and should therefore be restricted by every feasible means, lest it cause other similar tragedies. Such a man was not at all acceptable to the moderate wing of the Liberal Party, which had sponsored outgoing President Olaya Herrera. But when the party officially nominated López, good Liberals could scarcely do less than assure him of their support.

THE CONSERVATIVE BOYCOTT. The Conservatives were in an even more difficult position than their opponents. They knew full well that they had lost the confidence of the people and that any candidate they might select would be defeated by a considerable margin. So, rather than accept the humiliation of certain defeat, they decided not even to indicate their choice for the presidency. Of course, they gave a very different reason for this decision. They said that the Liberals would not permit an honest election, and that any man they might nominate would be cheated out of his triumph. Their only recourse, they declared, was to boycott the election in protest, and they called on all Conservatives to stay away from the polls. The obvious effect of this policy was to give the Liberals a victory by default; but, since they would undoubtedly have won anyway, the price may not have been too great. It saved the necessity of many embarrassing post-election explanations.

LAUREANO GÓMEZ. The man primarily responsible for the strategy of the Conservative boycott was the party leader, Dr. Laureano Eleuterio Gómez y Castro, a trained engineer who had devoted many more years to politics than to engineering.[9] At the time of the 1934 election he was forty-five years old and had served with distinction as senator, cabinet minister, and diplomat. He was thought to be the Conservative ideal of

[9] Russell Fitzgibbon presents an excellent character study of Laureano Gómez in his article, "Colombian Gadfly," published in *Inter-American*, February, 1945 (Vol. IV, No. 2), pp. 15–17.

a statesman. Wealthy, highly cultured, and intensely Catholic, he defended with great vigor the cause of the landed aristocracy, though he was sufficiently intelligent to know that a twentieth-century aristocrat must pay at least passing attention to the needs of the working class. Dr. Gómez could almost have been called a professional apologist for the Catholic Church. He never criticized it in any way, except to blame it for relinquishing a small measure of its authority in a concordat with the Colombian government. To him, every proposal for separation of church and state was the product of atheism. Every suggestion to increase religious freedom was heresy. And, it might be added, any really substantial expansion of the system of social security was communism.

Dr. Gómez was a very clever and determined fighter. At one time some of his sharpest arrows were reserved for the United States. He never forgot the part played by the "Colossus of the North" in the loss of Panama, and he often insisted that the United States was still just as imperialistic as it had been at that time. Good Colombians, he declared, must be prepared to resist it at every turn. Later, however, Laureano Gómez seemed to lose much of his Yankeephobia. His family-owned newspaper, *El Siglo* (The Century), proved an effective vehicle for the circulation of his ideas. Colombia's press laws were notoriously liberal, almost to the point of laxness, when Dr. Gómez was the leader of the opposition, and he took advantage of that fact to make violent charges against successive Liberal administrations. Many of his attacks seemed to fall just short of treason.

LIBERALISM OF LÓPEZ. The 1934 election provided no real test of Liberal strength, for the Conservatives boycotted it as Gómez had planned. The only opponent of Alfonso López was a Communist, who received merely a handful of votes. The new President took office on August 7, 1934, and promptly proceeded to confirm the worst fears of the moderates within his own party. He proposed extensive social legislation, and urged the adoption of so-called "soak-the-rich" laws. Some of his suggestions were adopted by Congress, but others met the determined resistance of the moderates and failed to secure the majority necessary for passage. By 1937 President López had grown so weary of congressional opposition that he threatened to resign unless the legislators would assume a more co-operative attitude. Thereupon the Workers' Union staged a strike as a demonstration of solidarity with President López and his policies. Apparently the strike had little effect, however, for Congress continued its hostility and the President did not resign. As a matter of fact, some progressive labor laws were enacted during these years, and other problems of major importance were solved in a satisfactory manner. A reciprocal trade agreement with the United States assured the sale of Colombian coffee in the American market and the sale of American manufactured goods in Colombia under favorable conditions. The result was a marked improvement in the economic life of the country. In 1936 the constitution was amended very extensively, making it a much more liberal document.

NOMINATION OF EDUARDO SANTOS. The presidential term, changed many times in the course of Colombian history, had finally been fixed at four years, with no immediate re-election. The year 1937 was, therefore, one of intense political activity, with another presidential election scheduled for the following May. The moderate wing of the Liberal Party was determined that the presidential candidate should be a man of less radical views than López, and it had its way. In the national convention of the party it secured the nomination of a distinguished newspaper publisher, Dr. Eduardo Santos. At this time he was fifty years of age, and had achieved an enviable reputation for scrupulous honesty. Unlike the Conservative leader, Dr. Gómez, he did not become a newspaper publisher to further his political ambitions. Instead he chose newspaper work as a career, and drifted into politics almost by accident. He studied in Paris as a very young man, and then joined his brother in an important venture, the publication of the Bogotá daily, El Tiempo (Time). The paper soon became recognized as an interpreter and leader of liberal thought, and made a handsome profit for its owners. Today it is one of the great newspapers of Latin America.

When President López first heard that Santos was being considered as his successor, he went out of his way to denounce the choice. The man was the tool of reactionary interests, he said, and would never fight for true liberalism. But this dire warning had no effect. It is an interesting commentary on this era of Colombian politics that the president of the nation did not necessarily name his successor—in fact, did not always approve of his own party's nominee.

The 1938 election was merely a form. The Conservatives persisted in their policy of non-participation, and even the Communists decided that a campaign was not worth the effort. So Eduardo Santos was the only candidate. He succeeded to the presidency on August 7, 1938, and immediately showed his intention of modifying the radical López policies. Labor conditions should be improved, he said, and labor unions should be encouraged, but there must be no violence and no union interference in politics. These words were not kindly received in labor circles. The new administration's first serious difficulties were created, however, by university students.

STUDENT UPRISING. In Colombia, as in all Latin America, the students of the universities take an active part in the political life of the country, and also insist upon a voice in the management of university affairs.[10] They sometimes go on strike because a popular professor is dismissed or an unpopular professor is retained. They make strenuous protests against anything they do not like—too difficult examinations, too short vacations, too crowded classrooms. Sometimes they stage demonstrations that cause considerable damage to property. Then, if the police are called out, they barricade themselves in the university buildings and defy the police force to dislodge them. Sometimes the challenge is accepted. The 1938 student strike in Colombia, called only two weeks after the inauguration of President Santos, was a protest against university entrance requirements. It led to considerable violence. Public buildings were sacked, and jails were raided. Students broke into banks and liquor stores, and were aided by others who welcomed the opportunity to plunder. The President ordered the police to restore order, and his prompt action forced the students to abandon their violent methods. Then the government issued an order prohibiting public demonstrations of any kind.

CO-OPERATION WITH THE UNITED STATES. For many years the government of Colombia had followed a policy of suspicion and unfriendliness in its dealings with the United States, but President Santos changed this official point of view. He had long been a warm admirer of the great Republic of the North, and from the very beginning of his administration he adopted a program of close co-operation. In November of 1938 it was announced that the United States would send a naval aviation mission to Colombia to aid in the training of Colombian fliers. Eight months later President Santos announced that his country would take all possible steps to prevent the use of Colombian soil as a base for foreign attacks on the Panama Canal and to aid the United States in the canal's defense. The first step in the fulfillment of this pledge was the signing of an agreement which permitted the American government to build an air base at Urrao, Colombia, about three hundred miles from the canal. A little later the United States showed its appreciation of this co-operation by making a substantial loan to Colombia.

[10] For a discussion of the Argentine government's troubles with university students, see page 62.

Severance of relations with the Axis. Meanwhile war had broken out in Europe, and there was obvious danger that the United States might become involved. A large part of Colombia's commercial aviation was in the hands of a German company, which employed German pilots and technicians almost exclusively. American military men shuddered at the thought that these German fliers might suddenly be transformed into officers of the German army in the event of war between Germany and the United States, and that their first military mission might be the bombing of the Panama Canal. This danger was discussed with the Colombian government, which agreed that the German company should be dissolved. The German fliers were replaced by pilots and instructors of Pan American Airways. In December of 1941, when the Japanese treachery at Pearl Harbor finally plunged the United States into war, Colombia responded promptly by breaking relations with the Axis powers. It was a very different story from the First World War, when Colombia had remained neutral.

RE-ELECTION OF LÓPEZ. December of 1941 found the Colombians less concerned with war, however, than with the exciting game of politics. Another presidential election was only a few months away, and so a suitable successor to President Santos must be found. The only Liberal leader, other than Santos himself, who seemed able to capture the imagination of both the politicians and the voters was former President Alfonso López. Under the terms of the constitution he was once more eligible for the presidency, and his many supporters eagerly urged his candidacy. The moderate wing of the Liberal Party was against him, of course. So was President Santos. But Santos was powerless to block the swing to López, just as López had been unable to prevent Santos' nomination four years earlier. The national convention of the Liberal Party enthusiastically named Alfonso López as its presidential candidate. Some dissident Liberals bolted the convention, declaring that they would cast their votes for a prominent Bogotá lawyer named Carlos Arango Vélez. The Conservatives, following their well-established policy of non-participation in elections, refused to present a candidate, but agreed to give Arango Vélez their support. He was well known and respected; his father had been a distinguished diplomat. But certainly he lacked the political appeal of the popular López. So not many persons were surprised when López was declared the victor by a margin of two hundred thousand votes.

WAR PROBLEMS. On August 7, 1942, President López was inaugurated for his second presidential term. It proved to be even more turbulent than his first. Congress blocked his liberal labor policy at every turn and thus fanned the dissatisfaction of the workers. When pro-labor legislation was enacted, as sometimes happened, congressional leaders usually shaped it along somewhat different lines from those suggested by the President, and then claimed all the credit. President López received fresh criticism, especially from Conservative sources, when he continued his predecessor's pro-United States policy. In 1943 Colombia declared war on Germany. There were not enough boats at this time to carry the usual quantities of Colombian coffee to the United States or to bring to Colombia badly needed supplies of manufactured goods. So the Colombian people suffered some of the minor inconveniences of a war that they did not really regard as their own, and their natural reaction was to blame the government. Cabinet ministers came and went. Within one period of eight months there were five complete turnovers in the cabinet.[11]

POLITICS AND UPRISINGS. In 1943 occurred a political scandal that rocked the López administration to its very foundation. The body of a local Negro prizefighter of unsavory reputation was found in a Bogotá park, riddled with knife wounds. In addition to prizefighting, the dead man had published a small radical newspaper called *The Voice of the People*, though very few people had ever paid much attention to the *Voice*. The whole affair seemed relatively trivial—just another routine murder to be cleared up by routine police methods. But a young judge, who happened to be a Conservative, decided to make a thorough investigation. Soon he had produced enough evidence to involve many Liberals in high places. The ex-director of the national police and the police chief of Bogotá were arrested; so was a former secretary of the President. Finally a high officer in the police force confessed that he had ordered the killing and had arranged with a sub-lieutenant to attend to all the necessary details.

To the Conservatives this was manna from heaven. They transformed the murdered prizefighter into a Conservative martyr and pictured the entire Liberal government as a gang of assassins. The Gómez newspaper *El Siglo* declared that even the Minister of the Interior had known what was happening and had tried to block the investigation. To this charge the Minister of the Interior replied by bringing a suit for libel against Dr. Gómez. But the Conservative leader refused to defend the suit and finally he was thrown into jail for contempt of court. The Conservatives promptly rioted and tried to release him. There was serious fighting in the streets of

[11] See Kathleen Romoli's article, *López of Colombia*, in the May, 1942, issue of *Inter-American*, pp. 9 ff.

Bogotá. Before long, however, Gómez was free once more on a technicality. The government obligingly found the technicality for him, rather
than permit him to continue his campaign of martyrdom. But the disturbances continued in various parts of the country. Four revolutionary
attempts were crushed by the government within a single year. On one
occasion the President was kidnapped, but he was promptly released.

RESIGNATION OF LÓPEZ. The strain of his office began to tell on President
López. His intimate friends said that he was worn out and would like
to resign. On November 16, 1943, he asked the Senate for permission to
leave the country for ninety days.[12] The ostensible reason for the journey
was that the President's wife required medical treatment in the United
States, but many people predicted freely that López would never again
assume the burdens of the presidency. They were wrong. He did return
to Bogotá and his duties. No sooner had he arrived, however, than he
said publicly that he would like to quit. A few days later he said the same
thing in Medellín. But he remained at his post until July 19 of the following year (1945), when he finally sent his resignation to the Senate,
which at first refused to accept it but later decided that it had no alternative.
Dr. Alberto Lleras Camargo, former ambassador to the United States, then
assumed the presidential duties for the remaining year of López' term.

THE LIBERALS SPLIT. Already the party leaders were beginning to lay
plans for the next presidential election, to be held early in 1946. The
Liberals nominated Gabriel Turbay, a distinguished diplomat who had
served as his country's foreign minister and also as ambassador to Washington. This choice was very displeasing to the leftist members of the
Liberal Party, for Turbay held moderate views on economic questions. He
belonged more or less to the same school of thought as former President
Santos. Another serious objection to Turbay, in the opinion of many
Colombians, was his Syrian ancestry. He was, they said, a *turco,* meaning
a person with Levantine blood in his veins. Of course, this term was an
expression of contempt. It was used freely throughout the campaign to
discredit everything that Turbay said or did. A cartoonist for a Conservative newspaper portrayed him in fez and flowing robes, astride a camel.

POLITICAL MANEUVERS. The radical wing of the Liberal Party refused
to give its support to Turbay. Instead it named its own candidate, Jorge
Eliecer Gaitán, who had once served as minister of labor and had seized
every opportunity to favor the trade unions in their disputes with big

---

[12] Such permission had to be obtained before a president might leave Colombian soil.
Constitution of 1886, Art. 122.

business. Gaitán was a popular man with the masses, and it seemed that he might be able to win a large share of the regular Liberal following. The Conservatives, of course, thoroughly enjoyed the spectacle of two Liberal candidates campaigning against each other. Unfortunately for their own peace of mind, however, they could not present an entirely united front. One of Lleras Camargo's first acts as president had been to issue an appeal for national unity. As evidence of the sincerity of his intentions he offered a number of cabinet posts to prominent Conservatives, and some of them accepted. Their acceptance roused the wrath of the Conservative Party leader, Laureano Gómez, who declared emphatically that there must be no "traffic with the enemy." But the new cabinet ministers stuck by their guns, and two members of the party's executive committee resigned in order to be free to support them. The election seemed to promise more than the usual amount of confusion, with both parties badly divided.

NOMINATION OF OSPINA PÉREZ. Eventually, however, it became clear that the Conservatives could set their own house in order for the presidential campaign. Conservative leaders of both factions agreed upon the urgent need for compromise. They realized that if only they could unite in choosing a suitable candidate, they might actually hope to win an election for the first time in many years. On March 24, 1946, only six weeks before election day, they abandoned their policy of non-participation and nominated a presidential candidate by the overwhelming vote of three hundred and sixty to three. Nothing could have indicated more clearly that the Conservatives had really succeeded in patching up their differences. The Conservative nominee was a wise choice. His name was Mariano Ospina Pérez, and he was a wealthy man of good family who had graduated in engineering from Louisiana State University. His political views, which he set forth in unmistakable language during the campaign, could easily have been accepted by the Turbay-Santos wing of the Liberal Party. Therefore these Liberals spent most of their time attacking Gómez and the Conservative diehards. After all, as they pointed out, Gómez was still the party leader. Ospina Pérez might talk like a Liberal, but as president he would be obliged to follow the Conservative party line. So the Liberals argued, but many voters were undoubtedly impressed by Ospina Pérez' promise of "a more liberal conservatism."

OSPINA'S VICTORY. On May 5, 1946, one and one-quarter million Colombians went to the polls. Ospina Pérez received only forty-two per cent of the total vote, but it was enough. He had one hundred thousand more votes than Turbay, the official Liberal candidate, and nearly two hundred thousand more than the dissident Liberal, Gaitán. It was the first Conservative victory in a presidential election in twenty years. But the new President understood that he had a difficult task. The election returns showed that he did not possess the confidence of a majority of the people. They showed, also, that the Liberals would control both houses of the new Congress. And of course there remained the problem of the reactionaries within the Conservative Party, who had contributed to the final result and certainly expected to reap the fruits of victory.

CONCILIATORY TACTICS. From the very beginning of his administration President Ospina Pérez made clear that he would not permit himself to be unduly influenced by the reactionaries. His campaign speeches had called for many social reforms, such as the extension of the social security laws to agricultural workers and more effective medical care for all wage earners. and he asked that Congress make these matters an early order of business. He also proposed a "cabinet of national unity" including Liberals as well as Conservatives. The Liberals, he said, would receive more posts than the Conservatives had been given under Lleras Camargo. He did in fact give them six ministries, exactly equal to the number held by his own Conservatives. But the reactionary Laureano Gómez became foreign minister.

POLITICAL QUARRELS. Despite President Ospina Pérez' much publicized desire to govern in the public interest, he had a difficult time. The Liberals gave grudging co-operation, but only on their own terms. Even the President's own Conservatives showed scant respect for the principle of national unity; they took advantage of every real or alleged mistake of the Liberals to make political capital. In November, 1947, the Liberal statesman Gabriel Turbay died in Paris of a heart attack. He was only forty-six years old. Undoubtedly his passing strengthened the influence of Jorge Gaitán, his principal rival for the leadership of the Liberal Party. The two Liberal factions had already composed most of their differences. They seemed determined to prevent another disastrous split in their ranks. With renewed vigor they forced their program upon the President, and as a result the coalition cabinet disintegrated in March, 1948.

ASSASSINATION AND MOB VIOLENCE. In April the Liberal leader Jorge Gaitán was assassinated. As he crossed a street in downtown Bogotá on his way to lunch a young man slipped up behind him and fired four shots into his neck and shoulders. Gaitán fell heavily to the ground, but the murderer was unable to make his getaway. A near-by vendor of lottery tickets seized him and someone from an adjacent café smashed a chair over his head. A mob gathered almost at once, and literally kicked and pommeled the assassin to death. Then it began to search for other persons on whom to wreak its vengeance. The rumor spread that Laureano Gómez had plotted the crime, so the rioters rushed to the national capitol in search of him. Not finding him there, they wantonly destroyed furniture and records.

In mid-afternoon, when word came from the Central Clinic that Gaitán was dead, the fury of the greatly augmented mob rose to new heights. It roamed through the city, looting and doing great damage. It set fire to the building in which the Gómez newspaper was published. It attacked government offices and even private stores and homes, doing almost unbelievable damage. The police, who seem to have been sympathetic to the rioters, made little effort to interfere. Army troops stationed in Bogotá were not sufficient to control the situation, and necessary reinforcements did not arrive until the next day. That first night, therefore, was filled with terror for all law-abiding citizens. Even after large numbers of troops arrived, sporadic outbursts occurred. The labor unions added fuel to the flames by calling a general strike, which lasted for several days. Gradually, however, order was restored, though not until at least five hundred persons had lost their lives. Darío Echandía, the recognized lieutenant of Gaitán in the Liberal hierarchy, spoke over the radio and strongly urged his followers to refrain from further violence.

A COMMUNIST PLOT? Strictly speaking, the uprising following Gaitán's assassination was not a revolution. It was simply a spontaneous demonstration by an infuriated people against the government that it believed responsible for the death of its beloved leader. It had no political significance; in fact, the leaders of both major parties condemned it in the strongest possible terms. To the Colombian government, however, it caused profound embarrassment, for it occurred during the sessions of the Ninth International Conference of American States, which was attended by leading statesmen from every nation in the Americas. For a few days the sessions of the Conference were suspended. Then discussions were resumed in a Bogotá school building, because the capitol, where the Conference had been opened, was too badly damaged to be of further use for many months to come. The Colombian government tried to place the blame for the rioting on the Communists. It arrested a number of Communist leaders and severed diplomatic relations with the Soviet Union. A little later, however, the Communists were released when a judge ruled that there was no evidence to connect them with the incident. There was, in fact, no evidence whatever to show that any Communists had plotted the assassination or its aftermath. Certainly, however, the chain of events suited them perfectly. If they did not arrange the affair, at least they took full advantage of their opportunity to encourage mob violence. They had long threatened to disrupt the Inter-American Conference.

UNSUCCESSFUL COALITION GOVERNMENT. One result of the tragic 1948 riots was the return of the Liberals to the cabinet, largely on their own terms. Once more they received six cabinet posts. Darío Echandía became minister of the interior. Laureano Gómez resigned as minister of foreign affairs, and his place was taken by another Conservative who was more acceptable to the Liberals. But this uneasy truce did not long continue. It was marred by violence in many parts of the country. Armed bands of civilians frequently attacked the police and even detachments of the regular army. Homes of prominent Liberals were burned to the ground, and homes of prominent Conservatives were burned in retaliation. Liberal army officers complained that the government was subjecting them to unfair discrimination. Some of them deserted, taking with them whole companies. After a time there were enough of these rebels to form a "Free Republic of Colombia." They hid in the hills, and made raids on communities that were generally known as Conservative strongholds. The government called these rebels "bandits," but many Liberal leaders defended them on the ground that they had been virtually forced to revolt. Passions flared on both sides, and the Conservatives took advantage of the troubled situation to enact a series of repressive measures. Thereupon the Liberals resigned from the cabinet, saying that they could no longer participate in a government based so largely on force.

SUPPRESSION OF LIBERTIES. As the time of the 1949 presidential election approached, the "moderate Conservative" President, Mariano Ospina Pérez, showed himself in new colors—much less moderate and much more conservative. He used army and police forces to protect Conservatives and to harass Liberals. He instituted a strict censorship of press, radio, and other means of communication. When the Liberals announced their intention of impeaching him, he dissolved Congress and placed the nation under martial law, thus blocking any attempt at impeachment. At the same time he issued a decree requiring a three-fourths majority of the supreme court for judgments involving constitutional questions. This decree was in violation of the plain letter of the constitution, but it prevented any interference with Conservative plans by the court's Liberal majority. The national convention of the Conservative Party met to select its presidential candidate, and promptly named Laureano Gómez, the arch-conservative whose very name was anathema to all Liberals. The Liberal Party responded by nominating its leader, Darío Echandía. Later, however, as the Conservative government made increasingly clear its intention of winning at any cost, Echandía withdrew his candidacy and announced that the Liberals would not take part in the election.

PRESIDENT GÓMEZ. November 28, 1949, was election day. Laureano Gómez was elected president, of course, and the Conservatives declared that his margin of victory was the greatest in the history of the country. Nine months later Gómez was inaugurated in a solemn ceremony boycotted by the Liberals. The nation was still under a state of siege, and Congress and the departmental assemblies were forbidden to meet. The new President strengthened the restrictions on civil liberties, and also increased the power of the Catholic Church. These policies could easily have been predicted. Totally unexpected, however, was Gómez' attitude toward the United States. Instead of denouncing its "overbearing imperialism," as he had done so often in the past, he praised the American defense of democracy in Korea, and suggested that Colombian troops might soon be fighting at the side of their United States neighbors. Later a Colombian batallion was sent to Korea. It was the only Latin American unit on the Korean front.

DISSIDENT FACTIONS. Both of the major parties soon developed dissident factions within their ranks. Some Liberals complained that the official Liberal policy of nonco-operation merely played into the hands of the Conservatives. So these dissatisfied Liberals formed a separate group— the Popular Liberals. In the congressional election of 1951 they nominated candidates and conducted a vigorous campaign, but received only about one per cent of the vote. The main body of the Liberals, of course, stayed away from the polls in protest against Colombia's dictatorial regime. Even some of the Conservatives thought that the government had gone too far in suppressing individual liberties. The leader of one such faction was Gilberto Alzate, so his followers called themselves "Alzatistas." Their protests sounded very much like the complaints of the Liberals, but there was no tendency for the "Alzatistas" and the Liberals to combine forces. Some Conservatives believed that their best choice for a presidential candidate in the next election would be Mariano Ospina Pérez, the man who had presided over the dissolution of the nation's democratic institutions. Apparently Ospina Pérez was most anxious to receive the nomination, but government forces led by President Gómez were bitterly opposed.

DECLINE OF DEMOCRACY. By 1952 Colombia was virtually in a state of civil war. Armed bands roamed the countryside, and the government seemed powerless to suppress this violence. In fact, it bred new violence by hunting out and persecuting Liberal leaders. Meanwhile the Conservatives, despite the quarrels within their own ranks, strengthened their hold on the nation's political life. They made plans for the adoption of a new and less liberal constitution, with longer terms for the president and members of Congress, and indirect election of many officers formerly chosen by the people. President Gómez took a leave of absence because of ill health, but his policies were continued by the acting president. Censorship remained as strict as ever, and strenuous efforts were made to intimidate the opposition.

REVOLUTION. On June 13, 1953, Laureano Gómez, faced with increasing opposition within his own party, resumed the presidency. Thereupon the army took a hand. It acted on the command of its chief, Lieutenant General Gustavo Rojas Pinilla, who had been threatened with dismissal, apparently because of undue friendliness with dissident Conservatives. Tanks surrounded the Presidential Palace, and troops seized all government offices, virtually without opposition. Within a few hours General Rojas was able to announce over the official radio that he was the new president of the nation. His position was speedily strengthened by the endorsement of the Constitutional Assembly and the Catholic Church. Deposed President Gómez and his family left the country, to take up exile in New York.

PRESIDENT ROJAS. Meanwhile President Rojas, a fifty-three-year-old professional soldier who once earned an engineering degree from the University of Michigan, surrounded himself with moderate Conservatives who had opposed the Gómez administration. Ospina Pérez became president of the Constitutional Assembly. President Rojas promised a government "for all the people of Colombia," but did not invite any Liberals to join his cabinet. He guaranteed honest elections, but did not set any date. He spoke glowingly of freedom of the press, though retaining the strict newspaper censorship that had been one of the causes of complaint against Gómez. Today, therefore, some doubt exists as to the exact goals of the Rojas regime. It has certainly put an end to the bloody repression of Liberal sympathizers, and perhaps it intends to restore Colombian democracy. Perhaps, on the other hand, it is planning to substitute a mild, middle-of-the-road Conservative dictatorship for the ruthless right-wing absolutism of Laureano Gómez. The entire story cannot yet be told.

The Structure of Government

THE CONSTITUTION. It is correct, but somewhat misleading, to say that the present constitution of Colombia was adopted in 1886. There have been so many amendments to the original document that the men who drafted it would scarcely recognize it in its present form. It has been modified on fifteen different occasions—seven of them since 1930. In 1936 thirty-five articles were added, modifying or annulling forty-seven separate clauses. The overhauling job of 1945 was very thorough, also; it altered seventeen articles.[13] And now a Constitutional Assembly is preparing a fresh set of amendments. Such constant tinkering with the fundamental law is not at all necessary; the constitution is a relatively short document and confines itself almost exclusively to fundamentals, which presumably should stand for many years. But amendment is very easy. In normal times it requires only the favorable action of Congress, by an absolute majority in both houses, during two successive legislative sessions.[14] The present revolutionary government, which is functioning without Congress, will probably accept the amendments proposed by the Constitutional Assembly. In theory the president has nothing to do with the amending process.

Church and state. Although the present constitution was adopted at the insistence of the mildly anti-clerical Liberals, its preamble recognizes the Almighty in the following words: "In the name of God, fountain of all authority, and with the purpose of promoting the national unity and assuring the ends of justice, liberty and peace, we have met together to decree, and we do decree, the following political constitution of Colombia." All forms of religion are tolerated, but the privileged position of the Roman Catholic Church is still recognized in a concordat with the Vatican. This concordat has been revised several times. It contains clauses which the Catholic Church must have accepted with regret—for example, the requirement that bishops and archbishops must be Colombian citizens who have sworn allegiance to their country.

Bill of rights. The bill of rights contains the traditional guarantees, such

[13] The constitutions of Colombia have been brought together in convenient form, with suitable editorial comment, by William Marion Gibson in his recent volume, *The Constitutions of Colombia.*

[14] Constitution, Art. 209.

as freedom of speech and press, immunity from arbitrary arrest, freedom from retroactive penalties, and the like. It also includes a number of the newer "social" guarantees: everyone is guaranteed the right (though not necessarily the opportunity) to work; public welfare is a function of the state; monopolies shall not exist unless permitted by law. "Property is a social function which implies obligations," declares the constitution.[15] Restrictions of various kinds are attached to nearly all the guarantees. The press is assured freedom under the laws *as long as it is heedful of the honor of individuals, the social order, and the public tranquility.*[16] The right of assembly for the redress of grievances is guaranteed, *but the government may dissolve every public meeting that degenerates into a riotous mob or obstructs the public highways.*[17]

State of siege. There is the usual provision for suspension of guarantees, by means of a state of siege, in case of foreign war or internal commotion.[18] The president is given very broad powers in this matter. He may declare a state of siege without consulting Congress, even if it is in session. He may suspend any laws that interfere with the performance of his functions, and he may continue his arbitrary rule indefinitely. The constitution declares that he shall lift the state of siege when the war has ended or the uprising has been suppressed; but, since he is the sole judge of the existence of internal commotion, this restriction is not very effective. Not much more significant are other limitations: that he must secure the approval of the members of his cabinet (whom he appoints) to every declaration of a state of siege, and that he shall be responsible (when public order has been restored) for abuse of his authority.

SUFFRAGE AND ELECTIONS. Only male citizens may vote. They must be literate and at least twenty-one years of age. The preparation of the ballots is left to the political parties, as in most countries of Latin America. The law merely specifies their size, color, and shape, so as to produce substantial uniformity. When a Colombian voter goes to the polls, therefore, he normally accepts the ballots of all the parties (so as not to reveal the way he intends to vote), takes an official envelope from the authorities at the polling place, and enters a private voting booth. In secret he selects the ballot of his party and places it in the official envelope, discarding the other ballots. Thus he is almost compelled to vote a straight ticket. It is pos-

[15] Art. 26.
[16] Art. 36.
[17] Art. 42.
[18] Art. 117.

sible for a voter to split his vote, after a fashion, but the process is complicated. If the ballot contains several lists prepared by the party—one for senators, let us say, one for representatives, and one for members of the assembly of the department—a voter may separate these lists by tearing his ballot into two or more strips. He may then place in the official envelope the Liberal list (let us assume) of senatorial candidates, but the Conservative list of nominees for the Chamber of Representatives and the departmental assembly. He must, of course, vote the complete list of the party for senators *or* deputies *or* assemblymen. Split voting is very rare. A system of proportional representation has been in operation since 1937. Ever since 1905, however, there has been some form of minority representation.

THE PRESIDENT: *Selection, term, qualifications, salary.* In normal times the president of the nation is elected by direct vote of the people for a term of four years and is not eligible for immediate re-election. The constitution states that he must have the same qualifications as a member of the Senate. These qualifications are rather unusual. They include not only such commonplace requirements as Colombian citizenship by birth and a minimum age of thirty years, but also an annual income which, in terms of American money, amounts to about seven hundred and fifty dollars. A 1945 amendment declares further that every senator (and therefore the president) must have served the nation in some important public post, such as congressman, cabinet minister, judge of a high court, or chief of a diplomatic mission, or else must be a university professor or other professional man with a university degree. This is one way to assure the selection of distinguished—or at least well educated—men for such high offices as president and senator. But of course it runs counter to the widely accepted theory that every elective public office should be open to every voter. The president's salary, which is only about twenty thousand dollars a year (American money), does not even begin to cover the expenses of his office.

Powers. At present the powers of the president are virtually unlimited, since he is accountable only to the armed forces. But even in ordinary times, when he is restricted by the constitution, his authority is very broad, though not quite so extensive as in some nations of Latin America. The president appoints and dismisses at his pleasure virtually every civilian officer in the public service, including of course the members of his own cabinet. But army officers above the rank of lieutenant colonel must be approved by the Senate. Judges of the supreme court are chosen by the two houses of Congress [19] from lists submitted by the president. He directs and controls Colombia's relations with foreign nations, receiving their emissaries and also negotiating treaties, which must be approved by Congress. War is declared with the authorization of the Senate. The president may assume active command of Colombian forces in time of war, but if he leaves Bogotá in order to do so he must renounce his other presidential powers until he returns. He may grant pardons for all offenses against the laws of the nation.

The president plays an important part in lawmaking. He opens and closes the ordinary sessions of Congress,[20] calls special sessions with the approval of an administrative court known as the Council of State,[21] and submits to Congress each year an annual message, plus such additional messages as may be required. He has the customary right to introduce bills. The clauses of the constitution dealing with the president's veto power contain a number of unusual features. First, he is given a variable number of days to decide whether he will accept or reject a measure, depending on its length.[22] Second, his veto may be overridden by an absolute majority in each house of Congress, rather than the customary two-thirds. This clause is by no means unique, but it is sufficiently rare in Latin America to warrant comment. There is still another unusual aspect of the president's veto power: if he objects to a legislative proposal because he believes it to be unconstitutional, the question is decided by the supreme court, and its opinion may not be overridden by Congress.[23]

Presidential succession. The constitution of 1886 originally provided for a vice-president, but this office was abolished in 1905 because of the danger that the vice-president would conspire to make himself president. Congress now elects first and second "presidential designates" at the beginning of each regular session. Since their term of waiting is but a single year, there is thought to be less likelihood that they will play an active part in the president's sudden demise or indisposition. If both of the designates should be unavailable—a situation that actually occurred in 1945, because both men had resigned before President López finally left office—the first and second designates of the preceding year then become eligible in turn.

[19] The details of this arrangement are explained on pages 414–415.
[20] Congress may function without his summons, however.
[21] See page 415.
[22] Six days, if the bill does not contain more than fifty articles; ten days, if the number of articles is between fifty and two hundred; and fifteen days for still longer measures.
[23] Arts. 80–84.

And if they too are unable to serve, the presidential mantle falls on the several members of the cabinet, in the order indicated by law. The constitution even contemplates the possibility that all the cabinet ministers may also be dead or disabled; it decrees that under such circumstances the governors of the several departments, one by one, shall inherit the presidency, *in the order of the proximity of their department capitals to Bogotá*.[24] These italicized words are not so strange as they may seem. It must be remembered that no governor of a department succeeds to the presidency unless the president and sixteen other persons are unable or unwilling to serve. Such a circumstance is likely to mean only one thing —revolution; and when revolutionary forces are menacing the very existence of the government, the presidential power should certainly be exercised by the responsible official who is best able to get to the national capital.[25] In the June, 1953, revolution the armed forces took the precaution of seizing the governorships in most of the departments as well as the presidency of the nation.

THE CABINET. The framers of the constitution wisely omitted all detailed references to the president's cabinet, stating only that "The number, nomenclature, and precedence of the several ministries or administrative departments shall be determined by law." [26] A cabinet minister must have the same qualifications as a member of the Chamber of Representatives—that is, he must be a citizen and voter, and have attained the age of twenty-five years. The constitution declares that every presidential order shall be countersigned by the head of the appropriate department, "who by that act makes himself responsible." [27] The question may well be asked: Responsible to whom? And the answer seems to be that he is responsible only to the president, who appoints him and dismisses him at will. Congress may summon him to explain any act of which it disapproves, but it is expressly forbidden to adopt a formal resolution of censure. Under such circumstances cabinet responsibility is a meaningless phrase.

NATIONAL ADMINISTRATION. The cabinet now consists of thirteen members—the ministers of government, foreign relations, finance, justice, war, national economy, agriculture, labor, hygiene, education, mines and petroleum, public works, post office and telegraph. Little comment is required concerning their principal activities. It might be remarked, however, that the minister of government directs the nation's internal administration,

[24] Art. 124.
[25] See Chap. VIII of *Derecho Constitucional Colombiano,* by Francisco de Paula Pérez.
[26] Art. 128.
[27] Art. 120.

supervising the governors and minor officials of the departments into which Colombia has been divided. He also assumes responsibility for the national police force (*gendarmería nacional*), which maintains order in all parts of the republic. Unlike the Chilean *carabineros*,[28] however, the Colombian *gendarmería* shares its authority with local police forces. The minister of national economy is responsible for the efficient utilization of the nation's lands and mineral resources, and for the development of commerce and industry. He administers the laws under which foreign companies are permitted to do business in Colombia.[29] There is no central civil service commission. The merit system is not used extensively in the selection of public personnel.

CONGRESS: *Organization.* The Palace of Congress, on one side of the Plaza Bolívar, is an imposing brownstone building situated in a two-and-one-half acre park. Long, graceful colonnades at the entrance to the congressional chambers are reminiscent of Athens. Congress is composed of the customary two houses. The Senate has sixty-three members, chosen by direct vote of the people for a term of four years. Until 1945 the senators were selected by the departmental assemblies. Each department has a number of senators roughly equivalent to its population. The less populous departments are somewhat favored, however, by the proviso that no department shall have fewer than three senators, or more than nine.

When the departmental assemblies chose the senators, they customarily named two alternates for each post. Now, however, the number of alternates elected by the voters in each department is exactly equal to the number of the department's senators, and they are no longer personal alternates. In other words, they have been designated as first alternate, second alternate, and the like, and the first alternate of the Liberals, let us say, takes the place of the first Liberal senator from the department to die or resign. Under the old plan Senator Fulano de Tal[30] had his two personal alternates, just like every other senator; and the first alternate of Fulano de Tal had to await Fulano's death or resignation before taking up the duties of senator. The Chamber of Representatives has one hundred and thirty-two members, chosen by direct popular vote for a two-year term. Representatives, like senators, are chosen at large from the several departments. Each representative has his two personal alternates. Both senators and

[28] See page 333.
[29] The organization and work of the several administrative departments is described by Carlos H. Pareja in his *Curso de Derecho Administrativo,* 2nd ed., Vol. I, Chap. 6.
[30] Fulano de Tal is well known in Spanish-speaking countries. He is John Doe, or Mr. So-and-So.

representatives are paid the same salary—the equivalent of about thirty-five hundred American dollars a year, plus about twelve dollars for every working day.

Sessions. The next session of Congress must await new elections, which have not yet been scheduled. But in normal times Congress meets in regular annual session on July 20 (the national independence day). The length of the regular session is always exactly one hundred and fifty days, regardless of the volume of business. In 1936 the constitution was amended to provide for two regular congressional sessions a year. The first was to begin February 1 and continue for three months; the second was to commence July 20 and last for four months. Under this arrangement, therefore, Congress was in session more than half of every year. The plan proved unpopular and was abandoned after two years. Congress has no power to call itself in special session, even by an extraordinary majority of its members. It must wait for a presidential summons, and during the special session it must confine itself to those matters listed by the president as urgent.

Procedure. Both houses of Congress usually meet three times a week, from four in the afternoon until eight in the evening. Longer hours are sometimes the rule toward the end of a session. Each house chooses its own presiding officers, and also a steering committee (*mesa directiva*), which prepares the order of business. One third of the membership of each house is a sufficient number to do routine business, but a majority is necessary for final passage of bills. The presiding officers name the permanent committees, subject to the approval of the respective chambers. There are forty permanent committees in the Senate, and ninety-two in the Chamber of Representatives. The influence of these committees on legislation is considerably less than in the Congress of the United States. Every bill reaching the floor of the Senate or the Chamber of Representatives receives three readings—one to decide general principles and the other two to consider details. In most cases the third reading is merely a formality.[31]

A bill may be introduced by any member of Congress, or—says the constitution—by any member of the president's cabinet. Since it is inconceivable that a cabinet minister would propose a law contrary to the president's program, this clause really confers on the president the power to initiate legislation. The general statement that any bill may be introduced by any member of Congress is subject to two exceptions. First,

[31] See the 3rd edition of *Táctica Parlamentaria*, by Eduardo Rodríguez Pinares.

every bill for raising revenue must originate in the Chamber of Representatives—a restriction that first originated in England and has now found its way into the fundamental laws of nearly all the Latin American countries, by way of the constitution of the United States. Second, every proposal dealing with civil justice or judicial procedure must be initiated by one of the permanent committees of Congress or by a cabinet minister. The framers of the constitution imposed this unusual restriction because they feared that individual congressmen engaged in private lawsuits might introduce bills to change the law temporarily in their own favor. Several commentators on the Colombian constitution [32] have proposed that this limitation be extended to include criminal justice, but this change has not yet been made. Disagreements between the two houses are adjusted by informal conferences of the party leaders.

Powers. The constitution lists the powers of Congress in twenty-one separate clauses, but adds nothing to the preliminary statement that "Congress shall have power to make the laws." [33] Each house, of course, has its own special authority. The Chamber of Representatives, through a special committee, makes an annual audit of the public accounts. It also brings charges of impeachment against the president and other high officers. As usual, the Senate hears these charges, a two-thirds vote being required for conviction. The Senate has the power to restore citizenship to those who have lost it through conviction of crime or otherwise. It permits the movement of foreign troops within the territory of the nation—assuming, of course, that the foreign troops await such permission. And it performs a number of other functions that have already been mentioned, such as authorizing the president to declare war, passing upon his nominations to high-ranking posts in the armed forces, and permitting him to leave the country. There is no permanent committee of Congress, as in Mexico,[34] to act as a check upon the executive while Congress is in recess.

THE COURTS: *Supreme court.* The judicial system of Colombia follows the usual Latin American pattern. Juries are used, however, for cases involving very serious crimes. Although the jury system has been used for nearly a century, it has never proved satisfactory and there have been numerous proposals to abolish it. The supreme court is composed of twelve judges, chosen for five years and eligible for immediate re-election. Six of the judges are elected by the Senate from a list of three names sub-

---

[32] See, for example, Tulio Enrique Tascón, *Derecho Constitucional Colombiano,* 2nd ed., p. 166. Tascón is recognized as a leading authority on the Colombian constitution.

[33] Art. 69.

[34] See pages 272–273.

mitted by the president for each vacancy. The other six are chosen in a similar manner by the Chamber of Representatives. The court selects one of its own number to serve as president. Although the law says that he shall be chosen annually, custom decrees that he shall continue to serve as long as he desires to do so.

Every justice of the supreme court must be native born and at least thirty-five years of age. He must also have practiced law for at least five years, or have served as a lower court judge or a professor of law in one of the universities. Vacancies on the supreme court bench, as in Congress, are filled by alternates. The president of the nation makes the appointments necessary to fill unexpired terms when no alternates are available. The supreme court is divided into four chambers, which correspond to its major functions. One chamber deals with criminal appeals from the lower courts; another handles appeals in civil cases; the third deals with a number of miscellaneous matters under the head of "general business," and the fourth is responsible for the court's original jurisdiction, involving chiefly high officers of the state and the diplomatic representatives of foreign powers. The supreme court is specifically authorized to declare laws unconstitutional.

Inferior courts. Each department has its superior court, whose judges are chosen by the supreme court from lists submitted by the departmental assemblies. The qualifications for these judges are not so high as for justices of the supreme court—native born, thirty years of age, and a lawyer for not less than three years. On the lower levels of the judicial hierarchy are the circuit judges and the justices of the peace. To be a circuit judge, one must be a citizen and a lawyer. To be a justice of the peace, one must be a citizen.

Administrative courts. In addition to the regular courts of law, Colombia has a number of administrative courts. Their task is to hear civil suits brought by private persons against the government or its officials. This system, borrowed from the French, is not unknown in other parts of Latin America, but Colombia has established a more complete hierarchy of administrative courts than other countries. It even has a supreme administrative tribunal—the Council of State—which is supposed to be the equal of the supreme court, though of course the sphere of its activities is much more restricted. The Council of State has had a stormy history. It was first established in 1831, abolished in 1843, set up once more in 1886, legislated out of existence for the second time in 1905, and finally re-established in 1914. Its troubles arose in part from the fact that it was created to hear the appeals of lower administrative courts long before these inferior courts were established. For many years, therefore, it performed only certain duties not directly connected with its main purpose. These secondary duties still consume a considerable part of its time and attention.

The Council of State checks all government contracts in excess of five thousand pesos, to make certain that legal requirements have been met. It advises the president on administrative matters, though he is not obliged to accept its suggestions. It studies the codes of law and proposes necessary changes. Special sessions of Congress may not be called without its consent.[35] The seven members of the Council of State must have the same qualifications as judges of the supreme court. Three members are chosen by the Senate and three by the Chamber of Representatives. The seventh member, who is named by the president, presides over the Council. The term of office is four years. The Council of State names the judges of the lower administrative courts.[36]

THE DEPARTMENTS. The internal administration of Colombia follows in general the lines that we have already observed in Chile and Peru.[37] There are sixteen departments,[38] and each of them is headed by a governor who is appointed by the president of the nation. The governors are political appointees, of course; they serve the party as well as the nation. They choose their own subordinates and supervise all phases of departmental administration. Their direct responsibility is to the minister of government. Each department has its popularly elected assembly, whose members serve for two years. The size of the assembly, which is fixed by national law, varies with the population of the department. Although the assembly is the local lawmaking body, it has very little authority. Its acts must not conflict with the laws of Congress, which has already legislated on almost all matters of importance. Moreover, every proposal of the assembly is subject to the absolute veto of the governor. The law declares that this veto may be exercised only for reasons of unconstitutionality or illegality; but, since there is no way of contesting the governor's decision that a measure is illegal, this restriction is not very significant.

Until recently the departments were divided into provinces, but the

[35] See page 410.

[36] For a discussion of the Council of State, see Tulio Enrique Tascón's previously cited work, pp. 241–250. There is a much more detailed discussion in the revised edition of Arcesio Aragón's *Jurisprudencia Administrativa*.

[37] See pages 339–341, 382.

[38] Colombia also has eight intendencies and commissariats, which include very sparsely settled territory and are governed from Bogotá without any attempt to provide popular representation in local assemblies.

provinces have now been eliminated. Professor Tascón thinks that the departments should also be abolished, leaving no units of government between the municipalities and the nation. "The existing departments," he declares, "do not arise from historical needs, nor do they reflect racial differences, which do not exist among us, nor economic interests. . . . They require a great outlay of public funds. We have fourteen [39] governors with their cabinets; fourteen assemblies, which are really little Congresses; and an enormous list of minor employees." [40]

THE MUNICIPALITIES. The municipalities are the most important units of local self-government. Even here, however, the national authorities exercise a large measure of control. The mayor is appointed by the governor of the department and may be removed by him at any time. Thus the governor has a close check on municipal administration. The municipal council, which is chosen by the voters, has a membership of five to fifteen, depending on population. It chooses its own presiding officer and enacts local ordinances, but has no voice in administrative matters. The governor has an absolute veto over its acts, either for illegality or inexpediency.[41] Bogotá, the national capital, is governed in exactly the same manner as the other cities. There have been many proposals to give it the status of a special district, and in 1945 the constitution was amended to authorize such an arrangement "in conformity with the law." But Congress has not yet enacted the necessary legislation. Small neighboring municipalities are strongly opposed to the plan, for they fear that eventually they may be swallowed up by the metropolis.

SELECTED REFERENCES

Bonilla Gutiérrez, Alfonso, *El Seguro Social y su Implantación en Colombia,* Bogotá, Aguila, 1940.

Corte Suprema de Justicia de Colombia, *Les Garantías Constitucionales en el Proceso Penal,* Bogotá, 1941.

Du Val, Miles P., Jr., *Cadiz to Cathay: The Story of the Long Struggle for a Waterway Across the American Isthmus,* Palo Alto, Calif., Stanford Univ. Press, 1940.

Espinosa, Augusto, *Pensamiento Económico y Político en Colombia,* Bucaramanga, Imp. del Departmento, Colombia, 1942.

García Avendano, Jesús, *Apuntes a la Decentralización,* Medellín, Colombia, Universidad de Antioquia, 1941.

[39] Now sixteen.
[40] *Op. cit.,* p. 36.
[41] Carlos H. Pareja's previously cited work contains an excellent summary of departmental and municipal administration. See Vol. I, Chaps. VII and VIII. For a more detailed survey, see *La División Departmental y los Orígenes del Municipio en Colombia,* by Carlos García Samudio.

García Samudio, Ramón, *La División Departmental y los Orígenes del Municipio en Colombia*, Bogotá, 1940.

Gibson, William M., *The Constitutions of Colombia*, Durham, N.C., Duke Univ. Press, 1948.

Gómez Botero, Evelio, *Nociones de Derecho Constitucional*, Bogotá, Co-operativo Nacional de Artes Gráficas, 1947.

Gómez Fernández, Miguel, *Tratado de Economía Colombiana*, Bogotá, Librería Editorial la Gran Colombia, 1943.

Henao, J. M., and G. Arrubia, *A History of Colombia* (translated by J. Fred Rippy), Chapel Hill, N.C., Univ. of North Carolina Press, 1938.

Herrnstadt, Ernesto, *Derecho Social Colombiano*, Bogotá, Antena, 1942.

Linke, Lilo, *Andean Adventure; A Social and Political Study of Colombia, Ecuador and Bolivia*, London, Hutchinson & Co., Ltd., 1945.

Núñez, Rafael, *La Reforma Política en Colombia*, Bogotá, Biblioteca Popular de Cultura Colombiana, 1944.

Ospina Racines, Eduardo, *La Economía del Petroleo en Colombia*, Bogotá, Editorial Minerva, 1942.

Parks, E. Taylor, *Colombia and the United States, 1765–1934*, Durham, N.C., Duke Univ. Press, 1935.

Pérez, Francisco de Paula, *Derecho Constitucional Colombiano*, Bogotá, Librería Voluntad, 1942.

Pérez, Luis Carlos, *Los Delitos Políticos; Interpretación Jurídica del 9 de Abril*, Distribuidora Americana de Publicaciones, 1948.

Pérez Rincón, Antonio, *Apuntaciones Históricas sobre el Derecho Administrativo Colombiano, 1784–1941*, Bogotá, Editorial Kelly, 1941.

Plata Uricoechea, Fernando, *El Régimen Constitucional en Colombia y en los Estados Unidos*, Bogotá, Editorial Cromos, 1943.

Puentes, Milton, *Historia del Partido Liberal Colombiano*, Bogotá, Tall. Gráf. Mundo al Día, 1942.

Rippy, J. Fred, *The Capitalists and Colombia*, New York, Vanguard Press, 1931.

Rodríguez Piñeres, Eduardo, *Táctica Parlamentaria*, 3rd ed., Bogotá, Librería Colombiana, 1937.

Romero Aguirre, Alfonso, *El Partido Conservador ante la Historia*, Bogotá, Librería Americana, 1944.

Romoli, Kathleen, *Colombia, Gateway to South America*, New York, Doubleday, Doran, 1941.

Ruís de Montoya, Antonio, *Tratado de Derecho Constitucional*, Bogotá, 1941.

Salazar, Mardonio, *Proceso Histórico de la Propiedad en Colombia*, Bogotá, Editorial ABC, 1948.

Sánchez Gómez, Gregorio, *Sociología Política Colombiana*, Cali, Colombia, Sánchez Gómez Hnos., 1943.

United Nations, Department of Economic Affairs, *Public Finance Information Papers: Colombia, 1950*, New York, Columbia University Press, 1951.

Vallejo, Alejandro, *Hombres de Colombia: Memorias de un Colombiano Exilado en Venezuela*, Caracas, Avila Gráfica, 1950.

CHAPTER 16

VENEZUELA

~~~~~~

The Land and the People

POPULATION, AREA, RACES. Venezuela is the eighth country of Latin America in both area and population. Its three hundred and fifty thousand square miles are approximately the equivalent of the area of Texas and Oregon combined, but in population (five million) it is not quite two thirds as large as Texas. There are many persons of pure white stock. Most of them are descendants of the original Spanish conquerors, though there are some more recent arrivals from various European countries. The government now encourages European immigration, and has permitted the entry of many thousand displaced or dissatisfied persons since the close of the Second World War. Indians are still to be found in the more remote sections, and some of them occasionally make their way to the market places of the larger cities. The far west of the country is the home of a savage tribe—the Molitón—which has never been conquered, and still hunts with bow and arrow.[1] The population includes also some Negroes, especially in the seaport towns. But the large majority of the people are *mestizos*—the sons and daughters, many generations removed, of the conquerors and the Indian women.

PHYSICAL HANDICAPS. Venezuela suffers from serious physical handicaps. It is situated in the heart of the tropics, only a few degrees north of the equator, and most of its territory is hot and unhealthful. There are, of course, some sections where the heat is tempered by altitude, and these

[1] See the interesting article by Stanley Ross, "They Want to Be Alone," in the May, 1945, issue (Vol. IV, No. 5) of the *Inter-American*.

regions are the heart of Venezuelan civilization. But they constitute only a very small part of the total area. Moreover, their development has been impeded by an exceedingly difficult terrain. Railroad and highway construction has proved very expensive, in money and sometimes in human life.

HIGH COST OF LIVING. The cost of living is higher in Venezuela than in any other country of the New World. Even United States prices seem modest by comparison. To some extent, of course, the present cost of living reflects the inflation which is currently plaguing nearly all countries, but high prices are not a new phenomenon in Venezuela. They were established long ago as a seemingly permanent part of the national economy. The basic reason for high prices is the predominant position of the petroleum industry. Venezuela is the world's second largest oil producer. And, as the world demand for petroleum products has increased year after year, more and more Venezuelans have left their former occupations to find jobs in the comparatively well-paid oil industry. The inevitable result has been a substantial curtailment of agriculture and stock farming. The country does not produce enough food for its own needs, so food must be imported at considerable cost. The government is trying to combat this situation by extending a special welcome to European immigrants who are experienced farmers. The high cost of almost everything in the country would make very little difference to Venezuelans if wages and salaries were at a correspondingly high level. Unfortunately they are not. They are the highest in Latin America, except perhaps Argentina, but even this wage level is not sufficient to compensate for the cost of living. Most of the people are desperately poor.

THE MARACAIBO BASIN. The oil industry centers around Lake Maracaibo, in the northwest corner of the country. It is scarcely a lake, despite its name, for it connects with the sea through a nine-mile-wide strait. But this entrance is shallow and partially blocked by shifting sandbars, so that deep-draught vessels cannot enter. Lake Maracaibo is a large body of water, extending nearly one hundred miles from north to south and fifty miles from east to west. On its northern shore is the city of Maracaibo, oil metropolis of the nation. It has two hundred and thirty thousand people, many fine buildings and other improvements, and a mean temperature of eighty-five degrees. No other major city of Latin America is so hot so much of the time. But there is oil in abundance, so the people are prepared to accept this climatic inconvenience.

Not until 1920 were large quantities of petroleum exported from Venezuela, but after that year the output increased at an amazing rate. Foreign capital poured into the Maracaibo basin, with the result that the oil fields are now almost exclusively in foreign hands. American companies are the principal owners, but the Royal Dutch Shell Corporation, which is partly Dutch and partly British, also has an important stake. The oil is carried, mostly in crude form, by shallow-draught tankers across the sandbars at the lake's entrance to the Dutch islands of Curaçao and Aruba, which lie just off the Venezuelan coast. Here great refineries have been constructed. There are large oil fields in the eastern part of the country, also, and they are becoming more important every year. The government imposes very heavy taxes on the oil industry, obtaining most of its revenue from this one source. Sometimes the oil companies complain that their tax burden is entirely too great, but they know that their problems would be much more serious if the Venezuelan government should ever follow Mexico's example and order outright confiscation of all foreign holdings.[2] The large returns from taxes on oil have enabled Venezuela to keep its finances in enviable condition. There is no long-term external debt and the internal debt represents only about two dollars per person. New issues of government bonds are always heavily oversubscribed.

There is some agriculture in the Maracaibo basin, despite the climatic handicaps. Large sugar plantations border the southern shores of the lake and parallel the banks of the Zulia River, which flows into the lake at its southern tip. But the land is poorly drained and provides a breeding place for mosquitoes, so that the plantation laborers are commonly victims of malaria. Almost without exception they are a shiftless lot. If they were not so utterly lacking in ambition they would be off to the oil fields, and the labor supply of the Maracaibo sugar plantations would be even smaller than at present. Somewhat similar conditions handicap the growth of other crops in the region. But there is some cotton, and also cacao, from which the cocoa and chocolate of commerce are derived. Cattle, sheep and goats graze on the dry lands north of the oil centers. Lumbering operations are carried on in the far south of the basin. But the Maracaibo area is not very important, except for oil. Most of the men who own the land live elsewhere, leaving their crops or herds to the care of paid overseers.

NORTHERN HIGHLANDS: *Caracas.* The northern highlands are where most of the people live. The oil industry has drawn off some of their population, but has not seriously menaced their dominant position in

[2] See page 207.

Venezuelan life. "My heart's in the highlands," says the average Venezuelan, and there his home is also. The northern highlands cover only
a small part of the total area of the country. They extend from the Colombian border eastward for about six hundred miles, some distance south
of the Maracaibo basin. In general the highlands are not very high; they
vary from one thousand to four thousand feet above sea level, with only a
few exceptions. Thus they provide sufficient altitude to break the intense
heat of the tropics, without the chilliness of such highland cities as Colombia's Bogotá or Peru's Cuzco.

The capital and chief city of Venezuela is Caracas; it lies in a cup-shaped
valley, ringed with mountains, at an elevation of only twenty-six hundred
feet. Its altitude and moderate rainfall give it an almost perfect climate—
a perpetual late spring or early summer, with flowers blooming in great
profusion throughout the year. Like so many cities of Latin America,
it is a quaint blending of old and new. Churches erected in the colonial
era stand beside modern skyscrapers. The narrow streets of the old
quarter contrast sharply with the broad boulevards of the new. But Caracas is essentially a modern metropolis. A view of its skyline from some
neighboring mountain slope reveals the number and size of its multi-
storied modern buildings. The population of its metropolitan area is
nearly seven hundred thousand.[3]

The seaport of Caracas. Caracas is only nine miles from the sea, in a
straight line. Unfortunately, however, straight lines have very little to
do with the construction of railroads and highways in the Venezuelan
highlands. The mountains are rugged, and the intervening valleys are
broken by the spurs of mountain chains; therefore roads must be built
over steep gorges at almost impossible angles and at very undesirable
grades. The highway from Caracas to its seaport, La Guaira (and to the
airport, which is a few miles nearer the capital, but also at sea level), winds
over a mountain pass and then makes its hazardous descent to the sea.
For many years it was a narrow road, marked by dozens of treacherous
turns. Pilots of the air lines, who had to travel over the road before every
flight, often declared that they had no fear of an accident in the air after
riding safely in a motor car "down the hill." Nothing, they said, could
be worse than that short journey. Now, however, the road has been
widened, and some of the worst curves have been straightened out. There

---

[3] Olga Briceño's book, *Cocks and Bulls in Caracas,* presents a very interesting picture of life
in the Venezuelan capital. The author is one of those rare persons who has an established
literary reputation in two languages.

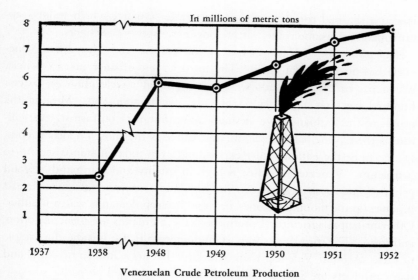

In millions of metric tons

Venezuelan Crude Petroleum Production

Based on information obtained from *United Nations Monthly Bulletin of Statistics*, March, 1953.

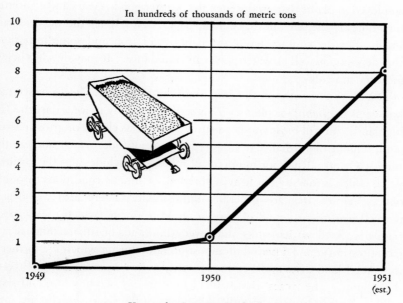

In hundreds of thousands of metric tons

Venezuelan Iron Ore Production

Based on information obtained from *United Nations Statistical Yearbook, 1952.*

is also a railroad connecting Caracas and La Guaira, which follows approximately the same route. It no longer transports passengers.

Agriculture and industry. Except for Caracas and Maracaibo, Venezuela has no important cities. The third largest urban center, Valencia, which lies in the highlands west of Caracas at an elevation of sixteen hundred feet, has a population of only seventy thousand. Most of the people of the highlands live in small communities or on farms. Agriculture is their principal occupation, and coffee is the most important crop. It used to be the nation's chief export, and even today it stands second to petroleum. Venezuelan coffee is high in quality and commands a good price. Some cacao is grown in the highlands, also, though only a short distance up the mountain slopes, because the crop demands warm weather. Other principal agricultural products of the highlands are tobacco, cotton, and corn. The corn is very important domestically, for it is the chief staple of diet. Around Valencia there is a large livestock industry. Meat and dairy products are sold locally, and hides are shipped abroad.

Manufacturing has not acquired great importance in Venezuela, but it is developing slowly. The two principal manufacturing centers are Caracas and Valencia. Most of the factory workers are engaged in the making of beverages or the processing of foods, but a considerable number are employed in plants that produce textiles, leather goods, cigars and cigarettes for domestic use, chemicals, cement, paper. Nearly all the factories are small. But the country has vast quantities of iron and some important coal deposits, as well as water power in abundance. It may develop heavy industry some day.

THE *llanos.* South of the important highland area lies a vast tract known as the *llanos,* or plains. This section is nearly twice as large as the highlands, but still mostly undeveloped. It consists chiefly of grass-covered land, seldom more than five hundred feet in altitude, which borders the mighty Orinoco River for hundreds of miles. It includes also the Orinoco delta, which is marshy but heavily forested. Climatic conditions throughout the entire area are generally unfavorable. There are two clearly marked seasons—a period of very heavy rain, during which the Orinoco regularly overflows its banks and covers thousands of square miles of adjacent territory; and a period of almost no rain, during which the formerly inundated land dries and becomes parched. Not so many people live in this region. The largest city, Ciudad Bolívar, lies two hundred and sixty miles from the Orinoco's mouth. The delta of the river is totally unsuited to the development of any city, so river steamers usually begin their upstream journey from Port of Spain on the British-owned island of Trinidad, which lies just off the coast. Until recently Ciudad Bolívar had a population of less than thirty thousand, but today it is booming. This change has been brought about by the discovery of one of the world's largest and richest iron ore deposits at Cerro Bolívar, only a few miles away. American steel companies have obtained permission to develop the area, and are shipping the ore to steel mills in the United States. Before the discovery of iron ore, the only important industry of the *llanos* was cattle raising. But tropical diseases have always affected the cattle and also the *llaneros* (cowboys) who tend them. At market time the cattle are driven to the northern highlands, where they must be fattened before they can be sold.

GUIANA HIGHLANDS. South of the Orinoco are the Guiana highlands. They are far larger than any other section of the country, and far less important. The mountains are very rugged, though not very high. In fact, the terrain is so broken that it is almost impossible to cover any great distance on foot. The area is excessively hot and rainy. Few parts of the world are less inviting, and few have been less carefully explored. Yet Venezuelans have high hopes for the ultimate development of this territory. They knew that it probably contains large reserves of coal, iron, and other metals. Gold is already mined in considerable quantities.

The Pattern of Politics

A VOLATILE HISTORY. Venezuela has had a volatile history. Revolution, bloodshed, and anarchy are to be found on almost every page. At the beginning of its independence it was a part of Bolívar's Great Colombia,[4] but when that union fell apart in 1830 Venezuela entered a period of confusion and distrust. The dictator of that time was José Antonio Páez, one of Bolívar's generals, who managed to dominate the country directly or through his henchmen for nearly two decades. Even during this era, however, there were five major rebellions against the government in addition to several minor uprisings. When at last Páez was exiled, the government fell into the hands of other dictators. And of course revolutions continued to sweep across the land. Some of the bitter disputes of the period dealt with the form of government. There were centralists and federalists, just as there were in Colombia at that time. But the federalists eventually had their way in Venezuela and adopted a succession

[4] See page 390.

of constitutions based on the principle of decentralization. Even the federalist leaders paid very little attention to this principle, however, when they were in power.

GUZMÁN BLANCO. In 1870 General Guzmán Blanco climaxed a brilliantly executed uprising by capturing Caracas and making himself the president of the nation. But there were many to dispute his authority. One of them was a former Blanco lieutenant named Salazar, who led a revolt that ended in dismal failure. Salazar was captured and shot. Two years later Blanco crushed another rebellion. It had become clear by this time that he was no ordinary *caudillo,* but a man of great skill in military and political maneuvers. He was also a capable administrator. For eighteen years he controlled the nation. Most of that time he was president. The nation prospered, and so did Blanco. He dictated a number of important reforms dealing with finance, education, and the church. The peace that he succeeded in imposing on the country during most of his regime facilitated the development of agriculture and commerce. But critics pointed out that Blanco's personal fortune grew much more rapidly than the national wealth, and challenged him to prove his honesty. They issued the challenge from exile, however; within Venezuela the people had learned that the only safe policy was to obey the government and extol the dictator. Those who learned the lesson too slowly paid with their liberty or their lives. Freedom of speech and press ceased to exist. No newspaper dared to print a single word that seemed to suggest the faintest criticism of the Blanco regime; no person dared to say—in public—that the president was less than perfect. Grandiloquent praise was heaped upon him. He was hailed as the "Illustrious American" and the "Regenerator of Venezuela."

CHAOS. Not all his countrymen shared the apparent enthusiasm for Blanco, however. In 1888 a number of rival chiefs staged another revolution, and eventually they succeeded in driving Blanco into exile. His long reign was over, but it was followed by virtual anarchy. Fresh revolts broke out and presidents succeeded one another in rapid succession. During all these years there were new constitutions adopted from time to time, but of course they had very little effect on the political life of the nation.

RISE OF GÓMEZ. In 1909 the presidency was seized by one of the most remarkable men whose name appears upon the scroll of Latin American history. He was called Juan Vicente Gómez, and he remained the absolute despot of Venezuela for twenty-seven years, until his death in 1935. Most of the time he was president; occasionally he was content to be merely the head of the army, while one or another of his subordinates held the presidential title. Few men have ever held a nation more tightly in their grip.

EARLY YEARS OF GÓMEZ. It seems that Juan Vicente Gómez was not even born in Venezuela, and that Gómez was not his name. He was born just across the Colombian border, the son of a well educated gentleman of Spanish blood and his illiterate Indian mistress. But the woman soon tired of her cultured lover and deserted him for an ignorant farmer named Pedro Gómez, taking her small son with her. The Gómez farm was near the small Andean town of San Antonio, Venezuela, and here Juan grew to young manhood. The record, in fact, shows that he was born in San Antonio, on the birthday of the great liberator Simón Bolívar, but Daniel Clinton, who has written the standard biography in English of the Dictator,[5] says that the record was falsified after Gómez had risen to power. The elder Gómez died when young Juan was only fourteen years of age. But he was the eldest of eleven children, and the management of the farm fell on his shoulders. He taught himself to read and write, for he had been given no formal education. Gradually he made himself a power in the community, though he showed little or no interest in politics. The farm took all his time.

YEARS IN EXILE. When he was thirty-six years old Gómez talked with a number of revolutionaries, who promised him large rewards if he would join forces with them. He accepted their offer, but the uprising was crushed. So Gómez and his friends were forced to flee across the Colombian border. They spent six years in Colombia and during that time Gómez made a small fortune in the cattle industry. He also learned the clever phrases of the better educated revolutionary leaders, who talked sweepingly of "new ideals, new men, new methods." In 1899 the revolutionists decided to try again. This time they were successful, and Gómez was rewarded for his part in the enterprise by appointment as governor of Caracas. He was then forty-two years old, shrewd and forceful but completely ignorant of the processes of government. The leader of the revolutionary movement, General Cipriano Castro, became president of the nation.

REVOLUTIONS. During its first five years the new regime had a difficult time. Its enemies were powerful and determined and on more than one occasion they nearly gained complete victory on the field of battle. Their failure to do so must be attributed almost exclusively to the military skill of

[5] *Gómez, Tyrant of the Andes,* by Thomas Rourke. "Thomas Rourke" is Clinton's pen name.

Juan Vicente Gómez, who proved himself an outstanding leader. In five years of fighting the rebels were finally crushed. By that time Gómez had become vice-president of the nation.

SEIZURE OF POWER BY GÓMEZ. In 1908 Gómez had his big chance. President Castro had been seriously ill for some time and finally, on the advice of physicians, he sailed for Europe to try to regain his shattered health. Gómez, the trusted adviser and family friend, arranged everything. He bought the tickets, obtained the necessary letter of credit, and went to the boat to bid the Castro party good-bye, promising to remain on the alert for possible uprisings. Then, twenty-eight days later, he sent Castro a cable informing him that his health would undoubtedly be better if he remained in Europe permanently. The same day he issued a proclamation making himself president of the nation. The people accepted the news calmly. President Castro had never been popular and there were many who hoped that the new regime would be more responsive to public opinion. They were destined to bitter disappointment.

BRUTAL TYRANNY. The Gómez dictatorship began on December 20, 1908. It lasted until December 17, 1935, when the old man died of natural causes. No one was strong enough to wrest control of the government from his hands, though many tried. During those twenty-seven years Venezuela had a number of presidents and three new constitutions. But not one of the puppet presidents even attempted to assert his independence. Not one of the constitutions made any real change in national powers or policies. Gómez was the government, and his will was law. Within a year after his rise to power he instituted a reign of terror. Those who openly criticized him, or even gave the slightest reason to suppose that they might be in opposition, were brutally murdered or consigned to slow death in the Venezuelan prisons. Their prison rations were barely enough to keep them from utter starvation. Their days and nights were spent in leg irons, so closely fitted that they could scarcely move. In time these leg irons distorted the ankles so badly that gangrene often set in. Some of the prisoners were then saved for further torture by the amputation of their legs. More fortunate opposition leaders managed to escape to foreign lands, where they were kept under close surveillance by a corps of spies maintained by the Venezuelan government at considerable expense.

SPIES AND SYCOPHANTS. At home Gómez established a most elaborate spy system. It included all sorts of persons—barbers, shopkeepers, chauffeurs, waiters. No one could be sure of his friends or his servants. Some found that they could not trust the members of their own families. The

Dictator paid well for information, and vast sums were taken secretly from the public treasury for this purpose. So not one word of criticism of the Gómez regime was ever heard in public places. Not a single objection to any of its acts ever appeared in the newspapers. Gómez was compared to God, somewhat to the detriment of the Almighty. Pictures of the Dictator were displayed prominently in every store and home. The people regarded this public homage as a form of life insurance.

PERSONAL FORTUNE OF GÓMEZ. As the years of the dictatorship passed, the personal fortune of General Gómez grew rapidly. He acquired some of the finest haciendas in the country, usually by legal means, but always at bargain prices. If a man did not wish to sell, there were ways of compelling him. Gómez would hire the best legal talent to find laws that would justify his acts. If no such laws could be found, they would be enacted speedily. Sometimes intimidation would be used. Large landowners who preferred to retain their properties would often change their minds after learning of the sudden death or disappearance of neighbors who had rejected offers from the Dictator's agents. In later years, when petroleum had become Venezuela's biggest industry, Gómez managed to divert a considerable part of the payments of the foreign companies to his own pockets. When he died in 1935, he left a fortune estimated at two hundred million dollars. It included cattle ranches, coffee plantations, industrial plants, and an amazing assortment of magnificent private homes. From a poor boy he had become one of the world's richest men.

GÓMEZ' MANNER OF LIVING. The Dictator's manner of living required a very large income. He had a number of fine homes in almost every part of the country, completely outfitted to meet all his needs, even as to clothing, and completely staffed by large retinues of servants. He had a large family—brothers, sisters, and cousins, children by a succession of mistresses, and a large number of grandchildren. One estimate, which is probably conservative, places the number of his children at ninety. Many members of the Gómez clan were given lucrative jobs in the public service. One brother became vice-president of the nation, and held this office until his death at the hands of an assassin. Another brother was made inspector general of the army. A foster brother, who had been convicted of murder and sent to jail for fifteen years, was released and placed in charge of the penitentiary where he had been a prisoner. The Dictator took care of his own.

ACCOMPLISHMENTS OF GÓMEZ. There were, of course, some things to be said for Juan Vicente Gómez. One of his apologists, who had been appointed minister to the United States, wrote a book in the General's defense and devoted many pages to a detailed enumeration of the accomplishments of the regime. First on his list was the maintenance of peace. The name of General Gómez, he said, would be "included on the scroll of benefactors of humanity for a single accomplishment, if for no other reason: namely, the establishment of peace in a country where the longest previous period of tranquility was the nine years which elapsed between the revolutions of Farfán in 1837 and of Rangel and Zamora in 1846." [6]   But there were other blessings that must not be overlooked. Good roads were built for the first time in the nation's history; public sanitation received far greater attention than ever before; and the national debt was practically eliminated.

Some of these words of praise are undoubtedly deserved. Gómez was a competent administrator. Though almost illiterate, he surrounded himself with trained advisers. Moreover, he normally took their advice unless his own native shrewdness suggested a different course. He did keep the peace, though it was a peace imposed by terror. He did guide the nation to new heights of material prosperity. The elimination of the national debt was made possible by the development of the petroleum industry rather than any financial wizardry. But Gómez did make certain that the national interest would be adequately protected before permitting the foreign oil companies to begin operations.

PRICE OF THE GÓMEZ REGIME.   In presenting the balance sheet of the Gómez regime, it is necessary to ask whether Venezuelans paid too high a price for these benefits. Practically all impartial observers think that they did. They paid with the loss of their liberty, and some of them paid with their lives. They forfeited the right to speak their own thoughts and to read the thoughts of others. They lost even the small measure of popular government that they had occasionally enjoyed in earlier years. They almost forgot the theory of a "loyal opposition," operating under the protection of the law.

LÓPEZ CONTRERAS' SUCCESSION TO PRESIDENCY.   As the year 1935 drew to a close it became generally known that General Gómez was seriously ill. His death was rumored from time to time. Then, on December 17, the rumor was officially confirmed. The old tyrant was dead at last, at the age of seventy-eight. The cabinet met hastily and chose one of its own members— Minister of War Eleazar López Contreras—to serve as provisional president. The new chief executive was a tall, thin man, forty-nine years of age, who had studied military science in foreign countries and risen to high rank

[6] Pedro Manuel Arcaya, *The Gómez Regime in Venezuela and Its Background*, p. 119.

on sheer merit. He was generally thought to be fair and honest, though a strict disciplinarian; and he enjoyed a considerable amount of popularity in both military and civilian circles. But he had been a trusted associate of Gómez, and it was generally assumed that he would continue the repressive policies of the old regime.

For two days following Gómez' death the people did nothing. They seemed to be stunned by the news that the Despot was gone at last. But then a storm of popular resentment against the dictatorship burst throughout the country. The people could not be stopped, and the new President was wise enough to let them have their way—within reasonable limits. There was singing and dancing in the streets, and a good deal of drinking. There was some looting, too. The mobs attacked the offices of the most servile newspapers and wrecked them. They tore down every picture of Gómez that they could find and burned them all. They practically destroyed some of the homes of the Gómez family. But when they marched into the Plaza Bolívar, in the heart of Caracas, shouting *vivas* for liberty and democracy, the police suddenly opened fire. Several demonstrators were killed, and a number of others were wounded.

THE NEW ORDER. Some persons thought that the police fusillade against the rioters was the new President's answer to those who dared to raise their voices for liberty. Nothing could have been further from the truth. López Contreras promptly announced that liberty would be the cornerstone of the new government, and he proved his intentions by taking a number of important steps. First, he removed the officer who had given the order to fire on the crowd. Then he emptied the jails of their political prisoners and invited all the exiles to come home. Some of them were given important posts in the new government. Freedom of speech and press were guaranteed. The newspaper editors took the President at his word. They printed the strongest kind of criticism of Gómez, and even included some harsh words about the new regime. Somewhat to their surprise, they found themselves still at liberty. Labor was guaranteed the right to organize and to strike. Labor organizers sprang up as if by magic, and some workers went on strike in order to enjoy the novelty of the experience. Rioting continued sporadically for several months. Some critics of López Contreras say that he did not use sufficient firmness in dealing with the mobs. They cannot say, however, that he used the repressive tactics of the old order.

RESTORATION OF FREEDOM. It cannot be emphasized too strongly that López Contreras charted his new course as a matter of conviction rather than expediency.   He believed in freedom, and he restored it to the people. Nothing would have been easier for him than to continue the dictatorship. The army was ready to give its support.   Governors and lesser officials throughout the country—all appointed by Gómez—were strongly in favor of the *status quo*.   Congress was composed chiefly of Gómez' personal friends and political henchmen.   The people, of course, were against the old order, almost to a man.   But they had never been able to make themselves heard while Gómez was alive, and they could readily have been silenced after his death.   The old methods of torture were still effective. But López Contreras deliberately renounced them.   He guided his nation toward democracy.

Mob violence against the Gómez clan.   As might well have been expected, the members of the Gómez clan were shocked at the President's lack of respect for the dead Dictator and his policies.   Eustoquio Gómez, the murderous foster brother who had been promoted from prisoner to prison commandant, arrived in Caracas with a few followers, vowing revenge on the "traitor" López Contreras.   But the people soon learned that another Gómez was in town.   They killed him and burned his car. López Contreras sent word to other members of the clan, and to a few other persons who had been responsible for the worst excesses of the old regime, that he could not protect them from the anger of the people. He advised them to leave the country at the earliest possible moment, and placed a gunboat at their disposal.   Nearly one hundred of them sailed the next day.

Massacre and its aftermath.   Early in February, 1936, occurred an incident that rocked the country to its political foundations.   The Gómez sympathizers still remaining in the government had been made the target for increasingly bitter attacks by the press.   One of them finally responded with an order for strict censorship of press and radio.   The labor unions protested by calling a general strike.   Thousands of the people of Caracas poured into the Plaza Bolívar to listen to impassioned orators who denounced the government in no uncertain terms.   Suddenly soldiers appeared on the second floor of the Government Palace, overlooking the plaza, and without warning of any kind fired several volleys into the crowd.   Two hundred persons were wounded and at least a dozen were killed.   It was a repetition of the massacre that had occurred in the same spot two months earlier.   This time, however, there was much less provocation, for the people had every reason to believe that the government would tolerate their demonstration.

That afternoon a great throng marched to the President's home. It contained not only the workers, who had precipitated the general strike and suffered most from the brutality of the soldiers, but also business and professional men, housewives, and even children. It was a true cross section of the people of the capital. President López Contreras greeted the leaders, and then spoke over the radio to the crowd. He promised them everything that they asked. There would be freedom of the press and of speech. The official who had given the order for the massacre would be arrested and tried for murder. The crowd listened, and then dispersed quietly. Before long it learned that the President was as good as his word. He restored the liberties demanded by the people. He dismissed more of Gómez' followers from the government, replacing them chiefly with opposition leaders who had spent years in prison or exile. And he indicated that an election for a new president would be held at the earliest possible moment.

López Contreras continues in power. Under the terms of the Venezuelan constitution, "election of the president" meant selection by Congress, instead of by the people. Congress was still in the hands of Gómez sympathizers, and there is little doubt that its members had been alienated from López Contreras by his liberal methods. But when the time came to name a new executive, in April, 1936, Congress found that it had virtually no choice. López Contreras was the man of the hour, the favorite of the turbulent masses. So the congressmen quietly elected him for a full presidential term. Any other action would undoubtedly have precipitated a great popular uprising.

A new constitution. In July, 1936, a new constitution was adopted for the nation. It was a remarkable document—remarkable for its adherence to the old ways, despite the avowedly pro-democratic sentiments of its authors. It retained the clause of the old constitution providing for the election of the president by Congress. It specified that senators should be chosen by the state legislatures, and that deputies should be named by the councils of the municipalities. Judges of the supreme court were to be selected by Congress. Under the new constitution, therefore, the people were excluded from direct participation in the government just as completely as they had been in the days of Gómez. But there were other clauses that marked a definite break with the old tradition. The president's term was fixed at five years, instead of seven, without eligibility for immediate re-election, and his powers were reduced slightly. At the same time a new labor law was adopted. It established the eight-hour day and a system of social insurance. Employers were directed to share the profits of their enterprises with their employees. The trade unions were placed on a firm legal basis, and the principle of collective bargaining was recognized as a part of national policy.

DISSATISFACTION OF THE RADICALS. President López Contreras sponsored the new labor legislation, but he refused to endorse all the demands of the trade union leaders. Before long, therefore, he lost the support of the more radical elements. A wave of strikes swept the country. There was a general strike in June, called to protest a new law which seemed to restrict individual liberties. During 1937 industrial unrest increased steadily. The President declared that Communists and alien agitators were responsible and took drastic steps to reduce their influence. A law passed in July, 1937, restricted the period of time that tourists and transients might remain in the country and required other foreigners to obtain identity cards. This law was applied with special severity to aliens who were prominent in the trade union movement.

GOVERNMENT POLICIES. Early in 1938 the President announced a three-year plan with which he hoped to bring increased prosperity to Venezuela. The plan had a number of important features: improvement of shipping facilities, development of tourist travel, encouragement of desirable immigration, improvement of public health and education. Some of these goals were attained almost at once. Colonists were brought from Denmark, though in small numbers. Large sums were set aside for health and education, and special attention was paid to the training of teachers. Venezuela signed with the United States a new commercial treaty permitting the importation of American products under somewhat more favorable conditions than formerly. López Contreras announced that there would be no change in the old Gómez policy of avoiding foreign debt. He also clung to some less popular survivals of the Gómez regime—restrictive decrees that he considered necessary for the preservation of public order. The trend toward democracy, though unmistakable, was entirely too slow for many persons.

LACK OF POLITICAL PARTIES IN 1936. During the long reign of Juan Vicente Gómez, political parties had ceased to exist. Gómez himself had declared that the people should stay out of politics, and had done everything in his power to make certain that they did so. When, therefore, Congress was required to choose a new president in 1936, its members were almost completely ignorant of the techniques of party politics, as generally understood in democratic nations. Venezuela had no functioning political parties. Some prominent politicians did in fact band themselves together in loose units which they called Bolívar Civic Groups, but their sole purpose was the support of López Contreras. They were generally known as the President's Party. The opposition was completely unorganized.

BIRTH OF DEMOCRATIC ACTION. By 1940, however, politically minded Venezuelans were ready to stage a real campaign. Opposition leaders had set up a political party under the name *Democratic Action*. This party was well to the left of center; it relied chiefly on labor and on the intellectuals, whose leadership had been almost completely lacking during the days of Gómez. The time was at hand for the election of a successor to López Contreras, who had indicated quite clearly that he intended to respect the constitution's one-term-at-a-time restriction. Democratic Action's leaders canvassed the field, and finally decided to support the distinguished author Rómulo Gallegos. They could scarcely have made a better choice. Gallegos was then fifty-eight years of age, a onetime college professor and former minister of education. Throughout the Spanish-speaking world he was known as the author of *Doña Bárbara,* one of the great novels of modern times. His reputation for honesty was unimpeachable.

THE HEIR APPARENT. In spite of his excellent qualifications, there was very little reason to suppose that Gallegos would be the next president of Venezuela. The campaign was almost certainly lost, even before it began. For López Contreras had already named the man to succeed him, and everyone knew that his nod of approval was the equivalent of election. The final decision would be made by Congress, of course, but that body had long since been purged of its Gómez majority, and reflected faithfully the will of the President. The heir apparent was General Isaías Medina Angarita, who had many things in common with the retiring President. He too was a professional soldier and former minister of war, and he came from the western Andean region where López Contreras had been born. But he was as stout as López Contreras was thin. At this time Medina Angarita was forty-three years of age.

MEDINA ANGARITA CHOSEN PRESIDENT. Congress met in joint session for the election of the president in late 1940 and voted almost unanimously for Medina Angarita. The new President took office the following January and promptly accelerated the movement toward complete democracy. On frequent occasions he participated in public demonstrations and mingled freely with the people, to the great annoyance of the army officers assigned as his bodyguards. He took care to respect the laws guaranteeing free speech and a free press, even when his own policies were under attack. The Communists were permitted to speak their minds freely, though some Nazi newspapers were suppressed after Venezuela broke relations with the Axis powers in 1941. Medina's program included an income tax, much to the disgust of the great landowning families, and also new legislation to strengthen the government's hand in its dealings with the foreign oil companies. Civilians were generally preferred to army officers for important jobs, and the army began to realize that it was no longer a dominant factor in the government.

POLITICAL ACTIVITY. At first President Medina tried to take the middle of the political road, in contrast with López Contreras, who had followed a path slightly to the right. Congress was willing to give its almost solid support. But there were a number of groups that offered more or less articulate opposition. On the right they included the friends of the popular and powerful López Contreras, the politically discredited but still wealthy former adherents of Gómez, and almost all the wealthy landowners and industrialists. On the left they were represented chiefly by Democratic Action, which sponsored a program of moderate socialism. Many of the workers, though possibly not a majority, were sympathetic to this group. Such a combination of opponents might have seemed sufficient to make the President's position almost untenable. But it must be remembered that these opposition groups were by no means united. On the contrary, some of them were at opposite extremes of political thought. Their only common desire was for a change in the government. Moreover, Medina Angarita possessed one advantage that his enemies could scarcely hope to overcome without revolution: he controlled the government. He had the power of political life and death over thousands of public employees, who were never allowed to forget this fact. In 1943 he decided to consolidate his position by creating a new political party. Originally it was called *The Partisans of Government Policy*—so that there would be no doubt as to its purposes, explained Medina. Later it changed its name to Venezuelan Democratic Party. Everyone in the government service was required to sign up, or explain his "disloyalty."

SHIFT TO THE LEFT. As Medina's term drew to a close he veered more to the left, apparently hoping to reap a rich harvest of labor support. The war had driven Venezuela's already high prices to new levels, and strikes were spreading throughout the country. The government usually gave its support to the unions in these disputes, thus earning the further distrust of the business interests. In August of 1944 the street transportation workers of Caracas announced their intention to strike. The government promptly intervened and named a three-man arbitration committee to decide the issues involved. But the arbiter who was supposed to represent the company soon withdrew, claiming that his side had not received a fair hearing. Thereupon the other two members of the committee, who had been selected as spokesmen for the union and the public, agreed to practically every one of the workers' demands. Wage increases up to fifty per cent were granted. The transportation company said that it would not abide by this two-man decision and threatened to carry the issue to the supreme court. Meanwhile the union staged a huge demonstration in support of the government's policy. Its banners read: "With Medina against the bus owners." Police broke up the parade and arrested the head of the union. But the government insisted on enforcing its award, even when the company announced that it would sell its holdings rather than submit. President Medina evidently desired to retain the appearance of impartiality, without sacrificing the labor following that he had worked so hard to win.[7]

ELECTIONS OF 1944. October 22, 1944, was election day in Venezuela. The principal officers to be elected were municipal councilmen and state assemblymen. It must be remembered that these assemblymen and councilmen were to choose the members of Congress who in turn would name the next president. So of course the election assumed an importance out of all proportion to the offices directly involved. Political activity took on greater proportions than Venezuelans had ever known. The official Venezuelan Democratic Party brought food to Caracas from the neighboring agricultural areas, and sold it at low prices in the poorer districts. Airplanes were used to drop showers of campaign literature. The Communists, who had not been able to muster sufficient strength to name their own candidates, agreed to support the nominees of the government. Some of Medina's close associates urged him to repudiate this questionable alliance, but he ignored their advice. Meanwhile Democratic Action waged a strenuous campaign against the government and all its works. But when the votes were counted the Medina forces had a comfortable majority. There seemed to be no doubt that the President could name his successor, without more than scattered opposition in Congress.

EXPECTATIONS OF LÓPEZ CONTRERAS. Among politically minded Vene-

[7] The October, 1944, issue of *Inter-American* (Vol. III, No. 10), contains an interesting unsigned commentary on the labor situation during this period.

zuelans, one question was uppermost: Who will be Medina's choice? López Contreras seems to have assumed that he would be the man. No other possible candidate could match his prestige. He had guided the nation through its troubled years after the death of Gómez and set its feet on the path toward democracy. He had ruled as a constitutional president, when dictatorship was within his grasp. Certainly the country owed him a great debt. Medina Angarita owed him a debt, too, for he had made Medina president. To López Contreras and to many other Venezuelans it seemed that Medina could do no less than return the favor.[8]

MEDINA'S CHOICE. But President Medina considered himself in no way obligated to return his predecessor to power. He passed along the word that the next president was to be sixty-four-year-old Diógenes Escalante, who was then in Washington as his country's ambassador. In many ways it was a fortunate choice. Escalante was able and popular, and though he had long been associated with the governments of Venezuela, he was known to have liberal tendencies. Equally important, he was a civilian. The nation had not been governed by a civilian for more than half a century, and it was weary of military men. When, therefore, the leaders of Democratic Action, the opposition group, learned that Escalante was to be the official candidate, they were agreeably surprised. They even considered the possibility of endorsing him, instead of naming their own candidate. Finally they decided to send two members of their group to the United States for the purpose of talking with Medina's candidate and learning his views. Escalante received them cordially, and promised to support their program of reform. The two representatives of Democratic Action returned to Caracas with glowing accounts of the official candidate, so the party agreed to support him. Meanwhile the government's Venezuelan Democratic Party officially ratified the choice already made by President Medina Angarita.

But López Contreras and his friends were not willing to accept Medina's decision. They hastily set up a new organization to promote the former President's candidacy. The mouth-filling name they adopted was *Group in Favor of the Presidential Candidacy* (*Agrupación Pro-Candidatura Presidencial*)—meaning, of course, the presidential candidacy of López Contreras. Large landowners and businessmen, as well as many army officers and intellectuals, lent their names to the movement. It was clear

---

[8] *Inter-American* published an analysis of the political situation at this time, calling López Contreras "the people's choice," and declaring its inability to see how he would avoid "being drafted into the candidacy and elected." July, 1945 (Vol. IV, No. 7), p. 11.

that López Contreras still had a substantial following, though scarcely large enough to win an election against the government's candidate. One veteran politician predicted that only thirty-two congressmen—less than one fourth of the total number—would give López their support.

MEDINA'S BREAK WITH DEMOCRATIC ACTION. With election results already forecast, the political situation took an unexpected turn. Diógenes Escalante, who had returned to Venezuela to campaign for the presidency, suffered a nervous breakdown and was compelled to announce his withdrawal from the race. President Medina Angarita then indicated that the government's support would be given to Minister of Agriculture Angel Biaggini. The new candidate was a colorless figure, known chiefly for his faithfulness in performing small jobs. As president he was almost certain to be Medina's tool. The leaders of Democratic Action, bitterly disappointed, refused to give him the support that they had promised to Escalante. Yet they were in a difficult position. Any candidate of their own choosing would almost certainly be defeated. Finally they approached the President with the proposal that all the parties unite to name a neutral candidate, who would take office with the understanding that he would serve but a single year. During that year a new constitution could be written, providing for direct popular election of the president. The new constitution could then be put into effect at once, and the people would not have to wait five years or more for the chance to name their chief executive.

Medina pointed out that such a suggestion ignored the established procedure for changing the form of government; if adopted, it would really be a *coup d'état*. Democratic Action did not deny its revolutionary nature, but said that since it would be a peaceful *coup d'état,* staged with the consent of all the political parties, its irregularity might well be overlooked. The leaders of Democratic Action did not add that the proposal represented their one chance of getting control of the government by peaceful means, but of course there was no need for them to underline the obvious. The President understood quite clearly that he was being urged to forego the advantages of the political machine he had built with great care, and he saw no reason to do so. His answer to Democratic Action, therefore, was a definite *no.*

REVOLUTION PLANNED. The opposition leaders had to decide whether they would accept the President's refusal to name a provisional government. Many of them thought that they should not do so, but instead should put their trust in armed force. So they talked with young army officers and learned that they too were dissatisfied, though for different reasons. Army influence with the President was surprisingly small, considering his military background. Army salaries were very low, despite the largest budget in Venezuelan history. Everyone knew that the government was riddled with graft, and many army officers thought that the existing budget could easily provide them with higher salaries if the graft were eliminated. For more than a year they had talked of revolution, and when the leaders of Democratic Action approached them with a proposition to overthrow the Medina government, they readily agreed.

THE OVERTHROW OF MEDINA. The uprising was scheduled for the end of 1945. Before all the plans were completed, however, the President learned of the plot and arrested a number of suspects. It was clear that the other revolutionaries must act at once. Hastily they changed their plans and attacked on October 18, 1945, at least two months ahead of the original date. Some units of the army remained loyal and there were a number of bloody encounters. Nearly three hundred persons were killed, and an equal number died from lack of proper medical care. The total number of wounded probably exceeded fifteen hundred. But it was all over in twenty-four hours. Medina surrendered and signed his resignation. He was hurried into exile, together with most of his principal advisers. López Contreras also was told that he must leave the country.

THE REVOLUTIONARY JUNTA. A seven-man junta assumed responsibility for the government of the nation, and set to work with promising vigor. It had little difficulty in restoring order, for the people seemed to have no desire to repeat the wild orgy of looting and destruction that had marked the end of the Gómez regime. Decrees and proclamations followed one another in rapid succession. It was stated that civilians and military men in the junta would work together for the common welfare. The remaining obstacles to complete democracy would be removed. A constitutional assembly would be called at the earliest possible moment to draft a new constitution along more democratic lines. Steps would be taken to relieve the serious economic situation.

These declarations were well received by most Venezuelans, who noted with relief that the junta seemed to be dominated by civilians. Only two of its seven members were army men, though they held important posts— minister of internal relations and minister of national defense. The president of the junta, who thus became virtually the president of the nation, was Rómulo Betancourt, stocky, forty-year-old lawyer and economist who had long been active in the opposition to earlier regimes. Gómez had exiled him, and even Medina Angarita had ordered his deportation, but he had managed to remain in Venezuela during the Medina regime, hiding in the homes of various friends. At one time he had joined the Communist Party. Later, however, he severed this affiliation and became a severe critic of communism, though retaining his radical point of view. For many years he had been closely associated with the labor movement.

POLITICAL AND ECONOMIC REFORMS. The revolutionary junta announced that the members of the constitutional assembly would be chosen directly by the people, and that women would be permitted to vote for the first time in Venezuelan history. There would be no literacy test. The original plan was to hold the election within six months after the new government seized power, but six additional months were required to complete all necessary arrangements. Meanwhile the junta continued to govern by decree. Its ambitious program called for expropriation of large estates, construction by the government of low-cost houses, and development of a publicly subsidized merchant marine. Almost at once it took a number of small steps toward the accomplishment of these reforms. It decided to enrich the public treasury by imposing a heavy excess profits tax on 1945 earnings above—approximately—two hundred and seventy-five thousand American dollars. This tax was aimed directly at the foreign oil companies, which paid about ninety per cent of it. Maximum prices were fixed for foodstuffs and other essentials.

THE CONSTITUTIONAL ASSEMBLY. As the campaign for the election of members of the constitutional assembly got under way, it was obvious that Democratic Action would have almost a clear field. Its leaders controlled the government. Its principal rivals were exiled. When all the votes had been counted, it was found that Democratic Action had won one hundred and seven of the one hundred and sixty seats. Thirty other seats went to independents who had promised to support the government program, though not running on the official ticket. Nineteen seats were won by a small opposition group known generally as *Copei*—a word formed by the initials (in Spanish) of its full title, Committee Organized for Independent Elections. This group was generally sympathetic to the revolution, but critical of the government's socialist policies. It regarded some of the educational reforms as anti-clerical, and favored a more sympathetic attitude toward the Catholic Church. The leader of Copei was Rafael Caldera, a brilliant young lawyer who had served for a short time as attorney general under the junta. His revolutionary record was unimpeachable. Two of the remaining seats in the constitutional assembly were held by the Republican Democratic Union, whose leaders held approximately the same views as Democratic Action, but thought that they could further their political ambitions by forming a separate faction. The other two seats were gained by the Communists.

A MORE DEMOCRATIC CONSTITUTION. With an overwhelming majority in the constitutional assembly, Democratic Action had little difficulty in framing a constitution to its own taste. But the task proved unexpectedly tedious. One reason was the sharp disagreement among the majority members on many points. President Betancourt did not attempt to impose his will on the assembly; he said repeatedly that he believed in party responsibility, and on many occasions he allowed himself to be overriden by the other party leaders. Some of the delay in completing the constitution could be traced to the assembly's bad habit of including—and needlessly debating— many matters that should have been covered by ordinary laws. In some respects the finished document almost resembled a legal code. The assembly occasionally took time off from its constitutional labors to pass laws for the country, though most matters were still regulated by the junta's decrees. Finally, however, the new constitution was completed. It was by far the most democratic document in the nation's history. The assembly then adjourned, on October 21, 1947, after authorizing the junta to continue in power until the inauguration of a new president. It had already enacted an election law, which it patterned after the decree providing for the election of its own members.

PENALTIES AGAINST FORMER OFFICIALS. While the constitutional assembly was studying the needs of the future, another body was examining the deeds and misdeeds of the past. It was called the jury of civil and administrative responsibility, and it was appointed by the junta for the express purpose of determining whether high officials in previous administrations had misappropriated public funds or illicitly acquired wealth. The estates of Gómez had been expropriated shortly after his death, and this act undoubtedly furnished a precedent. When the work of the jury was completed, its list contained the names of more than one hundred malefactors. Some of them were former associates of Gómez, who had never been molested in the enjoyment of their great wealth. But the majority were men who had served in more recent administrations. López Contreras and Medina Angarita headed the list; each of them was fined the equivalent of four million American dollars. Since their wealth was almost entirely in Venezuela, this act left them virtually penniless. It should be emphasized that the jury of civil and administrative responsibility was not a judicial body, and that its decision was never reviewed by any court. Some persons thought that the imposition of heavy penalties against the two former presidents was a mistake, since it provided an additional incentive for either or both of these men to plot a counterrevolution.

DISCONTENT. Within less than two months after the revolutionary junta seized power, a rebellion of dissatisfied army officers broke out in the western part of the country but was quickly suppressed. Other plots were nipped in the bud. Some uprisings assumed serious proportions before they were finally brought under control. Meanwhile the Communists added to the government's troubles by fomenting a wave of strikes. The oil workers presented to the foreign companies a list of demands which included, among other things, pay at eighteen times the normal rate for work on certain holidays, and food, housing, and medical care for all relatives of workers up to third cousins. The government finally persuaded the workers to accept a substantial increase in wages and withdraw their other demands.

PRESIDENTIAL CAMPAIGN OF 1947. It was finally announced that election day would be December 14, 1947. On that date the voters would choose a new president and a new Congress. There were five candidates for the presidency. Democratic Action nominated Rómulo Gallegos, who had been its standard-bearer against Medina Angarita in 1941.[9] Copei and the Republican Democratic Union chose their respective leaders, Rafael Caldera and Jovito Vallalba. The Communists, whose party membership was only twenty thousand, selected Gustavo Machado. The fifth candidate, an eccentric named Ramiro Nava, had no substantial following. It was clear that only death or revolution could keep Gallegos from the presidency. When all the votes had been counted, it was announced that he had received more than two thirds of the total. Democratic Action was equally successful in electing members of Congress; it won three fourths of the seats in the Chamber of Deputies, and more than four fifths of the Senate seats. The Communists made a sorry showing, with but three seats in the lower house and one in the Senate. Impartial observers agreed that it was an honest election.

RISE AND FALL OF RÓMULO GALLEGOS. President Gallegos took office on February 15, 1948. The new Congress was already in session. In his inaugural address the President promised to represent the entire nation, regardless of politics, but subsequently he showed little inclination to com-

[9] See page 435.

promise with minority groups. Nor was there any obvious reason for him to do so, in view of his party's overwhelming control of Congress. Before long, however, the President committed the serious error of alienating the army officers who had made possible his party's triumph. Some of his reforms were entirely too radical for army conservatives. He even talked of transforming the army into a police force. Finally the army decided that it must play a more important part in shaping government policy. It demanded six cabinet posts—one half of the total number—for high army officers and leaders of conservative Copei. President Gallegos flatly refused, and at the same time cabled a request for the immediate return of his friend Colonel Mario Vargas, inspector general of the army, who was in New York State receiving treatment for serious illness. Vargas reached Caracas in a few days, but after talking with other army leaders announced that he too opposed the President's policies. Gallegos still refused to yield, however, so the army took matters into its own hands.

On November 24, 1948, tanks and trucks rumbled into action. Within a few hours the revolution was a complete success. Most of the leaders of Democratic Action were arrested. Rómulo Gallegos went into exile. A three-man military junta, consisting of the minister of national defense and the chief and assistant chief of staff, assumed responsibility for governing the nation. Lieutenant Colonel Carlos Delgado Chalbaud, the minister of national defense, who had formerly been one of Gallegos' most trusted advisers, was named provisional president.

GOVERNMENT BY JUNTA. The new government promised to respect democratic principles, and announced that it would soon hold an election, so that the people might "name a president and other officers whom they really desire." This statement ignored the plain fact that the people had already expressed an unmistakable desire for the candidates of Democratic Action, only to have their votes nullified by force. Passing months made abundantly clear that the new regime had very little interest in democratic processes. It suppressed those portions on the constitution dealing with individual liberties, and finally suspended the constitution itself, announcing that new elections, when held, would be regulated by the less liberal fundamental law of 1936. The Confederation of Venezuelan Workers was dissolved by decree. Those leaders of Democratic Action who had not fled the country were sent to a concentration camp in the Guiana area. Democratic Action itself was officially labeled a subversive movement. So was the Communist Party. In November of 1950, two years after the rise to power of the military junta, its president, Carlos

Delgado Chalbaud, was assassinated by a mild-mannered man who had once plotted the overthrow of the tyrant Gómez. The two remaining members of the junta promptly declared a state of siege, and arrested scores of persons who were said to be implicated in the plot. They then named a civilian as the third member of the junta, and even called him its president. But the new president seems to have possessed very little authority. Most of the decisions were made by another member of the junta, Colonel Marcos Pérez Jiménez, who was beginning to emerge as Venezuela's new strong man.

FARCICAL ELECTION. The long-promised election for a constitutional assembly was finally set for November 30, 1952, more than four years after the junta had seized control of the government. An honest election was promised, but of course the people were given no opportunity to vote for Democratic Action, which had previously been the overwhelming favorite. The government organized an official party, which it called the Independent Electoral Front. The opposition was confined to four small parties, of which the most important were the conservative Copei and the more liberal Republican Democratic Union. These opposition groups were handicapped by numerous restrictions that the government did not enforce against its own Independent Electoral Front, but no attempt was made to compel the voters to accept the official slate. Evidently the junta believed that its candidates could win an honest election with Democratic Action out of the way. The first returns, however, were a great shock to the government. They indicated that the candidates of the Republican Democratic Union were ahead in almost every state, and that they were leading the government's candidates throughout the nation by a margin of two to one. Evidently Democratic Action's followers had almost all voted for the Republican Democratic Union. The final results seemed certain to indicate a complete repudiation of the government. But the junta decided not to wait for final results. Instead it placed the nation under a state of siege, and prohibited the publication of all newspapers. Even the radio was silenced. For two days the outside world was kept in complete ignorance of developments in Venezuela. Then, on December 2, came the official announcement that the government's Independent Electoral Front had won the election. In fact, said the statement, it had gained more seats than all its opponents combined, despite the early trend to the contrary. This amazing declaration was coupled with the news that Pérez Jiménez had been named provisional president of the nation. Thus the new President, who had hoped that he could offer tangible evidence of popular support for his regime, acquired office through a display of naked force. It was a crude maneuver, but few Venezuelans dared to challenge it. The leaders of the Republican Democratic Union were arrested immediately after the election and deported a short time later. Early in January, 1953, the new constitutional assembly confirmed Pérez Jiménez as president of the nation, and three months later it completed its task of preparing Venezuela's new constitution. Today, therefore, a tight military dictatorship is in the saddle. It is trying to erase the memory of Venezuela's brief experiment with democracy.[10]

The Structure of Government

THE CONSTITUTION. The United States of Venezuela, as it is officially known, has a scheme of government that shows marked traces of American influence, and also unmistakable evidence of its own turbulent history. The present constitution, the nineteenth in a long succession, is only about twice the length of the constitution of the United States, and therefore quite short by Latin American standards. It is, in fact, only about half as long as the constitution of 1947. It is also much less democratic, as reflected at the very outset by the *Preliminary Declaration*. This clause states that the primary reason for the nation's existence is "the maintenance of its moral and historic patrimony, the defense of its dignity, the conservation and defense of its territory, and the use of its riches for the welfare of its inhabitants." [11] The corresponding clause of the fundamental law of 1947 had referred instead to "the spiritual, political, and economic liberty of man, founded on human dignity, social justice, and the equitable participation of all the people in the benefits of the nation's riches." [12] In the 1953 version social justice and the liberty of man are conveniently forgotten.

Individual and social guarantees. The new constitution devotes about eleven hundred words to individual and social rights and duties. Almost as much space is needed for restrictions and qualifications as for the actual enumeration of rights. The inhabitants of the nation are assured religious liberty, for example, but "under the supreme right of inspection of all cults by the national executive power, in conformity with the law." [13]

10 See W. Donald Beatty's article, "Venezuela: Rich Abroad—Poor at Home," in the March, 1953, issue of *Current History*, pp. 149–155.
11 Constitution of 1953, Art. 1.
12 Constitution of 1947, Art. 1.
13 Constitution of 1953, Art. 35, Cl. 6.

The inviolability of the home is guaranteed, but not with regard to police inspection for reasons of public security.[14] The right of property is assured in four words, and restricted in one hundred and four.[15] Some of the newer social guarantees are included, but always "in conformity with the laws."

State of siege. Even the narrowly restricted guarantees of the constitution must yield to the state of siege, which may be declared by the president *in case of national or international emergency.*[16] During a state of siege persons may not be put to death, or sentenced to imprisonment for more than thirty years, but otherwise this important presidential power is restricted only by the necessity of securing cabinet approval—a mere formality. No attempt is made to limit the duration of the state of siege, except to say that it shall cease when the circumstances that necessitated it have disappeared. The president, of course, is the sole judge of the existence of such circumstances and of their disappearance. No constitution of Latin America places arbitrary power more completely in the hands of the chief executive.

Amendment of the constitution. The procedure for amending the constitution is much the same as in the United States. Every proposal must be approved by Congress and the state legislatures. An ordinary majority in each house of Congress is sufficient, but two thirds of the state legislatures must approve, by vote of an absolute majority of their members. An amendment may be proposed not only by Congress but also by the state legislatures. If the state legislatures take the initiative (two thirds of the total number of legislatures being necessary), the measure then goes to Congress, which may reject it or offer any number of modifications. The changes proposed by Congress must be accepted by the legislatures before the amendment becomes a part of the constitution.[17]

SUFFRAGE AND ELECTIONS. The right to vote extends to all men and women, literate or illiterate. Even foreigners may be permitted to vote, says the constitution, if Congress should so decide.[18] There is a separate ballot for each party, but these ballots are prepared by the government. The task of voting is made easier for illiterates by the use of different colors for the several parties. The parties have welcomed the idea of colored ballots. During political campaigns they have carefully associated them-

[14] Art. 35, Cl. 3.
[15] Art. 35, Cl. 9.
[16] Art. 36.
[17] Arts. 140–142.
[18] Art. 39.

selves with their respective colors, and have urged the people: Vote white! Vote green! Vote red! When the voter appears at the polling place, he presents his registration card. He is then handed the cards—in other words, the ballots—of all the parties, plus an official envelope. In the secrecy of the voting booth he then places the card of his choice in the envelope, discarding the others in a convenient receptacle. The election officials mark his little finger with indelible green ink, which will not come off for several days. This practice has proved very effective in keeping repeaters away from the polls. At first the voters objected to the stain; later they came to regard it as an evidence of their good citizenship. The Venezuelan electoral system does not permit a split vote. Proportional representation of the several parties is used for members of Congress and the state legislatures.

THE PRESIDENT: *Selection, qualifications, term, salary.* The president must be a native-born citizen, at least thirty years of age, and not a member of the clergy,[19] conditions that should not prove difficult for anyone who aspires to be the head of the nation. The constitution of 1947 broke with its predecessors by providing for direct popular election of the president, and the fundamental law of 1953 contains a similar clause.[20] The candidate receiving the largest number of votes is declared the winner; it is not necessary to have an absolute majority. The president's term is five years. Formerly he was ineligible for immediate re-election, but the present constitution imposes no such restriction. The salary of the president is the equivalent of twenty thousand dollars a year, which is totally inadequate in high-priced Venezuela. The law requires every retiring chief executive to go before a federal judge and make a public declaration of his assets and liabilities. Ex-President Betancourt swore that his net worth on leaving office was three hundred and forty-three dollars. Although the nation gives the president such a small salary, it provides him with a magnificent residence—Miraflores Palace, about four blocks from Plaza Bolívar in the center of the city. The palace has a beautiful patio and gardens, and its public rooms contain choice paintings and furniture carved from native woods. The *Casa Amarilla,* or Yellow House, which was the president's official home for many years, is now occupied by the Ministry of Foreign Affairs.

Executive powers. The constitution states that "the president of the Republic is the representative of the nation and the chief of the national

[19] Art. 103.
[20] Art. 104.

VENEZUELA

executive power."[21] He appoints and removes the members of his own cabinet and all other administrative officers and employees of the national government, either directly or through appropriate subordinates. He is not required to secure the consent of the Senate or any other body. For appointment to high office in the military service, however, Senate approval is necessary. The president has no part in the selection of judges. Treaties must receive the concurrence of both houses of Congress. The president is the commander in chief of the armed forces and may "assume the direction of" a war.[22] He may also declare war, but only when authorized by Congress.[23]

Legislative powers. The president plays an important part in lawmaking. He has the usual power to introduce bills and to present his views to Congress by means of messages. His veto of legislative proposals may be overridden by a two-thirds majority in each house. The presidents of Venezuela have been accustomed to governing the nation by decree, and there is every reason to suppose that this practice will be continued under the present regime. The constitution authorizes the chief executive to "create new public services . . . and to abolish or modify existing services."[24] It also permits the withdrawal of funds from the public treasury by executive order.[25] The president has the usual power of pardon.

Presidential succession. Venezuela has no vice-president. In case of the president's death, disability, or resignation, the cabinet selects one of its own members to serve as the chief executive of the nation until such time as Congress chooses a new president for the remainder of the term. Congress must make its selection within ten days, if it is already in session; otherwise it must convene at once and then decide within ten days.[26]

THE CABINET. The fundamental law of 1947 made a determined effort to establish a system of parliamentary government, but the present constitution sweeps away all traces of parliamentarism. It states very specifically that "the president of the republic is responsible for the acts of his administration."[27] Cabinet ministers must have the same legal qualifications as the president. The number of ministries is fixed by law. At present there are fourteen: Foreign Relations, Internal Relations, Finance, National Defense, Public Works, Development, Agriculture, Sanitation

[21] Art. 102.
[22] Art. 108, Cl. 22.
[23] Art. 108, Cl. 21.
[24] Art. 108, Cl. 3.
[25] Art. 108, Cl. 5.
[26] Art. 106.
[27] Art. 110.

and Public Assistance, Labor, Education, Communications, Justice, Mines and Petroleum, Federal District. Most of these titles are self-explanatory. It might be pointed out that "Federal District" refers to the city of Caracas and its environs. This area has been made a special district under the direct control of the nation, and its governor has a seat in the president's cabinet. In the federal service the merit system is not generally used and not seriously contemplated.

CONGRESS: *Selection, terms, qualifications.* Congress consists of two houses, as in most countries. The Senate has forty-two members. Two senators are chosen from each of the twenty states, by their respective state legislatures, and two from the federal district by its municipal council. The Chamber of Deputies has one hundred and four members, apportioned among the states, the federal district, and the territories on the basis of population, and chosen by direct vote of the people. Both senators and deputies serve for five years. Vacancies are filled by alternates elected at the same time. There is no system of partial renewal. Because the terms of congressmen coincide with that of the president, there is relatively little danger that he will be compelled to work with a hostile Congress for part of his term. Senators must be citizens by birth, and at least thirty years of age. Deputies also must be citizens by birth, but the minimum age is twenty-one.

Place of meeting. The capitol, which was built in 1885, is somewhat weather-beaten but still impressive. Its extensive gardens are very beautiful. Rooms have been set aside for the two houses of Congress in the south wing, and various government offices occupy adjacent parts of the building. In the north wing is the famous elliptical hall, which is used for presidential receptions and other major affairs of state. It contains some excellent paintings based on patriotic themes, and also the bronze urn in which the declaration of independence is preserved.

Sessions; organization. Congress meets in regular annual session on the 19th day of April, and adjourns one hundred days later. No provision is made for extension of regular sessions, but special sessions may be called by the president of the nation. They may deal only with matters specified in the presidential summons, except that matters of "obvious urgency" may also be considered. Two thirds of the membership of each house must be present at the preliminary meetings when officers are chosen and rules adopted. In subsequent meetings a majority is sufficient to do business. Each house chooses a president and a first and second vice-president, who serve but one year. The regular standing committees—thirty-five in the Senate and fifty-two in the Chamber of Deputies—are named by the presiding officers. Congress usually meets five days a week. Members are not provided with secretaries or private offices.

Procedure. Legislative proposals may originate with any member of either house of Congress, or with the president of the nation. Venezuela, unlike most countries, does not require bills for raising revenue to receive their first consideration in the Chamber of Deputies. Each bill receives the customary three readings. When it has been passed in different form by the two houses, they meet in joint session and decide the matter by majority vote. This is the simplest possible method of resolving such conflicts, but of course it favors the Chamber of Deputies, which has more than twice as many members as the Senate.[28]

Joint sessions. For most purposes, of course, the two houses of Congress meet as separate bodies. But there are times when they sit jointly—not only to resolve their own disputes, as noted above, but also to authorize the president to declare war or negotiate peace, to approve treaties and contracts, and to sanction the national budget.

THE COURTS. The supreme court of the nation is composed of ten judges, chosen by Congress for five-year terms. This arrangement permits every new Congress to decide whether it will select another panel of supreme court justices or renew the terms of those already serving. It was copied directly from earlier constitutions. Every member of the court must be a lawyer, and in addition must have the same qualifications as the president of the nation. The court chooses its own presiding officer and divides itself into chambers to hear different kinds of cases. It is specifically authorized to declare laws unconstitutional. Below the supreme court are courts of appeal and district courts. The judges of these lower tribunals are named by the supreme court—also for five years—and must have substantially the same qualifications. Juries are not used.[29]

THE STATES. The United States of Venezuela has a federal form of government, at least in theory. There are twenty states, and they are given all powers not reserved to the nation or the municipalities. The list of national powers is very extensive, however—much more so than in the United States of America. It includes control of elections, education, health, agriculture, and labor. Congress is empowered to enact codes of

[28] There is a good chapter on the organization and work of Congress in Ernesto Wolff's *Tratado de Derecho Constitucional Venezolano,* Vol. I, pp. 219–261. This work was published in 1945, however, so unfortunately large parts of it are out of date.
[29] Ernesto Wolff's previously cited work gives a detailed description of judicial organization. See Vol. II, pp. 311–349.

civil and criminal law, which must be enforced by the courts of both states and nation. Almost all forms of taxation are in the hands of the national government, but a substantial part of federal tax receipts is apportioned annually among the several states. The states in turn are required to allocate a portion of this subsidy to the cities. State budgets must conform to the general fiscal scheme of the national government. State borrowing is narrowly restricted by the federal constitution and the laws of Congress. There are other federal powers, also: control of banking and currency, protection of natural resources, regulation of all forms of transportation and communication. And, to make sure that nothing has been forgotten, the constitution authorizes the central government to promote the general welfare of the nation.[30]

The states are declared to be autonomous, and are guaranteed the right to regulate their own affairs. But these words mean almost nothing. Previous constitutions said the same thing, even while successive dictators controlled every aspect of both national and state activity.[31] The true position of the states is made clearer by some of the detailed provisions of the present constitution. State governors are said to be the agents of the nation and are directed to enforce national laws and decrees, as well as state legislation, within their respective jurisdictions. In order to make certain that they will play their part without insubordination, the constitution specifies that they shall be appointed by the president and may be removed by him at his discretion. The legislative assemblies of the states are unicameral and are chosen by direct vote of the people. Their term is three years.

THE CITIES. Unlike the states, the cities of Venezuela have been given a certain measure of autonomy. The constitution devotes about three hundred and fifty words to municipal affairs. It declares that municipal officials shall be free from federal and state interference in the performance of their duties, and that municipal ordinances shall not be vetoed or declared invalid, except by the courts of law. Certain kinds of taxes and license fees are designated as proper sources of municipal revenue. In addition, as we have already seen, the cities receive a share of the subsidy to the states from the federal treasury. City councils are comparatively small, varying in size from five members to twenty-two, according to population. The mayors of cities are chosen by the councils. Both mayors and councilmen serve for three years. As in many countries, the capital city is sub-

[30] Art. 60, Cl. 1.
[31] See the article by Chas. C. Griffin, "Regionalism's Role in Venezuelan Politics," in the *Inter-American Quarterly*, Oct., 1941, pp. 21–35.

jected to a larger measure of central control. With its suburbs it constitutes a federal district, and the administrative affairs of the district are in the hands of a governor appointed by the president of the nation.[32] There is a popularly elected council, as in other cities, but its powers are restricted. The governor may veto its proposals, and Congress may invalidate its ordinances by the simple process of enacting conflicting legislation.

SELECTED REFERENCES

Allen, Henry J., *Venezuela: A Democracy,* New York, Doubleday, Doran, 1940.

Baptista, Octavio, *Venezuela, Su Historia y Sus Métodos de Gobierno,* Guadalajara, Mex., Tall. Gráf., 1942.

Betancourt, Rómulo, *Problemas Venezolanos,* Santiago, Chile, Editorial Futuro, 1940.

Briceño, Olga, *Cocks and Bulls in Caracas,* Boston, Houghton Mifflin, 1945.

Celis Briceño, Pablo, *Elementos de Derecho Constitucional,* Caracas, Editorial Elite, 1943.

Clinton, Daniel J., *Gómez, Tyrant of the Andes,* New York, W. Morrow, 1936.

Colmenares Peraza, J. R., *Venezuela y sus Inmigraciones,* Caracas, Bolívar, 1940.

Gil Fortoul, José, *Historia Constitucional de Venezuela,* 3rd ed., Caracas, Parra León Hnos., 1942.

Granados Aguirre, Jesús, *Legislación del Trabajo en Venezuela,* Caracas, Editorial Elite, 1944.

León, Ramón David, *De Agro-Pecuario a Petróleo,* Caracas, Tip. Garrido, 1944.

Oropeza, Ambrosio, *Evolución Constitucional de Nuestra República,* Caracas, Cecilio Acosta, 1944.

Osorio, Luis Enrique, *Democracia en Venezuela,* Bogotá, Editorial Litografía Colombia, 1943.

Parra, Francisco J., *Consideraciones acerca del Sistema Arancelario,* Caracas, Tip. Americana, 1944.

Perera, Ambrosio, *Historia Orgánica de Venezuela,* Caracas, Editorial Venezuela, 1943.

Roosevelt, Nicholas, *Venezuela's Place in the Sun,* New York, Round Table Press, 1940.

Ruggeri Parra, Pablo, *Derecho Constitucional Venezolano,* Caracas, Editorial Cecilio Acosta, 1944.

—— *Historia Política y Constitucional de Venezuela,* Caracas, Editorial Universitaria, 1949.

—— *La Supremacia de la Constitución y su Defensa,* Caracas, Tip. Venezuela, 1941.

United Nations, Department of Economic Affairs, *Public Finance Information Papers: Venezuela, 1951,* New York, Columbia University Press, 1952.

Wise, George S., *Caudillo: A Portrait of Antonio Guzmán Blanco,* New York, Columbia University Press, 1951.

Wolff, Ernesto, *Tratado de Derecho Constitucional Venezolano,* 2 Vols., Caracas, Tip. Americana, 1945.

[32] See page 450.

CHAPTER 17

ECUADOR

~~~~~~

The Land and the People

ECUADOR is an exotic land. The colorful costumes of its rural Indians contrast sharply with the sophisticated dress of its city folk. Its ancient churches stand beside modern apartment houses and office buildings. In some parts of its territory the snow never melts; in other sections it never falls. There are steaming jungles and barren plateaus. Although Ecuador lies directly athwart the equator, from which it derives its name, a large part of its area is distinctly chilly at all times. Altitude, of course, provides the contrasts of climate.

POPULATION, AREA, RACES. The country is small—no larger than New Mexico. It has only about three million people and a population density of about twenty-four per square mile. Ninety per cent of the people have some Indian blood. About forty per cent are pure-blooded Indians, living in isolated valleys of the high plateau or lowland jungles in much the same way as their forefathers did before the Spanish conquest. They are miserably poor, of course, and their agricultural methods are amazingly primitive. The white ten per cent of Ecuador's population represents almost entirely the descendants of the old Spanish families. There are, however, some recent immigrants. The government attempts to exclude all prospective settlers who are not likely to make a worth-while contribution to the nation's economy.

THE COASTAL STRIP. Ecuador, like Peru, is divided into three main sections by the great Andean mountain chain. The western coastal strip, between the mountains and the sea, is slightly wider than in Peru, but

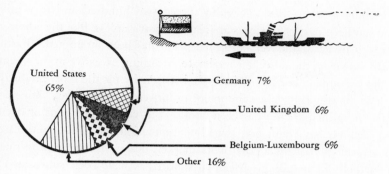

Ecuadorian Imports from Principal Countries (1951)

United States 65%

Germany 7%

United Kingdom 6%

Belgium-Luxembourg 6%

Other 16%

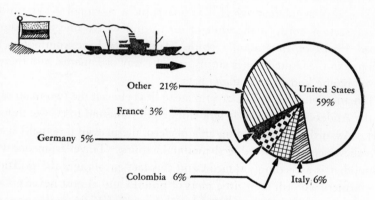

Ecuadorian Exports to Principal Countries (1951)

Other 21%

France 3%

Germany 5%

Colombia 6%

United States 59%

Italy 6%

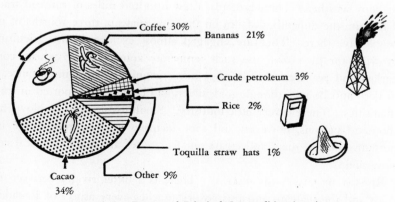

Ecuadorian Exports of Principal Commodities (1951)

Coffee 30%

Bananas 21%

Crude petroleum 3%

Rice 2%

Toquilla straw hats 1%

Other 9%

Cacao 34%

Based on information from the May, 1953, issue of *International Financial Statistics,* a publication of the International Monetary Fund.

practically nowhere does its width exceed two hundred and fifty miles. The southern part of this coastal area is almost rainless, like the adjoining territory in Peru, and very little irrigation has been attempted. Farther north, however, the rainfall is moderate, becoming excessive in the vicinity of the Colombian border. The coastal strip is by far the most productive area of the country. Here the major export crops are grown. For many years the principal crop has been cacao. But careless methods of drying and packing have damaged Ecuador's reputation for high-quality cacao. As a result it has lost a part of its market, despite recent improvements in methods of handling. Meanwhile bananas have been substituted in some areas, and have become one of the leading exports. Coffee is even more important. Sugar, rice, and cotton are also grown in the coastal area, as well as tobacco, which is a government monopoly. The Indians in the section north of the Gulf of Guayaquil weave fine hats from the broad leaves of the toquilla palm. These hats have commonly been shipped to the United States and Europe by way of Panama, and therefore have become known as Panama hats.

THE HIGH PLATEAU. The great plateau lies between the two main ranges of the Andes and varies in height from eight thousand to twelve thousand feet. As in the corresponding area of Peru, the plateau is actually a series of valleys separated by rugged mountain spurs. Travel from one valley to another is exceedingly difficult and this fact encourages the isolation of the farmers who till their little plots of ground and almost never go as far as the next valley. No well-developed system of highways connects the commercial and agricultural centers. Most of the roads are impassable in rainy weather. There are only a few hundred miles of railroad track.

Despite the difficulties of life on the high plateau, three fourths of the people live there. They are engaged almost exclusively in agriculture, growing for their own use such temperate zone crops as wheat, corn, barley, and potatoes. Mining has never acquired major importance, as in Peru and Bolivia, though gold, silver, and copper are exported in small quantities. There is very little industry. Small textile mills employ a few thousand persons, however, and shoe factories are becoming more important. Drugs, soap, and cigars and cigarettes are made for local consumption.

RIVALRY OF COAST AND PLATEAU. There is a bitter rivalry between the coast and the plateau, and this rivalry touches every aspect of Ecuador's political life. Both areas must be given suitable recognition. If the president comes from one section of the country, the vice-president must come

An Ecuadorian Indian from the country pauses briefly at a street intersection in Quito.
(Photograph by the author)

from the other.   If some cabinet members are from the coast, others must be from the highlands.   Even the members of the supreme court must be chosen with geography in mind.[1]

THE EASTERN LOWLANDS.   Beyond the Andes lies the region known as the eastern lowlands.   Much of this territory was lost to Peru in 1942,[2] but a large area still remains in Ecuadorian hands.   It is a part of the Amazon basin—hot, wet, and covered with heavy forests.   Most of its inhabitants are savage Indians, some of whom still cut off the heads of their enemies, remove the bones, and then use a secret formula to shrink the heads to a fraction of their original size.   The government of Ecuador tries to prevent the exportation of these heads, lest foreigners gain the impression that all Ecuadorians are savages; but many heads find their way into the channels of trade, nonetheless—usually from Brazil by way of the Amazon River. The principal commercial product of the eastern lowlands is rubber, and it is not very important.   At present, therefore, this area is almost a total loss.   Politically as well as economically it is unimportant.

POVERTY.   Ecuador is a poor country.   Because it has no highly developed mineral resources and very little manufacturing, it relies almost entirely on agriculture for its trade with the other nations of the world. And since so large a part of the agriculture has never risen above the subsistence level, Ecuador has very little to offer other countries.   Therefore it must depend to a very considerable extent on its own limited resources. The inevitable result is an extremely low standard of living.   Only one person in three hundred has a telephone; only one in two thousand has a motor car.   Two thirds of the population is illiterate, despite the determined efforts of successive governments to improve the educational system.

PRINCIPAL CITIES.   The capital city, Quito, lies only nine miles south of the equator, but at an altitude of ninety-three hundred feet.   It is a picturesque city, retaining most of its colonial charm despite the encroachments of modern architecture.   Indians from the country, dressed in their primitive costumes, press themselves against the sides of buildings to permit the passage of automobiles along the narrow streets.   Flowers are in bloom every month of the year, for, as the residents like to boast, it is always spring in Quito.   The city's eternal springtime is always cool, and often rainy—much like April in England; but at least there are no sud-

---

[1] See George I. Blanksten's excellent work, *Ecuador: Constitutions and Caudillos.*   This 1951 volume will doubtless be the standard treatise on Ecuador for some years to come.

[2] See page 355.

den extremes of heat or cold. Quito is a comparatively small city. Its population is only two hundred and fifteen thousand. Unlike any other capital of Latin America, it is not the largest city of the nation. That honor goes to Guayaquil, the principal port of the country, which lies on the Guayas River thirty miles from its mouth. But Guayaquil has only seven thousand more inhabitants than Quito. The rivalry between the two cities is intense.[3]

CHURCH AND STATE. Ecuador is known as the land of churches. This phrase indicates the traditional strength of the Catholic Church. At one time it exercised a large measure of control over almost every aspect of Ecuadorian life. It owned more than half of the land and buildings in Quito and other principal cities. It monopolized education as well as religion. All schools were Catholic, and all other worship was forbidden. In more recent years, however, the church has lost a great deal of its influence. Extensive church holdings have been nationalized and religious freedom is now guaranteed. The government has established a system of public schools. Catholic schools are permitted also, but they are subject to public supervision.[4]

The Pattern of Politics

TROUBLED HISTORY. Ecuador was the smallest and weakest of the triumvirate of nations comprising Bolívar's Great Colombia.[5] It withdrew from the confederation in 1830 and almost immediately plunged into civil war. Revolution and bloodshed have been its unhappy lot ever since. Dictator has followed dictator, usually to the accompaniment of gunfire. More than half of the nation's chief executives have been forced out of office before the expiration of their terms. There have been twenty-two presidents in the last thirty years. Under such circumstances, of course, democratic government is virtually impossible. The army can make and break presidents at its pleasure. It is the most important factor in Ecuadorian politics. Yet virtually all the political leaders of the nation deplore this state of affairs, and pay at least lip tribute to public opinion. Democracy is their avowed goal.

FREQUENT REVOLUTIONS. For many years the two traditional parties of Ecuador—Liberals and Conservatives—engaged in a bitter rivalry for control of the government. The Conservatives had the better of the argument

[3] See George I. Blanksten's previously cited work.
[4] Ludwig Bemelmans gives a lyrical account of Ecuadorian life in *The Donkey Inside.*
[5] See page 390.

for a long time, but in 1895 the Liberals staged a successful revolution and installed their leader, General Eloy Alfaro, as president of the nation. The Conservatives did not fully recover from that blow for nearly half a century. Within the Liberal Party, however, there were several dissident factions, which occasionally tried to make their influence felt by force of arms. Other uprisings were fomented by the Conservatives, though with little success. Ecuador experienced serious revolutions in 1906, 1913, 1925, 1931, and 1932. Finally, in 1933, a bitter dispute between the president and Congress culminated in the president's impeachment, conviction, and removal from office. The acting president thereupon set December 14 as the date for the election of a new chief executive. It was a quiet election, and surprisingly honest. When all the votes had been counted, it was announced that the winner was the Conservative candidate, a distinguished lawyer named José María Velasco Ibarra.

The new President undoubtedly faced serious economic problems, and he proposed drastic reforms in an effort to solve them. Congress, however, refused to support his program. When President Velasco Ibarra found that he could not get the kind of laws he wanted, he submitted his resignation to Congress, together with a message blaming its members for the plight of the nation. But Congress refused to accept the resignation. At this point the President seems to have lost all interest in quitting his job. Apparently he decided that he should stay in office and fight for his beliefs. Most of his countrymen applauded this decision, but they were quite unprepared for the President's new tactics. He broke completely with Congress and told its members that their services were no longer needed. He ordered the police to arrest his political opponents. And he called a constitutional assembly whose principal function was to be the legalization of his dictatorship. The people were outraged. Even more important, the army was dissatisfied with this turn of events. Several of its leaders engineered a *coup d'état* and sent a detachment to arrest the President, with word that this time his resignation would be accepted. Velasco Ibarra found that he had no choice. He resigned on August 20, 1935.

UNSETTLED CONDITIONS. The new President remained in office just thirty-seven days. He was succeeded by Frederico Páez, another army favorite, who managed to keep his job more than two years. During that time, however, he had to suppress three major revolts. Finally, on October 22, 1937, he surrendered the presidency to General Alberto Enríquez, who promptly named a cabinet composed chiefly of army officers. Enríquez lasted ten months; his successor remained in office an even shorter time.

Then came Aurelio Mosquera Narváez, who died in November of 1939 after an emergency operation.

ARROYO DEL RÍO. Upon the death of the Chief Executive, the president of the Senate became provisional president of the nation. His name was Carlos Arroyo del Río, and he was a lawyer and educator who had served as rector of the national university. Undoubtedly he possessed great ability and many Ecuadorians regarded him as the man most likely to establish orderly processes of government. When, therefore, the Liberal Party nominated him as their presidential candidate in the election scheduled for the following January, his triumph was virtually assured. One of the opposing candidates was former President Velasco Ibarra, who organized a revolt as soon as Arroyo del Río's election was announced. This uprising was easily suppressed, however, and Velasco Ibarra was exiled. He went to Chile, where he obtained a professorship in the University of Santiago.

POLITICAL AND ECONOMIC DIFFICULTIES. President Arroyo del Río found the task of governing the nation far from easy. Prices were rising steadily and foreign goods were becoming increasingly scarce as a result of the European war. Ecuador was forced by Peru to relinquish its claims to large areas in the eastern lowlands. Many persons blamed the President for this fiasco. He could have disputed Peru's claims more effectively, they said, if he had not hoarded guns that might have been used against himself. Actually, Ecuador had no first-rate military equipment, but the story gained wide credence. Arroyo's answer to these libelous charges was an ironclad censorship. Newspaper editors who continued to print stories that even remotely suggested criticism of the government were thrown into jail, and the doors of their establishments were padlocked. "Enemies of the state," which meant all persons who openly disagreed with the President's policies, were made the victims of police brutality. Some were tortured unmercifully.

THE UNDERGROUND OPPOSITION. As the opposition was driven underground, its numbers increased rapidly. The leaders of almost all political faiths, except the dominant Liberals, united in their determination to rid themselves of the hated Arroyo del Río. They formed a loose coalition which they called the Democratic Alliance. It included the far right and the far left, and almost everything between these two extremes. Even the Communists were represented. Meetings were held secretly to plan the strategy of the Alliance. Anti-government leaflets were printed in great numbers and widely distributed, despite the efforts of the police to locate the printing shops from which they came.

VELASCO'S CAMPAIGN. The presidential candidate finally chosen by the motley Alliance for the 1944 election was former President Velasco Ibarra. Everyone remembered the man's high ideals and seemingly forgot the dictatorial tactics that he had used during his brief term. To thousands of persons he became the embodiment of the democratic ideal. The double V (*Viva Velasco!*) was scrawled on walls and buildings in all parts of the country. At this time Great Britain and the United States were using the V sign (made by two upraised fingers) to symbolize ultimate victory over the Axis, and Velasco sympathizers speedily adapted it to their own purposes.

Meanwhile the government made vigorous efforts to stamp out the growing enthusiasm for the former President. It imprisoned or exiled large numbers of persons who had managed to escape the attention of the police during earlier investigations. It built up the *Carabineros*—the national police force—as a counterbalance to the army. It announced its official candidate for the presidency—a former minister of the interior who had once served briefly as provisional president. Velasco Ibarra, still in exile, was denied permission to return to Ecuador to conduct his campaign. He did in fact visit Ipiales, Colombia, just across the border and not more than one hundred miles from Quito. From this vantage point he hurled verbal broadsides against the Arroyo del Río regime and its dictatorial methods. The government responded by sending squads of secret police to the border to make sure that Velasco did not get across. Apparently there was no way, short of revolution, for the popular Velasco to win the presidency. The government was determined to prevent his election at any cost.

SUCCESSFUL REVOLUTION. Under the circumstances, revolution was inevitable. The leaders of the Democratic Alliance had taken the wise precaution of obtaining army support, and plans were laid to overwhelm the government before its forces could strike back. Operations proceeded on schedule. Firing broke out a little before midnight on May 28, 1944, just five days before the election. Army units moved quickly against strategic locations, pausing only long enough to hand out rifles and ammunition to eager civilians. Some troops remained loyal, but most of the government's support came from the *Carabineros*. They proved to be no match for the army and its civilian friends. The revolution triumphed in less than three days, with comparatively little loss of life, and Velasco entered Ecuador in triumph. Seldom has a revolution been more genuinely popular. The masses of the people—even those who had suffered very little from Arroyo del Río's tyrannical methods—welcomed Velasco Ibarra with genuine respect and affection. They seem to have regarded him as the savior of their country.

A POOR BEGINNING. Unfortunately for the hopes of the people, President Velasco was no worker of miracles. He was not even a very good administrator. And his erratic political course eventually alienated many of his staunchest supporters. At the outset, however, nearly everyone was willing to credit him with great ability as well as fine intentions. His only important opponents were the bankers and industrialists who had grown rich supporting the old regime, and they were speedily thrown into jail. A constituent assembly was elected to prepare a new constitution. It wrangled over this task for many months, occasionally taking time off to enact ordinary legislation for the nation. One law confiscated the properties of former President Arroyo del Río, deprived him of his citizenship, and sentenced him to sixteen years in jail. Since Arroyo was safe in Colombia, the jail sentence did not seriously affect his well-being.

QUARRELS AMONG GOVERNMENT SUPPORTERS. The Democratic Alliance, which had held together so many discordant elements in opposition to the Arroyo regime, proved incapable of accepting the responsibilities of victory. Within a few months it disintegrated, while the leaders of the various political groups angrily debated the proper course of public policy. A number of radicals had been elected to the constituent assembly, and they sponsored a bill designed to impose a strict censorship on the predominantly conservative press. The measure seemed to have enough supporters to assure its passage. When, however, President Velasco threatened to resign unless its most objectionable features were rewritten, the assembly hastily bowed to his wishes. The President was still the popular hero.

VELASCO, THE UNPREDICTABLE. The constituent assembly finally completed its task in March, 1945, after seven months of almost constant quarreling. Its members returned to their homes, leaving behind a large collection of unworkable laws, a budget fifty per cent larger than any other in the nation's history, and a general conviction that the assembly's work had been badly done. One resolution prohibited Congress from meeting for more than a year. The obvious purpose of this unusual bit of lawmaking was to prevent any tampering with the radical laws that had just been enacted. One of its effects—probably not intended—was to leave Velasco Ibarra in undisputed control of the government.

The President proceeded to alienate almost everybody by his bewildering shifts of policy. When the radicals endorsed his course of action, he promptly abandoned it for a more moderate program. When the conservatives indicated their pleasure at the change, he immediately veered sharply to the left. His moods were as unpredictable as his policies. He publicly reprimanded a provincial governor for jailing a newspaper editor who had criticized the government. Only a week later, when another editor printed somewhat the same criticism, Velasco furiously ordered the man's arrest. One day he made a speech promising full respect for constitutional liberties; the next, he swept them ruthlessly aside. More and more people began to feel the weight of the President's displeasure and to suffer the same penalties that had been their fate under Arroyo del Río and earlier tyrants. Velasco's official explanation was that these "precautions" were necessary to protect the nation against the threat of revolution, but cynical Ecuadorians remembered that dictatorship had often been justified in just such terms.

LOSS OF POPULARITY. When Congress finally met, its members were highly critical of the President's program and unwilling to pass the laws that he proposed. Their unco-operative attitude complicated an already difficult situation. Prices were rising steadily and wages were still very low. Shortages of food and other essentials fanned the flame of popular dissatisfaction. One newspaper, published and distributed clandestinely, accused the Velasco government of "beating up students, using sabers and bullets on workmen, attempting to murder a radio announcer, sacking and breaking into homes, jailing women, burning written thought, destroying a free press, persecuting, jailing, and exiling the nation's highest dignitaries and peaceful citizens." The President's democratic protestations were labeled as sheer hypocrisy. "In addition to the grabber of power, we have the penitent who beats his chest over the atrocities that he himself commits." [6]

VELASCO DISCREDITED. By 1946 President Velasco was completely discredited. He still talked of democracy, but completely ignored its fundamental principles. Early in the year he announced that the nation's constitution, adopted only two years earlier, was totally unsuited to existing conditions (which indeed it was) and would no longer be enforced. At the same time he substituted by decree the fundamental law of 1906 and made arrangements for the election of delegates to a new constitutional convention. The Conservatives and their friends won this election, largely as the result of tactics that Velasco Ibarra would have been the first to condemn when he was in exile. Most of the opposition's leaders

[6] Quoted in *Inter-American*, June, 1946 (Vol. V, No. 6), p. 32.

were imprisoned and its political rallies were broken up by the police. No attempt was made to give even the appearance of a fair election. Public opinion was so inflamed that even the President's intimates deserted him. Galo Plaza, the Ecuadorian ambassador to the United States, resigned his post and urged Velasco to follow his example "for the good of the country." But the President hung on doggedly, still upbraiding his political foes and proclaiming his own democratic faith. The constitutional convention met and drafted a new fundamental law. As might well have been expected, it was a much more moderate document than its predecessor.[7]

ANOTHER REVOLUTION. The time was ripe for revolt, just as it had been in 1944. And, as in 1944, the revolution was not long delayed. On August 24, 1947, Colonel Carlos Mancheno, the minister of defense, suddenly seized control of the government and proclaimed himself president. There was no bloodshed. Velasco Ibarra quietly wrote out his resignation and, for the second time in his career, went into exile. Later, when he had arrived safely in Colombia, he repudiated his resignation on the ground that he had been forced to sign it. No one was much interested in such details, however. Velasco had dissipated his popular support and apparently had no chance of regaining power.

AND STILL ANOTHER. One of Colonel Mancheno's first acts as chief of state was to set aside the 1946 constitution. He then proceeded to govern by decree, flooding the country with drastic rules and regulations. The jails were soon emptied of Velasco's political prisoners and filled almost at once with his former supporters. Mariano Suárez Veintimilla, who had been vice-president under Velasco, was told that he too must resign. When he refused, his arrest was ordered. Mancheno named a cabinet of Liberals and Socialists, but some Socialist leaders refused to participate.

Meanwhile it became clear that the army was by no means unanimous in its support of the new regime. Troops in several of the smaller cities rose in counterrevolt and attracted many followers. Colonel Mancheno issued a statement contemptuously describing the movement as a "small, seditious outbreak," but it was clearly more than that. The rebels had large numbers of troops massed at Riobamba, one hundred miles south of the capital. Against them Mancheno sent a strong detachment of tanks and several motorized units. But the rebels managed to keep up a running battle, though they had only rifles and machine guns. After a time the

[7] See H. B. Murkland's article, "Crisis in Ecuador," in the July, 1946, issue of *Current History*, pp. 20–24.

tanks ran out of ammunition and gasoline, and their crews were forced to surrender. Thereupon the anti-government forces streamed into Quito, gathering recruits as they went. Army planes swooped low over the capital, informing Mancheno that he must resign or be bombed out. The dictator promptly resigned and fled to the safety of the Venezuelan embassy. That was on September 2, just nine days after he had seized control of the government.

Suárez Veintimilla, released from prison, announced that he would restore the 1946 constitution and govern the country in accordance with its principles. At the same time he promised to resign as soon as Congress could meet and elect his successor. This turn of events seems to have received popular approval. Crowds gathered in several of the principal cities, shouting *"Viva la constitución!"* When the news reached Velasco Ibarra, who had gone to Buenos Aires, he boarded a plane bound for Quito, evidently hoping to return in triumph. In Lima, however, he was cautioned that the people were "not yet" ready to receive him, so he returned to Argentina.

INTERREGNUM. Suárez Veintimilla, the acting President, was as good as his word. He called a special session of Congress for September 15. During the interim he governed the country with a coalition cabinet, consisting of four Conservatives and four Liberals. As soon as Congress met, he submitted his resignation. Congress accepted it and chose as provisional president a distinguished banker and philanthropist named Carlos Julio Arosemena, who assumed his new duties at once. The new President's chief aim was to reconcile all dissident factions. He included in his cabinet both Conservatives and Liberals, as Suárez Veintimilla had done. He made every effort to respect the wishes of Congress and he governed within the letter of the constitution. Yet his brief regime was not entirely peaceful. An armed revolt challenged his authority less than eight weeks after his inauguration. It was quickly suppressed, however.

PRESIDENTIAL CAMPAIGN OF 1948. The presidential election was set for June, 1948, and within a short time the political parties were waging a furious campaign. The Liberals, whose prestige had suffered from their support of the tyrant Arroyo del Río, had reorganized as the Liberal-Radical Party. Most of its new leaders were men who had opposed the government in the final days of the Arroyo regime. As their presidential candidate they chose General Alberto Enríquez, who had been president for several months in the unsettled year 1938. Mariano Suárez Veintimilla, the recognized head of the Conservatives, refused to be a candidate, so the

Party nominated instead a former cabinet minister, Manuel Elicio Flor. Some of the country's civic leaders, dissatisfied with both nominees, united to form a middle-of-the-road party which they called the Independent Citizens. As their presidential candidate they selected Galo Plaza, the former ambassador who had once had the temerity to urge Velasco Ibarra to resign.[8] The government promised an honest election, but obviously could give no guarantee that the official returns would be respected. President Arosemena was asked whether the election would be followed by a revolution, and is said to have replied: "Why not? There are three candidates, and only one of them can win." [9] As a matter of fact, there was no revolution. The election, which was comparatively honest, resulted in the triumph of the Independent Citizens' candidate, Galo Plaza.

PRESIDENT GALO PLAZA. The new president, who had once studied at the University of California, soon made clear that he intended to follow a moderate course. His first goal was the improvement of Ecuador's living standards through better methods of farming. Public health received his constant attention, with emphasis on the fight against tuberculosis and malaria. Major highways were constructed or improved in many parts of the country. The President made a determined effort to keep down the cost of living, though with only moderate success. Throughout his entire term he gave strong support to liberal democracy. Galo Plaza governed Ecuador in the same spirit as his father, a former president of the nation, who had once arranged to secure additional newsprint for a newspaper that was grossly maligning him. The people gave him their ungrudging respect, and as a result he served his full four-year term—the first Ecuadorian president to do so in more than a quarter of a century. There were three revolutions during his administration, but they were suppressed without difficulty.

PRESIDENTIAL CAMPAIGN OF 1952. Late in 1951 Ecuador's loosely knit political parties began to plan their campaign strategy. The National Democratic Alliance, which represented not only Galo Plaza's Independent Citizens but also six other parties, chose as its presidential candidate a lawyer-diplomat named Educardo Salazar Gómez. Almost at the last minute, however, Salazar Gómez withdrew his candidacy, leaving the Alliance without any suitable candidate. Meanwhile three other presidential aspirants were campaigning vigorously. Among them was José Velasco Ibarra, Ecuador's on-and-off president who seemed to have a knack

[8] See page 465.
[9] *Time,* May 3, 1948, p. 3

of inspiring popular confidence when out of office and destroying it with his dictatorial ways whenever he acquired power. In 1952 he campaigned as an independent, and he soon gained the support of many powerful friends. President Galo Plaza displayed a determined neutrality. On one occasion he demanded the recall of the Argentine ambassador for speaking out too strongly in favor of Velasco; another time he warned the clergy that they had been too active on behalf of Velasco's principal opponent. All candidates were assured complete freedom of assembly and of the press. The election was orderly and honest.

RETURN OF VELASCO IBARRA. A complete count of the votes showed that Velasco Ibarra had won a great personal triumph. For the third time he assumed the presidency. But almost from the outset he has been embroiled in political squabbles. Some of his principal advisers, who were allied too closely with a militant Catholic youth movement, have been forced from office. The Liberal-Radical Party, which endorsed Velasco before the election, has withdrawn its support and directed its members to resign from government posts. A majority of the members of Congress are hostile to President Velasco. Revolt has already broken out, though without success. Opposition newspapers have been closed, and their editors thrown into jail. There may be some reason, therefore, to wonder whether Velasco Ibarra will be any more successful than in his previous attempts to round out a full presidential term.

The Structure of Government

THE CONSTITUTION: *Individual guarantees.* The 1946 constitution of Ecuador, the fifteenth in the nation's history, is nearly three times as long as the constitution of the United States. It omits a preamble and begins with a number of fundamental declarations concerning the sovereignty of the people, the inalienability of the national territory, and the principle of good neighborliness in international relations. The bill of rights, for some obscure reason, is placed at the end of the constitution instead of the beginning. Three thousand words are required to list all the guarantees of individual liberty and social justice. There shall be no arbitrary imprisonment, no unreasonable searches or seizures, no denial of the right to assemble and petition peacefully for the redress of grievances.[10] The death penalty is absolutely forbidden. Freedom of religious belief is assured. So, too, is freedom of the press, though in such cautious terms as

10 Art. 187.

to amount almost to a denial of such freedom. In fact, virtually all these guarantees are hedged with qualifications and restrictions. Most common is the phrase: "with such exceptions as the law may indicate."

Social guarantees. As in most of the recent constitutions, a great deal of space is devoted to social reform. Work is declared to be an obligation. The work week is fixed at forty-four hours, annual vacations with pay are assured, minimum wages are prescribed, and the right to strike is guaranteed, "with such exceptions as the law may indicate." Women shall be entitled to full pay without work for a suitable period before and after the birth of their children; the employment of minors under the age of fourteen years is prohibited (except in those cases permitted by law); employers must establish a suitable number of apprenticeships.[11] The constitution devotes a great deal of space to family relationships. Illegitimate children, equally with legitimate offspring, have the right to receive shelter and education from their parents, and to inherit property.[12]

Suspension of guarantees. The president is authorized to suspend the guarantees of the constitution in case of foreign war or internal commotion. He must, however, receive the consent of Congress if it is in session. If not, he must have the approval of the Council of State.[13] This body, whose functions are largely advisory, is composed of representatives of the several branches of the government—two members of Congress, the attorney general and controller general of the nation, a high officer of the armed forces, the president of the supreme court, and so on. It includes also two private citizens chosen by Congress.[14] The framers of the constitution endeavored to make certain that the president would never act solely on his own responsibility in suspending constitutional guarantees. They evidently tried their best to prevent dictatorial abuse of power. Their best, unfortunately, was not good enough.

Amendment of the constitution. The constitution is easily amended. Congress takes the initiative, passing the proposed amendment in exactly the same manner as any other law. The proposal is then put aside temporarily, until there has been another congressional election. This involves a delay of at least several months, and perhaps nearly two years. But during this interval the people have a chance to study the suggestion, and they can elect congressmen pledged to support or oppose it. The new

[11] Art. 164.
[12] Art. 164.
[13] Art. 94.
[14] Art. 145.

Congress then decides the matter.[15]   This method of amending the constitution, it will be noted, is almost exactly the same as in Peru.[16]

SUFFRAGE AND ELECTIONS.   The right to vote extends to both men and
women who have reached the age of twenty-one years.   Illiterates are
excluded, and so are members of the armed forces.   Priests and nuns are
permitted to vote, however; they are an important element of conservative
strength at every election.   The constitution declares that voting shall be
obligatory for men, and optional for women.   In practice penalties are
never enforced for failure to go to the polls.   The ballots are prepared by
the government from lists submitted by the several parties.   No provision
is made for an official envelope, as in most Latin American countries.
Arrangements designed to insure secrecy are not very satisfactory.

THE PRESIDENT: *Selection, term, qualifications, salary.*   The president of
the nation is chosen by direct popular vote for a term of four years, and is
not eligible for re-election, or election to the vice-presidency, until four years
have passed.   He must be a native-born citizen, at least thirty-five years of
age.   The constitution contains a long list of persons who may not be
chosen president—relatives of the retiring chief executive by blood or marriage, the retiring vice-president and cabinet ministers, as well as their
relatives, and those persons who have been cabinet ministers within six
months of the election.[17]   The salary of the president—about forty-five
hundred dollars a year, American money, plus trifling allowances—is
absurdly small, even for a poor country.   But the presidential residence is
the imposing Palace of Government, a two-story stone building dating from
colonial times, which faces the Plaza Independencia in the center of Quito.

Executive and legislative powers.   As might well be expected, the president's powers are extensive.   He appoints and removes all administrative
officers and employees,[18] including the members of his own cabinet, without the necessity of consulting anyone.   He appoints and removes, also,
the members of the diplomatic and consular service and high officers of
the army and navy, but with the approval of Congress.   The Council of
State passes upon these appointments if Congress is not in session.   The
president plays no part in the selection of judges.   His control of foreign
relations follows the usual pattern.   He makes treaties, which must be sub-

[15] Art. 190.
[16] See page 373.
[17] Art. 85.
[18] Except the attorney general, controller general, and superintendent of banks.   These officers are chosen by the two houses of Congress, sitting as a single body, from lists submitted
by the president.

mitted for ratification to the two houses of Congress sitting as a single body. In this form Congress also declares war, though its course is really set for it by the chief executive through his dealings with other nations. Bills may be presented to Congress by the president. Most of the important laws do in fact come from this source. The president has the customary ten days in which to decide whether he will sign or veto a measure presented by Congress. His veto may be overridden by the two houses of Congress, sitting as a single body. An ordinary majority is sufficient for this purpose. If, however, the president objects to a bill on the ground that it is unconstitutional, instead of merely inexpedient, it must go to the supreme court after repassage by Congress. The supreme court's decision is final. The president may call special sessions of Congress, and may then limit its discussions to matters listed in his summons.

The power of pardon. The pardoning power of the chief executive is narrowly restricted. He may not grant forgiveness for criminal offenses without a previous recommendation from a court of law and endorsement of this recommendation by the Council of State. Under no circumstances may he grant a pardon before trial and conviction. Congress, however, may pardon individuals or groups for political offenses, and may even grant general amnesty for common crimes. The constitution specifies that such action may be taken only "when some grave reason demands it," [19] but permits the legislative body to determine the existence of a grave reason.

Vice-president; presidential succession. The vice-president of the nation is chosen at the same time as the president, in the same manner, and for the same term. He must, of course, possess the same qualifications. His only active duty is to preside over the Senate. The order of presidential succession, below the vice-president, is: president of the Chamber of Deputies, vice-president of the Senate,[20] and vice-president of the Chamber of Deputies. These officers are chosen by their respective houses.

THE CABINET. The number of cabinet ministers is not specified in the constitution. At present there are eight: government, foreign relations, education, economy, national defense, public works, social security, and treasury. Each minister is required to be a natural-born citizen, at least thirty years of age. The constitution establishes—at least on paper—a modified form of parliamentary government. Every presidential order must be countersigned by the appropriate minister, who thereby makes himself responsible. Congress, sitting as a single body, may censure any

[19] Art. 53, Cl. 16.
[20] The vice-president of the nation is the president of the Senate.

cabinet minister. He must then resign, and may not assume another cabinet post for two years. In practice Congress has not acquired the habit of forcing the removal of ministers. It has preferred to strike directly at the president, compelling his resignation by legal or extralegal means.

CONGRESS: *Selection, terms, qualifications, salaries.* Congress is composed of the customary two houses. The Senate has forty-four members. In general there are two senators from each province, but the sparsely populated eastern provinces and the Galápagos Islands (which did not acquire the status of a province until 1945) are permitted only one senator apiece. The total number of senators chosen from the several provinces is only thirty-three; the eleven remaining members of the upper chamber are known as "functional" senators, and represent various economic or cultural groups. The universities, for example, elect their own representatives; so do the schools maintained by the Catholic Church. There are senators representing the agricultural, commercial, industrial, and labor interests of the coastal strip, and other senators representing the corresponding interests of the high plateau. These senators are chosen by the official spokesmen of their respective groups—agricultural associations, labor unions, and the like. All senators serve for four years, and are eligible for immediate re-election. Save for the functional members, they are elected by direct vote of the people. Senators must be native-born citizens, at least thirty-five years of age. They have, therefore, the same minimum qualifications as the president. The Chamber of Deputies has fifty-six members, chosen by direct popular vote for two-year terms. They too must be native-born citizens, but the minimum age is twenty-five years. The salary for both senators and deputies is approximately nine American dollars per working day.

Sessions. Congress meets in regular annual session on August 10, and continues for sixty days. It may, however, extend the session an additional thirty days by vote of a majority of its members. Special sessions may be called not only by the president of the nation, but also by the president of Congress (that is, the vice-president of the nation). The president of Congress may not act, however, unless presented with a written request signed by two thirds of the total membership of the two houses. This is a virtually impossible requirement. In practice, therefore, the president of the nation determines whether special sessions are necessary. For many years he has commonly decided that they were not.

Organization and procedure. Each house chooses its own officers and assistants—except, of course, that the Senate has no voice in the selection of its president. The officers normally serve but one year and are not re-elected. Together they form a steering committee (*mesa directiva*), which names the regular standing committees. These committees do not play a decisive part in the enactment of laws. They must report on all measures, and their recommendations are frequently disregarded. Debate presents no unusual features. Disagreements between the two houses are decided by a joint meeting, in which every member has one vote.

Joint sessions. Although Congress has two houses, the constitution speci-fies many occasions on which they shall meet as one. Some of the matters requiring joint consideration have already been mentioned: approval of treaties, declaration of war, censure of cabinet ministers, consideration of bills over the president's veto, reconciliation of divergent legislative pro-posals. There are others also: election of judges of the supreme and superior courts; election of the attorney general, the controller general, and the superintendent of banks; consideration of presidential appoint-ments requiring the consent of Congress; enactment of the annual budget; final action on proposed constitutional amendments; acceptance or rejection of the president's resignation; consideration of any proposal to declare the president physically or mentally incapacitated.[21] In no other country of Latin America does Congress meet in joint session for so many different purposes. Even in Ecuador, however, joint sessions are the exception rather than the rule.

THE COURTS. The judicial system follows the customary Spanish pat-tern. Juries are used in criminal cases, however, but the jurors are lawyers. The courts are specifically forbidden to declare laws unconstitu-tional, except in those cases where the president and Congress hold conflict-ing views.[22] The supreme court has fifteen members, chosen by Congress, as we have just seen. Their term of office is six years, and they are eligible for immediate re-election. For most matters the supreme court sits in three divisions. Each division has five judges, and handles all types of cases, instead of specializing in different aspects of the law. Below the supreme court are eight superior courts, whose principal task is to hear cases on appeal from the lower tribunals. The judges of these courts, also, are selected by Congress. They serve for four years. Then there are the courts of first instance, whose judges are chosen for two-year terms.

INTERNAL ORGANIZATION. Each one of Ecuador's seventeen provinces has a governor appointed by the president for an indefinite period. The gov-

---

[21] Art. 55.
[22] See page 471.

ernor has a threefold task: to administer the internal affairs of the province, to enforce national laws, and to guide local political activity into "approved" channels, keeping a sharp watch for possible revolutions. The governor regulates most matters by decree. Although there is a popularly elected assembly in each province, its duties are relatively unimportant. The provinces are divided into cantons, and there are eighty-six cantons in all Ecuador. Each rural canton is governed by a political chief, who is appointed by the president of the nation. An urban canton, however, acquires the status of a municipality, and then receives a certain measure of self-government. Its voters normally choose their own mayors and councils, who perform a considerable number of routine functions. Below the cantons are the smallest units of local government—the parishes. In urban cantons the parishes are unimportant, but in rural cantons they are the centers of local government. The principal officer of a rural parish is the political lieutenant, who is appointed by the president of the republic upon the recommendation of the provincial governor. The political lieutenant represents authority for the uneducated masses. "He is nothing less than the conquistador in twentieth-century dress. He is government as no president ever was." [23]

SELECTED REFERENCES

Bemelmans, Ludwig, *The Donkey Inside,* New York, Viking Press, 1941.

Blanksten, George I., *Ecuador: Constitutions and Caudillos,* Berkeley, University of California Press, 1951.

Estrada, Víctor Emilio, *La Tragedia Monetaria del Ecuador,* Guayaquil, Ecuador. Litografía La Reforma, 1945.

Franklin, Albert B., *Ecuador; Portrait of a People,* New York, Doubleday, Doran, 1943.

Gallegos, Luis Gerardo, *Defendiendo a la Patria,* Riobamba, Ecuador, Imp. del Colegio Maldonado, 1945.

Lasso, Raphael V., *The Wonderland of Ecuador,* New York, Alpha-Ecuador Publications, 1944.

Linke, Lilo, *Andean Adventure; A Social and Political Study of Colombia, Ecuador and Bolivia,* London, Hutchinson, 1945.

López Arteta, Fidel Alberto, *La Reforma del Seguro Social en la República del Ecuador,* Montreal, Canada, International Labor Office, 1944.

Moreno, Julio, *El Sentido Histórico y la Cultura,* Quito, Litografía Romero, 1941.

Partido Socialista Ecuatoriano, *Un Año de Lucha Socialista,* Quito, Editora Socialista, 1942.

Paz y Miño, Luis Telmo, *La Población del Ecuador,* Quito, Tall. Gráf. de Educación, 1942.

[23] George I. Blanksten's previously cited work, p. 156.

Pino Ycaza, Gabriel, *Derecho Territorial Ecuatoriano,* Guayaquil, Ecuador, Universidad de Guayaquil, 1945.

Reyes, Oscar E., *Los Ultimos Siete Años,* Quito, Tall. Gráf. Nacionales, 1933.

Robalino Dávila, Luis, *Orígenes del Ecuador de Hoy,* Quito, Tall. Gráf. Nacionales, 1948.

Unión Nacional de Periodistas, *Realidad y Posibilidad del Ecuador,* Quito, Imp. del Ministerio de Hacienda, 1946.

von Hagen, Victor Wolfgang, *Ecuador and the Galápagos Islands,* Norman, University of Oklahoma Press, 1949.

Zevallos Reyre, Francisco, *Lecciones de Derecho Constitucional,* 2nd ed., Guayaquil, Impr. de la Universidad, 1947.

CHAPTER 18

URUGUAY

~~~~~~

The Land and the People

UNUSUAL FEATURES. Uruguay is a utopian land. The soil is fertile, the climate good, the people literate, friendly, and prosperous. In many ways Uruguay is different from almost all the other nations of Latin America. It is the only one that lies entirely within the temperate zone, and this fact enables it to escape many of the health problems of its tropical neighbors. Sanitary conditions are certainly as good as in any part of Latin America, and very much better than in most countries. The death rate is low and there is not a great amount of communicable disease. Uruguayans are justifiably proud of their health record, though they readily admit that their temperate-zone location gives them a great advantage. They are proud, too, of their educational system, which is at least as good as any in Latin America. The law establishing compulsory education at the primary level is really enforced, so that almost everyone can read and write. Special emphasis is placed on vocational training for the masses, but cultural education is not neglected. The national university is highly regarded in other countries.

AREA, POPULATION, TERRAIN, TRANSPORTATION. Uruguay is the smallest country of the South American continent; its seventy-two thousand square miles are just about equal to the area of North Dakota. But it has more people (two and one-quarter million) than Paraguay. And though its area is limited, almost every square mile can be put to good use. There are no great mountains, as in most of Latin America. Instead there are gently rolling grass-covered hills, ideal for grazing. In 1519, when the great Portuguese navigator Magellan sailed up the Río de la Plata, it is said that a member of his crew cried out in Portuguese: "Monte vide eu!" ("I see a mountain!"). From this incident Montevideo received its name. But the "mountain" seen by the sailor was only a high hill, where a lighthouse stands today. The flatness of the terrain has greatly facilitated the nation's development. There are none of the problems that Andean countries must face in building railroads and highways. And as a result Uruguay has more miles of roads, in proportion to its area, than any other nation of Latin America. In Montevideo and its vicinity they are paved. Dirt roads are still used extensively in the interior, but they are maintained in good condition and can be used even in wet weather. The Uruguayan railroads are all built on the same gauge—a most unusual feature south of the United States.

CLIMATE. Although Uruguay is in the temperate zone, it escapes the severe winters of less favored lands. In Montevideo, the capital city, frost is practically unknown, though excessively high temperatures are almost equally rare. Other parts of the country are very nearly as fortunate. The annual rainfall is about forty inches, distributed more or less evenly throughout the year. Except in unusually dry years, therefore, water supply presents no problem.

RACES. The population of the country is almost exclusively white. There are a few mestizos and Indians in the interior, and an even smaller number of Negroes, most of whom have come from Brazil. The whites are mainly of Spanish origin, but the Italians represent a very substantial minority. There are also a good many Swiss, Germans, and English, as well as Brazilians and Argentines. The 1890s and early 1900s were eventful in Uruguayan life; they witnessed a great wave of immigration from Europe, which has had a marked influence on the nation's development.

STOCK RAISING. Stock raising has always been the chief industry. Nearly all the land is devoted to pasture. Uruguay supplies almost one fifth of the world's meat exports, as well as large quantities of wool and hides. The most recent livestock census shows that there are at least nine sheep for every man, woman, and child. Cattle are less numerous, but they play an important part in the economic life of the nation. In the early days, when both sheep and cattle were small and of inferior quality, wool and hides were most important. The meat was salted and sold as jerked beef. But just before the turn of the present century the Uruguayans began to observe the success of the Argentines in selling frozen meat to Europe. The first step in this success story had been the improvement of Argentine herds; large numbers of pure-bred cattle had been imported from Europe at great expense. Meanwhile the mechanical processes for transporting meat had been perfected. And as a result Argentine meat exports had risen rapidly, bringing great wealth to the nation. So Uruguay decided to adopt similar tactics. Its first modern plant for freezing meat began operations in 1904. Its registrations of imported stock multiplied sixfold between 1903 and 1908. And soon its exports of frozen and canned meat, like those of Argentina, took a sharp swing upward.[1] Together with wool exports, they now dominate Uruguay's export trade almost completely. The decline of meat and wool exports since 1950 has had some unpleasant effects on the economy of the nation.

AGRICULTURE AND MINING. Agriculture deserves brief mention, though it pales into insignificance when compared with stock raising. It provides a living for not more than five per cent of the people. Wheat, oats, and corn are grown, though not always in sufficient quantities to supply domestic needs. Vegetables are raised for the local market. The only major export crop is linseed, which is extremely important in the manufacture of paints. Mining plays a very small part in the Uruguayan economy. There are some known deposits of coal—mostly of low quality—and some traces of silver, gold, copper, manganese, and iron. Vast mineral riches are not likely to be unearthed.

INDUSTRY. Manufacturing has developed slowly, but is becoming steadily more important. The government has encouraged this growth by permitting machinery and raw materials to enter free of duty, while imposing heavy tariffs on most manufactured goods. As might well be supposed, the products of the meat industry are first by a wide margin. But wine, beer, and denatured alcohol are made in large quantities. The woolen textile industry has grown rapidly in the last ten years. Leather goods represent a substantial part of the total. Chemical and glass factories have been opened recently. There are a few small iron and steel plants, but the future of heavy industry seems to hold little promise, despite the adoption of plans for the large-scale development of hydroelectric power.

TOURISTS. The tourist trade provides a substantial part of the national income. There are nearly two hundred miles of fine beaches, and many excellent hotels. Wealthy Argentine families like to spend the summer months at Uruguayan shore resorts, so as to escape the oppressive heat of Buenos Aires. Even Brazilians come to Uruguay in the summer, es-

[1] The development of the meat industry is discussed by Simon G. Hanson in his excellent volume, *Utopia in Uruguay*, Chap. XII.

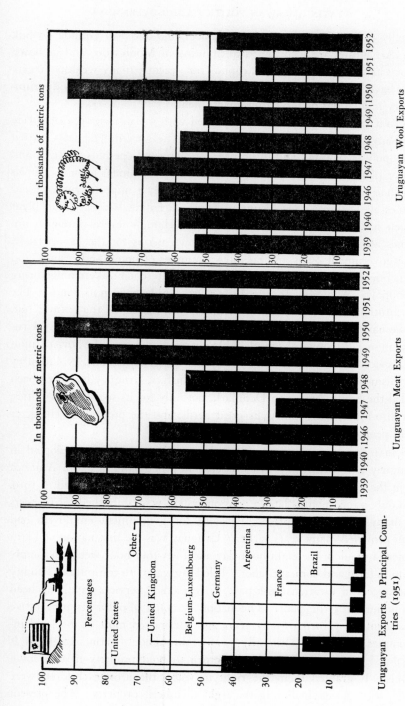

In thousands of metric tons

Uruguayan Wool Exports

1939 1940 1946 1947 1948 1949 1950 1951 1952

In thousands of metric tons

Uruguayan Meat Exports

1939 1940 1946 1947 1948 1949 1950 1951 1952

Percentages

United States

United Kingdom

Belgium-Luxembourg

Germany

Other

Argentina

France

Brazil

Uruguayan Exports to Principal Countries (1951)

Based on information obtained from the May, 1953, issue of *International Financial Statistics*, a publication of the International Monetary Fund.

pecially from the southern states of São Paulo and Rio Grande do Sul. The Argentines are accustomed to thinking of Montevideo and its beach resorts as suburbs of their own capital, but recently many wealthy Argentines have been deterred from making their annual pilgrimage by discriminatory regulations of the Perón government.

SOCIALISM. Uruguay has experimented with socialism more extensively than any other nation of Latin America. The government has a virtual monopoly of banking and insurance. It owns and operates the light and power plants, and also the telephones. One government agency controls the state monopoly of cement, alcohol, and fuel; it imports crude oil and refines all Uruguay's petroleum. There is a national refrigeration plant which has a monopoly on domestic meat, though several foreign companies are permitted to maintain their own plants for the export trade. The government owns and operates a number of hotels and casinos, and even one night club. It has established a state chemical manufacturing monopoly. About one fourth of the railroad mileage is in its hands. The constitution declares that all mineral deposits belong to the nation; but, as we have already seen, they have not been developed extensively. Uruguayan socialism is not the result of bloody revolution, as in the Soviet Union or Mexico. It resembles more nearly the quiet, democratic, evolutionary socialism of the Scandinavian countries. In fact, Uruguay has often been called the South American Denmark, not only for its socialistic activities, but also for its flat country, its great herds, and the progressive character of its people.

SOCIAL REFORMS. An extensive social security program was adopted in Uruguay long before it was considered in other parts of Latin America or in the United States. An old age assistance law was adopted in 1919, and only a few months later a pension system was established for workers in many private enterprises. Pensions for government employees had been provided many years earlier. Uruguay was the first nation of Latin America to adopt the eight-hour day and forty-four-hour week, and apply them to farm and domestic labor. It led the way with compulsory liability insurance and vacations with pay. Free medical services have long been maintained for the poor. The nation is noted also for its progressive treatment of women. Many years ago it removed most of the legal inequalities that still commonly persist throughout Latin America. It legalized divorce and permitted women to hold property in their own names. It granted them the right to vote. Illegitimate children were given legal status, including the right to inherit property. The present children's code provides for obligatory investigation of paternity. Uruguay's progressive record is surprising, for it was established at a time when most of the neighboring countries were highly conservative.[2]

MONTEVIDEO. Montevideo, the capital city, dominates almost completely the life of the nation. It is the leading port because it has by far the best harbor, strategically located at the junction of the Río de la Plata and the Atlantic Ocean. It is the hub of the railroad and highway system. Within its borders or close at hand are virtually all the nation's manufacturing plants. So are the national university, the national museums of history and fine arts, the national library, the great theaters. Every phase of national life finds its center in Montevideo. It has seven hundred and fifty thousand people—more than one third of the entire population of the country. No other city in the world dominates a nation so completely. The second city, Paysandú, is only one fourteenth as large. Montevideo is essentially a modern city; its newer sections have broad, tree-lined avenues and palm-shaded gardens and plazas. But there still remains the old quarter, where the colonial atmosphere has never disappeared. Here the houses have grilled windows, red-tiled roofs, and colorful patios. For the American tourist Montevideo has less to offer than big, brilliant Buenos Aires, just across the Río de la Plata. But for its residents it offers as pleasant living as any city in the world.

INTERNATIONAL RELATIONS. Uruguay is a buffer state, and this fact has conditioned its entire history. Wits sometimes say that it is an Argentine province in Brazilian territory—a description that contains more than a grain of truth. In the first days of independence it was a part of the Argentine confederation,[3] long before the establishment of a true Argentine nation. Later it was incorporated with Brazil under the name of the Cisplatine Province. After several years of bitter fighting it again became a part of Argentina, and finally, in 1828, an independent nation.

Uruguay owes its independence largely to the fact that neither Argentina nor Brazil is willing to see it become a part of the other. Uruguayan statesmen must continually bear in mind that they are sandwiched between two great powers. They must remember that the country has neither the men nor the resources to defend itself in a protracted struggle. It is for this reason that Uruguay has always been a leader in plans for mutual defense within the American hemisphere. In 1945, at the Conference

---

[2] See Mary M. Cannon's *Social and Labor Problems of Peru and Uruguay*, published in 1945 by the Women's Bureau of the United States Department of Labor.

[3] The confederation was then known as the United Provinces of La Plata.

of Chapultepec, it joined with Colombia and Brazil in calling for an agreement to prevent, by armed force if necessary, any attack upon the territory or political integrity of an American nation. The following year it proposed collective action by the nations of the Western Hemisphere against any American country defaulting on its international obligations or denying to its own people "the elementary rights of man and of citizen." These suggestions never reached the form of binding treaties, but they underscore the Uruguayan point of view. Like most small nations, Uruguay is interested in internationalism.[4]

The Pattern of Politics

FIRST DECADES OF INDEPENDENCE. The modern history of Uruguay as an enlightened democratic nation does not begin until 1903. Prior to that time there was the usual succession of dictatorships and civil wars. More than a century ago the political differences of rival factions led to the formation of two political parties, the Colorados (Reds) and Blancos (Whites), and even today these two parties dominate the life of the nation. The Colorados were the liberals; they opposed the great power of the landed aristocracy and the Catholic Church. The conservative Blancos, of course, wished to retain the old order. Rather than submit to change, they threw in their lot with the Argentine Dictator Juan Manuel de Rosas, and agreed that Uruguay once again should join the United Provinces of La Plata. In 1843 the Blanco forces, together with an Argentine army, began the so-called nine years' siege of Montevideo, which was interrupted by the arrival of English and French troops seeking satisfaction for the bad treatment of their citizens. The siege was permanently lifted in 1851, when Brazil sent an army and a fleet to aid the Colorado cause. The Brazilian forces were completely successful, and Argentina abandoned its attempts to force Uruguay to join the confederation.

But peace did not come to the little republic. Within three years it plunged into another bloody civil war which continued sporadically for more than twenty years. During this period both Brazil and Argentina occasionally took a hand in Uruguayan affairs, often at the urgent request of some Uruguayan president or would-be president. Between 1865 and 1870 Uruguay joined forces with Argentina and Brazil in a war against Paraguay.[5] The Colorado leader, General Venancio Flores, returned to

---

[4] See George Pendle's compact but interesting work, published in 1952, *Uruguay: South America's First Welfare State.*

[5] See pages 512–514.

Montevideo before the end of the struggle in order to resume the duties of the presidency, but only a few months later he was assassinated. Thereupon the civil war flared anew. Both Colorados and Blancos seemed to assume that the field of battle was the only place to settle their differences.

REVOLUTIONS. In 1876 General Lorenzo Latorre proclaimed himself president of the nation. He had the support of the army, so opposition leaders were in no position to contest his authority. After a few years, however, he lost some of his army support and was forced to resign. Other presidents came and went in rapid succession. Another revolution broke out in 1891, but was quickly suppressed. In 1897 there was another uprising, which at one time seemed on the point of overthrowing the government. Before its final collapse the president was assassinated. The new provisional president thereupon dissolved Congress, and declared himself dictator. In 1899 he managed to have himself elected president for a full four-year term. But his anti-clerical reforms were unpopular in many circles and he narrowly escaped assassination.[6]

BATLLE Y ORDÓÑEZ: *Early years.* Dictatorship, revolution, civil war— these played major roles in the history of Uruguay until 1903. There was no evidence that the nation stood on the threshold of a new period of peace, prosperity, and liberal democracy. Nor did the events of the next eighteen months indicate such a happy transformation, for they were marred by another civil war. But the new order was just around the corner. It was largely the work of one man—José Batlle y Ordóñez, who was elected president in 1903 by the Colorado Party.[7] Batlle soon proved himself one of the outstanding statesmen of Latin America. He had already made a distinguished record in public and private life. The son of a former president, he had served as governor (*jefe político*) of one of the departments, and also as senator from Montevideo. He studied law, but journalism was his chosen profession. When still in his teens he served as editor of a Montevideo newspaper, *La Nación.* At the age of twenty he founded *El Día,* and soon made it the most widely read and influential paper in the country.

Fight for social justice. At this time the Colorado Party controlled Uruguay, as it had for many years. There were several departments domi-

---

[6] Pablo Blanco Acevedo traces the history of this period in great detail in his massive *Historia del Uruguay,* published in six volumes. A more concise account is *Historia de la Independencia de la República Oriental del Uruguay,* by Pedro Riva-Zucchelli.

[7] The late Percy A. Martin published an excellent article, "The Career of José Batlle y Ordóñez," in the November, 1930, issue of the *Hispanic American Historical Review* (Vol. X, No. 4), pp. 413–428.

nated almost completely by the Blancos, but the Colorados always succeeded in naming the president. Whether their choice represented the will of the people was quite immaterial. The Colorados were in the saddle and meant to stay there. Although José Batlle was a Colorado, he had no patience with this viewpoint. He constantly urged his belief that the Colorado Party must adopt democratic ways and make itself worthy of popular support. It must strive for social justice. It must revise its political system. It must make Uruguay a progressive modern nation, instead of a semifeudal land. This was the message that he constantly spread across the pages of his newspaper.

First term. In 1903 the Colorados made Batlle president. He was then thirty-eight years of age. But he had little opportunity to establish political or social reforms, for almost at once his authority was challenged by the Blancos. The rebellion was costly in lives and money, but it was finally crushed in a decisive battle on the first day of September, 1904. The Blanco leader was wounded so severely that he died a few days later. The rest of President Batlle's term was required to restore normal conditions throughout the nation. By his conduct in war and peace he had greatly enhanced his prestige, and many persons thought that he should offer himself for re-election, despite a constitutional prohibition of two successive terms. But Batlle was not the man to abandon his belief in orderly constitutional government. He refused to permit his name to be considered by the General Assembly (the Congress of the nation) which chose the president in those days. Instead he gave his support to Dr. Claudio Williman, who was elected with ease. Batlle might easily have remained the power behind the throne. Instead he sailed for Europe and remained there the next four years, thus giving his successor a free hand. President Williman proved himself a capable and enlightened executive. He secured the adoption of some of Batlle's reforms, especially in the field of education.

Second term. As the time drew near to choose a new president, the Colorados announced that once again they would support Batlle y Ordóñez. There was no other candidate who could match his prestige and the General Assembly elected him without serious opposition. His second term extended from 1911 to 1915. During those years he forced through the General Assembly, almost by the sheer weight of his personality, the social reforms that had long been a part of his creed. The eight-hour working day was established at this time; so were compensation for industrial accidents and government inspection of factories. The death penalty for crime was abolished; probation and parole were made a part of the system of Uruguayan justice. The nation embarked upon its extensive program of public ownership. The conservatives were outraged, of course. Some of them openly questioned Batlle's sanity. But the President had his way, and Uruguay became one of the leaders of the modern trend toward state socialism.

Political reform. Batlle's restless mind concerned itself also with the structure of government. While he was in Europe, in the interval between his two terms, he had time to consider the unhappy history of his beloved country, and he wondered why it had been afflicted with so many civil wars. Finally he decided that the presidential system must be to blame. Every president was virtually a dictator, for neither the General Assembly nor the courts could offer effective resistance to his policies. Every president had the opportunity to name his own successor and thus perpetuate the rule of his own clique. The opposition was powerless to combat the president by peaceful means; therefore it turned inevitably to revolution. So the only solution, as Batlle saw it, was to eliminate the all-powerful president. But what could be put in his place? In Switzerland Batlle found the answer he had been seeking. Switzerland had a plural executive—a federal council of seven members, who jointly performed all the functions that would normally be the responsibility of a president. One of its members was designated as president of the council, but he served in that capacity for but a single year and had virtually no more authority than the other members. Here, thought Batlle, was an ideal arrangement. If only he could transplant it to Uruguay, he would solve the nation's basic political problem.

Plural executive? When, therefore, he assumed the presidency for the second time, he promptly announced his sponsorship of a project to eliminate the office of president and substitute an executive council, whose members would be chosen by direct vote of the people. The first reaction of the people to this suggestion was shocked disbelief. The first reaction of the politicians was utter scorn. Most of the newspapers published editorials and cartoons ridiculing the idea; the only important exception was Batlle's own paper, *El Día*. One of the other important dailies conducted a survey among lawyers, professors, and publicists, and found them overwhelmingly opposed. Most of the leaders of the Colorado Party, despite their desire to support their own president, called the scheme visionary. But Batlle refused to admit defeat. Through the columns of his influential paper he constantly urged the elimination of the presidency. A number of younger statesmen in the Colorado Party finally endorsed the scheme. People were undoubtedly influenced by the force of Batlle's personality, if not the force of his arguments. By the end of his second term he had succeeded in making the plural executive a major issue in the nation's political life.

A hotly debated issue. The next president, who had been endorsed by Batlle, continued his predecessor's progressive policies. But social and educational reforms were almost forgotten as Uruguayans debated the burning question: Should the nation change its form of government? There was general agreement that some modifications were necessary, for the constitution had been adopted in 1830 and had been amended only once. Many of its clauses reflected the spirit of an age long dead. So the General Assembly passed a law providing for the popular election of the members of a constitutional convention, which was to meet in Montevideo in the early months of 1917. Batlle and his friends thereupon renewed their demands for a plural executive. The Blancos, who habitually opposed Batlle's projects, raised strenuous objections. So did a good many Colorados, though they were willing to accept the ex-President's leadership in most matters. Feeling ran so high within the Colorado Party that it finally split into two factions. Those remaining loyal to Batlle were generally known as Colorados Batllistas. The others called themselves the Colorados Riveristas, taking their name from José Fructuoso Rivera, a Uruguayan patriot of the early days.

Compromise. When all the votes had been counted, it became clear that the Batlle faction had suffered a decisive defeat in its attempt to gain control of the constitutional convention. But its leaders were not willing to accept this popular verdict. Instead they tried to find some way to turn their loss into victory. Finally they announced that Batlle would seek a third presidential term, from 1919 to 1923. The Blancos, or Nationalists, as they now commonly called themselves, were aghast at the mere thought of four more years of the hated radical. Yet they knew that there was no way to stop his election, short of revolution, for his followers still controlled the General Assembly, which named the president. In a short time, however, it became clear that Batlle did not really wish a third term. He would be willing to withdraw his name as a presidential candidate, if the constitutional convention would accept his conditions. At last a compromise was reached. A majority of the delegates agreed to restrict the powers of the president, and even to establish some sort of executive council. Batlle and his friends reluctantly abandoned their hope of abolishing the presidency. And the third term movement was quietly dropped.

Reform of the presidency. In its final form, the compromise concerning the executive was exceedingly strange. Some students of government have called it almost fantastic. Executive power was divided between a president and a National Council of Administration. The president was to be elected by the people for a term of four years, without eligibility for immediate re-election. The nine members of the National Council, also popularly chosen, were to serve for six-year terms, one third of the membership being renewed every two years. It was further provided that at every biennial election for members of the Council, the party receiving the largest number of votes should receive two of the three seats, while the remaining seat should go to the leading minority party, regardless of the number of votes it might poll. The obvious purpose of this clause was to assure three of the nine seats on the National Council to the Blancos, even if they did not succeed in winning one third of the total vote. The National Council was to have charge of many phases of the public administration—education, health, public works, industrial relations. It was also to assume responsibility for preparing the national budget. The president, on the other hand, was to control foreign relations, national defense, agriculture, and a number of other matters. Thus no one person—not even one group of persons—was to be responsible for all administrative activities.

Other constitutional features. After the adoption of this compromise, the constitutional convention had little difficulty in writing the other provisions of the new constitution. Members of the Chamber of Deputies should be popularly elected, but senators should be chosen through the medium of an electoral college. The units of local government—departments and municipalities—should be given a considerable measure of local autonomy. The secret ballot should be used in all elections. Church and state should be separated, for the first time in Uruguayan history. In brief outline, then, this was the new constitution that the convention prepared. It was submitted to the people on November 25, 1917, and received the necessary majority. Early in 1919 it went into effect.[8]

PRESIDENT BRUM. At the same time that the new constitution was adopted, Dr. Baltasar Brum became president of the nation. He was one of Batlle's closest associates and had been a leader in the fight for a plural

[8] See the previously cited article by Percy A. Martin in the *Hispanic American Historical Review.*

executive. Indeed, he did not abandon this idea, even as president. In 1922 he proposed that the presidency be abolished and its functions transferred to the National Council of Administration. But his suggestion aroused no popular response. The issue had been decided and few people seemed disposed to reopen it. At the time of his election, President Brum was only thirty-six years of age. He had already served with distinction as minister of foreign affairs, and had made substantial contributions to the cause of Pan Americanism. As president he continued Batlle's progressive policies and took a number of important steps that improved the country's financial condition. He was an excellent administrator and a statesman of great vision.

DICTATORSHIP. The 1920s were quiet and relatively uneventful. The Colorados, though continuing to fight among themselves, managed to retain control of the government. Elections were honest, and the people were happy with a comparatively high standard of living. By 1933, however, there was considerable unrest. The world depression had shaken Uruguay's economic structure to its very foundations. Prices of meat and wool had dropped sharply, and wages had been similarly reduced. The president of the nation at this time was Gabriel Terra, a lawyer with a flair for politics. Like his predecessors for many years, he was a member of the Colorado Party. The great Batlle was dead. People were becoming increasingly critical of President Terra's policies, and the General Assembly was displaying unwonted independence. The National Council of Administration, as usual, was carrying on its own activities with almost no regard for any of the other branches of the government. Its six Colorados and three Blancos were quarreling continuously with one another.

On March 31, 1933, a serious uprising occurred—the first major disturbance in nearly thirty years. President Terra suppressed it with a firm hand, and then used this incident as an excuse to establish a dictatorship. He ordered the arrest of his political opponents, and the police were soon busy with their unaccustomed task of rounding up all prominent enemies of the regime. Some were thrown into jail; others managed to escape to Argentina or Brazil. Former President Brum committed suicide. The nation was governed largely by decree. Yet the dictatorship was exceedingly mild by Latin American standards. Most people continued to say what they thought about the government, without fear of molestation. Some mass meetings of protest were held without interference from the police. Meanwhile President Terra appointed eight prominent citizens to assist him in the task of governing the nation. At the same time he announced that the new regime was only temporary. It would be replaced by constitutional government as soon as a new constitution could be prepared and adopted.

CONSTITUTION OF 1934. A constitutional convention worked on the draft of the new document for several months and finally submitted its work to a popular plebiscite on March 21, 1934. The voters expressed their approval by a substantial majority. The new constitution, which largely reflected the ideas of President Terra, made substantial changes in the structure of government. The National Council of Administration was abolished and its powers transferred to the president, who thus became once more the dominant figure in the nation's political life. But the opposition was still assured a voice in the government by two very unusual provisions. First, the president must select three of the nine members of his cabinet from the leading minority party. Second, this party must be given one half of the seats in the Senate, thereby acquiring the opportunity to block all legislation. Nowhere else in the world has it been thought necessary to protect the rights of the minority by placing it on an equal footing with the majority in one branch of the legislature. The plan was foredoomed to failure.

GOVERNMENT BY DECREE. One of the last acts of the constitutional convention was to re-elect President Terra for another term of four years. Obviously it had no authority to do so; neither the constitution of 1919 nor the new document contemplated any such method of choosing the chief executive. But Terra controlled both the army and the civil administration, so there was little opportunity for plain citizens to protest effectively. The President disregarded the new constitution almost as completely as he had ignored the old. When he could not force his legislative proposals through the General Assembly he governed by decree. He was a confirmed socialist, and he used his broad powers to expand the scope of the government's economic activities. Finally his enemies rose in revolt, but the uprising was poorly planned and President Terra crushed it without difficulty. Shortly afterward his life was menaced by a political adversary, but he escaped with a leg wound.

RETURN TO DEMOCRACY. With the President apparently invulnerable to physical violence, it seemed that the opponents of the regime had no choice but to wait until 1938. President Terra let it be known that he would respect the clause of the constitution prohibiting another term. As the time approached, political activity reached a new peak. The two leading candidates were Terra's brother-in-law and son-in-law. The brother-in-law won. His name was Alfredo Baldomir, and he was an architect who had served in the army for many years and risen to the rank of general. Politics was also one of his major interests; he had served as minister of war and as chief of police of Montevideo. At the time of his election he was fifty-four years old, tall and gray haired, with the bearing of a professional soldier. Throughout the campaign he constantly stressed Uruguay's need for true democracy. He never quite said "a return to democracy"; that would have been too direct a criticism of President Terra. But he left no doubt in the minds of his listeners that he was promising a very different way of life. And, as soon as he had been inaugurated, he tried to fulfill that promise. He pardoned all political prisoners. He made a determined effort to work with the General Assembly. He even restored the National Council of Administration, thus restricting his own authority. Uruguay was learning once again the democratic way of life.

NAZI ACTIVITIES. The war in Europe brought fresh problems to the tiny nation. European markets for its products were partially shut off and it was unable to obtain many of the manufactured goods on which it normally depended. On December 13, 1939, the German pocket battleship *Graf Spee* was driven into Montevideo harbor by British warships. The Uruguayan government refused to permit it to make an extended stay, so it soon sailed away and was sunk by its own crew. Germany protested that Uruguay had been guilty of "unfriendliness." Meanwhile a Uruguayan fascist party had made its appearance and soon began an extensive propaganda campaign with funds obtained in part from the German embassy. The Uruguayan government answered this threat by adopting compulsory military service and modernizing its armaments. In June, 1940, it announced that it had unearthed a plot to transform the country into a German colony. Further revelations of Nazi activities led to a determined hunt for fifth columnists and the arrest of many suspects.

CO-OPERATION WITH THE UNITED STATES. The anti-Nazi policy led almost inevitably to closer co-operation with the United States. Uruguay agreed to establish naval and air bases for the defense of the Americas, and the United States promised to supply both money and technical skill in completing these projects. There was, of course, considerable opposition to these plans. Luis Herrera, the leader of the Blanco Party, advanced all the traditional arguments of the isolationists and spoke vehemently against "Yankee imperialism." The Blancos used their strategic position in the National Council of Administration and the Senate to prevent the enactment of badly needed laws. At every turn President Baldomir found himself handicapped by legal restrictions, some of which he had insisted on restoring to the constitution. In this atmosphere of crisis the date of the 1942 presidential election drew near. The Blancos offered sharp criticism of the government's "inaction," for which they were largely responsible. They campaigned with great vigor, apparently assuming that Baldomir would not attempt to prolong his term in some unconstitutional manner, as Terra had done.

POSTPONEMENT OF ELECTIONS. In January, 1942, one month after the Japanese attack at Pearl Harbor, Uruguay severed relations with the Axis powers. This was the signal for renewed demonstrations by Nazi sympathizers and Blanco adherents. In late February, with the election only a few weeks away, President Baldomir suddenly announced that it had been indefinitely postponed. This action was necessary, he explained, to combat the subversive forces that were trying to sap the strength of the nation. But postponement of the election was only temporary; he promised that it would be held at the earliest possible moment. Meanwhile he took vigorous steps to strengthen his own power. He replaced the Blanco members of his cabinet with his own supporters, in direct defiance of the constitutional requirements that three cabinet ministers must be members of the leading minority party. He told Congress that its services were no longer needed, and proceeded to govern by decree. At the same time he arranged for the preparation of a new constitution—the third in a little more than two decades. Baldomir the democrat had become Baldomir the dictator. But he still insisted that democracy was his true love; he was merely "clarifying" the political situation in order to make Uruguay safe for democracy.

PRESIDENTIAL ELECTION OF 1942. By late 1942 the political situation seems to have been sufficiently clarified for a resumption of popular government. November 29 was set as the new date for the presidential election, and the interrupted campaign got under way once more. The man picked by Baldomir as his successor was Juan José Amézaga, a sixty-one-year-old lawyer whose private practice had netted him a small fortune. Though scarcely a professional politician, he had served as assemblyman and cabinet minister and for a short time had represented his country in the League of Nations. He was known to be a thoroughgoing liberal and a firm friend of the United States. As president it was generally assumed that he would continue the progressive policies of the outgoing administration. The Blancos (or Nationalists) nominated their leader, Senator Luis Herrera, whose ringing pronouncements against the United States had brought him a certain following. There were other candidates also—an Independent Nationalist, two representatives of dissident factions of the Colorado Party, and a Communist. But everyone knew that the real fight would be between Amézaga and Herrera. The Uruguayan election law, written by the Colorado Party, provided that votes cast for candidates of a party's different factions would be pooled, and given to the party's candidate who stood highest in the balloting. This arrangement gave the Colorados a substantial advantage over the Blancos, whose two major factions were recognized as separate parties. When all the votes had been counted, it was announced that Amézaga had a margin of more than two to one over his principal opponent. The Colorados also captured both houses of the General Assembly, and a substantial majority of local offices throughout the country.

CONSTITUTIONAL CHANGES. The constitutional amendments submitted to the voters at the 1942 election were designed to take from the minority party its power to stalemate the government. One amendment provided for the abolition of the National Council of Administration, which Baldomir had insisted upon re-establishing at the beginning of his term, only to learn from bitter experience that it prevented co-ordinated control of the national administration. Another amendment specified that the political parties should be represented in the Senate in direct proportion to the number of votes received, thus eliminating the peculiar arrangement that gave to the minority one half of the total number of places. These changes were given popular approval, and the constitution thus lost some of its more obvious idiosyncracies.

ARGENTINE INFLUENCE. President Amézaga continued Uruguay's close co-operation with the United States throughout the war. This policy displeased not only the Blancos, who constantly urged a policy of strict neutrality, but also the military dictatorship that had seized control of the Argentine government. When Uruguay made its proposal for collective action against New World aggressors,[9] the Argentine ambassador called this act "a stab in the back." The Argentine government was further incensed by Uruguayan hospitality to Argentine political refugees.[10] When, therefore, the 1946 election drew near, President Perón threw the full weight of his influence against the Amézaga government. He emphasized his power by withholding from Uruguay its normal supply of Argen-

[9] See pages 481–482.
[10] See pages 55–56.

tine wheat, thus creating a bread shortage in the tiny nation. The ostensible reason for this step was the desperate plight of Europe, which undoubtedly needed as much Argentine wheat as it could obtain. But at the same time Perón made clear that more wheat could be found for a "friendly" Uruguay. "I'll give bread to the Uruguayan people," he declared, "but not one crumb to the politicians." He meant, of course, that he would not help the "wrong" politicians. For the "right" politicians he had unstinted praise—and, even more important, the promise of bread. Chief among these admirers of the Perón regime were the leaders of the Blanco Party, who urged close co-operation with Argentina instead of the United States.

PRESIDENTIAL CANDIDATES. The 1946 presidential candidate of the Blancos was their aged leader, Luis Herrera, who had been defeated on two previous occasions. The Colorados were badly split, as usual. Amézaga's faction, whose members called themselves the Colorados Batllistas and claimed to be the true political heirs of the great Batlle, chose Tomás Berreta as their presidential nominee. Born of poor parents on a small farm, Berreta never had the opportunity to obtain much education. He worked for a time as a common laborer and later as a rural policeman. But he joined the Batlle movement before it became the dominant force in Uruguayan politics, and rose gradually to important office as Batlle became the leader of the nation. In 1929 he was elected to the National Council of Administration; four years later he was forced to leave the country as President Terra systematically jailed or exiled his political opponents.[11] Later Berreta returned to Uruguay, and was elected a senator. He served as Amézaga's minister of public works. A humble man who had demonstrated unusual skill in picking competent subordinates, he made a strong appeal to the average voter. The chief objection to his candidacy was the precarious state of his health. At the time of his nomination he was seventy-one years old.

Because of the danger that Berreta might not survive four strenuous years as president, the Colorados Batllistas knew that they must exercise great care in selecting a vice-presidential candidate. They finally chose Luis Batlle Berres, the fifty-year-old favorite nephew of the late Batlle y Ordóñez. Luis Batlle possessed a number of assets in addition to a great name. For twenty-five years he had been a successful politician. He owned one of Montevideo's principal radio stations and had made its facilities available to Argentine refugees in defiance of Perón. There were

[11] See page 488.

other candidates also. One of them was former President Baldomir, who had quarreled with Amézaga over domestic policies, and now headed a dissident faction of the Colorado Party.

BERRETA AND BATLLE. The election was held on November 24, 1946. Berreta and Batlle were declared the winners, since the combined Colorado vote exceeded that of the Blancos by a substantial margin. The dominant government faction (Batllista) of the Colorados received the total party vote, of course, though many Colorado voters cast their ballots for other factions. In February, 1947, President-elect Berreta visited the United States and renewed his nation's pledges of close co-operation in continental defense. In March he was inaugurated as chief executive, but in August he died after a brief illness, and was succeeded by the vice-president. Thus another Batlle became president of Uruguay. But he governed with the uncertain support of a divided party, and never equaled the reputation of his distinguished uncle.

PRESIDENTIAL ELECTION OF 1950. As the presidential campaign of 1950 got under way, the Colorados were as badly split as ever. They failed to agree upon a single presidential candidate, despite numerous attempts to find someone who would be acceptable to all factions. Finally they decided to present three separate slates of presidential and vice-presidential nominees, all representing the Colorado Party and all advocating the same platform, with the understanding that the slate receiving the greatest number of votes would be credited with all the votes of the Colorados. This strategy was successful, as usual. Luis Herrera, the perennial presidential nominee of the Blancos, received more popular support than any one of the Colorados, but he lost the election because he could not match the combined Colorado strength. The winner was Andrés Martínez Trueba, leader of the Colorados' Batllista faction.

ABOLITION OF THE PRESIDENCY. In his inaugural address President Martínez Trueba revived a proposal that had previously agitated the nation—abolition of the office of president and creation of a plural executive. Batlle Ordóñez had advocated such a change, with only partial success. So had Baltasar Brum, without awakening any popular interest.[12] But Martínez Trueba struck a more responsive chord. He won the support of Luis Herrera, the opposition leader, and soon arranged for an unofficial bipartisan commission to work out the basic principles of constitutional reform. Congress then devoted two months to the details of the proposed change. So extensive were the amendments that they

12 See pages 485–487.

amounted to a new constitution. On December 16, 1951, this constitution was submitted to the voters, who approved it by an extremely narrow margin. The following March the new nine-member National Council of Government became Uruguay's plural executive, replacing the president of the nation. Martínez Trueba, the president who had deliberately talked himself out of a job, immediately acquired a new position. He was elected president (chairman) of the National Council of Government.[13]

The Structure of Government

THE CONSTITUTION: *Individual guarantees.* Uruguay's 1951 constitution is about three times as long as the constitution of the United States. Like so many of the fundamental laws of Latin America, it contains a great many details that might better have been left to ordinary legislation. There is no preamble. Instead the constitution begins with a statement of the nature of the state, and then proceeds to the usual lengthy enumeration of individual and social guarantees. The death penalty is forbidden. Prisons shall be regarded as places to re-educate criminals instead of punishing them.[14] The spoken and written word shall be inviolable, but abuses of this right shall be punished according to law.[15] Arbitrary arrest is prohibited; there shall be no unreasonable searches or seizures; freedom of movement in all parts of the nation is assured. And, as might well be expected, the usual qualification accompanies almost all these guarantees: they shall be exercised in such manner and with such exceptions as the law may determine. Equality of treatment is assured to all religions. Uruguay, which separated church and state in 1919,[16] nonetheless confirmed the title of the Catholic Church to all its properties used for religious purposes, even if built with public money. A large fund was raised by popular subscription at that time and turned over to the Church, in order to compensate it for its loss of public support.

Social guarantees. The so-called social guarantees, which have no place in the constitution of the United States, represent Uruguay's political philosophy of the present century. "The law will protect children from physical, intellectual, or moral neglect, and will prohibit their exploitation or abuse."[17] "Parents have the same obligation toward their natural chil-

---

[13] See "Adoption of a Collegiate Executive in Uruguay," by Russell H. Fitzgibbon, in the *Journal of Politics,* Nov., 1952, pp. 616–642.

[14] Art. 26.

[15] Art. 29.

[16] See page 487.

[17] Art. 41.

dren as toward those born within the bonds of wedlock." [18] "All the inhabitants have the duty of caring for their own health, and the obligation to seek aid or to assist themselves in case of illness. The state will assist those whose finances do not permit adequate medical care." [19] "Labor receives the special protection of the state. Every inhabitant of the republic, without prejudice to his liberty, has the duty of applying his physical or mental energy in such manner as to redound to the general welfare." [20] "The law will promote the organization of trade unions." [21] "Social security laws will be enacted in such form as to assure to all workers adequate financial protection from cases of accident, illness, or forced unemployment." [22] "Primary education is free and compulsory." [23]

Emergency powers. There is no clause specifically providing for the suspension of guarantees in time of emergency. The National Council of Government is authorized, however, to take such measures as may be necessary for the protection of the nation in case of foreign attack or domestic commotion. It may order any person's arrest or transfer from one part of the country to another, but may not impose punishment for alleged crimes. Any steps taken under this emergency power must be reported to the General Assembly within twenty-four hours—or, if it is not in session, to its Permanent Committee. Uruguay has an enviable reputation for respecting individual liberties.

Amendment of the constitution. The constitution may be amended in a number of different ways. If the proposal for change is submitted by the National Council of Government or by a member of the General Assembly, that body considers the matter and gives or withholds its approval. Should it approve, a constitutional convention is summoned to consider not only the original project but any other suggestions for constitutional change that may be presented. The people then pass upon the convention's work. Members of the convention are chosen by direct popular vote. Amendments may also be initiated by two fifths of the total membership of the General Assembly (thus eliminating the need for a constitutional convention), or by means of a petition signed by ten per cent of the total number of voters; in all cases the final decision is then made by the electorate. Uruguay is almost the only Latin American nation to re-

[18] Art. 42.
[19] Art. 44.
[20] Art. 53.
[21] Art. 57.
[22] Art. 67.
[23] Art. 70.

quire popular participation in the process of amending the constitution.[24]

SUFFRAGE AND ELECTIONS. The right to vote is extended to all citizens who have reached the age of eighteen years, without distinction of sex. Even illiterates may vote. So, too, may foreigners who have resided in the country at least fifteen years. The law declares that voting is not only a right but an obligation, and imposes a fine for failure to go to the polls without valid excuse. In practice, however, this statute is not enforced, and large numbers of persons absent themselves at every election. The ballots are prepared by the parties under state supervision. The usual official envelope is provided. A list system of proportional representation is used for legislative offices. Electors may indicate their preferences within the list of a single party, but may not split their votes among several parties.

THE NATIONAL COUNCIL OF GOVERNMENT. Under the terms of the 1917 constitution the president shared his powers with a National Council of Administration. The fundamental law of 1934 conferred upon him greater authority, but not enough to make him a really strong executive.[25] And then, in 1951, the office of president was abolished and its place was taken by a National Council of Government. This Council is composed of nine members, chosen by direct vote of the people for four years, and not eligible for immediate re-election. They must be natural-born citizens, at least thirty-five years of age. A double number of alternates is elected to take care of possible vacancies. Six of the Council's seats are reserved for the majority party; the other three go to the opposition.[26] One member of the Council is designated as its president, but he is merely the presiding officer, and serves in that capacity for only one year. The Council decides all questions by majority vote. It possesses the powers that are normally assigned to the president in other countries. It appoints all civil and military officials and employees of the government, including the members of the diplomatic service. For virtually all appointments to higher offices, however, it must have the consent of the Senate. Dismissals, also, are subject to Senate approval. The General Assembly, sitting as a single body, approves treaties and declares war. It may also override the National Council's veto of proposed legislation, a three-fifths vote being

[24] It should be noted, however, that Cuba's temporarily suspended constitution of 1940 makes provision for submitting proposed constitutional changes to the people under certain circumstances.

[25] See the privately printed monograph of Philip B. Taylor, Jr., *The Executive Power in Uruguay.*

[26] Arts. 151, 152.

necessary for this purpose. The National Council is not authorized to legislate by decree. Its members must secure the consent of the General Assembly before leaving the country for more than seven days.[27]

THE CABINET. In Switzerland, which obviously furnished the inspiration for the Uruguayan plural executive, the members of the Federal Council head the various ministries. In Uruguay, however, the members of the National Council of Government merely exercise a general supervision over the national administration, and jointly choose the cabinet ministers. The constitution declares that there shall be nine members of the cabinet, but adds that this number may be increased by a two-thirds vote of the General Assembly. To date the Assembly has made no attempt to change the number fixed by the constitution. The nine ministries are: Foreign Relations, Interior, Finance, National Defense, Public Instruction and Social Assistance, Agriculture and Stock Raising, Industry and Labor, Public Works, Public Health. The 1951 constitution, like its immediate predecessor, provides for the interpellation of ministers and for their resignation when the General Assembly votes *no confidence*. Either house of the General Assembly may present a resolution of censure, which is then considered by the two chambers sitting as a single body. The motion may be directed against one of the ministers or against the entire cabinet; if it is adopted by an absolute majority of the full membership, the minister or ministers are expected to resign.[28] But, obviously, the real object of legislative censure, in most cases, would be the National Council of Government, and its members cannot be reached by a vote of *no confidence*.

PUBLIC PERSONNEL. Selection of public personnel is largely on a spoils basis, as in most of Latin America, but there are elaborate safeguards against the dismissal of minor employees for political—or almost any other —reasons. There is no civil service commission.

GENERAL ASSEMBLY: *Selection, terms, qualifications.* The two houses of the General Assembly are known as the Senate and the Chamber of Representatives. The Senate has thirty-one members, chosen by direct vote of the people through a list system of proportional representation. All senators are chosen at large, the entire nation comprising the voting district. The Chamber of Representatives has ninety-nine members. They too are popularly elected, but by departments.[29] Each department has at least two representatives. Both senators and representatives serve for four

[27] Art. 170.
[28] Arts. 147, 148.
[29] As in many countries, the departments are units of local government.

years and are eligible for immediate re-election. Senators must be at least thirty years of age and native-born citizens or naturalized citizens with a minimum standing of at least seven years. For representatives the minimum age is twenty-five, and five years of citizenship are sufficient. Vacancies are filled by alternates, who are chosen at the regular election.

Meeting place, sessions, organization. The Legislative Palace, in which the General Assembly holds its sessions, is the pride of Uruguay. Completed in 1925 at a cost of over twelve million dollars, it is built of many different varieties of marble. Its magnificent interior contains a profusion of hardwoods, mosaics, and stained glass. A great granite stairway leads to the upper floor, where the legislative chambers are situated. Here the senators and deputies meet in regular session for nine months every year, beginning the fifteenth day of March. Because of the unusual length of the regular session, special sessions are scarcely necessary. They may be called by the National Council of Government, however, and at such times the General Assembly must limit itself to a consideration of the council's proposals. Under certain circumstances special sessions may also be called by the Permanent Committee. Meetings are normally held two days a week, beginning at five in the afternoon and continuing for three or four hours. The president or presiding officer of the Senate is the person who headed the majority party's winning list of candidates. He has one vote as a senator, and a second vote in case of a tie. Each year the Senate chooses its other officers, including a president *pro tempore* to preside in the absence of its president. The Chamber of Representatives, of course, has a presiding officer (president) chosen in the same manner as the president of the Senate. Committees in each house are named by the presiding officer, but must receive the approval of the entire membership.

Procedure. Legislation may be proposed by the National Council of Government or by any member of the General Assembly. There are certain matters, however, that may be initiated only by the National Council. The list includes virtually everything that increases the national debt, creates new jobs in the public service, or increases salaries or pensions. It includes also the annual budget. The solvency of the nation is further safeguarded by the requirement that every bill involving extra-budgetary expenditures must indicate the revenues from which they are to be met. Bills approved by the two chambers, but with some variations, are then considered by the membership of both chambers, sitting as a single body. A two-thirds vote is necessary for adoption under such circumstances. The two-thirds requirement obviously reduces—but does not completely eliminate—the danger that the more numerous Chamber of Representatives will always be able to dominate the Senate.

Permanent committee. As in many of the Latin American countries, there is a Permanent Committee of the General Assembly. It is composed of four senators and seven representatives, chosen by their respective chambers, and it meets at regular intervals during the three months of legislative recess. The principal task of the Permanent Committee is to keep a watchful eye on the National Council and cabinet ministers, and caution them whenever they violate the constitution or the laws. If they continue to act in an illegal manner, even after two such warnings, the Permanent Committee may then summon the General Assembly to meet in special session and decide what shall be done.[30]

THE COURTS: *Supreme court.* The usual hierarchy of courts has been established for the administration of justice. Juries are used in criminal cases. The supreme court has five members, who are chosen by the two houses of the General Assembly sitting as a single body. The judges serve for ten years and are ineligible for re-election until five years after the expiration of their terms. This strange restriction on re-election has no logical justification. Supreme court justices are not likely to use their exalted position to gain control of the government and transform themselves into dictators. Even if they had the desire to take such a step, they would be in no position to do so. The constitution establishes relatively high qualifications for members of the supreme court: they must be at least forty years of age, natural-born citizens or naturalized citizens of ten years' standing, and lawyers with ten years' experience in the practice of their professions or eight years' service on the bench. Like all judges in Uruguay, they must retire at the age of seventy. The original jurisdiction of the supreme court extends to all cases arising on the high seas or involving the principles of international law, as well as civil actions brought by foreign diplomats. Other cases reach the highest tribunal on appeal. It exercises general supervision over the entire judicial system. Its right to declare laws unconstitutional is specifically recognized.

Appellate courts. Below the supreme court are five courts of appeal, located in the principal urban centers. Each of these tribunals has three members, appointed by the supreme court with the consent of the Senate. The qualifications are somewhat lower than for judges of the supreme court: a minimum age of thirty-six years, citizenship by birth or by naturalization of at least seven years' standing, and eight years of legal practice

[30] Constitution, Arts. 127–132.

or six years as a judge. Oddly enough, the justices of the appellate courts have life tenure (or until age seventy), in contrast with the ten-year terms of members of the highest tribunal. Elsewhere it is the almost invariable practice to give the supreme court judges at least as long terms as any other members of the judicial system.

Inferior courts. Every important municipality has a circuit court, which tries all criminal cases and all civil suits involving substantial sums. The judges of these tribunals are appointed by the supreme court with Senate approval; they too serve during good behavior. But the supreme court is authorized to transfer them from one jurisdiction to another, or even to assign them to tasks involving reductions in salary. Undesirable transfers must be approved by four of the supreme court's five members; other changes may be ordered by three of the justices. Qualifications of circuit court judges are not high. They must have legal training, however. Even a knowledge of the law is not necessary for the justices of the peace,[31] who serve in all the cities and towns of the nation. They handle legal disputes that are too inconsequential for the circuit courts. Like the other judges of inferior tribunals, they are named by the supreme court. Their term of office is four years.

Administrative tribunal. In addition to the regular courts of law, there is also an administrative tribunal whose five members are chosen in the same manner as supreme court justices, for the same term, and with the same qualifications. This court has jurisdiction over suits involving the infringement of private rights by public officials, and also conflicts of authority among minor government agencies. It may suspend certain minor officials for abuse of authority.

THE DEPARTMENTS. The territory of Uruguay has been divided into nineteen departments, which possess a relatively large measure of self-government. The legislative body of each department is called a board, and its members, who are popularly elected, legislate without central interference on many matters of local interest. The chief executive of the department has long been known as the *intendente,* but in 1955 this individual is to be replaced by a five-member council.[32] Thus the idea of a plural executive is carried into the sphere of local government. Members of the departmental council, like the *intendente* before them, are to be popularly elected. Such a concession to local opinion is very unusual in Latin America. Yet the national authorities keep a reasonably firm grip

[31] Except in Montevideo.
[32] Except in Montevideo, where the council is to have seven members.

on departmental affairs. Local police are appointed by the minister of the interior, and are responsible directly to him. Local finances are subject to central control. The constitution of 1917 gave to the departments a considerable measure of fiscal autonomy, but the plan worked badly and was abandoned in 1936. Today the departments derive their revenues largely from taxes on real estate. There are other sources of local revenue, also, but they may be changed from year to year by the laws of Congress.

The constitution prescribes in detail the qualifications of the members of departmental boards and councils, their term of office (four years), and powers.[33] The council has the right to propose legislation. Its veto may be overridden by a three-fifths vote of the board. In Montevideo the departmental board has sixty-five members; elsewhere it has thirty-one. There is no general scheme of municipal government below the department level, as in most countries. Some of the more important communities have been permitted to have their own governing bodies, however. In most cases these local officials merely administer the laws of the department and the nation, without attempting to function as lawmaking bodies in their own right.[34]

SELECTED REFERENCES

Arias, José F., *Organizando una Nueva Enseñanza,* Montevideo, Dirección General de la Enseñanza Industrial, 1941.

Cannon, Mary M., *Social and Labor Problems of Peru and Uruguay,* Washington, D.C., Women's Bureau, U.S. Department of Labor, 1945.

Castro, Julio, *El Analfabetismo,* Montevideo, Imp. Nacional, 1940.

Díaz Peluffo, Zola, *Los Impuestos Municipales de Herencia Están Vigentes,* Montevideo, C. García, 1943.

Erserguer, Enrique V., *Cosas del Uruguay,* Montevideo, A. Monteverde, 1943.

Frugoni, Emilio, *La Mujer ante el Derecho,* Montevideo, Editorial Indoamericana, 1940.

Gallinal, Gustavo, *El Uruguay hacia la Dictadura,* Montevideo, Editorial Nueva América, 1942.

Hanson, Simon, *Utopia in Uruguay,* New York, Oxford Univ. Press, 1938.

Juega Farrulla, Arturo, *Las Tres Constituciones de la República Oriental del Uruguay, 1917–1930–1934,* Montevideo, Librería Perkin, 1941.

[33] Arts. 262–306.
[34] There is a good brief discussion of Uruguayan local government in Sebastián Morey Otero's *Constitución Anotada de la República Oriental del Uruguay.* The author's annotations relating to this section of the constitution are found on pp. 305–346. For a more detailed description, see the two-volume work by Benjamín Pereira Bustamante, *El Régimen Municipal Vigente.* It must be remembered that both of these works antedate the new regime.

Llana Barrios, Mario, *El Juicio Político; Estudio Constitucional Histórico-Político*, Montevideo, Impresora Moderna, 1942.

Pendle, George, *Uruguay: South America's First Welfare State*, New York, Royal Institute of International Affairs, 1952.

Pérez, Silvestre, *Filosofía del Federalismo en el Río de La Plata*, Montevideo, Tip. Atlántida, 1948.

Pivel Devoto, Juan E., *Historia de los Partidos Políticos en el Uruguay*, Montevideo, C. García, 1942.

Rodríguez Fabregat, Enrique, *Batlle y Ordóñez, el Reformador*, Buenos Aires, Editorial Claridad, 1942.

Salom, Miguel, *Seguro Obligatorio Social*, Montevideo, Editorial La Casa del Estudiante, 1943.

Salterain Herrera, Eduardo de, *Enseñanza Secundaria Uruguaya*, Montevideo, Casa A. Barreiro, 1942.

Taylor, Philip B., Jr., *The Executive Power in Uruguay*, Berkeley, California, mimeographed, 1951.

Williman, José Claudio, *Una Comedia Política, 1937–1943*, Montevideo, Imp. Moderna, 1943.

Zum Felde, Alberto, *Evolución Histórica del Uruguay*, 3rd ed., Montevideo, M. García, 1945.

CHAPTER 19

PARAGUAY

~~~~~~

The Land and the People

THE names *Paraguay* and *Uruguay* are almost alike, causing a certain amount of confusion among the uninitiated. Yet the two countries are totally different. Though separated by only nine hundred miles, they belong to two different centuries. Uruguay is mid-twentieth century— modern, alert, progressive. Paraguay is still a part of the early nineteenth century. Its people are not very different from their ancestors in speech, in dress, in manner of life, or in form of government. Paraguay lies astride the Paraguay River, the important waterway that flows into the mighty Paraná and thus connects with the Río de la Plata. The journey northward from Buenos Aires to Asunción, the Paraguayan capital, requires four hours by plane, a little over two days by the weekly train, and three and one-half days by river boat. Anyone who takes the boat trip up the Paraguay River is impressed by the contrast in the appearance of the settlements on the two banks of the stream. The west side, which is Argentine, has clean towns, progressive agricultural methods, and a white population. The Paraguayan side has squalid communities, primitive farming methods, and a large admixture of Indian blood.

AREA, POPULATION, RACES. Paraguay is a small country. Its area is one hundred and seventy-five thousand square miles, making it only slightly larger than the state of California. Its population is said to be about one million, though no one really knows. In any event, it certainly has far fewer inhabitants than any other nation of South America. Some of the people are full-blooded Indians, the descendants of the Guaranís who lived in Paraguay before the coming of the white man. Some of the inhabitants are white. But the overwhelming majority are *mestizos*—the product of the blending of the two races. Negroes are virtually unknown. There are some colonies of refugees. Among the most important are the Mennonites, whose systematic refusal to accept governmental authority has made them unwelcome in most countries. Paraguay has given them refuge in the more remote parts of its territory. There they have developed and managed their own settlements.[1] Other colonies have been established, also; they include Czechs, Austrians, and other displaced persons. Some of these colonies have collapsed, because neither the people nor their leaders had any realization of the hardships involved.

ILLITERACY AND ILLEGITIMACY. Although Spanish is the literary language of the country, thousands of Paraguayans have never learned it. They still speak Guaraní, the language of their ancestors. Even the children of the best families learn Guaraní from the servants and use it at times. Illiteracy is amazingly high. Some careful observers have estimated that at least eighty-five per cent of the people are unable to read and write, despite laws prescribing compulsory elementary education. At one time four children out of every five were illegitimate, but it is said that the figure is now somewhat lower. The government has conducted several extensive propaganda campaigns emphasizing the importance of the marriage ceremony, and has decreed that couples who marry may thus legitimatize their natural children. It should be emphasized that such widespread illegitimacy does not imply a corresponding degree of immorality. In many cases it means only that the costs of the marriage ceremony are too high for poor people, or that the civil registry is too distant. An additional complicating factor is the great excess of women. Successive wars have so depleted the male population that at times it has been necessary to resort to polygamy in order to repeople the nation.

POVERTY. The line between rich and poor is as sharply drawn in Paraguay as anywhere in the world. For poor people the standard of living is very low. Most of them work on the great estates where their fathers and grandfathers worked. They are paid only a few *centavos* a day. Their food consists of what they can grow easily and quickly. Corn, cassava, and rice are standard products, and jerked beef can often be obtained without great difficulty. The rich, of course, have their great estates and fine homes. But even they are affected by the general poverty of the country,

[1] See Morill Cody's article, "Refuge in the Chaco," published in the July, 1943, issue of *Inter-American* (Vol. II, No. 7), pp. 10–13.

for they lack the income to buy many of the imported goods that add to the luxury of wealthy living in most parts of Latin America. It has been said that no family in the entire country possesses a fortune in excess of two hundred thousand dollars. Very much less is needed, however, for a magnificent estate and a great retinue of servants, provided one's taste for foreign luxuries is kept in check.

ASUNCIÓN. The casual visitor to Asunción, the nation's capital, is apt to receive a false impression of economic conditions throughout Paraguay. It is a picturesque city, with broad tree-lined avenues and perpetually blooming gardens. There are many fine homes. The cathedral and the government buildings, though very old, are quite impressive. But Asunción is not typical of the nation. Like other capitals of Latin America, it contains far more than its share of wealth and culture. Its educational facilities are vastly superior. It is the home of at least seventy-five per cent of the nation's physicians. Most of the people in the rural sections are completely without medical care. Asunción has a population of about two hundred thousand. No other city is even half as large.

CLIMATE. One third of Paraguay lies within the tropics. There are no great mountains or high plateaus, so the entire country suffers the inconvenience of a tropical or subtropical climate. Temperatures above one hundred degrees are common. In the warmer months government employees normally report for work at five o'clock in the morning and leave for the day at least an hour before noon, thus escaping the intense midday heat. Yet there are sharp variations in temperature in some parts of the country, especially in the west. Paraguay suffers from the usual tropical diseases—malaria, hookworm, amoebic disorders.

THE CENTRAL BELT. Most of the people live in a comparatively small belt that runs through the central part of the country along the east bank of the Paraguay River. The principal cities are in this area; so are nearly all the cultivated lands. Cotton is grown in considerable quantities and is a major export crop. Some tobacco is grown for export also, as well as the corn and other crops that provide the chief staples of the nation's diet. Food must be imported in most years, despite a climate and soil that lend themselves readily to agricultural production. The chief difficulties are lack of transportation and an inadequate labor supply. Paraguay has less than eight hundred miles of railroad track and almost no roads that can be used in wet weather. There are only six persons per square mile.

THE CHACO. West of the Paraguay River lies the vast area of undulating plains known as the Chaco. The far northwest of this region is a steaming jungle, where Paraguayans and Bolivians fought a senseless war not many years ago.[2] Most of the Chaco is not jungle, however; it is good grazing land and offers substantial advantages for cattle raising. But the disadvantages are even more numerous, as Argentine and American cattle interests have discovered. The insect life is abundant and persistent. Clouds of mosquitoes are sometimes so thick that they virtually obscure the sun. Ants are found everywhere. There is not sufficient water, except during a small part of the year when the rain often comes in such quantities as to cause major damage. Yet the livestock industry manages to make a fairly creditable showing. Canned meat, hides, and meat extract represent an important part of the nation's exports.

THE SOUTHEASTERN FORESTLAND. The other major region of Paraguay is the heavily forested area in the southeast. Here there are virtually no cities and few towns. Yet this territory plays a major role in the economic life of the nation. Its most important product is quebracho, a wood whose hardness may be judged by the fact that its name is derived from the Spanish words for axe-breaker. Quebracho trees grow wild in great numbers throughout this part of the country; they provide the extract that is used in tanning hides. They are useful also for railroad ties, furniture, and, in Argentina, for fence posts on the boundless *pampa*. The hard wood is almost completely immune to the attacks of insects. At present the quebracho forests are being demolished at a rapid rate, and virtually no thought is given to reforestation. This is extremely unfortunate, for the trees grow slowly. The other major product of this region is yerba maté, or, as it is often called, Paraguay tea. This is the favorite drink of millions of South Americans. The plant grows wild in Paraguay and also in adjacent sections of Brazil and Argentina. The leaves are picked, cured for about three days, and then made into powder. The tea is prepared by placing the powdered leaves in a dried gourd and pouring hot water over them. It is drunk through a metal tube known as a bombilla, or little pump.

MINING AND MANUFACTURING. There is almost no mining in Paraguay, and probably very little mineral wealth. Some iron and copper have been reported, however, and small quantities of manganese are known to exist. The Chaco may perhaps have important petroleum deposits. American oil companies have concessions in the region and have already made a substantial outlay. Inadequate transportation facilities are a serious handicap to large-scale production. Manufacturing is not much more important

[2] See pages 514–515.

than mining. It is limited chiefly to the elaboration of domestic raw materials. Meat is canned; quebracho extract is prepared and bottled; cotton is ginned; sugar is made into rum or industrial alcohol. The manufacturing plants are small. Most of them are in or near Asunción.[3]

DEPENDENCE ON ARGENTINA. In economic matters Paraguay is almost completely dependent on Argentina. It is shut off from direct contact with the sea, and its main avenue of commerce is the Paraguay-Paraná river system, which flows through Argentine territory for hundreds of miles. The primitive condition of Paraguay, in contrast with the modern development of Argentina, makes Argentine domination of its small neighbor almost inevitable. Argentines own and operate the steamship companies that connect Paraguay with the outside world. The Argentine government owns seventy-five per cent of the Paraguayan Central Railroad, which is the only railroad worth mentioning. Much of Paraguay's wheat comes from Argentina, and Argentines own most of the Paraguayan bakeries. They control the quebracho industry and have a considerable stake in yerba maté. The Paraguayan *guaraní,* which is the unit of currency, is tied to the Argentine peso, and foreign exchange is obtained through Buenos Aires. The average Paraguayan regards Buenos Aires as the center of the universe, in much the same manner as Argentines look to Paris. The Paraguayans are sometimes called tenants in their own land. They owe economic allegiance to the Argentines and political allegiance to a little group of Paraguayan politicians.

The Pattern of Politics

RISE OF FRANCIA. Paraguay has not yet entered the democratic era. It has been ruled by dictators through most of its independent life, and today's government follows the familiar pattern. The land has been bled white by senseless conflicts. Never has it been permitted the opportunity to develop a peaceful, prosperous manner of life. Its story is as tragic as that of any nation. Independence from Spain was won without difficulty and the leading citizens entrusted the task of preparing a constitution for the new nation to a lawyer named José Gaspar Tomás Rodríguez Francia. That was in 1811. Francia drafted a constitution, which provided that the executive power should be divided between two consuls, so that neither of them might secure unlimited authority. There was to be a Congress, meeting annually. This constitution was adopted in 1813, and Francia was

[3] There is an interesting article by Sylvia Martin, "Riverfront Nation," in the July, 1945, issue of *Inter-American* (Vol. IV, No. 7), pp. 24-26.

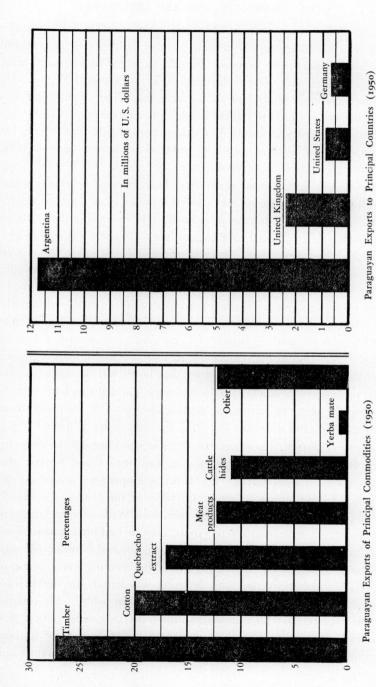

Paraguayan Exports of Principal Commodities (1950)

Paraguayan Exports to Principal Countries (1950)

Based on information obtained from the May, 1953, issue of *International Financial Statistics*, a publication of the International Monetary Fund.

named one of the two consuls. His colleague was General Fulgencio Yegros, who had been the outstanding military figure of the revolution. Within a very short time, however, Francia managed to imprison, exile, or kill all persons who stood in his way, including General Yegros. He then seized complete control of the government. The constitution was speedily forgotten. In 1816 he had himself proclaimed perpetual dictator and ruled the country as an absolute despot until his death in 1840. He was known as *El Supremo,* and his subjects worshiped him abjectly, either through admiration or terror.

EARLY YEARS. All writers agree that Francia was a strange man. Descended from one of the country's oldest families, he was sent to Argentina as a youth to study for the priesthood. He never completed his religious studies, but returned to Paraguay with advanced degrees in philosophy and theology. Soon he was appointed counsel to the royal treasury; a little later he became a member of the city council of Asunción; and after the abdication of the Spanish monarch in 1811 he was appointed a delegate to the Congress in Buenos Aires that was supposed to decide the future course of the Viceroyalty of the Río de la Plata. This appointment marked him as the leading citizen of Paraguay; his commission to write the new constitution of the nation was further proof of his distinguished position. It was but natural, therefore, that he should be named one of the two consuls. The strange part of the story was that this lawyer, without military training or experience, could gain control of the government in a military age and dominate the army throughout his lifetime.

ABSOLUTE DESPOTISM. It seems that Francia was obsessed by a lust for power. Personally he was incorruptible, and would not tolerate dishonesty among his colleagues. He never attempted to amass a great fortune. He lived simply—almost austerely—in the Governor's House, attended by an orderly and two women servants. Without wife, family, or even pets, he may have been a lonely man. But he had little time to think of such matters, for all his waking hours were devoted to affairs of state. From his office he issued detailed instructions covering every phase of Paraguayan government and life. Nothing was left to the initiative of others. And no one dared to question his lightest whim. He ordered wholesale executions of his enemies and filled the jails with political prisoners. His constant fear of assassination caused him to take unusual precautions against attack. Any person suspected of plotting against him was promptly put to death.

ISOLATION. Francia had a fixed notion that Paraguay was superior to all other nations and that this superiority could best be preserved by shutting it off completely from the rest of the world. He was a confirmed isolationist who carried his belief to its logical conclusion. The Paraguay River was closed to commerce. Imports and exports were prohibited and this prohibition was rigidly enforced. Mail service with foreign countries ceased. Aliens were not admitted, whatever the nature of their business. For nearly a quarter of a century Paraguayans lost contact with the rest of mankind.[4]

FROM FRANCIA TO THE ELDER LÓPEZ. In 1840 Francia had a fit and died. His secretary tried to keep the death a secret and continued to issue orders in the Dictator's name. But this fraud was soon discovered and the secretary committed suicide. There followed a period of virtual anarchy. Dictators were put up and pulled down by the army in rapid succession. Between September, when Francia died, and the following January there were eleven abortive attempts at dictatorship. Finally, however, two consuls assumed joint control of the government. One of these consuls—Carlos Antonio López—is said to have been a nephew of Francia, though such relationships were somewhat obscure in Paraguay. In any event, López seems to have had the old Dictator's forceful character. He soon forced the other consul from power and became dictator in his own right. For nineteen years, until his death in 1862, he managed to keep himself in power. But he tried to give his regime some semblance of legality by summoning Congress to confirm his authority from time to time. Actually he was no more dependent on Congress or any other agency or person than Francia had been.

BENEVOLENT TYRANNY. López was a kindly man and he governed in a wise and benevolent manner. He abolished slavery, but with some regard for the interests of the former slaveholders. The Francia closed-door policy was reversed, and the outside world was invited to resume communications and trade. Foreigners were made welcome. These years were among the best in the nation's history. The people were prosperous and happy. Unfortunately, however, they were not to be permitted many more years of happiness. Carlos López was succeeded by his son Francisco, who promptly gave the nation the bloodiest and most terrifying dictatorship that it had ever known.

FIRST YEARS OF THE YOUNGER LÓPEZ. The younger López was born in

---

[4] See the interesting article, "José Gaspar de Francia, Dictator of Paraguay," by Justo Pastor Benítez, published in the November, 1940, issue of the Bulletin of the Pan American Union, pp. 737–742.

Ascunción in 1827. Although he was the second son, he seems to have been generally regarded as the heir apparent. His education was supplied chiefly by a Jesuit priest, who later became one of his principal executioners. As a youth Francisco López was made a general in the army, though he never had any kind of military training and never voluntarily exposed himself to enemy fire. His father decided that young Francisco should go to Europe to study military tactics, but such matters seem to have left him completely disinterested. In Paris, however, he did find many things to his taste. He returned to Asunción after a few years, bringing with him a mistress who was, in her way, a very remarkable woman. Her name was Alice Lynch, and she had been born in Ireland. Most of her life had been spent in Paris, however, and she seems to have considered herself French. At the age of fifteen she had married a minor employee of the French government, but that marriage had ended disastrously before she met Francisco López. By that time she was twenty years old, and ready for further adventure. Young Francisco fell madly in love with her, and would almost certainly have married her if she could have secured an annulment of her existing marriage. But her husband, who was a devout Catholic, refused to give his consent and the matter could not be arranged. Nonetheless she became the companion of López, bore his sons, and remained faithful to him until his death.

WAR AGAINST NEIGHBORING STATES. When the elder López died, in September of 1862, Francisco summoned Congress and directed its members to name him dictator. They did so without objection, little knowing the tragedy that lay ahead for them and for all the people of Paraguay. It soon became clear that the new ruler was inordinately ambitious. He seems to have considered himself a superdictator, dominating not only his own nation but also neighboring states. In 1864, when Uruguay had a dispute with Brazil, López offered himself as mediator. The two governments refused and the people of both countries laughed at his pretensions. Newspaper editors and cartoonists pictured him as the half-civilized dictator of a half-civilized nation, trying to interfere in matters that he did not even understand. López was deeply offended, and satisfied his vanity by declaring war on Brazil. In order to gain a military advantage he then asked Argentina for permission to take his troops across its territory. The Argentine government refused, as it should have done, and López countered with a declaration of war. Uruguay joined Brazil and Argentina in the fight to crush the Paraguayan Dictator.

A PROTRACTED STRUGGLE. The war should have ended in a few months.

Paraguay had only a small population and its army was equipped with wornout rifles. The allies, on the other hand, had excellent weapons, including a supply of heavy artillery. The Brazilian navy even had some gunboats. Yet Paraguay managed to prolong the struggle for six years. In part it maintained such a successful resistance because of the mistakes of the allied generals, who frequently failed to press a hard-won advantage, thus giving the Paraguayans time to reform their scattered lines. The people of the little nation displayed amazing courage. Often they continued to fight when the situation seemed hopeless. López originated and gave wide circulation to the story that the allies put all their prisoners to death with horrible tortures, and this belief undoubtedly stimulated the fighting spirit of the Paraguayan troops. Moreover, they seem to have had no idea that the war was going against them. They knew only what they were told, and the official communiqués were always reporting glorious victories on other fronts.

INDESCRIBABLE CONDITIONS. As the war went from bad to worse, conditions in Paraguay became almost indescribable. So many men were slaughtered that it became necessary to obtain fresh recruits from the very young and the very old. Eventually the ranks included all males from ten to sixty years of age. Even women were recruited during the last few months, though it is doubtful whether many of them saw front-line service. Food supplies were almost completely exhausted. The domestic animals had been killed in the early years of the war and almost no persons were left to till the fields. People were forced to live on roots. Even salt was unavailable. Meanwhile, however, López and his family continued to live luxuriously on vast supplies of hoarded food. At every meal they had champagne, of which the Dictator was inordinately fond. When the army retreated, they retreated too, always keeping well behind the lines and taking with them their precious food supply.

INCREDIBLE TORTURES. The cruel tortures devised by the Tyrant are almost beyond belief. Some poor unfortunates had their fingers smashed with mallets. Others had their eyelids cut off; they were then bound hand and foot and placed face upward in the burning sun. Some victims were put in anthills, to be eaten alive. Many were flogged to death, or put in red-hot fetters. At first López used these methods only against his known enemies or against deserters. Later, however, he decided that almost everyone was conspiring against him. Virtually all his friends and advisers incurred his hatred and suffered terrible deaths. Even the members of his own family were caught in this orgy of wanton cruelty.

The Tyrant had his brothers put to death, and tortured his mother and sisters unmercifully in an attempt to learn the details of an alleged plot against his life. One of his last official acts was to sign his mother's death warrant.

END OF THE WAR. The Dictator's reign ended abruptly on the first day of April, 1870. The remnants of his army had finally been dispersed, and he was surrounded by Brazilian troops and killed by a common soldier. His mistress and one of his sons dug his grave with their hands. Thus Paraguay was freed of its tyrant, but its economy was almost completely destroyed. Scarcely thirty thousand able-bodied men remained alive, and most of these survivors were very old. There was no livestock. Agricultural lands had been allowed to return to a wild state. It is possible that no nation in history ever paid a heavier price for the cruelties of a mad tyrant. Despite the pitiable condition of the country, Brazil at first insisted upon trying to collect a huge indemnity. But other nations of South America finally persuaded it to abandon this attempt, and Brazilian troops were withdrawn.[5]

POLITICAL CHAOS. Once again the people of Paraguay were free to shape their own destiny, and once again they demonstrated their complete incapacity to meet the situation. There were new presidents, new revolutions, and new assassinations. A constitution adopted in 1870 remained in force for seventy years, though it was more honored in the breach than in the observance. During those seventy years there were fourteen full-scale civil wars, and numerous minor uprisings. Only a very few presidents succeeded in serving their full terms, and some of them lost their lives in the attempt. Factional rivalries were still decided on the field of battle. Meanwhile two political parties competed for control of the government. They were the Colorados (Reds) and the Azules (Blues). In general the Colorados included the more liberal and anti-clerical elements, while the Azules represented the large landowners and the devout Catholics. But there was no sharp line between Reds and Blues; each side was more interested in gaining power than in upholding fundamental principles. The political campaigns and the civil wars centered mainly around the personalities of rival *caudillos*.

WAR AGAINST BOLIVIA. In 1932 Paraguay plunged into another sanguinary war, this time with Bolivia. The dispute concerned the boundary

[5] There are many good accounts of the López dictatorship. One of the best is *Woman on Horseback*, by Wm. E. Barrett. Another is *Portrait of a Dictator*, by R. B. Cunninghame Graham. A collection of important documents of the period was published in Buenos Aires in 1871 under the title: *López—El Tirano Pintado por Sí Mismo*.

PARAGUAY   515

between the two nations in the area known as the Chaco.⁶ For three
generations the matter had been argued. So many young men in both
countries had earned higher university degrees by writing theses "proving"
the claims of their respective countries that wags sometimes called them
"doctores en Chaco." But the quarrel was well beyond the academic
stage by 1932. There had already been some desultory fighting between
the forces of the two nations, and it finally developed into full-scale warfare.
The League of Nations and various individual nations, including the
United States, tried to find some satisfactory formula for a compromise,
but without success.

   In the first stages of the war everything seemed to favor the Bolivians.
They had larger, better equipped armies, trained by German officers. The
Paraguayans were so poorly armed that sometimes they had to ambush and
kill their enemies before they could obtain the guns and ammunition necessary for modern warfare. Yet the Paraguayan troops had one marked
advantage: they were fighting on ground they knew, under conditions that
approximated their everyday life. Most of the Bolivians, on the other hand,
came from the high plateau, and they fell easy prey to jungle diseases as
well as the stratagems of their adversaries. Before the end of the war
Paraguay had captured most of the disputed territory. An armistice was
finally arranged in 1935, through the efforts of the United States and
several of the immediate neighbors of the warring powers, but the formal
treaty of peace was not signed until 1938. Both sides lost heavily in the
war. For Paraguay, especially, this fresh loss of manpower was a national
catastrophe, but Paraguayans could boast of victory. The peace treaty
awarded them about three-fourths of the area for which they had fought,
though Bolivia was assured a navigable outlet on the Paraguay River.⁷

   REVOLUTIONS. The terms of the 1935 armistice with Bolivia, involving
the withdrawal of Paraguayan troops from some positions that they had
won after hard fighting, aroused widespread indignation in Paraguay,
especially among the leaders of the army. They plotted to overthrow the
President, and set February 17, 1936, as the date for the uprising. Everything happened exactly as planned. The President, caught completely by
surprise, fled on a gunboat and radioed his resignation. Thereupon the
revolutionaries installed Colonel Franco as chief executive. He was a war
veteran with socialistic ideas. His program included expropriation of

   ⁶ See pages 506–507.
   ⁷ Woolsey, L. H., "The Settlement of the Chaco Dispute," *American Journal of International Law,* Vol. XXXIII (1939), pp. 126–129.

the great estates and distribution of the land to the landless poor. The government was to be fashioned after that of Nazi Germany, with both capital and labor subordinated to the total state. Colonel Franco counted not only on army support, but also on the aid of students, intellectuals, and workers. Representatives of these different groups had already banded together in a loose organization known as the National Front. But dissatisfaction with Franco was widespread, and he was forced out of office by another revolution in less than six months.

His place was taken by Dr. Félix Paiva, the president of the University of Asunción. Even this change did not bring peace. There were two rebellions against the new President in less than six months. He managed to suppress them, however, and remained in office until 1939, when another president was elected. This election was peaceful, but scarcely democratic. In fact, there was only one candidate—General José Félix Estigarribia, a Chaco war hero who had once served as minister to the United States. He was the choice of the Liberal Party (the onetime Blues). Since this party controlled the government and obviously intended to win, whether by honest means or otherwise, the National Republicans (Colorados) announced that they would boycott the election.

CONSTITUTION OF 1940. President Estigarribia was inaugurated on April 15, 1939. The early months of his administration were marked by increasing unrest, despite his attempt to liberalize the government. Finally, on February 17, 1940, Congress resigned in order to give the President a free hand "in combating anarchy." Estigarribia then declared himself dictator of the nation. In a radio address he explained, however, that the dictatorship was only temporary, and that he would call a constitutional convention to reform the 1870 document as soon as the people were ready for self-government. They seem to have been ready in an amazingly short time, for only a few months afterward the convention was called. It was packed with Estigarribia's supporters and produced the kind of constitution that he desired—highly centralized, vesting great power in the president, and authorizing a large measure of government activity in economic and social matters. The President made a bow to public opinion by ordering a plebiscite on the new fundamental law. This plebiscite was held on August 4, 1940, and of course it resulted in a favorable vote of overwhelming proportions. Estigarribia was clearly the master of the nation. Five weeks later he and his wife were killed in an airplane accident while en route to their country estate.

ANOTHER TYRANNY. The cabinet met this crisis by designating a provisional president—Minister of War Higinio Morínigo, a forty-three-year-old professional soldier of mixed blood and little education. It was assumed, of course, that Morínigo would hold office for a few months at most, until arrangements could be made for the election of his successor. But the new President had other ideas. He announced that no election would be held until February, 1943, and that during the intervening two and one-half years he would retain control of the government. The exact nature of that control soon became apparent. It involved one of the strictest censorships in Latin America. Civil liberties were ignored, and the opposition was suppressed with complete ruthlessness. No one dared utter a word against the new regime. No newspaper could print a word of criticism. It was necessary to get a police permit for a birthday party at a private home.

It was a repetition of the old Francia-López story. In fact, the new Dictator even paid public tribute to the nineteenth-century tyrants, and declared that he would like to see a revival of the warlike tradition of that earlier day. One can scarcely believe that those words were spoken only two years after the end of the bitter war with Bolivia, in which Paraguay lost proportionately as many men as did France in the First World War. But if the people did not share the Dictator's sentiments, they certainly had no opportunity to express a contrary opinion. Morínigo announced that he would "orient, once and for all, the Paraguayan revolution." In order to make this meaningless phrase still more confusing, he explained that the new regime would be based on "selective democracy."

MORÍNIGO'S ADVISERS AND OPPONENTS. The chief victims of Morínigo's tyrannies were the leaders of the Liberal Party. They had controlled the government under Estigarribia and had been responsible for the selection of his successor. They had every reason to suppose, therefore, that the new President would be guided by their advice and make certain that they retained control of the government. Instead he turned to a group of young army officers—"boy heroes," as some Paraguayans derisively called them—who represented the more reactionary elements of the Colorado Party. Under their influence Morínigo swung more and more to the right. Estigarribia's aids disappeared from public life. Some managed to get out of the country, but many were thrown into jail. There they were joined by rebellious students and labor leaders.

A FARCICAL ELECTION. Morínigo had promised that there would be a presidential election in 1943. He kept that promise. There was an election, and he was the only candidate. No registration of voters was required, since any persons who took the trouble to vote twice would simply multiply the number of votes for the Dictator. The election was held on different days in different parts of the country, presumably to permit a concentration of police and army strength in each region when the votes were cast. In the face of such precautions, the result was scarcely in doubt.

One Paraguayan is said to have talked with an American citizen, who boasted of the efficient devices used in the United States to bring election returns to the people promptly. "We turn on our radios after the polls close," declared the American, "and by bedtime we know the name of our next president."

"We do much better than that," replied the Paraguayan. "We know the name of our next president three months before the election."

OPPOSITION. During 1944 there was considerable political activity in Paraguay. The followers of former President Franco, who had been exiled, set up a rudimentary party organization and called themselves the *Febreristas* (because the 1936 revolution that made Franco president had occurred in the month of February). Their appeal was primarily to the underprivileged; they urged extensive social legislation and a curtailment of the privileges of the rich. There were some persons—primarily liberal intellectuals and students, as well as some labor leaders—who endorsed in general the Febreristas' program, but thought that their leader, General Franco, was scarcely the man to execute it. What the country needed, they said, was a civilian president. These men called themselves the *Tiempistas,* because their principal mouthpiece was the newspaper *El Tiempo.* Morínigo, who seems to have been amused by these political maneuvers, did not attempt to suppress them. When, however, the dissidents called a rally to be held in the auditorium of the national university and succeeded in drawing a great crowd which adopted resolutions denouncing the government, the Dictator decided that the time had come to act. Censorship was enforced with renewed vigor and hundreds of new political prisoners filled the jails. Included in this group were leading intellectuals who had signed a petition for the restoration of civil liberties. University students held a meeting of protest in Asunción's Plaza Uruguaya and were attacked by mounted police. Those who resisted were thrown into the already overcrowded prisons.

LABOR POLICIES. Labor was slow to organize in Paraguay, but by 1945 the trade union movement had succeeded in attracting large numbers of workers, especially in the meat-packing and tanning industries. There had been a number of strikes, which had produced some slight improvement in wages and hours of work. Every president since Franco, not excepting Higinio Morínigo, had sponsored some social legislation. In February of 1945 the President issued a decree placing all unions under strict government supervision and deducting three per cent from wages for a social security fund. The union leaders, who preferred to control their own affairs and suspected that the social security fund would be used for political purposes, promptly declared the Paraguayan equivalent of a general strike. It was not general, because the country's workers were not sufficiently organized, but it did affect a large number of industries. The government took stern retaliatory measures against the unions. It raided union headquarters, arrested labor leaders and their families, and finally decreed that all trade unions were dissolved.

ARMY DISCONTENT. Within the army there were sharp differences of opinion concerning the wisdom of Morínigo's policies. Three reactionary army colonels were widely credited with framing these policies; one writer went so far as to call the Dictator a "cipher"—a manager for this three-man board of directors.[8] But by June of 1946 the President decided that he could safely break with his too-powerful associates. He made one of them the chief of the Paraguayan mission to attend the inauguration of Perón in Buenos Aires, and thus removed him from the country. While he was away, Morínigo moved on a strategic garrison commanded by the absent colonel and captured it almost without bloodshed. The other members of the triumvirate heard the news before Morínigo could arrest them, and quickly took to their heels. Thus the Dictator broke the power of the one group of men that seemed to offer any serious challenge to his authority. A few weeks later he invited the Febreristas to participate in a coalition government and they accepted. But this arrangement lasted only six months. Morínigo then governed solely with the support of the Colorado Party. Eventually all other political groups were outlawed.

REBELLION. During the first seven years of the Morínigo regime there were twenty-six revolutions. The twenty-sixth, which began in the early part of 1947, and continued for several months, almost succeeded in overthrowing the government. At least a thousand men died, and thousands of others were seriously wounded. The first news reaching the outside world seemed to indicate that the rebels were gaining steadily; at one time they established a provisional government and announced that victory had been won. But the announcement was premature. Government forces regained one stronghold after another, and finally succeeded in killing

[8] See Sylvia Martin's previously cited article, p. 25.

the revolutionary leaders or driving them from the country. Morínigo's position seemed to be more secure than ever after this display of strength.

ANOTHER CONTROLLED ELECTION. The Dictator's term of office was due to expire in 1948, and Paraguayans wondered whether he would seek re-election. In October he announced that he would not. Thereupon the leaders of the Colorado Party made plans for a convention to choose their candidate, who would be elected as a matter of course, since there was no legal opposition. The man who seemed most likely to win the nomination was Federico Chaves, the popular minister of foreign affairs. Many prominent party members had endorsed him. The official newspaper of the Colorado Party gave its blessing to his candidacy. When, therefore, President Morínigo announced that he favored another candidate—Minister of Finance J. Natalicio González—the party leaders were taken completely by surprise. Many of them declared that they would still support Chaves and thus brave the Dictator's disapproval.

The party convention was set for November. Just before the opening session the capital was flooded with posters and other propaganda for Morínigo's candidate, González. Overnight the galleries were packed with González sympathizers. The first test of strength in the convention came with the selection of a chairman. The delegates defeated the Morínigo-González candidate for this post by a narrow margin. Thereupon the galleries demonstrated their displeasure by disrupting the meeting. Even bricks were thrown. As soon as order had been restored the Morínigo-González forces took control and announced that their defeated candidate for the chairmanship had been elected. Delegates who objected were expelled forcibly from the building. Then the remaining delegates "acclaimed" the presidential candidacy of González. The party's newspaper was seized and the editor removed. Foreign Minister Chaves was placed under "forced residence" at a nearby resort.

RISE AND FALL OF GONZÁLEZ. J. Natalicio González was assured of the presidency; he was the only candidate in the election, which was held on February 14, 1948. He received ninety-six per cent of the votes cast. The other four per cent represented ballots that had been invalidated in one way or another, since it was impossible to vote for any other person. The principal result of the election was to strengthen Morínigo's power. President-elect González emphasized this fact by announcing that General Morínigo would remain as chief of the army. From this position, of course, he could continue to dominate the government.

The prospect of Morínigo as the power behind the presidency proved highly unsatisfactory to other high-ranking army officers. They laid a careful plot to depose the Dictator, and carried it out so well that there was almost no bloodshed. Morínigo was forced to leave the country. An interim government was then established under the chief justice of the supreme court, but the victorious army leaders promised that González would be permitted to assume the presidency on August 15 as originally planned. That promise was kept, and thus Natalicio González became president in his own right. In less than six months, however, he was deposed by a group of his own advisers, and General Raimundo Rolón, who was also a member of the Colorado Party, assumed the presidency. Rolón lasted just twenty-eight days. Then the army removed him in an almost bloodless coup, and installed as president a dentist named Felipe Molas López. In April, 1949, an election was held. The Colorados were the only official party, and Molas López was the only presidential candidate. He won, of course, but within four months he was deposed by an act of Congress. Thereupon Federico Chaves, the popular ex-foreign minister who had almost achieved the presidency in 1948, became the new master of the country.

DICTATORSHIP OF CHAVES. Since 1949 Chaves has managed to hang onto the presidency. He has kept Paraguay almost continuously in a state of martial law, and has imprisoned or exiled his opponents. Leaders of the Liberal Party, speaking from the safety of Buenos Aires, declare that Paraguayan jails are filled with political prisoners. Opposition groups within the country are denied access to press or radio, but some of them use mimeographing machines to turn out their propaganda, and circulate it furtively from hand to hand. The government has tried to combat this practice by ordering the registration of mimeographing machines. Public gatherings of all kinds are forbidden, except with the authorization of the police. In this atmosphere the people of the nation conduct their daily affairs. President Chaves has added a touch of legitimacy to his position by winning the usual kind of election, with one party and one candidate. Paraguay's story is indeed tragic, and the end of that tragedy is not in sight.

The Structure of Government

THE CONSTITUTION. There is, of course, no need to describe in great detail the structure of Paraguayan government. All power rests in the hands of a president. His word is law. Constitutional provisions have no more significance than he chooses to give them. Nonetheless, a brief glance at the theory of government may be worth while, if only to emphasize the wide gulf between theory and practice. The present constitution, adopted in 1940, is one of the shortest in Latin America. Its seventy-six hundred words make it only fifteen per cent longer than the terse constitution of the United States. There is a preamble, which uses flowery language to invoke the blessing of Almighty God. The list of individual and social rights is as impressive as in any country. These rights may be swept away by the president in time of emergency, of course, but he is required to report his acts to the Chamber of Representatives,[9] which is the Paraguayan Congress, since the constitution makes provision for only one legislative chamber. The right to vote extends to all males, literate and illiterate, who have reached the age of eighteen.

THE PRESIDENT. The constitution states that the president shall be elected by direct vote of the people. His term is five years, and he may be re-elected immediately for one additional period.[10] He must be a native-born citizen, a Roman Catholic, and at least forty years of age.[11] His appointing power is most extensive, including all administrative officers and employees, all army officers, all diplomats, all archbishops and bishops of the Catholic Church, and all judges. For many of these appointments he must have the approval of the Council of State, which consists of the members of his cabinet plus a number of other prominent persons, such as the rector of the National University, the archbishop of the nation, and the president of the central bank. For the most part this Council of State acts in an advisory capacity.[12]

THE CABINET. The constitution does not fix the number of cabinet ministries, but nine have been established. Each minister must be a native-born citizen, at least thirty years of age, and must enjoy the reputation of honesty and familiarity with public affairs.[13] Every presidential act must be countersigned by the appropriate minister, who thereby becomes responsible.[14] This clause, of course, is utterly meaningless.

CHAMBER OF REPRESENTATIVES. The Chamber of Representatives has fifty members, popularly elected for five years. Representatives must be natural-born citizens, at least twenty-five years of age. Bills may be intro-

9 Constitution, Art. 52.
10 Art. 47.
11 Art. 46.
12 Arts. 62–66.
13 Art. 60.
14 Arts. 59–61.

duced by any member. They may also be introduced by the president; in fact, they *must* come from this source if they deal with taxes or the recruitment or mobilization of troops. The president's proposals must be considered during the session in which they are submitted. If the Chamber of Representatives adjourns without acting upon them, its approval is assumed. The president is specifically authorized to issue decree-laws while the Chamber of Representatives is in recess, though these decrees must later be submitted for legislative approval. The president's veto is absolute, unless it refers only to items or parts of a bill, in which case it may be overridden by a two-thirds vote. Special sessions may be called by the president, and he may dissolve the Chamber of Representatives at any time, subject to the necessity of calling elections for a new Chamber within two months.[15] Even this brief summary of the lawmaking process, as envisioned by the constitution, indicates the dominant position of the president in the scheme of government. When there is no Chamber of Representatives to hamper him, of course, his authority is even more complete. Such a situation prevailed throughout the Morínigo regime.

THE COURTS. The supreme court has three members. Their term, like that of the president, is five years, so that each new chief executive may have the opportunity to name his own court.[16] There are no courts of appeal between the highest tribunal and the courts of first instance.

INTERNAL ORGANIZATION. The eastern section of Paraguay, where almost all the people live, has been divided into twelve departments (not including Asunción and its environs). Each department is governed by a delegate, who is appointed by the president. There is no local self-government. The affairs of Asunción are handled directly by the minister of the interior.

SELECTED REFERENCES

Baliarda Bigaire, L., *José Gaspar Rodríguez de Francia, Primer Dictador Perpetuo Sud Americano*, Buenos Aires, Editorial "Urbe," 1942.
Bellani Nazeri, Rodolfo, *Morínigo, un Hombre de América*, Santiago de Chile, Editorial "Revistas de las Américas," 1946.
Cardozo, Ramón I., *La Pedagogía de la Escuela Activa*, Asunción, La Colmena, 1939.
Chaves, Julio C., *El Supremo Dictador; Biografía de José Gaspar de Francia*, Buenos Aires, Editorial Difusam, 1942.
Cunninghame, Graham R. B., *Portrait of a Dictator*, London, W. Heinemann, Ltd., 1933.

[15] Arts. 67–79.
[16] Arts. 80–82.

De Ronde, Philip, *Paraguay, A Gallant Little Nation*, New York, Putnam, 1935.

Garay, Blas, *Tres Ensayos sobre Historia del Paraguay*, Asunción, Editorial Guaraní, 1942.

García, Emilio, *Economía Política*, Asunción, La Colmena, 1942.

González, Juan Natalicio, *Como se Construye una Nación*, Asunción, Editorial Guaraní, 1949.

—— *El Paraguayao y la Lucha por su Expresión*, Asunción, Editorial Guaraní, 1945.

Méndez, Epifanio, *Batallas por la Democracia*, Asunción, Editorial Guaraní, 1950.

Oddone, Rafael, *Esquema Político del Paraguay*, Buenos Aires, Editorial Asunción, 1948.

O'Leary, Juan Emiliano, *El Legado Cívico de Héroe*, Asunción, Biblioteca "Blas Garay," 1944.

Pastore, Carlos, *La Lucha por la Tierra en el Paraguay*, Montevideo, Editorial Antequera, 1949.

Pérez Echeguren, José Antonio, *Relieve y Categoría de la Revolución Paraguaya*, Asunción, Imp. Nacional, 1940.

Sanabria, Salustiano, *Organización Política del Paraguay*, Asunción, Editorial Guaraní, 1946.

Stefanich, Juan, *El Paraguay Nuevo*, Buenos Aires, Editorial Claridad, 1943.

Warren, Harris G., *Paraguay*, Norman, University of Oklahoma Press, 1949.

CHAPTER 20

BOLIVIA

~~~~~~

The Land and the People

AREA AND POPULATION. Bolivia has an area of four hundred thousand square miles, which makes it the sixth largest country of Latin America. It is approximately the same size as the eastern seaboard of the United States, from Maine to Florida. Formerly it was even larger, but it lost considerable territory in two disastrous conflicts—the War of the Pacific, in which it forfeited its outlet to the sea,[1] and the more recent Chaco War.[2] There are only three and one-half million people within the present extensive boundaries of Bolivia. Its population density of nine per square mile is lower than that of any other Latin American nation except neighboring Paraguay.

THE HIGH PLATEAU. It is scarcely surprising that Bolivia has so few people. Nature has imposed upon it almost insurmountable handicaps. The western plateau, where the population is largely concentrated, has many peaks that rise more than twenty thousand feet above sea level. The principal mountain passes are mostly at thirteen or fourteen thousand feet. Lake Titicaca, the great body of water that lies athwart the Bolivian-Peruvian boundary, has an altitude of more than twelve thousand feet. At such heights the maintenance of human communities is extremely difficult. The plateau is cold and barren, changing scarcely at all from season to season. Driving storms sometimes leave it white with snow. High temperatures are virtually unknown, but there are great differences be-

[1] See page 286.
[2] See pages 514–515.

tween night and day. The northern part of the plateau has so little rainfall that it scarcely supports agriculture; the southern section has even less, and is virtually a desert. There are no trees anywhere on the plateau; therefore there is no wood and no coal. The principal fuels are llama dung and fungus growths, which are used even in steam boilers. The rarified air makes the slightest exertion difficult for visitors. Even the natives experience a tendency to apathy and an appalling susceptibility to respiratory diseases. The poorer classes face approximately the same problems as the poor of Peru's high plateau, and solve them in the same manner—by drugging themselves with coca leaves.[3]

PRIMITIVE CONDITIONS. Only the hardiest crops can be grown on the Bolivian plateau. Barley and potatoes are most common, with smaller yields of wheat and oats. The farming methods are incredibly primitive in most sections, following the pattern of life before the Spanish conquest. Transportation presents many difficult problems. The roads are dirt for the most part and unfit for use by motor cars in wet weather, though some hard-surface mileage has been built in and near the larger cities and near some of the more important mines. Railroads provide a more satisfactory method of travel; there are several lines, and almost all use the same gauge. Those lines coming from the coast must conquer steep grades. One of them even uses a cograil system for twenty-two miles. A large part of Bolivia's commerce still moves on the backs of llamas and burros. In the entire country there are only about seven thousand telephones and not more than six thousand motor cars. These facts give some slight indication of the nation's intense poverty.

TWO CAPITALS. Years ago the capital of the country was declared to be Sucre, which lies on the eastern slope of the Andes. But most Bolivians thought that Sucre was inaccessible and refused to make it the seat of their government. Today, therefore, Bolivia is a nation with two capitals. The legal capital is still Sucre; the supreme court sits here, and the archbishop makes the city his residence. But all other governmental activity centers in La Paz. Here Congress holds its sessions; here are the presidential palace and all the ministries. It is the nation's capital for all practical purposes, despite legal provisions to the contrary. La Paz has a very unusual setting. It lies in a deep gorge, two miles wide, which has been cut into the high plateau by the La Paz River. In order to reach the city by airplane, therefore, it is necessary to land on the plateau at an elevation of more than thirteen thousand feet and then descend by motor car into the

3 See page 347.

canyon. Yet La Paz is more than twelve thousand feet above sea level. With a population of three hundred thousand, it is the highest big city in the world. Its location within the canyon provides a measure of protection from the chill winds that sweep the high plateau.

EASTERN SLOPES. East of the plateau, on the slopes of the Andes, are other regions that provide more pleasant living conditions. At altitudes of seven or eight thousand feet the air is warm and springlike throughout the year and there is ample rain for agriculture. Bolivia's second city, Cochabamba, is situated in this area at an elevation of eighty-five hundred feet. It has a population of sixty thousand. Farther south, but at the same altitude, is the capital city of Sucre. These warmer regions permit the cultivation of a much wider variety of crops than is possible on the plateau. Corn is grown, and also sugar. But the principal crop is coca, which the Indians find so necessary to their mode of life.

EASTERN PLAINS. Below the mountains are the foothills and plains of the Amazon and Paraguay Rivers. They comprise more than one half of Bolivia's total area, but contribute very little to its economy. Some of the land is suitable for grazing; much of it is heavily forested. It contains some rubber, which has been exported in small quantities. Here, too, is the petroleum that Bolivia hopes to make the basis for a major industry some day. The region is sparsely settled and has few cities of any consequence.

RACES. The percentage of Indian blood is probably higher in Bolivia than in any other country of Latin America. About fifty-five per cent of the people are of pure Indian stock. Most of the others are *mestizos* (or *cholos*, as half-breeds are called in this part of South America). Not more than fifteen per cent—perhaps not more than ten per cent—are white. The overwhelming majority of the whites are of Spanish stock, but there are some Italians and Germans. There has been very little immigration to Bolivia, despite government policies intended to encourage newcomers. The whites and cholos control the country. Some have great estates; a few have important financial interests in the mines. Many more are the managers of the estates, or skilled workers, or minor government officials. The Indians are the laboring class. Most of them are engaged in agriculture. If they do not have their own small plots of ground, they work on the estates where they are virtually serfs. From sun to sun they toil, in exchange for the mere right to exist. They receive almost no money wages; their health and education are neglected. Yet nothing could induce them to move from the place that they have always known as home.

MINING.   The economy of Bolivia is based on mining.   Silver was taken from the mines in fabulous quantities during the colonial period; the group of mines at Potosí was recognized as the richest in the world.   Some silver is still produced, but the richest deposits seem to have been depleted. Today tin is by far the most important metal; it represents about two thirds of the nation's total exports.   There are virtually no facilities for major smelting operations; therefore the ore is shipped to the coast and taken by boat to the United States or Europe.   Unfortunately for Bolivia, the ore is comparatively low grade.   For many years it was able to meet the competition of Malaya only because of artificially high tin prices, which were maintained by an international cartel.   During the Second World War, when Malaya was occupied by the Japanese and the Bolivian mines were the only important sources of tin available to the United States and its allies, the demand reached unprecedented proportions.   Now, however, the competition of Malaya has again made itself felt and Bolivia's economy has suffered some severe shocks.   There are, of course, other minerals also—antimony, tungsten, bismuth, and zinc, as well as gold and copper; but they are of minor importance.

Cheap labor.   For many years Bolivian tin mining was in private hands, and was based on a system of cheap labor.   The wages were low and housing conditions inadequate.   Company stores supplied necessities to the workers at prices that were calculated to keep them in perpetual debt. Yet there was some gradual improvement in recent years, due largely to the efforts of Bolivia's political leaders.   Model labor laws were enacted; they established maximum hours of work and minimum wages, and made provision for compulsory education and free health services.   But they were not systematically enforced, and most of the private owners contended that enforcement was not economically feasible.   In some instances the owners of small mines even abandoned operations when faced with government insistence on improved living conditions for the workers.   The profit margin was so small, said these owners, that they could not afford to make the additional outlay.[4]

The Patiño interests.   During the days of private ownership there were a few companies that controlled almost all the tin mines.   These companies were largely foreign-owned.   Most important were the Patiño interests.   Simón Patiño, the founder of this tin empire, was born in southeastern Bolivia in the mid-sixties of the last century.   Mostly of Indian blood, he had almost no education.   But he managed to accumu-

[4] See Olen E. Leonard's 1952 monograph, *Bolivia: Land, People and Institutions.*

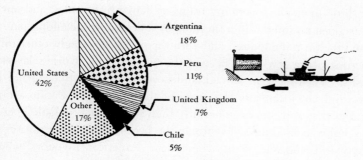

Bolivian Imports by Country of Origin (1950)

Based on information obtained from the *Foreign Commerce Yearbook, 1950*, a 1952 publication of the United States Department of Commerce.

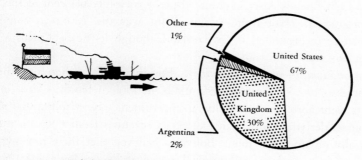

Bolivian Exports by Country of Destination (1950)

Based on information obtained from the *Foreign Commerce Yearbook, 1950*, a 1952 publication of the United States Department of Commerce.

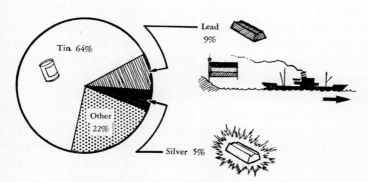

Bolivian Exports of Principal Commodities (1950)

Based on information obtained from the May, 1953, issue of *International Financial Statistics*, a publication of the International Monetary Fund.

late a little money by operating trains of llamas and mules, and one day he was given an interest in a tin mine by a debtor who couldn't pay. He worked the tin mine himself and with the profits he bought other mining properties. In a few years he was the owner of the world's largest tin deposits. Then he went abroad, and never returned. But absence from Bolivia did not mean loss of control of the tin mines. Patiño arranged the cartel that kept prices sufficiently high to permit profitable operation of his Bolivian holdings. Eventually he became known as the tin king of the world, and one of its richest men. American investors bought a substantial interest in his holdings.

Hochschild and Aramayo. Two other groups shared control of Bolivian tin with the Patiño family. One was headed by Mauricio Hochschild, a German of Argentine nationality. His company, which had its headquarters in Buenos Aires, dominated perhaps twenty per cent of the total tin production. Not quite so important was the Aramayo company, which was incorporated in Switzerland, though its head—Carlos Víctor Aramayo—was a Bolivian.

Nationalization of the tin mines. For many years, therefore, the tin resources of the nation were essentially in foreign hands. Most of the profits went abroad. The Bolivian government took a substantial share, of course, deriving more than half of its revenues from taxes on metals, especially on tin. But many Bolivians believed that their nation could never be free—economically as well as politically—as long as foreigners dominated the main source of national wealth. So in 1952 the government expropriated the tin mines and placed them under the direction of a seven-man board, five of whose members were to be chosen by the president and the other two by the labor unions. The present policy of nationalization is highly popular with the Bolivian masses, but only time can tell whether it will bring a larger or smaller measure of prosperity to the impoverished nation. Bolivian tin must still be sold abroad, and it must still compete with the superior tin of Malaya.[5]

PETROLEUM. In the hot lands of the Bolivian Chaco are petroleum deposits that may become extremely important some day. These deposits were first developed by an American oil company, but considerable friction between company representatives and government officials developed during the Chaco War. The Bolivian government contended that the company's failure to increase production seriously hampered the war effort.

[5] For a further discussion of tin nationalization, see page 541.

The company replied that inefficient Bolivian labor and unsatisfactory transportation facilities prevented further development. Finally the Bolivian authorities ordered the confiscation of the American oil properties. That was in 1937. The company offered no serious objection to the loss of its concession, which had proved unsatisfactory in many ways, but it requested a reasonable compensation for the large investment already made. Bolivia paid this compensation in 1942 and the incident was closed. There can be little doubt that the Bolivian government's willingness to adjust the matter so promptly was occasioned by its desire to obtain a loan from the United States. The oil fields are now a government monopoly. A pipe line carries the crude oil to refineries in Cochabamba.

INDUSTRY. Like most nations of Latin America, Bolivia is interested in industrialization as a means of raising its present low standard of living. There are, however, great difficulties, such as the lack of coal, the inadequacy of transportation facilities, and the almost complete absence of technical skills in the population. Some factories have been established, nonetheless. They produce chiefly goods that can be easily fabricated and sold locally, such as cement, flour, leather goods, cotton textiles, foodstuffs, and beverages. Local substitutes for beer and whisky are made in large quantities. The manufacturing plants are located almost exclusively in the cities of La Paz and Cochabamba. The prospect for heavy industry seems to be almost hopeless.

The Pattern of Politics

A BLOODY SAGA. Bolivia, like so many nations of Latin America, has had a tragic history. Blood is spilled across almost every page. Dictators have succeeded one another with monotonous regularity. Many have died violent deaths. Fourteen constitutions have been adopted without substantially changing the political pattern. Throughout the nineteenth century the traditional conservatives and liberals fought for control of the government, though neither group had any clear-cut program. Leaders were more important than principles. The army dominated the nation.

REFORM GROUPS. During the early years of the present century a number of civilians were elected to the presidency. Some of them tried to respect the forms established by the constitution; others openly flouted constitutional provisions and governed as dictators. But all governed in the interest of the wealthy tin magnates and landowners. All had the support of the

army—or, losing it, forfeited their power and sometimes their lives. Bolivia had somewhat the aspect of a company town, with the entire economy
of the nation revolving around tin. The oppressed masses lived as they
had always lived, without comforts and without hope. But the crushing
defeats of the Chaco War focused attention on the ineptitude of the administration. Young army officers were openly contemptuous of their
own officers and of the civilian politicians. Young intellectuals who had
read of revolutionary movements in other lands began to talk of nationalizing the tin mines and confiscating the great estates. These reformers were
communist fellow travelers, if not openly converts to the communist faith.
They formed a political party which they called the Revolutionary Party
of the Left—or, to give it the initials of its Spanish name, PIR. Another
group of intellectuals banded together to form the Nationalist Revolutionary Movement, or MNR. They were strongly nationalistic, and interested
in the fascist experiments of Hitler's Germany and Mussolini's Italy.
Their hatred seemed to be reserved especially for the "imperialistic" United
States.

THE 1936 REVOLUTION. The conservative administrations that controlled
the country made some concessions to the new order. President José Luis
Tejada Sórzano, who had seized control of the government in 1934, when
the then President was absent from La Paz on a visit to the Chaco battle
front, issued a decree providing compensation for industrial accidents.
But the workers were not satisfied. On May 15, 1936, they began a general
strike that threatened to disrupt the economic life of the nation. Jobless
Chaco War veterans gave them strong encouragement. Two days later
the army seized control of the government in a swift, bloodless *coup d'état*.
The acting chief of staff, Lieutenant Colonel Germán Busch, became provisional president, but only for a single day, until a government could be
formed. The leaders of the uprising were radicals, and they promptly
announced that the new president would be another army officer, Colonel
David Toro, who was known to be sympathetic to their socialistic aims.
Toro promptly suspended the constitution and eliminated all civilians from
important posts in the government. He abolished all political parties except the National Socialist, which had been responsible for placing him
in power.

LABOR POLICIES. One of President Toro's first acts was to settle the general strike. He also provided pensions for the jobless veterans. These
pensions were not large, but considerably more than the men had been
paid as soldiers. Thus they were confirmed in their belief that socialism

would provide a solution to all their difficulties. A little later, however, they had a rude awakening. The shortage of jobs proved to be only temporary. Men were needed in the mines and in industry. Moreover, the government did not have the money to pay the promised pensions. So President Toro told the pension holders that they must go out and get jobs; if they did not, they would be assigned to work at the prevailing wage. Many veterans did refuse to go to work, despite the official decree, so they were rounded up and sent to the mines. This was a different brand of socialism from what the workers had been led to expect. It reduced the popularity of the government to the vanishing point.

RISE AND FALL OF GERMÁN BUSCH. With widespread resentment of the administration's policies, another revolution was inevitable. It occurred on July 13, 1937, only a little more than a year after the uprising that had put Toro in power, and it was directed by Germán Busch, who had led the previous *coup d'état.* This time, however, Busch was determined to retain the presidency more than a single day. He had the army behind him. He announced that the nation would abandon its socialistic experiments and "return to democracy." The constitution, which Toro had suspended, was declared once more in effect.

Colonel Busch was the son of a German doctor and an Indian woman. He had been born in one of the more remote jungle areas of the country and had grown to know and love this region. When, therefore, he was called upon to fight in the Chaco War, he found himself in the same kind of country that had always been his home. That gave him a great advantage over most of his countrymen, who had come from the high plateau. So perhaps his excellent war record was partly a matter of luck. In any event, he found himself a popular hero at the war's end. His forceful personality made him a natural leader. But he was young—only thirty-three years of age at the time he became president—and very ignorant. He had received just a rudimentary education, and of course he knew nothing about the management of public affairs. He listened first to one adviser and then to another, and changed the policies of state after almost every interview. First he called a constitutional convention and encouraged it to prepare a liberal document. Later he discarded this constitution and ruled as a dictator. In the early days of his administration he encouraged criticism; afterward he wearied of it and jailed or exiled his critics.

But none of his measures brought prosperity to the country; in fact, matters seemed to be going rapidly from bad to worse. So President

Busch took the advice of the nationalists and issued a decree requiring the tin companies to turn over to the government the full value of their exports, receiving Bolivian currency in exchange. The purpose of this decree was to compel the companies to invest their earnings in Bolivian enterprises. Actually it had no such effect. The tin cartel threatened to retaliate by stopping all mining operations, and it was in a position to carry out its threat. If it did so, of course, the principal source of the Bolivian government's revenue would dry up overnight. The government could seize and operate the mines, but it would have to send the ore to England for smelting. And then it would discover that the cartel owned not only the mines but also the smelters. It was a most unhappy situation for Bolivia. What made it especially unhappy for President Busch was that he could not safely rescind his decree. Bolivians of all political faiths united to praise him for his fearless stand against foreign monopoly. Even the newspapers that had been most determined in their opposition— before the strict censorship—announced that they were completely in favor of the President's policy. Eventually, of course, the decree had to be revoked, but President Busch was not alive to take this step. On August 23, 1939, after a night of riotous drinking, he shot himself through the head. That, at least, is the official story. And no one could doubt that he was dead.[6]

PRESIDENT PEÑARANDA. The older and more conservative army leaders promptly seized control of the government. The chief of staff declared himself provisional president and announced that he would continue in office until arrangements could be made for an election. One candidate was expelled from the country two months later. In March, 1940, the election was finally held. There was only one candidate and he was a general on whom the older army officers had agreed. His name was Enrique Peñaranda; his principal qualification for the presidency seems to have been a willingness to take orders. Unfortunately, however, the orders that he received from his army associates merely increased the disordered state of the nation's economy. Prices rose steadily while wages lagged far behind, thus bringing the prospect of actual starvation to many workers. Peñaranda managed to stay in office for three and one-half years, however, despite increasing discontent. But the opposition was becoming constantly more numerous and more critical. Peñaranda was said to be a tool of the tin magnates and the Yankee "imperialists." When he car-

---

[6] See the interesting article by Laurence Duggan, "Background for Revolution," in the September, 1946, issue (Vol. V, No. 9) of *Inter-American*, pp. 15–17 and 31–32.

ried the nation into war at the side of the United States, in April of 1943, these charges were made with redoubled vigor. Young army officers began to organize themselves in secret lodges, where they planned a *coup d'état*. Associated with them in this enterprise were the civilians of the MNR. The PIR, though equally critical of the President's policies, regarded the other opposition groups as too conservative.

THE VILLARROEL REGIME. The uprising occurred in the early morning hours of December 20, 1943. It was highly successful. Peñaranda was permitted to leave the country, and the army officers chose one of their own number, Major Gualberto Villarroel, to be president. The MNR was invited to take a hand in forming the new government and promptly accepted. At first the PIR hoped to be included, also, but this hope was doomed to disappointment. So the PIR joined the opposition, thus aligning itself uncomfortably with the mine owners and the other deposed conservatives.

THE QUESTION OF RECOGNITION. When the United States State Department examined the records of the men who were responsible for the revolution, it decided that the whole affair must be a German or Argentine plot to draw Bolivia into the orbit of the Axis powers. The conclusion was not warranted, but it did have a certain plausibility. MNR leaders were known to have printed the German version of the news in their papers, and even to have accepted German subsidies. So the United States announced that it would not recognize the new regime. President Villarroel and his friends viewed this decision with dismay. They knew that Germany could not win the war and they wanted to be on the winning side. Moreover, the Allied nations were the only ones that could buy Bolivian tin, and Bolivia had to sell its tin or starve.

It was clear that the pro-Nazi stigma must somehow be removed from the new government. The President protested his friendship for the United States and his determination to continue his country's part in the war effort. To prove his sincerity, he removed from his cabinet several members of the MNR, including those who had been most outspoken in their criticism of American policies. One of the victims of this purge was the MNR's acknowledged leader, Víctor Paz Estenssoro. The United States government took several months to decide whether the Villarroel administration had experienced a change of heart—though of course it continued without interruption its purchases of tin—and finally decided that the conversion was genuine. On June 23, 1944, it extended recognition. Nine days later elections were held for members of Congress and the MNR was swept back into power. Also elected was José Antonio Arze, the leader of the PIR, but he was attacked by an assassin who sent a bullet through his left lung. After recovering, he left the country.

CONCILIATORY ATTITUDE TOWARD LABOR. The new regime made a determined effort to win the support of the workers, thus undermining the opposition PIR which also made its strong appeal to the laboring class. Laws and decrees improving working and housing conditions were issued at frequent intervals. Public housing was undertaken on an extensive scale. Wage boards were created to hear workers' complaints. Labor was encouraged to organize, and several government employees were assigned to the task of promoting trade unions. The mine owners naturally disapproved of these policies but accepted the situation with good grace when they found their properties were not to be expropriated.

A REIGN OF TERROR. While wooing the workers, the Villarroel government attempted to silence the opposition and strengthen its own position by establishing a reign of terror. Its attacks were directed primarily against the PIR, but no one was safe if he uttered a word of criticism or complaint. Newspaper editors, union leaders, and even members of Congress were arrested and thrown into jail. Sometimes they were beaten brutally by the police. One prominent congressman was attacked by three men in civilian clothes only a few minutes after leaving the Palace of Congress. He was finally rescued by onlookers, though not before he had received a severe beating. One of the three attackers was captured by friends of the congressman who happened to be close at hand; he turned out to be a police officer who had discarded his uniform for the occasion. When asked why he had taken part in the assault, he replied that he was acting under orders. No one doubted him. Tin magnate Mauricio Hochschild was kidnaped, but managed to escape with his life. Instances of calculated police brutality multiplied rapidly. In November, 1944, fifteen leaders of the opposition were murdered. The list of victims included two senators and two former cabinet members. Other prominent persons hastily made plans to leave the country.

DISSENSION WITHIN THE GOVERNMENT. Rumors of revolution were everywhere. The government did not know whom to trust and usually solved this difficulty by killing or exiling any person who might possibly be plotting to make trouble. Even within the Villarroel administration there were sharp differences of opinion which could not always be suppressed. Some of the army officers were highly critical of the civilian element, represented by MNR. In June, 1946, several of these officers launched a revolution, and used their planes in an attempt to bomb the presidential palace. The uprising was suppressed, but it emphasized the insecurity of the government. Successful revolution was only a matter of time.

RIOTS AND MASSACRES. The final rebellion that led to the destruction of the Villarroel regime seemed at first to be only a minor incident. The miserably underpaid schoolteachers of La Paz struck for higher salaries and organized a demonstration which was joined by a number of students. Even before they reached the presidential palace the government gave its answer. A detachment of police fired into the unarmed crowd, killing one student and wounding many other persons. That was on July 13, 1946. The next day there was another demonstration, which included Bolivians of every social class. Teachers' salaries were forgotten in the demand for freedom of expression and freedom from fear. This time the police held their fire. When, however, a group of students stormed the central police station in an effort to obtain arms and ammunition, they were mowed down unmercifully. Thereupon the survivors attacked and captured the government radio station. In a short time they were broadcasting an appeal for help. The help came from all quarters, though weapons of war were still conspicuously lacking. By the afternoon of July 19 a crowd of at least thirty-five thousand persons had gathered in the Plaza Murillo, before the presidential palace, singing the national anthem and shouting for liberty. Once again the government replied with a crude display of force. Troops armed with machine guns fired into the mob from the windows and roofs of surrounding buildings. A tank charged across the plaza, firing in all directions. The demonstrators fled in wild disorder, while soldiers hastily dragged away the bodies of the dead.

A POPULAR VICTORY. For once, however, the government had under-estimated the determination of the people. They met in little groups in every section of La Paz, trying to decide how they could secure arms. On Sunday, July 21, they made another attack on the central police station. This time they managed to capture the building, despite heavy losses. Soon they were handing out rifles, pistols, and even machine guns. At last they could meet the police and the army on fairly equal terms. Their next point of attack was the national penitentiary, which they speedily captured. Hundreds of political prisoners were freed and given arms. Then the mob headed once more for the presidential palace. President Villarroel tried desperately to escape to a nearby airfield where a warmed-up plane was waiting. But he was driven back by heavy gunfire. At eleven in the morning he broadcast his resignation. The mob continued its advance on the palace. Some regiments of troops joined the attackers. Within a short time the palace doors were battered in, and the people poured into the building, searching for the leaders of the hated regime. They found Villarroel cowering in the basement, riddled his body with bullets, carried it to a third-floor window, and threw it to the crowd below. Eventually the late President made his final public appearance, dangling by the neck from a lamppost. Some of his associates were accorded similar treatment. Others were arrested and held for trial. Many managed to escape. The crowds soon dispersed quietly, without the looting that often accompanies such uprisings.

The people of La Paz had won a major victory, though they were not quite sure what should be done next. In other parts of the country the news of the revolution was received with mixed emotions. Some of the tin workers even talked of beginning a counterrevolt. But they soon abandoned this idea, and peace returned to the unhappy nation.

PRESIDENTIAL ELECTION OF 1947. The leaders of the uprising were unanimous in their belief that the provisional president must be a civilian. Finally they agreed upon Dr. Tomás Monje, the respected president of the superior court of La Paz. But Monje was ill at the time, so another judge served temporarily in his place. As soon as Monje was able to take office, he appointed an all-civilian cabinet to help him govern the nation and invited the political exiles to return. Hundreds of them did so. Announcement was made that an election for president and members of Congress would be held at the earliest possible moment. That election was held on January 4, 1947.

There were two principal candidates. One of them was Enrique Hertzog, a highly respected surgeon of French descent who had served in the front lines during the Chaco War. He had a record of consistent opposition to the unpopular regimes that had caused the nation so much suffering. Six times during the course of his political career he had been exiled and seven times he had been imprisoned. The scars on his body were evidence of the treatment he had received. A coalition of parties was formed to promote Hertzog's candidacy. The most important element in the coalition was the Republican Socialist Union Party (PUSR), which had been organized the previous year. Its program was slightly left of center, including such planks as better living and working conditions for the masses and opposition to foreign control of Bolivia's natural wealth.

The other principal candidate was Luis Fernando Guachalla, the popular scion of an old La Paz family, who had once served as ambassador to the United States. Guachalla also had the support of a coalition, which included the radical PIR, and also the conservative but misnamed Liberal Party. It was a strange alliance, held together only by dislike of Hertzog. The elements of dissension became apparent when the coalition tried to prepare a program. Finally it succeeded, but only after the PIR's leader, José Arze, who had returned from exile, managed to convince his Liberal colleagues that they could not possibly hope to win the election except by steering to the left of the radical PUSR. A third candidate, General Félix Tavera, had no substantial following and was not expected to win more than a few votes. The MNR, of course, was not permitted to participate. Most of its leaders were dead or exiled.

AN UNEASY PEACE. The election was honest, probably for the first time in Bolivian history. Hertzog beat Guachalla by only two hundred and eighty-nine votes. This was not sufficient to give him a popular majority, so Congress had to decide the matter. Before it met, however, the two leading candidates made a deal that seemed to give satisfaction to both sides. Hertzog was to become president, but was to govern with a coalition cabinet drawn from both of the major political groups. All the Guachalla congressmen whose seats had been challenged were to be seated, thus assuring them substantial representation. Congress respected this arrangement and named Hertzog president. Guachalla was appointed foreign minister and Arze became president of the Chamber of Deputies. For a time, therefore, President Hertzog had the nominal support of virtually every important political group.

But this harmony was only surface-deep. The members of the PIR constantly urged the adoption of more radical reforms, and openly expressed their dissatisfaction with the President's policies. The miners, who had received glowing promises of future benefits from Villarroel, found the Hertzog administration unable or unwilling to renew these pledges. So they began a series of strikes which disrupted the nation's economy and brought it dangerously close to bankruptcy. The government finally found a formula to settle these strikes, but the PIR refused to accept this arrangement. Its cabinet members resigned their portfolios in August, 1947, and joined the opposition. José Arze, the PIR leader, was forced out as president of the Chamber of Deputies. Therefore President Hertzog had to govern the nation with a coalition of his own Republican Socialists and the conservative Liberals, who voted against him in the 1947 election. This alliance gave him a substantial majority in both houses of Congress, but the situation was explosive.

ELECTIONS AND REBELLIONS. In May, 1949, elections were held for members of Congress. President Hertzog's PUSR managed to maintain its majority, but the MNR showed surprising strength. Its supporters were so elated by their unexpected popularity that they tried to storm the presidential palace, but were repulsed by loyal troops. After that the MNR made several unsuccessful attempts to take over the government by force. In 1949 its partisans actually succeeded in capturing Cochabamba and setting up a revolutionary government in Santa Cruz. Víctor Paz Estenssoro, the forty-four-year-old ex-college professor who had been directing the activities of the MNR from his exile in Montevideo, was named as president of the revolutionary regime. But the uprising was finally suppressed with severe loss of life on both sides. Meanwhile Hertzog had become ill, and on October 21 he decided to resign the presidency. His place was taken by Vice-President Mamerto Urriolagoitía. A number of other plots to overthrow the government were discovered, and strikes were rampant in all parts of the country, with frequent fighting in the streets. Bolivia was almost continuously under a state of martial law. Yet the government proceeded with its plans to hold a new presidential election on schedule.

The election took place on May 6, 1951, and resulted in a sweeping victory for the MNR. Víctor Paz Estenssoro was compelled to conduct his campaign from exile, yet he won forty-one per cent of the total vote. This was far more than the vote for any other candidate. Since it fell short of an absolute majority, however, the final decision had to be made by Congress. MNR supporters talked of installing Paz Estenssoro in the presidential chair by force of arms if Congress should dare to choose some other nominee. At this juncture, however, anti-MNR elements in the army decided to take charge. President Urriolagoitía was forced to resign, and his place was taken by a military junta, which promptly announced that the recent presidential election was invalid. Supporters of the MNR protested vehemently, but to no avail.

TRIUMPH OF THE MNR. For months the leaders of the MNR plotted against the government, and on April 9, 1952, they finally struck. Revolt broke out simultaneously in all seven of Bolivia's major cities. The fighting was intense for two days, and more than three thousand people were killed. The damage to property was extensive. Finally, however, the government forces were obliged to concede defeat, and the members of the military junta took refuge in foreign embassies. On April 15 Dr. Paz

Estenssoro returned to La Paz in triumph, and the following day he was sworn in as president of the nation. Almost at once he announced radical measures for strengthening the nation's economy. Large landholdings were to be broken up, and agriculture diversified. Basic foodstuffs were to be imported by a government agency, so as to keep prices as low as possible. And, most important of all, the mines were to be nationalized. The nationalization decree was signed in October, 1952; it formally transferred title from the private owners to a government mining corporation. President Paz Estenssoro has said that just compensation will be paid to the mine owners, but apparently he intends to pay for nothing more than the surface installations because, as he points out, the government already owns everything below the surface of the ground. The mines are still operating, but on a greatly reduced scale. Meanwhile the MNR is using severe repressive measures to force its opponents into line or into exile. Opposition newspapers have been closed. All ten members of the supreme court have been replaced by MNR partisans. An attempt has been made to win greater popular support by extending the suffrage to illiterates, and by telling women that they may vote in national as well as local elections. The radical PIR has now become officially the Communist Party of Bolivia, and has thrown in its lot with the MNR. Its leaders have been given important posts in the government. But the opposition has not readily accepted this turn of events. Already it has staged a number of revolts. Still other plots have been discovered before they reached the stage of open rebellion, and the army has been purged of "unreliable" elements. Peaceful democratic ways do not come easily to a nation that is poverty-stricken, largely illiterate, and torn by political feuds.

The Structure of Government

The constitution. The present constitution of Bolivia was adopted in 1938 and modified substantially in 1945. It is a document of moderate length—much longer than the fundamental laws of the United States and Paraguay, but considerably shorter than the constitutions of Mexico and Venezuela. It seems to offer a firm basis for democratic government. The casual reader would never guess that it had been framed under one dictatorship and amended to its present form under another. The first four articles take the place of a preamble. They declare that sovereignty resides in the people, who govern through their properly elected representatives; that any armed group attempting to govern in the name of the people is guilty of sedition; and that the official religion of the nation is Roman Catholicism, though other faiths are respected.[7]

Bill of rights. Then follows a two-thousand-word enumeration of rights and guarantees. Every person has the right to express his ideas freely, to petition the government individually or in the company of others; and to obtain release under a writ of *habeas corpus* in case of illegal detention.[8] Such guarantees must be a source of bitter mirth to the thousands of Bolivians who have suffered under the ruthless tyrannies of successive dictatorships. As in many recent Latin American constitutions, the authors take the opportunity to express their economic and social philosophy. All mineral wealth is declared to be the property of the state, as well as all lands that are not in a state of cultivation.[9] This clause was made the basis for expropriating the mines. The government is authorized to establish a public monopoly over any product designed for export and to control the importation of any article necessary for the nation's industrial economy.[10] Workers are guaranteed the right to organize, to strike, and even to participate in the profits of the companies that employ them.[11]

State of siege. Nearly one thousand words are used to authorize the declaration of a state of siege and to restrict its operation to cases of genuine necessity. The president, with the approval of his cabinet, may decree a state of siege whenever there is grave danger to the welfare of the nation because of a domestic upheaval or foreign war. He must report his action to Congress at the earliest possible opportunity, however. The state of siege ends automatically at the end of ninety days, unless Congress has specifically authorized its continuance or unless the nation is actually engaged in civil war or armed conflict with another nation.[12] "Neither the Congress nor any gathering of the people may grant to the chief executive extraordinary powers, the sum total of public authority, nor any power that will place the lives, the honor, and the property of Bolivians at the mercy of the government, or of any person."[13] These are brave words, but Bolivians have found them of little value.

[7] Bolivia did not adopt a policy of religious toleration, however, until 1906. See N. A. N. Cleven's *Political Organization of Bolivia*, pp. 189–206.

[8] Arts. 6 and 7.

[9] Art. 108.

[10] Art. 110.

[11] Arts. 126 and 127.

[12] Arts. 34–37.

[13] Art. 38.

Amendment of the constitution. The constitution may be amended by Congress, but only by an extraordinary majority and after a certain lapse of time. First there must be a two-thirds vote favoring the amendment in each house; then the proposal must be set aside until after the next congressional election. Only one half of the deputies and one third of the senators are chosen at any one election; therefore a large percentage of the total membership is sure to remain unaltered. Nonetheless, Congress may now proceed to a second consideration of the proposed reform, and if it again votes its approval by a two-thirds margin, the amendment becomes a part of the constitution. The president, according to the letter of the constitution, has no part in the amending process.[14]

SUFFRAGE. The right to vote in national elections is extended to all citizens at the age of twenty-one if unmarried or eighteen if married. Until 1952 inability to read and write was supposed to be a bar to voting, but many illiterates were permitted to cast ballots, especially in the rural districts. Women were first permitted to vote in municipal elections only; this reform was adopted in 1947. In the municipal elections of that year a woman was chosen mayor in one small city, and several other women were elected to municipal councils. Now unrestricted suffrage has been granted to both sexes.

ELECTIONS. Each party prepares its own list of candidates and, as in most Latin American countries, these printed lists take the place of official ballots. They must conform, of course, to government regulations concerning their shape, size, and color. In most cases the voter merely accepts the ballot of his favorite party and deposits it in the ballot box. He may, however, take the ballots of several parties and place them all in the official envelope, after crossing out on each ballot the names of candidates whom he does not favor. In this way he may split his vote. Proportional representation is not used. A simple plurality is sufficient to elect, except in the case of the chief executive.

THE PRESIDENT: *Selection, term, qualifications, salary.* The president is chosen by direct vote of the people. A majority is sufficient to elect, but, if no one has a majority, then Congress shall make its choice from among the three highest candidates. That, at least, is what the constitution declares. But many Bolivian presidents, as we have seen, have attained that high office in somewhat informal fashion. The term of office is six years, without the privilege of immediate re-election. The president, according to the constitution, must have the same qualifications as a senator—in other

[14] Arts. 174–177.

words, he must be a natural-born citizen, at least thirty-five years of age, who has completed his period of compulsory military training and is enrolled on the list of voters. Even for a poor country, Bolivia pays its president an absurdly small salary—the equivalent of about fourteen hundred American dollars a year. To this is added, however, a small amount for entertaining and miscellaneous expenses. The presidential palace is a magnificent structure overlooking the Plaza Murillo in the center of La Paz.

Executive powers. The constitution confers upon the president very extensive authority. He is as powerful in theory as in fact. His power of appointment and removal extends to all administrative officers and employees—including, of course, the members of his own cabinet. It extends also to diplomats and consular agents. For these appointments and removals the president does not need to have the consent of the Senate or any other body.[15] He appoints also the archbishops and bishops of the Roman Catholic Church, but from a list of three names submitted by the Senate for each vacancy. He selects high officers of the army, with Senate approval. He does not name the judges of the courts.[16] As in all countries, he exercises general control over the conduct of foreign relations. Congress approves treaties and declares war. Papal bulls and decrees must be approved by the president and the Senate before taking effect in Bolivian territory.

Legislative powers. The president plays an important part in lawmaking. He may propose laws, and these proposals must receive the prompt consideration of Congress. Certain types of legislation ordinarily originate with the chief executive. The list includes all tax measures and all proposals affecting administrative offices and the salaries of administrative employees. Under certain circumstances, however, Congress may initiate tax legislation. If either house believes that new taxes should be imposed, or that existing taxes should be increased, it may request the president to prepare suitable proposals. If he does not act within twenty days, Congress may then consider measures presented by its own members.[17] The president may veto laws, but his veto may be overridden by a two-thirds vote in each house. He may call Congress in special session.

Other powers. The remaining powers of the president follow more or less the usual pattern, but with some variations. The constitution declares

---

[15] There are, however, two exceptions—the auditor general and the attorney general. They are appointed by the president from lists presented by the Senate.

[16] See page 547.

[17] Art. 59.

that he shall have the title of Captain General of the Army, but further states that he shall appoint a commander-in-chief to conduct actual military operations. There is a Supreme Council of National Defense, of which the president is the presiding officer.[18] The power to grant pardons for ordinary crimes rests with Congress instead of the president, and may be exercised only upon the recommendation of the supreme court. But either the president or Congress may grant amnesty for political offenses, and the president may commute the death penalty, whether for political or other crimes.[19]

Vice-president; presidential succession. There is a vice-president of the nation, who is chosen in the same manner as the president and for a similar term. He must, of course, possess the same qualifications. His only duty, while he awaits the president's death or disability, is to preside over the Senate. After serving a term as vice-president, he is not eligible to be either vice-president or president until six years have passed. Below the vice-president, the line of presidential succession extends first to the president *pro tempore* of the Senate, and then to the president of the Chamber of Deputies, but these officers serve as president of the nation only until a new election can be held, unless at least half of the presidential term has expired.[20]

THE CABINET. The size of the president's cabinet is fixed by law. There are now twelve ministries: Foreign Affairs, Government, Finance, National Defense, Education, National Economy, Public Works, Labor and Social Welfare, Agriculture, Public Health, Rural Affairs, Mines and Petroleum. Each minister must be a native-born citizen, at least twenty-five years of age. The constitution declares that every presidential order must be countersigned by the appropriate minister, who thus endorses the decree and assumes responsibility for it. Actually this clause has no significance. It is just a form, as in so many countries of Latin America. Some years ago, however, Bolivia did experiment with the parliamentary system and cabinet responsibility. The 1931 constitution established the right of Congress to interpellate cabinet ministers and to compel their resignation by a vote of censure. But the presidents of that period were disinclined to accept legislative interference, and the right of censure remained largely a form.[21]

18 Arts. 168–173.
19 Arts. 59 and 94.
20 Art. 91.
21 For a contrary view, see N. A. N. Cleven's previously cited work, p. 113. Professor Cleven's volume contains much factual information, but shows a singular lack of understanding of the actual operation of Bolivian government.

In 1938, with the adoption of the present constitution, parliamentary government was abandoned. Congress is still authorized to request (not compel) the attendance of ministers at legislative sessions, and it may adopt a vote of censure against any minister or the entire cabinet "for the purpose of obtaining a modification of the policy that has caused the censure." [22] But there is no suggestion that the cabinet ministers thus censured must resign, nor is there even a hint of the manner in which Congress may actually procure a modification of ministerial (in other words, presidential) policy. Everything depends on the relations of Congress and the executive, and on the political power of each branch of the government. A congressional majority hostile to the president might readily compel some respect for its wishes by blocking his legislative program, but this power is inherent in the nature of constitutional government and has nothing whatever to do with the interpellation or censure of ministers.

CONGRESS: *Selection, terms, qualifications.* The two houses of Congress have been given the usual names—Senate and Chamber of Deputies. The Senate has twenty-seven members, three from each of the nation's nine departments. They serve for six years, one third retiring every second year. The Chamber of Deputies has one hundred and five members, whose term is four years, with renewal of one half of the membership every two years. Both senators and deputies are chosen by direct vote of the people. The qualifications are approximately the same—natural-born citizenship and fulfillment of the obligation of compulsory military service —but the minimum age is thirty-five years for senators and only twenty-five for deputies.

Place of meeting; sessions. The Palace of Congress, like the presidential residence, faces the central Plaza Murillo. It is a low, flat-roofed building with marble columns and an oddly proportioned dome. Here Congress meets in regular annual session the sixth day of August (Bolivia's independence day). The session continues for at least ninety days and may be prolonged an additional thirty days by action of Congress itself or of the president. Special sessions may be called by the president of the nation, or by the president of the Chamber of Deputies upon the request of a majority of the members of Congress. Bolivian political theorists attach great importance to the fact that Congress may meet independently of a summons from the executive.[23] Almost all the constitutions of the nation

[22] Art. 63.
[23] See, for example, Manuel Ordóñez López, *Constitución Política de la República de Bolivia*, Vol. II, p. 407.

have conferred this privilege. In practice, however, Congress seldom meets in special session, and never without a call from the president.

Organization and procedure. Each house chooses its own officers, who serve for but a single year. In the Chamber of Deputies the members elect a president, two vice-presidents, and two secretaries. This group forms a steering committee (*mesa directiva*), which prepares the legislative calendar and exercises general supervision over the work of the Chamber. The president of the lower house is its presiding officer; he possesses wide powers in connection with the recognition of speakers and the restriction of debate. He names the regular standing committees. All his decisions, however, are subject to the confirmation of the Chamber's membership. In the Senate the organization is much the same, except that the vice-president of the nation presides. He unites with the president *pro tempore* and the secretary to form the steering committee. There are nineteen permanent committees in the Chamber of Deputies, and ten in the Senate. The rules require them to report on all bills—within a certain number of days, in the case of important measures.[24] Disagreements between the two houses are settled at a joint session, in which every member has one vote.

THE COURTS: *Supreme court.* The supreme court of Bolivia has ten members. They are chosen by the Chamber of Deputies from a list of three names submitted by the Senate for each vacancy. Their term is ten years—unless, of course they are the victims of political manipulation—and they may be re-elected indefinitely. They must be native-born citizens, at least thirty-five years of age, who have practiced law "in a creditable manner" for ten years or more.[25] The supreme court is divided into two chambers, one for criminal cases and the other for civil affairs. Its president, who is chosen by the justices from their own membership, serves for only one year. Every member of the court is thus assured its presidency before the end of his ten-year term. Most cases reach the supreme court on appeal. The court exercises original jurisdiction, however, over disputes involving foreign diplomats and important officials of the Bolivian government. The list of these officials includes not only the president and the members of his cabinet, but also the prefects of departments, judges of the lower courts, and principal officers of the national university.

Inferior courts. Each of Bolivia's nine departments has a superior court,

[24] Each house of Congress publishes its *Reglamento,* which prescribes in great detail the procedure of the house and its committees.
[25] Art. 142.

which hears cases chiefly on appeal, though exercising a limited original jurisdiction. In the more populous departments the superior tribunal has five members; elsewhere it has only three. Below the superior tribunals are the courts of first instance. Superior court justices serve for six years, while judges of the lowest courts serve for four. All judges below the supreme court level are chosen by the high tribunal and are responsible to it for the proper performance of their duties.

DEPARTMENTS, PROVINCES, CANTONS. There is the usual division of the nation's territory into smaller administrative units. Bolivia's nine departments vary greatly in population, area and importance. The Department of La Paz, which includes the city of the same name, has one fourth of all the people in the country and a population density of twenty-one per square mile. El Beni, which lies in the Amazon basin, has nearly twice as much territory as the Department of La Paz, but only one fiftieth as many people. Its density of population is much less than one per square mile. Despite these differences, all the departments are governed in exactly the same manner. The chief officer is a prefect, who is appointed by the president. His term is four years, but he may be removed at the president's pleasure. Since there is no departmental assembly with which he must share his authority, the prefect assumes full responsibility for the department's government and administration. In 1931 a new constitution was adopted, which bestowed upon the people of the departments a substantial measure of self-government. Departmental assemblies were set up, and their members were chosen by direct popular vote. One writer called this measure "the most important achievement of the revolution of June, 1930." [26] Seven years later, with the advent of another constitution, the assemblies were abolished and the "most important achievement" became merely a footnote to the history of the nation. The departments are divided into provinces, and each province has a subprefect, who is appointed by the president upon the prefect's recommendation. Below the provinces are cantons; they are governed by *corregidors,* who are named by the prefects upon recommendation of the subprefects. There are no local legislative bodies in either the provinces or the cantons. The administrative hierarchy centering in the minister of government issues the necessary decrees and also enforces them.

MUNICIPALITIES. In the cities a certain amount of self-government is permitted. Each municipality has a popularly elected council, which varies in size from five members to twelve, according to the city's popula-

[26] N. A. N. Cleven, *op. cit.,* p. 181.

tion. This council legislates concerning matters of local concern. Its ordinances must be approved by the Senate of the nation if they deal with taxes or grant special privileges. Members of the council serve for two years. The municipal administration is in the hands of the mayor (*alcalde*), who is chosen by the president of the nation from a list of three names submitted by the municipal council. One of the names on the list, however, must represent the wishes of the minority members.[27] This very unusual proviso is designed to prevent a municipal council which happens to be dominated by the national opposition from submitting only the names of its own sympathizers and thus forcing the president to make an unwelcome choice. Sucre, the legal capital, and La Paz, the actual seat of government, are treated exactly the same as other cities.

SELECTED REFERENCES

Alcázar, Moisés, *Crónicas Parlamentarias,* La Paz, Editorial Fénix, 1946.

Ardúz Eguía, Gastón, *Legislación Boliviano del Trabajo y de la Previsión Social,* La Paz, Imp. "Eléctrica," 1941.

Arze, José Antonio, *Bolivia bajo el Terrorismo Nazifascista,* Lima, Empresa Editora Peruana, 1945.

Capriles Rico, Remberto, and Gastón Ardúz Eguía, *El Problema Social en Bolivia,* La Paz, "Editorial Fénix," 1941.

Cleven, N. A. N., *The Political Organization of Bolivia,* Washington, D.C., Carnegie Institution of Washington, 1940.

Cornejo, Alberto S., *Leyes y Decretos sobre Jubilaciones en Todos los Ramos,* La Paz, Imp. Universitaria, 1944.

Donoso Torres, Vicente, *Reformas Constitucionales,* La Paz, Tall. Gráf. A. Gamarra, 1947.

Leonard, Olen E., *Bolivia: Land, People and Institutions,* Washington, D.C., Scarecrow Press, 1952.

Linke, Lilo, *Andean Adventure; A Social and Political Study of Colombia, Ecuador and Bolivia,* London, Hutchinson & Co., Ltd., 1945.

Pinilla, Claudio, *Estudios Comparables de la Constitución Boliviana con las de los Otros Países de América Meridional,* La Paz, González y Medina, 1927.

Ríos, Cornelio, *Bolivia en el Primer Centenario de su Independencia,* Buenos Aires, Imp. Mercatali, 1925.

Saavedra, Bautista, *La Democracia en Nuestra Historia,* La Paz, González y Medina, 1921.

Thompson, R. W., *Land of Tomorrow,* New York, D. Appleton–Century, 1937.

Urquidi, Carlos W., *La Reforma Constitucional en Bolivia,* La Paz, Editorial Universo, 1939.

Zaconeta, José Víctor, *La Democracia de Bolivia en el Primer Centenario de su Gloriosa Independencia,* Oruro, Imp. "La Favorita" de D. Teran Miranda, 1925.

[27] Constitution, Art. 148.

CHAPTER 21

CUBA

~~~~~~

The Land and the People

STRATEGIC IMPORTANCE. Cuba stands at the crossroads of the Caribbean Its northern shore lies only one hundred and ten miles from the Florida coast. Its eastern tip is washed by the waters of the Windward Passage, along the main route between northern Europe and the Panama Canal. Only a few hundred miles of open sea separate Cuba from the Canal and this fact gives the island great strategic importance in the defense plans of the United States. The principal American naval base in the Caribbean area is located at Guantánamo Bay, on Cuba's southeastern coast. The United States has leased from the Cuban government a section of land surrounding the bay and installed strong fortifications.

AREA AND POPULATION. Cuba is the largest island of the West Indies, and one of the most beautiful. It richly deserves the title that the Spaniards bestowed upon it—*Pearl of the Antilles*. Only in relation to its neighboring islands, however, does it seem large. Its area is forty-four thousand square miles, which is no greater than that of Pennsylvania. Its population is only five and one-half million, as against Pennsylvania's ten and one-half million. This comparison is of little value, however, without a reminder that the Keystone State is chiefly industrial, whereas Cuba is primarily agricultural and therefore unable to maintain as large a population in any degree of comfort. Actually Cuba is one of the most densely populated nations of Latin America. It has one hundred and twenty-five persons per square mile—more than any of the other countries except Haiti and El Salvador.

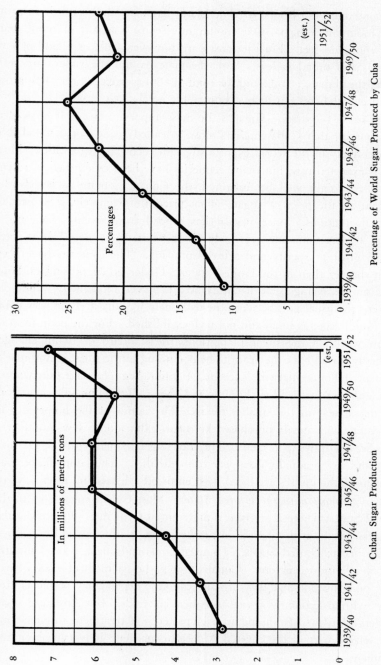

Cuban Sugar Production

Percentage of World Sugar Produced by Cuba

Based on information obtained from *United Nations Statistical Yearbook, 1952* (U.S.S.R. excluded from world figures).

TOPOGRAPHY AND CLIMATE. The island has many hills and three principal mountain ranges. One mountain rises to a height of more than eight thousand feet. For the most part, however, Cuba is a land of low plateaus and broad valleys. Both the plateaus and the valleys are very fertile; the climate is mild and the rainfall not excessive. Crops will grow almost everywhere. In such a country life is relatively easy.

THE SUGAR ECONOMY. Sugar is the most important crop. It is, in fact, so important that Cuba might almost be called a one-crop nation. No other country in the world exports sugar in such large quantities. Most of it is exported raw, but many refineries have been established in recent years. As might well be imagined, the Cuban economy is largely dependent on the price of sugar. That price, unfortunately, is subject to sharp fluctuations. Since 1920 it has ranged from twenty-two cents a pound to less than one cent.[1] In those years, therefore, Cubans have known great prosperity and acute depression. The contrasts have been much sharper than in the United States. Under no circumstances, however, can the average Cuban family be called even moderately well-to-do. There is the usual gulf between the extremely wealthy and the very poor. The middle class is small and not well established. For the poor, most of whom work on the sugar plantations, the standard of living changes markedly throughout the year. The beginning of the sugar season marks a new period of regular employment. Families begin to make purchases of meat and rice, as well as clothing and shoes. Traveling salesmen from Havana appear in the smaller towns. The lamps of the homes are lit once more with newly purchased kerosene. But after a few months the sugar season draws to its close. The traveling salesmen return to Havana. Meat and rice gradually disappear from the diet. The lamps flicker out. Once more the masses are faced with enforced idleness and utter poverty.

Arrangements with the United States. Most Cuban sugar goes to the United States, where it is given a preferential tariff rate. It receives also a regular quota in the American market, along with cane and beet sugar grown in the United States. These arrangements have proved unsatisfactory to almost everyone. Cubans protest the payment of even a small duty, pointing out that they are an economic dependency of the United States with an economy geared to American needs. But American sugar growers ask why Cuba should be given preferential treatment, thus enabling it to seize a part of the coveted American market. It is a never-ending argument.

[1] These prices are for crude sugar in the New York market, before duty has been added.

OTHER AGRICULTURAL PRODUCTS. There are, besides sugar, other Cuban exports. Tobacco is native to the island, and stands high in world reputation. In colonial days it was a crown monopoly. About half of the crop is consumed domestically; most of the remainder went to Europe before the Second World War, but now goes to the United States. Coffee, which was once an important export, is now grown in relatively small quantities. Fruits and vegetables are shipped to the United States in considerable quantities. Corn is widely grown, but almost exclusively for domestic use.

OTHER RESOURCES. A flourishing livestock industry has grown up since 1930. Prior to that time prepared beef was imported in large quantities, but more recently the situation has been reversed. There is abundant grazing land and pests are less of a problem than in most tropical countries. Forestry is relatively unimportant. Cuba was once heavily forested, but many of the trees have been cut down in order to provide more land for sugar plantations. The island's mineral resources are extensive. Large deposits of iron, copper, manganese, and nickel have been discovered; some of them are in close proximity to the seaports. Unfortunately, however, many of these deposits are of inferior quality. Extraction costs are correspondingly high.

INDUSTRY. Cuban industry has made great strides in recent years, yet even today it centers around sugar and tobacco. Alcohol and rum are made from the sugar crop. Tobacco is made into cigars and cigarettes. There are, however, other industries, which have received the benefit of high protective tariffs. Nearly half of the cotton textiles used in the island are the product of local mills. Other factories produce shoes, hats, foodstuffs and beverages, rope, cement, and a long list of other articles. But most of the factories, aside from those that specialize in the products of the sugar and tobacco plantations, operate on a small scale. There is no immediate likelihood that Cuba will become an industrialized nation.

TOURISTS. Tourists provide an important source of revenue. Most of the boats from New York to South America stop at Havana. During the winter season there is frequent service by boat and airplane between Havana and Miami. The Cuban metropolis has captured the imagination of America's smart set, and has built some of the world's finest (and most expensive) hotels to meet their requirements. For persons of moderate means there are more modest hostelries. Innumerable restaurants cater to American appetites by offering American food with Spanish names. Plans have been laid to improve the highway system, which is already fairly good, and to cover the island with motels in imitation of the United States.

POSITION OF LABOR.   Labor is relatively strong in Cuba.   Trade unions boast of large memberships.   Since 1933 the government has been openly pro-labor and has encouraged this development.   Labor has become a powerful political force.   Its leaders have used strikes for political as well as economic purposes—sometimes with great success.   Jurisdictional disputes have weakened labor's position on more than one occasion, however. Communist and anti-Communist groups have waged a constant struggle for power, with the Communists having the better of the argument until the fall of 1947, when the government intervened in favor of the anti-Communist faction.[2]   It must be recorded in all fairness that only a small part of the people of Cuba accept Communism, and that the present government is making a determined effort to check its spread.

SOCIAL LEGISLATION.   Advanced social legislation has been enacted by the government in recent years.[3]   The work week has been fixed at forty-four hours; one month's vacation with pay is assured for every eleven months of work; accident insurance has been made compulsory; minimum wages have been established; provision has been made for the protection of the health of women and children engaged in industry.   Collective bargaining is regulated by law; the constitutional and legal provisions designed to protect workers' associations have accomplished this purpose so well that they place employers under a substantial handicap.[4]

EDUCATION.   Cuba is one of the few nations of Latin America that has a reasonably satisfactory record of literacy.   The Spaniards made elementary education compulsory in 1880, when they still controlled the island, but very little was done to enforce this decree.   In the early years of independence the schools were few and poorly equipped and the government lacked the funds necessary to make substantial improvements. More recently, however, great strides have been taken.   Schools have been opened in remote parts of the island and some attempt has been made to enforce the compulsory attendance laws.   Increased emphasis has been placed on teacher training.   In Cuba, as everywhere in Latin America, very few persons continue their education beyond the primary grades.   Secondary schools—*colegios* or *institutos*—are designed chiefly to prepare students to enter the university.   But there has been a recent trend

[2] See pages 566–567.
[3] See H. E. Friedlaender's *Historia Económica de Cuba,* which was published in 1944.
[4] See the International Bank for Reconstruction and Development's 1951 *Report on Cuba.*

in Cuba, as in some of the other progressive nations, toward commercial schools paralleling the *institutos*. Older boys and girls may now specialize in such subjects as English, typewriting, stenography, bookkeeping, domestic science, and manual arts. Most of these commercial schools are in or near Havana, however. The University of Havana was founded in 1721 and is highly respected. More than thirteen thousand students are enrolled in its many professional courses.

HEALTH. Cuba has a comparatively good health record. Its location in the tropics, with all important cities at or near sea level, seriously complicates the health problem. Such common tropical scourges as malaria and amoebic disorders are still widespread, especially in the rural districts. But many other diseases that once menaced the island have now been brought under control. Part of the credit for improved health conditions may properly be claimed by the American forces that have occupied Cuba a number of times in recent decades. Cuban leaders have been anxious for the success of the work, however, and have co-operated zealously with American officials in the adoption of better methods of sanitation. Many Cuban health officers have been trained in the United States.

RACES. When the Spaniards first came to Cuba, they followed their usual policy of reducing the native population to slavery. But the Indians could not thrive under such conditions and eventually they died off. So Negroes were brought from Africa to take the Indians' place. Today, therefore, there is a substantial admixture of Negro blood in the population of the island. Perhaps one person in three is colored. Yet Cuba is more nearly white than other Latin American nations, with only a few exceptions. The color line is very thinly drawn. Negroes and mulattoes are free to enter any business or profession. They are not deliberately excluded from the social life of the better families, though few of them actually mingle with the social aristocrats on terms of equality. In Cuba it is a matter of wealth or breeding, rather than race.

HAVANA. The capital city of Havana, with its population of eight hundred thousand, is about the size of Washington, D.C. No other Cuban city is more than one fourth as large. Havana owes much to its location; it has one of the world's finest natural harbors. But man's efforts have added greatly to the bounty of nature. Broad boulevards, generous open spaces, and fine modern buildings combine to give the city an air of magnificence. Yet its old quarter still has the narrow, twisting streets and one-story structures of a day long past. Fortresses and monasteries are only a short distance away from the business center. Undoubtedly Havana is a charming place. It is, also, a center of industrial and commercial activity. Almost all the nation's imports, and a large part of the exports, pass through its harbor. Almost all the factories are situated within its borders or close at hand. So are the national university, the national library, and the Academy of Science. To millions of vistors Havana and Cuba are practically synonymous.

The Pattern of Politics

FREEDOM GAINED AND LOST. Cuba was almost the last of the Latin American republics to achieve independence.[5] When Napoleon overthrew the Spanish government in 1808, the Cubans declared their loyalty to the legitimate monarch, Ferdinand VII. Instead of joining the revolt against Spanish rule that was sweeping a large part of the New World, they threw in their lot with the Spanish crown. But the mother country rewarded this loyalty—as soon as it was able to do so—by enacting a series of repressive measures that kept the people of Cuba ignorant and poverty-stricken for many years. Such treatment naturally inspired hatred of Spain in all parts of the island. There were numerous revolts, but they were suppressed with great cruelty. One of these uprisings lasted for ten years. It gave every promise of success, for the Spaniards were busy with their own affairs. So the Cubans declared the independence of their country, created a republic, and elected a president. They even adopted a constitution, which guaranteed freedom of worship and abolished slavery. But eventually Spain succeeded in regaining control of the island and promptly imposed burdensome new taxes to pay for the war. That was in 1878.[6]

THE FINAL VICTORY. Spain did indeed make some effort to win once more the loyalty of the Cubans. It gave them representation in the Spanish Parliament and permitted them to elect some of their local officials, though taking care that these officials should have no real authority. But these few grudging concessions were not enough. Many Cubans had gone to the United States and there they plotted a revolt that would free their island from Spanish tyranny for all time. The acknowledged leader of this movement was José Martí, who had been exiled from Cuba because of his revolutionary activities. By 1895 all arrangements had been completed and the uprising began. Martí was killed early in the struggle,

---

[5] The only exception is Panama.

[6] For a detailed discussion of these years, see Willis Fletcher Johnson's *History of Cuba*, published in five volumes in 1920.

but there were others to carry on his work. For three years the war continued in indecisive fashion. Then, early in 1898, occurred the incident that changed the entire course of Cuban history. The American battleship *Maine,* which was in Havana harbor for the purpose of protecting the lives and property of United States citizens, sank as the result of an explosion. The cause of that explosion was not then known, and has not since been determined with absolute certainty, but American public opinion was inflamed against Spain. There was general approval, therefore, when Congress subsequently passed a joint resolution recognizing Cuban independence and demanding the withdrawal of Spanish forces from the island. Such a resolution, of course, was tantamount to a declaration of war. The resultant struggle ended with Spain's complete defeat and its relinquishment of all claims to sovereignty over Cuba.

THE UNITED STATES AS TRUSTEE. The island was free at last, yet it was in no condition to govern itself. The people were starving; disease was rampant; civil government had virtually disappeared. Under the circumstances the United States had no choice but to act as trustee for the Cuban people. It accepted the responsibility and began the tremendous task of rehabilitation on the first day of 1899. Many persons in Europe, and even in the United States, were inclined to question the value of the American promise to restore Cuba's government to its own people at the earliest possible moment. The promise was kept, however. On May 20, 1902, Major General Leonard Wood, who had served as governor-general of Cuba with conspicuous success, turned over the government to Tomás Palma, the newly elected president of the nation. Roads had been rebuilt, sanitary conditions vastly improved, and the school system completely reorganized.

THE PLATT AMENDMENT. The United States had no intention of leaving the Cubans entirely to their own devices, however. It had already notified the convention preparing a new constitution that certain important clauses must be included in the document. Among other things, it must guarantee the right of American forces to intervene in Cuban affairs at any time for the purpose of preserving the nation's independence or maintaining a stable government. The framers of the constitution, though grateful to the United States for its decisive part in freeing the island, were unwilling to accept these conditions. So they simply ignored them and adopted a fundamental law that made no reference to Cuban-American relations. Thereupon the government of the United States took matters in its own hands. Congress attached an amendment to the army appropriation bill of 1904, affirming in considerable detail the right of intervention that the Cubans were unwilling to grant. This codicil was sponsored by Senator Thomas Platt and therefore became known as the Platt Amendment. For thirty years it formed the basis of the relations between the two nations. Eventually it became an appendix to the Cuban constitution.[7] It assured the right of the United States to lease land for naval bases and also to land troops on Cuban soil. It also forbade the Cuban government to impair the sovereignty of the island in any manner or to assume indebtedness in excess of its ability to pay.

AMERICAN INTERVENTION. The United States did not hesitate to use its right of intervention. In 1906, after a hotly contested election in which President Palma was re-elected for another four-year term, the leaders of the opposition rose in rebellion. The government found itself unable to cope with the situation and finally requested the United States to take a hand. Thereupon American representatives tried to find a satisfactory compromise, but their proposals were not acceptable to either side. Finally the President resigned, and the United States once more assumed the responsibility of governing the island. It remained in control for about two and one-half years. During that time its policies were bitterly criticized by Cubans of all political faiths; indeed, there is strong evidence that the provisional governor, Charles Magoon, made some serious mistakes.[8] Yet he introduced important reforms in matters of health and education, and established by decree a new electoral law. Under this law elections were held in 1908, and the Liberals were generally successful. Their candidate, General José Miguel Gómez, was inaugurated as president the following January. The Conservatives managed to win a substantial minority of the seats in Congress, however; they also gained control of some of the municipalities. After the new government had been installed, American forces were withdrawn and the Cubans were left once more in control of their country.

ELECTIONS, REVOLTS, AND INTERVENTIONS. President Gómez was a strong leader, but he could not appease all the dissatisfied elements in the population. Moreover, his administration was said to be hopelessly corrupt. So revolt flared in various parts of the island. The situation was almost out of control. At this point the United States again landed American troops for the purpose of preserving order. But the Cuban government

---

[7] The matter is discussed at length by A. G. Robinson in *Cuba and the Intervention*, which was published in 1905.

[8] See D. A. Lockmiller's valuable monograph, *Magoon in Cuba*.

finally managed to suppress the uprising, and the American forces were withdrawn. That was in 1912. Shortly afterward another presidential election was held. The Liberals received a majority of the popular vote, but they divided their strength between two rival presidential candidates and as a result the Conservative nominee, General Mario García Menocal, was elected to the presidency. He took immediate steps to eliminate graft and improve the condition of the public treasury. Under his guidance the economic position of the island was greatly strengthened. When, therefore, the President indicated his desire for re-election in 1916, the Conservatives nominated him as a matter of course. But the Liberals offered strong opposition and the result was so close that second elections were necessary in some communities. Before they could be held, however, the Liberals decided to settle the matter by force of arms. Once again revolt swept the island, and once again American marines landed to preserve order. The uprising collapsed almost as quickly as it had begun, and President Menocal took office for a second term.

Cuba experienced unparalleled prosperity during the next two or three years. The First World War had shut off most of the world from its supplies of German beet sugar and thus increased the demand for cane sugar. Cuban production expanded rapidly, and the income of Cuban planters was higher than ever before. When, however, unsettled world economic conditions marked the aftermath of the war, the bubble of Cuban prosperity burst with startling suddenness. The government was obliged to take drastic steps in order to prevent the complete collapse of the nation's economy.

POLITICAL MANEUVERS. During the postwar depression President Menocal's term expired. He was ineligible for re-election, since the constitution prohibited more than two successive terms. But he gave his support to Dr. Alfredo Zayas, who had been his principal opponent in the election of 1912. Zayas was endorsed by a coalition of Conservatives and dissident Liberals. The principal Liberal faction nominated former President Gómez. Zayas won an easy victory, but the Gómez forces refused to concede defeat. Instead they made the usual charges of fraud, and asked the United States to take a hand. The American government refused to send troops at this time, but it did direct General Enoch Crowder, who had been responsible for a thoroughgoing revision of the Cuban election laws, to investigate the matter and try to obtain a satisfactory compromise. General Crowder ordered additional elections in some of the disputed districts, and finally reaffirmed the election of Dr. Zayas, who was thereupon recognized by the United States and duly inaugurated. That was in 1921. It was becoming increasingly clear that no one could become president of Cuba without the endorsement of the United States.

AMERICAN INFLUENCE. The Cuban government was anxious to float a large loan in the United States, but first, under the terms of the Platt Amendment, it was required to put its financial house in order. General Crowder remained in Cuba to help with this difficult task. He proposed a number of important economies, which were promptly adopted. He even suggested the names of certain distinguished Cubans whose support would strengthen the government, and these men were appointed to cabinet posts. The United States then approved the proposed loan, and Cuba's financial position was greatly improved. The part played by the United States in the determination of Cuba's internal policies was strongly resented—perhaps not without reason—by many Cuban patriots. Yet they could scarcely deny that their country had received great material benefits as a result of this interference.

The extent to which the United States had forced honest and efficient government upon the Zayas administration became glaringly apparent in 1923, when General Crowder's rank was changed from special agent to ambassador. This new title sounded more impressive than the old, but it really meant the adoption by the United States—at least temporarily—of a "hands off" policy. Cuba was once more the master of its own destiny. President Zayas celebrated the occasion by dismissing from the government most of the men who had made major contributions to the success of his administration. He then replaced many of them with his own relatives. Graft became so widespread that many civic leaders united to form an Association of Veterans and Patriots for the purpose of restoring honest government. Even the Cuban Minister to London raised his voice in protest against the orgy of government waste and was promptly dismissed from the diplomatic service. The Veterans and Patriots then staged a revolution, but their cause was doomed to failure by the American policy of denying them arms and ammunition, while permitting the sale of war materials to the Cuban government.[9]

DICTATORIAL TACTICS. By 1924, when a new presidential campaign was getting under way, it was obvious that President Zayas could not hope to be re-elected. He had already been nominated by a so-called Popular Party, but he withdrew in favor of General Gerardo Machado y Morales,

[9] This period is well covered by Charles E. Chapman in his *History of the Cuban Republic.*

who had the support of the Liberals. Meanwhile the Conservatives chose ex-President Menocal, but he had lost much of his former popularity. He was defeated by a substantial margin and did not even attempt to organize a revolution. President Machado was inaugurated on May 20, 1925. During his campaign he had promised not to be a candidate for re-election, but long before the expiration of his term he experienced a change of heart. Not only did he run for a second term in 1928; he made certain of victory by systematically persecuting all possible opponents. He adopted the usual tactics of an unscrupulous dictator, suppressing free speech, imprisoning or deporting hundreds of persons, and even closing the national university. And he arranged to have the constitution amended so as to increase the presidential term from four years to six.

SECRET POLICE AND SECRET OPPOSITION. Under the threat of dictatorship, revolution was inevitable. It broke out in August of 1931, but was soon suppressed. Meanwhile the supreme court declared unconstitutional many of the acts of the Machado regime. The dictator's reply was to declare a state of siege, thus depriving Cuban citizens of their right to appeal to the courts. Terrorism became the order of the day. A newly organized secret police arrested thousands of persons who were thought to be too sympathetic to the opposition. Many of these suspects were shot "while trying to escape." The enemies of Machado retaliated by plotting his overthrow. They formed a secret society, the ABC, which included many of the nation's leading professional men and large numbers of the students. (The letters ABC had no significance.) There was talk of American intervention, but the United States was loath to continue its policy of interference, which had gained it nothing but criticism. Moreover, the American ambassador was friendly to President Machado.

A SUCCESSFUL REVOLT. In the summer of 1933 a crisis was precipitated by a general strike. Only a week later the army revolted. It was clear that the existing regime could no longer continue, and the newly appointed American ambassador proposed a "leave of absence" for President Machado. Thereupon Machado and his cabinet hastily left the country. Everyone knew that the "leave of absence" was permanent. For the moment, however, Cuba was without a strong hand at the helm. The new provisional President remained in office only three weeks; then he was forced to resign by a five-man committee which soon turned over the executive power to a distinguished physician named Ramón Grau San Martín. The United States carefully refrained from using its armed forces to influence the course of events. It did, however, withhold recognition of Grau San Martín's government, on the ground that it represented only one of the many factions that had opposed Machado and played a part in his overthrow.

LABOR TROUBLES. The real boss of Cuba following Machado's departure was not President Grau San Martín, but a tough young Army ex-sergeant named Fulgencio Batista, who had promoted himself to the rank of colonel at the time of the 1933 revolution and demoted others of higher rank. Batista was genuinely interested in improving the lot of the common people and willing to work with radical reformers in order to accomplish this result. As a boy he had scarcely had enough to eat; his brother had died of tuberculosis from lack of a proper diet and adequate medical care. So Batista naturally favored a strong pro-labor policy, including the enactment of advanced social security laws.

In this matter Batista and Grau San Martín saw eye to eye, but the Colonel soon discovered that the new President possessed neither the tact nor the administrative ability to produce desired results. So he forced Grau from office and installed as president another physician named Carlos Mendieta y Montúfur, who had been active in the movement against Machado. The new executive tried to restore normal conditions throughout the island, but he experienced great difficulties. Labor agitators, frequently inspired by Communist propaganda, fomented strikes almost incessantly. First the telephone workers walked out; then the gas, water, and street car workers caused trouble. Mendieta, like Batista, was sympathetic to labor, but unwilling to permit a state of virtual anarchy. He ordered the army to replace the strikers in some cases, and Batista made certain that the order was obeyed. Then students joined the strikers. There were frequent riots, and a number of bombings. The President declared a state of siege, whereupon the agitators loudly protested this suspension of constitutional guarantees.

The situation was clearly out of hand. Many Cubans said that the real ruler of the island was the American ambassador, though the United States had formally abolished the Platt Amendment in the first part of 1934, thus voluntarily relinquishing its right of intervention and retaining only the important naval base at Guantánamo Bay. The opposition to President Mendieta grew steadily as his government became more arbitrary. By March of 1935 Havana had been placed under martial law. Almost all schools were closed and many business houses had closed their doors in protest against the government's policies. In December the President finally resigned, declaring that it was his patriotic duty to do so. Thousands

CUBA 563

of Cubans heartily echoed this sentiment. His successor, who had been the minister of state, served only long enough to permit the election of a new president. The balloting took place on January 10, 1936. Women voted for the first time in Cuban history.

BATISTA UNOFFICIALLY IN POWER. The presidential winner was Miguel Mariano Gómez, but the power behind the throne was still Colonel Fulgencio Batista, as subsequent events abundantly proved. At first the two men were on most cordial terms. The new President outlined a program that had Batista's hearty endorsement: a more equitable distribution of the nation's wealth, a betterment of the relations between capital and labor, a more efficient system of public sanitation, and an improvement of the nation's credit. Nothing was said about schools, but everyone knew that one of Colonel Batista's favorite projects was the establishment of rural schools taught by army officers. At first President Gómez endorsed this plan. Later, however, he tried to prevent the enactment of a sugar tax bill that was to provide sufficient revenue for the rural school program. That decision marked the end of Gómez' political career. Batista would permit no interference with his cherished plan—not even from the president of the nation. He brought pressure to bear on his friends in Congress, and they began impeachment proceedings against President Gómez. He was convicted on the charge of undue interference with the legislative branch and removed from office. Vice-President Federico Bru then succeeded to the presidency for the unexpired term. He accepted Batista's orders without question and thus managed to stay in office. While Cuba was experiencing these difficulties, the United States merely played the role of an observer. It seemed clear that the former policy of intervention had really been abandoned.[10]

BATISTA OFFICIALLY IN POWER. Late in 1939, as the time approached for a new presidential election, the rumor circulated that president-maker Batista would like to be the next president of the nation. As chief of staff of the army, however, he was ineligible for the presidency. The rumor became a fact when Congress received a bill permitting the chief of staff to retire and become a presidential candidate. Many persons objected to this proposal, but it was approved by Congress and the President. Thereupon Batista became the candidate of a coalition of parties, which included the Liberals and even the Communists. Former President Grau San Martín

[10] There are many works that deal with the relations of Cuba and the United States. For a concise summary, see Graham H. Stuart's *Latin America and the United States*, 3rd ed., Chaps. VIII and IX.

was nominated by the Cuban Revolutionary Party. Another ex-president, Mario Menocal, received the support of several ultraconservative groups. Meanwhile a constituent assembly had been chosen, and had begun its task of preparing a new constitution for the nation. This document went into effect in October, 1940. The presidential election was twice postponed. When, however, the votes were finally cast and counted, Batista was declared the winner. He took office on October 10. After seven years as Cuba's boss, he was still only thirty-nine years old.

WAR PROBLEMS. One of the planks of Batista's platform had been the maintenance of Cuban neutrality in the European war. When, however, the United States became involved in the struggle, Cuba promptly declared war against the Axis powers, and permitted the establishment of numerous American bases. It also co-operated fully with the United States in combating subversive elements. In some ways the war proved a boon to Cuba. It stimulated the demand for Cuban sugar and raised sugar prices. But it also produced serious shortages and started a dangerous spiral of inflation. Thousands of port workers were thrown out of work by the lack of ships. These and other factors were responsible for a steady decline in the President's popularity. Labor was not satisfied with the treatment it received. Democratically minded citizens objected to the government's habitual disregard of constitutional guarantees. Widespread graft was a source of annoyance to almost everyone—except, of course, the beneficiaries.

POLITICAL PARTIES. It was widely supposed that Batista would find some way to extend his power beyond 1944, when his term of office expired. But in 1943 he made clear that he had no such intention and told the nation's political leaders to get ready for the forthcoming campaign. They took him at his word. Even some of the members of the President's cabinet resigned in order to begin active campaigning. Batista had no intention of remaining neutral, however. He threw his support to Carlos Saladrigas, a well-known lawyer, who had the backing of a group of parties known as the Democratic Socialist Coalition. This coalition included the oldtime Liberal Party, which had once dominated Cuban politics but had lost most of its prestige because of its support of the tyrant Machado. Not until 1940 did it recover from that blow. Another faction in the government bloc was the ABC Party, which had been Machado's nemesis. Also included were the Democratic Party and the Communists, who called themselves the Popular Socialist Party. Arrayed against this combination was the Republican Authentic Alliance. The "Republican" part of this coalition was composed chiefly of oldtime Conservatives. The *Auténticos* had been in existence since the last days of the Machado regime and had played a major part in the selection of Grau San Martín as president in 1933. Since that time Grau had been their recognized leader, and his nomination as the candidate of the Alliance was accepted as a matter of course.

CAMPAIGN OF 1944. Presidential candidate Ramón Grau San Martín was an unusual man. Even his bitterest opponents admitted that he had some enviable characteristics: an intense devotion to his country and its people, a steadfastness of purpose, and a high standard of personal honesty. But he was said to be a fanatical dreamer, incapable of directing the public administration in an efficient manner. Critics recalled his four months in office in 1933, and pointed out that they had been marked by social upheaval and bloody riots. To elect Grau, they said, would be to invite similar trouble. But the masses were unimpressed by such arguments. Grau had become their idol. They remembered the social legislation of 1933, but not the bungling manner in which it had been administered. The rumor spread that if Grau were elected he would repeal all taxes and forbid landlords to collect rent.[11] Under such circumstances his election was a foregone conclusion, if Batista would permit an honest election.

Few persons supposed, however, that the election would be honest. Batista had been the virtual dictator of Cuba for eleven years, and probably had acquired a lust for power. Certainly he could swing the election to his own candidate, if he so desired. He controlled the election machinery. He had the backing of a powerful political organization that had been in power for many years. He enjoyed the support of the army. Yet Grau San Martín and his friends never seemed to think that their cause was hopeless. They campaigned with fervor. Grau himself appeared at innumerable public meetings, always receiving a tumultuous welcome. His followers seem to have regarded him as almost a messiah.

GRAU AND CONGRESS. Election day was June 1, 1944. When all the votes had been counted, it was announced that Dr. Grau had won, carrying five of the six provinces. The miracle had happened. Batista had permitted an honest election and had accepted with good grace the defeat of his own candidate. Overnight he found himself almost as much of a popular hero as Grau San Martín. The two men met and publicly exchanged greetings. Then Batista quietly made preparations for an extensive vacation outside of Cuba, while Grau organized his new administration. It seemed at

[11] See the interesting article, "Return Engagement," by R. Hart Phillips, in the December, 1944, issue of *Inter-American* (Vol. III, No. 12), pp. 16 *ff*.

first that the President and Congress might spend most of their time fighting each other, for Batista's Democratic Socialist Coalition had won a majority of the seats in both the Senate and the Chamber of Representatives. But the various groups comprising the Coalition could not work in unison and before long some of them threw their support to President Grau. First the Popular Socialists (Communists) agreed to work with the government. Then the ABC Party followed suit, and its leader became a member of the cabinet. These shifts gave the President a working majority in the Senate, but not in the Chamber of Representatives. When, however, congressional elections were held in the spring of 1946, the administration obtained a clear majority in both houses. This result was interpreted as a vote of confidence for President Grau.

ECONOMIC AND POLITICAL DIFFICULTIES. In spite of public approval, the President was having his troubles. Prices were rising steadily and food supplies were low. There was an extensive black market in hundreds of major commodities. Workers were asking for sharp increases in wages and going out on strike when their almost prohibitive demands were refused. Crime was becoming widespread in all parts of the island and the police seemed powerless to cope with it. In two years there were nearly fifty political murders. Graft was as common as it had ever been in the history of the nation. Meanwhile President Grau shifted his cabinet ministers at frequent intervals, apparently trying to find a combination that would produce satisfactory results. Some ministers quit their posts after noisy quarrels. Those persons who had questioned Grau's administrative ability adopted an "I-told-you-so" attitude. Hardly anyone suggested that the President was profiting personally from the corrupt practices of lesser officials, but that scarcely seemed to excuse his apparent indifference. More and more politically influential citizens joined the opposition. "Honesty is not enough!" was their cry. They minimized or ignored the administration's solid achievements, which included the construction of many new schools and the inauguration of an elaborate housing program.

OPPOSITION. In the spring of 1947 Senator Eduardo Chibás, who had been one of Grau's principal apologists, finally broke with him and promptly organized a new political party—the P.P.C. (Cuban People's Party). The leaders of the ABC Party disbanded their organization and joined the P.P.C. Meanwhile the Communists moved into the ranks of the opposition. The President, who had accepted their support for more than two years and repaid it with many favors, finally found sufficient courage to break the loose alliance. He openly encouraged the anti-Communist Confederation of Cuban Workers and finally recognized its executive committee as the head of the Cuban labor movement. The police were ordered to break up strikes by Communists.

A GOVERNMENT VICTORY. As a result of these shifts of allegiance, the government lost control of both houses of Congress. It faced the possibility of defeat in the 1948 elections. Grau himself was ineligible for re-election, but he gave his blessing to one of his cabinet ministers, Carlos Prío Socarrás, who had been the principal figure in the fight against the Communists. The Auténticos thereupon made Prío their candidate. The more conservative elements nominated a physician named Ricardo Núñez Portuondo, whose father had been a revolutionary hero. And of course the P.P.C. chose its founder and recognized leader, Eduardo Chibás. The election was held on June 1. A final tabulation of the results showed that the government forces had won an impressive victory. Prío Socarrás became the new president of the nation, with an Auténtico majority in Congress to support him. The people still had faith in Grau and his friends. Before long, however, Grau and President Prío came to a parting of the ways. Grau began to criticize the government for its wasteful inefficiency. Shortly afterward he was formally indicted on a charge of stealing nearly two hundred million dollars of public funds. The trial dragged on inconclusively. On one occasion masked gunmen stole seven thousand pages of evidence, which had to be gathered a second time. Finally, however, the ex-President was cleared of the charges against him.

POLITICAL RIVALRIES. By the beginning of 1952 the political scene had become badly confused. Former Dictator Fulgencio Batista had formed a new party—Progressive Unitary Action—and announced that he would be a candidate for president at the next election. Two other political groups agreed to support him. Eduardo Chibás, the popular founder of the P.P.C., committed suicide, leaving his party without any leader of similar stature. The government-sponsored Auténticos, trying desperately to strengthen their position, made agreements with a number of rival groups. Even Grau San Martín was induced to co-operate once more with the government coalition. In February of 1952 Cuba had nine political parties, but new deals were made or rumored almost every day. The situation was chaotic.

RETURN OF BATISTA. Early on the morning of March 10, 1952, Batista led a revolution that took three lives and lasted exactly two hours and sixteen minutes. At the end of that time the ex-Dictator was once more the unchallenged boss of the island. He won over the Cuban Federation of

Labor by assuring its leaders that they would be allowed to stay in their jobs, and he calmed the fears of the business community by promising to respect all internal and international agreements. A state of siege was decreed for forty-five days, but not extended beyond that time. Opposition leaders were permitted to leave the country. When students of the University of Havana rioted in protest against the new regime, Batista ordered the police not to interfere. But members of Congress who tried to hold a previously scheduled meeting were forcibly prevented from entering the national capitol.

ABSOLUTE DICTATORSHIP. One of Batista's first official acts was to suspend the constitution of 1940. A few weeks later he decreed a new provisional constitution, which modified the fundamental law in a number of important respects. All executive and legislative powers were concentrated in the president and his cabinet. The nearest approach to a legislative assembly was a powerless Consultative Council, whose members were to be chosen by the president. Existing political parties were dissolved. Batista soon made quite clear, however, that these changes were not intended to be permanent. Political parties would be permitted to reorganize as soon as a new election law could be drafted. Elections for president, members of Congress, and other public officials would be held at the earliest possible moment. And then the constitution of 1940 would be restored. Eventually November 1, 1953, was set as the date for the next election. Batista announced that he would be a candidate for the presidency, and that his party would shorten its name to Progressive Action. Opposition political groups immediately began a feverish search for candidates and platforms that would have a wide appeal. Then, without warning, the government suddenly announced that it was postponing the elections until June 1, 1954. Even at that date, moreover, the people would be allowed to choose only congressmen, governors, and local officials. The new president would be elected later in 1954, or perhaps in 1955. The newly elected Congress would decide when to restore the constitution of 1940. Today, therefore, Cuba is ruled by a virtually absolute dictator. The comparative mildness of his regime does not completely conceal its arbitrary nature. He has promised a return to legitimate constitutional government within a short time, but no one can say whether he intends to keep that promise. His enemies, who have already been foiled in several counter-revolutionary plots, would certainly prefer not to rely solely on the Dictator's integrity.[12]

[12] See "Batista: Master of the Coup d'Etat," by J. Losada, in *United Nations World*, April, 1953, pp. 31–35.

The Structure of Government

THE CONSTITUTION. The constitution of 1940 is still presumed to be Cuba's fundamental law, despite its temporary suspension. It contains nearly twice as many words as the massive constitution of Mexico. In fact, it is one of the longest ever adopted by any nation. There is, of course, no good excuse for such verbosity. The constitution begins with a brief preamble, which sets forth its noble purposes: to assure liberty and justice, maintain order, and promote the public welfare. The blessing of God is invoked, although church and state have long been separated. Nine thousand words are devoted to an elaborate enumeration of fundamental rights. As in most of the newer constitutions, there are sections dealing not only with individual liberties, but also such matters as education, the family, labor, property. There are the usual clauses guaranteeing freedom of speech and press, freedom of religion, liberty to assemble and petition for the redress of grievances, immunity from arbitrary arrest, and the like. These guarantees may be suspended in time of crisis by law of Congress or executive decree; but, if the president takes the initiative, he must summon Congress to meet within forty-eight hours. Congress then decides whether the state of siege shall remain in force.[13] At present, of course, there is no Congress, so the provisional constitution authorizes the president to suspend the guarantees of individual liberty.[14]

Social guarantees. The section of the constitution of 1940 dealing with labor has almost the prolixity of a code of law. It reflects the social philosophy of recent Cuban governments. There are guarantees of maximum hours of work and minimum wages, with compensation for industrial accidents. Everyone is entitled to a paid annual vacation of one month. The principle of equal pay for equal work is established, without regard to sex. But women and children are given special protection, and children under the age of fourteen years may not be employed.[15] The clauses of the constitution dealing with property reflect the fundamental law of Mexico. The institution of private property is recognized, but the subsoil is said to be owned exclusively by the state, which may make concessions for its exploitation. All property must be used with due regard for the public welfare.[16]

Amendment of the constitution. The clauses of the 1940 constitution

[13] Constitution of 1940, Art. 41.
[14] Art. 120, Cl. g.
[15] Arts. 60–86.
[16] Arts. 87–96.

dealing with the method of amendment are quite complicated. There are, in fact, several ways in which amendments may be adopted. One way involves only the action of Congress, and this is the plan that will probably be used to the exclusion of more cumbersome alternatives. Under its terms, an amendment may be proposed by one fourth of the members of either house. The two houses then meet in joint session and decide the matter by a two-thirds vote of the total membership. If the necessary two-thirds vote is obtained, Congress waits until a subsequent legislative session, and then finally accepts or rejects the proposal. As before, there must be a two-thirds vote for adoption. The constitution also permits popular participation in the amending process. It states that an amendment may be initiated by the people, the signatures of one hundred thousand literate voters being required. Congress then decides whether to call a constitutional convention or to submit the proposal to a popular plebiscite. Certain parts of the constitution, which have been designed to protect the nation's sovereignty or to prevent dictatorship, cannot be altered without popular approval.[17] The effectiveness of these restrictions may be judged in the light of Batista's 1952 *coup d'état*. It is interesting to note that the present provisional constitution requires nothing more for its amendment than a two-thirds vote of the president's cabinet, which is officially known as the Council of Ministers.

SUFFRAGE AND ELECTIONS. Both men and women vote when they reach the age of twenty years. There is no literacy requirement. Voting is compulsory, and the government makes a serious effort to enforce this requirement. Fines are frequently imposed for failure to appear at the polls without valid excuse. Unlike most of the other countries of Latin America, Cuba has copied its election procedure largely from the United States. Candidates are nominated by party conventions, and the government prints the official ballots from the party lists. There is a separate column for each party, headed by a symbol that is designed primarily to guide illiterate voters. One column is left blank, so that the electors may write in the names of persons who lack regular party support. Minority representation is assured by a system of limited voting.

THE PRESIDENT: *Selection, term, qualifications, salary.* The president of the nation is chosen by vote of the people, according to the constitution of 1940. As in the United States, however, there is a system that makes possible the election of a minority candidate. Each province has a number of electoral votes equal to its congressional representation, and gives them

17 Arts. 285, 286.

all to the candidate winning a popular majority *in the province.* In theory, therefore, it would be possible for a presidential nominee to win the election by receiving a bare majority of the votes in a number of key provinces, even though his defeat in the other provinces was so thorough as to give him a smaller number of popular votes throughout the nation than one of his rivals. In practice this danger has not materialized. The president must be a natural-born Cuban, at least thirty-five years of age. He serves for four years and is not eligible for re-election until eight years after the expiration of his term. His salary is seventy-two thousand pesos a year. The Cuban peso circulates on a par with the American dollar. The president's official residence is an imposing domed structure which was built at a cost of two million dollars.

Parliamentary government in theory. The constitution gives only a partial clue to the importance of the president. In fact, a literal reading might give the impression that he was largely a figurehead, dependent on the members of his cabinet or on Congress for permission to perform any official act. Nothing could be further from the truth. The president is the master of the nation even in normal times. He dominates every aspect of its political life. The men who wrote the present Cuban constitution had in mind a parliamentary scheme of government. They not only adopted the customary Latin American clauses requiring ministerial countersignature of all the president's acts, but also specified that one member of the cabinet should serve as prime minister. Either house of congress was given the right to summon cabinet ministers for questioning and to force their resignation by a vote of lack of confidence. Ministers thus censured might not be reappointed immediately to the same posts.

In practice congressional censure has had very little effect on presidential policies. It has indeed forced the resignation of certain ministers, but the chief executive has not permitted such incidents to alter his course of action. In 1947 Congress voted formal censure of the minister of education. It did so at five o'clock one afternoon. By eight o'clock that evening the minister had resigned, and by eleven o'clock he was back in the president's cabinet as minister without portfolio. The provision of the constitution creating the office of prime minister has no greater significance. The prime minister is merely a member of the cabinet. He possesses no special powers, though his title does carry a certain measure of added prestige.[18]

Executive powers. The president's power of appointment is extensive.

[18] See Enrique Hernández Corujo's excellent work, *Lecciones de Derecho Constitucional Cubano,* pp. 73–81.

He names the members of his own cabinet and lesser officers in the administrative service, members of the diplomatic corps, and judges of the supreme court. For diplomats and judges, however, according to the terms of the 1940 constitution, he must have the approval of the Senate. His choice of judges is further restricted by the proviso that he must make his selections from lists presented by a special commission.[19] Administrators and diplomats serve only at the president's pleasure. He exercises the customary control over foreign affairs and military matters. Congress has the power to declare war, and Senate approval is required for treaties. At present, of course, the lack of a Congress makes these clauses meaningless, but they will regain their former significance when the constitution is restored. The president may grant pardons to persons convicted of crime.

Legislative powers. As in other Latin American countries, the chief executive has the right to introduce bills in Congress. The constitution says that he may veto legislative proposals and that his objections cannot be overridden except by two thirds of the total membership of each house —not just two thirds of those present, as in most countries. Presidential vetoes have, in fact, almost never been overridden. The president is authorized to call Congress in special session, and at such a time it may consider only those matters set forth in the presidential summons. In Cuba the influence of the legislative branch has been greatly weakened by the practice of regulating almost everything through executive decrees. Every president has followed this custom to some extent, but Batista carried it to extremes in the days when he was the constitutionally elected president. Using the war as an excuse, he secured from Congress a law granting him special powers to issue decree-laws. Grau continued the practice, even after the war had ended. In 1946 he issued more than three thousand decrees, while Congress enacted only twenty laws.[20] The annual budget of the nation has consistently been put into effect by decree, despite detailed constitutional provisions calling for its enactment by Congress.

Vice-president; presidential succession. In normal times there is a vice-president, chosen at the same time as the president and in the same manner. His only task, other than the duty of awaiting the president's death or disability, is to preside over the Senate. As usual, he has no vote unless there is a tie. The constitution names only one person to succeed to the presidency in case of the unavailability of both the president and vice-

[19] See page 577.
[20] According to the Havana publication, *Bohemia,* June 15, 1947, p. 69.

president. That person is the supreme court justice with the longest record of service. He does not fill out the unexpired term, however, unless there is less than one year remaining. When the vacancy occurs earlier in the period, he must call a special election, so that the people may choose another president.

THE CABINET. The cabinet consists of thirteen ministers with portfolio, plus the president's secretary, who serves also as the secretary of the cabinet. This number may be increased by the addition of a prime minister serving without portfolio, or the prime minister may accept responsibility for one of the administrative departments. He is authorized to preside over cabinet meetings in the absence of the chief executive, but this clause has little significance, for the cabinet would never think of taking the initiative with regard to any matters of major importance. The thirteen cabinet portfolios are: State, Treasury, Interior, National Defense, Justice, Public Works, Commerce, Agriculture, Labor, Public Education, Health and Welfare, Communications, Information. It will be noted that the official directly responsible for the conduct of relations with other countries is called the minister of state—not the minister of foreign affairs, as elsewhere in Latin America. This terminology, like so many other things in Cuba, reflects the influence of the United States. The minister of the interior, however, does not perform approximately the same duties as the American secretary of the interior. Instead he corresponds to the ministers of the interior or government in other parts of Latin America and in continental Europe. His principal task is to supervise the relations of the nation with the provinces and municipalities.[21]

PUBLIC PERSONNEL. Cuba was the first nation of Latin America to introduce the merit principle for the selection of public employees. Since 1909 it has had a civil service commission, which administers examinations for positions in the public service. Unfortunately, however, this system has not given satisfactory results. It has been weakened by the practice of marking thousands of positions as "political" or "confidential," and exempting them from the classified service. For these positions, therefore, no examinations are needed and no adequate protection is given against arbitrary dismissal. Even in the classified service many appointments seem to be made on a political basis. There is one well-authenticated case of a young resident of Havana who took the examination for teacher of English in the public schools. She received the fifth highest grade, but was told that she had no chance for an appointment, even though there

[21] See *Derecho Administrativo*, by Antonio Lancís Sánchez.

were twenty vacancies. Meanwhile another young lady—a friend of the minister of education—stood eighty-ninth on the examination list and was promptly appointed.

CONGRESS: *Selection, term, qualifications, salaries.* Although Cuba is now governed without benefit of Congress, there is reason to believe that this state of affairs is only temporary. The best plan, therefore, is to describe Congress as it functioned under the temporarily suspended constitution of 1940. The Cuban Senate has fifty-four members—nine from each of the six provinces. They are elected by direct vote of the people for terms of four years. There is no system of partial renewal. Every senator must be a natural-born citizen, at least thirty years of age. Army officers are ineligible if they have been on active duty within two years of their nomination. The Chamber of Representatives is larger than the upper house, of course. Its one hundred and thirty-six members are chosen in the same manner as the members of the Senate, but each province has representation in direct proportion to its population. The term of representatives is four years, and one half of the total number is chosen every second year. Naturalized citizens may be elected, if they have ten years of continuous residence in Cuba after the date of naturalization. The minimum age for representatives is twenty-one years. Congressional salaries have been fixed at thirty-six hundred pesos (or American dollars) a year, plus another thirty-six hundred for expenses.

Meeting place. The national capital, where Congress holds its sessions in normal times, is the pride of Cuba. A beautiful granite and marble building resembling the capitol of the United States, it was completed in 1929 at a cost of twenty million dollars. Its dome is the third highest in the world. Directly below this dome, in the floor of the rotunda, is the famous twenty-four-carat diamond from which all distances on the central highway are measured. This diamond was mysteriously stolen in 1947 and returned just as mysteriously by parcel post several months later. The capitol contains the magnificent Hall of Lost Steps, where the president of the nation is inaugurated. It contains also the beautiful Martí Hall, which is used for state banquets.

In the wings of the capitol are the meeting places of the senators and representatives. The representatives' chamber is arranged in a great arc; the seats of the members rise in tiers from a central pit, where a circular table has been placed for the convenience of newsmen. The president of the chamber and the secretaries sit on a raised platform at the front of the hall. There is a gallery with space for five hundred visitors. Every member of the Chamber of Representatives has a spacious desk. He is equipped with a bell to summon pages, and also a set of headphones to hear the addresses, which are delivered into conveniently placed microphones. The arrangements in the Senate chamber are almost identical, but the hall is considerably smaller. Both representatives and senators have private

The Cuban national capitol, where Congress holds its sessions. (Photo, Courtesy Pan American World Airways System)

offices and publicly paid secretaries—luxuries that are almost unknown in Latin American legislative circles.

Sessions, organization, procedure. Congress normally holds two regular sessions every year, beginning the third Monday in September and the third Monday in March. Each session must be at least sixty days in length, but the two combined may not total more than one hundred and forty days. We have already noted that the calling of special sessions is a

prerogative of the president.[22]   Each house chooses its own officers,[23] and
they form the usual steering committee, which assumes responsibility for
the routine conduct of legislative business.   Committees are named by the
entire membership of each house, upon the recommendation of the steering
committee.   The Chamber of Representatives has thirty-seven permanent
standing committees, which deal with a wide variety of subjects—foreign
affairs, commerce and industry, and labor, among others.   There is one
committee to consider the problems of the sugar industry, another for
tobacco, and still another to ponder means of promoting the tourist trade.
No committee has fewer than twenty-three members; those dealing with
foreign affairs and the budget have fifty members apiece.   The minority is
given substantial representation on every committee.   Because of the large
number of committees, every member of the Chamber of Representatives is
assigned to six or seven.   This means that he must necessarily neglect some
of his committee duties.   The situation is much the same in the Senate,
except that there are thirty-nine committees, with an average membership of seventeen.   Since there are only fifty-four senators, each of them
must sit on ten or eleven committees and thus carry a most unreasonable
burden.   The committees are not ordinarily required to return to their
respective chambers the measures of which they disapprove.   It is generally
understood, however, that the president's proposals may not be buried in
committee.   Disagreements between the two houses of Congress are compromised by specially appointed conference committees, as in the United
States.   Each conference committee consists of five senators and five representatives.[24]

THE COURTS: *Supreme court.* The Cuban judicial system follows the
traditional Spanish pattern.   In 1900, when the United States controlled
the government of Cuba, it introduced the jury system.   But this institution did not work well, and was abandoned by the Cubans as soon as they
became their own masters.   The supreme court of the nation has twenty
members, divided into chambers for the more efficient handling of various
types of cases.   Although the constitution of 1940 contemplates one chamber devoting its entire time to questions of unconstitutionality, this chamber has not yet been established by law, so all the judges sit as a group to
decide whether legislative acts or executive decrees violate the constitution.

[22] See page 572.
[23] Except, of course, the presiding officer of the Senate, who is the vice-president of the
nation.
[24] The 1940 constitution of Cuba, unlike the fundamental laws of most Latin American
nations, makes no mention of the manner in which disagreements between the Senate and
the Chamber of Representatives are to be compromised.   The matter is covered by a law of
Congress, which was signed by President Grau on October 25, 1946.

The constitutionality of laws and decrees may be challenged, not only by persons whose interests have been adversely affected, as in the United States, but also by any group of twenty-five citizens who are sufficiently interested to raise the issue. Judges of the supreme court must be natural-born citizens, at least forty years of age, who have had ten years' experience as practicing attorneys or judges or professors of law. Although the president appoints them, with Senate approval, his choice is narrowly restricted. He must make his selections from lists—three names for each vacancy—prepared by a special commission. This commission has nine members. Four of them are chosen by the supreme court itself, three by the president, and two by the faculty of law of the University of Havana. This arrangement produced excellent results until its suspension by Batista in 1952.

Lower courts. Below the supreme court are six superior courts—one for each province. They exercise a very limited original jurisdiction, devoting most of their time to appeals from the lower tribunals. These lower courts fall into two categories, civil and criminal. The same courts do not hear both kinds of cases. The president is nominally responsible for the selection of justices of the superior courts and courts of first instance, as well as the members of the supreme tribunal. Under the constitution and laws, however, he must make his appointments on the basis of proved ability and experience. Vacancies in the higher courts are normally filled by promotion from the courts immediately below.

THE PROVINCES. The six provinces of Cuba vary widely in population and area. Havana Province, which includes the capital city, has only a little over three thousand square miles, but one and a half million inhabitants. Camagüey, a rich sugar-producing province in the eastern part of the island, has three times as much territory and only one third as many people. The nation has been unusually generous in granting self-government to the provinces. In normal times each province has a popularly elected governor, and also a provincial council, composed of the popularly chosen mayors of the municipalities. The governor is the agent of the nation, and is responsible for the enforcement of national laws, but he is not removable at the president's pleasure. In fact, he may even challenge the constitutionality of the acts of national officials on the ground that they interfere with provincial autonomy. In such cases the issue is decided by the supreme court. The provincial council meets in regular session once every two months and at such other times as the governor may indicate. It is scarcely a lawmaking body; instead it serves as an advisory agency to the governor and the other administrative officers of the province.

The governor regulates most provincial affairs by decree. He is required to be a Cuban citizen by birth, or by naturalization of ten years' standing, and to have attained the age of twenty-five years.[25]

THE MUNICIPALITIES. The constitution of 1940 devotes four thousand words to the subject of municipal government. "The municipality is autonomous," it declares. "The municipal authorities possess all the powers necessary to regulate local affairs."[26] Subsequent clauses make clear that this is not a grant of home rule, in the American sense. It is, however, a fairly generous bestowal of authority—much more so than in most of the other nations of Latin America. The municipalities are specifically authorized to establish and administer schools and libraries, make and enforce local sanitary regulations, and condemn land needed for public works. They are permitted to adopt their own budgets, though with due regard for the national system of finance. Public loans must be approved not only by the voters, but also by the national Tribunal of Accounts.

The constitution of 1940 declares that every municipality may choose its own form of government, selecting one of three plans: mayor-council, commission, or council-manager. Here the influence of the United States is very clear. No other Latin American country has even considered the possibility of experimenting with these American schemes of government. To date, however, Cuban municipalities have not been given the options promised them by the constitution because Congress has failed to pass the necessary enabling act. The present statute recognizes only the traditional mayor-council form of government, and makes it obligatory for all Cuban municipalities. Both the mayor and the members of the council are elected by direct vote of the people, for terms of four years. They must be Cuban citizens, at least twenty-one years of age. The mayor supervises the local administration, and issues decrees that have the force of law. He is paid a regular salary. The councilmen, who meet at regular intervals to enact necessary local ordinances, serve without pay. As in most of the Latin American countries, the municipalities are not exclusively—or even primarily—urban areas. They correspond to counties in the United States. Every square foot of Cuban soil lies within one of the one hundred and twenty-six municipalities into which the island has been divided.[27]

[25] The constitution of 1940 regulates provincial government in considerable detail. Arts. 233–250.

[26] Art. 212.

[27] See *Curso de Historia de las Instituciones Locales de Cuba*, by Andrés Angulo y Pérez. See also the same author's *Derecho Municipal Comentado y Comparado*.

CUBA

579

SELECTED REFERENCES

Angulo y Pérez, Andrés, *Curso de Historia de las Instituciones Locales de Cuba,* Havana, Cultural S.A., 1943.

Baroni, Aldo, *Cuba, País de Poca Memoria,* Mexico, D.F., Ediciones Botas, 1944.

Cabús, José D., *Batista; Pensamiento y Acción Reportaje Histórico,* Havana, Prensa Indoamericana, 1944.

Calderío, Francisco, *Los Fundamentos del Socialismo en Cuba,* Havana, Editorial "Páginas," 1944.

Davis, J. Merle, *The Cuban Church in a Sugar Economy,* New York, Dept. of Social & Economic Research & Counsel, 1942.

Escanaverino, Andrés, *Leyes del Trabajo,* Havana, Editorial "Alfa," 1938.

Farias y Lazcano, Jesús Daniel, *Ley de Jubilaciones y Pensiones del Poder Judicial,* Havana, Editorial Lex, 1944.

Fitzgibbon, Russell H., *Cuba and the United States, 1900–1935,* Menasha, Wis., George Banta, 1935.

Friedlaender, H. E., *Historia Económica de Cuba,* Havana, J. Montero, 1944.

Gutiérrez y Sánchez, Gustavo, *Código Electoral,* Havana, Editorial Lex, 1944.

Hernández Corujo, Enrique, *La Acción Pública en Materia de Inconstitucionalidad en Cuba,* Havana, Imp. y Papelería de Rambla, Bouzá y Cía., 1935.

—— *Lecciones de Derecho Constitucional Cubano,* Havana, Cía. Editora O'Reilly, 1942.

Infiesta, Ramón, *Historia Constitucional de Cuba,* Havana, Editorial Selecta, 1942.

International Bank for Reconstruction and Development, *Report on Cuba,* Washington, D.C., The Bank, 1951.

Lancís Sánchez, Antonio, *Derecho Administrativo,* Havana, Universidad de la Habana, 1942.

—— *El Recurso de Alzada ante el Presidente de la República,* Havana, Editorial Lex, 1944.

Leal y González, Antonio, *Jurisprudencia Electoral Cubana,* Havana, Editorial Selecta, 1941.

Lockmiller, D. A., *Magoon in Cuba,* Chapel Hill, N.C., Univ. of North Carolina Press, 1938.

Montagú y Vivero, Guillermo de, *El Juez ante la Norma Injusta,* Havana, Editorial Lex, 1944.

Nelson, Lowry, *Rural Cuba,* Minneapolis, University of Minnesota Press, 1950.

Pereda, Diego de, *El Nuevo Pensamiento Político de Cuba,* Havana, Editorial Lex, 1943.

Raggi Ageo, Carlos M., *Condiciones Económicas y Sociales de la República de Cuba,* Havana, Editorial Lex, 1944.

—— *Seguridad Social en Cuba,* Havana, Editorial Lex, 1944.

Ramírez Olivella, Gustavo, *Jurisprudencia Constitucional,* Havana, J. Montero, 1945.

Roig de Leuchsenring, Emilio, *Los Grandes Movimientos Políticos Cubanos en la República,* Havana, Molina y Cía., 1943.

CHAPTER 22

The Island of HAITI

~~~~~~

Lands and Peoples

TOPOGRAPHY AND CLIMATE. In November of 1492 the Columbus expedition discovered a beautiful Caribbean island and gave it the name of Española. The natives called it Haiti—meaning, in their tongue, high place. It is indeed very mountainous; in some places the mountains extend almost to the edge of the sea. Therefore a considerable part of the island is unsuited for agriculture. So the people of Haiti, like the people of the Japanese Empire, are concentrated in the fertile valleys and along some of the lower mountain slopes. The island lies just east of Cuba, and shares to some extent its climate and problems. But the rugged terrain presents additional problems that the Cubans have never had to face. There are great variations in rainfall in different parts of the island. Some sections receive only about fourteen inches a year, and therefore are almost desert; in other areas the annual rainfall is as much as ninety inches.

TWO SEPARATE NATIONS. Two separate nations comprise the island of Haiti. In the western—and smaller—part of the island is the Republic of Haiti, which is about the size of the state of New Hampshire, but has six times as many people. The Republic of Haiti is the smallest nation of the New World and by far the most densely populated; its two hundred and seventy-five persons per square mile are far more than it can support without forcing them virtually to the level of starvation. It is at this level, therefore, that most of the people spend their lives. The Dominican Republic comprises the eastern two thirds of the island. It has only two million persons, as compared with Haiti's three millions. So the pressure

580

of population is not so great and the standard of living is correspondingly higher.

HAITI: *Negro republic*. The Republic of Haiti differs in two important respects from the Dominican Republic. In fact, it differs from all the other nations of Latin America. It is the only Negro republic and the only one where French is spoken. In other parts of Latin America there is a certain admixture of Negro blood, but in Haiti the overwhelming majority of the people are black. There are only a few thousand whites— mostly recent arrivals—and no Indians. The people are divided sharply into two social groups, and color tends to mark the dividing line. The upper classes are, for the most part, what we would call mulattoes, though this word is repugnant to the Haitian people. And, indeed, some members of the elite have quite dark skins, whereas some of the masses are relatively light in color. Yet it cannot be denied that a large majority of the aristocrats have lighter skins than the general population.

Castes. Skin color is by no means the only test of social class, however. The manner of life provides a more nearly infallible clue. The aristocrats do not work with their hands. Instead they engage in politics, practice the learned professions, hold commissions in the army, or direct large agricultural or business enterprises. All these careers are closed to the masses. Although the well-born comprise not more than three per cent of the country's population, they dominate completely every aspect of the nation's life. They live in comfortable homes and many of them own fine estates. Their womenfolk devote their lives to the rearing of children and the management of servants. Membership in the elite involves at least a minimum of education and a reasonably high standard of personal appearance.

The lower classes are unconcerned with such matters. Most of them are agricultural laborers. Both men and women work in the fields. They can afford neither comfortable homes nor decent clothing. Nor can many of them obtain even the rudiments of an education. The law declares that primary education shall be free and compulsory, but peasant children cannot be spared from the fields long enough to go to school. One foreign observer, who had been asked how to distinguish between the two classes of the Haitian people, replied: "The elite wear shoes." [1] That is true enough, but of course it fails to reach the heart of the matter.

Vodun. The official religion of the nation is Roman Catholicism. The

[1] James G. Leyburn, *The Haitian People*, p. 5. Dean Leyburn's book contains a searching analysis of Haitian life.

upper classes are Catholics or agnostics. For the masses, however, Catholicism is at best a superficial faith. Their true allegiance is to the folk religion that their ancestors brought from Africa. In the United States it is generally known as voodoo, but its proper name is Vodun. It consists largely of sorcery. Its devotees believe that the evil forces of nature, such as parching sun, poisonous weeds, snakes, and hurricanes, are all leagued against them. Moreover, their human enemies desire to cast spells upon them. Should they succeed, the unfortunate victims will surely die. But even this is not their greatest misfortune, for they will be raised from the dead in the form of zombies, they will be alive and yet not alive; and, in this uncomfortable and somewhat ambiguous condition, they will be forced to work as slaves. To persons from other countries these dangers seem highly imaginary, but to the ignorant Haitian peasants they are very real. Steps must be taken to secure protection against the evil forces. The witch doctor knows what to do, of course, and therefore he is a very important person in the community. The Haitian government has taken steps to combat these superstitions. The Catholic Church is strongly opposed to them. Yet they still persist, even among great numbers of peasant families that call themselves Catholics.[2]

Language. Although French is the official language of Haiti, it is used only by the upper classes. The vast majority of the people speak Creole, which is a variation of the seventeenth century Norman dialect of French with African and Spanish overtones. Even the aristocrats know Creole; they learn it as children from the servants and necessarily use it in all their contacts with the lower orders. But among themselves they speak French and take great pride in the purity of their diction. The ability to speak the French language correctly is one of the most obvious signs of membership in the aristocracy.

Crops. Haiti is almost a one-crop country. The crop is coffee; it represents nearly three fourths of the value of all exports. For many years the coffee went almost exclusively to France, which re-exported some of it to other European nations. France in turn received favorable tariff treatment from Haiti. Thus the economic ties between the two nations were strong, supplementing the cultural bonds that had existed since colonial days. Even before the Second World War, however, France abandoned its large-scale purchases of Haitian coffee, and most of the crop then went to the United States.

The Haitian government is endeavoring to develop some of the other

2 See Zora Neale Hurston's *Tell My Horse.*

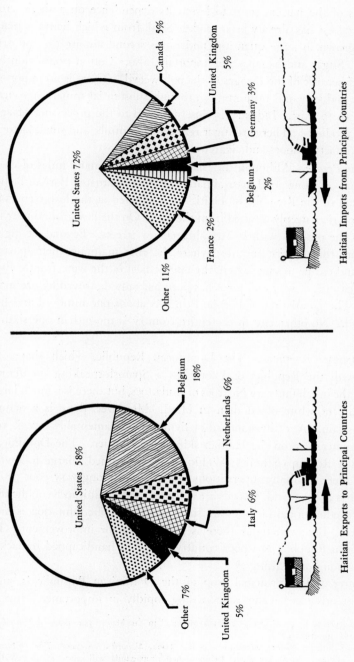

Haitian Imports from Principal Countries

United States 72%

Canada 5%

United Kingdom 5%

Germany 3%

Belgium 2%

France 2%

Other 11%

Haitian Exports to Principal Countries

United States 58%

Belgium 18%

Netherlands 6%

Italy 6%

United Kingdom 5%

Other 7%

Based on information obtained from *Economic and Commercial Conditions in Haiti*, July, 1952, one of a series of Overseas Economic Surveys published for the Commercial Relations and Exports Department of the Board of Trade by Her Majesty's Stationery Office, London, 1953.

resources of the nation, so as to lessen its dependence on a single crop. Some progress has already been made. Sisal, from which hemp is made, is now grown in large quantities and ranks second among the country's exports. Sugar and bananas are important, also. Cotton production has fallen off because of the ravages of the boll weevil. There is no important livestock industry and little mining, though substantial mineral resources are known to exist. Industry is closely related to the processing of agricultural products. There are sugar refineries, sawmills, and small factories that manufacture shoes and cigarettes.

Port-au-Prince. Although the island of Haiti has many miles of coastline, it has only one good natural harbor. Here is situated Port-au-Prince, the capital of the Republic of Haiti. It is situated at the lower end of a valley and rises steeply upward from the bay. On the low ground near the water is the old city with its straight, narrow streets. Beyond, at higher levels, are the modern suburbs, where the elite maintain their spacious homes and escape to some extent the intense heat of the waterfront. Even the old city is not very old, for it has been partially destroyed by fire many times. The population of Port-au-Prince is about one hundred and fifty thousand. No other city in the entire country is more than one sixth as large.[3]

DOMINICAN REPUBLIC. The Dominican Republic, which shares the island with the Republic of Haiti, has a Spanish-speaking population. Most of the inhabitants are Negroes or mulattoes, but there is a much larger admixture of white blood than in Haiti. Moreover, there is a definite Indian strain. And the standard of living, while lamentably low, is very much higher than on the Haitian side of the frontier. The Dominicans are mostly Roman Catholics; Vodun has never gained a large following, though there are many superstitious practices, as among very poor people in all parts of the world. Roads are better in the Dominican Republic than in Haiti; educational facilities are superior; and public sanitation is more advanced. But even today there is great room for improvement. The Dominican Republic is a poor country, and it is handicapped by lack of funds, among other things.[4]

Resources. The principal crop of the Dominican Republic is sugar. Coffee stands second and is increasing rapidly in importance. But the

[3] See the article by T. Koeves, "Haitian Mosaic," in the May, 1952, issue of *United Nations World*, pp. 16–19.

[4] In 1928 Sumner Welles wrote an excellent book, *Naboth's Vineyard: The Dominican Republic.* Those who do not object to unabashed propaganda will enjoy Stanley Walker's little volume, *Journey Toward the Sunlight,* which was published in 1947.

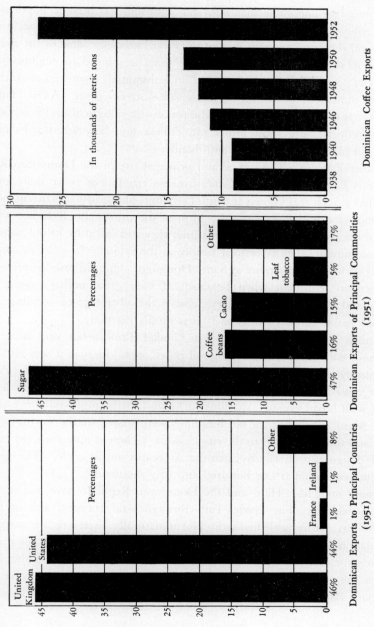

Dominican Exports to Principal Countries   **Dominican Exports of Principal Commodities**   **Dominican Coffee Exports**
(1951)   (1951)

Based on information obtained from the May, 1953, issue of *International Financial Statistics*, a publication of the International Monetary Fund.

585

third crop, cacao, is far less important than formerly. Tobacco and corn are entitled to honorable mention. Stock raising has become important in recent years, largely because of the establishment of a meat packing plant and the improvement of transportation facilities. Most of the meat is sold in the domestic market, though some is shipped to neighboring countries. Gold has been produced in substantial quantities, but the known mineral resources of the nation are not very great. As in Haiti, industry is concerned chiefly with the processing of agricultural products. Sugar refineries are most important. There are, however, textile and chemical plants, shoe factories, and distilleries.

Ciudad Trujillo. The capital and principal city of the Dominican Republic is Ciudad Trujillo. (*Ciudad* means *city*.) For more than four hundred years it was known as Santo Domingo, but in 1936 it was renamed in honor of the nation's dictator. Most of the inhabitants have not welcomed the change, however. Sometimes they still call it by its old name; more commonly they refer to it simply as the capital. In years to come it may be known once more as Santo Domingo. One old priest expressed the general sentiment when he said: "If your grandmother's name is Mary, and always has been Mary, what is the advantage of deciding, in her old age, to call her Margaret? It is simply not done." [5]

It must be confessed that modern Ciudad Trujillo has very little in common with the Santo Domingo of other days. In 1930 it was almost completely destroyed by a wild hurricane and had to be rebuilt. Advantage was taken of this opportunity to lay out the new city on modern lines, with broad avenues, spacious parks, and vastly improved port facilities. Many of the historic old buildings were spared by the storm, however, and today they add to the city's charm. There is a magnificent new hotel, designed primarily to catch the American tourist trade. The city's present population is one hundred and fifty thousand. [6]

BORDER DISPUTES. Haiti and the Dominican Republic have had many border disputes. The border runs through wild country, and in the past it was not too well marked. Not unnaturally, therefore, the surplus population of Haiti sometimes swept across the frontier, looking for work or, in some cases, looking for loot. There were many bloody clashes between the citizens of the two nations. In 1937, when another wave of Haitians came across the border seeking jobs in the sugar fields, the out-

[5] Stanley Walker, *op. cit.,* p. 222.

[6] See O. P. Newman's article, "The Land Columbus Loved," in the February, 1944, issue of the *National Geographic Magazine,* pp. 196–224.

raged Dominicans fell upon them with machetes and literally cut them to pieces. At least seven thousand persons lost their lives. The news of this massacre eventually reached Port-au-Prince and caused great indignation. There was even talk of war. But the Dominican government expressed its regret and paid a substantial indemnity. Today Haitian farmers think twice before wandering into Dominican territory. The Dominican government has tried to secure its side of the frontier by establishing settlements all along the line. Even convicts have been paroled, in order to permit them to make homes in this remote area.

THE ROLAND AFFAIR. In 1949 the Haitian government accused its own minister to Ecuador, Colonel Astrel Roland, of plotting revolution, and ordered him to return home to explain his activities. He set out from Ecuador, but when he got as far as the Dominican Republic he was given the use of the official radio in order to launch bitter attacks against the president of Haiti and other high officials. Frequently he called for an uprising of the Haitian people. The government of Haiti indignantly accused the Dominican Republic of "moral aggression," and laid its case before the Organization of American States, which appointed a special commission to investigate the matter. The report of this commission placed the blame squarely on the Dominican Republic, despite Dominican counter-charges. The two nations have now signed a treaty designed to prevent similar unfriendly acts, but even today this treaty is not strictly observed.[7]

The Pattern of Haitian Politics

BUCCANEERS AND SLAVES. For several centuries the territory that now comprises the Republic of Haiti belonged to France. French buccaneers established bases in the western part of the island, from which they harassed the ships of Spain and England. The governors sent from France actually encouraged these illicit ventures. Gradually, however, the territory became a thriving agricultural colony, with only vague memories of its rough beginnings. Spain had recognized French sovereignty over the western area in 1697, and shortly afterward it was discovered that large profits could be made from such prosaic enterprises as the raising of sugar, coffee, and cacao. But labor was needed in great quantities, and the Indians soon died off, so Negro slaves were brought from Africa. More than a million

[7] See the report of the Special Committee for the Caribbean, in the *Annals of the Organization of American States*, Vol. II, No. 4, 1950.

were imported during the eighteenth century, though many of them were unable to survive the harsh conditions of slave life. As the eighteenth century drew to a close, a rigid class system had already grown up in the colony. There were the wealthy whites, who owned the great plantations and the more important commercial enterprises, and served as the chief officials of the government; the "little whites," [8] as they were generally known—tradesmen and artisans, small planters, and ne'er-do-wells; and Negroes or mulattoes who had been given—or perhaps had been able to purchase—their freedom. The Negro slaves were not included in the class system, even at its lowest level. They were scarcely considered human.

RACE TROUBLES. In time the free mulattoes became almost as numerous as the whites. Some of them became quite prosperous, owning large plantations and many slaves. This prosperity aroused the jealousy of the whites, who proceeded to enact discriminatory legislation. They forbade the mulattoes to hold any major public offices, to engage in certain lucrative businesses and professions, even to wear the same clothes as whites or to sit in the same sections of churches and theaters. These restrictions naturally inflamed the passions of the mulattoes, who had been accustomed to mingling with their white neighbors almost on terms of equality. Hatred flared on both sides. Then, in 1789, came the French Revolution and the Declaration of the Rights of Man. These events had sharp repercussions in the colony. The wealthy whites petitioned the French Assembly for complete autonomy, on the ground that only they knew how to solve the difficult problem of white-mulatto relations. But the mulattoes strenuously demanded political equality and even offered to present to the French Republic one fifth of all their wealth. Finally, after many protracted debates, the French Assembly passed an ambiguous resolution which satisfied no one. When it later adopted another resolution confirming some of the demands of the mulattoes, the whites refused to permit its enforcement. For the mulattoes it seemed that only revolution was left. Before they could act, however, the Negro slaves staged one of the bloodiest uprisings in history. They slaughtered every white man, woman, and child on whom they could lay their hands, burning the plantations as they went. Some planters and their families managed to escape to the comparative safety of the capital. That was in August of 1791.

INDEPENDENCE. The years following the Negro uprising were marked by chaos. Virtually all the whites left the island as soon as possible. The

---

[8] Literally, *petits blancs*.

Spaniards invaded the colony by land, and the English attacked it from the water. Meanwhile mulattoes and blacks were working at cross purposes. In August of 1793 the French commissioner on the island formally proclaimed the abolition of slavery. Thereupon a pure-blooded Negro named Toussaint l'Ouverture, who had been raised as a slave but had escaped to the Spanish part of the island and risen to high rank in the Spanish army, deserted his Spanish friends and united the blacks to defeat both the Spaniards and the English. Thus France gained at least nominal control of the entire island, though Toussaint was its real ruler. On July 1, 1801, he declared Haiti independent of the mother country and made himself president for life. Political equality was guaranteed to all persons. By this time, however, Napoleon had become master of France and he was determined to regain the nation's lost colony. He sent thirty thousand troops to accomplish this purpose, yet found it necessary to resort to treachery to capture Toussaint l'Ouverture. The Negro died in a French dungeon in 1803. His death did not mark the end of the struggle, however. Other black leaders replaced him and eventually the French were forced to surrender. Their rule was at an end, though they did not formally recognize the independence of the new nation for another two decades.

Two GOVERNMENTS. After the withdrawal of the French, the new leader of the Haitian people was General Jean Jacabo Dessalines, who had struck the final blow for freedom. His officers made him governor-general for life, but this modest title was not good enough. Within a few months he declared himself emperor, taking the title of Jacques I. He was a capable man, but very ruthless, and his harsh policies made many enemies. As a Negro he hated the mulattoes and tried to break their influence, though frequently declaring himself indifferent to the color of a man's skin. The mulattoes returned this hatred. Their idol was Alexandre Pétion, who had been born of free parents and educated in France.

In 1806, when Dessalines was murdered, his place was taken by another black named Henri Christophe, who called himself King Henri I. The followers of Pétion refused to accept Christophe's authority, however, and established a republic in the southern part of the island. Pétion was its president, of course. For a number of years, therefore, the island had two governments. Not only the mulattoes favored Pétion; many Negroes fled to his part of the island because of the rumor that life was easier. There was, indeed, a measure of truth in this report. Christophe made and enforced rules that compelled hard work, because he thought that it was the only way to restore prosperity to the island after the devastating years of warfare. The easygoing Pétion followed a less rigorous and more popular path.

UNION AND DISUNION. In 1818 Pétion died, and was succeeded by his devoted follower, General Jean Pierre Boyer. Two years later Christophe committed suicide. This led to the union of all the French-speaking parts of the island under Boyer's rule. In the east, however, Spain had regained control of its former colony, only to lose it once more in the wars of independence. For a time this eastern section was associated with Bolívar's Great Colombia, but in 1822 it was conquered by Boyer and the whole island became known as the Republic of Haiti. Finally, in 1844, the people of the east asserted and won their independence, calling their new nation the Dominican Republic.

CHAOS. The people of Haiti consistently demonstrated their complete incapacity for self-government. They followed blindly a long succession of despots. Revolution followed revolution, each new leader seemingly determined to outdo his predecessor in ruthless disregard of human rights. President Boyer ruled the nation until 1842, when he was driven into exile.[9] During the next seventy-five years only one chief executive completed his prescribed term. Fourteen were forced from office as a result of armed uprisings, one was blown up, one was poisoned, and another was hacked to pieces by an infuriated mob. Three others died in office—presumably from natural causes. Most of the time the blacks managed to control the government, though the mulattoes maintained their superior economic and social status.[10]

AMERICAN INTERVENTION. One of the results of Haiti's political disturbances was the almost complete depletion of its economic and financial resources. The little country had borrowed large sums from several European nations, but was in no position to repay them or even to continue interest payments. Great Britain, France, and Germany demanded that corrective steps be taken; Germany even sent a battleship into the harbor of Port-au-Prince, with a demand for control of the customs. The outbreak of the First World War in 1914 temporarily eased the pressure, but Haiti knew that after the war the demands of the victorious powers would be presented with increasing vigor. So, too, did the United States. It could not permit European governments to interfere in Haitian affairs without abandoning the Monroe Doctrine. On the other hand, it was

---

[9] See J. E. Baur's article, "Mulatto Machiavelli; Jean Pierre Boyer and the Haiti of His Day," in the July, 1947, issue of the *Journal of Negro History*, pp. 307–353.

[10] For a more detailed account of the events of these years, see the 3rd edition of H. P. Davis' *Black Democracy; the Story of Haiti*.

forced to admit the justice of the European claims. So it proposed to the Haitian government an agreement permitting American officials to take over the customs and put the country's finances in order. The Haitian president refused to consider this suggestion. Shortly afterward, however, he was killed. The next president, Villbrün Guillaume Sam, proved to be one of the bloodiest tyrants in Haitian history. One of his first acts was to order the execution of one hundred and sixty of his political opponents. Such brutality inflamed the people of Port-au-Prince, and they retaliated by assassinating the President. Mobs roamed the streets, looting and rioting. Before the end of the day American marines landed in the capital to protect the legation; they then took over the customs and other public services.

American forces remained in virtual control of the island for the next nineteen years. First they supervised a presidential election. The winner was Sudré Dartiguenave, the first mulatto to occupy the presidency in many years. Then the representatives of the United States presented to the Haitian government a proposed treaty that would transform the little republic into an American protectorate. American officials would remain in control of the customs and would supervise the nation's finances; American marines would organize and direct a native constabulary; Haiti would guarantee not to cede its territory to other nations. President Dartiguenave signed the treaty at once, but it encountered strong opposition in the Haitian Senate. Gradually, however, the senators began to realize that the United States had come to stay and they were powerless to alter the situation. American officials emphasized the point by announcing that the funds collected at the customs house would not be available to pay Haitian salaries until the treaty had been ratified. On November 11, 1915, the Senate finally gave its reluctant consent, and the United States could finally boast that it was maintaining its forces in the island under an agreement with the Haitian government.

DISCONTENT. President Dartiguenave and his successor, another mulatto named Louis Borno, co-operated closely with the United States. There was every reason for them to do so, for in all probability neither of them could have stayed in office without American support. Americans supplied the government with funds—primarily through the administration of the local customs; and Americans maintained order. A new American-made constitution was adopted. It called for a popularly elected Congress, but the Congress never met. The president ruled the nation, and American officials ruled the president.

It is easy to understand, therefore, why the American occupation was highly unpopular. Haitians of all classes were united in opposition. Some of their leaders made serious charges against the occupation forces. They said that no attempt had been made to pay the foreign debt, although that was the principal reason alleged for American intervention. They accused American marines of using forced labor on the roads and, in some cases, torturing and killing Haitian citizens. So loud and persistent were these complaints that eventually they attracted attention in Washington. Several investigations were ordered. The Senate investigating committee explored the situation carefully and submitted a report that was fairly critical of American policy. Most of the charges made by the Haitians were conceded to be true, though they represented isolated instances. The chief fault of the United States government, in the opinion of the committee, was its failure to select officials who would try to understand the Haitian viewpoint and establish cordial relations. On the other hand, the occupation had achieved some highly desirable results. It had taught the Haitians the elements of public sanitation, improved schools, and roads, and—above all else—it had maintained the peace. Under the circumstances, therefore, the committee thought that American representatives should remain in the island.[11]

END OF AMERICAN OCCUPATION. American officials did remain for a number of years, but the United States government tried to correct some of its earlier mistakes. It appointed a high commissioner to deal with the Haitian authorities and also to exercise a close supervision over the American treaty officials. The results seem to have been beneficial, but most Haitians continued their complaints that their country was still ruled by a foreign power. In the latter part of 1929 the general dissatisfaction took the form of strikes of protest. Finally a mob attacked American marines in Port-au-Prince. When the marines defended themselves, more than thirty of the rioters were killed or wounded. Emotions rose to fever pitch. In all Haiti scarcely a person could be found—other than President Borno and his immediate associates—who would say a good word for the forces of occupation.

One of the results of the incident was the appointment by President Hoover of a commission to study the situation once more and make fresh recommendations. After several months of investigation it proposed complete withdrawal of American troops and civil officers by 1936, and gradual

[11] See Senate Report No. 794, 67th Cong., 2nd Sess.

removal prior to that time.[12] These suggestions were not acceptable to the government of Haiti, but they formed the basis for further negotiations. When President Roosevelt took office in the spring of 1933, he indicated his desire to end the American occupation at the earliest possible moment. The last American troops were withdrawn in the summer of 1934, and one year later the Haitian government resumed control of its own finances under the terms of an agreement with the National City Bank of New York. Some members of the Haitian Senate opposed this financial transaction, but when the president of the nation submitted it to a popular referendum, it received overwhelming approval. Thus the United States terminated a trusteeship that had gained for it very little except ill will.[13]

STÉNIO VINCENT. In 1931 a lawyer and editor named Sténio Vincent was elected to the presidency. He was chosen by the legislative branch—not by the people, for the constitution specified this manner of selection. Like his immediate predecessors he was a mulatto and a firm believer in the continued supremacy of his own group. Unlike them, however, he dared to speak out strongly against American occupation, and in this way he made himself popular with Haitians of all classes. A new constitution was adopted in 1932, only to be replaced by still another in 1935. The 1935 document contained a special clause extending President Vincent's term until 1941. Both the constitution and its special clause were submitted to a popular plebiscite. The government counted the votes and announced that an overwhelming majority had given approval. During President Vincent's ten years in office he proved himself a capable administrator, improving Haiti's domestic conditions and world position. Many times he went out into the fields and talked with the peasants, urging them to rotate their crops and adopt other modern farming methods. But he permitted no interference with his plans. He kept the legislative branch in the subordinate position that it had occupied during most of the nation's history. He showed scant respect for civil liberties. And he maintained himself in power through a close alliance with the Haitian Guard—the military constabulary trained by American marines.

ELECTION OF LESCOT. As President Vincent's term drew to a close in 1941, he indicated that he would not seek a further extension of his term. Instead he threw his support to light-skinned Elie Lescot, who had served

[12] The complete recommendations are available in the *Report of the President's Commission for the Study and Review of Conditions in the Republic of Haiti.*

[13] The story of American occupation is well told by Arthur C. Millspaugh in *Haiti Under American Control.*

as minister to the United States. Presidential endorsement was equivalent to election,[14] so Lescot was chosen without serious opposition and continued Vincent's policies without substantial modifications.[15]

REVOLUTION. The new President had a difficult time, however. After the attack at Pearl Harbor, Haiti went to war on the side of the United States. For a time its usual markets and also its usual sources of supply were cut off. Prices were rising steadily, as in other countries, and wages showed an unfortunate tendency to lag behind. The people blamed the government, riots became so violent that the Haitian Guard was unable to maintain order. In January, 1946, President Lescot was forced to abandon his post and leave the country. Thereupon a military junta took charge of the government. Major Frank Lavaud, a leader of the group, announced that a new Congress would be elected on May 12 and charged with the duty of naming a new president and preparing a new constitution. Military men were forbidden to be candidates.

ESTIMÉ AND MAGLOIRE. The congressional election was held as scheduled and the legislative branch then chose the new president of the nation: Dumarsais Estimé, a forty-six-year-old lawyer who had worked as a farmer and rural schoolteacher. Estimé was a black, but he was known as a moderate. Neither he nor anyone else supposed that he could suddenly sweep away all the economic and social privileges of the mulattoes and eliminate the nation's caste system. His announced goal, however, was to improve the desperate living conditions of the impoverished masses. He financed his extensive program by means of an income tax—the first in the nation's history. In 1950 President Estimé, who evidently desired to continue in office beyond the expiration of his six-year term, announced that he favored abolition of the prohibition against immediate presidential succession. The army promptly responded by deposing Estimé, and turning the government over to a military junta headed by Colonel (later Brigadier General) Paul Magloire. Five months later Magloire was elected president. The choice was made by the people, rather than by the legislative branch, as formerly. Haiti has had two new constitutions recently—one in 1946 and the other in 1950. The 1950 document seems to be somewhat more democratic than any of its predecessors, but it has not really changed the dictatorial pattern of Haitian life. The fact is that Haiti is not yet ready for the responsibilities of democracy.

[14] See Russell H. Fitzgibbon's article, "*Continuismo* in Central America and the Caribbean," in the July, 1940, issue of the *Inter-American Quarterly,* pp. 56–74.

[15] See G. E. Simpson's article, "Haitian Politics," in the May, 1942, issue of *Social Forces,* pp. 487–491.

The Structure of Haitian Government

THE CONSTITUTION. Haiti has had nineteen constitutions during its
troubled history. The present document, which contains about twelve
thousand words, is relatively short. About one sixth of the total space is
devoted to a statement of civil and political liberties. Even a casual reading of this section is sufficient, however, to make clear that civil rights are
not held in high esteem. Freedom of speech and press are guaranteed,
under such conditions and in such manner as the law may indicate. Haitians may assemble peaceably to petition for the redress of grievances, in
conformity with the laws that regulate the exercise of this right. And so
the constitution continues for page after page. Men shall be free, it states
in effect, at such times and to such extent as the law may permit. The
law has never permitted much freedom, or for long periods. It is interesting to note that all the constitutions of Haiti, not excepting even the present
document, have remained largely untouched by the modern tendency to
include guarantees of social welfare. The liberties they enumerate are
mostly the liberties of the American Bill of Rights and the French Declaration of the Rights of Man.[16]

Amendment of the constitution. Amendments to the constitution may
be proposed by the president or either house of the legislative branch.
The two houses then meet in joint session to decide the matter. Two
thirds of the total membership must be present and a two-thirds vote is
necessary for adoption. Whenever the two houses meet jointly, whether
to consider constitutional amendments or for other purposes, they are
known as the National Assembly. Otherwise they are called simply the
legislative branch; the term *Congress* is not used.

SUFFRAGE AND ELECTIONS. Men who have attained the age of twenty-one
years are permitted to vote. Until 1946, however, both the president and
the members of the Senate were chosen indirectly, so that the people voted
only for members of the Chamber of Deputies and local officials. Until
1950 they were not allowed to choose the president of the nation. Political
parties, in the democratic sense, are scarcely known. Candidates are
either for the president or against him. Most of them are for him. The
law declares that voting shall be secret. Even under the most favorable
circumstances, however, such a provision could scarcely be enforced in a
country where ninety per cent of the people are illiterate. Very little
attempt is made to enforce it, except in the capital. The rural leaders of

16 The bill of rights of the present constitution is found in Arts. 3–31.

the well-entrenched political machine usually collect the registration cards of their unlettered followers—paying a small sum for this privilege—and then vote these cards in batches. This system has been used for so many years that no one thinks to challenge it.

THE PRESIDENT: *Selection, term, qualifications, salary.* The president completely dominates the political life of the nation. No one can challenge his authority successfully without recourse to violence. Neither the legislative branch nor the courts can be regarded as a co-ordinate part of the government. We have already observed that the president is now chosen by direct vote of the citizens of the nation. The president must be a natural-born citizen, at least forty years of age. His term is six years. In 1935 the constitutional prohibition against two successive terms was removed for President Vincent's special benefit,[17] but in 1946 it was restored. The chief executive's salary is approximately thirty thousand a year, in terms of American currency. For a very poor country this is a generous allowance. The presidential palace faces the Place l'Ouverture, in the center of the capital.

Executive powers. The president's appointing power is virtually unlimited. He names all officers and employees of the administrative services, including of course the members of his own cabinet. He appoints all the officers of the armed forces. He chooses all the members of the diplomatic service, and all judges. For none of these appointments does he require the consent of the National Assembly or either of its chambers. His power of removal is equally unlimited, except with regard to judges, who are assured a definite tenure. Declarations of war and treaties must be approved by the National Assembly.

Legislative powers. The president is given the right to introduce bills in the legislative branch. In fact, he alone may introduce appropriation measures, and the legislature may not increase his estimates. The veto, however, follows conventional lines, two thirds of each house being sufficient to override the president's objections. Legislation by decree is the rule rather than the exception. Some of the most important reforms in Haitian history have been made by presidential order. The president may adjourn the legislative branch for a limited time. He may also convene it in special session, at which time it may consider only the proposals that he chooses to submit.

Presidential succession. There is no vice-president, but the constitution establishes an order of presidential succession—first the president of the

[17] See page 593.

nation's highest court, then the vice-president of the court, and finally the judge of the court who has the longest period of service. The person thus assuming the presidency must make arrangements immediately for the popular election of a new chief executive.

THE CABINET. There is the customary provision for countersignature of the president's acts by the appropriate ministers, and the usual declaration that they are responsible for every act to which they give their consent. These statements have no significance. Haiti does not have parliamentary government, and never has had a system even remotely approaching it. Two of the earlier constitutions did in fact seem to establish ministerial responsibility, but their clauses dealing with this matter were never enforced.[18] The cabinet does not even have the status that is accorded it in most countries using a presidential system. Its seven members are little better than clerks, performing routine tasks while the president decides all major matters of policy.[19]

THE LEGISLATIVE BRANCH. Under the constitution of 1935 the president named nearly one half of the members of the Senate, and submitted a list from which at least some of the other senators were likely to be drawn. Today, however, the members of both houses of the legislative branch are elected by vote of the people. The Senate has twenty-one members; the Chamber of Deputies has thirty-seven. Both senators and deputies must be natural-born citizens, and residents of the districts they represent. Minimum age limits are thirty and twenty-five years, respectively. Senators serve for six years, and deputies for four. Their salary is approximately four thousand American dollars a year—a fairly substantial sum in Haiti. The legislative branch meets in regular session each year on the second Monday in April. The length of the session is usually three months, but this period may be extended for two additional months by the legislature itself or by the president. As usual, each house chooses its own officers. The number of permanent standing committees—seven—is the same in both the Senate and the Chamber of Deputies. Haiti, like Cuba, is one of the few Latin American countries that makes use of conference committees to adjust differences of opinion between the two chambers of the legislature.

THE COURTS. The supreme court of the nation—the Tribunal of Cassation, as it is officially known—has nine judges. They serve for ten-year

18 Wm. S. Stokes, "Parliamentary Government in Latin America," in the June, 1945, issue of the *American Political Science Review,* Vol. XXXIX, no. 3, p. 528.
19 James G. Leyburn, *op. cit.,* p. 231.

terms. Below the high tribunal are three courts of appeal whose justices also serve for ten years. Then there are the courts of first instance. Their judges have seven-year terms. And, finally, there are the justices of the peace—one in every community—serving for an indefinite period and administering local affairs in addition to trying petty cases. All members of the judiciary are appointed by the president. Except for justices of the peace, they are removable only by process of impeachment. That, at least, is the theory of the constitution. But in the early days many Haitian presidents summarily dismissed judges who displeased them. Therefore the Tribunal of Cassation prudently developed the habit of discussing important cases with the chief executive before submitting its opinions.

INTERNAL ORGANIZATION. Haiti's system of internal administration follows the French pattern to some extent, though not so completely as the use of French names might indicate. There are five departments, twenty-seven arrondissements, and one hundred and fourteen communes. The departments are not important units of government, however. They are useful chiefly for clerical and statistical purposes. Very different are the arrondissements, which serve as the principal units of local administration. Every arrondissement is in charge of a prefect—a politician, usually connected with the military forces, who has been appointed by the president and holds office at his pleasure. The prefect is responsible for the administration of public services within the arrondissement. He issues necessary local decrees. There is no legislative assembly. In the communes, however, there are popularly elected councils. Their measure of authority is very small. The affairs of the commune are administered chiefly by a local magistrate, or justice of the peace, who is appointed by the president. This magistrate is responsible directly to the minister of the interior, a member of the president's cabinet.

The Pattern of Dominican Politics

A TRAGIC HISTORY. The history of the Dominican Republic as an independent nation has been quite as tragic as that of its sister republic. There have been innumerable dictatorships, revolutions, and counterrevolutions. Foreign nations have intervened on several occasions. Almost insoluble economic and social problems have beset the nation. At times even the forces of nature seem to have wreaked their vengeance upon it.

SANTANA AND BÁEZ. In 1844 the Dominicans won their independence from Haiti, but the Haitians were not content to accept this decision as final. On several subsequent occasions they sent large forces to capture the eastern part of the island, though without success. Meanwhile the ambitious leaders of the new nation could not agree among themselves. Two of them—Pedro Santana and Buenaventura Báez—almost wrecked the country with their quarrels. General Santana was the first president, but his regime was troubled by domestic uprisings and foreign invasions. He managed to triumph over all his enemies and round out his term of office, though of course he could give scarcely a thought to the urgent problems of economic reconstruction. His successor lasted only a few months; then Santana led a successful revolution and installed himself in the presidency once more. This time he did not even bother to give lip worship to the established forms of constitutional government. In 1849 Buenaventura Báez was chosen president, and began his first term. Before the completion of this period, however, Santana staged a *coup d'état,* and once again became president-dictator. In 1856 Báez again assumed the presidency; in 1858 Santana drove him once more from power. Not until 1866 did Báez again become the nation's chief executive, and when he did, a triumvirate soon managed to expel him. The life of Buenaventura Báez seemed to be a succession of violent removals and triumphant returns.

PROTECTORATE PLANS. While Báez rose and fell in power, the Dominican Republic's other strong man, General Santana, became convinced that the tiny country could scarcely defend itself against Haiti. So he hit upon the plan of placing it under the protection of one of the great powers. Both France and Spain were approached, with this end in view. Finally, in 1861, Spain gave its consent to the proposals, and thus the Dominican Republic became once more a Spanish colony. Santana was made its governor-general. The United States protested that this action violated the Monroe Doctrine, but it was busily engaged in the Civil War, and could take no steps to make its protest effective.[20] Before long, however, the Dominicans took matters into their own hands. Spanish rule had proved as inept as in earlier years and just as indifferent to colonial interests. So Dominican patriots raised an army which drove the Spanish forces from the island for all time and re-established the republic. The idea of a protectorate persisted, however. President Báez, once more in power,

[20] See C. C. Hauch's article, "Attitudes of Foreign Governments towards the Spanish Reoccupation of the Dominican Republic, 1861," in the May, 1947, issue of the *Hispanic American Historical Review,* pp. 247–268.

tried to arrange for the annexation of the Dominican Republic to the United States. President Grant strongly favored this proposal, but Congress refused to give its consent.[21]

AMERICAN FINANCIAL SUPERVISION. In 1882 a young Negro named Ulises Heureaux succeeded in making himself master of the nation. He ruled it for seventeen years. After the manner of strong dictators, he gave it a measure of peace and relative prosperity, but at the sacrifice of human rights. All opposition was suppressed with savage fury. Finally Heureaux was assassinated. In the next six years there were four major revolutions and five presidents. Civil liberties were completely ignored, property was wantonly destroyed, and thousands of lives were sacrificed to serve the vanity of rival *caudillos*. Normal business relations were almost at a standstill and the nation's economy was disintegrating rapidly. Under such circumstances it could scarcely hope to remain solvent.

Its virtual bankruptcy was a matter of deep concern to the United States, because an American corporation—the San Domingo Improvement Corporation—had become involved in the collection of the small republic's customs duties. Meanwhile both French and Italian creditors were demanding payment of long-due claims and their governments were threatening to use force. So the American government arranged with the Dominican authorities to take over the customs houses, turning over forty-five per cent of the receipts to the Dominican treasury and using the remainder for interest charges and debt reduction. It is interesting to note that under American administration the Dominican government received more from its share than the total amount it had previously been able to collect. Nonetheless there were many Dominicans who objected to American interference. Even in the United States there was considerable opposition to the arrangement. The treaty between the two countries, authorizing American control of the customs, was ignored by the United States Senate when first presented by President Theodore Roosevelt in 1905. But American officials continued to function under a *modus vivendi* until 1907, when Senate approval was finally obtained.

AMERICAN OCCUPATION. Although American control of the customs resulted in larger revenues, it had no effect on the island republic's unstable political conditions. In 1911 the president was assassinated, and his successor was forced to resign after only a few months. Meanwhile the United States was becoming more deeply involved in Dominican affairs.

[21] For a detailed discussion of this incident, see *The United States and Santo Domingo, 1798–1873*, by C. C. Tansill.

It supervised two presidential elections and landed several hundred marines to preserve order. When a new president was chosen in 1916, the American government refused to extend recognition until a new treaty was signed providing, among other things, for the appointment of an American financial adviser and the creation of a Dominican constabulary under American officers. Not unnaturally, the Dominican president refused to accept these terms. Thereupon the United States announced that it could not turn over customs revenues to unrecognized authorities. Thus it virtually forced the government into bankruptcy. A few months later, on November 29, 1916, it announced that the Dominican Republic was under the military administration of the United States. Rear-Admiral Knapp, in charge of the American forces of occupation, suspended the Dominican Congress and virtually assumed the powers of a dictator. This intervention came only a little more than a year after the establishment of American control in Haiti.[22] Thus the entire island came under the military rule of the United States.

RESULTS OF THE OCCUPATION. The story of American occupation was much the same in the Dominican Republic as in Haiti. Roads were built, unsatisfactory sanitary conditions were corrected, educational facilities were greatly expanded, public finances were placed on a firmer basis—and the people constantly showed their resentment of improvements imposed by a foreign power. In fact, they had many legitimate grievances. Persons were imprisoned without valid reason, and occasionally tortured. A strict censorship was maintained. American military courts were sometimes slow in meting out justice. Dominicans had experienced such evils throughout most of their history, but at least they had suffered under their own rulers. To the average Dominican this difference was important.

END OF AMERICAN OCCUPATION. Even in the United States there was strong sentiment against the occupation. Secretary of State Hughes recognized the justice of this sentiment when, in 1924, he said: "It is the belief of many that the military occupation would never have occurred had President Wilson had the opportunity or the time in the excitement of that period, to become fully cognizant of the causes of the situation existing in the Dominican Republic. Likewise it is improbable that he was informed of many of the occurrences which took place in the Dominican Republic during the earlier years of the American occupation—occurrences deeply to be regretted by every American citizen."[23] By the time

[22] See page 591.
[23] Quoted by Graham H. Stuart in *Latin America and the United States*, 3rd ed., p. 299.

the Secretary uttered these words, however, the American occupation was almost at an end. The Dominicans were encouraged to prepare a new constitution for their country, which was adopted in June, 1924. A new president was inaugurated in July, and in September the American marines were withdrawn. Representatives of the United States government continued to control the customs, however. This arrangement was not finally terminated until 1940.[24]

RISE OF TRUJILLO. General Horacio Vásquez began his term as president in 1924 by filling government positions with his friends and relatives. In 1927 he arranged for the adoption of a new constitution, which increased his term from four years to six. These maneuvers caused a great deal of dissatisfaction, but the President proved more than a match for his opponents. When, however, he went to the United States for medical treatment in the fall of 1929, other Dominican leaders fell to quarreling among themselves. Vásquez returned and adjusted these differences, but by this time he was too old and feeble to direct public affairs with a firm hand. When, therefore, dissatisfied army officers and politicians rose in revolt, they were quickly successful. President Vásquez resigned and a provisional government was established. That was in February, 1930. Three months later new elections were held. They swept into power General Rafael Leonidas Trujillo Molina, one of the strong men of the Americas, who still dominates the affairs of the Dominican Republic.

EARLY YEARS. Trujillo was born in 1893 near the little town of San Cristobal. His father dealt in cattle, and, according to rumor, was not too particular as to the means by which he acquired them. Young Rafael grew up to be a powerful man, useful on the sugar plantation where he worked because he could keep order. When the American marines came to the Dominican Republic, he joined their newly formed constabulary and soon rose to the rank of captain. He proved himself adept at killing his fellow countrymen who were waging guerrilla warfare against the occupation forces. When, however, the marines left the country, the change did not interfere with his career. He simply transformed the Dominican Guard into an effective army. First he became colonel, and then general. By the time Vásquez was overthrown, in 1930, Trujillo was chief of staff. The army was ready to carry out whatever orders he might issue.

TRUJILLO ELECTED PRESIDENT. Trujillo was eager for the presidency.

[24] For a careful and impartial analysis of American occupation, see Sumner Welles' previously cited work.

So was the provisional president who had led the 1930 revolution. But Trujillo persuaded him to accept the vice-presidential nomination. Then began a campaign of intimidation such as the nation had not seen in many years. Armed thugs roamed the countryside, breaking up the meetings of the opposition and beating the leaders unmercifully. When necessary, they did not hesitate to resort to murder. At least one hundred persons were killed because they persisted in expressing their opinions. Such tactics proved extremely effective. Trujillo became president of the nation with scarcly an audible objection. At the time of his inauguration he was still only thirty-seven years of age.

ECONOMIC PROGRESS. Hardly had Trujillo taken office when a great hurricane struck the island, devastating the capital and doing vast damage elsewhere.[25] It was tragedy for the people, but a stroke of good fortune for the new chief executive, for it enabled him to display his undoubted talent as an organizer and administrator. He kept order in the face of great difficulties, preventing almost completely the looting that usually accompanies such events. Then he set about the task of rebuilding the capital and repairing the damage in other parts of the island. To his credit it must be reported that he did an excellent job. In other ways, also, he bettered conditions throughout the country. He reduced the national debt, improved the school system, built miles of irrigation ditches, and built the first really adequate harbor in the history of the republic. Foreign visitors to Italy used to say of Mussolini that he made the trains run on time. The Dominican Dictator has performed just as substantial miracles for his country.

THE PRICE OF TYRANNY. Like Mussolini, however, Trujillo has exacted a high price for his services. He has not only ruled the nation as an absolute despot, but has used harsh methods in perpetuating his rule. At least three thousand of his enemies have been quietly liquidated, according to reports from many reliable sources. There has been an ironclad censorship, not only of newspapers and magazines but also of private mail. A secret police pries into the innermost lives of Dominican citizens, looking for the faintest hint of rebellion. Meanwhile Trujillo has found many ways to increase his private fortune. He has monopolized—as his private business—the salt and tobacco industries. He has taken personal control of most forms of insurance. Vast estates have fallen into his hands. Today, therefore, he is a very wealthy man. Some estimates place his private income as high as five million dollars a year. In any event, it can

[25] See page 586.

be said with certainty that he has made a large profit from his position as president of the nation.[26]

EXTRAVAGANT PRAISE. The politicians and the people have been compelled—or have thought it wise—to heap extravagant adulation upon the Dictator. Congress has given him the following titles: Benefactor of the Fatherland, Restorer of Financial Independence, Liberator of the Nation, Generalissimo, Admiral of the Navy, Protector of Fine Arts and Letters. The name of the capital, as we have already seen, has been changed in his honor. Public buildings bear plaques reading: *Era of Trujillo*. Automobile license plates are marked: *Viva Trujillo!* His picture occupies a prominent place in every hotel lobby, every store, and almost every private home. The three newspapers try to outdo one another in singing his praises.

A PUPPET PRESIDENT. Trujillo prefers to pay some attention to constitutional forms, instead of merely sweeping away the constitution and the legislative branch. Congress still continues to function, though of course it takes its orders from the Dictator. In 1947 Trujillo even went to the trouble of having a new constitution adopted. Every few years, when his term has expired, he goes through the form of holding an election and having himself declared the victor. The forms of democracy must be preserved at all costs.

In practice, of course, democracy is completely ignored. After Trujillo had first been elected, in 1930, he abolished all existing political parties and transformed the Dominican Republic into a one-party state, with all its members pledged to his support. The new party was called the *Partido Dominicano,* or Dominican Party, and everyone was supposed to belong to it. Practically everyone did. In 1934, when Trujillo proclaimed himself the Dominican Party's candidate for a second term, no one dared to challenge him. By 1938, however, the Dictator seems to have decided that it would be more fitting for someone else to assume the presidency for a term. Under his orders, therefore, the Dominican Party nominated his personal dentist and longtime political ally, Dr. Jacinto B. Peynado, who was elected without opposition. Trujillo thereupon assumed active command of the army. Dr. Peynado was so grateful for the honor conferred upon him that he installed on his home a large neon sign which read:

26 See Albert C. Hicks, *Blood in the Streets.* See also an interesting article by George Kent, "God and Trujillo," published in the March, 1946, issue of *Inter-American,* Vol. V, no. 3, pp. 14 ff.

"God and Trujillo." Some wags expressed surprise that the Deity should have been placed before the Dictator.

OPPOSITION TO ORDER. President Peynado did not serve out his full term. Early in 1940 he died of a leg infection, and his place was taken by the vice-president, Dr. Manuel Jesús Troncoso de la Concha, whose loyalty to Trujillo was equally intense. In preparation for the 1942 election, the Dictator organized another political party, which assumed the name of *Partido Trujillista,* or Trujillo's Party. It was not to be a rival political organization, however, but rather a club for the elite of the political world, within the framework of the Dominican Party. Both parties nominated Trujillo for president, of course, and as usual he won without opposition. The army and the secret police worked side by side to make certain that potential rivals would cause no trouble. By 1947, when President Trujillo was ready for his fourth term, he decided that a little opposition might be desirable, in order to convince the United States and other democracies that the Dominican Republic was not really a dictatorship. So he ordered the creation of two "opposition" parties, which promptly came into being. Each nominated a presidential candidate and then calmly awaited the news of the Dictator's victory. They made no attempt to influence the voters; in fact, the two candidates supposedly challenging Trujillo did not deliver a single address or write a single letter in their own behalf throughout the campaign. When the votes were counted, Trujillo modestly claimed only ninety-two per cent of the vote.[27] He then took office for another term. And in 1952, when that term expired, he arranged for the "popular election" of his forty-four-year-old brother, Héctor Bienvenido Trujillo, as president of the nation. Dictator Rafael Trujillo then assumed the title of head of the armed forces, just as he had in 1938, when another of his henchmen became president. Rafael's eldest son is now chief of staff of the navy and the air force. Thus the most influential jobs are safely in the Trujillo family. Brother Héctor, the new president, has discreetly announced that he intends to continue Rafael's beneficent policies.

OPPONENTS IN EXILE. The people have not remained entirely prostrate under the Trujillo tyranny, however. Some of them have acted anonymously to rouse the latent opposition. Leaflets reciting the government's brutalities have occasionally been printed and distributed clandestinely. The police have rounded up suspects from time to time, and some of these unfortunate persons have then disappeared. Most of the opposition, how-

[27] See R. J. Alexander's article, "Dictatorship in the Caribbean," in the May, 1948, issue of the *Canadian Forum,* pp. 35 ff.

ever, comes from Dominicans who have succeeded in escaping to other Latin American countries or to the United States. Their revolutionary plots occasionally come to light. But Rafael Trujillo seems to be complete master of the situation. He is too resourceful a man to be overthrown with ease.

The Structure of Dominican Government

THE CONSTITUTION. The present constitution was adopted in 1947. It is the tenth constitution of the nation, and gives no indication that all the power of the government is vested in one man. On the contrary, it seems to be quite a democratic document. Like the 1946 constitution of Haiti, it is relatively short—only about eleven thousand words. Without introduction or preamble, it proceeds at once to a number of general statements concerning the democratic nature of the government and the inalienability of the national territory. Then comes an imposing list of guarantees of individual liberty. There are very few restrictive clauses; anyone who did not know the recent history of the Dominican Republic might well assume that human rights were carefully respected.[28] The usual provision for suspension of guarantees in time of emergency is included, of course. It authorizes the president to declare a state of siege when Congress is not in session.

Amendment of the constitution. Amendments to the constitution may be proposed, but only by two thirds of the membership of either house of Congress. If the other chamber concurs in these suggestions—also by a two-thirds vote—the voters then elect delegates to a constituent convention, which proceeds to a consideration of the proposed changes. The convention may not discuss any other amendments. The president, according to the letter of the constitution, plays no part in the amending process.[29]

SUFFRAGE AND ELECTIONS. Both men and women have the right to vote when they reach the age of eighteen—or even earlier, if they are married. Literacy is not necessary. Foreigners who have resided in the republic for at least five years are permitted to vote in local elections. The government prepares an official ballot. No attempt is made to insure secrecy. Voting is compulsory. Each voter comes to the polling place with an identification card which contains his photograph and fingerprints. He is supposed to carry this card with him at all times; in fact, such a precau-

[28] See the Constitution, Arts. 6–11.
[29] Arts. 108–112.

tion is absolutely necessary if he plans to travel from town to town. After the voter has established his identity to the satisfaction of the election officials, he is handed a ballot and a blue crayon. The ballot must be marked in the presence of the officials. It is then folded and placed in the ballot box. Policemen are always nearby, but their services are seldom required.

THE PRESIDENT: *Selection, term, qualifications, salary.* The president is chosen by direct vote of the people—according to the constitution. He must be a natural-born citizen, not less than thirty years of age. It might be remarked, in passing, that thirty years is the legal minimum for virtually all officers of the national government. The president is elected for five years, and there is no constitutional restriction to prevent any number of subsequent terms. Although the presidential salary is only eight thousand dollars, that fact seems to have caused the present chief executive no serious hardship.

Powers. The powers of the president, as enumerated in the fundamental law, are no more extensive than in most other Latin American nations. He appoints the members of his own cabinet and other administrative officers, as well as diplomats. Only for the selection of diplomats must he secure the consent of the Senate. Dismissals are solely in his hands. He has no part—officially—in the naming of judges. As usual, he directs foreign affairs. He must, however, have congressional approval for treaties. Congress declares war. With regard to lawmaking the president's authority is not at all unusual, except that he is specifically permitted to issue decree-laws. He may introduce bills in Congress and may veto congressional proposals. Ordinarily he has eight days to consider measures that have been presented for his signature, but this period may be reduced to three days if the legislative branch marks a bill as urgent. A two-thirds vote in each chamber is necessary to override the president's veto. He has the sole power to call Congress in special session.

Presidential succession. The office of vice-president was abolished in 1947. If the president dies or becomes incapacitated, his place is taken by the president of the supreme court, who serves until Congress meets in joint session and chooses the nation's new chief executive. If, however, the president's absence from his office is only temporary, his place is taken by the secretary of war and navy. The constitution also names two other cabinet ministers, who complete the order of succession.[30] There are eight members of the cabinet. No attempt is made to establish the forms of parliamentary government. The constitution does not contain even

---

[30] Art. 51.

the usual stipulation that the president's acts must be countersigned by the appropriate ministers.

CONGRESS. The Senate has eighteen members—one for each of the nation's seventeen provinces and one for the District of Santo Domingo, which includes the capital. The Chamber of Deputies has a membership of forty, apportioned on the basis of population. All members of Congress are chosen by direct vote of the people and serve for five years. There is no system of partial renewal of membership before the end of the five-year period. Congress meets in regular session twice a year—in February and August. Each session normally continues for ninety days, but may be prolonged for an additional sixty days. Special sessions, as we have already noted, may be called only by the president. Each house functions through the usual standing committees, which are appointed by the *mesa directiva,* or steering committee. Disagreements between the two houses are adjusted by informal discussions of congressional leaders.

THE COURTS. The supreme court has seven members, who sit as a group and decide cases by majority vote. Below the high tribunal are three courts of appeal. Every judicial district has a judge of first instance, and every commune has a justice of the peace. All judges are chosen by the Senate and serve for five years. They are eligible for any additional numbers of terms. Judges of the supreme court must be natural-born citizens— a requirement that is not imposed for any other office except that of president.

INTERNAL ORGANIZATION. The system of internal administration is highly centralized. Each of the seventeen provinces has a governor, appointed by the president and removable at his pleasure. The governor assumes responsibility for all provincial affairs. There is no provincial assembly. Ciudad Trujillo and its environs have been made a special district. The provinces have been divided into communes, and each commune has its popularly elected council, which possesses few powers.

SELECTED REFERENCES

Baguidy, Joseph D., *Considérations sur la Conscience Nationale,* Port-au-Prince, H. Deschamps, 1945.

Brookings Institution, *Refugee Settlement in the Dominican Republic,* Washington, D.C., The Brookings Institution, 1942.

Bellegarde, Dantès, *La Nation Haïtienne,* Paris, J. de Gigord, 1938.

Cassa Logrono, José, *Estudio acerca de la Inconstitucionalidad de la Ley,* Ciudad Trujillo, Montalvo, 1940.

Cooper, Page, *Sambumbia,* New York, Caribbean Library, 1947.

Craige, John Houston, *Black Bagdad*, New York, Minton, Balch, 1933.

Davis, H. P., *Black Democracy*, New York, L. Macveagh, Dial Press, 1928.

Franco Ornes, Péricles, *La Tragedia Dominicana*, Santiago, Chile, Federación de Estudiantes de Chile, 1946.

Hicks, Albert C., *Blood in the Streets; The Life and Rule of Trujillo*, New York, Creative Age Press, 1946.

Hurston, Zora Neale, *Tell My Horse*, Philadelphia, Lippincott, 1938.

Jean-Jacques, Tales, *Histoire du Droit Haitien*, Port-au-Prince, Imprimerie N. Telhomme, 1936.

Jimenes Grullón, Juan Isidro, *La Propaganda de Trujillo al Desnudo*, Havana, "Unión Democrática Antinazista Dominicana," 1944.

Jones, Chester Lloyd, *The Caribbean Since 1900*, New York, Prentice-Hall, 1936.

Knight, Melvin M., *The Americans in Santo Domingo*, New York, Vanguard Press, 1928.

Leyburn, James G., *The Haitian People*, New Haven, Conn., H. Milford, Oxford Univ. Press, 1941.

Logan, R. W., *The Diplomatic Relations of the United States with Haiti*, Chapel Hill, N.C., Univ. of North Carolina Press, 1941.

Millspaugh, Arthur C., *Haiti Under American Control*, Boston, World Peace Foundation, 1931.

Montague, Ludwell, *Haiti and the United States*, Durham, N.C., Duke Univ. Press, 1940.

Moscoso Puello, Francisco, *Los Servicios de Asistencia Pública en la República Dominicana*, Ciudad Trujillo, Editora Montalvo, 1944.

Niles, Blair, *Black Haiti*, New York, Putnam, 1926.

President's Commission for the Study and Review of Conditions in the Republic of Haiti, *Report*, Washington, D.C., U.S. Govt. Printing Office, 1930.

Ravelo A., Oscar, *El Correo en Santo Domingo*, Ciudad Trujillo, Imp. "La Opinión," 1944.

Seabrook, W. B., *The Magic Island*, New York, Harcourt, Brace, 1929.

Tansill, C. C., *The United States and Santo Domingo, 1798–1873*, Baltimore, Johns Hopkins Press, 1938.

Walker, Stanley, *Journey toward the Sunlight*, New York, Caribbean Library, 1947.

Welles, Sumner, *Naboth's Vineyard: The Dominican Republic*, New York, Payson & Clark, 1928.

CHAPTER 23

CENTRAL AMERICA

~~~~~~

CENTRAL AMERICAN FEDERATION. Between Mexico's Isthmus of Tehauntepec and the Colombian border lies a strip of territory known as Central America. It is only about thirty per cent larger than California and has fewer people; yet it includes six independent nations. There is, of course, no valid economic reason why these countries should be independent of one another. Their importance in world affairs would be greatly strengthened by union. But such rational considerations seldom determine political boundaries. The people of every country, big or little, take pride in their national sovereignty and hesitate to surrender it, even to improve their way of life.

In Central America, however, the leaders of the several nations have not been ignorant of the need for federation or indifferent to its advantages. The five independent states of the region actually joined in a federal republic in 1823, with Guatemala City as the capital.[1] But the president and Congress were constantly quarreling; Conservatives and Liberals were at each other's throats; and in 1840 the federation collapsed. A little later El Salvador, Honduras, and Nicaragua agreed to form a loose union, but the plan failed almost as soon as it was established. Various Central American states seriously contemplated federation with their neighbors in 1845, 1847, 1849, 1862, 1876, 1885, and 1886. In 1895 Nicaragua, El Salvador, and Honduras adopted a plan which vested control of the foreign affairs of the three nations in a three-member council, but this arrangement was

---

[1] Panama was not included, of course. It did not gain its independence until eighty years later.

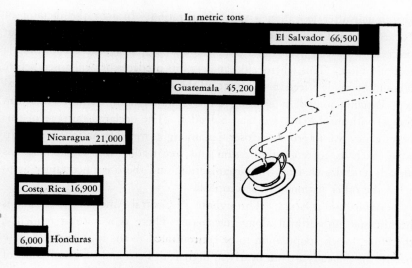

In metric tons

El Salvador 66,500

Guatemala 45,200

Nicaragua 21,000

Costa Rica 16,900

6,000 Honduras

Coffee Exports from Central American Republics (1950)

Based on information obtained from the November, 1951, issue of the *Monthly Bulletin of Food and Agricultural Statistics,* a publication of the Food and Agriculture Organization of the United Nations.

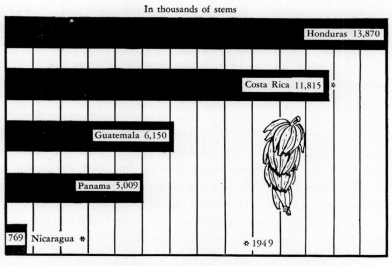

In thousands of stems

Honduras 13,870

Costa Rica 11,815 *

Guatemala 6,150

Panama 5,009

769 Nicaragua *

* 1949

Banana Exports from Central American Republics (1950)

Figures for Costa Rica, Nicaragua, and Panama based upon information obtained from *Foreign Commerce Yearbook, 1950;* figures for Guatemala and Honduras based on information obtained from the May, 1953, issue of *International Financial Statistics,* a publication of the International Monetary Fund.

abandoned after less than a year of operation. In 1907 the dictator of Nicaragua tried to achieve Central American union by force, but without success. Fourteen years later four nations signed a pact establishing a federal union. This scheme, like many of its predecessors, collapsed before it could be made effective. In 1951 all the nations of Central America except Panama joined in creating an Organization of Central American States, with headquarters in San Salvador. The declared purpose of this new agency was to promote closer ties among its member nations in various ways, such as currency unification and free trade. But Guatemala has already withdrawn from the organization, and there is uncertainty as to what the other nations can accomplish.

ALTITUDE AND CLIMATE. Throughout all Central America the climate is humid and unhealthful along the coast. There is a natural tendency, therefore, for the population to be concentrated in the highlands. Fortunately, the plateaus are not nearly so high as in Peru and Bolivia. Most of the centers of Central American civilization are at altitudes of from two thousand to five thousand feet. San Salvador is two thousand feet above sea level; Tegucigalpa, three thousand; San José, four thousand; and Guatemala City, five thousand. At such heights, in the tropics, the climate is always like late spring. There are only two seasons and they vary little in temperature. But winter (from May until October) is likely to be rainy, whereas summer is reasonably dry. Rainfall is heavier on the Atlantic slopes of the mountains than on the Pacific side. Coffee flourishes in the wetter areas. It should be pointed out that Panama has less high ground than its neighbors and that its principal cities are practically at sea level. Therefore its life is geared to the pace of the tropic lowlands.

TRANSPORTATION. Transportation has always presented serious difficulties in Central America. The terrain is broken, necessitating steep grades and sharp curves in the construction of railroads and highways. For the most part the railroad in each country runs from the capital city to the coast; therefore the quickest way to get from one capital to another, until recently, was to take the train to the principal seaport, go by boat to the seaport of the other country, and from there take the train to the capital. Recently, however, there have been great changes. The airplane, of course, has transformed travel for the well-to-do, and even for those in comparatively modest circumstances. Also the Pan American highway, when completed, promises to perform a similar miracle for more humble folk. Already it connects some of the principal cities.[2]

[2] For a discussion of the Pan American highway under wartime conditions, see "Middle

DISCRIMINATION AGAINST FOREIGN BUSINESS. In many parts of Central America, as in a substantial number of other Latin American countries, there is a marked tendency to discriminate against foreign business houses. Most of these enterprises are owned by Americans and there is strong resentment against "American imperialism"—meaning, in this case, the employment of Americans and the funneling off of locally earned profits to American investors. In Costa Rica only citizens may engage in business or hold shares of stock in business enterprises. This law has not been enforced against commercial houses already in existence, but it effectively prevents new undertakings by foreigners. In El Salvador ninety per cent of the employees of every business must be citizens. Guatemalan law says eighty-five per cent. Panama has approximately the same requirement, but its percentage is seventy-five and it counts as citizens, for this purpose, those aliens who have married Panamanian women or have lived in the country for many years. "Our country for ourselves" is a popular slogan in Latin America today. It is multiplying the difficulties that foreigners previously encountered in doing business.[3]

Guatemala

THE LAND AND THE PEOPLE. Every country of Central America has certain outstanding characteristics. Guatemala has more people than any of the others—a total of just under three million. It has, also, a larger percentage of Indians; most of the inhabitants are of unmixed Indian blood. In the smaller rural communities they still live in much the same manner as their primitive ancestors, dressing in picturesque traditional costumes and using native dialects instead of Spanish. In the fields the crops are still grown by crude methods and in the homes the garments of the family are woven on hand looms.[4] Roman Catholicism, which is at least the nominal religion of almost all the people, seems to have affected but slightly the Guatemalan Indians. In Chichicastenango, a small highland town that has become a tourist center, American visitors are fascinated by the spectacle of Guatemalan Indians worshiping their Mayan gods outside

American Lifeline," by Barbara Trigg Brown, in the August, 1943, issue of *Inter-American,* (Vol. II, No. 9), pp. 19–24. For more recent developments, see "Pan American Roller Coaster," by J. Lear in the January 25, 1947, issue of the *Saturday Evening Post,* pp. 12 *ff.,* and "Inter-American Highway," by A. Williams, in the September, 1947, issue of *United Nations World,* pp. 36–39.

[3] Reference should be made to Charles Morrow Wilson's excellent work, *Middle America,* which was published in 1944.

[4] See *Public Finance and Economic Development in Guatemala,* by J. H. Adler and others.

the Catholic Church and then making obeisance to the Christian Deity within the church's portals. The local priest has with difficulty persuaded them not to bring their Mayan idols into the church.[5]

Ninety per cent of the working population of Guatemala is engaged in agriculture. Coffee is the most important crop; it represents about two thirds of the country's exports. Bananas are grown also, but they are less

Guatemalan highlanders on their way to market. (Photograph by the author)

important than formerly. In recent years the government has encouraged the development of new crops, such as cinchona, from which quinine is derived, and also abaca, whose fibers can be woven into hemp. Cotton has recently become a major crop. Corn and wheat are grown for local consumption.

Mining is not very important. Industry follows the pattern of most agricultural countries, consisting chiefly of the elaboration of readily ac-

[5] See D. Reynolds' article, "Guatemalan Market Day," in the June, 1942, issue of the *Yale Review*, pp. 731–746.

cessible raw materials—the manufacture of textiles, the making of shoes, the production of foods and bottled beverages. No city of Central America is very large. Guatemala City has a population of two hundred and twenty-five thousand. It is a pleasant city, almost completely modern. Successive earthquakes have destroyed most of its colonial buildings.[6]

THE PATTERN OF POLITICS: *Conservatives* versus *Liberals*. Like so many nations of Latin America, Guatemala has had a troubled history. There have been many revolutions and many dictators. The Conservatives, traditionally sympathetic to the large landowners and the Catholic Church, have often been pitted against the anti-aristocratic, anti-clerical Liberals, but the struggle has reflected the personal ambition of rival *caudillos* much more often than it has dealt with the broad principles of economic and religious life. Even before the complete collapse of the Central American federation in 1840, Guatemala had withdrawn and established itself as an independent nation. The strong man of that period was an ignorant mestizo named Rafael Carrera, who soon made himself dictator with the support of the Conservatives. He was chosen president a number of times, and from 1854 to 1865 he served with the title of *president for life*. During these years there were frequent revolutions, however, as well as wars with other Central American nations.

Dictators and revolutions. In 1871 the Liberals came into power. President Justo Barrios energetically pressed their advantage by depriving many wealthy Conservatives of their properties and forcing others into exile. Religious orders were expelled from the country. President Barrios was killed in battle against El Salvador in 1885; after his death there were other revolutions and other wars. The assassination of the president in 1898 was significant chiefly because it brought into power a young mestizo, Manual Estrada Cabrera, who had been serving as vice-president. He ruled the nation as an almost absolute despot for the next twenty-two years, suppressing revolt with a firm hand. Like most other Guatemalan dictators, he paid scant attention to human rights. Yet every one of the many constitutions guaranteed individual liberty in very specific terms. In 1920 one of the chronic uprisings was successful, and Cabrera was driven into exile. He died four years later.

Rise of Ubico. The next strong man after Cabrera to seize and hold dictatorial power was General Jorge Ubico, who became president in 1930. He suppressed all opposition, using a secret police force to uncover possible plots against his regime. No one dared to utter a word of criticism, even

[6] See Chester Lloyd Jones' excellent work, *Guatemala, Past and Present*.

in the privacy of his own home, without first making certain that no servants were within earshot.[7] Yet Ubico brought to the country a certain
degree of prosperity. The world depression had struck at the very beginning of his regime, and he resolutely set about the task of reducing its
effects. He arranged for the free entry of Guatemalan coffee into the
United States, as part of a reciprocal trade agreement between the two
countries; and he increased exports of Guatemalan cotton to Italy. When
the Second World War engulfed the New World, President Ubico
promptly brought his country into the conflict on the side of the United
States. Coffee plantations owned by wealthy Germans were confiscated,
even though some of these foreigners had lived in the country for many
years and had married Guatemalan women.

Overthrow of Ubico. There can be no doubt that Ubico was responsible
for many material improvements. He built more roads than all his
predecessors combined, and he greatly expanded the school system. Most
Guatemalans readily admitted these benefits, but thought that they were
paying too high a price for them. In whispers they talked of revolution. When the dictator of neighboring El Salvador was forced out of
power by a general strike in May of 1944,[8] Guatemalans began to ask—
in somewhat more audible tones—why they couldn't do likewise. President Ubico learned of these dangerous conversations, and promptly declared a state of siege. Thereupon students from the national university
held street meetings in protest. The Dictator responded with machine
guns. The people were so outraged that they joined in a general strike.
Storekeepers kept their shops closed. Even judges refused to sit on the
bench. Priests shut the doors of the churches. The army tried to restore
normal conditions, but without success. It was clear to Ubico that he
had lost control of the country. Without delay, therefore, he submitted
his resignation.

Another revolt. With the withdrawal of Ubico, three army officers
then took control of the government, and one of them—General Federico
Ponce—became provisional president, promising free elections at an early
date. It soon became apparent, however, that the new regime was merely
a pale reflection of the old. Ponce still took orders from Ubico, who
remained quietly in the background. The press censorship was almost
as rigid as before. One editor who dared to publish stinging editorials

[7] See the article by L. and S. Martin, "Four Strong Men and a President: Little Napoleon,"
in the September, 1942, issue of *Harper's Magazine,* pp. 418–420.

[8] See pages 623–624.

against the government was murdered. Other outspoken critics disappeared. Finally, on October 19, 1944, the leaders of the democratically minded people decided that they had suffered enough. They staged a revolution which swept General Ponce from power and forced Ubico to seek the safety of the British legation.

Election of Arévalo. A triumvirate of revolutionaries, calling itself the Committee of Liberation, announced that the presidential election would be held on schedule and without government interference. First, however, there would be elections for a new Congress. Almost all the old congressmen were known to be Ubico's henchmen. Political activity soon reached fever pitch. There were a number of presidential candidates, but the leading contender seemed to be Juan José Arévalo, who had the support of the newly formed Revolutionary Action Party. There was no doubt that Arévalo, a forty-two-year-old teacher just returned to Guatemala after ten years in Argentina, had managed to capture the popular imagination. His opponents declared—apparently with good reason—that he had acquired Argentine citizenship during his long absence from Guatemala and therefore was ineligible for the presidency. Without answering this charge, however, Arévalo continued his vigorous campaign. He received ninety-two per cent of the total vote and took office on March 15, 1945. Meanwhile Congress had passed a law removing any doubts as to his citizenship. A new constitution was prepared and put into effect just forty-eight hours before the inaugural ceremony.[9]

The Arévalo regime. It developed soon after the election, however, that President Arévalo was not completely master in his own house. His finance minister, Jorge Toriello, who had been one of the leading spirits of the revolution, seemed to fancy himself as a dictator of the nation. He openly criticized the President in radio addresses and even countermanded some presidential orders. When Arévalo took to the radio to complain of his finance minister's conduct, Toriello did not resign. Apparently he counted on his friendship with high army officers to keep him in office. But the President gradually strengthened his own position with all elements, including the army, and eventually forced Toriello to submit his resignation. That was in March of 1946. After that date there was no doubt as to Arévalo's control of the government. He dealt competently with the economic problems arising from high prices and commodity shortages. But he imposed a press censorship almost as strict as in

---

[9] See "Schoolteacher President," by Carleton Beals, in the August, 1946, issue of *Asia,* pp. 363–367.

Ubico's day. Dissident elements throughout the country were effectively denied the opportunity to voice their opposition. The chief of the armed forces, a conservative who seemed lukewarm toward some of Arévalo's radical policies, was assassinated. Thereupon the friends of the dead man started a revolution, but they were defeated by loyal government forces.

President Arbenz and the Communists. As the time drew near for the 1950 election, more than one hundred persons announced that they were candidates for the office of president. But only one had any real chance of success—Colonel Jacobo Arbenz Guzmán, the thirty-seven-year-old radical whom Arévalo had personally chosen as his successor. The other candidates were never given an adequate opportunity to present themselves to the voters, so Arbenz achieved an easy victory. He was inaugurated on March 15, 1951. The new president has said repeatedly that he is not a Communist, but he has certainly encouraged the Communists to take over control of the government. The Communist Party, which calls itself the Labor Party, operates quite openly despite a constitutional prohibition against such activity. All anti-Communist movements have been officially labeled subversive, and have felt the heavy hand of the police. Congress has enacted a considerable number of Communist-sponsored statutes, including an "agrarian reform" law that nationalizes all uncultivated land, except for very small holdings. One of the principal victims of this legislation has been the United Fruit Company; it has lost more than two hundred thousand acres, despite appeals to the president and to the courts. The Guatemalan government offers payment for the confiscated land, but only on its assessed value, which is far below actual worth, and only in long-term government bonds, instead of cash. Today, therefore, the Communists are more firmly entrenched in Guatemala than in any other country of Latin America.[10]

BELICE. One issue that has united all the people of the country is the dispute with Great Britain over the territory known in Britain and the United States as British Honduras, but called Belice by the Guatemalans. This area, which adjoins Guatemala, was seized by the British at the end of the eighteenth century, and remained under their rule while the Spanish colonies of the New World were transforming themselves into independent nations. Guatemala laid claim to the territory, but the British indicated that they had no intention of relinquishing it. Finally, in 1859, Guatemala formally ceded the disputed area to Great Britain. There were

[10] See Charles C. Cumberland's article, "Guatemala: Labor and the Communists," in the March, 1953, issue of *Current History*, pp. 143–148.

a number of conditions attached, however, one of which was the construction of a road from the coast to Guatemala City. This road has never been built. Guatemala contends, therefore, that the British claim to Belice is void. Great Britain, on the other hand, justifies its position by pointing to its continuous occupation of the territory for more than a century and a half. There seems to be little reason to suppose that Guatemala can change the *status quo,* but at least the issue provides a perennial opportunity for Guatemalan statesmen to display their patriotism by disputing British claims.[11]

THE STRUCTURE OF GOVERNMENT: *The constitution.* Guatemala's present constitution is a long document, though not quite so voluminous as the constitutions of Mexico and Venezuela. Adopted in 1945, its bill of rights reflects the modern trend by including so-called social and cultural guarantees. The list of individual liberties follows the usual pattern, but always "with such exceptions as the law may make." The first step in the process of amending the constitution is a two-thirds vote of the total membership of Congress. A constituent assembly is then chosen by direct vote of the people to pass upon the congressional proposals. If, however, the amendment deals with the president's term of office, it may not be ratified by the constituent assembly until six years after Congress has acted—in other words, not until another president has been installed.

Suffrage and elections. The minimum voting age is eighteen years. Literacy is required of women, but not of men, apparently on the theory that an ignorant male knows as much as an educated female. The parties prepare their own ballots and the government supplies an official envelope. There is no opportunity for a voter to divide his vote among the candidates of several parties.

The president. The president is chosen by direct vote of the people for a term of six years, and may not be re-elected until twelve years have passed. There is a long list of persons ineligible for the presidency; it includes relatives of the outgoing president, cabinet ministers and other important public officers, and members of the clergy. The president must be a natural-born citizen, at least thirty-five years of age. He receives a salary of sixty thousand dollars a year, which is ample for a country with Guatemala's standards and living costs.

The president's power of appointment is extensive. He must secure

---

[11] See *Inglaterra y sus Pactos sobre Belice,* by José Luis Mendoza. See also the article by J. L. Kunz, "Guatemala *versus* Great Britain *in re* Belice," in the April, 1946, issue of the *American Journal of International Law,* pp. 383–390.

the consent of Congress, however, for nominations to the diplomatic service and high posts in the army. He plays no part in the selection of judges. Foreign affairs are directed by the president, but treaties require congressional approval, by a two-thirds vote. Congress declares war. As might well be supposed, the president has a major role in lawmaking. He may introduce bills, and his proposals always receive first consideration. His veto may be overridden by a two-thirds vote of Congress.

Guatemala has no vice-president. In case of the president's death or disability, the president of Congress (chosen by that body) assumes the rank and duties of chief executive. After him come the two vice-presidents of Congress, and then the president of the supreme court.

The cabinet. The cabinet has nine portfolios—foreign affairs, national defense, government, agriculture, public works and communications, finance, economy and labor, education, public health. An attempt has been made to establish parliamentary government in limited form. The constitution specifies that a congressional vote of *no confidence* shall ordinarily cause the resignation of a cabinet minister. If, however, the president believes that public opinion does not support the action of Congress, he may refuse to accept the minister's resignation. In that case, a two-thirds vote of the total membership of Congress is necessary to compel the minister's removal. It is highly doubtful that any member of the cabinet would ever be removed in such a manner. If, however, he should be forced from office, there would be nothing to prevent the president from appointing a new minister to continue the policy to which Congress had already objected.

Congress. The world's national legislative bodies are bicameral, with very few exceptions. Six of the exceptions are in Latin America, however, and five of them are in Central America. In Guatemala the Congress is unicameral. The sixty-three members of the one house are chosen by direct vote of the people for terms of four years and, as in Mexico, may not be re-elected immediately. One half of the membership is renewed every second year. Congressmen must be natural-born citizens, at least twenty-one years of age. There are two ordinary sessions of Congress each year. Each session is supposed to last two months, but may be extended for an additional month. Special sessions may be called by the president, or by the Permanent Committee of Congress upon the request of fifteen congressmen. The Permanent Committee is composed of nine members; it sits during the recess of Congress and gives provisional approval to certain presidential acts.

The courts. The supreme court has seven members, chosen by Congress for a term of four years. For certain matters they sit as a group, but ordinarily they divide into two chambers, which specialize in civil appeals and criminal appeals. Judges of the lower tribunals are named by the supreme court. Juries are used in criminal cases.

Internal organization. Guatemala is divided into twenty-two departments, each of which has a governor appointed by the president for an indefinite term. There is no departmental assembly. The municipalities have a measure of self-government. They have their own popularly elected mayors and councils.[12]

El Salvador

THE LAND AND THE PEOPLE. El Salvador has the smallest area of any of the Central American nations. In fact, it is not much bigger than Maryland. But it has more people—nearly two million—than any of its neighbors except Guatemala, and its population density of one hundred and forty-seven per square mile is almost the highest in Latin America.[13] There is also another distinguishing feature of El Salvador: it is the only country of Central America without both Atlantic and Pacific coastlines. It fronts only on the Pacific and this fact has undoubtedly handicapped its development.

There are comparatively few pure-blooded Indians and not very many whites. Almost all the people are mestizos; they speak Spanish and ignore the traditions of their Indian ancestors. El Salvador, therefore, does not have the problem, as in Guatemala and Mexico and Peru, of dealing with large numbers of persons who live within the country yet are almost completely untouched by the main current of its civilization. Coffee is El Salvador's principal export; corn is the main crop for local use. The capital city, San Salvador, has a population of about one hundred and twenty-five thousand.[14]

THE PATTERN OF POLITICS: *Unsettled conditions.* The history of El Salvador parallels that of Guatemala and most of the other nations of Central America. There have been innumerable revolutions and many wars with neighboring states. Dictatorship has been the rule. Even

[12] There is a recent but not very satisfactory work dealing with Guatemalan government— *Derecho Constitucional Guatemalteco*, by Buenaventura Echeverría.

[13] Only Haiti's population density is greater.

[14] See L. Marden's article, "Coffee Is King in El Salvador," in the November, 1944, issue of *National Geographic Magazine*, pp. 575–616.

today there seems to be no assurance of permanent peace or real democracy. El Salvador withdrew from the Central American federation in 1839 and became an independent nation. Before long, however, it fell under the influence of Guatemala, whose President-Dictator Rafael Carrera established one of his henchmen in the position of commander-in-chief of the Salvadorean army. This puppet, the Conservative Francisco Malespín, made and unmade presidents according to his fancy. But eventually he was driven from power by the Liberals, aided by troops from Honduras. Later the Liberals were defeated in battle by the Conservatives, with the help of Guatemala. Time after time other Central American nations interfered in the affairs of El Salvador, instead of permitting it to work out its own destiny. Several times El Salvador joined with some of its neighbors in an attempt to establish a federal union, but none of these schemes proved permanent.

The present century brought no substantial changes in the political habits of the little nation. There was a short war with Guatemala in 1906, and one with Nicaragua, which began in 1907 and continued for two years. In 1913 the president was assassinated.

Hernández Martínez. The year 1931 was eventful in El Salvador's history. A distinguished engineer named Arturo Araujo had been duly elected to the presidency and had completed almost one year of his term. But there was considerable dissatisfaction because of low prices and widespread unemployment, so the army decided to take a hand. It removed President Araujo and installed the vice-president as chief executive. His name was Maximiliano Hernández Martínez, and he proved to be one of the bloodiest tyrants in Latin American history. For thirteen years he ruled the nation. He was determined to win the support of his fellow countrymen, and for this purpose he found machine guns the most suitable instruments of persuasion. Several thousand persons were arrested and shot during the first year of his regime. The President's excuse for instituting this reign of terror was that he was stamping out communism. It soon became clear that anyone who criticized the government, or even dared to wander about the streets after dark, automatically made himself a Communist, and therefore liable to liquidation. The government controlled the press, and permitted nothing but praise of its policies. There were numerous uprisings, but they were suppressed promptly and vigorously. Those revolutionary leaders who did not manage to escape to the safety of neighboring countries were executed. Hernández Martínez had no patience with the idea that he would be safe from trouble if his political opponents were in exile. Execution seemed to be a much surer procedure.[15]

For two years the United States did not recognize the Hernández Martínez government, but finally it extended recognition—not as a gesture of approval, but as an acknowledgment of the obvious fact that it was the established government of the nation.

In 1934, as the end of the President's term drew near, he took steps to make certain of another term. First he resigned and permitted one of his henchmen to become provisional president. Then he was sworn in as minister of war, and with the aid of his troops supervised the election. No one was surprised to learn that he had been elected. In 1939 the Dictator did not even bother to hold an election. He simply ordered the constituent assembly, which was then preparing a new constitution, to extend his term until 1945. It did so without delay. In 1944 this procedure was repeated, with only slight variations. Another constituent assembly was writing another constitution. It adopted a clause authorizing Congress to choose the president of the nation. Then it transformed itself into the national Congress, elected Hernández Martínez for another term extending until 1949, and promptly returned to its original role of constituent assembly. It was a most amazing feat of legerdemain.

By 1944, however, there was serious opposition to the Dictator—not only among the people but also in the army. Revolt flared on April 2. The revolutionary leaders had managed to obtain tanks and planes, and they made a desperate effort to capture a number of strategic points. But the President was more than a match for them. He too had tanks and planes, and he used them effectively. The rebels were routed after a two-day battle and several of their leaders were captured and put to death. It seemed that Hernández Martínez was more firmly in the saddle than ever.

Yet only a few weeks later he was finally driven from power by the passive resistance of the outraged people. Students began the movement by printing and distributing leaflets calling for a general strike. Then they walked out of their classrooms. Workers laid down their tools. Businessmen closed the doors of their shops. Even government employees failed to report for work. Doctors stayed away from the hospitals. Trains and street cars stopped. Garbage was not collected. The economic pulse of the nation abruptly ceased to beat. Perhaps in all history no strike was

[15] See the article by L. and S. Martin, "Four Strong Men and a President: The Fox," in the September, 1942, issue of *Harper's Magazine*, pp. 420–422.

ever more truly general. The President, accustomed to using harsh measures against his opponents, found that he could not direct them against an entire nation. Completely bewildered, he asked the members of his cabinet what to do, and they advised him to resign. So he grudgingly submitted his resignation and left for Guatemala. At once the people returned to work.

Postwar instability. Unfortunately, however, the desire to get rid of Hernández Martínez seemed to be almost the only point of agreement among the political and military leaders of the country. The army installed General Andrés Menéndez as provisional president, over the objections of many civilians. Another revolt soon broke out, and though it was quickly suppressed, General Menéndez resigned "for reasons of health." Thereupon Colonel Osmín Aguirre Salinas became the nation's chief executive. To many civilians this was a bitter disappointment. They had formed a liberal political party, the Democratic Union, and had hoped to place their leader, a young professor named Arturo Romero, in the presidency. Aguirre Salinas soon made clear, however, that he would do nothing to help the Democratic Union. He did indeed agree to hold a free election at an early date, but in the meantime he used the police to break up the Union's meetings. Dr. Romero prudently remained in exile. The promised election was held in January, 1945. There was just one candidate—General Salvador Castañeda Castro, an aging conservative who was expected to take orders from Aguirre without asking for explanations. After his election, however, newly elected President Castañeda proved a deep disappointment to the Aguirre faction. He proceeded to govern the nation according to his own ideas and even found a considerable number of army officers who were willing to support him. Colonel Aguirre, bitterly resentful of such "ingratitude," staged a revolution in the summer of 1945, which the President promptly suppressed.

President Castañeda apparently made a serious effort to give the country good government. He introduced a number of major reforms, especially with regard to education and labor. He made a serious effort to work with the legislature. But he systematically disregarded constitutional liberties. Many of his opponents were arrested, though they were exiled and not shot. Many opposition newspapers were forced to close their doors. Finally President Castañeda announced that an election would be held for a new president in December, 1948. Fourteen political groups promptly sprang into being, each of them presenting its own nominee for the approval of the voters. As election day approached, however, it became increasingly clear that the President was reluctant to step aside, and therefore few people were surprised when the National Assembly announced indefinite postponement of the election, on the ground that the national interest required Castañeda to remain in office. Revolt flared immediately. Castañeda and his friends were swept from power, and a military junta seized control of the government, promising a new presidential election and a new constitution at the earliest opportunity.

The election was finally held on March 26, 1950. The winner was Major Oscar Osorio, who had headed the military junta for more than a year. A majority of the members of the new legislature were Osorio's supporters. In September of 1950 a new constitution was adopted. President Osorio seems to have tried to respect the forms of democratic government, yet he has declared a state of siege on several occasions. The government contends that it must restrict individual liberties because of the almost constant threat of revolutionary violence. Opposition parties reply that the government's talk of threatened uprisings is merely a cloak to justify its own policy of force and fraud. In any event, there is little reason to believe that El Salvador has entered an era of political stability.[16]

THE STRUCTURE OF GOVERNMENT: *The constitution.* The constitution of 1950, which now serves as El Salvador's fundamental law, is a fairly long document. It has about eighteen thousand words. The guarantees of individual liberty are very complete and stated in absolute terms. They may be swept away in times of emergency, however, by means of a declaration of the customary state of siege. Such a declaration may be issued by the National Assembly, or by the president when the Assembly is not in session. Amendment of the constitution requires a two-thirds vote in two successive Assemblies, plus the approval of a specially elected constituent congress.

Suffrage and elections. Both men and women may vote when they reach the age of eighteen, even if they cannot read and write. The government prepares the ballots from lists presented by the parties. Voters have no opportunity to divide their preferences among the candidates of different groups.

The president. The president of the nation is chosen by direct vote of the people for a term of six years. He is not eligible for immediate re-election. He must be a natural-born citizen, at least thirty years of age.

[16] An important work is Francisco Gavidia's *Historia Moderna de El Salvador.* It does not cover the developments of recent years, however. See the enthusiastic article by J. Quetglas, "El Salvador Discovers Democracy," in the September, 1951, issue of *United Nations World,* pp. 44–45.

His powers are not at all unusual. He makes all appointments in the administrative, diplomatic, and armed services of the nation, without the necessity of securing legislative consent. But the National Assembly names the judges of the higher courts. War is declared by the National Assembly and treaties must receive its approval. The president has the customary power to propose legislation. His veto of bills passed by the National Assembly may be overridden by a two-thirds vote.

Presidential succession. There is a vice-president, with the usual powers —or lack of them. Each year the National Assembly designates three persons, who succeed to the presidency in the event of the death or disability of the president and vice-president.

THE CABINET. The cabinet consists of but five members. Two of the portfolios, however, represent a large number of activities. Thus there is a minister of treasury, public credit, industry, and commerce, and also a minister of government, development, agriculture, labor, and social welfare. The three remaining ministers have but a single service apiece— foreign relations, national defense, public education. No attempt has been made to establish a system of parliamentary responsibility.

The National Assembly. The legislative branch—the National Assembly—is unicameral. Its members are chosen by direct vote of the people and serve for two years. Each of the nation's fourteen departments has three representatives in the Assembly, thus making the total membership forty-two. As usual, there is a system of alternates, elected at the same time and in the same manner. Members of the Assembly are known as deputies. Every deputy must be a citizen by birth or naturalization, and must have attained the age of twenty-five years. The Assembly meets in regular session twice a year, and each session continues for as many months as may be necessary. This means that the legislative branch sits almost continuously. Under such circumstances, special sessions are almost never required. They may be called by the president, however, if he so desires.

The courts. The National Assembly chooses the nine members of the supreme court, who serve for but three years, though they are eligible for additional terms. The court is divided into civil and criminal chambers, but all its members sit as a group for certain types of cases. Below the high tribunal are six appellate courts—one for civil affairs and one for criminal matters in the capital, and four in other parts of the country, hearing all classes of cases. The justices of these appellate courts are named by the National Assembly; they too serve for three years. Then there are the judges of first instance and the justices of the peace; these minor members of the judiciary are appointed by the supreme court. Juries are used in criminal cases.

Internal organization. The fourteen departments of El Salvador are merely administrative and political areas; no attempt has been made to give them even a small measure of self-government. Each department is controlled by a governor, who is appointed by the president on a political basis. There is no departmental assembly. Each municipality, however, has its popularly elected mayor and council.

Nicaragua

THE LAND AND THE PEOPLE. Nicaragua is the largest country of Central America, though its area is no greater than that of North Carolina. In population it stands fourth, with approximately one million, one hundred thousand inhabitants. It is a land of great scenic beauty. Within its borders are seventeen volcanoes—many of them active—and numerous large lakes. For years it has been considered as a possible route for an Atlantic-Pacific waterway rivaling the Panama Canal.

As in El Salvador, the people are mostly of mixed white and Indian blood. There are, however, some white families, descended mostly from the Spaniards of colonial times, and a substantial sprinkling of Indians, as well as a considerable number of Negroes along the coast. Coffee is the principal export crop. The capital city, Managua, has about one hundred and forty thousand inhabitants.[17]

THE PATTERN OF POLITICS: *Walker expeditions.* The story of Nicaragua is much the same as that of its neighbors. There has been the usual procession of dictators and the usual amount of civil and foreign strife. In 1854 the Liberals invited a number of adventurers from the United States to help them overthrow the Conservatives. This group of filibusters was so successful that its leader, a young newspaperman named William Walker, eventually managed to have himself elected president of Nicaragua. He had the support of important American business interests, which desired to monopolize the transportation of travelers and supplies across the Nicaraguan isthmus. Other American interests already possessed this monopoly, however, and they threw their influence against Walker. The situation was further complicated by the intervention of Costa Rican troops. Eventually Walker's forces were defeated and he was compelled

---

[17] See J. Zacala's article, "Vulcan's Land," in the March, 1952, issue of *Americas*, pp. 20–23.

to leave the country. But he was back in a short time with a new force, only to suffer defeat once more. In 1860 he attempted an invasion of Honduras. This time he was captured and shot.[18]

American intervention. During the years there were several bitter wars among the Central American states. Nicaragua was usually involved. The United States assumed the role of mediator, though with only partial success. Finally, in 1909, it broke off relations with President Zelaya and virtually assured the success of an uprising against his regime by forbidding government forces to bombard the Nicaraguan port of Bluefields, which had been made the headquarters of the revolutionists. The United States Department of State justified this attitude by pointing out that Americans, as well as other foreigners, would be among the chief victims of a bombardment. A little later, when a president favored by the United States had been safely installed, arrangements were made for a loan by American banks to the Nicaraguan government. An American was put in charge of the customs, in order to make certain that this loan would be repaid. But conditions were still unsettled and the United States government finally landed marines, who aided the government forces in suppressing a fresh rebellion. That was in 1912. From that date, for more than two decades, Nicaragua was virtually a protectorate of the United States. No man could be elected president of the little nation without American support. American marines supervised the elections. The forces of the United States were withdrawn in 1925, except for a small legation guard, but in less than a year they returned to deal with a fresh revolution. They did not finally leave the country until 1933.

American influence. During the years of American supervision the established governments were friendly to the United States, as indeed they were required to be in order to stay in power. Throughout the country, however, there was a great deal of opposition to the dominant position of the United States. The acknowledged leader of this opposition was César Agusto Sandino, whose guerrilla forces plundered towns and villages and killed many persons, including a number of Americans. The government of Nicaragua, as well as the government of the United States, called Sandino a bandit, but to thousands of his fellow countrymen he was a hero. When the American marines ultimately left Nicaragua in 1933, the Sandino forces soon reached an agreement with the government and laid down their arms. Sandino himself announced that he

[18] See W. O. Scrogg's interesting work, *Filibusters and Financiers.*

would become a farmer. Only a short time later, however, he was killed by members of the Nicaraguan Guard.

The American occupation accomplished the same results as in Haiti and the Dominican Republic—better schools and roads, improved health conditions, and deep popular resentment at foreign interference.[19] There can be little doubt that American interest in the tiny republic was greatly stimulated by the possibility of building a canal across the Nicaraguan isthmus. At one time the Nicaraguan route was considered as an alternative to that of Panama; more recently, since the Panama Canal's construction, the need for a second canal by way of Nicaragua has been discussed. Since 1916 the United States has had a treaty with Nicaragua guaranteeing exclusive American rights to such territory as may be necessary for the construction and operation of a canal.

The Somoza regime. In 1937 General Anastacio Somoza, who already controlled the army, became president of Nicaragua. He has ruled the country ever since, either as president or president-maker. In 1939 a new constitution was adopted, extending his term for eight years. Somoza tried to win popular favor by adopting a number of social reforms and working desperately to keep living costs within reasonable limits. But he incurred the wrath of thousands of influential persons by his dictatorial methods and utter disregard of the liberties guaranteed by the constitution.[20] By the summer of 1946, therefore, with a presidential election only a few months away, he decided not to be a candidate for re-election. Instead he proposed as his successor a seventy-one-year-old relative by marriage, Dr. Leonardo Argüello. The Nationalist Liberal Party, composed of Somoza's henchmen, was already trying to decide between two other aspirants, but it promptly obeyed orders and nominated Argüello. The Conservatives also agreed to give him their support. Only the Independent Liberals refused to accept Somoza's candidate—and, since they controlled neither the election machinery nor the army, it was unreasonable to suppose that they could make a good showing. As a matter of fact, they did not. A final tabulation of the votes gave Argüello a majority of two to one. The government also secured an overwhelming

[19] See Harold N. Denny's *Dollars for Bullets, The Story of American Rule in Nicaragua.* See also Henry L. Stimson's *American Policy in Nicaragua.*

[20] See the article by L. and S. Martin, "Four Strong Men and a President: Big Shot," in the September, 1942, issue of *Harper's Magazine,* pp. 423–425. See also "All Nicaragua Is His Hacienda," by O. Gondi, in the March, 1948, issue of *United Nations World,* pp. 30–33.

majority of the seats in Congress. The opposition charged fraud, but could do nothing except complain.

Somoza still dictator. President Argüello took office on May 1, 1947. During his campaign he had frequently made the statement that he would take orders from no one. This was thought to be mere campaign oratory, but apparently the new President meant what he said. From the very outset he ignored Somoza's suggestions and governed the country according to his own ideas. Then, enraged by the long-time Dictator's constant interference, he ordered him to leave Nicaragua within twenty-four hours. Somoza responded with characteristic decisiveness. He got the members of Congress together at three o'clock in the morning and had them declare Argüello "incapacitated" by virtue of his inability to maintain public order. Then he went to the presidential palace, awoke the sleeping President, and told him that he—not Somoza—was going to leave the country, without even twenty-four hours' notice. Argüello fled to the safety of the Mexican embassy. Seven months later he died in Mexico, of natural causes. Meanwhile Somoza's uncle, Víctor Román y Reyes, was named president by a pliant constituent assembly which was busily preparing a new fundamental law for the nation. Somoza became minister of war, navy, and aviation, and commander of the Nicaraguan Guard. Before long, however, the new President had to go to the United States for medical treatment, and in May of 1950 he died of cancer. So Congress named Somoza to fill the unexpired term. Two weeks later a presidential election was held. Somoza was a candidate, and of course he won. It seems that nothing short of revolution can break his hold on the nation. Even the principal opposition party now co-operates smoothly to maintain his dictatorship.

THE STRUCTURE OF GOVERNMENT: *The constitution.* The present constitution of Nicaragua, adopted in 1951, gives very little indication of the dictatorial nature of the government. In fact, it pays lip worship to the accepted forms of democracy. There is a long list of guarantees of individual freedom, though these liberties may be enjoyed only "in conformity with the laws." A group of so-called social guarantees has been included, after the fashion set by Mexico. These regulate hours of work, wages, and other matters of interest to labor. They also impose numerous restrictions on the right to own property. In times of emergency the president may declare a state of siege, and thus sweep away constitutional guarantees, if Congress is not in session. Amendments to the constitution may be proposed by the president or any ten members of Congress. If passed by absolute majorities in both houses of Congress, they go to the president for his signature. The president may veto proposed constitutional amendments, however, just as he would veto ordinary legislation, but final action is not taken until the next session of Congress. At that time Congress may override the presidential veto by absolute majorities in both houses. A completely new constitution may not be adopted before 1961.

Suffrage and elections. Both men and women are permitted to vote. The minimum voting age for literates is eighteen years; for illiterates it is twenty-one. Each party prepares its own list of candidates. No opportunity is provided for voters to divide their preferences among the candidates of different parties. Members of the Chamber of Deputies are chosen by a system of proportional representation.

The president. The constitution declares that the president shall be chosen by direct vote of the people, that he shall serve for six years, and that he shall not be immediately eligible for another term. He must be a native of Nicaragua, and the son of a Nicaraguan father or mother. In addition he must be at least twenty-five years of age, a resident of the country for not less than five years prior to his election, and not a member of the priesthood.

The president appoints all the administrative officers of the government and all members of the diplomatic corps. Theoretically, at least, he plays no part in the selection of judges. He directs the relations of Nicaragua with other nations. Treaties must be approved by Congress. If they deal with the Central American Union, or with the nation's boundaries or the construction of a canal, they must receive a two-thirds vote. Congress declares war or authorizes the president to do so. The provisions of the constitution concerning the president's power to propose legislation, and to veto the acts of Congress, follow the usual pattern.

Presidential succession; the cabinet. There is no vice-president. As in El Salvador,[21] Congress annually prepares a list of three alternates, who succeed to the presidency in case of the chief executive's death or disability. The cabinet has ten members—the ministers of interior, foreign affairs, war, public education, agriculture, health, finance and public credits, public works, economy, national district. The minister of the national district regulates the affairs of Managua, the capital city. The president's secretary sits regularly with the cabinet. Members of the cabinet are not responsible to Congress and cannot be removed by a legislative vote of censure.

[21] See page 626.

Congress. Unlike the other nations of Central America, Nicaragua has a bicameral Congress. The Senate has sixteen popularly elected senators—one from each of the nation's sixteen departments—plus three former presidents of the nation.[22] The elective senators have six-year terms; the former presidents serve for life. In addition, the membership of the Senate includes the defeated presidential candidate—that is, the person who stood second in the balloting. He has a six-year term. There are forty-two members of the Chamber of Deputies, who also have terms of six years. The minimum age for deputies is twenty-five years; for senators it is thirty-five years, as contrasted with the twenty-five year minimum of the president. Congress meets in regular annual session on the fifteenth day of April and normally completes its business within sixty days, though it may extend the session an additional thirty days. Special sessions may be called by the president and must be devoted to such matters as he may indicate.

The courts. The two houses of Congress, in joint session, select the five justices of the supreme court, and also the judges of the five courts of appeal. Lower court judges and justices of the peace are named by the supreme court. Judicial terms are relatively short—six years for members of the supreme court, four years for appellate judges, two years for judges of the courts of first instance, and one year for justices of the peace. Since the president and members of Congress serve for six years, every new administration has an opportunity to remake the personnel of the judiciary.

Internal organization. There is no attempt to give the smaller units of government even a slight degree of autonomy. Each of the sixteen departments has a governor appointed by the president. Each municipality has a mayor, who is chosen in a similar manner. There are no departmental assemblies and no municipal councils; therefore the people of the departments and municipalities have no voice in the management of their own affairs. The capital city, as we have already noted, has been set apart as a national district, under the control of the president through a member of his cabinet.

Honduras

THE LAND AND THE PEOPLE. Honduras has fewer outstanding characteristics than most of the other nations of Central America. It is not the largest or most densely populated or best governed or most beautiful or

[22] Only former presidents who were popularly elected are entitled to seats in the Senate.

most prosperous. It is, however, the largest banana producer among the so-called "banana republics." Disease has played havoc with the banana crop, as in neighboring countries, but spraying and dusting have now brought the pest at least partially under control. The great plantations are owned chiefly by American companies. In Honduras, and also in neighboring countries, the United Fruit Company has great holdings; it grows the bananas and ships them to the United States on its own boats. For many years the United Fruit Company has been the target for a great deal of criticism by Central American political leaders, who sometimes claim that its sole interest is in quick profits, regardless of the welfare of the workers or the ultimate condition of the land. But the company has tried hard to live down this reputation. Among other activities, it has established in Honduras a school of tropical agriculture where outstanding Central American youths are trained in modern farming methods. There are, of course, other Honduran exports in addition to bananas. Among them are coffee, tobacco, citrus fruits, and mahogany. The capital city—Tegucigalpa—which has a population of only one hundred thousand, is no larger than Waterbury, Connecticut, or Peoria, Illinois.

THE PATTERN OF POLITICS. Like the other countries of Central America, Honduras has suffered from the rivalries of ambitious political leaders. Blood is spilled across every page of its history. From the very first days of independence there have been sanguinary conflicts, often involving a large part of the population. At first there was intense rivalry between the two principal towns. The people of Comayagua, which had been the seat of the Spanish government, supported the aristocratic, clerical Conservative Party, while the inhabitants of Tegucigalpa, the present capital, aided the Liberal cause.

From 1823 to 1838 Honduras was a part of the Central American federation, but even during those years its internal quarrels did not cease. The Liberals finally managed to suppress their enemies and take control of the government. In 1840, however, President Carrera of Guatemala supported a Honduran revolution which placed the Conservatives in power. General Francisco Ferrer was a leader in that uprising; he managed to dominate the country, either as president or commander of the army, for thirteen years. Since that time there have been other dictators, other revolutions, other wars with neighboring countries. Presidents have been assassinated, or have been driven from office by rival *caudillos*—not infrequently with the aid of Guatemalan or Nicaraguan troops. Liberals and Conservatives have alternated in power. Only a few presidents have been able to complete their prescribed terms. New constitutions have been adopted from time to time, without substantially improving the lot of the unhappy country.[23]

Dictatorship. In 1932 a strong man appeared on the Honduran scene. He was General Tiburcio Carías Andino, an ignorant mestizo who succeeded in winning the election from the dominant Liberals by a judicious combination of bribery and force. Thereupon he suppressed all opposition with an iron hand. He responded to numerous uprisings with declarations of martial law and soon compelled the surrender of the various rebel factions. In 1936 a new constitution was adopted; the constituent assembly obediently voted to extend the president's term to 1943. A subsequent amendment extended it still further—to January 1, 1949. Thus Carías Andino was assured of sixteen years in office without the inconvenience of seeking re-election—assuming, of course, that revolutionists could be kept in check. The constituent assembly, almost all of whose members were congressmen, also voted to keep the existing membership of Congress unchanged. For President Carías Andino this arrangement was most fortunate, since every legislator was a member of his National Party (the oldtime conservatives).

The government made some concessions to public opinion by establishing agricultural colonies for the landless and developing a new program of public education. But it refused to tolerate even the mildest criticism. Newspaper editors were jailed for failure to show sufficient enthusiasm in their discussion of the government's policies. Prominent opposition leaders were exiled or shot. Rebellion continued to break out sporadically, though without success. In 1946 hundreds of Honduran exiles swept across the border from El Salvador, capturing a number of towns and attracting many recruits. But government planes machine-gunned their headquarters and government troops drove them into the hills. It was one of many such ill-fated attempts.[24]

Election of 1948. In the spring of 1948, as Carías Andino's protracted term drew to a close, he indicated that he would not be a candidate for re-election. Thereupon the National Party, acting on his orders, nominated a prominent attorney named Juan Manuel Gálvez, whose long

[23] For a detailed history of Honduras during these years, see Rómulo Enrique Durón y Gamero's *Bosquejo Histórico de Honduras, 1501 a 1921.*

[24] See the article by L. and S. Martin, "Four Strong Men and a President: Butch," in the September, 1942, issue of *Harper's Magazine,* pp. 422–423. See also the letter written by Julian R. Cácares, Honduran Ambassador to the United States, and published in the February, 1945, issue of *Inter-American,* pp. 47–48. In this letter Ambassador Cácares takes the editors of *Inter-American* to task for calling Dictator Carías Andino a dictator.

career of public service included the offices of judge, deputy, ambassador, cabinet minister, and secretary to the President. The opposition Liberal Party, relying on Carías Andino's promise of an honest election, hastily drew together its scattered forces and announced that its presidential candidate would be Angel Zuñiga Huete, a distinguished lawyer and writer who had been defeated by Carías Andino at the last election, in 1932. Before long, however, it became clear that Carías Andino had no serious intention of permitting an opposition victory. Political rallies of the Liberals were broken up by the police, and newspaper editors who supported the Liberal cause were thrown into jail. So Zuñiga Huete withdrew his candidacy, and the Liberals announced that they would boycott the election. Thereupon all the candidates of the government-sponsored National Party were elected without opposition. A revolution staged by Liberal partisans was quickly suppressed, and President-elect Gálvez took office on the first day of 1949.

President Gálvez. The last few years have witnessed a number of important changes in the policies of the government. President Gálvez has made a determined effort to govern within the framework of the constitution. He has worked with Congress more closely than any other Honduran president in many years. He has shown unusual respect for the constitutional guarantees of individual liberty. He has even encouraged the organization of Honduran labor. And he has devoted a large part of his time to the problem of improving the school and highway systems. Many disgruntled politicians have appealed to Carías Andino to reverse some of the decisions of the President, but the old man has refused to interfere. If he persists in that attitude—and, possibly, even if he does not—Juan Gálvez is the master of the nation.

THE STRUCTURE OF GOVERNMENT: *The constitution.* The present constitution of Honduras, adopted in 1936, presents no unusual features. It is a document of moderate length. About one fifth of its space is devoted to various guarantees of liberty and equality, but there is virtually no mention of the recent "social guarantees" dealing with labor and welfare. Almost all the individual rights established by the constitution are said to be subject to the restrictions of the law. The president may declare a state of siege when Congress is not in session. Constitutional amendments require a two-thirds vote in two successive annual sessions of Congress.

Suffrage and elections. Women have never been given the right to vote. The minimum voting age for men is twenty-one years, unless they can read and write, in which case it is eighteen. Each party prepares its own ballot. The government, which has never been greatly concerned with legal provisions concerning secret voting, does not bother to provide an official envelope.

The president. The constitution declares, with unconscious humor, that the president of the nation shall be chosen by direct vote of the people, that his term shall be six years, and that he shall not be eligible for immediate re-election. It states further that he must be a natural-born citizen, at least thirty years of age.

The powers of the president follow more or less closely the customary pattern. He appoints all administrative and diplomatic officials, and most of the officers of the armed forces. Congress declares war and passes upon the treaties presented for its approval. The president has the right to introduce legislation, and also to veto the acts of Congress. The customary two-thirds vote is necessary to override his veto, and in addition the supreme court must pass upon any legislative proposal vetoed on constitutional grounds.

Presidential succession; the cabinet. There is a vice-president. After him, the line of presidential succession extends to the president of Congress, and then to the president of the supreme court. There are six cabinet ministers. The constitution of 1924 provided for parliamentary responsibility, and several ministers were actually forced to resign by adverse votes in Congress.[25] Under the present constitution, however, neither theory nor practice permits parliamentary control of members of the president's cabinet.

Congress. The unicameral Congress has forty-five members. They are chosen by direct vote of the people—or so the constitution declares—and their term of office is six years. Every member must be a natural-born or naturalized citizen, at least twenty-five years of age. Congress meets once a year for a sixty-day session, which may be extended for forty more days if necessary. Special sessions may be called by the president, or by the presiding officer of Congress upon the request of two thirds of its members.

The courts. Congress chooses the five judges of the supreme court, who serve for six years and sit as a group to hear all cases. The supreme court names the justices of the four courts of appeal, and also the magistrates of the twenty-six courts of first instance. These judges have no fixed terms; they are supposed to serve during good behavior, but may

---

[25] Wm. S. Stokes, "Parliamentary Government in Latin America," in the June, 1945, issue of the *American Political Science Review* (Vol. XXXIX, No. 3), pp. 528–529.

be removed at any time for political or other reasons. The judges of the courts of first instance appoint the justices of the peace within their respective jurisdictions.

Internal organization. The country has been divided into seventeen departments, and each department has a governor appointed by the president. There is no departmental assembly. In the municipalities, however, the people are permitted to elect the members of the legislative councils. The mayors are popularly chosen in the small towns, but appointed by the government in the larger cities.

Costa Rica

THE LAND AND THE PEOPLE. Costa Rica has a number of distinctive features. It is the only predominantly white country of Central America, the only one with a long record of practicing democracy, and by far the most literate nation of the group. At least three fourths of the people are white; most of them are descended from Spaniards who came from Galicia many years ago. Most of them can at least read and write. The official figures declare that eighty-eight per cent of the adult population is literate; this estimate is probably too high, but certainly comes within striking distance of the truth. For years Costa Rica liked to boast that it had more school teachers than soldiers—a most unusual situation in Latin America. Today there is no Costa Rican army; it has been officially disbanded.

Although Costa Rica is very small (no larger than West Virginia), it has important natural resources and some of the most spectacular scenery in the New World. There is an abundance of hydroelectric power. Coffee is the leading crop, but bananas and cacao are grown in large quantities. The chief mineral export is gold. Industry follows the usual pattern of the region. San José, the capital, is a charming city with a population of about ninety thousand.[26]

THE PATTERN OF POLITICS: *Civil wars.* Costa Rica has had its share of dictators and revolutions. Throughout the nineteenth century there were frequent uprisings. As recently as 1948 the little nation experienced the bloodiest civil war in its history. Yet it has gradually learned to understand and accept the democratic way of life. With only a few exceptions, recent elections have been honest and comparatively peaceful.

[26] See *Costa Rican Life*, by John and Mavis Biesanz. See also *Costa Rica: A Study in Economic Development*, by Stacy May and others.

THE MODERN ERA. The modern era began in 1902, with the election to the presidency of Ascensión Esquivel, who introduced new standards of honesty and efficiency in government. His immediate successors were men of similar caliber. In 1914, however, the election was clouded by charges of fraud. The successful candidate, Alfredo González Flores, introduced a number of economic reforms that caused widespread dissatisfaction, and in 1917 he was overthrown by force of arms. It was Costa Rica's first major revolution in many years, but less than three years later revolt again spread throughout the country.

SOCIAL REFORM. In 1940 Dr. Rafael Calderón Guardia was elected president. He was the candidate of the National Republican Party, a liberal group that had dominated Costa Rican politics for some time and had been responsible for some progressive legislation. President Calderón Guardia was not satisfied, however, with the social progress that had been made. He called for sweeping reforms, including paid vacations, unemployment insurance, and free clinics. The money for these costly innovations was to come in part from an income tax. Labor was to be assured the right to strike and to bargain collectively. These proposals met determined opposition from the Conservatives, most of whom belonged to the Democrat Party, but the President had his way. The Communists were understandably jubilant; their leader rode with President Calderón in a parade and hailed him as a great statesman. Even the Archbishop gave his blessing, for the President was known to be a devout Catholic.

Election of 1944. When the time drew near for the 1944 election, the National Republicans nominated Teodoro Picado Michalski, an able lawyer who had been serving as president of the Legislative Assembly. Picado promised to continue and extend the government's reforms, whereupon he received the endorsement of the Communists, who had meanwhile sought to gain greater popular support by changing the name of their party to Popular Vanguard. Against this coalition the Democrats endorsed former President León Cortés, who had been a National Republican before the party swung so far to the left. The final count indicated that Picado had won the election. Cortés charged fraud, though he made no effort to foment a revolution. The Communists did not formally enter the cabinet, but many of their leaders were given good jobs in the public service and they were encouraged to take control of the rapidly growing labor unions. Thus the government paid its political debt.

Liberals versus *moderates.* In the summer of 1947, as the time drew near for another presidential election, the country's moderates made a determined effort to win popular support. Their candidate was Otilio Ulate, the publisher of the nation's most widely read newspaper, whose liberal views were so well known that the government could not convincingly portray him as "a tool of reaction," though it made every effort to do so. To offset Ulate's popular appeal the National Republicans nominated former President Calderón Guardia, who had started the sharp leftward trend. The Communists, of course, agreed to support him. Meanwhile Congress changed the election law to provide separate ballots for presidential and other candidates, so that the Communists could vote for Calderón while supporting their own nominees for minor offices.

Politics and civil war. The 1947 campaign was exciting. The government seems to have made little effort to maintain even a semblance of impartiality. The police interfered so frequently with Democrat rallies that Ulate raised strenuous objections. Finally he called a protest strike, which brought virtually all business to a standstill. The government declared its intention to break the strike by force, if necessary, but finally compromised the issue by agreeing to place the police under the control of a commander selected by the election board. The election, which was held on February 8, 1948, was tense but quiet. It resulted in a substantial victory for Ulate and the Democrats. Calderón Guardia conceded defeat, but charged "shameless fraud," despite the fact that his friends had been in control of the election machinery. On March 1 the "lame duck" legislature, composed chiefly of Calderón sympathizers, declared the election void. The police then arrested Ulate and a number of the other leaders of the Democrat Party, but released most of them after a night in jail.

Then the storm broke. From the mountains came word that rebels led by Colonel José Figueres were gathering in force and would soon be ready to move against the troops of the government. Over a portable broadcasting set the Colonel sent an urgent plea for recruits. They came by the thousands, bringing their own weapons. Meanwhile neighboring countries interfered, as they had often done in earlier days. Nicaraguan troops were sent to support the faltering Picado government. Honduran pilots and mechanics helped to keep government planes flying. Guatemala, on the other hand, dispatched planes, guns and ammunition to the revolutionary forces.

Victory of the moderates. Within seven weeks the civil war ended, after great loss of life and substantial damage to property. Picado and Calderón were forced into exile, together with the Communist leaders. Thereupon the victorious revolutionists installed a provisional president to serve until May 8, when Otilio Ulate was to begin his regular term of office. But Ulate announced that he preferred to defer his assumption of power until such time as a regular legislature could be elected and a new constitution adopted. The election for members of the Legislative Assembly was held in October, 1949, and Ulate's Democrat Party won a sweeping victory. A few weeks later a new constitution was adopted, and the following day—November 8, 1949—Ulate became president of the nation. He governed in the best democratic tradition, but not without considerable criticism from the extreme left and also the extreme right.

Presidential campaign of 1953. As the time drew near for the next presidential election, the principal candidate was forty-six-year-old José Figueres, the revolutionary hero who had driven the radicals from power in 1948 and served as temporary head of the nation until President Ulate began his regular term of office. Supporting Figueres was a new political group that called itself the National Liberation Party. Its platform called for sweeping reforms that would bring a large measure of socialism to Costa Rica. Opposing Figueres was a sixty-eight-year-old millionaire agriculturist named Fernando Castro, who pledged himself to the preservation of the country's "traditional" way of life. President Ulate promised that the government would be completely neutral, and he kept his word. The election was held on July 26, 1953. It resulted in a sweeping victory for Figueres and the National Liberation Party. There seemed little doubt that Costa Rica's new government would move sharply to the left, though not toward communism.

THE STRUCTURE OF GOVERNMENT: *The constitution.* The present constitution of Costa Rica, adopted in 1949, is one of the shortest in Latin America, though its thirteen thousand words make it twice as long as the Constitution of the United States. The bill of rights includes not only the traditional guarantees of individual liberty, but also the newer social guarantees dealing with labor and property. There is the usual provision for suspension of constitutional rights in time of emergency. The president is authorized to declare a state of seige if the Legislative Assembly should be in recess, but under such circumstances the Assembly is directed to meet within forty-eight hours and determine whether to uphold the chief executive's action. Constitutional amendments may be adopted by the Legislative Assembly, but only by a two-thirds vote in two successive annual sessions.

Suffrage and elections. Both men and women are permitted to vote in Costa Rica when they become twenty years of age. Literacy is not necessary. Each party prepares its own ballot, and the government provides an official envelope. The election law assures to each party a number of seats in the Legislative Assembly proportional to its voting strength.[27]

The president. The president is elected by direct vote of the people for a term of four years, and is not eligible for immediate re-election. He must be a natural-born citizen, at least thirty years of age, and not a member of the priesthood.

The president's powers require no special comment. He appoints and removes administrative officials and minor officers of the army, without the necessity of securing legislative consent. For the appointment of high army officers and all members of the diplomatic corps, however, the approval of the Legislative Assembly is required. The president has the customary right to initiate legislation, and to veto bills submitted by the legislature; but, as usual, his veto may be overridden by a two-thirds vote.

Presidential succession; the cabinet. Costa Rica has two vice-presidents, chosen in the same manner as the president. Below the vice-presidents the presidential succession extends to the president of the Legislative Assembly. The president's cabinet consists of eight members, who hold the following portfolios: foreign affairs; agriculture and industry; economy, finance and commerce; education; interior, police, and justice; labor and social welfare; public health; public works. No attempt has been made to establish a system of parliamentary responsibility.

The Legislative Assembly. The Legislative Assembly is a unicameral body. Its forty-five members, together with fifteen alternates, are chosen by direct popular vote for terms of four years, with partial renewal every two years. Every deputy must be a literate citizen, at least twenty-one years of age. The regular annual session of the Legislative Assembly is divided into two parts, and each part continues for three months. Special sessions may be called by the president.[28]

The courts. The supreme court has seventeen members, divided into four chambers for different classes of business. These justices, who serve for eight years, are chosen by the Legislative Assembly. They in turn name the judges of the four appellate tribunals and the courts of first instance. Justices of the peace, however, are appointed by the minister

[27] See Wm. Redin Woodward's note in the September, 1946, issue of the *National Municipal Review* (Vol. XXXV, No. 8), p. 432.

[28] There are several works dealing with Costa Rican constitutional law. One of the best is *Principios de Ciencia Constitucional*, by Elias Leiva Quiros. More recent is *Secciones de Ciencia Constitucional y Constitución de la República de Costa Rica*, by Marco Tulio Zeledón.

of government, acting for the president of the nation. All members of the judiciary below supreme court judges have four-year terms. They are, of course, eligible for additional periods. Juries are not used in Costa Rica.[29]

Internal organization. The nation has been divided into seven provinces. Each province has a governor, who is appointed by the president and made directly responsible to the minister of government. There is no provincial assembly. In the municipalities, however, the people choose their own mayors and the members of their local councils.[30]

Panama

THE LAND AND THE PEOPLE. In many ways Panama is different from its neighbors. Its independence was attained much more recently. Its small population—about eight hundred thousand—is less than that of St. Louis, Missouri. People from every quarter of the earth have settled here. There are Frenchmen, Italians, Greeks, East Indians, Poles, Turks, Spaniards—to mention only a few. About sixty per cent of the inhabitants are mestizos. There are, however, a good many Negroes.

The life of the country revolves about the canal. It is the most important fact in Panama's existence. The canal cuts the nation approximately in half. It provides a means of livelihood for at least half of the population, either as workers in the Canal Zone or domestic servants in the homes of Americans or merchants dependent on the tourist trade or the requirements of passing ships. The very existence of the canal compels close cooperation between the governments of Panama and the United States. The United States requires fortifications on Panamanian soil, and Panama depends in no small part on canal revenues to balance its budget. Bananas are the nation's chief export. Some abacá is grown, however, and also cacao. There is a small livestock industry. Panama City, the capital, has a population of about one hundred and twenty-five thousand.

THE PATTERN OF POLITICS: *Influence of the United States.* Panama's history as an independent nation has been short but troubled. The existence of the canal has necessitated close relations with the United States, though the little country has sometimes complained of unfair treatment. In 1903, when freedom from Colombia had just been won, Panama

---

[29] See *Ley Orgánica del Poder Judicial,* by Antonio Picado G.
[30] See *Dispociones Legales Relacionadas con el Gobierno Municipal,* complied by Máximo Quesada Picado.

signed a treaty granting to the United States a strip of land ten miles wide across the isthmus for the construction of a canal. Such other land as might be necessary for the canal's construction, operation, or protection should also be subject to American occupation. In return the United States promised to maintain Panama's independence, and to make annual payments of two hundred and fifty thousand dollars in gold, in addition to an initial grant of ten million dollars.

This treaty, which made Panama virtually a protectorate of the United States, furnished the excuse for occasional interference in the tiny republic's internal affairs. As early as 1908 American marines supervised the presidential election. From time to time Panama protested what it termed the excessive condemnation of land by the United States in connection with the protection of the canal. It objected, too, to the establishment of American commissaries in the Canal Zone, because these stores deprived local merchants of a large part of their retail trade. When, in 1933, the United States devalued the dollar and offered to pay its annual canal subsidy in this depreciated currency, Panama had further cause for complaint. It pointed to the stipulation of the 1903 treaty that payments should be in gold. Finally, in 1936, these differences were settled by four separate treaties. The United States agreed to renounce further land grants and to restrict the activities of its commissaries. It also adjusted the annual subsidy in such manner as to satisfy Panama for the moment.[31]

American bases. In 1939, following the outbreak of war in Europe and the possibility of American involvement, the government of the United States requested the use of a number of strategic areas outside the Canal Zone for air bases and other defensive purposes. Panama's reply was delayed by the death of the president and the excitement inevitably surrounding the subsequent presidential election. When the newly elected chief executive, Arnulfo Arias, was pressed for a decision, he displayed strong hostility toward the United States. He did indeed grant permission to use the necessary sites, though after delaying still further and imposing a number of conditions. But he took occasion to speak bitterly against "Yankee imperialism," and in many ways he hampered the American defense effort. One example of his antagonism was his refusal to permit the arming of American-owned vessels sailing under the flag of Panama.

A successful revolution. When, however, President Arias went to Havana for a short visit in October of 1941, his enemies seized this op-

[31] See Wm. D. McCain's scholarly study, *The United States and the Republic of Panama.* See also N. J. Padelford's *The Panama Canal in Peace and War.*

portunity to force him from power. Pointing out that he had failed to
secure the National Assembly's permission to leave the country, as required
by the constitution, they declared the presidency vacant and installed
Ricardo Adolfo de la Guardia as the new chief executive. Many persons
charged that the United States had secretly plotted this *coup d'état,* especially when they learned that de la Guardia was an enthusiastic exponent
of close co-operation between the two nations. The rumor reached such
widespread proportions that Secretary of State Cordell Hull finally issued
an official denial. The United States, he said, had not aided the plotters
either directly or indirectly, and had not even known of the plot. Yet
there was no doubt that the change of presidents proved pleasing to the
American government.

The war years. Throughout the war Panama continued its cordial
co-operation with the United States. Meanwhile President de la Guardia
tried to assure himself of a long term by inducing the National Assembly
not to name presidential alternates, as provided in the constitution. Since
no one could constitutionally claim the right to succeed him, no one could
challenge his indefinite tenure. So, at least, he reasoned. But the opposition kept insisting that alternates should be selected. As the time
approached for the next session of the National Assembly, on January 2,
1945, word reached the President that alternates were finally to be chosen.
Since de la Guardia's own rise to power had been highly irregular, the
first of these alternates would automatically become president. Thereupon de la Guardia acted in an unconstitutional but very effective manner.
He canceled the Assembly's session—only four days before it was scheduled
to convene; suspended the constitution; and announced that an election
would be held in May for delegates to a new constitutional convention.
The opposition protested these highhanded tactics, but found itself powerless to make the protest effective.

A new president and a new constitution. The election for convention
delegates was held as promised on May 5, 1945. Many different parties
and factions were represented, but the liberal elements united to choose
a provisional president of the republic. His name was Enrique A.
Jiménez, and he had formerly served as ambassador to the United States.
Thereupon de la Guardia retired to his private life as a newspaper publisher and Jiménez assumed the duties of the presidency. Meanwhile the
constitutional convention proceeded with the preparation of a new fundamental law, occasionally pausing in its task to enact ordinary legislation.
When the constitution was finished, the convention voted to transform

itself into the National Assembly—the country's regular legislative body—and to continue the terms of its members until October 1, 1948. Meanwhile the followers of former President Arias staged an abortive revolt, which resulted in the killing of several policemen and the arrest of the plot's ringleaders. Arias himself denied any knowledge of the affair, but was taken into custody nonetheless.

The bases become an issue. As the year 1947 drew to a close, the United States expressed a desire to retain some of its wartime bases, in order to provide full protection for the canal. President Jiménez sympathized with this viewpoint and signed a treaty granting the United States continued authority over these areas. When this treaty came before the National Assembly, however, there was considerable opposition. A number of rallies were staged in protest. The police broke up one of these rallies, using unnecessary violence, and thus transformed the agitators into martyrs. Feeling against the cession of Panamanian territory was so intense throughout the country that hardly any of the political leaders dared to speak in the treaty's defense. It was finally rejected by the National Assembly.

This action had unexpected repercussions in the United States. Several Senators said in effect: "If we can't get the territory necessary to defend the Panama Canal, we certainly should not think of expanding it. Let's turn instead to Nicaragua, where we already have treaty rights." Thereupon General Anastacio Somoza, Nicaragua's dictator, eagerly announced that the United States could have all the land it desired for a canal in his country, without unnecessary quibbling over terms. The American government began to withdraw its troops from the disputed bases in Panama, although the existing treaty still had some time to run. These developments evidently surprised Panamanian officials, who seem to have assumed that the rejection of the treaty would merely be the starting point for new negotiations.

Election of 1948. A presidential election—the first in eight years—was scheduled for May 9, 1948. Panama's welter of parties finally produced five nominees. The official candidate was aged Domingo Díaz Arosemena, who had been defeated for the presidency in 1936. One of the principal contenders was ex-President Arnulfo Arias, the anti-Yankee politician deposed in 1941. The government promised free elections, but the opposition charged official interference with its campaign. All the candidates stressed the need for cordial relations with the United States, though insisting that Panama must be treated as an equal. Arias seemed to be especially successful in rousing the voters with his ever-popular theme, "Panama for the Panamanians." A preliminary count of the ballots indicated that he had been elected president. Early in July, however, the National Assembly met in special session and, by a margin of one vote, chose Controller General Obarrio as president of the nation. The Assembly's action was clearly unconstitutional, and was promptly set aside by the supreme court. But the resulting confusion provided a sufficient excuse for President Jiménez to declare a state of siege and issue a number of emergency decrees strengthening his own position. Arnulfo Arias hastily left the country, declaring that he had been cheated out of the presidency. On August 7, 1948, virtually three months after the election, the national election board announced that the official candidate, Díaz Arosemena, had been chosen president by a scant margin of twenty-four hundred votes. He took office in October. Nine months later he suffered a severe heart attack, and took a temporary leave of absence, turning the government over to Dr. Daniel Chanis, the first vice-president.

Turbulent times. In August of 1949 President Díaz Arosemena died. Dr. Chanis thus became president of the nation, and he promptly ordered the removal of the chief of the national police, José Antonio Remón, whose business dealings had been tinged with scandal. Remón responded by sending his police—the only armed force in Panama—to surround the presidential palace. Chanis was forced to resign, and the second vice-president then assumed the presidency. But Chanis suddenly appeared before the National Assembly with a declaration that he was still president. His resignation, he said, had been obtained under duress, and therefore could not be considered valid. The issue was referred to the supreme court, which upheld Chanis. At this point, however, Police Chief Remón came forward with former President Arnulfo Arias, whose loss of the 1948 election had almost certainly been due to fraud. Arias, said Remón, should be considered the legitimate president of Panama. Thereupon the National Election Board, hastily summoned to recount the 1948 returns, announced that Arias had indeed been the victor. His alleged defeat, said the Board, had been "the greatest fraud in the history of the country." So Arias took over the presidency, and governed with the aid of Remón's national police. Opposition groups were rigorously repressed. Newspaper editors and others who dared to criticize the President were thrown into jail, and court orders for their release were ignored. "Voluntary" contributions were forced from public employees. Meanwhile President Arias had become increasingly uncertain of Remón's support, and had set up his own secret police to match the national police. Clashes between the two groups were not infrequent.

From Arias to Remón. Finally Arias went so far as to dissolve the National Assembly, suspend the supreme court, and set aside the constitution. These arbitrary acts were too much for the people. On May 8, 1951, they responded to a call for a general strike. Fifteen thousand men and women marched to the headquarters of the national police, and called upon Chief Remón to help them. Remón answered their appeal by turning against Arias, whom he had installed in office. The "dissolved" National Assembly passed a resolution deposing the President, and this resolution was upheld by the "suspended" supreme court. The first vice-president became the new chief executive. Plans were soon made for another presidential election, and Police Chief Remón became the candidate of a five-party coalition. Four other parties united to select their own nominee, but they soon discovered that the government would not permit them to campaign freely against the favored Remón. Few persons were surprised, therefore, when José Antonio Remón defeated his principal opponent by a margin of two to one. He was inaugurated on October 1, 1952, and chose his cabinet from the parties that had supported him in the election.

THE STRUCTURE OF GOVERNMENT: *The constitution.* The present constitution of Panama, adopted in 1946, has twenty-two thousand words, and may therefore be classed as one of the bulkier constitutions of Latin America. About one fourth of its total space is devoted to various guarantees, which are listed under a number of main headings, such as fundamental guarantees, the family, labor, national culture, and public health. There are the usual assurances of personal liberty, plus numerous detailed declarations of public policy on a wide variety of subjects. "It is a function of the state to safeguard the welfare of the individual." "Primary education is free and compulsory." "Labor is a right and a duty." And so the constitution continues, for thousands of words. The president may declare a state of siege in time of emergency, but only when the National Assembly is not in session. Constitutional amendments may be enacted by the National Assembly like ordinary legislation, but must be passed at two successive annual sessions. The president may veto these proposed constitutional reforms; his veto may be overridden by the legislature by a two-thirds vote.

Suffrage and elections. Both men and women may vote when they reach the age of twenty-one years. Literacy is not a requirement. The parties prepare their separate ballots and, as in most Latin American countries, the government provides an official envelope. A system of proportional representation is used for the election of members of the National Assembly.

The president. The constitution declares that the president shall be elected by direct vote of the people for a term of four years, and shall not be re-eligible until the expiration of two additional terms. He is required to be a natural-born citizen, at least thirty-five years of age. His power of appointment extends to all the usual officers; legislative approval is required only for judges and members of the diplomatic service. The president may veto items of bills, if he so desires, without disapproving of them in their entirety. His veto may be overridden by a two-thirds vote of the National Assembly; but, if his objections are based on constitutional grounds, the issue is finally decided by the supreme court.

Presidential succession; cabinet. There are two vice-presidents. After them the presidential succession extends to the cabinet ministers, in the order designated by law. There are seven members of the cabinet. They are supposed to resign if two thirds of the legislature votes lack of confidence. This clause is so new that its ultimate effect cannot yet be known.

National Assembly. The unicameral National Assembly has fifty-one members, popularly elected for four-year terms. They meet once a year for a regular ninety-day session, and may be called into special session by the president. They must be citizens who have attained the age of twenty-five years. The National Assembly declares war and gives its approval to treaties. A Permanent Committee, composed of five members of the Assembly, continues to function when the Assembly is not in session.

The courts. The supreme court has five members, who sit as a body. They are appointed by the president, with the approval of the Assembly, for terms of ten years. One of their duties is to name the judges of the lower courts.

Internal organization. There are seven provinces, whose governors are appointed by the president. No provincial assemblies have been established. In the municipalities, however, a measure of self-government is now permitted. The people choose their local mayors and councilmen.

SELECTED REFERENCES

Adler, J. H., and Others, *Public Finance and Economic Development in Guatemala,* Stanford, California, Stanford University Press, 1952.

Aguilar, J. Humberto, *Vida y Muerte de una Dictadura,* 2nd ed., Mexico, D.F., Lino-tipográfica Nieto's, 1944.

Benedetti Benedetti, Eloy, *Los Derechos Individuales y Sociales; Estudio Crítico de la Constitución de Panamá, Comparada con la Constitución de Chile y Demás Cartas Políticas Americanas,* Santiago, Chile, Imp. Simiente, 1942.

Biesanz, John and Mavis, *Costa Rican Life,* New York, Columbia Univ. Press, 1944.

Cordero Reyes, Manuel, *Nicaragua bajo el Régimen de Somoza, a los Gobiernos y Pueblos de América,* San Salvador, Imp. Funes, 1944.

Coto Romero, Rafael, *Visión de Centro América,* San Salvador, Tip. La Unión, 1946.

Ealy, Lawrence O., *Panama in World Affairs, 1903–1950,* Philadelphia, University of Pennsylvania Press, 1951.

Echeverría S., Buenaventura, *Derecho Constitucional Guatemalteco,* Guatemala City, Tip. Nacional, 1944.

Greenbie, Sydney, *The Central Five,* Evanston, Ill., Row, Peterson, 1943.

Hernández, Daniel, *La Tributación en Honduras,* Tegucigalpa, Talleres Tip.-Lito, 1947.

Holleran, Mary P., *Church and State in Guatemala,* New York, Columbia University Press, 1949.

Inman, Samuel G., *A New Day in Guatemala: A Study of the Present Social Revolution,* Wilton, Connecticut, Worldover Press, 1951.

International Bank for Reconstruction and Development, *The Economic Development of Guatemala,* Washington, D.C., The Bank, 1951.

Krehn, William, *Democracia y Tiranías en el Caribe,* Mexico, D.F., Unión Democrática Centroamericana, 1949.

May, Stacy, and Others, *Costa Rica: A Study in Economic Development,* New York, Twentieth Century Fund, 1952.

Mendoza, José Luis, *Inglaterra y sus Pactos sobre Belice,* Guatemala City, Tip. Nacional, 1942.

Rochac, Alfonso, *El Crédito Rural,* San Salvador, El Banco Hipotecario de El Salvador, 1942.

Rodríguez, Cristóbal, *Para la Historia; Un Año de Secretaría General de la Presidencia,* Panama City, 1942.

Rojas Suárez, Juan Francisco, *Costa Rica en la Segunda Guerra Mundial,* San José, Imp. Nacional, 1943.

Samayoa, Julio, *Ensayos sobre Problemas de lo Porvenir,* Guatemala City, Tip. Sánchez & de Guise, 1944.

Stokes, William S., *Honduras: An Area Study in Government,* Madison, University of Wisconsin Press, 1950.

Suslow, Leo, *Aspects of Social Reforms in Guatemala,* Hamilton, New York, Colgate University, 1949.

Wallich, Henry C., and J. H. Adler, *Public Finance in a Developing Country: El Salvador,* Cambridge, Massachusetts, Harvard University Press, 1951.

Wilson, Charles Morrow, *Middle America,* New York, W. W. Norton, 1944.

Zeledón, Marco Tulio, *Lecciones de Ciencia Constitucional y Constitución Política de la República de Costa Rica,* San José, Imp. Nacional, 1945.

CHAPTER 24

LATIN AMERICA and the UNITED STATES

GROWING INFLUENCE OF THE UNITED STATES. The rise of the United States to first place among the nations of the world has greatly changed its relations with Latin America. A century ago the people of Latin America were scarcely aware of the existence of their northern neighbor, and most of them were supremely indifferent to its words and deeds. To-day, however, they cannot afford to be indifferent. The United States takes more than one third of all Latin American exports, and supplies nearly two thirds of the goods that Latin America buys abroad. United States loans, public and private, have played an important part in the development of Latin American resources. United States leadership has been largely responsible for the growth of an effective inter-American organization. Whether or not Latin Americans like the United States, therefore, they must recognize its influence. They cannot ignore the facts of political life.

THE SPHERE OF UNITED STATES INFLUENCE. There can be no doubt, however, that the influence of the United States is much greater in some parts of Latin America than in others. Mexico and the Caribbean area lie well within the shadow of the United States, partly because of their proximity to the great Republic of the North, and partly because of their strategic importance to the Panama Canal, which the United States is determined to defend at all costs. More than four fifths of the Mexican export-import trade is with the United States, and United States purchases of Mexican silver help to stabilize the Mexican economy. In most of the other Caribbean countries the picture is very similar. Brazil and Chile, also, carry on extensive trade with the United States. But Argentina had comparatively little trade with the United States until the dislocations of war changed the economic picture. There is no doubt that Argentina would like to reduce its purchases of United States goods.

Early Latin American Policy of the United States

ISOLATION. In the early years of the eighteenth century, when the United States had just won its independence, it did not aspire to leadership in the Americas. It was in no position to do so. It was in fact a very weak nation, surrounded on three sides by the territories of European powers and not at all certain that it could defend itself against possible attack. Yet the new nation possessed one major asset. It was separated by three thousand miles of ocean from Europe, and thus able to escape most of the Old World's apparently endless troubles. This advantage seemed priceless to the statesmen who guided the destinies of the United States in the first years of its independence. They believed that the young nation could best protect its own security by keeping clear of European affairs. In 1796, when President Washington delivered his Farewell Address to the people of the United States, he said:

The great rule of conduct for us, in regard to foreign nations, is, in extending our commercial relations, to have with them as little political connexion as possible. . . . Europe has a set of primary interests, which to us have none, or a very remote relation. Hence she must be engaged in frequent controversies, the causes of which are essentially foreign to our concerns. Hence, therefore, it must be unwise in us to implicate ourselves, by artificial ties, in the ordinary vicissitudes of her politics, or the ordinary combinations and collisions of her friendships or enmities. . . . Our detached and distant situation invites, and enables us to pursue, a different course. . . . Why forego the advantages of so peculiar a situation? . . . 'Tis our policy to steer clear of permanent alliances with any portion of the foreign world. . . .[1]

Fifteen years later Thomas Jefferson expressed the same thought when he advocated "peace, commerce, and honest friendship with all nations, entangling alliances with none."[2] For more than a century the fear of "entangling alliances" dominated political thought in the United States, and exerted a powerful influence on foreign policy.

NO-TRANSFER RESOLUTION OF 1811. The United States greatly strength-

[1] *American State Papers, Foreign Relations*, Vol. I, pp. 34 ff.
[2] *Ibid.*, p. 56.

ened its position in 1803 by purchasing the vast Louisiana Territory from France. Thus it secured its western frontier. To the south, however, Florida remained in Spanish hands. The government of the United States did not greatly fear trouble with Spain, which was on the verge of losing much of its territory and more of its prestige, yet there was always the danger that Great Britain might obtain Florida by negotiation, and use it as a base of operations against the United States. In 1810, therefore, President Madison directed American troops to seize West Florida. Both Spain and Great Britain protested vigorously, though to no avail. Meanwhile the government of the United States was worried lest East Florida come into the possession of Great Britain. President Madison sent a secret message to Congress in January of 1811, requesting authority to seize East Florida if necessary. Congress unhesitatingly gave this authority, and at the same time expressed its belief that the United States could not "without serious inquietude see any part of the said territory pass into the hands of any foreign power." [3] This No-Transfer Resolution had no direct effect, for Spain sold the entire peninsula of Florida to the United States a few years later. But every student of world politics should note that the United States went on record, as early as 1811, against the transfer of New World possessions from one European power to another. That "no-transfer" principle is still a fundamental part of the foreign policy of the United States.

MONROE DOCTRINE. The first few years of the nineteenth century were fateful years for Spain. In 1808 Napoleon managed to place his brother upon the Spanish throne, and this incident led to widespread revolt in Spanish America. In rapid succession the Spanish colonies in the New World declared themselves independent of the mother country, though not immediately renouncing their allegiance to the dethroned Spanish monarch, Ferdinand VII. A few years later, however, when Ferdinand regained the Spanish throne and attempted to restore his autocratic rule in the New World, the colonists denied his authority and began a determined struggle for freedom. By 1824 the success of the movement for independence was assured, though another two years elapsed before all Spanish troops were driven from the soil of the new republics.

Meanwhile the government of the United States manifested a sympathetic interest in the revolutionary efforts of its southern neighbors. In 1815 it accorded the new governments the status of belligerents, and it

[3] *Annals of Congress,* 11th Congress, 3rd Session, 1810–1811, Col. 374.

would probably have recognized their independence except for the fear that such an act would prejudice the pending Florida treaty with Spain. In fact, the United States did recognize the new republics in 1822, only fifteen months after the signing of the Florida treaty. The revolutionary successes in Spanish America caused general alarm among the absolute monarchs of Europe. Their so-called Holy Alliance seriously considered ways and means of aiding Ferdinand VII to regain his lost colonies. But Great Britain refused to back this project, for it knew that restoration of Spanish rule would mean the loss of British trade with the new nations of Spanish America. In an effort to block the plans of the Holy Alliance, therefore, Britain's foreign minister proposed a joint Anglo-American declaration opposing the seizure of Spain's former colonies by other European powers. President Monroe and most of the members of his cabinet were inclined to look favorably upon such a joint declaration, but Secretary of State John Quincy Adams argued that the United States should speak for itself, instead of accepting the leadership of Great Britain or any other nation. In the end Adams had his way, and the United States made its own pronouncement of foreign policy.

The occasion for this declaration was the message that President Monroe sent to Congress on December 2, 1823. The President was concerned not only with the efforts of the Holy Alliance to regain the lost Spanish colonies in the New World, but also with the menace of Russian expansion on the Pacific coast of North America. He discussed the world situation at length, and explained the position of the United States in some detail, but two sentences in widely separated paragraphs form the gist of what came to be known as the Monroe Doctrine:

. . . the American continents, by the free and independent condition which they have assumed and maintain, are henceforth not to be considered as subjects for future colonization by any European power. . . .

We owe it therefore to candor, and to the amicable relations existing between the United States and those [European] powers, to declare that we should consider any attempt on their part to extend their system to any portions of this hemisphere, as dangerous to our peace and safety. With the existing colonies or dependencies of any European power, we have not interfered, and shall not interfere. But with the governments who have declared their independence, and maintained it, and whose independence we have, on great consideration, and on just principles, acknowledged, we could not view any interposition for the purpose of oppressing them, or controlling in any other manner, their destiny, by any European power, in any other light, than as the manifestation of an unfriendly disposition towards the United States.[4]

European reactions. The governments of continental Europe, to no one's surprise, sneered openly at the brave words spoken by the President of the United States. The Vicomte de Chateaubriand expressed the general sentiment in the chancelleries of Europe when he declared that the Monroe Doctrine "should be resisted by all the powers possessing either territorial or commercial interest in" the New World. The British foreign minister might have been expected to welcome the new American declaration, since it fitted in so closely with his own plans, yet even he expressed annoyance at the presumption of the United States. Before long he forgot his irritation, however, and talked as if the Monroe Doctrine were due directly to his own efforts. "I called the New World into existence," he boasted, "to redress the balance of power of the Old."[5]

Latin American reactions. In Latin America, of course, the revolutionary leaders generally welcomed the Monroe Doctrine. Two of the new republics gave it their official endorsement, and several of them proposed formal alliances with the United States. The Colombian minister in Washington presented a memorandum asking for a precise statement of just what the United States intended to do in order to prevent European aggression in the New World. To all these proposals and inquiries the government of the United States gave evasive answers. The truth of the matter was that the United States could do virtually nothing unless it had the active support of the British navy. In time the Latin American leaders learned this elementary fact, and lost their enthusiasm for the Monroe Doctrine.

Early violations of the Monroe Doctrine. In the years immediately following the announcement of the Monroe Doctrine, the United States permitted without protest a number of violations by European powers. In 1833, for example, a British warship seized the Argentine-governed Falkland Islands, which lay only a few hundred miles off the Argentine coast. Argentina protested loudly against this British action, invoking the Monroe Doctrine in partial justification of its position. But the British replied that their rights to the Islands were based on an old treaty with Spain, and the government of the United States accepted this explanation. Its

[4] William K. Manning, *Diplomatic Correspondence of the United States Concerning the Independence of the Latin American Nations,* Vol. I, p. 146.

[5] Harold Temperley, *The Foreign Policy of Canning,* p. 130.

readiness to do so may have arisen from the fact that American fishermen in the waters surrounding the Falkland Islands had been badly treated by the Argentine authorities only a few years earlier.[6]   Between 1838 and 1850 the governments of France and Great Britain interfered in Argentine affairs on several occasions, blockading Argentine territory and even landing troops on the shores of the Plata estuary. The United States assumed an attitude of almost complete indifference to these acts. Not once did it suggest that they might be a violation of the Monroe Doctrine. But it must not be supposed that Americans had forgotten their cherished doctrine. They were merely too busy with the problems of their own territorial expansion to challenge European power in a distant quarter of the world.

Violations during the Civil War. Only one month after the outbreak of the American Civil War, Spain announced the reannexation of Santo Domingo, which had been independent for many years. In justification of this act the Spanish government explained that it was merely carrying out the will of the inhabitants of Santo Domingo. It did indeed have the support of the Dominican president, who wrote a flowery letter to Queen Isabella of Spain assuring her of the people's affection and loyalty. The exact extent of that affection and loyalty were indicated shortly afterward, when the people rose in spontaneous and bloody revolt against Spanish rule. Meanwhile the government of the United States protested vigorously against this clear violation of the Monroe Doctrine. But Spain ignored the protest, and the United States was too busy with the problems of its own Civil War to take more drastic action. By 1865, however, Spanish troops had suffered such losses in Santo Domingo—partly from popular resistance and partly from disease—that Spain decided to relinquish its claim to the colony. Thus the incident ended without any direct intervention by the United States.[7]

In 1864 Spain violated the Monroe Doctrine in another part of the world. It seized the Chincha Islands off the coast of Peru, announcing that this act was in reprisal for the maltreatment of some Spanish subjects. The Spanish naval officer in charge of the expedition explained that Spain was entitled to the islands, since it had never recognized Peru's independence. Presumably this same line of reasoning would have justified the Spanish government in annexing all Peru. The United States made known its objections in blunt language, and received prompt assurances

[6] See *The Struggle for the Falkland Islands*, by Julius Goebel, Jr.
[7] See page 599.

from the Spanish prime minister that his government would not challenge the Monroe Doctrine. Eventually Peru made a satisfactory settlement of Spanish claims, and Spain withdrew its troops from the Chincha Islands.

By far the most serious threat to the Monroe Doctrine, however, arose from the French attempt to place a puppet emperor upon the throne of Mexico. The trouble arose from Mexico's failure to continue payments on its foreign debt. The nation had just been ravaged by civil war, and its treasury was virtually empty. Nonetheless France, Britain, and Spain, the principal creditors, insisted upon regular interest payments, and prepared to enforce their demands by sending armed forces to seize the chief Mexican ports. But France was not satisfied with the mere collection of customs. Its grandiose plans included the pacification of the Mexican nation and the establishment of the Archduke Maximilian as its titular head. For a time these plans went well; French forces met with little effective opposition, and some Mexicans were even persuaded to establish a monarchy and to offer Maximilian the crown. Meanwhile Britain and Spain withdrew from the undertaking, but France pressed on. The United States, of course, was in no position to take any effective action. The seizure of Mexico City by the French occurred during one of the most desperate periods of the American Civil War; in fact, the Battle of Gettysburg was fought just three weeks later. Yet the House of Representatives of the United States took time from its war problems to pass a resolution deploring French activities in Mexico and condemning "any monarchical government erected on the ruins of any republican government in America under the auspices of any European power."[8] After the end of the Civil War the government of the United States was in a position to take an even firmer stand. It did so, and shortly afterward the French withdrew their forces. Thereupon Maximilian's regime collapsed, and the unfortunate emperor was executed by a firing squad.[9]

Venezuelan boundary dispute. By 1895 the United States had become a powerful nation. Its domain extended from coast to coast. Its population was large and constantly growing. Its neighbors were comparatively weak. When, therefore, another incident arose concerning the Monroe Doctrine, the American government acted more boldly than ever before. Great Britain and Venezuela had argued for many years about the exact boundaries of British Guiana without finding a satisfactory compromise.

[8] John Bassett Moore, *Digest of International Law*, Vol. VI, p. 496.

[9] The story of the French invasion of Mexico is well told by J. H. Latané in his *The United States and Latin America*, Chap. V.

Finally the United States insisted upon arbitration. It pointed out that powerful Britain might otherwise seize territory belonging to Venezuela, and thus increase British holdings in the New World in direct violation of the Monroe Doctrine. At first, however, the British government refused to admit that the Monroe Doctrine was involved in any way. Why, it asked, should outsiders interfere in a dispute that involved only Britain and Venezuela? Did anyone seriously think that Britain would try to seize territory not rightfully its own? Apparently the United States did think so, and perhaps not without reason. American statesmen could remember the boundary dispute between Great Britain and Guatemala many years earlier, a controversy that had ended by doubling the territory of British Honduras. At that time, it is true, the United States had uttered no word of protest. By 1895, however, it had a clearer understanding of the Monroe Doctrine, and a stronger will to enforce it. So Great Britain finally accepted the contention of the United States. An arbitration commission was appointed, and held a number of meetings in Paris. Its award was not substantially different from the original British demands, but at least the United States had made its point that governmental disputes in the New World involving European powers must be settled by peaceful means.[10]

Paramount interest of the United States. It was in connection with the Venezuelan boundary dispute that Richard Olney, then Secretary of State of the United States, restated the Monroe Doctrine in much stronger language than that originally used by President Monroe.

The United States has proclaimed itself the protector of this western world, in which she is by far the stronger power, from the intrusion of European sovereignties. She can point with proud satisfaction to the fact that over and over again has she declared effectively, that serious indeed would be the consequences if European hostile foot should, without just cause, tread those states in the New World which have emancipated themselves from European control. She has announced that she would cherish as it becomes her the territorial rights of the feeblest of these states. . . .

After summarizing the history of the Monroe Doctrine, Olney added this confident boast: "Today the United States is practically sovereign on this continent, and its fiat is law upon the subjects to which it confines its interposition." [11] Monroe had told the European powers that they

---

[10] See Charles C. Tansill's competent work, *The Foreign Policy of Thomas F. Bayard, 1885–1897.* Bayard was American ambassador to Great Britain at the time of the Venezuelan boundary dispute.

[11] John Bassett Moore, *op. cit.,* Vol. VI, p. 535.

must keep out of the affairs of the Americas; Olney added the postscript that only the United States was competent to decide what were American affairs.

Caribbean interventions. Only a few years after the boundary dispute with Great Britain, Venezuela found itself embroiled in another international controversy. This time ten nations were involved. The trouble began when the Venezuelan dictator failed to meet the nation's foreign debt obligations. Many foreign nationals residing in Venezuela lost their property through arbitrary government action, and were unable to secure justice in the Venezuelan courts. Thereupon they appealed to their own governments for protection. At least three European powers—Germany, Great Britain, and Italy—decided to take forcible action. The German government, anxious to avoid any misunderstanding with the United States, presented to the American Department of State a note carefully explaining its plans, and disclaiming any intention of acquiring territory in the New World. This note was delivered on December 11, 1901. As a matter of fact, President Theodore Roosevelt had already indicated that he would pursue a hands-off policy. In his message to Congress, delivered eight days earlier, he had said: "We do not guarantee any state against punishment if it misconducts itself, provided that punishment does not take the form of the acquisition of territory by any non-American power." [12]

Thus reassured as to the position of the United States, Germany and Great Britain, together with Italy, engaged in warlike operations against Venezuela. Five of the principal ports of Venezuela were blockaded, three of its gunboats were sunk, and two coastal forts were shelled. The Venezuelan dictator quickly proposed arbitration. Apparently the United States had not realized that the situation would assume such serious proportions. In any event, President Roosevelt seemed to forget his earlier indifference. He strongly urged the blockading powers to accept the Venezuelan suggestion that the whole controversy be submitted to arbitration. Germany promptly agreed. So did Britain and Italy. These three nations insisted, however, that the claims of their citizens should take priority over the claims of Belgians or Spaniards or other foreigners. In effect the three blockading nations said: "We have borne the brunt of this dispute. We have forced an unreasonable dictator to assume a reasonable attitude. Therefore our nationals should have first claim on all available assets." Venezuela replied that all creditors should be treated alike, and

[12] *Foreign Relations of the United States, 1901,* p. XXXVI.

of course the nations that had not engaged in the blockade accepted this view. Early in 1904 the Hague tribunal handed down a decision recognizing the preferred status of German, British, and Italian citizens.[13] This award was clearly an invitation to European powers to use force in the collection of New World debts. It imposed a heavy penalty on those nations that failed to do so.

The Roosevelt Corollary. Public opinion in the United States began to look with increasing disfavor upon European interventions in the affairs of the Latin American states. Such interventions might readily begin as an attempt to collect just debts, and end as permanent seizure of the territory of defaulting nations. British or German or other European troops landed to take "temporary" possession of a few customhouses might find themselves obliged to take more extensive measures, until they reduced independent nations to the status of colonies. Thus the Monroe Doctrine might be violated in the name of law and order. The most obvious way for the United States to keep the Monroe Doctrine intact was to insist that non-American powers must not use force against an American state, regardless of the circumstances. But President Roosevelt believed that the United States could not conscientiously tell aggrieved European nations to keep hands off unless it offered to act in their stead. He thought that if the Monroe Doctrine imposed an obligation on Europe not to intervene in Latin American affairs, it also imposed on the United States the absolute duty of intervening in Latin America whenever necessary to do justice. In his annual message to Congress, dated December 6, 1904, Roosevelt declared:

> If a nation shows that it knows how to act with reasonable efficiency and decency in social and political matters, if it keeps order and pays its obligations, it need fear no interference from the United States. Chronic wrongdoing, or an impotence which results in a general loosening of the ties of civilized society, may in America, as elsewhere, ultimately require intervention by some civilized nation, and in the Western Hemisphere the adherence of the United States to the Monroe Doctrine may force the United States, however reluctantly, in flagrant cases of such wrongdoing or impotence, to the exercise of an international police power.[14]

This Roosevelt Corollary, as it came to be known, was indeed a far cry from the original doctrine of Monroe. The doctrine of 1823 had merely told the European powers that they must not intervene in Latin American

13 For a full report of the case, see *Senate Documents,* 58th Congress, 3rd Session, No. 119.
14 J. Reuben Clark, *Memorandum on the Monroe Doctrine,* p. 174.

affairs. The corollary of 1904 added this postscript for the benefit of investors: "Don't worry; we shall intervene in Latin America on your behalf."

Dollar diplomacy. Latin American scholars and diplomats were not slow to point out that the United States almost invariably used its newly discovered "international police power" for the benefit of United States investors. British and German and French investors might also be helped, as indeed they were on numerous occasions, but certainly the rights of American citizens were not neglected. The immediate occasion for the birth of the Roosevelt Corollary was the virtual collapse of the government of the Dominican Republic. The country was virtually bankrupt, and foreign investors were clamoring for their money. The rumor spread that Italy was about to use force to protect the rights of its nationals. So the government of the United States arranged to take over the Dominican customhouses. Eventually it took over the entire country.[15] This story was repeated, with minor variations, in other small republics of the Caribbean area. In every instance, of course, the United States was able to justify its acts by calling attention to the deplorable instability of the local government. In every instance, too, it was able to point with pride to necessary reforms instituted by its own forces. But the fact remained that American investors were among the principal beneficiaries of some American interventions. In some cases the United States even refused to recognize newly established governments unless they would agree to resume payments on the foreign debt. And, since United States recognition sometimes meant life or death to the new governments, they had no choice but to obey. Unfriendly foreign critics were quick to exaggerate the mercenary motives of the American government. They pictured the State Department as a tool of Wall Street, and the United States Marine Corps as a debt collection agency. *Dollar diplomacy* was the phrase they coined to describe the Latin American policy of the United States. Many of these criticisms were unfair. There seems to be little doubt that the American government was much more deeply concerned with the danger of European domination in the New World than with the danger of impaired American investments. The Monroe Doctrine was still uppermost in the minds of American statesmen. Yet no one can deny that the Monroe Doctrine of the early twentieth century had become something very different from the doctrine enunciated by James Monroe in 1823.

THE PANAMA CANAL. A great deal of the foreign policy of the United

[15] See pages 600–602.

States, especially with regard to Latin America, has centered around the Panama Canal. Spanish explorers conceived the idea of such a canal as early as 1515, and interested the King of Spain in their project. A number of surveys were made in the effort to find a suitable route, but nothing was accomplished. Throughout the years, however, the plan was kept alive, and by the first part of the nineteenth century it had fired the imagination of some farseeing leaders in the United States. Both Henry Clay and Andrew Jackson spoke of the manifold advantages of a canal connecting the Atlantic and Pacific oceans. But the American public seemed to have no great interest in the scheme. After the Mexican War, however, public interest suddenly kindled. California and Texas had become parts of the United States, and it was obvious that something should be done to shorten the sea route between the nation's Atlantic and Pacific coasts.

Clayton-Bulwer Treaty. By the middle of the nineteenth century other nations were also considering the possibility of an artificial waterway connecting the Atlantic and Pacific oceans. Great Britain was especially active; its agents busily sought control of the route across Nicaragua. Finally, in 1850, Britain and the United States decided to end their rivalry concerning the canal. They signed an agreement—the famous Clayton-Bulwer Treaty [16]—which placed any future canal or railway across the Isthmus under joint Anglo-American control, assured equal transit charges for the citizens of both nations, and prohibited the erection of fortifications. This treaty seemed to represent a substantial victory for the United States. It said in unequivocal language that Great Britain, a mighty naval power, should not build a canal across the Isthmus, fortify it, and exclude the ships of the United States. Thus American statesmen apparently had good reason to believe that they would be able to turn to their pressing domestic problems without fear that the Isthmus would slip entirely from their grasp.

The French debacle. By 1879, however, the French had begun to interest themselves in the canal project. It is true that the work was financed with private capital and directed by a private engineer; but the capital was French, the engineer—Ferdinand de Lesseps—was French, and the company was organized under French law. No American statesman could safely overlook the possibility that the French government might find some excuse to take over the activities of the private company, and eventually

[16] Named for John M. Clayton, the Secretary of State of the United States, and Sir Henry Bulwer, special Ambassador of Great Britain.

claim sovereignty over the Isthmus of Panama in direct violation of the Monroe Doctrine. As a matter of fact, American statesmen were keenly alive to this danger. Secretary of State Blaine declared in 1881 that the United States could not permit any European power (as distinct from a private company) to control a canal across the Isthmus. Eventually it transpired that the fears of the United States were groundless. The French company had grossly underestimated the cost of the project, and also the physical difficulties. It had actually bribed French officials and subsidized French newspapers in an effort to suppress the news of its troubles. By 1889, however, the complete story of inefficiency and corruption became generally known, and the company collapsed. Only a small part of the work had been completed. A new French company was organized some years later, but it never carried on extensive operations. Eventually it sold its holdings to the United States.

The Hay-Pauncefote Treaty. Meanwhile the advantages to the United States of the Clayton-Bulwer Treaty had become increasingly nebulous. The proposed canal was still unbuilt. The Pacific Coast had become an important part of the American domain, and urgently required some shorter means of water communication with the Atlantic seaboard. Britain, on the other hand, seemed to have lost its interest in the canal project, and no longer offered serious rivalry to American ambitions. By 1898, therefore, the Clayton-Bulwer Treaty had assumed a very different aspect. Its importance no longer lay in the fact that Great Britain could not build a canal without the United States, but rather in the fact that the United States could not build a canal without Great Britain. Such a situation was completely unacceptable to the American people and to their leaders. John Hay, the Secretary of State of the United States, began negotiations with Great Britain to amend the Clayton-Bulwer Treaty so as to permit the United States to build and operate a canal across the Isthmus, without the necessity of accepting British partnership. No one said in so many words that the United States was determined to have complete control of the proposed canal, treaty or no treaty. No one openly threatened to ignore the provisions of the old treaty unless Britain agreed to some sort of modification. But British statesmen were not slow to sense the temper of the American public. Nor did they forget the value of American friendship. So they consented readily to the suggestion of the United States State Department that a new agreement be prepared to replace the outmoded Clayton-Bulwer Treaty.

Both time and patience were required, however, to work out the details of the new treaty. Britain naturally desired to retain most of the advantages of the old agreement. It insisted that any canal across the Isthmus, even though built with American funds and operated by American personnel, must be open on equal terms to the ships of all nations, in war as well as peace. "All nations" clearly included even the enemies of the United States. Moreover, said the British, there must be no fortification of the canal. Such conditions were obviously unsatisfactory from the standpoint of the United States, yet Secretary Hay accepted them and actually seems to have believed that he had achieved a diplomatic triumph. Other Americans, however, were quick to point out that the United States was about to lose more than it would gain. Henry Cabot Lodge and other Senators spoke strongly against the treaty, and it never received the Senate's approval. New negotiations were necessary, therefore, and they finally resulted in another agreement more favorable to the United States. The right to fortify and defend the canal, though not specifically mentioned, was clearly implied, especially in the light of earlier discussions. This new agreement, officially known as the Hay-Pauncefote Treaty,[17] was ratified by the United States Senate early in 1902. It greatly strengthened American influence in the Caribbean.

Negotiations with Colombia. There were many aspects of the complicated negotiations that preceded the construction of the Panama Canal. Many interests were involved. Great Britain's willingness to waive its original treaty rights was important, of course, but other difficulties remained. After all, Great Britain did not own the canal route. The privately controlled, French-financed Panama Canal Company had already completed about forty per cent of the canal, and it possessed valuable properties and franchises. Its directors were anxious to abandon the project, but they insisted upon a large sum for their holdings. Finally, however, in the spring of 1902, they came to terms with the United States, and thus removed one more obstacle to American control of the canal route. Yet not even the Panama Canal Company could confer sovereign rights upon the United States. The proposed route stretched across the territory of the Republic of Colombia, and only the government of that country could cede the necessary strip of land. Colombia decided to strike a hard bargain. The Colombian minister, presumably acting on orders from Bogotá, sent evasive or unsatisfactory replies to American requests for a treaty and finally left Washington. Eventually, however, a treaty was prepared and signed by the representatives of both countries. It authorized

[17] Lord Pauncefote was British Ambassador to the United States.

the United States to build a canal across the Isthmus of Panama, and to operate it for one hundred years, with the option of extending this period indefinitely. A strip of land three miles wide on each side of the canal was to be placed under American control, but Colombia was to have the right to transport vessels and troops over the canal at all times. In exchange for the privilege of using Colombian territory the United States was to pay ten million dollars at once, and two hundred and fifty thousand dollars a year thereafter. This treaty would not take effect, of course, until ratified by the Senates of both nations. The United States Senate gave its ratification promptly, but the Colombian Senate decided to hold out for better terms. Finally it rejected the agreement by a unanimous vote.

The Panama revolution. The people of the province of Panama, who had expected to benefit greatly from the construction of the canal, were bitterly disappointed at this turn of events. Some of their leaders talked freely of revolution, and they were encouraged to believe that the United States would aid their plans. The encouragement came from the former engineer of the Panama Canal Company, and not from American representatives. But this engineer seems to have been able to convince the revolutionaries that he had a secret understanding with the United States. He even learned of the sailing of an American cruiser, and cabled that it would arrive in two and one-half days to insure the revolution's success. When, therefore, the cruiser did arrive at the appointed time, the conspirators promptly declared the independence of Panama. Colombian troops were put ashore, but some of them were seized by the revolutionary forces. The Colombian commander then attempted to move the remainder of his forces to a more suitable location; he was prevented from doing so, however, by the action of American marines. The ostensible basis for this American interference was an old treaty with Colombia authorizing the United States to maintain the neutrality of the Isthmus and keep traffic open. But only a strained interpretation could justify the theory that Colombia had deliberately sanctioned the use of force against its own troops. In any event, the action of the United States marines made possible the revolution's success.

The timing of the incident is very significant. November 3, 1903, was the date of the uprising in Panama City. On November 4 American marines landed "to preserve order" and also to prevent the movement of loyal Colombian troops. On November 6 the United States recognized the government of Panama. And only twelve days later American representatives signed with the new government of Panama a treaty providing for the construction of a canal. This agreement was almost identical with the treaty rejected by Colombia. Its only important change was an extension of the American-controlled area from three to five miles on either side of the canal.

The role of the United States. Indignant Colombians contended that the revolution had been staged by the United States. The evidence seems to point the other way, but certainly no one can deny that the American government acted with precipitate haste in recognizing Panama. There had been other uprisings in the province, which had aroused virtually no interest in the United States. One of these rebellions—in 1895, just eight years before the final winning of independence—had continued for three months, only to be crushed by a large force of Colombian troops. At that time the United States did nothing. But when American interests were at stake, American marines virtually guaranteed the victory of the revolutionists and the United States extended recognition to the revolutionary government after three days of sporadic fighting. It is unfortunate that the American title to the Panama Canal should have been acquired in such a questionable manner, even though there is no doubt as to the canal's value to world commerce, and to the trade of Colombia itself.

Attempts to negotiate a settlement. Even the United States government tacitly admitted that Colombia had been wronged. Its replies to Colombia's repeated protests invariably stressed the correctness of the American position, but at the same time indicated a willingness to make some adjustment that would lessen the extent of the injury. In 1907, after negotiations among the representatives of the United States, Colombia, and Panama, it was agreed that the first ten annual payments from the United States to Panama should go instead to Colombia, and that Colombian ships and products should have special privileges in the use of the canal. It must be noted that the money to be paid to Colombia under this treaty was only one fourth of the sum originally offered by the United States and rejected by the Colombian Senate for the privilege of building the canal. Small wonder, therefore, that when the 1907 treaty was placed before the Colombian Senate, it too was rejected unanimously. Public opinion in Colombia ran so strongly against the agreement that the minister who had negotiated it was compelled to leave the country.

Improved relations. Failure to conclude this treaty did not end the "Panama incident," however. Another agreement was made during the Taft administration, and again spurned by the Colombian Senate. When Woodrow Wilson became president in 1913, negotiations were reopened, and Colombia was invited to state the terms that it would consider satisfactory. It did so, and listed three main points: an expression of regret from the United States, an assurance of free use of the canal, and an indemnity of fifty million dollars. Only the second of these three demands proved acceptable to the State Department of the United States. Instead of an apology for American conduct it offered an expression of regret that the friendly relations between the two countries had been marred in any way—which was something quite different, of course, from what Colombia had in mind. Instead of fifty million dollars it offered twenty-five million. And even these terms proved unsatisfactory to the American Senate, which refused to give its consent. Later, however, at the urgent request of President Harding, the Senate did in fact agree to offer substantially these terms to Colombia, which accepted them in 1922. The so-called apology clause was quietly eliminated. Thus the "Panama incident" was finally settled, after nearly three decades. It must be admitted that the desire of American oil interests to secure important concessions in Colombia undoubtedly influenced the government of the United States in its policy of conciliation.[18]

The Nicaragua route. The possibility of a canal across Nicaragua from the Atlantic to the Pacific has been considered many times. In 1899, when the United States was seriously considering the canal problem, President McKinley appointed a commission to determine the best possible route. This commission decided in favor of a canal across Nicaragua, though its choice was undoubtedly influenced by the difficulty of making satisfactory arrangements with the Panama Canal Company. Almost immediately the Company indicated its willingness to sell at a much lower figure, and the commission thereupon changed its opinion in a supplementary report. So Panama was chosen in preference to Nicaragua, and became the site of the canal. Throughout the years, however, the possibility of a Nicaragua route has continued to attract attention. After the Second World War many persons, influenced by the increase in the volume of canal traffic and the vulnerability of the canal to air attack in case of another war, discussed the need for a second canal. The merits of the Nicaragua route once again received wide publicity. President Somoza of Nicaragua promptly announced that he would be willing to cede a suitable strip of land to the United States at any time. The price of such a strip was not

---

[18] The story of the canal incident has been told many times. Some of the more important books on the subject are *History of the Panama Canal*, by W. J. Abbott, and *Cadiz to Cathay: The Story of the Long Struggle for a Waterway across the American Isthmus*, by Miles P. DuVal, Jr.

mentioned, but everyone knew that price would be a minor consideration if the United States were determined to complete the project. There is no certainty, however, that anything will be done.

THE OVERSEAS EMPIRE. The Caribbean policy of the United States has been strongly influenced, not only by the Panama Canal, but also by the American overseas empire. For more than a hundred years of its national life the United States had no distant island possessions and no apparent interest in acquiring them.[19] Its efforts were directed toward the development of its great western territories, extending eventually to the shores of the Pacific. But the war with Spain in 1898 created new problems and a new point of view. It led directly to the annexation of Puerto Rico, Guam, and the Philippines, which Spain ceded to the United States by the treaty of peace. At the same time Cuba became virtually a protectorate of the United States—a status that it did not lose for many years. The Hawaiian Islands, also, were annexed in 1898. Within a few months, therefore, the United States acquired a substantial overseas empire. This empire was important in many ways. It provided bases in widely scattered parts of the world for the rapidly growing American navy; it offered new markets for American products; and it greatly enhanced American prestige. There were some Americans who decried the march of empire beyond the continental limits of the United States. They professed to see the seeds of conflict in these new island possessions. But they did not represent the prevailing sentiment of the American people, who generally regarded the new imperialistic policy of their government as manifest destiny.

MEXICO AND THE UNITED STATES: *The Mexican War*. The relations of Mexico and the United States are amicable today, but there have been many stormy years. Mexicans are loath to forget that they have lost to the United States approximately one half of their original territory. First it was Texas, which had been settled by Americans and later declared itself an independent republic after repeated difficulties with the Mexican government. The United States promptly recognized the new republic—too promptly, according to Mexico—and when Mexican troops tried to reconquer Mexican territory Americans helped to defend it. War between Mexico and the United States became inevitable. And as a result of that war Mexico lost half a million square miles, including the territory then

---

[19] For a brief reference to the proposed American annexation of the Dominican Republic, see pages 599–600. The matter is considered at greater length in the 4th edition of Graham H. Stuart's *Latin America and the United States*, Chap. XI.

known as New Mexico and Upper California.   The United States did in fact pay fifteen million dollars for this vast empire, and also agreed to pay certain claims of its own citizens against the Mexican government.   But fifteen millions—or ten times that amount—did not even approximate the value of the land taken.   Mexicans were understandably bitter.   Yet many Americans, including some congressmen and members of President Polk's own cabinet, thought that the United States was entirely too lenient. They wanted us to annex all Mexico.[20]

Intervention.   On many occasions the United States has interfered in Mexican affairs.   It did so in 1914, when American forces shelled Vera Cruz and then landed troops who seized the city after sharp fighting. In 1916 it sent American troops into Mexico, without the consent of the Mexican government, for the purpose of capturing or destroying a band of Mexicans who had committed hostile acts against citizens of the United States.   Several times the United States has made or broken a Mexican revolution by granting or withholding recognition of the presidential claims of a Mexican general.   There has, of course, been considerable justification for American interference.   Most of it occurred during un-settled periods of Mexican history, when the Mexican government itself was not able or willing to protect the lives and property of foreigners.   But Mexicans are a proud people and they resent the implication that they cannot manage their own affairs, even when they cannot do so.   They prefer a policy that permits each nation to shape its own destiny without outside interference.

Inter-American Conferences

CONGRESS OF PANAMA.   The dream of an inter-American organization is even older than the independent nations of the Americas.   Nothing was done to realize this dream, however, until 1824, when Simón Bolívar, the great liberator of northern South America, sent letters to the independent nations of Latin America, inviting them to meet at Panama for a discussion of their common problems.   The United States was later included at the suggestion of Colombia, Mexico, and Central America.   The Congress of Panama assembled on June 22, 1826, and sat for about three weeks. Representatives of four states were present, and signed a number of agree-

[20] The early period of United States–Mexican relations is well covered in W. R. Manning's *Early Diplomatic Relations between the United States and Mexico.*   See also Miguel Re-bolledo's *México y los Estados Unidos.*

ments, which never went into effect for lack of ratification. The delegates of the United States did not reach Panama until after the Congress had adjourned. Although nothing of any consequence was accomplished, the Congress of Panama is significant as the first serious attempt to promote joint consideration of common problems among the American states.

LATIN AMERICAN CONGRESSES. For more than two decades after the Congress of Panama there was no similar meeting of American states. In 1847, however, delegates from five Latin American nations gathered in Lima and signed a number of treaties of confederation, commerce, and navigation. Only one of these agreements became effective. Nine years later the representatives of Chile, Ecuador, and Peru assembled in Santiago, but without any substantial results. In 1864 seven Latin American nations sent delegates to a congress in Lima, but it was as unfruitful as its predecessors. These various conferences established the habit of consultation, however, and strengthened the vague belief that some mechanism should be established for united action against common perils.

FIRST INTERNATIONAL CONFERENCE OF AMERICAN STATES. By 1881 the United States had begun to emerge as a great power, and it already felt the urge to leadership among the nations of the Americas. In that year, therefore, Secretary of State James G. Blaine extended invitations to all the independent governments of the New World to a conference to be held in Washington "for the purpose of considering and discussing the methods of preventing war between the nations of America." [21] The War of the Pacific, involving Chile, Peru, and Bolivia, was then in progress, so the delegates did not actually assemble until 1889. In that year, however, every independent nation of the New World except the Dominican Republic was represented. A loose inter-American organization was set up, and given an imposing title: *International Union of American Republics*. At the same time the Bureau of American Republics was established, which was to serve as the secretariat of the International Union; at the outset its primary task was to collect and distribute commercial information.

PAN AMERICAN UNION. As the years passed, the Bureau of American Republics became increasingly influential in the life of the Americas. It kept the records of inter-American conferences, developed an excellent library, and provided information both to governments and to the public concerning all aspects of co-operative activity in the Americas. It ac-

---

[21] Important excerpts from the correspondence concerning the First International Conference of American States have been published in James W. Gantenbein's *The Evolution of Our Latin American Policy*, pp. 49–58.

quired a magnificent home in Washington, D.C., through the generosity of the American millionaire Andrew Carnegie. In 1910 its name was changed to *Pan American Union*. At the same time the *International Union of American Republics* became more simply the *Union of American Republics*. The similarity of the names *Union of American Republics* and *Pan American Union* caused confusion among many persons, who never quite understood that the Union of American Republics was the official organization of the nations of the Americas, whereas the Pan American Union was its secretariat.

INTER-AMERICAN CONFERENCES. The Second International Conference of American States met in Mexico City in the fall of 1901. Since that time similar conferences have been held about every five years, though with some interruptions due chiefly to the exigencies of war. There have been several special conferences, also, such as the 1945 Inter-American Conference on Problems of War and Peace, in Mexico City. On four separate occasions the ministers of foreign affairs of the American republics have met to consider pressing problems. And there have been many technical conferences throughout the years, dealing with a wide variety of subjects from agriculture to radio. The first general inter-American conferences concerned themselves chiefly with nonpolitical matters, but by the 1920's political questions were cropping up with increasing frequency. Many Latin American nations were asking for a clarification of the Monroe Doctrine. Argentina was insisting that "no nation may intervene in the internal or external affairs of another." [22] The United States, of course, was not yet prepared to accept such proposals, and therefore the results of some of the inter-American conferences of this period were quite disappointing.

The Era of Distrust

It must be admitted that by the mid-1920's the United States was generally unpopular in Latin America. Part of this unpopularity could be attributed to misunderstandings; part of it was due to differences in the Latin and Anglo-Saxon cultures; and part undoubtedly arose from Latin American jealousy of the wealth and power of the United States. But these factors were not solely responsible. The Latin Americans had a number of specific grievances against the United States, which they never

[22] International Commission of Jurists, *Public International Law Projects*, 1927, p. 8.

tired of discussing with all who would listen. Yet these complaints had no apparent effect on American foreign policy.

UNITED STATES INTERVENTIONS. The occupation of some Caribbean republics by United States troops undoubtedly had a very unfortunate effect upon public opinion in all parts of Latin America. Newspaper editors and popular writers pictured the Republic of the North as a giant octopus, stretching out its greedy tentacles to grasp every independent nation of Latin America. "Today Haiti and the Dominican Republic and Nicaragua are at the mercy of the Yanquis," said the publicists. "Tomorrow it may be our turn. Who can tell where this menace will strike next?" Spokesmen for the United States answered these charges as best they could by pointing out that the American intervention was not purely arbitrary; it did not occur unless the government of a country had been reduced to virtual chaos by the acts of its own citizens. But such explanations did not satisfy the Latin Americans. They protested time and again that each nation was sovereign, that it must be free to run its own affairs in such way as it saw fit, and that if its way did not suit the rest of the world, then the rest of the world should wait patiently until conditions improved. The United States might declare its good intentions, as it did on numerous occasions, but its words fell on unsympathetic Latin American ears until every soldier of occupation was removed from Latin American soil.

DISTORTION OF THE MONROE DOCTRINE. The Monroe Doctrine in its original form was a declaration to European nations that they must keep hands off the New World. Almost any citizen of any nation in the Americas could endorse such a statement of policy. Even though promulgated essentially for the benefit of the United States, it seemed to provide a substantial measure of protection for every independent republic of the New World. As later interpreted, however, it proved to be the basis for United States intervention in the affairs of its neighbors. At the Sixth International Conference of American States, held in Havana in 1928, some of the Latin American nations proposed that the Conference formulate an exact interpretation of the Monroe Doctrine, so as to avoid any further "misunderstandings." Other nations suggested a joint restatement of the doctrine, making both the United States and Latin America responsible for its enforcement (and for determining when it had been violated). To both of these proposals the United States turned a deaf ear, its representatives explaining that the Monroe Doctrine was a part of American foreign policy and therefore could not possibly be interpreted by any other nation. Circumstances might indeed change the exact meaning of the doctrine, but in that even the United States must be free to assess the new circumstances and determine the new meaning. After all, no nation would permit other nations to frame its foreign policy. And as to the suggestion that enforcement of the Monroe Doctrine be made a joint affair, the United States replied that it preferred to accept the sole responsibility, though it had no objection to statements by other nations indicating their support of the Doctrine. Obviously the delegates of Latin America and the United States were far apart in their thinking. The inevitable result was the adoption of a resolution phrased so vaguely that it offended no one and accomplished nothing. The Monroe Doctrine remained a major source of irritation.

RECOGNITION AS AN INSTRUMENT OF IMPERIALISM. Although the use of armed force by one nation against another is the most obvious form of intervention, it is by no means the only form. Political and economic pressures may sometimes be exerted on a weak country by a powerful neighbor, and the result may be quite as effective as the shelling of the principal ports. Especially important is the act of granting or withholding recognition from a new government. When a nation like the United States refuses recognition of a Latin American regime that has just staged a successful coup d'état, the effect is often disastrous for the new government. Its prestige is weakened, its credit is impaired, its foreign trade is reduced, and its enemies are encouraged to continue resistance. When, however, a nation like the United States extends recognition, the new government finds that many obstacles have been removed from its path. So one can readily understand the position of those Latin American publicists who declare that unreasonable delay in recognizing a new government —at least, on the part of the United States—is a subtle form of intervention. It enables the United States to force concessions from the new governments as the price of recognition, and even to accomplish the overthrow of some new regimes that will not do its bidding. In Latin America the popular solution of this dilemma is universal acceptance of the general rule that any government able to maintain itself in power shall *automatically* be recognized as the government of the country. This is the essence of the Estrada Doctrine, which bears the name of a former foreign minister of Mexico. Other theories of recognition have been proposed by various Latin American statesmen and scholars, and some have even acquired a substantial following. But the Estrada Doctrine best represents the Latin American point of view. It denies the right of any nation to use recognition as a political instrument.

During the 1920's the United States frequently granted or withheld recognition in Latin America for political reasons. New presidents in Caribbean countries were sometimes told that they were completely unacceptable to the United States, and as a result they were forced from office. The United States did not fire a single shot or land a single marine in some instances, yet its influence was so great that it made and unmade governments. It did not have a clear and consistent policy; its reasons for granting or withholding recognition were not always the same. But certainly it was not ready to forego the advantages of bargaining with each new government. So it continued to apply pressures in various countries from time to time, and Latin Americans continued to grumble about indirect intervention.[23]

UNITED STATES DOMINATION OF THE PAN AMERICAN UNION. For many years the Pan American Union was dominated by the United States. Its director-general was always an American citizen. Its governing board consisted of the diplomatic representatives in Washington of the twenty Latin American nations, plus the secretary of state of the United States, who served *ex officio* as chairman of the board. There were, of course, some good reasons for the dominant position of the United States. It was the leading nation of the hemisphere. Its support was essential to the success of many of the Union's most cherished projects. Yet the fact remained that it was only one nation in a group of twenty-one. The Latin American republics were firmly committed to the principle of the equality of nations, and they regarded the Pan American Union as a good place to establish that equality.

It is easy to understand, therefore, why students of inter-American relations sometimes refer to the first three decades of the present century as an era of distrust. Most Latin Americans were suspicious of the motives of the United States. They emphasized the contrast between its high-sounding talk of democracy and its imperialistic activities.

The Era of Reconciliation

Even in the United States, by the late nineteen-twenties, many thoughtful persons began to realize that something was acutely wrong with inter-American relations, and to search for ways to correct this situation. A number of private organizations appointed committees to study specific aspects of the problem in Haiti or Cuba or Panama. One of Herbert

[23] See *Recognition of Governments in the Americas,* by William L. Neumann, Jr.

Hoover's first acts after his election to the Presidency of the United States —even before his inauguration—was to visit the principal countries of South America. Everywhere he spoke of the good intentions of the United States, and of the need for better understanding. Latin Americans were impressed by his words, but they awaited specific proof of his sincerity. The proof was not long delayed. Within a very few years the United States reversed almost completely its earlier Latin American policy. Herbert Hoover laid the foundations of this new course; Franklin D. Roosevelt accepted it, expanded it, and gave it a name—the Good Neighbor Policy. In most matters the Latin American viewpoint became also the viewpoint of the United States. One by one the old sources of irritation were removed.

RENUNCIATION OF INTERVENTION: *Withdrawal of troops.* The presence of large numbers of United States troops in some of the Caribbean countries had long been a source of anti–United States agitation in every part of Latin America. No genuine good feeling was possible between Latin America and Anglo-Saxon America while United States troops remained on Latin American soil. Their removal was one of the first prerequisites of good neighborliness. In 1924, under President Coolidge, United States occupation forces were ordered home from the Dominican Republic. The Hoover Administration took a number of steps toward the further withdrawal of United States troops, and greatly reduced their strength. But the process was not completed until Franklin Roosevelt took office. In 1933 the last occupation forces were removed from Nicaragua, and the following year they left Haiti. By 1934, therefore, Latin America was finally free of United States occupation forces. The American policy of intervention had been adopted in good faith; it had brought material benefits to several Caribbean republics; but it had scattered over a wide area the seeds of hatred and ill will.

The principle of non-intervention. Latin America was glad to see the last of United States soldiers of occupation, but it was especially anxious to make sure that they would not return. One of the primary aims of Latin American statesmen was to secure United States agreement to some sort of treaty specifically denying the right of intervention. At the Havana Conference of 1928 a committee dominated by Latin American delegates proposed this article: "No state may intervene in the internal affairs of another." The United States, of course, was in no position to accept this suggestion. Its troops were then intervening actively in the internal affairs of several other states. But it sturdily insisted that its sole purpose in sending troops into other countries was to insure the stability of their governments. Once this goal had been achieved, United States forces would speedily be withdrawn. As to the proposition prohibiting intervention, the delegates of the United States disputed its validity. Intervention, they said, might be of two kinds—permanent, for the purpose of acquiring new territory (even though the purpose might be disguised); or temporary, in order to protect lives or for other humanitarian reasons. Permanent intervention should be condemned, according to the United States delegates, but temporary intervention might actually be beneficial to all concerned. So the United States and its Latin American neighbors failed to agree upon a very crucial point.

The Seventh International Conference of American States met in Montevideo in 1933. Once again the Latin American nations insisted upon discussing the problem of intervention. A committee of the Conference presented a proposal somewhat similar to that rejected in 1928, but much more comprehensive. The new draft of 1933 prohibited intervention by any state, not merely in the *internal* affairs of another, but in its *internal or external* affairs. Perhaps this proposal went even further than its authors intended. It could have meant, as one careful student of the problem subsequently pointed out, that "if one of the sovereign and equal American republics should negotiate away its independence, no third state could step in to stop it, no matter how much the process might endanger the security of the third state." [24] At the time of the Conference, however, no one bothered to question the phraseology. Even the United States, which was in the process of withdrawing the last of its occupation forces from Latin America, seemed ready and willing to give substantial agreement. Yet Secretary of State Hull, speaking for the American delegation, still felt impelled to add conditions to his acceptance. He explained that the United States would not yield its rights under "the law of nations as generally recognized." Evidently the Secretary of State believed that this restriction was necessary to enable the United States to liquidate its former imperialistic policy. As he explained to the Conference, the American government was "doing its utmost, with due regard to commitments made in the past, to end with all possible speed engagements which have been set up by previous circumstances. There are some engagements which can be removed more speedily than others. In some instances dis-

[24] Samuel Flagg Bemis, *The Latin American Policy of the United States,* p. 272.

entanglement from obligations of another era can only be brought about through the exercise of some patience." [25] Translated from the language of diplomacy into the language of the street, these words meant that the United States was through with intervention, that it would never again intervene in the affairs of another nation, but that it must have a little more time to straighten out the diplomatic tangles inherited from a lustier day when the strong thought that they had a God-given right to regulate the affairs of the weak. Secretary Hull's words were reasonable, and his invocation of the law of nations may have been necessary, inasmuch as the withdrawal of American troops from foreign territory had not yet been completed, but the Latin American delegates were in no mood for conditional acceptance. They greeted Secretary Hull's explanation with silence, and then cheered one another heartily as delegate after delegate stressed his acceptance of the no-intervention policy *without reservations*.

In 1936 a special Inter-American Conference for the Maintenance of Peace was held in Buenos Aires. The Latin American delegates, not content with the manner in which the United States had agreed to the non-intervention pact of 1933, decided to raise the issue anew. This time they found the United States ready to concur without reservations of any kind. American foreign policy had already abandoned the principle of intervention, and, in Secretary Hull's phrase, had finally "disentangled itself from obligations of another era." American occupation forces were no longer in Latin America. So the delegates of the United States signed the non-intervention treaty, and the Senate of the United States ratified it without even a record vote. The era of intervention was gone forever.

Abrogation of the Platt Amendment. For many years Cuba was bound more closely to the United States than the other republics of Latin America. The Platt Amendment, which eventually became a part of the Cuban constitution, guaranteed the right of the United States to intervene in Cuban affairs "for the preservation of Cuban independence, the maintenance of a government adequate for the protection of life, property, and individual liberty," and for certain other purposes.[26] Therefore American intervention had a firmer legal basis in Cuba than in the other Caribbean republics. But legality did not prevent bitter criticism of American policy, in Cuba and elsewhere in Latin America. So in 1934, when the

[25] *Report of the Delegates of the United States of America to the Seventh International Conference of American States*, p. 114.
[26] See pages 557–558.

United States was abandoning the last vestiges of its earlier imperialism, it signed a treaty with Cuba renouncing the Platt Amendment.

United States reaction to defaulted debts. The Good Neighbor Policy met a severe test very shortly after its adoption. In the early 1930's the Great Depression was at its worst, and many governments were finding difficulties in meeting their obligations. Most of the nations of Latin America suspended payments on their foreign debts. The only two exceptions were Argentina, which had scrupulously refrained from borrowing in excess of its capacity to repay, and Venezuela, which had financed its activities by means of its oil revenues instead of foreign loans. There were many reasons, of course, for such widespread defaults in Latin America. In some cases greedy dictators had spent a large part of the borrowed money on their personal whims, and subsequently had been driven from power, leaving their several nations with heavy obligations but no corresponding gains. In other instances the loans had been contracted in good faith by honest officials, but had not always been used to the greatest advantage. Latin Americans frequently blamed their financial plight on the great New York bond houses, which had sometimes urged them to borrow more than they could afford. In many cases, it was said, the bond houses had sold Latin American securities to the general public in the United States without explaining the risks involved. And when the storms of depression broke, the bond houses were safely out of the Latin American market, leaving the American public with large quantities of practically worthless bonds.

Regardless of the truth of these charges and countercharges, the fact remained that almost all the Latin American governments owed money which they could not or would not pay, and private investors in the United States had no way of compelling them to do so. In earlier years such a situation might well have led to drastic action by the United States in order to protect the financial interests of its citizens, but in the era of the Good Neighbor Policy the United States did virtually nothing. It did not even protest when some Latin American governments deliberately permitted their bonds to sink to the lowest possible level, and then used surplus dollars to buy those bonds in the open market at bargain prices. Eventually, of course, a number of the Latin American countries resumed interest payments on their foreign debt, whereas others have never made any serious effort to honor their financial obligations. But in every instance the United States has carefully avoided any act that might be construed as economic retaliation.

United States reaction to expropriations. The United States has refrained from retaliation, also, with regard to expropriation of private holdings in Latin America. Most widely publicized was the confiscation by the Mexican government in 1938 of American—and also British—oil properties worth many millions of dollars. The confiscation order was the result of a long dispute between the companies and their workers, involving wages, pensions, and working conditions. Mexico did not deny the principle of compensation for the seized properties; on the contrary, it put itself on record as intending to indemnify the oil companies. But payment was to take place in the distant future, and the amount promised was only a small fraction of the reasonable value of the oil fields. In other days the American government would undoubtedly have brought strong pressure to bear in the oil companies' behalf. But in 1938 Secretary of State Cordell Hull merely hoped for "a fair and equitable solution." No hint of threat could be found in any of his notes. The American companies were encouraged to negotiate directly with the Mexican government. Great Britain, which would have been willing to take more drastic steps, found itself unable to do so because of our unwillingness to take similar action. Eventually, when commissioners from both countries agreed on the amount of compensation, the American oil companies declared that it represented only seven per cent of the value of their properties.[27]

In Bolivia, where expropriation of American oil properties had been ordered by the government in 1937, the United States was scrupulously careful not to interfere. The final payment by Bolivia to the American company for the loss of its properties was more generous than in Mexico. Bolivian tin mines, representing in part an investment of American capital, have been expropriated so recently that no one can yet predict the nature of the final settlement. But once again the United States is taking care not to intervene in Bolivian affairs.

Accusations of indirect intervention. Although charges of armed intervention can no longer be made against the United States, many Latin Americans contend that the United States government is intervening as actively as ever in Latin American affairs, though in a more subtle manner. They point to the efforts of the United States during the Second World War to induce the nations of Latin America to break diplomatic relations with the Axis powers, and later to declare war. They point out that in many other cases, also, the American government has driven home its argu-

[27] See Harlow S. Person's *Mexican Oil.*

ments by lending money or releasing scarce materials to countries that followed its lead, while assuming a less generous attitude toward nations that showed a greater degree of independence.

If indeed such a policy can fairly be called indirect intervention, then the United States is doubtless guilty. Like every nation, it is more disposed to help its friends than its enemies. Like every nation, it tries to induce others to share its point of view, in order to strengthen its position in the world. In this respect the United States is not different from the countries of Latin America; it is merely more powerful. Every nation uses whatever influence it may possess for the purpose of attaining its own goals and persuading others to travel in the same direction. The policies of the United States attract particular attention because they exert a powerful influence on its neighbors—and, indeed, on every nation in the world. If the United States brings pressure to bear on other countries by granting or withholding loans or tariff concessions, that may perhaps be called a form of indirect intervention. But certainly it is very different from the use of armed force. It bears little resemblance to the intervention of earlier days.

Collective intervention. In the fall of 1945 the issue of intervention was raised again, but in a new form. The tiny republic of Uruguay, which had long feared neighboring Argentina, sought to acquire a measure of protection against its powerful neighbor by proposing "collective multilateral action" against any American state violating the "basic rights of man." Such a suggestion, if incorporated in the inter-American system, would authorize the nations of the Americas to take action—presumably using armed force, if necessary—against any one of their number that ignored the fundamental tenets of democratic government. Such action would be intervention, of course, but it would be joint action by a majority of the American republics, and would be taken only after suitable consultations. According to Uruguay, it would be "really nothing more than the fulfilment of obligations freely assumed by the American republics, all of whom have proclaimed at inter-American conferences their devotion to democracy and the rights of man." The United States promptly announced its unqualified approval of the Uruguayan proposal. So did Guatemala, which had just succeeded in ridding itself of a hated dictator. But most of the other Latin American nations were definitely opposed. They had worked long and hard to win acceptance of the principle of non-intervention by one nation in another nation's affairs. They were not prepared to abandon that principle—not even if the intervention should be by many nations instead of one. Joint action might only make the matter worse. So the Uruguayan suggestion died a quiet death. There were few mourners.

COLLECTIVE SUPPORT OF THE MONROE DOCTRINE. The Monroe Doctrine has not been abandoned, but it has been stripped of its objectionable connotations. Moreover, it has been recognized as a part of the basic policy of all the nations of the Americas. As early as 1928 J. Reuben Clark, then Under Secretary of State of the United States, submitted to the Secretary of State a memorandum in which he specifically denied that the Roosevelt Corollary was justified by the terms of the Monroe Doctrine. In subsequent years, as American occupation troops were withdrawn from Caribbean republics, it became increasingly clear that the United States would no longer attempt intervention in the affairs of neighboring republics. The Monroe Doctrine, therefore, had been restored to its original status; it was merely a warning to non-American powers to keep out of the affairs of the Americas. In that form it was entirely acceptable to the Latin American republics. It was, in fact, an additional bulwark against intervention. When, therefore, the fall of France in 1940 presented the danger of German seizure of French territory in the New World for naval bases or other unfriendly purposes, the nations of the Americas acted promptly to check this menace. Their foreign ministers, meeting in Havana in the summer of 1940, unanimously agreed that

. . . any attempt on the part of a non-American state against the integrity or inviolability of the territory, the sovereignty or the political independence of an American state shall be considered as an act of aggression against the states which sign this declaration.

In case acts of aggression are committed or should there be reason to believe that an act of aggression is being prepared by a non-American nation against the integrity or inviolability of the territory, the sovereignty or the political independence of an American nation, the nations signatory to the present declaration will consult among themselves in order to agree upon the measures it may be advisable to take.[28]

These words certainly invoked the spirit of the Monroe Doctrine; they said "Hands off!" to Europe, and said it very plainly. Though they did not compel any nation of Latin America to take specific action against European aggressors in the New World, or restrain the United States from using its own forces against such aggressors, yet they implied that joint action would be the rule in the protection of the New World's frontiers.

[28] Second Meeting of the Ministers of Foreign Affairs of the American Republics, Report of the Secretary of State, p. 71.

Thus the Monroe Doctrine became a part of the inter-American system, without ceasing to be a pillar of the foreign policy of the United States.

UNITED STATES ATTEMPTS TO FORMULATE A SOUND RECOGNITION POLICY. The United States has not been completely successful in its attempts to formulate a sound policy concerning the recognition of new governments. For the most part it has granted or withheld recognition in recent years on the basis of two major factors: first, whether the new government is sufficiently stable to compel obedience to its orders; and, second, whether it is capable of meeting its international obligations. But this policy has not been followed with complete consistency. Sometimes other factors, such as the willingness of newly established governments to sever diplomatic relations with our enemies or to take stringent action against local Communists, have played a part in our decision. In recent years the United States has placed increasing reliance on consultations with other nations of the Americas before granting recognition to new American governments.

The issue of recognition has placed the United States in a particularly delicate position. Any recognition policy of the United States, no matter how well meant, apparently evokes criticism by some leaders of Latin American thought. It might seem that criticism could be avoided by recognizing all established governments, regardless of the circumstances involved. Such a policy would be merely a practical application of the Estrada Doctrine, which has been so widely endorsed in Latin America.[29] Unfortunately, however, every attempt by the United States to shape its recognition policy along such lines subjects it to bitter complaints. Latin Americans say that many of the governments recognized by the United States are dictatorships—which is not at all surprising, considering the number of dictatorships in Latin America. Whenever American arms and military supplies are made available to established governments, and withheld from revolutionaries, Latin Americans declare that the United States is helping dictators to suppress the revolutionary friends of liberty. In some cases, without doubt, these statements are true. But let us suppose that the United States should adopt a completely different policy. Let us suppose that it should withhold recognition—and all its accompanying advantages—from dictatorial regimes, throwing instead the full weight of its prestige and influence behind every democratic movement in Latin America. Such a course would immediately arouse frenzied charges of intervention from many Latin American sources. It must be remem-

29 See page 672.

bered that practically every government or revolutionary movement in Latin America claims to be democratic. Therefore the United States would be obliged to pass upon such claims before granting recognition. Its motives would inevitably be assailed. There seems to be no escape from the horns of this dilemma. American recognition policy, no matter what it may be, is certain to cause critical comment. But in all probability the criticisms will be fewer, and less easily justified, if the United States recognizes all established governments—or at least all established governments that meet their international obligations.

REORGANIZATION OF THE PAN AMERICAN UNION. Even before the inauguration of the Good Neighbor Policy the United States gave its consent to changes desired by the Latin American nations in the structure of the inter-American organization. In 1923 the secretary of state of the United States was stripped of his *ex officio* position as chairman of the Pan American Union's governing board, and that body was given the right to choose its own president and vice-president. Five years later the rules of the Union were changed to permit each nation to decide for itself whether its seat on the governing board should be occupied by its diplomatic representative in Washington or by a special delegate. In 1946 the Colombian statesman Alberto Lleras Comargo was named director general of the Pan American Union, following the tragic death in an automobile accident of Leo S. Rowe, who had served in that capacity for a quarter of a century. No longer could it be said, therefore, that the Pan American Union was too subservient to the United States. Only in one respect did the rules continue to favor the Republic of the North: Washington remained as the permanent home of the Pan American Union. But that arrangement could not readily be changed. Expensive buildings and equipment, including extensive library facilities, could not be moved from country to country.

ORGANIZATION OF AMERICAN STATES. Eventually it became clear that the Union of American Republics was too loose an organization to meet the responsibilities of inter-American co-operation. At the Bogotá Conference of 1948, therefore, the *Union of American Republics* became the *Organization of American States,* with new responsibilities, new duties, and new prestige. The new organization bears a strong resemblance to the old, however. Its secretariat is still the Pan American Union. The governing board, now known as the Council of the Organization of American States, still makes its headquarters in Washington, and still consists of the Secretary of State of the United States and one representative

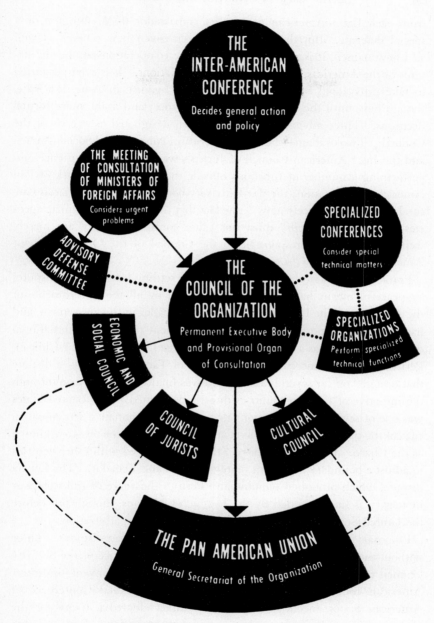

THE
INTER-AMERICAN
CONFERENCE
Decides general action
and policy

THE MEETING
OF CONSULTATION
OF MINISTERS OF
FOREIGN AFFAIRS
Considers urgent
problems

SPECIALIZED
CONFERENCES
Consider special
technical matters

ADVISORY
DEFENSE
COMMITTEE

THE
COUNCIL OF THE
ORGANIZATION
Permanent Executive Body
and Provisional Organ
of Consultation

SPECIALIZED
ORGANIZATIONS
Perform specialized
technical functions

ECONOMIC AND
SOCIAL COUNCIL

COUNCIL
OF JURISTS

CULTURAL
COUNCIL

THE PAN AMERICAN UNION
General Secretariat of the Organization

ORGANIZATION OF AMERICAN STATES

The International Organization of the 21 American Republics Established by the Charter
Signed at the Ninth International Conference of American States, Bogotá, Colombia, 1948.

Reproduced from *Organization of American States;* prepared by the Division of Education,
Department of Cultural Affairs, Pan American Union, Washington, D.C., 1949.

from each Latin American nation—its ambassador to Washington or a special delegate. But the Council has been given new powers as well as a new name. It is authorized to promote co-operation among the nations of the Americas, and with the United Nations. It is even permitted to take provisional steps to meet aggression against an American state, though only until the foreign ministers can meet and make more formal decisions. Three advisory bodies have been designated as organs of the Council. Two of them—the Inter-American Economic and Social Council and the Inter-American Council of Jurists—were already in existence and performing a number of functions outside the regular framework of Pan American organization; the third advisory body—the Inter-American Cultural Council—is entirely new. The fact that these three subordinate agencies are called "councils" must not cause confusion. They are merely technical committees responsible to the Council of the Organization of American States.

PEACE BY ARBITRATION. The desirability of settling international disputes by peaceful means has long been recognized by all the governments of the Americas. The United States has been a leader in this movement, and has played an important part in the adjustment of several international quarrels. It acted as a friendly and disinterested mediator in the Chilean-Peruvian dispute concerning the provinces of Tacna and Arica—a dispute that dragged on for several decades and was finally settled in 1929 through the initiative of the two countries directly concerned. The United States was one of several neutral nations that helped to negotiate a settlement in 1938 of the quarrel between Bolivia and Paraguay over the territory known as the Chaco. In 1941 the United States again joined with other neutrals to adjust a boundary argument involving Peru and Ecuador. The Leticia dispute, which brought Colombia and Peru to the verge of full-scale war in 1935, was finally settled by the League of Nations, though not before the United States had made a futile effort to arrange arbitration.

Proposals for compulsory arbitration of inter-American disputes, with or without the assistance of the International Court of Justice or the Security Council of the United Nations, have been made at many of the inter-American conferences. In 1923 the Fifth International Conference of American States, meeting in Santiago, Chile, adopted a treaty for the settlement of conflicts among the nations of the Americas. Provision was made for a commission of inquiry to investigate disputes, in order to avoid actual hostilities. Five years later a special International Conference of American States on Conciliation and Arbitration met in Washington and adopted two additional treaties.   Other agreements of a similar nature have also been adopted—one at Buenos Aires in 1936 and another at Bogotá in 1948.   The "Pact of Bogotá" was designed to cover virtually every kind of dispute that might arise among the nations of the Americas, and to make provision for peaceful settlement.   It was phrased so broadly that several nations, including the United States, refused to sign it without making certain reservations.   Even today there is no absolute guarantee that all inter-American disputes will be adjusted peacefully, but great progress has been made toward this goal.

INTER-AMERICAN CULTURAL AND SCIENTIFIC RELATIONS. Important co-operative relationships in cultural and scientific fields have been developed among the nations of the Americas in recent years.   Almost all these activities have been financed chiefly by the United States, because of its vastly superior resources.   Trips to the United States have been arranged for Latin American public officials and business and professional leaders, in order to let them observe for themselves what the United States is thinking and doing.   Opportunities have been provided for Latin American graduate students to take courses in American universities—and, on a smaller scale, for American students to visit Latin America.

United States binational centers have been established in almost all the larger cities of Latin America.   They are financed jointly by the United States and by the nations in which they are located.   Their primary purpose is to interpret life in the United States to the Latin Americans.   Courses are offered in United States government, history, art, literature, and music.   The most important activity of these cultural centers, however, is the teaching of English.   Thousands of Latin Americans, though they may have no particular interest in United States art or history, wish nonetheless to learn the English language.   So they take courses in English and indirectly learn something about the United States.   The binational centers have small libraries, and in a few of the metropolitan centers of Latin America additional libraries are maintained with United States funds.   One of the most important of these libraries—the Biblioteca Benjamin Franklin, in Mexico City—has a large collection of American books and periodicals, which it makes available to all who are interested.   Co-operation in the field of public health has been carried on for many years.

American health experts have worked in virtually every country of

Latin America, studying the problems of disease prevention, public health nursing, and sanitary engineering. Representatives of the United States Department of Agriculture have aided Latin American officials in the establishment of agricultural experiment stations and the development of new crops. Studies have been made of the conservation of wild life resources. These examples of co-operative relationships in cultural and scientific matters are merely suggestive; they make no pretense at completeness.

INTER-AMERICAN ECONOMIC RELATIONS. Co-operation in economic matters among the nations of the Americas was greatly stimulated by the Second World War. The Latin American nations had dozens of materials that were vital to the war effort of the United States—among them, tin, copper, tungsten, mica, quinine, balsa wood, flax, and sisal. These materials were made available to the United States and its allies in the greatest possible quantities at the greatest possible speed. The United States, for its part, made a determined effort to keep necessary civilian goods flowing to Latin America during the war years, and to prevent unreasonably high prices for these goods. In most cases, however, Latin American governments permitted their own merchants to sell scarce articles from the United States at whatever price they could get. The resultant inflation was generally blamed on the United States, and scarcely anyone bothered to explain the true situation.

Tariffs. For many years the United States followed a consistent high tariff policy. Latin Americans, who desired to expand their United States markets, often spoke bitterly against this policy, but their words had no effect. In 1934, however, largely through the efforts of Secretary of State Cordell Hull, the United States adopted a new tariff program designed to stimulate foreign trade by lowering tariff barriers. The law authorized the President to reduce custom duties as much as fifty per cent, but with the understanding that such concessions would not be granted to any country unless it would consent to make comparable reductions on goods imported from the United States. Any article on the tariff list could be made the subject of special bargaining. Thus the United States might agree to admit Venezuelan oil more cheaply if Venezuela would reduce its tariff on American motor cars. Since 1934 the United States has made reciprocal trade agreements with most of the Latin American nations.

For the most part, however, Latin America is not vitally interested in lower tariffs. It is too firmly convinced that its own high tariff barriers must be retained or even raised to new levels. Today Latin America is industrializing at a rapid rate,[30] and it desires to protect its infant industries from foreign competition. Even those countries that have not experienced the industrial boom prefer to keep their tariffs at a high level, because they are constantly in need of additional revenues, and custom duties provide a large share of government income.

Dollar surpluses and deficits. In many countries of Latin America there is a chronic shortage of United States dollars for purposes of foreign exchange. This shortage arises from the tendency of Latin American nations to buy more products from the United States than they can sell to it in exchange. During the Second World War, however, this dollar shortage was transformed into a dollar surplus. The United States was bolstering its war effort by buying more Latin American goods than ever before, whereas Latin America could not obtain more than a part of the United States goods it desired. So the dollar surplus continued to grow. At the end of the Second World War it had reached large proportions, and seemed to provide a comfortable cushion against the effects of any fresh unbalance in United States–Latin American trade. But inflationary trends soon increased the price of United States goods, and thus reduced the purchasing power of the Latin American dollar surpluses. Moreover, some Latin American governments permitted their excess dollars to be used for virtually any purpose, regardless of existing needs. In a very short time, therefore, the surpluses had shrunk sharply, or had disappeared altogether. The present trend in Latin America is toward strict regulation of exchange. Many countries will not permit articles to be imported unless they are essential to the national economy, or unless they can be obtained from nations that are sufficiently good customers. This plan has tended to work to the advantage of Europe and to the detriment of the United States.

Economic nationalism. In recent years there has been a wave of economic nationalism throughout Latin America. Popular sentiment has been roused against the great foreign companies that control so large a part of Latin American agriculture, industry, and commerce. The belief is widely held that these foreign companies enjoy special rights and privileges, enabling them to exploit local resources without giving anything in return. Many Latin American governments, therefore, have enacted laws designed to restrict the rights and privileges of the foreign companies and insure greater participation by local citizens in foreign enterprises. Some

[30] For a good discussion of Latin American industrialization, see *Industry in Latin America*, by George Wythe.

of these laws specify that at least seventy or eighty or even ninety per cent of the workers in any business must be citizens of the country. The employment of more than a small percentage of foreigners, even in those highly paid jobs requiring professional or technical skill, may be expressly forbidden. In some instances the law requires the use of certain local products; for example, it may specify that coal imported from abroad must be mixed with local coal, or that imported wheat flour must be blended with local manioca flour. Tax discrimination against foreign companies is widespread. The desirability of some of these restrictions, even from the standpoint of the countries imposing them, may perhaps be questioned, but there is no doubt that they are highly popular in Latin America.

Financing Latin American development. The rapid development of industry in Latin America, and the conviction of many Latin American governments that much greater industrialization is necessary to raise the general standard of living, have created a serious financial problem. Latin American statesmen must find large sums of money in order to finance their ambitious plans. The great families of Latin America have traditionally invested their wealth in land, and many of them prefer to continue this arrangement. Little by little the situation is changing, however, and larger funds from private Latin American sources are available today for investment in industry than ever before. Yet only a small part of the required total can be obtained in this way. The natural tendency of Latin American governments, therefore, is to look abroad for extensive loans. In the past they relied heavily on private American and European investors, but money from these sources is no longer so readily available. Private investors have been discouraged by the record of defaults and by recent restrictive legislation. So the present tendency in Latin America is to look to foreign governments—especially that of the United States—for the money needed to finance extensive development programs. At the Ninth International Conference of American States, held at Bogotá in 1948, many of the Latin American delegates made clear that they hoped for large-scale aid from the United States, similar to the Marshall Plan for Europe. But Secretary of State Marshall, who attended the Conference, made equally clear that the United States had no intention of duplicating its European aid program in Latin America. The money appropriated for Europe, as the Secretary pointed out, was to help it recover from the severe but temporary crisis caused by the ravages of war. The needs of Latin America were not at all comparable. They were of long standing, and not likely to disappear in a few years. For such needs the United States could not accept any major share of responsibility.

The United States government has by no means turned a completely deaf ear to Latin American requests for financial assistance, however. The United States Export-Import Bank, originally established in 1933 to increase exports from the United States, has since become a major lending agency. It has made funds available to the Latin American republics for a wide variety of purposes, including public works and industrial expansion. In June of 1950 President Truman's Point Four Program [31] was translated into law. It makes provision for co-operation in technical matters with other nations, not only in Latin America but in underdeveloped areas throughout the world, "in developing their resources and in improving their working and living conditions." [32]

Within the State Department there is an Institute of Inter-American Affairs, whose primary task is to study the means of developing industry in Latin America. It functions through national commissions which it has established. The members of these national commissions are usually business and financial leaders, and technical experts. Mention must also be made of the International Bank for Reconstruction and Development— the World Bank, as it is commonly known. This institution, which has been operating since 1946 with capital subscribed by nearly forty countries, sometimes makes loans to its members for the purpose of developing their productive facilities and untapped resources. All these lending agencies combined, however, have not provided more than a small part of the capital that Latin America could use to advantage. Since the end of the Second World War all twenty nations of Latin America have received financial aid from the United States totaling less than seven hundred million dollars. In that same period Europe has been given twenty-nine billions. The Netherlands has received twice as much as all Latin America, and Greece has been given three times as much. These statistics are regarded without enthusiasm in Latin America.

The Fruits of Good Neighborliness

NEW SPIRIT OF CO-OPERATION. Even today, after a quarter of a century of good neighborliness, the United States is far from popular in Latin

[31] So called because it was the fourth of several points made by President Truman in his inaugural address of January 20, 1949.

[32] For an impartial and penetrating analysis of the Point Four Program, see the 1953 publication of the Brookings Institution, American Foreign Assistance, by William Adams Brown, Jr., and Redvers Opie.

America. Yet a great change has occurred in the attitude of almost all the Latin American countries toward their North American neighbor. That change made itself clearly evident in the first days of the Second World War. In January of 1942, only six weeks after the Japanese attack at Pearl Harbor, the foreign ministers of the Americas met in Rio de Janeiro and adopted a resolution recommending the severance of diplomatic relations with Germany, Italy, and Japan. Mexico's foreign minister, Ezquiel Padilla, spoke in ardent support of the United States and pleaded for even more drastic action against its enemies. Forty-one declarations and resolutions were adopted by the Conference, looking toward political, economic, and even military collaboration with the United States. Many of these declarations and resolutions were translated into action. Strategic materials, as previously pointed out,[33] flowed from Latin America in vast quantities. Important sites for military and naval bases were made available to the United States. In 1945, when the war's end was in sight, the American republics that had actively assisted the Allied cause met in Mexico City for an Inter-American Conference on War and Peace. One of the most important results of this conference was the "Act of Chapultepec," [34] which provided for joint consultation in case of aggression against any American state. Two years later the representatives of all the nations of the Americas, meeting once more in Rio de Janeiro, strengthened the Act of Chapultepec by adopting a treaty of reciprocal assistance. "Reciprocal assistance," as everyone knew, implied chiefly assistance by the United States, because of its vast military power. But the Latin American nations no longer feared that the military power of the United States might be turned against them. They had learned to trust the Colossus of the North. Today the peace of the Americas is safeguarded by an Inter-American Defense Board, composed of representatives of all the republics of the Americas. The chairman of this board is an officer of the armed forces of the United States. The Board's task is to make recommendations for the defense of the Americas, including such military collaboration as may seem desirable. Eight Latin American nations [35] have signed agreements by which they receive direct grants of equipment and other assistance from the United States. Army, navy, and air force missions from the United States are helping to train the armed forces of almost all the Latin American countries.

[33] See p. 687.
[34] The conference was held in Chapultepec Palace.
[35] Brazil, Chile, Colombia, Cuba, Dominican Republic, Ecuador, Peru, Uruguay.

Latin America in Two World Wars

	First World War	Second World War
Argentina	Neutral	Broke relations January, 1944. Declared war March, 1945.*
Bolivia	Neutral	Broke relations January, 1942. Declared war April, 1943.
Brazil	Broke relations April, 1917. Declared war October, 1917.	Broke relations January, 1942. Declared war August, 1942.
Chile	Neutral	Broke relations January, 1943. Declared war April, 1945.*
Colombia	Neutral	Broke relations December, 1941. Declared war November, 1943.
Costa Rica	Broke relations September, 1917. Declared war May, 1918.	Declared war December, 1941.
Cuba	Declared war April, 1917.	Declared war December, 1941.
Dominican Republic	Broke relations September, 1917.	Declared war December, 1941.
Ecuador	Broke relations December, 1917.	Broke relations January, 1942. Declared war February, 1945.*
Guatemala	Broke relations April, 1917. Declared war April, 1918.	Declared war December, 1941.
Haiti	Broke relations June, 1917. Declared war July, 1918.	Declared war December, 1941.
Honduras	Broke relations May, 1917. Declared war July, 1918.	Declared war December, 1941.
Mexico	Neutral	Broke relations December, 1941. Declared war June, 1942.
Nicaragua	Broke relations May, 1917. Declared war May, 1918.	Declared war December, 1941.
Panama	Broke relations May, 1917. Declared war May, 1918.	Declared war December, 1941.
Paraguay	Neutral	Broke relations January, 1942. Declared war February, 1945.*
Peru	Broke relations October, 1917.	Broke relations January, 1942. Declared war February, 1945.*
El Salvador	Neutral	Declared war December, 1941.
Uruguay	Broke relations October, 1917.	Broke relations January, 1942. Declared war February, 1945.*
Venezuela	Neutral	Broke relations January, 1942. Declared war February, 1945.*

* Last-minute declaration, made in order to obtain an invitation to the San Francisco Conference organizing the United Nations.

PAN AMERICANISM AND THE UNITED NATIONS. Although the Organization of American States and its specialized agencies have taken many important steps for the prevention of war and the betterment of international relations, they do not intend to ignore or compete with another international organization—the United Nations—which is striving toward the same goal. On the contrary, every effort is made to insure the fullest co-operation between the world organization and its regional counterpart. The treaty establishing the Organization of American States makes frequent references to the United Nations, and specifically declares that "None of the provisions of this charter shall be construed as impairing the rights and obligations of the member states under the charter of the United Nations." After all, the Organization of American States is a regional agency within the United Nations. It is, however, much more than a branch of the world organization. It is the formal expression of a regional system much older than the United Nations—a system that is capable of continued existence if the United Nations should collapse. In a sense the Organization of American States is much stronger than the United Nations because the American republics have managed to adjust many of their basic differences. They have learned to work together.

POSITION OF ARGENTINA. It must be admitted, however, that in the midst of this atmosphere of Pan American co-operation and good will, the United States and Argentina have frequently failed to see eye to eye. Argentina aspires to leadership, at least in the southern part of South America, and it resents the dominant position of the United States. Geography has placed Argentina outside the sphere of strongest United States influence, and the southern republic has taken full advantage of that fact. On more than one occasion it has played an active part in rejecting the proposals of the United States at inter-American conferences; sometimes it has been almost alone in its opposition. The government of the United States has not known just how to handle this situation. Its recent attitude toward Argentina has ranged from open friendliness to scarcely concealed hostility. The truth of the matter is that the fundamental differences between the two nations cannot easily be reconciled.

RECENT DIFFERENCES: *Viewpoint of Latin America.* With regard to most of Latin America, however, the most serious obstacles to friendly co-operation have now been removed. Mutual suspicion and distrust no longer mar inter-American conferences. Yet there can be no doubt that the last four or five years have witnessed a slight but perceptible deterioration in the relations of Latin America with the United States. Many Latin Americans believe that the United States is too preoccupied with Europe. They complain that whereas Latin American difficulties once received primary consideration in Washington, they are now subordinated to the problems of the cold war against communism. In 1953 Latin American sensibilities were hurt when the Secretary of State of the United States visited a large part of the world to talk with the leaders of many nations, but failed to include any country of Latin America in his itinerary. The subsequent official Latin American tour of President Eisenhower's brother proved to be only partial compensation. Latin Americans are disturbed also by the long-term decline in the value of the products that form the bulk of their exports. They complain that the United States was glad enough to pay a "fair" price during the Second World War, when goods were in short supply, but that now it is disposed to haggle. A popular term in Latin America today is "economic democracy." This term, as some Latin Americans define it, means equality of opportunity for all—an equality that cannot be achieved while one nation in the Americas possesses the lion's share of the wealth. Only by "a more equitable distribution of wealth"—in other words, by vastly increased payments from the treasury of the United States to the nations of Latin America, *as a matter of right*— can economic democracy be established.

Viewpoint of the United States. Such Latin American ideas have found no widespread acceptance north of the border. Most residents of the United States would speedily reject the notion that Latin America was entitled to receive any substantial part of its revenues from the United States treasury. Most residents of the United States probably approve their public officials' attempts to secure raw materials from Latin America as cheaply as possible. They regard such activity as a legitimate protection of United States taxpayers, rather than a form of economic aggression. And though the people of the United States have no desire to offend Latin America, they will probably be preoccupied with the cold war against communism for many years to come.

NEED FOR GOOD WILL. In the foreseeable future, therefore, the statesmen of Latin America will probably not see completely eye to eye with the statesmen of the United States. Differences of opinion may never be removed completely; they are based not only on misunderstandings or variations in temperament, but also on differences in the fundamental interests of the nations involved. Yet divergent opinions need not necessarily prevent fruitful co-operation. A great deal depends on the willingness of all the statesmen of the Americas to subordinate their different policies and beliefs to the need for mutual good will.

SELECTED REFERENCES

Aikman, Duncan, *The All-American Front,* New York, Doubleday, Doran, 1940.

Alba, Pedro de, *De Bolívar a Roosevelt,* Mexico, D.F., Cuadernos Americanos, 1949.

Ball, M. Margaret, *The Problem of Inter-American Organization,* Stanford, California, Stanford University Press, 1944.

Barclay, Wade C., *Greater Good Neighbor Policy,* Chicago, Willett Clark, 1944.

Beals, Carleton, and Others, *What South Americans Think of Us,* New York, McBride, 1945.

Bemis, Samuel F., *The Latin American Policy of the United States,* New York, Harcourt, Brace, 1943.

Bernstein, Harry, *Origins of Inter-American Interest, 1700–1812,* Philadelphia, University of Pennsylvania Press, 1945.

Bidwell, Percy W., *Economic Defense of Latin America,* Boston, World Peace Foundation, 1941.

Brown, William Adams, Jr., and Redvers Opie, *American Foreign Assistance,* Washington, D.C., Brookings Institution, 1953.

Callcott, Wilfrid H., *The Caribbean Policy of the United States, 1890–1920,* Baltimore, Johns Hopkins Press, 1942.

Committee on International Economic Policy, *Inter-American Economic Relations: Problems and Prospects,* New York, The Committee, 1948.

Cooke, Juan I., *Acción Diplomática,* Buenos Aires, Ediciones del Mar, 1947.

Cox, I. J., *Nicaragua and the United States, 1909–1927,* Boston, World Peace Foundation, 1927.

Daniels, Walter M., *Latin America in the Cold War,* New York, Wilson, 1952.

Dávila, Carlos, and Clarence Senior, *Latin America and the Good Neighbor Policy,* New York, New York University Press, 1944.

Dean, Vera M., *Latin America and the War,* London, Oxford University Press, 1942.

DeConde, Alexander, *Herbert Hoover's Latin American Policy,* Stanford, California, Stanford University Press, 1951.

Duggan, Laurence, *The Americas: The Search for Hemisphere Security,* New York, Holt, 1949.

Easter, Allan W., *The United States and the A. B. C. Powers, 1889–1906,* Dallas, Southern Methodist University Press, 1952.

Fenwick, Charles G., *The Inter-American Regional System,* New York, Declan X. McMullen, 1949.

Gantenbein, James W., ed., *The Evolution of Our Latin American Policy,* New York, Columbia University Press, 1950.

Gordon, Wendell C., *The Economy of Latin America,* New York, Columbia University Press, 1950.

Green, Philip L., *Pan American Progress,* New York, Hastings House, 1942.

Guerrant, Edward O., *Roosevelt's Good Neighbor Policy,* Albuquerque, University of New Mexico Press, 1950.

Hanson, Simon G., *Economic Development in Latin America,* Washington, D.C., American Affairs Press, 1951.

Haring, Clarence H., *Argentina and the United States,* Boston, World Peace Foundation, 1941.

Herring, Hubert, *America and the Americas,* Claremont, California, Claremont Colleges, 1944.

James, Preston E., *Latin America,* rev. ed., New York, Odyssey Press, 1950.

Kaufmann, William W., *British Policy and the Independence of Latin America, 1804–1828,* New Haven, Yale University Press, 1951.

Masters, Ruth D., ed., *Handbook of International Organizations in the Americas,* Washington, D.C., Carnegie Endowment for International Peace, 1945.

Montague, Ludwell, *Haiti and the United States,* Durham, Duke University Press, 1940.

Navarro Andrade, Ulpiano, *Unión de las Naciones Americanas,* Quito, Impr. de la Universidad, 1949.

Neumann, William L., Jr., *Recognition of Governments in the Americas,* Washington, D.C., Foundation for Foreign Affairs, 1947.

Parks, E. Taylor, *Colombia and the United States,* Durham, Duke University Press, 1935.

Phillips, C. A., and D. K. Farthing, *Understanding the Latin Americans,* Chicago, Lyons and Carnahan, 1946.

Phillips, Henry A., *Argentina: Pivot of Pan American Peace,* New York, Hastings House, 1944.

—— *Brazil: Bulwark of Inter-American Relations,* New York, Hastings House, 1945.

Prewett, Virginia, *The Americas and Tomorrow,* Philadelphia, Blakiston, 1944.

Privitera, Joseph F., *The Latin American Front,* Milwaukee, Bruce, 1945.

Quintanilla, Luis, *Pan Americanism and Democracy,* Boston, Boston University Press, 1952.

Repetto, Nicolás, *Política Internacional,* Buenos Aires, Ediciones La Vanguardia, 1943.

Rippy, J. Fred, *Latin American in World Politics,* New York, Crofts, 1938.

—— *South America and Hemisphere Defense,* Baton Rouge, Louisiana State University Press, 1941.

Rojas Suárez, Juan Francisco, ed., *Costa Rica en la Segunda Guerra Mundial,* San José, Costa Rica, Imprenta Nacional.

Sáenz, Vicente, *Latin America against the Colonial System,* Mexico, D.F., Unión Democrática Centroamericana, 1949.

Sands, William F., and Joseph M. Lalley, *Our Jungle Diplomacy,* Chapel Hill, University of North Carolina Press, 1944.

Smith, C. Edmund, Jr., *Yankee Diplomacy: United States Intervention in Argentina,* Dallas, Southern Methodist University Press, 1952.

Soule, George H., and Others, *Latin America in the Future World,* New York, Farrar and Rinehart, 1944.

Stuart, Graham H., *Latin America and the United States,* 4th ed., New York, Appleton-Century, 1943.

Wartenbaker, Charles, *New Doctrine for the Americas,* New York, Viking Press, 1941.

Westerman, George W., *A Study of Socio-Economic Conflicts in the Panama Canal Zone,* Panamá, Liga Cívica Nacional, 1948.

White, John W., *Our Good Neighbor Hurdle,* Milwaukee, Bruce, 1943.

Wilgus, A. Curtis, ed., *The Caribbean at Mid-Century,* Gainesville, University of Florida Press, 1951.

Williamson, René de Visme, *Culture and Policy: The United States and the Hispanic World,* Knoxville, University of Tennessee Press, 1949.

Index